Studies in the History of Law and Justice

Volume 11

The purpose of this book series is to publish high quality volumes on the history of law and justice.

Legal history can be a deeply provocative and influential field, as illustrated by the growth of the European universities and the *ius commune*, the French Revolution, the American Revolution, and indeed all the great movements for national liberation through law. The study of history gives scholars and reformers the models and courage to question entrenched injustices, by demonstrating the contingency of law and other social arrangements.

Yet legal history today finds itself diminished in the universities and legal academy. Too often scholarship betrays no knowledge of what went before, or why legal institutions took the shape they did. This series seeks to remedy that deficiency.

Studies in the History of Law and Justice will be theoretical and reflective. Volumes will address the history of law and justice from a critical and comparative viewpoint. The studies in this series will be strong bold narratives of the development of law and justice. Some will be suitable for a very broad readership.

Contributions to this series will come from scholars on every continent and in every legal system. Volumes will promote international comparisons and dialogue. The purpose will be to provide the next generation of lawyers with the models and narratives needed to understand and improve the law and justice of their own era.

The series includes monographs focusing on a specific topic, as well as collections of articles covering a theme or collections of article by one author.

More information about this series at http://www.springer.com/series/11794

Aniceto Masferrer
Editor

The Western Codification of Criminal Law

A Revision of the Myth of its Predominant French Influence

Springer

Editor
Aniceto Masferrer
Faculty of Law, Campus dels Tarongers
University of Valencia
Valencia
Spain

ISSN 2198-9842 ISSN 2198-9850 (electronic)
Studies in the History of Law and Justice
ISBN 978-3-030-10129-9 ISBN 978-3-319-71912-2 (eBook)
https://doi.org/10.1007/978-3-319-71912-2

Printed on acid-free paper

This Springer imprint is published by Springer Nature
The registered company is Springer International Publishing AG
The registered company address is: Gewerbestrasse 11, 6330 Cham, Switzerland

Preface and Acknowledgements

This volume seeks to fill in a historiographical gap, dealing with the contribution of the tradition and foreign influences to the nineteenth-century codification of criminal law. More specifically, it focuses on the extent of the French influence—among others—in European and American Civil Law Jurisdictions. In this vein, the book aims at dispelling some myths concerning the real extent of the influence of the French model on European and Latin American criminal codes. The impact of the Napoleonic criminal code on other jurisdictions was real, but the scope and extent of such influence was less strong than it has sometimes been described. The overemphasis of the French influence on other civil law jurisdictions is partly due to a line of thought that defends the idea that modern criminal codes constituted a break with the past. The question as to whether modern criminal codes constituted a break with the past or just a degree of reform touches on a difficult issue, namely, the dichotomy between tradition and foreign influences in the criminal law codification process. Those who stress that the codes broke with the past, usually tend to overemphasize foreign influences on the criminal codes. Conversely, those who argue that codes did not constitute a break with the past and contained many traditional institutions have the opposite tendency, underrating the role of foreign models.

Since codes cannot come out the blue, the proportions of tradition and foreign influence need to be carefully explored. Familiarity with tradition is the best way to ascertain the weight of foreign influences, and, by the same logic, the study of the foreign influences enhances the recognition of the weight of tradition. Tradition and foreign influences are not mutually exclusive. It would be unwise to overlook that the codes, inasmuch as they consecrated the notions, categories, and principles of the *ius commune* tradition, had a "supranational" flavor, and simultaneously took the guise of "national" law once integrated into the tradition of *ius proprium*. A code is never purely a national product. This perspective enables us to assess the extent to which the codification process in a given jurisdiction brought with it a nationalization or denationalization of its criminal law. Scholarship had unduly ignored this important subject. The present volume aims at filling such scholarly gap.

This book has been undertaken in the context of two research projects entitled "La influencia de la Codificación francesa en la tradición penal española: su concreto alcance en la Parte General de los Códigos decimonónicos" (ref. DER2012-38469), and "Las influencias extranjeras en la Codificación penal española: su concreto alcance en la Parte Especial de los Códigos decimonónicos" (ref. DER2016-78388-P), both financed by the Spanish "Ministerio de Economía y Competitividad." From its very beginning, I envisaged the convenience of inviting a group of distinguished scholars who might contribute to such an important subject from a comparative perspective, including jurisdictions from Europe and Latin America. That was the goal I pursued, and I think it was achieved. Even more, I dare to say that the contributors to this volume went far beyond my original expectations. The merit of this book is due to them, not to me. The only merit I may fairly deserve is to have contacted them and persuaded them to embark in this project. I am grateful to all of them for their generous cooperation and academic excellence.

Most of the contributors had the chance to discuss and exchange their views in the context of two biannual conferences organized by the *European Society for Comparative Legal History* in Macerata (Italy) in 2014, and in Gdansk (Poland) in 2016. The results of the project were presented and debated in the context of an international conference that was held from 9 to 11 November at the Faculty of Law of the University of Valencia, with the title "The Influence of the *Code pénal* (1810) over the Codification in Europe and Latin America: Tradition and Foreign Influences in the Codification Movement," thanks to the financial support of the *Conselleria d'Educació, Investigació, Cultura i Esport* de la *Generalitat Valenciana*, and the cooperation of the *Institute for Social, Political and Legal Studies* (Valencia) and the *Instituto de Historia de la Intolerancia* (adscrito a la *Real Academia de Jurisprudencia y Legislación*). Almost all the contributors of this volume attended the Valencian conference, devoting some hours in the morning to communicate the results to first-year law students—whose questions reflected their sincere interest and their ability to follow and understand the presentations—and several hours after lunch to discuss and debate in a scholarly seminar the most difficult issues of our findings.

I wish to express my gratitude to Georges Martin and Mortimer Sellers, the editors of the series "History of Law and Justice", for agreeing to publish this book in this prestigious Springer's collection, to Neil Olivier, for suggesting to me in Macerata (July 2014) the possibility of publishing this project with Springer, and to Christie Lue, for their generous availability and assistance.

Valencia, Spain
March 2017

Aniceto Masferrer

Contents

Contributors

Alejandro Agüero Universidad Nacional de Córdoba, Córdoba, Argentina

Pedro Caeiro University of Coimbra, Coimbra, Portugal

Yves Cartuyvels University of Saint-Louis, Brussels, Belgium

Oscar Cruz Barney Instituto de Investigaciones Jurídicas, UNAM, México City, Mexico

Frederico de Lacerda da Costa Pinto NOVA University of Lisbon, Lisboa, Portugal

Karl Härter Max Planck Institute for European Legal History, Frankfurt am Main, Germany

Emilia Iñesta-Pastor Law Faculty, University of Alicante, Alicante, Spain

Aniceto Masferrer University of Valencia, Valencia, Spain

Diego Nunes Universidade Federal de Santa Catarina, Florianópolis, Brazil

Jorge A. Núñez CONICET (Consejo Nacional de Investigaciones Científicas y Tecnológicas), Buenos Aires, Argentine Republic; INHIDE (Instituto de Investigaciones de Historia del Derecho), Buenos Aires, Argentine Republic

Michele Pifferi University of Ferrara, Ferrara, Italy

Ignacio Maria Poveda Velasco University of São Paulo Law School, São Paulo, Brazil

Matías Rosso Universidad Empresarial Siglo XXI, Córdoba, Argentina

Martin P. Schennach University of Innsbruck, Innsbruck, Austria

Eduardo Tomasevicius Filho University of São Paulo Law School, São Paulo, Brazil

Isabel Ramos Vázquez University of Jaén, Jaén, Spain

Stefano Vinci University of Bari Aldo Moro, Bari, Italy

Part I
Introduction

Tradition and Foreign Influences in the 19th Century Codification of Criminal Law: Dispelling the Myth of the Pervasive French Influence in Europe and Latin America

Aniceto Masferrer

Abstract Any civil law student knows that most of provisions in any European or Latin American civil code derive from Roman law, that they were the outcome of a long and gradual scholarly elaboration extending from 12th century glossators to the natural lawyers of the 18th century. However, there is no such consensus about criminal law. The civil law tradition has doubtlessly committed more effort to the scholarly development of private law institutions than to those of public law, privileging civil law over criminal law. The main consequences of this fact are twofold: (i) 19th century criminal jurisprudence is sometimes presented as if had arisen out of the blue, or as if institutions contained in the 19th criminal codes broke with the past or bore no traces of Roman law; and (ii) since criminal codes supposedly broke with the past, the extent and scope of foreign influences—and the French in particular—on the criminal codes in Europe and Latin America are overemphasized. The chapter aims at dispelling this common place, and particularly the myth of the overall French influence in Europe and Latin America.

This work was undertaken in the context of two research projects entitled "La influencia de la Codificación francesa en la tradición penal española: su concreto alcance en la Parte General de los Códigos decimonónicos" (ref. DER2012-38469), and "Las influencias extranjeras en la Codificación penal española: su concreto alcance en la Parte Especial de los Códigos decimonónicos" (ref. DER2016-78388-P), both financed by the Spanish 'Ministerio de Economía y Competitividad.'

A. Masferrer (✉)
University of Valencia, Valencia, Spain
e-mail: aniceto.masferrer@uv.es

A. Masferrer (ed.), *The Western Codification of Criminal Law*, Studies in the History of Law and Justice 11, https://doi.org/10.1007/978-3-319-71912-2_1

1 Introduction

In 1994 James Gordley published a somewhat controversial article with a provocative title: "Myths of the French Civil Code."[1] In his view, the Napoleonic code simply laid down some liberal principles from the revolution (property, freedom of contract, torts) rather than set out new, individualistic ones. In fact, this seems to be what Jean-Étienne-Marie Portalis, the main drafter of the French civil code, thought about the *Code Civil* (1804), fully aware of the past's important role in drafting, interpreting, and applying the code.[2]

Any civil law student knows that many provisions in most European or Latin American civil code derive from Roman law, that they were the outcome of a long and gradual scholarly elaboration extending from 12th century glossators to the

---

[1]James Gordley, "Myths of the French Civil Code," 42 *Am. J. Comp. L.* 459, 488–489 (1994): "The Code did not rebuild the law of property, contract or tort on new and individualistic principles. Indeed, it was drafted in what one can only describe as the trough between two intellectual waves: a wave of natural law theory that crested in the 16th and 17th centuries, and a wave of individualistic will-centred theory that did not emerge clearly until the 19th century. To the extent the drafters were guided by general principles at all, they used those of the natural lawyers which were already old-fashioned. The principles of the Revolution that did influence the drafters were a republican vision of law and the principle of human equality. The republican vision, however, was rejected by the drafters themselves, and the principle of equality did not lead to a reshaping of private law. Although the Code is often said to have abolished feudal property, it is hard to find much of economic consequence that changed."

[2]Portalis, *Preliminary Address delivered on the occasion of the presentation of the draft of the government commission*, on 1 Pluviôse IX (21 January 1801) (available at http://www.justice.gc.ca/eng/rp-pr/csj-sjc/ilp-pji/code/index.html): "But what a great task is the drafting of a civil legislation for a great people! The endeavor would be beyond human powers, if it entailed giving this people an entirely new institution and if, forgetting that civil legislation ranks first among civilized nations, one did not deign to benefit from the experience of the past and from that tradition of good sense, rules and maxims which has come down to us and informs the spirit of centuries.

(…) The lawmaker does not exert an authority so much as a sacred function. He must not lose sight of the fact that laws are made for men, and not men for laws; that (…), rather than change laws, it is almost always more useful to present the citizenry with new reasons to love them; that history offers us the promulgation of no more than two or three good laws over the span of several centuries (…).

It is useful to protect all that need not be destroyed: laws must show consideration for common practices, when such practices are not vices. Too often one reasons as though the human race ended and began at every moment, with no sort of communication between one generation and that which replaces it. Generations, in succeeding one another, mingle, intertwine and merge. A law-maker would be isolating his institutions from all that can naturalize them on earth if he did not carefully observe the natural relationships that always, to varying degrees, bind the present to the past and the future to the present; and that cause a people, unless it is exterminated or falls into a decline worse than annihilation, to always resemble itself to some degree. We have, in our modern times, loved change and reform too much; if, when it comes to institutions and laws, centuries of ignorance have been the arena of abuses, then centuries of philosophy and knowledge have all too often been the arena of excesses."

natural lawyers of the 18th century.[3] However, there is no such consensus about criminal law.

The civil law tradition has doubtlessly committed more effort to the scholarly development of private law institutions than to those of public law, privileging civil law over criminal law. However, it would be naïve to think that 19th century criminal jurisprudence arose out the blue or that the institutions contained in the 19th criminal codes bore no traces of Roman law.[4] Such belief would require a leap of faith much greater than what is needed to believe in God, although not for those who replaced Him with the codes.[5] If codes be gods, then one might argue that they even preceded the beginning of the world and transcended Roman law and history altogether, with prophets announcing the gospel in the 18th century (Voltaire, Feuerbach, Beccaria, etc.), the alleged dawn of an entirely new criminal law. According to this view, no criminal law science antedated the 18th century, and the criminal codes, drafted in line with the Enlightenment and rationalist principles, broke utterly with the past and tradition. Far from consistent, this account is more a fairy tale than a credible account of the historical truth (to the extent history has—or should have—any relation to truth or objectivity), which is a bit more complex.

2 Criminal Law Reform and Codification: A Break with the Past?

> … [A] rule in which nothing was worthy of respect, or conservation: no part could be saved for the ordering of future society. All of it, entirely all, needed to be left behind (…) The cart of destruction and reform had to pass through the ruined building, because in it there was scarcely an arch, scarcely a column, that could nor should be saved … In Spanish criminal law there was only one legitimate and viable system, the system of codification, the system of absolute change.[6]

---

[3]On this matter, see the recent work by George Mousourakis, *Roman Law and the Origins of the Civil Law Tradition* (Heidelberg-New York, Dordrecht-London: Springer, 2015); see also Emilija Stanković, "The influence of Roman law on Napoleon's Code Civil," *'Ex iusta causa traditum': Essays in honour of Eric Pool* (Pretoria: Fundamina, 2005), pp. 310–315.

[4]On this matter, see Aniceto Masferrer, *Tradición y reformismo en la Codificación penal española. Hacia el ocaso de un mito. Materiales, apuntes y reflexiones para un nuevo enfoque metodológico e historiográfico del movimiento codificador penal europeo* (Jaén: Universidad de Jaén, 2003).

[5]See, for example, Shael Herman, "From Philosophers to Legislators, and Legislators to Gods: The French Civil Code as Secular Scripture," *University of Illinois Law Review* 1984, pp. 597–620; see also R.C. Caenegem, *Judges, Legislators and Professors: Chapters in European Legal History* (Cambridge University Press, 1993), p. 89 (explaining that the French Exegetical School treated codes as the bible: "…since it believed in a limited number of holy books containing the law and nothing but the law").

[6]Joaquín Francisco Pacheco, *El Código penal concordado y comentado* (1848; I use the 2nd ed.: 1856, in particular, the facsimilar edition with a preliminary study by Abel Téllez Aguilera, Madrid: Edisofer, 2000), p. 82.

I remember how surprised I was the first time I read this paragraph some years ago. I thought it could not possibly be correct. Even more, I was almost convinced that the author did not say what he really thought about the true role of the criminal law tradition in the codification enterprise. I am not saying he lied. I am just saying he did not show the whole picture, for it emphasized just one side of the "criminal problem"[7] in the late 18th century to the beginning of the 19th century.[8]

2.1 The Liberal System and the 'Constitutionalization' of Criminal Law Principles

As is well known, criminal law was in disarray at the turn of the 19th century. What is often overlooked is one aspect that explains many other features of criminal law before it was codified, namely, that the main problem of the criminal law was not scientific but political. This explains many aspects that otherwise cannot be properly grasped: that criminal legislation was so harsh; punishments so severe, even sometimes affecting those who did not commit the crime; some punishments were still theoretically in force, though rarely or inconsistently applied in practice (the confiscation of goods, infamy, some degrading punishments, the death penalty, etc.); the disproportionality between crimes and their punishments; the persistence of torture, despite its rare application in many territories; that the kind of punishment applied depended more on political circumstances or interest than on the

[7]Giovanni Tarello, *Storia della cultura giuridica moderna*, vol. I: Assolutismo e codificazione del diritto (Bologna, 1976), p. 383; for an interesting treatment of Enlightenement thought and criminal law, see pp. 383–483.

[8]A description of the Spanish criminal law in the 18th century can be seen in Isabel Ramos Vázquez, "Las reformas borbónicas en el Derecho penal y de Policía criminal de la España dieciochesca" (see http://www.forhistiur.de/zitat/1001ramos.htm); a 18th-century view of that period in criminal law can be found in Joaquín Cadafalch y Burguñá, *Discurso sobre el atraso y descuido del Derecho penal hasta el siglo XVIII* (1849); for an overview on the Codification of criminal in Spain, see Masferrer, *Tradición y reformismo en la Codificación penal española*, already cited; Aniceto Masferrer, "Codification of Spanish Criminal Law in the Nineteenth Century. A Comparative Legal History Approach", *Journal of Comparative Law* Vol. 4, no. 1 (2009), pp. 96–139; Aniceto Masferrer, "Liberal State and Criminal Law Reform in Spain", Mortimer Sellers & Tadeusz Tomaszewski (eds.), *The Rule of Law in Comparative Perspective*. Series: *Ius Gentium: Comparative Perspectives on Law and Justice*, vol. 3 (2010), pp. 19–40.

legislative prescription; that judges enjoyed—and sometimes misused, although less frequently than many suspect—excessive discretion; etc.

Ius commune lawyers had defended most of the modern criminal law principles that were claimed by authors like Beccaria, Montesquieu, Feuerbach, Lardizábal, among others. These include the legality of crime and punishment, the proportionality between crime and punishment, the individuality of punishment, favorable decision, favorable interpretation, and the presumption of innocence.[9]

It might seem that this is precisely what the French Revolution demanded and brought about, which is true. However, these criminal law principles were not an original product of the revolution. These principles were well known among scholars, although not politically recognized or implemented.[10] A new political system was needed to protect criminal law from misuse.[11] That was precisely the greatest contribution of the French Revolution to modern criminal law.[12]

---

[9]Jesús Lalinde Abadía, *Iniciación histórica al Derecho español* (1983), p. 669; on the presumption of innocence in Enlightenment thought and its roots in glossators' doctrine, see Joachim Hruschka, "Die Unschuldsvemutung in der Rechtsphilosophie der Aufklärung", in *ZStW*, CXII (1990), Heft 2, pp. 285–300.

[10]On this matter, see Masferrer, *Tradición y reformismo en la Codificación penal española*, pp. 69–91; Masferrer, "Codification of Spanish Criminal Law in the Nineteenth Century...", pp. 100–111; Masferrer, "Liberal State and Criminal Law Reform in Spain", pp. 23–40.

[11]The importance of the political context in explaining and reconstructing the historical development of criminal law should not be neglected; on this matter see, Masferrer, *Tradición y reformismo en la Codificación penal española*, pp. 53–54; Masferrer, "La dimensión ejemplarizante del Derecho penal municipal catalán en el marco de la tradición jurídica europea. Algunas reflexiones iushistórico-penales de carácter metodológico", *AHDE* 71 (2001), pp. 439–471, particularly pp. 446–450; R. C. Caenegem, "Criminal Law in England and Flanders under King Henry II and Count Philip of Alsace", *Actes du Congrès de Naples (1980) de la société italienne d'Histoire du Droit. Studia Historica Gandensia* 253, 1982 (republished in R. C. van Caenegem, ed., *Legal History: a European Perspective*, London, 1991, pp. 37–60), p. 254: "The conclusion is that no study of criminal law, in the past or in the present, can be conducted fruitfully without constant reference to the political situation and the power structure in society: criminal law is not the fruit of logical deductions from eternal principles formulated by unworldly scholars." This is particularly important in historical periods of political reforms, convulsions o revolutions, as the French historiography has clearly shown.

[12]On the close link between the political revolution (French Revolution) and the codification of criminal law in France, see Jean-Marie Carbasse, *Introduction historique au droit pénal* (Paris, 1990), pp. 329 ff.; Jean-Marie Carbasse, "Le droit pénal dans la Déclaration des droits", *Droits: Revue française de théorie juridique* VIII (1988), pp. 123–134; Renée Martinage, "Les innovations des constituants en matière de répression", *Une autre justice. Contributions à l'histoire de la justice sous la Révolution française* (dir. Robert Badinter) (Fayard, 1989), pp. 105–126; Jean-Marie Carbasse, "État autoritaire et justice répressive: l'evolution de la législation pénale de 1789 au Code de 1810", *All'ombra dell'Aquila Imperiale. Transformazioni e continuità istituzionali nei territori sabaudi in età napoleonica (1802–1814). Atti del convegno, Torino 15–18 ottobre 1990* (Roma, 1994), I, pp. 313–333; Pierre Lascoumes, "Revolution ou reforme juridique? Les codes penaux français de 1791 a 1810", *Revolutions et justice en Europe. Modeles français et traditions nationales (1780–1830)* (Paris: L'Harmattan, 1999), pp. 61–69; Bernard Schnapper, "Les Systemes repressifs français de 1789 a 1815", *Revolutions et justice en Europe. Modeles français et traditions nationales (1780–1830)* (Paris: L'Harmattan, 1999), pp. 17–35; Pierre

More specifically, both the *Declaration of the Rights of the Man and of the Citizen* (1789) and the first modern French Constitution (1791) instigated a remarkable legacy that I call the 'constitutionalization' of the main criminal-law principles, followed by their 'legalization,' whereby these principles were laid down in criminal codes or—to distinguish them from 'absolutist' theories—the 'liberal' codes.[13]

Lascoumes/Pierrette Poncela, "Classer et punir autrement: les incriminations sous l'Ancien Régime et sous la Constituante", *Une autre justice. Contributions à l'histoire de la justice sous la Révolution française* (dir. Robert Badinter) (Fayard, 1989), pp. 73–104; Antoine Leca, "Les principes de la revolution dans les droits civil et criminel", *Les principes de 1789* (Marseille, 1989), pp. 113–149; Georges Levasseur, "Les grands principes de la Déclaration des droits de l'homme et le droit répressif français", *La Déclaration des droits de l'homme et du citoyen de 1789, ses origines – sa pérennité* (Paris, 1990), pp. 233–250; Renée Martinage, "Les origines de la pénologie dans le code pénal de 1791", *La revolution et l'ordre juridique privé. Rationalité ou scandale? Actes du colloque d'Orléans (11–13 septembre 1986)* (Orléans, 1988), I, pp. 15–29; Renée Martinage, *Punir le crime. La repression judiciaire depuis le code pénal* (Villeneuve-d'Ascq, 1989); Germain Sicard, "Sur la terreur judiciaire a Toulouse (1793-AN II)", *Liber Amicorum. Etudes offertes à Pierre Jaubert* (Bourdeaux, 1992), pp. 679–700; Jean-Pierre Delmas Saint-Hilaire, "1789: un nouveau droit pénal est né…", *Liber Amicorum. Etudes offertes à Pierre Jaubert* (Bourdeaux, 1992), pp. 161–177.

[13]Pio Caroni, *Lecciones catalanas sobre la historia de la Codificación* (Madrid, 1996), pp. 69 ff.; see also Bartolomé Clavero, "La idea de Código en la Ilustración jurídica", *Historia. Instituciones Documentos* 6 (1979), pp. 49–88; Diego Silva Forné, "La Codificación penal y el surgimiento del Estado liberal en España", *Revista de Derecho Penal y Criminología*, 2º época, 7 (2001), pp. 233–309; Masferrer, "Codification of Spanish Criminal Law in the Nineteenth Century…", cited in the fn n. 8; Masferrer, "Liberal State and Criminal Law Reform in Spain", cited in the fn n. 8; Manuel Bermejo Castrillo, "Primeras luces de codificación. El Código como concepto y temprana memoria de su advenimiento en España", *Anuario de Historia del Derecho Español* 83 (2013), pp. 9–63; on the codification movement in the Early Modern Age, see Yves Cartuyvels, *D'où vient le code pénal?: une approche généalogique des premiers codes pénaux absolutistes au XVIIIe siècle* ([Montréal et al.]: Presses de l'Université de Montréal/Presses de l'Université d'Ottawa/De Boeck Université, 1996); Yves Cartuyvels, "Le droit pénal entre consolidation étatique et codification absolutiste au XVIIIe siècle", *Le penal dans tous ses Etats. Justice, Etats et Sociétés en Europe (XIIe-Xxe siècles)* (Bruxelles, 1997), pp. 252–278; Yves Cartuyvels, "Eléments pour une approche généalogique du code penal", *Déviance et Société* 18 (1994), 4, pp. 373–396; Stanislaw Salmonowicz, "Penal codes of the 16th–19th centuries. A discussion of models", *La codification européene du Moyen-Age au siècle des Lunières. Etudes réunies par Stanislaw Salmonowicz* (Warsawa, 1997), pp. 127–141; Katarzyna Sójka-Zielinska, "Über den modernen Kodifikationsbegriff", *La codification européene du Moyen-Age au siècle des Lunières. Etudes réunies par Stanislaw Salmonowicz* (Warsawa, 1997), pp. 9–19; Yves Castan, "Les codifications penales d'Ancien Régime", *Le penal dans ses Etats. Justice, Etats et Sociétés en Europe (XIIe-XXe siècles)* (Bruxelles, 1997), pp. 279–286; Benoît Garnot, "L'évolution récente de l'Histoire de la criminalité en France à l'époque moderne", *Histoire de la Justice* 11 (1998), pp. 225–243; Benoît Garnot, "Justice, infrajustice, parajustice et extrajustice dans la France d'Ancien Régime", *Crime, Histoire et Societés* 2000, vol. 4, n. 1, pp. 103–120.

The aforementioned principles can be found in articles 4–8 of the *Declaration of the Rights of the Man and of the Citizen*,[14] of which the last two are particularly relevant to criminal justice:

Art. 7: "No person shall be accused, arrested, or imprisoned except in the cases and according to the forms prescribed by law. Any one soliciting, transmitting, executing, or causing to be executed, any arbitrary order shall be punished. But any citizen summoned or arrested in virtue of the law shall submit without delay, as resistance constitutes an offense."

Art. 8: "The law shall provide for such punishments only as are strictly and obviously necessary, and no one shall suffer punishment except it be legally inflicted in virtue of a law passed and promulgated before the commission of the offense."

It is highly likely this was the greatest contribution to modern criminal law system from France and the French Revolution.[15] Moreover, France constituted the first continental country that 'constitutionalized' the criminal law principles that *ius commune* lawyers had claimed some centuries before the French Revolution.

From this perspective, Pacheco was right in asserting that criminal law needed a clean break, but the shift from the *ancien régime* to a liberal system that occurred in France during the revolution was more political than scientific. This permitted a new criminal law system to emerge whose main principles were 'constitutionalized' thanks to political will that was incompatible with 18th century absolutist monarchies. The same process would soon recur throughout the Continent. As the American colonies achieved political autonomy from the metropolis, so too did Latin America.

From the political point of view, the criminal law system clearly broke from tradition. This is evident in various European constitutions, some articles of which established the principles of the new concept of justice in criminal law.[16]

[14]Art. 4 *DRMC* 1789: "Liberty consists in the freedom to do everything which injures no one else; hence the exercise of the natural rights of each man has no limits except those which assure to the other members of the society the enjoyment of the same rights. These limits can only be determined by law."

Art. 5 *DRMC* 1789: "Law can only prohibit such actions as are hurtful to society. Nothing may be prevented which is not forbidden by law, and no one may be forced to do anything not provided for by law."

Art. 6 *DRMC* 1789: "Law is the expression of the general will. Every citizen has a right to participate personally, or through his representative, in its foundation. It must be the same for all, whether it protects or punishes. All citizens, being equal in the eyes of the law, are equally eligible to all dignities and to all public positions and occupations, according to their abilities, and without distinction except that of their virtues and talents."

[15]On this matter, see the bibliography cited in the footnote n. 7.

[16]For the Spanish and German constitutionalism, see Aniceto Masferrer, "El alcance de la prohibición de las *penas inhumanas y degradantes* en el constitucionalismo español y europeo. Una contribución histórico-comparada al contenido penal del constitucionalismo español y alemán", *Presente y futuro de la Constitución española de 1978* (Valencia: tirant lo blanc, 2005), pp. 515–544.

The shift from the *ancien régime* to a liberal system occurred in all European countries, and its main consequence in the realm of criminal law was always the same, namely, the 'constitutionalization' of several criminal law principles (legality of crime and punishment, the proportionality between crime and punishment, the individuality of punishment, favorable decision, favorable interpretation, and the presumption of innocence). Whereas the fall of the *ancien régime* followed a revolution in some countries (e.g. France), in others it was the result of an inconstant process that lasted several decades (e.g. Spain).

The Spanish case consequently defies comparison with other European jurisdictions. Spain's singular historical circumstances, especially its relation with France, make this case peculiar. As is well known, Spain fought France for seven years (1808–1814), a period in which the *Cortes* (a representative body or parliament) of Cádiz adopted many liberal reforms and principles. In the field of criminal law, several provisions of the 1812 Constitution innovated criminal law principles: the principle of legality[17]; the principle of the individuality of punishments,[18] the abolition of infamy the offspring of convicted traitors[19] and the confiscation of

[17]The 1812 Constitution was the only one not to incorporate this principle explicitly, but it can be inferred from the interpretation of some provisions. In other Spanish constitutions: art. 9, 1837 Constitution: "No Spaniard can be tried or sentenced except by a judge and a court having jurisdiction under previous laws and [for a] crime in the manner prescribed by law"; art. 9, 1845 Constitution: "No Spaniard can be tried or sentenced except by a judge and a competent court, pursuant to law prior to the crime and in the manner prescribed by law"; art. 10, 1856 Constitution (never promulgated): "No Spaniard can be tried or sentenced except by a judge and jurisdiction, pursuant to law prior to the crime and in the manner prescribed by law"; art. 11, 1869 Constitution: "No Spaniard may be tried or sentenced except by a judge and a court with knowledge and competence in the manner prescribed by law, pursuant to law prior to the crime. Extraordinary courts may not create special commissions to hear any crime"; art. 16, 1876 Constitution: "No Spaniard can be tried or sentenced except by a judge and a competent court, pursuant to law prior to the crime and in the manner prescribed by law"; art. 28, 1931 Constitution: "Only deeds determined prior to their commission are punishable by law. No one shall be tried except by a competent court and in accordance with legal procedures"; 1978 Constitution: "The Constitution guarantees the rule of law …" (art. 3); "No one can be convicted or sentenced for actions or omissions which when committed did not constitute a crime, misdemeanor or administrative offense under the laws then in force." (art. 25.1); on the this matter, see Masferrer, *Tradición y reformismo en la Codificación penal española*, pp. 75–76; Masferrer, "Codification of Spanish Criminal Law in the Nineteenth Century…", pp. 103–104; Masferrer, "Liberal State and Criminal Law Reform in Spain", pp. 28–31; for a more specific and exhaustive view, see Matthew C.Mirow, "The Legality Principle and the Constitution of Cádiz", *Judges' Arbitrium to the Legality Principle: Legislation as a Source of Law in Criminal Trials* (Anthony Musson/Georges Martyn/ Heikki Pihlajamäki, eds.) (Duncker & Humblot, 2013), pp. 189–205 (available at http://papers.ssrn.com/sol3/papers.cfm?abstract_id=1844486).

[18]Art. 305, 1812 Constitution: No penalty imposed for any crime whatever shall have no effect on the family of the convicted, but shall have its full effect on precisely he who deserves it.

[19]Aniceto Masferrer, *La pena de infamia en el Derecho histórico español. Contribución al estudio de la tradición penal europea en el marco del ius commune* (Madrid: Dykinson, 2001), pp. 373 ff.; and by the same author: "La pena de infamia en la Codificación penal española", *Ius fvgit. Revista interdisciplinar de estudios histórico-jurídicos* 7 (1998), pp. 123–176.

goods[20]; and the principle of due process.[21] These constitutional principles outline the modern criminal law system from which the codes stemmed. This was the initial influence of the French model on the modern Spanish (read: liberal) criminal justice system. Specifically, this influence shows the close relationship between the introduction of a liberal system, the 'constitutionalization' of the modern criminal law principles, and the 'legalization' of these principles using code. Just as the *Code pénal* reflected the criminal law principles laid down in the *Declaration of the Rights of the Man and of the Citizen* (1789) and the 1791 Constitution, 19th-century Spanish codes echoed the Spanish constitutions (1812, 1837, 1845, 1869, 1876).

In fact, this occurred in all European countries, not just Spain. This perspective might obscure the particularity of the Spanish case, since modern criminal law principles were 'constitutionalized' and 'legalized' through codes even in common law jurisdictions.[22]

---

[20]Art. 304 1812 Constitution: The punishment of confiscation of goods shall not be imposed. In other Spanish Constitutions: Article 10, 1837 Constitution: "There will be never imposed the penalty of confiscation of property, and no Spaniard will be deprived of his property, but for cause of public utility, subject to appropriate compensation"; art. 10, 1845 Constitution: "There will be never imposed the penalty of confiscation of property, and no Spaniard will be deprived of property except on justified grounds of public utility, subject to appropriate compensation"; art. 12, 1856 Constitution (never promulgated): "Nor shall the penalty of confiscation of property be imposed for any offense"; the 1869 Constitution did not expressly prohibit the enforcement of the penalty for the confiscation of property, although it could be implied from art. 13: "No one shall be temporarily or permanently deprived of their property and rights, or disturbed in the possession of them, except by court order. Public officials who, under any pretext violate this requirement shall be personally liable for damage caused ..."; art. 10, 1876 Constitution: "The penalty of confiscation of property will be never imposed and no one shall be deprived of his property except by competent authority and for cause of public utility, subject always appropriate compensation", art. 44, 1931 Constitution: "the penalty of confiscation of property shall be imposed in no case"; the current 1978 Constitution does not contain any provision expressly laying down such a prohibition, in the area of taxation, not penal, art. 31.1 provides that "all contribute to sustain public expenditure according to their economic (...), which in no case shall be confiscatory in scope." On this punishment, see Miguel Pino Abad, *La pena de confiscación de bienes en el Derecho histórico español* (Córdoba: Universidad de Córdoba, 1999); on the legal development of the death penalty in Spain, see also Juan Sainz Guerra, *La evolución del Derecho penal en España* (Jaén: Universidad de Jaén, 2004), pp. 349–352.

[21]Arts. 286 ff., 1812 Constitution. In other Spanish Constitutions: arts. 7 and 63 ff., 1837 Constitution; 7 and 66 ff., 1845 Constitution; 8 and 67 ff., 1856 Constitution (never promulgated); arts. 2-4 and 12, 1869 Constitution; 4-8, 16, 17, 76; and 79, 1876 Constitution; arts. 29, 42 and 94 ff., 1931 Constitution, arts. 17.2-4, 24.2 and 117.1, 1978 Constitution.

[22]On this matter, see Aniceto Masferrer, "The Principle of Legality and Codification in the 19th-century Western Criminal Law Reform", *From the Judge's Arbitrium to the Legality Principle: Legislation as a Source of Law in Criminal Trials* (Georges Martyn, Anthony Musson and Heikki Pihlajamäki, eds.) (Duncker & Humblot, 2013), pp. 253–293.

2.2 *Criminal Codes and Legalization of 'Liberal' Criminal Law Principles: The Legality Principle*

A number of political criminal law reforms that originated on the political or constitutional levels and eventually introduced into the codes were included largely without the influence of the French code. This was the case for the principle of legality (concerning both the crime and its punishment), the proportionality of crime and punishment, the individuality of punishment, favorable decision, favorable interpretation, and the presumption of innocence, all of which I mentioned above.[23]

Instead, the influence of the principle of legality over all European jurisdictions was mainly caused by modern constitutions, especially that of France in 1791 and the *Declarations* (particularly that of 1789).[24] However, once this principle was adopted in the French code, this legal source did contribute to expanding its effect to other jurisdictions.

Despite this, it should be emphasized that the generalization of the principle of legality in the Western legal tradition was the result of a broader movement that encompassed several European codes. The early codes observed the principle of legality without accepting all of its consequences, as was the case of the Prussian Code of 1721 (*Verbessertes Landrecht*),[25] the Swedish Law of the Realm of 1734, the *Codex juris criminalis* of Bavaria (1751) and the Austrian Code of 1769 (*Constitutio Theresiana*).

The first European criminal code that unambiguously established the principle of legality, expressly forbidding both judicial discretion and analogy, was the Austrian Code of 1787 (*Allgemeine Gesetz über Verbrechen und Strafen*), enacted by Joseph II.[26] The French code of 1791 established a regime of legality that was too

---

[23]See the fn n. 9, and its main text.

[24]On this matter, see Masferrer, "The Principle of Legality and Codification in the 19th-century Western Criminal Law Reform", cited in the fn n. 22.

[25]In fact, it could be argued that the Prussian code of 1721 was actually a typical traditional law ("land law") that, comprising many different provisions, was only subsidiary to the *ius commune* and not based on (or did not fully comply with) the principle of legality.

[26]That was the opinion of Karl Ludwig von Bar, *A History of Continental Criminal Law* (originally published: Boston: Little, Brown, and Company, 1916; reprinted 1999 by The Lawbook Exchange), p. 252; see Jerome Hall, "Nulla Poena sine Lege," (1937–1938) *Yale L. J.* 168; in Ancel's view, the Tuscany code of 1786 "drawn up by a commission headed by Beccaria," would be the first that contained a consistent recognition of the principle of legality, constituting "historically the first legislative codification expressing the new penal law of continental Europe" (Ancel, "The Collection of European Penal Codes…", p. 344); in 1803, this code was revised, preserving the principle of legality.

inflexible with fixed punishments without any possibility of pardon. Such inflexibility was corrected by the Napoleonic criminal code (1810).[27] The Bavarian code of 1813,[28] which was inspired—if not drafted—by Feuerbach,[29] also introduced the principle of legality with all of its consequences, thus excluding any judicial discretion or analogy in theory, not in practice, and affirming this principle "more strongly than ever."[30] From then on, many European criminal codes, some partly

---

[27]The French criminal code of 1810 adopted, however, the principle of legality in a more flexible way, giving judges a legal minimum and a maximum within which they could act. This model was introduced in a number of European countries; on the relationship between the French criminal codes of 1791 and 1810, see Aniceto Masferrer, "Continuismo, reformismo y ruptura en la Codificación penal francesa. Contribución al estudio de una controversia historiográfica actual de alcance europeo", *AHDE* 73 (2003), pp. 403–420; see also Ancel, "The Collection of European Penal Codes…", p. 345.

[28]On this code and its relationship with Feuerbach, see Karl Geisel, *Der Feuerbachsche Entwurf von 1807: sein Strafsystem und dessen Entwicklung. Ein Beitrag zur Entstehung des Bayerischen Strafgesetzbuches von 1813* (Göttingen, 1929); Edwin Baumgarten, "Das bayerische Strafgesetzbuch von 1813 und Anselm von Feuerbach", *Der Gerichtssaal* 81 (1913), Stuttgart, pp. 98 ff.; Karl Arnold, "Erfahrungen aus dem bayerischen *StGB* vom Jahre 1813 und Betrachtungen hierüber", *Archiv des Criminalrechts*, Halle 1843, pp. 96 ff., pp. 240 ff., 377 ff., 512 ff.; 1844, pp. 190 ff.

[29]Paul Johann Anselm von Feuerbach, *Lehrbuch des gemeinen in Deutschland gültigen peinlichen Rechts* (Gieβen, 1801); Paul Johann Anselm von Feuerbach, *Über die Strafe als Sicherungsmittel vor künftigen Beleidigung des Verbrechers. Nebst einer näheren Prüfung der Kleinischen Strafrechtstheorie* (Chemnitz, 1800), that was Feuerbach's answer to the work written by Ernst Ferdinand Klein, *Grundsätze des gemeinen deutschen und preußischen peinlichen Rechts* (Halle, 1796); on Feuerbach, see the—classical works—written by Karl Binding, "Zum Hundertjährigen Geburtstage Anselm Feuerbachs", *Strafrechtliche und Strafprozessuale Abhandlungen* I (1915), pp. 507–521; Max Grünhut, "Anselm von Feuerbach und das Problem der strafrechtlichen Zurechnung", *Hamburgische Schriften zur gesamten Strafrechtswissenschaft* (Hamburg, 1922); Herbert Blohm, *Feuerbach und das Reichsstrafgesetzbuch von 1871* (Breslau, 1935); Eberhard Kieper, *Johann Paul Anselm Ritter von Feuerbach, sein Leben als Denker, Gesetzgeber und Richter* (Darmstadt, 1969); Gustav Radbruch, *Paul Johann Alselm Feuerbach. Ein Juristenleben* (Göttingen, 1969); Mario A. Cattaneo, *Anselm Feuerbach, filosofo e giurista liberale* (Milano, 1970).

[30]Ancel, "The Collection of European Penal Codes…", p. 345; Hall, "Nulla Poena sine Lege", pp. 169–170.

influenced by the criminal codes of France (1810) and Bavaria (1813),[31] laid down the principle of legality.[32]

Nonetheless, it is important to keep in mind that, even before Feuerbach coined his famous expression *nulla poena sine lege, nulla poena sine crimine, nullum crimen sine poena legali* ("No punishment without law, no punishment without crime, no crime without a criminal law") in the Bavarian criminal code (1813),[33] the principle of legality had been constitutionally recognized through the

---

[31]Ancel, "The Collection of European Penal Codes…", pp. 346 ff.

[32]See, among others, the following 19th-century codes: Code of *Grand-Duché d'Oldemburg* 1814 (*Das Strafgesetzbuch für die Herzoglich–Oldenburguischen Lande von 10. September 1814*, Oldenburg, 1814), Polish criminal Code of 1818, Code of the Two Sicilies of 1819, Parma criminal Code of 1820, Spanish Code of 1822, Russian Code of 1832 (coming into force in 1835), Greek criminal Code of 1834, *Das Strafgesetzbuch für das Königreich Sachsen vom 30. März 1838…*(Dresden, 1838), Sardinia criminal Code of 1839 (governing Piedmont and Sardinia), *Das Strafgesetzbuch für das Grossherzogthum Sachsen-Weimar-Eisenach vom 5. April 1839…* (Eisenach, 1840), *Das Strafgesetzbuch für das Königreich Württemberg vom 5. September 1839* (Stuttgart, 1839), *Allgemeines Criminal-Gesetzbuch für das Königreich Hannover vom 8. August 1840* (Hannover, 1851), *Criminalgesetzbuch für das Grossherzogthum Sachsen-Altenburg vom 3. Mai 1841…*(Darmstadt, 1841), *Strafgesetzbuchs für das Grossherzogthum Hessen vom 17. September 1841…*(Altenburg, 1841), Norwengian Code of 1842, Russian Code of 1845, *Strafgesetzbuch für das Großherzogthum Baden vom 6. Märch 1845…*(Karlsruhe, 1845), Polish criminal Code of 1847 (coming into force in 1848), *Das Straf-Gesetzbuch für die Frei Stadt Frankfurt und deren Gebiet in seinem Entwurfe vom Jahre 1848 nach dem am 1. Januar 1857 dahier in Kraft tretenden Straf-Gesetzbuch für das Großherzogthum Hessen* (Frankfurt am Main, 1856), Spanish Codes of 1848 and 1850, Prussian Code of 1851 (*Das Strafgesetzbuch für die Preussischen Staaten…vom 14 April 1851*, Berlin, 1851), Austrian Code of 1852 (*Das Strafgesetz über Verbrechen, Vergehen und Übertretungen, die Strafgerichts-Competenz-Verordnungen und die Preßordnung vom 27. Mai 1852 für das Raiserthum Österreich*, Wien, 1852), Portugal Code of 1852, Tuscan Code of 1853, Sardinia criminal Code of 1859 (governing Piedmont, Sardinia and Lombardia), *Criminalgesetzbuch für das Königreich Sachsen vom 11. August 1855…*(Leipzig, 1862), *Das Strafgesetzbuch für das Königreich Bayern vom 10. November 1861* (München, 1861), Swedish Code of 1864, Rumanian criminal Code of 1864, Danish Code of 1866, Belgian Penal Code of 1867, Spanish Code of 1870, *Das neue Strafgesetzbuch für den Norddeutschen Bund… vom 31. Mai 1870* (Berlin, 1870), German Code of 1871 (*Das Strafgesetzbuch für das Deutsche Reich*), Hungarian Code of 1878, Dutch Code of 1881; Portugal Code of 1886, Zanardelli Code of 1889; Finland Code of 1889, Bulgarian Code of 1896; see also the first 20th-century criminal code of Europe: the Norwegian Code of 1902.

[33]Feuerbach's main merit, however, consisted in the legal recognition of the principle of legality within the political context of an absolutist state. While in France the principle of legality was recognized in the context of a political revolution to set up a liberal system, in Bavaria the principle was legally—not constitutionally, like in France—recognized in the absolutist system. On the Bavarian criminal code of 1813, see the classical works written by Ludwig von Jagermann, *Das neue Badische Strafgesetzbuch mit systhematischen Übersichten, Competenzbezeichnungen, Parallelstellen, Register u.s.w., zur Erleichterung des Gebrauchs, besonders für Beamte und Geschworne* (Karlsruhe, 1851); Karl Scheickert, *Das badische Strafedikt von 1803 und das Strafgesetzbuch von 1845. Ein Beitrag zur Geschichte der deutschen Partikularstrafgesetzgebung im 19. Jahrhundert* (Freiburg, 1903); see also Hall, "Nulla Poena sine Lege", pp. 169–170.

Declaration of the Rights of Man and of the Citizen (1789)[34] and the *French Constitution* of 1791.

The principle of legality was not conceived in the 18th and 19th centuries, for it had historical antecedents,[35] nor was the dissemination of the legality principle mainly due to the influence of the French code over other European jurisdictions. In the 19th-century Spain, for example, the criminal codes reflected the principle of legality after all constitutions (1812, 1837, 1845, 1869, 1876) prescribed it,[36] though the text of Cádiz did not expressly recognize the legality principle.[37]

---

[34]Art. 8 Bavarian criminal Code: "No one can be punished except under prior law and legally applied to the crime"; see also Hall, "Nulla Poena sine Lege", pp. 169–170.

[35]On the history of this principle, see J. Ballesteros Llompart, "La Historia y la Historicidad del principio jurídico *nulla poena sine lege*", *Estudios en honor al prof. José Corts Grau* (Valencia, 1977), I, pp. 521–537; César Camargo Hernández, "El Principio de legalidad de los delitos y de las penas", *Revista de la Facultad de Derecho de la Universidad de Madrid*, vol. III, nº5, 1959; Christos Dedes, "Sobre el origen del principio «nullum crimen nulla pena sine lege»," *Revista de Derecho Penal y Criminología*, 2ª Época, nº 9 (2002), pp. 141–146; J. Guallart/L. de Goicoechea, "El principio «Nullum crimen, nulla poena sine previa lege» en los Fueros de Aragón," *Homenaje a la memoria de Don Juan Moneva* (Zaragoza, 1954), pp. 659–682; on the history of this principle in the Spanish historiography, Aniceto Masferrer, "La historiografía penal española del siglo XX. Una aproximación a sus principales líneas temáticas y metodológicas", *Rudimentos Legales* 5 (2003), footnote n. 199; in the German historiography, see A. Schottländer, *Die geschichtliche Entwicklung des Satzes: Nulla poena sine lege* (Ruprecht-Karls-Universität Heidelberg, 1911) (*Strafrechtliche Abhandlungen* 1, Heft 132, 1911); Volker Krey, *Keine Strafe ohne Gesetz. Eine Einführung in die Dogmengeschichte des Satzes "nullum crimen, nulla poena sine lege"* (Berlin-New York, 1983); Rolf Sprandel, "Ivo von Chartres und die moderne Doktrin «nulla poene sine lege»," *Zeitschrift der Savigny-Stiftung für Rechtsgechichte.* Kanonistische Abteilung 47 (1961) pp. 95–108; in the Anglo-American historiography, see Hall, "Nulla Poena sine Lege", pp. 165–193; Stanislaw Pomorski, *American Common Law and the Principle Nullum Crimen sine Lege* (Elzbieta Chodakowska trans., 2nd ed., 1975); Aly Mokhtar, "Nullum Crimen, Nulla Poena Sine Lege: Aspects and Prospects," (2005) *Statute Law Review* 26: 41.

[36]Only the Constitution of 1812 did not expressly mention this principle, although it can be deduced from the interpretation of certain precepts: Article 9, Constitution 1837; Article 9, Constitution 1845; Article 10, Constitution *nonnata* (1856); Article 11, Constitution 1869; Article 16, Constitution 1876; see also Article 28, Constitution 1931; Articles 3 and 25(1), Constitution of 1978.

[37]On the evolution of this principle in Spanish constitutionalism, see Agustín Ruíz Robledo, "El principio de legalidad penal en la historia constitucional española", *Revista de Derecho Político* XLII (1997), pp. 137–169; see also Mirow, "The Legality Principle and the Constitution of Cádiz", cited in the fn n. 17; Matthew C. Mirow, "Codification and the Constitution of Cádiz", *Estudios Jurídicos en Homenaje al Professor Alejandro Guzmán Brito* (Patricio-Ignacio Carvajal and Massimo Miglietta, eds.) (Edizioni dell'Orso, 2014), vol. 3, pp. 343–361 (available at http://papers.ssrn.com/sol3/papers.cfm?abstract_id=1844438); see also Alejandro Agüero & Marta Lorente, "Penal enlightenment in Spain: from Beccaria's reception to the first criminal code" (15. Noviembre 2012), *forum historiae iuris*, nn. 36 & 47 *in fine* (available at http://www.forhistiur.de/2012-11-aguero-lorente/; it has also been republished in *The Spanish Enlightenment revisited*, Jesús Astigarraga, ed., Voltaire Foundation–University of Oxford, 2015).

This also occurred in the Germany[38] and probably in many other European countries.

3 Criminal Law Development and Criminal Codes as Continuity and Legal Reform

As mentioned above, from the political point of view the 19th century criminal law system experienced a clear 'break' from tradition, not because of the novelty of its principles, but because of its introduction in both national constitutions ('constitutionalization') and codes ('legalization').

On the contrary, speaking strictly from the perspective of criminal law jurisprudence, both 'continuity' and 'reform' are better terms to describe the development of criminal law from the 18th century to the 19th century. This explains why modern criminal law codes, adopting the 'constitutionalized' criminal law principles, contained many criminal law notions, categories and institutions that stemmed from the tradition. Therefore, I must refute Pacheco's claim that codification was "the system of absolute change".[39]

The *Code pénal* was not the first European criminal code. Several criminal law statutes and codes had been enacted in 18th-century Europe: the Bavarian code of 1751 (Joseph III),[40] the Austrian criminal ordinance of 1768 (Marie Therese),[41] the code of Catherine II (never in force), the Tuscan code of 1786 (Leopold II),[42] the Austrian

[38]In Germany, for example, Art. 103. 2 of the current German constitution is a clear provision in line with German constitutional history itself, considering some of their constitutions, namely, that of Hessen (17.XII.1820, §105); the *Constitution of the Prussian state* (5.XII.1848, §§7–8) within both the *oktroyierte Verfassung* (1848–1850) and *reidierte Verfassung*, respectively; and the Weimar Constitution (11.VII.1919, art. 116); among others; see the *Dokumente zur Deutschen Verfassungsgeschichte* (Herausgegeben von Ernst Rudolf Huber), 1961. I use the 3rd edition of W. Kohlhammer Verlag, Stuttgard-Berlin-Köln-Mainz, Band 1: *Deutsche Verfassungsdokumente 1803–1850* (1978); Band 2: *Deutsche Verfassungsdokumente 1851–1900* (1986); Band 4: *Deutsche Verfassungsdokumente 1919–1933* (1991); see also Fritz Hartung, *Deutsche Verfassungsgeschichte vom 15. Jahrhundert bis zur Gegenwart* (Stuttgart: Koehler, 9th ed., 1969), pp. 310–342; on this matter, see Masferrer, "The Principle of Legality and Codification in the 19th-century Western Criminal Law Reform", cited in the fn n. 22.

[39]See the footnote n. 6.

[40]*Codex Iuris Bavarici Criminalis de anno MDCCLI* (München, 1751); that code was a traditional *ius commune* type of code such as the famous Carolina of 1532; thus it was not a comprehensive code since many other laws complemented it; one might even argue that it was not a real code from a modern perspective.

[41]*Constitutio Criminalis Theresiana oder der Römisch-Kaiserl. zu Hungarn und Böheim* etc. *König. Apost. Majestät Maria Theresia Erzherzogin zu Oesterreich* etc. *Peinliche Gerichtsordnung vom 31. Dezember 1768* (Wien, 1769).

[42]*Riforma della legislazione criminale Toscana del di 30 novembre 1786* (Siena, 1786); there is a French version: *Nouveau Code criminel pour le Grand-Duché de Toscane* (Lausanne, 1787).

criminal code of 1787 (Joseph II),[43] the French Code of 1791 (General Assembly),[44] the Prussian *Allgemeines Landrecht* of 1794 (Frederick William II),[45] and the Austrian criminal code of 1803,[46] among others.[47] Although some were more humanitarian and enlightened than others,[48] all (except France's) were drafted in similar political contexts in that they were enacted by monarchs rather than parliaments. This led some scholars to distinguish between 'enlightened codes' and 'liberal codes,'[49] which may account for some of the (political) "absolute change" of which Pacheco spoke.

However, whether they were 'enlightened' or 'liberal', most of the notions, categories and institutions they contained came from the same tradition. While *ius commune* lawyers defended the majority of the criminal law principles that enlightened figures later regarded as 'modern', the codes' drafters resorted to the classic categories and institutions had been in force for several centuries and seen scholarly development by lawyers from the 14th century onwards.[50]

This is not to deny the codification movement's positive contribution to the development of criminal law. That contribution can be synthesized in three words: systematization, humanization and secularization. Indeed, the whole codification process entailed gradual and clear processes of systematization, humanization, and secularization.[51]

[43] *Allgemeines Gesetz über Verbrechen und derselben Bestrafung vom 13. Januar 1787* (Wien, 1787). A German-Polish version was also edited (Wien, 1787).

[44] *Code pénal des 25 septembre–6 October 1791*, in *Collection des lois, décrets, ordonnances, réglements et avis du Conseil d'Etat, publiée sur les editions officielles*...par J.B. Duvergier, t. III; it was also edited in H. Remy, *Les principes généraux du code penal de 1791* (Paris, 1910), pp. 242 ff.

[45] *Allgemeines Landrecht für die Preussischen Staten vom 5. Februar 1794*, Bd. I-IV (Berlin, 1794); it has also been edited as *Allgemeines Landrecht für die Preußischen Staaten von 1794*. Mit einer Einführung von Dr. Hans Hattenhauer und einer Bibliographie von Dr. Günther Bernert. 2. Auflage. Neuwied-Kriftel-Berlin, 1994; see also Arno Burschmann, *Textbuch zur Strafrechtsgeschichte der Neuzeit. Die klassischen Gesetze* (München, 1998), pp. 272 ff.; the German historiography has considerably critizised this code, considering it as a 'dinosaur of the criminal law' (Klaus Volk, "Napoleon und das deutsche Strafrecht", *JuS* 1991, p. 282).

[46] *Strafgesetz über Verbrechen und schwere Polizei-Übertretungen vom 3. September 1803* (*JGS*, Wien, 1816, n. 626, pp. 313 ff.).

[47] Following the Austrian criminal code of 1787 (Joseph II), other codes were enacted by François II in the late 18th–early 19th centuries, namely, the criminal code of 1796 (*Stradgesetzbuch für Westgalizien vom 17. Junius 1796*, in *Gesetz und Verfassungen im Justizfache, Justizgesetzsammlung –JGS–*, Praghe, 1796).

[48] In this regard, it is clear than the code of 1786 and the Austrian criminal code of 1787 were more heavily influenced by the Enlightenment and enlightened humanitarianism than the Bavarian code of 1751 and the Austrian criminal ordinance of 1768; on this matter, see Leslau Pauli, *Peines corporelles et capitales dans la législation des États européens des années 1751–1903* (Warsawa-Krakow, 1986), pp. 10–15; Marc Ancel, "The Collection of European Penal Codes and the Study of comparative Law," (1957–1958) 106 *U. Pa. L. Rev.* 329, pp. 344–345.

[49] See the fn n. 13.

[50] On this matter, see, for example, Michele Pifferi, *Generalia delictorum. Il Tractatus criminalis di Tiberio Deciani e la "parte generale" di diritto penale* (Milano: Giuffrè, 2006).

[51] On this matter, see Masferrer, "Codification of Spanish Criminal Law in the Nineteenth Century...", pp. 111–139; Masferrer, "Liberal State and Criminal Law Reform in Spain", pp. 25–27.

Let me emphasize that the codification scheme was never generally understood as a legal tool to break from the past. It contributed to the consolidation of political criminal law reforms that had already been introduced by the liberal system previously laid down in the constitutions.

The question as to whether modern codes constituted a break with the past or merely reformed from a historical point of view has been extensively explored in France,[52] Germany[53] and Spain.[54] The developments in Belgium,[55] Italy,[56] and England,[57] among others,[58] have also seen smaller efforts.

---

[52]On this matter, see Masferrer, "Continuismo, reformismo y ruptura en la Codificación penal francesa…' cited in fn n. 26; see also X. Rousseau/M.-S. Dupont-Bouchat, "Revolutions et justice penale. Modeles français et traditions nationales (1780–1830)", *Revolutions et justice en Europe. Modeles français et traditions nationales (1780–1830)* (Paris: L'Harmattan, 1999), pp. 9–15.

[53]On the discussion about continuity and reform in nineteenth century Germany, see Karl Härter, "Kontinuität und Reform der Strafjustiz zwischen Reichsverfassung und Rheinbund", *Reich oder Nation? Mitteleuropa 1780–1815* (herausgegeben von Heinz Duchhardt und Andreas Kunz). *Veröffentlichungen des Instituts für Europäische Geschichte Mainz*, Abteilung Universalgeschichte, Beiheft 46 (Mainz, 1998), pp. 219–278; Regula Ludi, *Die Fabrikation des Verbrechens. Zur Geschichte der modernen Kriminalpolitik 1750–1850* (Frühneuzeit-Forschungen 5) (Tübingen, bibliotheca academica, 1999) (a review of this research can be found in Karl Härter, "Von der «Entstehung des öffentlichen Strafrechts» zur «Fabrikation des Verbrechens». Neuere Forschungen zur Entwicklung von Kriminalität und Strafjustiz im früheneuzeitlichen Europa", *Rechtsgeschichte. Zeitschrift des Max-Planck-Institut für europäische Rechtsgeschichte* 1 (2002), pp. 159–196); Karl Härter, "Reichsrecht und Reichsverfassung in der Auflösungsphase des Heiligen Römischen Reichs deutscher Nation: Funktionsfähigkeit, Desintegration und Transfer", *Zeitschrift für Neue Rechtsgeschichte* 28 (2006), Nr. 3/4, pp. 316–337.

[54]Masferrer, *Tradición y reformismo en la Codificación penal española*, cited in the fn n. 8.

[55]Fred Stevens, "La codification penale en Belgique. Heritage français et debats neerlandais (1781–1867)", *Le penal dans tous ses Etats. Justice, Etats et Sociétés en Europe (XIIe-Xxe siècles)* (Bruxelles, 1997), pp. 287–302.

[56]Mario Da Passano, "La codification du droit pénal dans l'Italie jacobine et napoleonienne", *Revolutions et justice en Europe. Modeles français et traditions nationales (1780–1830)* (Paris: L'Harmattan, 1999), pp. 85–99.

[57]Clive Emsley, "Law Reform and Penal Reform in England in the Age of the French Revolution", *Revolutions et justice en Europe. Modeles français et traditions nationales (1780–1830)* (Paris: L'Harmattan, 1999), pp. 319–331.

[58]On the influences exerted on the French codification, see Jacques Godechot, "Les influences étrangères sur le droit pénal de la Révolution française", *La revolution et l'ordre juridique privé. Rationalité ou scandale? Actes du colloque d'Orléans (11–13 septembre 1986)* (Orléans, 1988), I, pp. 47–53.

4 Tradition and Foreign Influences in the Codification of Criminal Law

The question as to whether modern criminal codes constituted a break with the past or just a degree of reform touches on a difficult issue, namely, the dichotomy between tradition and foreign influences in the criminal codes. Those who—like Pacheco—stress that the codes broke with the past, usually tend to overemphasize foreign influences on the criminal codes. Affirming that the codes broke with the past also discourages the study of the criminal law tradition.

Conversely, those who argue that codes did not constitute a break with the past and contained many traditional institutions have the opposite tendency, underrating the role of foreign models. According to them, the drafters did not feel the need to resort to foreign codes in drafting the codes. Since codes cannot come out of the blue, the proportions of tradition and foreign influence need to be carefully explored. This would enable assessments of the extent to which the codification process in a given jurisdiction brought with it a nationalization or denationalization of its criminal law.[59]

Scholars have unduly ignored this important subject. German historiography has dealt with the influence of the Napoleonic code over the German codification of criminal law. France occupied the left bank of the Rhine since 1797, and from that year onwards implemented French law in the former German territories which were formally ceded to France through the peace treaty of Luneville (1801).[60] This might partly explain the interest of German historiography in the French influence.[61]

---

[59]On this matter, see Aniceto Masferrer, "Codification as Nationalization or Denationalization of Law: The Spanish Case in Comparative Perspective", *Comparative Legal History* 4.2 (2016), pp. 100–130; see also Heikki Pihlajamäki, "Private Law Codification, Modernization and Nationalism: A View from Critical Legal History", *Critical Analysis of Law* 1:2 (2015), pp. 135–152 (available at http://cal.library.utoronto.ca/index.php/cal/article/view/22518).

[60]Reiner Schulze, "Rheinisches Recht im Wandel der Forschungsperspektiven", *ZNR* (2002), pp. 65–90, particularly p. 67; Elisabeth Fehrenbach, *Traditionale Gesellschaft und revolutionäres Recht: Die Einführung des Code Napoleón in den Rheinbundestaaten* (Göttingen, 3 edic., 1983); Stefan Kleinbreuer, *Das Rheinische Strafgesetzbuch. Das materielle Strafrecht und sein Einfluß auf die Strafgesetzgebung in Preußen und im Norddeutschen Bund* (Bonn, 1999); regarding both the private law and the procedural private law, see also Werner Schubert, *Französisches Recht in Deutschland zu Beginn des 19. Jahrhunderts. Zivilrecht, Gerichtsverfassungsrecht und Zivilprozeßrecht* (Köln, 1977).

[61]On this matter, see Von Kräwel, "Über die französischen Elemente im Preußischen Strafgesetzbuch", *Archiv für Preußisches Strafrecht*, Berlin I (1853), pp. 461 ff.; Fritz Hartmann, *Der Einfluß des französischen Rechts auf das Preußische Strafgesetzbuch von 1851 (Allgemeiner Teil)*. Göttingen, 1923; Volk, "Napoleon und das deutsche Strafrecht", pp. 281–285; Frank Zieschang, *Das Sanktionensystem in der Reform des französischen Strafrechts im Vergleich mit dem deutschen Strafrecht* (Berlin, 1992); Werner Schubert, *Der Code pénal des Königreichs Westphalen von 1813 mit dem Code pénal von 1810 im Original und in deutscher Übersetzung* (Frankfurt/Main: Peter Lang, 2001); Christian Brandt, *Die Entstehung des Code pénal von 1810 und sein Einfluß auf die Strafgesetzgebung der deutschen Partikularstaaten des 19. Jahrhunderts am Beispiel Bayerns und Preußens* (Frankfurt/Main: Peter Lang, 2002); on the codification of

A group of Spanish scholars have been working on this subject recently, and some results have been published. In the domain of criminal law, the outcomes have been revealing indeed.[62]

For example, chapters IV and V of an edited volume on foreign influences on the Spanish criminal codes of 1822 and 1848 show (i) scant doctrinal or historiographical references to foreign influences on either criminal text; (ii) the direct influence of the Napoleonic code was much slighter than one could expect, given with the received wisdom mentioned above, particularly on the 1848 criminal code; and (iii) drafters' careful examination of both the criminal law tradition and other (non-French) foreign models.[63]

4.1 *Tradition Versus Foreign Influence?*

Familiarity with tradition is the best way to ascertain the weight of foreign influences, and, by the same logic, the study of the foreign influences enhances the recognition of the weight of tradition.

It would be wrong to think that tradition and foreign influences are mutually exclusive. As has been argued elsewhere,[64] it would be unwise to overlook that the

---

criminal law in Germany, see Wolfgang Sellert, "Strafrecht und Strafrechtskodifikation im 18. und 19. Jahrhundert in Deutschland", *Rechtsgeschichtliche Abhandlungen. Publikationen des Lehrstuhls für Ungarische Rechtsgeschichte an der Eötvös-Loránd-Universität*, Redakteur Barno Mezey, Band 21 (Budapest, 1997), pp. 131–139; Jörg Engelbrecht, "The French Model and German Society: the Impact of the Code Penal on the Rhineland", *Revolutions et justice en Europe. Modeles français et traditions nationales (1780–1830)* (Paris: L'Harmattan, 1999), pp. 101–107; see also Masferrer, "Continuismo, reformismo y ruptura en la Codificación penal francesa…", cited in the fn n. 26.

[62]Aniceto Masferrer, "The Napoleonic *Code pénal* and the Codification of Criminal Law in Spain", *Le Code Pénal. Les Métamorphoses d'un Modèle 1810–2010. Actes du colloque international Lille/Ghent, 16–18 décembre 2010* (Chantal Aboucaya & Renée Martinage, coords.) (Lille: Centre d'Histoire Judiciare, 2012), pp. 65–98; Aniceto Masferrer (ed.), *La Codificación española. Una aproximación doctrinal e historiográfica a sus influencias extranjeras, y a la francesa en particular* (Pamplona: Aranzadi–Thomson Reuters, 2014). Aniceto Masferrer (ed.), *La Codificación penal española. Tradición e influencias extranjeras: su contribución al proceso codificador*. Parte General (Pamplona: Aranzadi–Thomson Reuters, 2017).

[63]I. Ramos Vázquez/J. Cañizares-Navarro, "La influencia francesa en la primera Codificación española: el Código penal francés de 1810 y el Código penal español de 1822", *La Codificación española. Una aproximación doctrinal e historiográfica a sus influencias extranjeras, y a la francesa en particular* (Aniceto Masferrer, ed.) (Pamplona: Aranzadi–Thomson Reuters, 2014), pp. 153–212; see also Aniceto Masferrer/Dolores del Mar Sánchez-González, "Tradición e influencias extranjeras en el Código penal de 1848. Aproximación a un mito historiográfico", *La Codificación española. Una aproximación doctrinal e historiográfica a sus influencias extranjeras, y a la francesa en particular* (Aniceto Masferrer, ed.) (Pamplona: Aranzadi–Thomson Reuters, 2014), pp. 213–274.

[64]Masferrer, "Codification as Nationalization or Denationalization of Law: The Spanish Case in Comparative Perspective", cited in the fn n. 58.

codes, inasmuch as they consecrated the notions, categories and principles of the *ius commune* tradition, had a 'supranational' flavor, and simultaneously took the guise of 'national' law once integrated into the tradition of *ius proprium*. A code is never purely a national product.[65]

It would therefore be pointless to hold that any influence or element arising from foreign models represented a 'denationalization' of the law or constituted a threat to the legal tradition. We should examine in each case whether an alleged foreign influence could have come from the doctrinal development of categories and principles of *ius commune* and become integrated into the tradition of *ius proprium* of several Spanish territories rather than from a genuine transplant or adoption of an institution foreign to the peninsular tradition. Hence, it would be unwise to hastily conclude that some articles of a code broke with tradition because they had been adopted from a foreign code. In the civil law domain, for example, it should be examined to what extent the articles about obligations and contracts implied a consecration of an old Spanish tradition thanks to the scholarly contributions of the French jurists Jean Domat (1625–1696),[66] Henri François D'Aguesseau (1668–1751)[67] and Robert-Joseph Pothier (1699–1772),[68] despite the similarity of their formulations among the French, Spanish and Italian civil codes, among others.

The same idea applies to criminal law. There was a 'supranational' criminal law science reflected in a number of treatises, which were well known and used by lawyers and judges all over Europe. Hence, it would be pointless to regard some categories as 'foreign' merely based on their origins in foreign codes. There are different ways to adopt an institution contained in a foreign code. Such a code might be perfectly in line with the target legal tradition. Moreover, legal transplants do not necessarily imply the rejection of the target legal tradition.[69] The *Kulturtransfer* or *transferts culturels* theory, for example, is a methodology that analyzes how foreign elements can be adopted in a given society and emphasizes how foreign elements can change in the course of adoption.[70]

---

[65]On this matter, see Bernardino Bravo Lira, "Fortuna del Código penal español de 1848. Historia en cuatro actos y tres Continentes: de Mello Freire y Zeiller a Vasconcelos y Seijas Lozano", *AHDE* 74 (2004), pp. 23–58, p. 24.

[66]Jean Domat, *Les lois civiles dans leur ordre natural*, 3 vols. (Paris, 1689–1694).a

[67]Henri F. D'Aguesseau, *Oeuvres complètes du chancelier d'Aguesseau*, 13 vols. (Paris, 1759–1789); Jean M. Pardessus edited a revised version in 16 vols (Paris, 1819).

[68]Robert Joseph Pothier, *Pandectae Iustinianeae in novum ordinem digestae*, 3 vols. (Paris, 1748–1752); *Traité des obligations*, 2 vols. (Paris, Orleans, 1761–1764).

[69]On this matter, see Alain Watson, *Legal Transplants* (Edinburgh, 1974; Athens, Ga., 1993, 2ª ed.); for the opposite view, see Pierre Legrand, "The Impossibility of 'Legal Transplants'" 4 *Maastricht Journal of European and Comparative Law* 1997, 111 ff.; Watson's answer to Pierre Legrand can be seen in Alain Watson, 'Legal Transplants and European Private Law' *Electronic Journal of Comparative Law* vol. 4.4 (December 2000) (available at http://www.ejcl.org/ejcl/44/44-2.html).

[70]M. Espagne & M. Werner, "Deutsch-französischer Kulturtransfer im 18. und 19. Jahrhundert. Zu einem neuen interdiszipliären Forschungsprogramm des C.N.R.S." (1985) 13 *Francia: Forschungen zur westeuropäischen Geschichte*, pp. 502–510; M. Espagne & M. Werner, "La construction d'une référence culturelle allemande en France: genèse et histoire (1750–1914)"

4.2 Types of Foreign Influences

In analyzing the scope of a foreign influence, it is important to distinguish between three different kinds of influences: (1) the idea of the code itself; (2) the formal or structural influence; and (3) the substantive influence.

4.2.1 The Idea of the Code Itself

The historiographical literature has ascribed such influence of the *Code pénal* of Napoleon over other European and Latin American jurisdictions due to its being the first modern criminal code in Europe. As mentioned above, several codes had been enacted in Europe during the late 18th century and early 19th centuries,[71] but the Napoleonic criminal code was the first that can be regarded as 'modern' or 'liberal'.[72] This expression refers to its promulgation within the context of a liberal system. More specifically, this entails: (a) its approval by a parliament, not a king; (b) the recognition of national sovereignty instead of absolute monarchy; and (c) the introduction of the liberal principles of legality and equality.

As the first modern, liberal code of Europe, the Napoleonic code was a reference point for other European countries on the road to codifying their criminal law. This yielded France the advantage of being the first continental country to experience a liberal revolution. From then on, hardly any country could codify its criminal law without consulting Napoleon's model. Not surprisingly, the French criminal code was translated into other languages: English,[73]

(1987) 42 *Annales. Économies, Sociétés, Civilisations*, 969–92; Michel Espagne, *Les transferts culturels francoallemand* (Paris: Presses Universitaires de France, 1999).

[71]See the footnotes n. 25 ff., and their main texts.

[72]Now I'm using the expression 'modern' as synonym of 'liberal.' This does not mean that I fully disagree with the Cartuyvles' notion of 'modern codes', referring to those that were promulgated in the second half of the 18th century and in the context of absolutist monarchies (Prussia, 1748; Bavaria, 1751; Russia, 1767; Toscania, 1786; Austria, 1787; Lombardia, 1791; and again Prussia, 1794). I agree that these codes can be regarded as 'qualitative' in the sense that were part of a new political and philosophical project based on state monism and natural law. However, 18th-century 'modern codes' (as Cartuyvels call them) could not compete with the 19th-century 'liberal codes' that were promulgated within a constitutional political context that implied the recognition of national sovereignty—instead of absolute monarchy—and the guarantee of the liberal principles of legality and equality; in other words, although they might be somehow regarded as 'modern' from a scholarly or jurisprudential perspective, political absolutism burdened them considerably; on this matter, see Cartuyvels, *D'où vient le code pénal?: une approche généalogique des premiers codes pénaux absolutistes au XVIIIe siècle*, and Cartuyvels, "Eléments pour une approche généalogique du code penal", both cited in the footnote n. 13.

[73]For English-speaking territories, there are several translations, including that of J. Fergus Belanger (1811); see also *The Penal Code of France, Translated into English*... (London: H. Butterworth, 1819); in the 20th century, see that of Jean F. Moreau & Gerhard O.W. Mueller, *The Penal Code of France* (1960; see a review of it on http://www.jstor.org/pss/3478667).

German,[74] and Spanish.[75] Nonetheless, one should note that French was then the most well-known language in Europe. It was read and used by many intellectuals from several European countries, as was explicitly recognized by Conde de Toreno, a member of the 1822 Spanish parliament.[76]

This explains why the Napoleonic code was used as a model, cited so frequently in the concordances of other codes and the parliamentary debates, as well as being used as a comparative-law reference.

Interestingly, this also happened in some common law jurisdictions outside the civil law tradition.[77] Despite the variety of codes enacted throughout Europe, the French codification has been erroneously regarded among common law lawyers as the 'continental model' of codification, perhaps because of its great influence.[78]

---

[74]There are several translations of the *Code pénal* into German: F. C. Flaxland/Faustin Hélie, *Criminal-Gesetzgebung des französischen Reichs 2. Pönal-Codex oder Gesetzbuch der Verbrechen und Strafen* (Straßburg: Treuttel 1810); *Strafgesetzbuch des französischen Reiches: nach dem offiziellen Texte übersetzt*/von Joh. Birnbaum, Richter zu Trier (Trier: J. J. Lintz, 1810); *Code pénal. Aus dem Franz. nach der officiellen Ausg. übers. von Wilhelm Blanchard* (Köln 1811; that was the official translation for the Rhineland); *Straf-Codex für das französische Reich. Übersetzt und mit Anmerkungen so wie mit einer Übersicht der neuen französichen Criminal-Prozess-Ordnung versehen von L. Hundrich* (Magdeburg 1811, ND 2006); *Napoleons peinliches und Polizey - Strafgesetzbuch. Nach der Original-Ausgabe übersetzt, mit einer Einleitung und Bemerkungen über Frankreichs Justiz- und Polizey-Verfassung, die Motive dieser Gesetzgebung und ihre Verhältnisse zu Oesterreichs und Preußens Gesetzbüchern von Theodor Hartleben* (Frankfurt a. M., 1811); Heinrich Gottfried Wilhelm Daniels, *Criminal-Gesetzbuch Frankreichs*, Tl. 1-2, 2. verb. und verm. Aufl. (Köln 1812); Johann Wilhelm August Rosenthal, *Wesentliche Grundzüge des Strafgesetzbuchs Frankreichs; übersichtlich und systematisch darstellt, und mit einem möglichst vollständigen Sachregister versehen, nebst einem, die besondern Gesetze und Decrete in alphabetischer Ordnung enthaltenen Anhange* (Hamburg: Bohn 1812); *Der Code pénal des Königreichs Westphalen von 1813 mit dem Code pénal von 1810 im Original und in deutscher Übersetzung, hrsg. und mit einer Einl. versehen von Werner Schubert* (Frankfurt am Main [u.a.] 2001); Schubert, *Der Code pénal des Königreichs Westphalen von 1813 mit dem Code pénal von 1810*...cit., pp. 12–13; on this issue, see K. Härter, "The Influence of the Napoleonic Penal Code of 1810 on the Development of Criminal Law in Central Europe," published in this volume.

[75]For Spain, see the *Código penal del imperio Francés, traducido en lengua española por el texto de la edición original y la unica que [...] publicado de oficio, por el jurisconsulto Don Benito Redondo,...* (Paris: P.-N. Rougeron, 1810); *Code pénal de l'empire français, traduit en langue espagnole sur le texte de l'édition originale et seule officielle*, par Don Benoit Redondo.

[76](Conde de Toreno) "La situación de la Francia con respecto á este asunto es diferente de la nuestra. Su idioma es general en toda la Europa, al paso que el nuestro es muy poco usado. Si allí se escribiese un periódico en lengua española, solo circularía aquí, y poco daño podría hacer a otras potencias, pero escrito en lengua francesa circularía por toda la Europa..." (DSC, Congreso, 24 de enero de 1822, p. 1984).

[77]On this matter, see my forthcoming article "French Codification and 'Codiphobia' in the Common Law Tradition", which describes the impact of the French codification in common law jurisdictions.

[78]On this matter, see, for example, William Tetley, "Mixed jurisdictions: common law v. civil law (codified and uncodified)", *4 Unif. L. Rev.* 591 (1999), pp. 600–601; Jean Limpens, "Territorial Expansion of the Code," Bernard Schwartz (ed.), *The Code Napoleon and the Common-Law World* (New York, 1956—I use the The Lawbook Exchange edition, Union-New Jersey, 1998), 93–109; see Schwartz book's review in Joseph Dainow, "The Civil Code and the Common Law"

In drafting criminal law reports,[79] it was difficult (if not impossible) to ignore the French model,[80] as some primary sources show.[81] However, this does not necessarily mean that the French code was particularly influential or a substantive exemplar, even when it was cited or mentioned. In Western Australia,[82] for

(1956–1967) 51 *Nw. U. L. Rev.* 719; an old, Anglo-American view on the impact of the French codification can be seen in Charles S. Lobinger, "The Napoleon Centenary's Legal Significance", (1921) 55 *Am. L. Rev.* 665.

[79]For a general view on the history of criminal law in nineteenth-century Britain, see William Rodolf Cornish/Jenifer Hart/A.H. Manchester/J. Stevenson, *Crime and Law in Nineteenth Century Britain* (Dublin: Irish University Press, 1978); Sir Leon Radzinowicz/Roger Hood, *A History of English Criminal Law and its Administration from 1750* (London: Stevens & Sons, 1986), vol. 5, pp. 723–740; John Hostettler, *The Politics of Criminal Law Reform in the Nineteenth Century* (Chichester: Barry Rose, 1992); David Bentley, *English Criminal Justice in the Nineteenth Century* (London: Hambledon Press, 1998); David J.A. Cairns, *Advocacy and the Making of the Adversarial Criminal Trial 1800–1865* (Oxford, 1998).

[80]As Hostettler shows, from the *Commissioner's First Report* (1834), it was clear that there was a will to draft a digest with Brougham in charge. Lord Wynford—not willing to follow the French code's example, since the brevity of Napoleon's code "almost put absolute power into the hands of the judges"—warned about the main difficulties of such an undertaking. The notions of code and digest started to get confused, and identifying the code with the French experience wounded British pride (Hostettler, *The Politics of Criminal Law Reform in the Nineteenth Century*, pp. 39–40). Later, Hostettler goes on, four kinds of codification were distinguished, namely, the Bentham Code, the French Code, Partial Codes, like the 1882 *Bill of Exchange Act* and the 1892 *Bill of Sale Of Goods Act*, and the Stephen Code (Hostettler, *The Politics of Criminal Law Reform in the Nineteenth Century*, pp. 210–211); see also M.D. Chalmers, "An Experiment in Codification" (1886) 2 *Law Quarterly Review* 125; the French civil code was immediately translated from French into English: *Code Napoleon; or The French Civil Code*. Literally translated from the original and official edition, published at Paris, in 1804. By a Barrister of the Inner Temple. Claitor's Book Store, Baton Rouge 2, La, 1969 Reprint; the American John Rodman, a prominent member of the metropolitan bar, translated the four French codes.

[81]Anthony Hammond, *A Letter to the Members of the Different Circuits* (London, 1826); *The Criminal Code. Coining*. London, Printed by George Eyre and Andrew Strahan, Printers to the King's Most Excellent Majesty, 1825; Anthony Hammond noted that "this Article of the Criminal Code contains a Digest of Judicial Decisions, a Consolidation of the Enactments, the Opinions of the Texts Writers, and the Law of Scotland and of France; the former from the Commentaries of Mr. Baron Hume, the latter from the Code Napoleon (p. III), see also The *First Report from his Majesty's Commissioners on the Criminal Law, 24th June 1834* (Ordered, by The House of Commons, to be Printed, 30 July 1834) contained as Appendix, several excerpts from both the Louisiana Code (pp. 43–49) and the French Code (pp. 49–51); see *First Report from his Majesty's Commissioners on the Criminal Law (24th June 1834)*. London, 1834, en *Reports from Commissioners*, 22 volumes (8), Session 4 February-15 August 1834, vol. XXVI (1834), pp. 117–177).

[82]On Western Australia, see R.G. Kenny, *An Introduction to Criminal Law in Queensland and Western Australia* (LexisNexis Butterworths, 2008), 7th ed., pp. 1–10; Enid Russell, *A History of the Law in Western Australia and its Development from 1829 to 1979* (University of Western Australia Press, 1980), pp. 233–238; Jeremy Finn, "Codification of the Criminal Law: the Australian Parliamentary Experience," B. Godfrey & G. Dunstall (eds.), *Crime and Empire 1840–1940. Criminal Justice in Local and Global Context* (Cullompton: William Publishing, 2005), 224–237 (also available at http://ir.canterbury.ac.nz/bitstream/10092/1828/1/12590980_Codification%20of%20the%20Criminal%20Law.pdf, which I consulted on August 20, 2016).

example, where a criminal code was enacted in 1902,[83] some references to France can be found in the parliamentary debates.[84] It does not seem to me that they had any relevance in terms of reflecting a particular influence of the *Code pénal* over the Western Australia criminal code.

4.2.2 Formal or Structural Influence

The second level of influence of any foreign code concerns its contribution from the formal or structural point of view. In fact, the greatest legacy of the modern codification was more formal than substantive, with the paramount example being the divide between the General Part and the Special Part.

The divide between a General Part and Special Part was not original to the French criminal code,[85] but its introduction in that code contributed greatly to its propagation in successive European codes. In Spain, for example, the parliamentary debates do not show any reluctance or controversy about this division in general terms or about some specific aspects in the General Part.

Some notions, concepts, categories and 1998 institutions of the French code's General Part certainly became relevant references for the drafters of other European codes, the Spanish one among them. This does not mean, however, that drafters slavishly followed the French paradigm. On the contrary, sometimes drafters

[83]*The Criminal Code of Western Australia, and the Criminal Practice Rules of 1902*, with Index to the Act (1 & 2 Edwd. VII., No. 14) and the Code of Criminal Law set forth in the First Schedule thereof. Perth, W.M. Alfred Watson, Government Printer, 1902; *An Act to Amend the Criminal Code* (Assented to, 20th December, 1902, Western Australia). Perth, W.M. Alfred Watson, Government Printer, 1902; *An Act to Amend the Criminal Code* (Assented to, 20th December, 1902, Western Australia). Perth, W.M. Alfred Watson, Government Printer, 1902 (it contains only a repeal of Subsection 5 of Section 19; and an Amendment of Section 319); *An Act to Amend the Criminal Code* (Assented to 14th December, 1906, Western Australia). Perth, W.M. Alfred Watson, Government Printer, 1902; the current code of Western Australia is the *Criminal Code Act* 1913.

[84]A. Jamenson, the Minister for Lands, in moving the second reading of the Criminal Code Bill, was fully aware of and emphasized the fact that "this is probably the most comprehensive Bill which has ever come before the House", and added: "It is a measure that simplifies and consolidates our criminal law, and thus is entirely in accordance with the progressive spirit of our time. Indeed, I think all progressive countries have a criminal code. I know that these remarks apply to France and Italy, and to all the Northern States of America. Both New Zealand and Queensland have a criminal code. Indeed, the criminal code of Queensland is really the source from which this code has been drawn" (Western Australian Parliamentary Debates, WAPD, vol. XX, p. 2446 [22 January 1902]).

[85]On this matter, see Friedrich Schaffstein, "Tiberius Decianus und seine Bedeutung für die Entstehung des Allgemeinen Teils im Gemeinen deutschen Strafrecht", *Abhandlungen zur Strafrechtsgeschichte und zur Wissenschaftsgeschichte* (Darmstadt: Scientia Verlag Aalen, 1986), pp. 199–226; see also F. Javier Álvarez García, "Relaciones entre la parte general y la parte especial del Derecho Penal (I)", *Anuario del Derecho Penal y de las Ciencias Penales* 46 (1993), f. III, pp. 1021–1023; Masferrer, *Tradición y reformismo en la Codificación penal española…*, pp. 114–117.

deliberately departed from the French model, as will be seen in analyzing the Spanish case.[86]

4.2.3 Substantive Influence

This kind of influence is the most important, since it reveals the extent to which the substantive criminal law contained in a foreign code was adopted in a given target code. More specifically, the substantive depth and breadth of the influence of the Napoleonic code over codifications in other European and Latin American jurisdictions can be difficult to assess. Thorough research is needed to provide such an assessment convincingly.

A complete analysis of a foreign code's influence over the codification in another jurisdiction requires detailed studies of each article, comparing it to the foreign text and looking at the materials used by the drafters.

Further, if the main contribution of the codification to 19th century criminal law could be summarized in its systematization, humanization and secularization, as argued above, another way to consistently explore the influence of a foreign criminal code over other European and Latin American countries would be to trace the development of these three categories that describe modernization in any jurisdiction.

While analyzing the Spanish case some years ago, I concluded that, whereas *Code pénal*'s influence was evident as a legal tool and formal model, the substantive influence was much weaker. I realized that the influence of the French code over the codification of criminal law in Spain was undeniable, but much less than one might have expected, particularly regarding specific criminal law-institutions whose regulation in the first criminal codes (1822 and 1848) revealed both their attachment to the Spanish legal tradition and the influence of other foreign codes, not all of them European (as with the 1830 Brazilian code's on the 1848 Spanish criminal code).[87]

The influence of the French model over other jurisdictions—both European and Latin American—might be weaker and narrower than one might expect. This explains why the French influence in Latin America was more indirect, through

---

[86]See my chapter entitled "The Myth of French Influence over Spanish Codification: The General Part of the Criminal Codes of 1822 and 1848," published in this volume.

[87]Masferrer, "The Napoleonic *Code pénal* and the Codification of Criminal Law in Spain", cited in fn n. 60; see also Emilia Iñesta-Pastor, "The influence of the 1819 criminal code of the Two Sicilies upon the Spanish criminal law codification and the parliament of the nineteenth century", *Culture parlamentari a confronto. Modelli della rappresentanza politica e identità nazionali* (Andrea Romano, ed.) (Bologna: CLUEB, 2016), pp. 245–259; on the weight of the tradition in the Latin American codification of criminal law, see Emilia Iñesta-Pastor, "Los delitos contra la propiedad en la codificación penal hispanoamericana: la pervivencia jurídica indiana," *Actas XVIII Congreso del Instituto Internacional de Historia del Derecho Indiano, Córdoba, Argentina, 2012* (Alejando Agüero & Pedro Yanzi Ferreira eds.) (Córdoba, Argentina, 2016), pp. 1287–1327.

other codes that had been somehow influenced by the French one.[88] Furthermore, historical research has shown that the influence of the Napoleonic criminal code radically decreased after the promulgation of the criminal code of Brazil (1830), whose main drafter, Bernardo Pereira de Vasconcelos, drew much more heavily upon the Austrian criminal code (1803) than the French one (1810).[89] According to this view, the French model was overcome by the superiority of the rational constructions of the Central European ones.[90]

If true, this claim would require reassessment of the notion that from 1830 onwards French influence over the criminal law in European or Latin American jurisdictions came through the Brazilian criminal code.

4.3 An Overview of French Influence Over European and Latin American Codifications of Criminal Law

The matter deserves, however, a much deeper and more exhaustive analysis, and this is precisely the purpose of the present volume, the scope of which extends beyond simply exploring the French influence on the Spanish codification of criminal law.

However, revisiting the commonplace regarding the influence of the French criminal code over Europe and Latin America might also be a fruitful way to dispel the myth and to ascertain the weight of tradition and foreign influences in European and Latin American codifications of criminal law.

---

[88]On this matter, see some works by Emilia Iñesta-Pastor, "La proyección hispanoamericana del Código Penal español de 1848," II, *Estudios, Actas del XIII Congreso del Instituto Internacional de Historia de Derecho Indiano* (González Vale, ed.) (San Juan de Puerto Rico, 2003), pp. 493–521; by the same autor, "El Código Penal chileno de 1874," *Revista Chilena de Historia del Derecho*, 19 (Santiago de Chile, 2006), pp. 293–328; Iñesta-Pastor, Emilia, "Antecedentes histórico-jurídicos del Código penal chileno de 1874", *Derecho, Instituciones y Procesos históricos, XIV Congreso del Instituto Internacional de Historia del Derecho Indiano*, III (José De La Puente Brunke y Armando Guevara Gil, eds.) (Lima: Instituto Riva Agüero, Universidad Pontificia de Lima, 2008), pp. 203–242; by the same author, "La reforma penal del Perú independiente: El Código Penal de 1863," *Actas XV Congreso del Instituto Internacional de Historia del Derecho Indiano*, II, *Córdoba, España, 2005* (Manuel Torres Aguilar, coord.) (Córdoba: Universidad-Diputación, 2008), pp. 1071–1098.

[89]On this matter, see Bravo Lira, "Fortuna del Código penal español de 1848…," pp. 40 ff.; Bernardino Bravo Lira, "Bicentenario del Código penal de Austria. Su proyección desde el Danubio a Filipinas", *Revista de Estudios Histórico-Jurídicos de Valparaíso* (Chile) 26 (2004), pp. 140–145.

[90]Bravo Lira, "Fortuna del Código penal español de 1848…," p. 57 (where the author resorts to the thesis of André-Jean Arnaud, *Origines doctrinelles du code civil français* (Paris, 1969): "Francia no estaba preparada en su conjunto para las construcciones racionalistas que gozaban de gran favor en Europa central. Los juristas franceses seguían adheridos al viejo plan tripartito de las *Instituciones*, con las antedichas aproximaciones al espíritu moderno. Otro tanto hicieron los codificadores").

The book is divided into 15 chapters. After the present introductory chapter—with the title "Tradition and Foreign Influences in the 19th century Codification of Criminal Law: Dispelling the Myth of the Overall French Influence in Europe and Latin America"—Chaps. 2–9 deal with European jurisdictions (Germany, Austria, Belgium, Portugal, Italy and Spain), while Chaps. 10–14 tackle three Latin American jurisdictions (Argentine, Brazil and México). Chap. 15 touches upon the European and US Influences on the 19th century Prison Reform.

Chapter 2 deals with the territories that are part of the present day Germany. With the title "[t]he Influence of the Napoleonic Penal Code on the Development of Criminal Law in Germany: Juridical Discourses, Legal Transfer and Codification", Karl Härter (Max Planck Institute for European Legal History—University of Darmstadt, Germany), points out that the Napoleonic Penal Code of 1810 (*Code pénal)* and its companion, the procedural code of 1808 (*Code d'instruction criminelle)*, which were partly based on the reform discourses of the Enlightenment and the French revolutionary codes of 1791/1795, had a strong and lasting impact on criminal law in Germany. He explains that after the dissolution of the Holy Roman Empire of the German Nation in 1806, the *Code pénal* in particular influenced the German juridical discourse on criminal law as well as the development of criminal codes and respective reform projects in many German states of the Confederation of the Rhine (1806–1813) and the German Confederation (1815–1866).

The chapter gives a systematic survey of these influences that focuses on general aspects of the perception, the transfer and the implementation of the *Code pénal* in exemplary German states under the conditions of cultural and political diversity, legal pluralism and the need to reform and codify criminal law. It outlines the discussion of the *Code pénal* in the contemporary German juridical discourse, depicts various modes of its implementation and adoption in some German territories/states (notably Bavaria and Prussia), and analyzes exemplary problems of the legal transfer: the trinity of punishable offences and the integration of police-contraventions, the penalty system and the purposes of punishment, as well as the infeasibility of a strictly codified conformity of offenses, penal system, and judiciary.

The results are presented by way of discussing which elements and characteristics of the *Code pénal* impeded or promoted its implementation and impact. Härter's analysis reveals characteristic problems with the transfer and implementation of the *Code pénal* in Germany through a 'scientific adjustment' by jurists in cooperation with governments. Whereas the former tried in vain to align their philosophical penal theories with the pragmatic utilitarian orientation of the *Code pénal*, the latter only pursued the interests of the state and rejected constitutional achievements, such as the jury and the public oral trial. Moreover, jurists and governments were reluctant to accept the consequences of codifying the police-contraventions and the respective powers of the police and the administration. With the rejection of 'foreign' French criminal law, the reform process to codify criminal law needed more than 25 years to produce new modern penal codes.

According to Härter, without the model and the direct push of the *Code pénal*, the broad and intense German codification discourse could not produce concrete legislative results. However, the influence of French criminal law continued in the former French territories of the Rhineland in which the *Code pénal* as well as elements of the trial and the judiciary remained in force or were still practiced. Most notably the inhabitants of these territories had accepted the French criminal justice system as the more reliable, efficient, and appropriate system in contrast to the diverse and hybrid German criminal law that still comprised elements of the former *ius commune*. Also the Prussian penal code (1851) adopted the structure and basic principles of the *Code pénal*, most notably in the general introduction that established the three systematically and hierarchically defined categories of crimes, delicts, and contraventions. It followed the penalty system of the *Code pénal* in its primary and supplementary penalties, a defined range of penalties, a system of mitigating circumstances, and discretionary powers of the judges to decide the range of punishment based on the code.

Thus, only in time did German jurists and governments realize the advantages of the *Code pénal*, which were still intensely discussed within the juridical discourse and justice administrations. Karl Härter holds that the main intent of German governments to implement or partly adopt the *Code pénal* from 1810 onwards was not to humanize criminal justice, nor to establish better legal protection for citizens or their civil rights, because they ultimately rejected a constitutional and a civil society as the political and social base of the code. Rather, modern French criminal law was to serve as a means to rationalize, homogenize, and nationalize criminal law, to establish a monopoly of legislative/jurisdictional power based on sovereignty and the nation-state, and to make criminal justice more effective in terms of deterrence, prevention, and state security. As a result, the Napoleonic penal code served as a means of state-building and of 'defensive modernization'. In this regard, the author concludes by affirming that the influence of the *Code pénal* on the development of criminal law in Central Europe underscores the ambiguous nature of the code itself.

In Chap. 3, Martin Paul Schennach (University of Innsbruck, Austria) analyzes the Austrian case with a revealing title: "Ignoring France? Possible French Influences on the Development of Austrian Penal Law in the 19th century."

Schennach argues that widespread evidence suggests that there was no significant reciprocal influence between French and Austrian penal law during the 19th century. First and foremost, the timeline makes any substantial impact of the French code on its Austrian equivalent impossible: the Austrian codification dates from 1803, and the French codification was passed several years later. In addition, there was no indication that the French code of 1791 had any impact on the process of Austrian codification. Clearly, the older Austrian penal code passed in 1787 by Emperor Joseph II was considered a modern and adequate basis, hence there was no need to pursue imported prototypes. There are noted similarities between the French and the Austrian codes—both adopted the principle of legality, threatened potential offenders with severe punishments and placed significant emphasis on crimes against the state –, but these similarities are attributed to common origins in rational law and the Enlightenment. It was only when the first attempt to revise the Austrian code commenced in 1817 that the leading legal scholar Franz von Zeiller explicitly referenced the French code. However, as these efforts led to no reform, this mention of the French Penal Code as a potential role model appears to have been an isolated occurrence. When the Austrian code was finally revised in 1852, the lead scholar, Anton Hye did not use foreign templates; moreover, the French statute would already have been outdated by the middle of the 19th century. Therefore, it is not surprising that the French codification played absolutely no role during the reform debates in Austria in the second half of the 19th century which led to various drafts of penal codes submitted to the Austrian Parliament from the 1860s onwards.

As far as Austrian legal science is concerned, the author gives evidence that none of the commentaries on the Austrian penal code published in the decades after 1803 mentions any French influences or considers French legal literature in a significant way. The same is true for the second half of the 19th century: when Austrian legal scholars adopted a comparative view, they regularly preferred to consult codifications and scientific literature originating from other German-speaking countries.

Chapter 4 touches upon Belgium. With the title "[t]he Influence of the French Penal Code of 1810 on the Belgian Penal Code of 1867: Between Continuity and Innovation," Yves Cartuyvels (University of Saint-Louis—Bruxelles, Belgium) explains that as soon as Belgium became independent, a will to reform the Napoleon Penal Code of 1810 emerged. In 1848, a reform commission initiated the reform process that led to the new Penal Code of 1867. In Cartuyvels' view, the penal reform was marked by multiple influences. The French heritage was analyzed and discussed against the background of legislative changes at work in France at the time and the desire to incorporate home-grown liberal political thought and new ideas of the neoclassical school regarding criminal law, which were blowing across Europe at the time. So, if the influence of France remained important, it was diluted in a movement emphasizing broader European ideas.

Under the direction of H. Haus, a penalist from the Ghent University, the revision process took a rather abstract and technical direction. The revision commission opted for remaining faithful to the main categories of the 1810 French Penal Code, that was considered clearer and more concise than its legislative rival, the Bavarian Penal Code of 1813. Very soon, Haus claimed that he did not intend to create "an entirely new code": it would indeed be "foolish to topple the substantive criminal code from top to bottom and replace it with an entirely different system, for the sake of creating national legislation only." It was therefore no longer a question of replacing the 1810 Penal Code system but merely "to correct its defective parts and to fill in its gaps."

As a consequence, the new penal Code of 1867 did not mark a clear rupture with the imperial Code of 1810. Cartuyvels argues that the text oscillated between reform and continuity, with a specific wish to correct the punitive excesses of the earlier text. However, a number of inflections are noticeable. Thus, the 1867 Code was structured in two parts and not four, as had been the case for the 1810 Code. Haus considered the Code as a logico-deductive whole, with a strong articulation between the general principles of Book I and the incriminations and penalties of Book II. In this perspective, the importance of Book I, dedicated to general principles, became essential, since its construction determined the application of incriminations and penalties *in concreto*. In addition, while the 1810 Penal Code was mainly devoted to the question of specific incriminations and penalties, the Code of 1867 "would reverse the order of priorities,"[91] demonstrating a central interest to the technical discussion of the general principles of criminal law contained in Book I.

Described as "a work of optimism and humanity, hope and faith in the perfectibility of man" (Prins), Cartuyvels points out that the new Code introduced rules that refined and generally softened repression. The 1867 Code deleted the term "afflictive and defamatory punishment", replacing it with "criminal penalty." Following the French penal reform of 1832, the 1867 Code officially abolished several "afflictive" corporal penalties. The author argues that such a softer penology was marked by a double influence. On the one hand, punishment was no longer conceived for its sole function of intimidation, as in the Penal Code of 1810. It now included a concern not only for the criminal's atonement, but also for "a new principle, namely the amendment of the condemned." This new corrective perspective required a radical change in the penal system, with the elimination of various 'cruel' and 'infamous' forms of punishments, which were incompatible with the amendment objective. On the other hand, the debate over the prison issue, which dealt with the execution of the sentence, changed the way to conceive sentencing. The choice made in favor of solitary confinement explains also a change in the scale and length of punishments, which were generally softened.

Although the Belgian Penal Code of 1867 was the result of a political initiative that dates back to the aftermath of the Belgian revolution, its political character was —in Cartuyvels' view—relatively weak. More than a political project, the text therefore bore the seal of neoclassical thought that dominated the legal debate in France and other European countries at the time.

In Chap. 5, Frederico de Lacerda da Costa Pinto (University of Lisbon) and Pedro Caeiro (University of Coimbra) deal with Portugal. With the title "[t]he Influence of the French Penal Code of 1810 over the 'General Part' of the Portuguese Penal Code of 1852: The Visible and the Invisible," the Portuguese authors point out that the influence of the *Code Pénal* 1810 on the 'general part' of the Portuguese Penal Code of 1852 is ambiguous: paradigmatically, contemporaneous literature criticized the Portuguese legislature for both merely copying and not copying closely enough his French counterpart. In fact, and in spite of significant similarities, there is no evidence that the *Code* was explicitly assumed by the Portuguese law makers as a model to be implemented.

Da Costa and Caeiro maintain that the comparison between the two codes results in a mixed picture, which is due to circumstances of a diverse nature. In the first place, the fact that forty years had elapsed since the *Code* had been published allowed for the adoption of other foreign references that came to light in that period

[91]Fr. Tulkens, M. van de Kerchove, Y. Cartuyvels, Ch. Guillain, *Introduction au droit penal. Aspects juridiques et criminologiques* (Diegem: Kluwer, 2014), p. 98.

(in the German States, Spain, Brazil, etc.). The critique of the French Code undertaken by the legal literature was also taken into consideration. In the second place, some of the principles brought by the Enlightenment had already been enacted in the Constitution(s) and other common laws. Finally, the Portuguese legislature recovered some of the proposals laid down by Mello Freire in his draft penal code (1786). Hence, the drafters of the Penal Code of 1852 tried to harmonize—with arguably doubtful success—the Portuguese tradition with solutions provided by several foreign legal traditions—in which the Code played a significant role.

According to Da Costa and Caeiro, a detailed analysis of the general part of the CP 1852 shows that the first section, which deals with the criminal act and its imputation, essentially tracks the Portuguese tradition (especially to Mello Freire's draft penal code) but, in several particular aspects, follows other foreign laws. In contrast, the section that regulates the penalties seems to have been mostly inspired by the French legislation in force at the time, especially by the laws that reformed the *Code* in 1832. In some cases, the Portuguese Code followed, with some adaptations, the solutions provided for by the *Code*, e.g., mitigating circumstances and the implementation of the special surveillance by the police, along with or after the enforcement of certain penalties. In other cases, the legislature plainly copied the French norms, even in cases where the same institution existed already under former Portuguese law. Yet in other cases, Portuguese law departed from the French punitive system, e.g., by referring to individual guilt in a way that could arguably be construed as a requirement and a limit to punishment and by rejecting the penalty of general confiscation.

Chapters 6 and 7 touch upon the codification of criminal law in Italy. In Chap. 6, with the title "An Autonomous Path for the Italian Penal Code of 1889: The Constructing Process and the first Case Law Applications," Stefano Vinci (University of Bari, Italy) claims—after a close examination of parliamentary acts and doctrinal works—that the 'national path' followed by the Italian penal science in the process of drafting the Criminal Code came to light—after a 30-year debate —in 1889. The author argues that the Italian criminal-law codification process reveals the efforts to abandon the 1810 Napoleonic model. However, the promulgation of the new code met with some real practical difficulties, owing to the persistent tradition of the old criminal laws among lawyers and judges.

Vinci's chapter is composed of five parts. The first two parts describe the very long process of codification of the Italian penal code, promulgated in 1889 by Minister Giuseppe Zanardelli. Part three examines the speech of general attorneys of the Court of Cassation which deals with the cultural problems of implementing the new code among lawyers and judges accustomed to the old criminal law. Finally, the last two parts deal with the examination of some practical cases decided by the Supreme Court in Rome, in order to highlight the difficulties encountered in applying the new code.

In the aftermath of Napoleonic rule, those seeking to codify criminal law in the region, a process which began prior to the unification of Italy following the Congress of Vienna, borrowed from many different criminal law traditions. The pre-unitarian Italian governments had introduced different criminal laws mostly modelled after the 1810 Napoleonic Code. The coexistence of these different laws in the various Italian provinces presented a serious obstacle to the consolidation of one unified criminal code. In any case, it became immediately apparent that it would be necessary to build a code having Italian characteristics rather than foreign ones, imported and badly adjusted to Italian customs and tendencies.

Vinci describes the intensive season of studies and proposals which legitimately absorbed Italian scholars and lawyers. In the parliamentary seats and through the pages of the most accredited journals and drafts printed freely, scholars and lawyers sought to contribute to draw up a penal code bearing consolidated and distinctive hallmarks. The obtained code was the result of the Italian liberal criminal law tradition, the postulate of which allowed the passing of a modern and balanced text arising from the remains of the Sardinian penal code—with its French style—and the Tuscan one—with its German style. Legislators aimed for the new text to be meticulous and succinct. The result was a code with concise definitions and which achieved a satisfactory proportion of parts and homogeneity of formulas, and avoiding any arid case records.

Vinci points out that the code was welcomed by a great number of Italian lawyers who had been waiting for the issuing of a new text for a long time. However, the text did not lead courts to abandon the old code. In fact, legal practitioners happened to enforce the new penal laws in compliance with the Italian and French old case law and doctrinal apparatus. These difficulties were clearly perceived by the Italian lawyers in using the new Code, as they called for a relevant contribution of the Italian judiciary in diligently defining and interpreting the new cases. The earlier case law interventions by the Court of Cassation were basic to steer the lawyers and the lower courts towards the application of the new Code which was soon followed by commentary works. This literature sorted out the most relevant legitimacy rulings, many of which were summarized and noted in the main sector journals that were increasing just in those years. In the first years, journals never lacked—in referring to the pre-existing codes—the comparison, which proved to be necessary to remove any doubt and uncertainty resulting from the several pre-existing codes which often led the lower courts into error.

This transitional period of the new penal code was completed only after the initial years of its application, when the references to the previous codifications by the Court of Cassation started becoming less frequent. In fact, judges started to focus their efforts on the principles of law based on the new rules, many of which were already consolidated in the Supreme Court's case law. Except for the offenses committed under the rule of the previous Sardinian code of 1859 (for which it would have been necessary to conduct an examination of the milder rule between the old and new law),[92] judges of the Supreme Court (Rome) believed the

[92]Corte di Cassazione di Roma, udienza 12 ottobre 1893. *Pres. De Cesare, Est. Onnis, Rc. PM e Forcellino*, "Il foro italiano", a. XIX (1894), vol. XIX, cc. 64–66; Corte di Cassazione di Roma, udeinza 28 dicembre 1893. *Pres. De Cesare, Est. Lucchini, Ric. Porzio*, ivi, cc. 99–100; Corte di Cassazione di Roma, udienza 21 gennaio 1895. *Pres. Canonico, Est. Basile, Ric. Carnevali e Menghini*, "Il foro italiano", a. XX (1895), vol XX, cc. 75–82.

continued comparisons with obsolete provisions or references to preliminary works or parliamentary reports to be unnecessary. Nevertheless, this tendency persisted in the notes accompanying the most relevant and innovative judgments, as a way to better explain the enunciated principle or to disagree with it.

Chapter 7, entitled "[t]he Roots of Italian Penal Codification: Nation Building and the Claim for a Peculiar Identity in Criminal Law," by Michele Pifferi (University of Ferrara, Italy), analyses the discourses used by Italian pre- and post-unitarian jurisprudence to corroborate the existence of a national genius of criminal law.

According to the author, after political unification, jurists were committed to penal codification, which they believed should not be based on foreign models and in particular on the Napoleonic Code (imposed to the Kingdom of Italy from 1811 to 1814), but should correspond to Italy's sophisticated and renowned ancient tradition of criminal law. In order to create—rather than simply recognize—such unitarian and independent tradition, some scholars, in particular Enrico Pessina, emphasised the pivotal role of a national legal history as a cultural means to pave the way to a prompt codification. In Pessina's view, the 'Italianness' of law and legal culture was part of a twofold approach: while, on the one side it looked to the future, in order to plan the legal order of the new state, it also looked to the past to find in long-established practices and principles those signs of continuity in which the 'Italian character' could be identified, despite transitory political fragmentations and regional differences. Therefore, the undisputed value of the Italian tradition of criminal law played, during the unifying process, a double role. On the one hand, its proud evocation was a key argument used by legal culture to avoid the fast imposition of the Sardinian penal code of 1859 to the entire country, because it was considered to be too much influenced by the French model and not corresponding to the most progressive national penal thought. On the other hand, the reference to the founding fathers of Italian criminalistics was exploited as a political strategy to make the differences uniform: it implied a long commitment in order to cast a criminal law community as truly consistent and driven by shared values within a highly diversified country, as well as to draft a feasible penal code embodying the *new* national legal tendency.

Conversely, other scholars, such as Francesco Carrara, Filippo Ambrosoli and Pietro Ellero, more realistically recognized the considerable differences between criminal law approaches as well as the lack of a theoretical identity. Following the Savignyan method, they proposed postponing the national codification until the gradual formation of a truly national criminal law doctrine, influenced neither by the French jurisprudence nor by the German doctrine. Not only did the three different penal codes simultaneously in force testify to the persistent legal fragmentation, but the enthusiasm for the building of the new state was also accompanied by a realistic acknowledgment of the lack of a unique school upon whose theories the penal code could be built. Under the surface of a celebrated Italian tradition, then, there was the criminalistics' diversified world, which, beyond rhetorical reference to common founding fathers, was culturally divided, largely dependent on foreign doctrine, and without any shared legislation or case-law. It was not just a matter of choice between different models—the French one of 1810, the German codes or a third Italian way still to be found—but the very opportunity to enact a code, and above all to do it quickly, was contested, in particular by Carrara and Ellero, who feared a regression in penal civilization caused by the quick imposition to all of the country of the Sardinian Penal Code of 1859, which retained capital punishment and was not inspired by the more modern liberal principles. This approach, claiming the opportunity to codify not until the gradual formation of a national and liberal school of criminal law, was successful. The Zanardelli code of 1889 was the final outcome of this hybrid past- and future-oriented attitude.

Chapter 8 deals with Spain and, more particularly, with—as the title reads—"[t]he Myth of French Influence over Spanish Codification: The General Part of the Criminal Codes of 1822 and 1848", by Aniceto Masferrer (University of Valencia, Spain). Departing from the views of some 19th century criminal lawyers who, like J.F. Pacheco, stated in the old criminal laws "nothing was worthy of respect, or conservation" and "there was only one legitimate and viable system, the system of codification, the system of absolute change," and recognizing that drafters were fully acquainted with the case of France, a jurisdiction that managed to turn its old laws—including the criminal ones—into modern codes (1804–1811), the chapter aims to explore the scope of the foreign influences, that of the French in particular, in the criminal codes of 1822 and 1848/50. In doing do, the author briefly presents the *status quaestionis* of the dichotomy between tradition and foreign influences in the 19th century codification of criminal law, then focuses on the scope of French influence in the criminal codes of 1822 and 1848/50, and concludes with some final considerations.

The results of the author's research dispel the myth of the pervasive French Influence in Spain. Without denying French influence, he argues that the sources, particularly the parliamentary debates, legal doctrine and historiography, enable a more balanced view that shows the specific scope of French influence. In doing so, he applies the abovementioned three levels or types of influence (the idea of the code itself, the formal/structural influence, and the substantive influence) in the context of Spain. In sum, while the French influence on *the idea of the code itself* is undeniable, and *the formal or structural one* was also present—although perhaps slightly weaker than the first one –, *the substantive influence* of the Napoleonic Code over 19th century Spanish criminal codes was much weaker. This was due to three reasons: (i) Spanish criminal law had a long and strong tradition both legally and doctrinally, which was reflected in the divergence of some criminal law institutions from the French model; (ii) the sources document the reluctance of many lawyers to resort to the French model when the Spanish tradition had comparable institutions of its own; and (iii) CP 1848 was the most important as the main model and reference for those that followed. This text shows much richer and diverse foreign influences than the 1822 one, particularly the 1830 Brazilian code, as well as a considerable debt to the Spanish legal tradition. Thus, Masferrer does not hold that French influence was totally absent substantively. It was present, but it was much weaker than it may seem, and weaker than usually maintained in Spanish historiography.

In Chap. 9, with the title "[t]he Influence exerted by the 1819 Criminal Code of the Two Sicilies upon nineteenth-century Spanish Criminal Law Codification and its Projection in Latin America", Emilia Iñesta-Pastor (University of Alicante, Spain) touches upon a particular foreign influence on the 1848 Spanish criminal code and beyond, describing its influence in Latin America.

It would be wrong to deny that 19th century Spanish criminal law codification found its inspiration—along with its own tradition—in foreign model codes. As highlighted by Emilia Iñesta-Pastor, the specific relevance of the 1819 Criminal Code of the Kingdom of the Two Sicilies in Spanish codification has only been studied to a limited extent. Nevertheless, its influence on the 1848 Spanish Criminal Code, considered the most important Criminal Code of 19th century Spain, becomes clearly visible both in the General Part and in the Special Part. Amongst the reasons for the projection of this Code of the Two Sicilies stands out the progress made therein with respect to the 1810 French Criminal Code as a result of the impact caused by the advanced Italian criminal doctrine. These advances will play a significant role in its adoption as a model by the drafters of the 1848 Spanish Criminal Code.

Iñesta-Pastor stresses the fact that the 1819 Criminal Code of the Two Sicilies derived not only from the influence exerted by the 1810 French criminal code but also from the complex political and legal evolution operated during Napoleonic rule and Murat's Government in the Italian territories of Naples and Sicily. The influence of Italian criminal law doctrine, with authors such as Beccaria, Filangieri, Pagano, Briganti and Romagnosi, most significantly contributed to the unique nature of the 1819 code, which in turn explains its projection amongst Italian pre-unitary codes.

The contributions made to the 1848 Spanish Criminal Code proved to be particularly relevant, as shown by their survival in the reformed edition of 1850 and in the subsequent Spanish Criminal Codes of 1870, 1928, 1932, 1944, the reforms of 1973 and 1983, and up to the 1995 Code, currently in force.

The mentioned influence did not imply a simple translation of the Code of the Two Sicilies into the 1848 Spanish Criminal Code, though. In this regard, some provisions on different matters (e.g., the distinction between accomplices, authors and accessories; the distinction between failed attempt and attempted offence, and recidivism; the catalogue of circumstances modifying responsibility, such as minority, dementia or insurmountable fear; preterintentionality; and legitimate defence) were improved by the 1848 Criminal Code on the basis of the Two Sicilies text, thus achieving greater consistency and coherence. The influence exerted by the Code of the Two Sicilies also becomes obvious in the context of penalties, and more specifically in the penalty determination system, as well as in the distinction of its scales and degrees. The Code of the Two Sicilies thus contributed to build the so-called Spanish 'arithmetic or metrics' system. This is one of the characteristic features of the 1848 Criminal Code that adopted one of the most legalist systems for the determination of penalties within the European context. The relevance of the 1819 Criminal Code of the Two Sicilies is equally evident in the Special Part of the

1848 Spanish Criminal Code, in offences committed by civil servants, in falsehood, in offences against property and in injuries, amongst others.

In addition, the influence exerted by the Neapolitan legislation is inseparable from the arrival of Italian criminal law doctrine in Spain. One cannot deny in this respect the relevance of the doctrine developed by Beccaria, and that of Filangieri, which inspired the first Spanish criminal code of 1822, along with those of Romagnosi and Pelegrino Rossi, whose influence determined the doctrinal orientation and criminal policy in the Criminal Code of 1848, which was maintained in its reform of 1850 and in the Criminal Code of 1870.

Finally, Iñesta-Pastor also highlights the relevance of the Code of Two Sicilies in Latin America, either directly, as it happened in the 1830 Brazilian Code, or indirectly, through the 1848 Spanish Criminal Code, giving rise to an important succession of Codes that can be referred to with the expression "*travelling codes*".

In the Latin American context, Chap. 10 contains a general approach. More specifically, with the title "[t]he 'Code Pénal' in the Itinerary of the Criminal Codification in America and Europe: 'Influence' and Circularity of Models," Diego Nunes (Universidade Federal de Santa Catarina, Brazil) aims to analyse the legacy of the French model in Latin America from the Brazilian perspective. The author's original idea was to verify whether the existence of some elements (general rules as well as crime species) of Napoleon's *Code Pénal de l'Empire Français* (French Empire's Criminal Code) of 1810 in the Latin American Criminal Codes of the 19th-century might be due to the dissemination of the *Codigo Criminal do Imperio do Brazil* (Brazilian Empire's Criminal Code) of 1830. Analysing the characters of the penal reforms—systematization, secularization and humanization –, Nunes emphasizes some differences in comparison with the criminal law of the *Ancién regime*, although there were also elements of continuity with the previous criminal jurisprudence. The author argues – following a line of thought that I also share—that 19th century codes are better described as tools for criminal law reform than criminal law revolution (or rupture). Political revolutions, which occurred before the promulgation of liberal codes, had consequences in the criminal law domain, but their introduction in the criminal codes was due to political—rather than just doctrinal (or jurisprudential)—reasons. According to Nunes, rationalism—in a modern view—pervaded most of the 19th century reforms.

The author explores the problems of the idea of 'influence.' How can be measured the extent to which a code might be a 'copy' of another, or rather, 'from where does it come?' In this regard, Nunes gives an account of the current historiography, so as to ask if 'how much' (in other words, influence) would matter more than 'how' (that means, the use of these models in each historical reality).

Nunes wonders whether it is possible to understand the Brazilian code by only reading the comparative models: from the French Penal Code to the Brazilian Criminal Code, passing through the Spanish penal code (1822); getting to the Spanish Code (1848), and from there onwards to the Latin American criminal encodings—and perhaps rediscover the Brazilian criminal code? One might intuit heredity, as did Bernardino Bravo Lira; or even measure it, as Vivian Costa. Did codes imply a break? In Brazil the answer is—in Nunes' view—affirmative, not in the sense that the Brazilian code implied a revolution in a dogmatic way, but because the Brazilian parliament used the codification process as a symbol of modernization. The myth of Imperial Criminal Code was fundamental to the State building and to create a legal tradition, giving rise to the 'nationalization' of legal thought or the birth of Brazilian criminal legal thought. It is undeniable that foreign models played a special role in this regard, but it is difficult to know where the ideas came from or, in short, verifying a clear itinerary of influence is problematic. In this regard, some "travel (criminal) codes", as the French one of 1810, the Spanish one of 1822, the Brazilian one of 1830 and the Spanish one of 1848, found a good way and moment for the circulation of ideas.

Having said this, Nunes maintains that determining from where a code comes—its origin—and then understanding where it goes—its influence –, does not seem so important to verify the way it has been living in every historical reality. He argues that the circulation of ideas and their use in each context is more relevant than the origin and influence of codes. In other words, he thinks that influence does not matter so much, considering that the sources are so similar and different itineraries can be chosen. According to the author, the circulation of the 'Enlightened' ideas is the best choice because they work in different contexts: Brazil was an absolutist monarchy but used a liberal discourse of criminal law; that was not a contradiction, but just a strategy to insert Brazil in the 'civilized nations' circle. In Nunes' account, the quality and intensity of ideas in circulation predominate over the quantification of influences.

Chapters 11 and 12 deal with the Codification of criminal law in Argentina. Alejandro Agüero and Matías Rosso (Univ. Nacional de Córdoba, Argentina) co-author Chap. 11, with the title "Codifying the Criminal Law in Argentina: Provincial and National Codification in the Genesis of the First Penal Code." They focus on the devious way that lead to the sanction of the first Argentinian Criminal Code, trying to show the difficulties that brought Argentina to a fact: it was one of the last countries of the region in undertaking the codification of criminal law.

Agüero and Rosso also try to understand the notion of codified law lawyers, judges and prosecutors had in mind. In doing so, they link that idea with the 'Code Culture.' According to Agüero and Rosso, the moderate role of Spanish reforms before independency constitutes a remarkable fact that brought with it an idea: moderation persisted during the first half of the 19th century. It was only after the Argentinian constitutional organization, an event that took place between 1853 and 1860, when the conditions for the codification of criminal law at a national level, were settled. But even in this context, the codification had to face the consequences of a constitutional hybrid system (half federal-half unitary). This system gave to the National Congress the faculty of enacting the substantive law codes for the whole Nation, while the provinces retained their own courts systems and the power of legislating in procedural matters. At the same time, the provinces kept the faculty of sanctioning substantive criminal laws as long as the Congress did not promulgate the national code. In virtue of this particular model, the provinces sanctioned provisional criminal codes until 1887, when the National Criminal Code began to rule.

The expounded reasons explain why Agüero and Rosso regard as highly important the study of the provincial dimension of the Argentinian criminal-law codification process, being an aspect that has been unfairly hidden by the national character that finally acquired the substantive criminal law in the Argentinian legal system. In this vein, the chapter focuses on the codification of criminal law in Córdoba, the second biggest district in the country, before the national codification. Using and analyzing a series of criminal process taken from the *Archivo Histórico de la Provincia de Córdoba* between 1881 and 1886, Agüero and Rosso show that the first experiences of codification did not end the normative pluralism and the judicial discretion inherited from the legal tradition of colonial times. In this sense, it rather represented—as some authors have suggested—a codification without a 'culture code'.

In addition, the codification process shows—according to Agüero and Rosso—that the first Argentinian criminal law codification did not imply an imposition process of a normative system deployed from the center of national power over the provinces. The main reason that led national authorities to choose a project in order to sanction it as a national criminal code was the fact that most of the provinces had already adopted that project as provincial criminal code. Considering the weight of this pragmatic argument, the authors suggest that this first Argentinean criminal codification was a process built upon from the base of provincial power.

Chapter 12 also deals with the Argentinian jurisdiction, but within a different chronological context. With the title "From Free Will to Social Defense (or from Cesare Beccaria to Cesare Lombroso): Julio Herrera and the Criminal Law Codification in Argentina (1903–1922)," Jorge Núñez (CONICET/INHIDE/Max Planck Institute for European Legal History, Argentina/Germany) seeks to scrutinize the views of Julio Herrera—one of the most prominent Argentine criminal law jurists of the first half of the 20th century, but oddly overlooked by legal historiography—on two criminal codes: one of them inspired by the ideas of the Classical School, and the other influenced by the Italian Positivist School.

In 1903, Herrera, a self-taught jurist, governor of Catamarca (a province in the north-east region of Argentina), a congressman and a senator, harshly questioned before the Senate the code in force at the time (styled 'Tejedor Code' after its author) for being based on the ideas of the Classical School of Criminology, and suggested a complete overhaul. Some years later, in 1922, during a series of lectures delivered in the universities of Buenos Aires and Córdoba, he praised the new criminal code (approved in 1921), which he considered to have been influenced by the ideas of the Italian Positivist School and the German Criminal Policy. Despite having given a favorable opinion on the recently-approved code's general provisions, he strongly criticized many of its specific sections.

Núñez believes that an analysis of Herrera's observations before the Senate and during lectures delivered at the two most prominent law schools in the country, as well as his written work, particularly *La reforma penal* (1911), might provide with some insight on the prevailing ideology at the time, the foreign influences, discussions and transformations of Criminal Law which Argentina was subject to during the first decades of the 20th century. Hence, Julio Herrera's views—which show only a partial view of things, of course—might be helpful to understand the transition that took place in Argentina from the (alleged) supremacy of the Classical School ideas (retributive nature of punishment, free will, crime as a legal abstraction, among others) to the partial dominance of principles formulated by the Italian Positivist School and the German Criminal Policy doctrine (social defense, individualization of punishment, reform and reeducation of offenders, incorrigibility, etc.).

According to Núñez, the chapter contributes to the development of legal historiography in two senses: first, by claiming the figure of a very distinguished man back in his time, though oddly unknown to both legal historians and criminal law scholars. Secondly, by placing into perspective totalizing notions regarding the predominance of different criminal law schools: neither were the *classical* tenets accepted completely by the legal community nor were the ideas of the Italian Positivist School adopted without criticism by such scientific community years later.

The Brazilian criminal code of 1830 is analyzed by Ignacio María Poveda Velasco and Eduardo Tomasevicius Filho (University of São Paulo, Brazil), who co-authored Chap. 13 entitled "The 1830 Criminal Code of the Brazilian Empire and its Originality."

In the history of the Latin American criminal law codification, there is an interesting fact concerning the 1830 Criminal Code of the Empire of Brazil. This fact consists—according to Poveda and Filho—in the divergence of opinions between Argentinian and Brazilian jurists about the real contribution and originality of this code and its influence for the Latin American criminal codes: Argentinian lawyers state the originality and importance of this criminal code, whereas Brazilian jurists state that this code has no scientific value. The chapter seeks to shed light on the importance of the criminal code of the Empire of Brazil (1830). Indeed, it was necessary and urgent to enact a criminal code for the young Brazilian nation, because criminal law as prescribed in Book V of the Portuguese Philippine Ordinations required the cruel punishments of death or deportation to Brazil. This latter punishment was, of course, impossible to apply it as a matter of logic. The 1824 Constitution ordered that a Civil Code and a Criminal Code should be drawn up as soon as possible, based on the principles of justice and equity. While the Brazilian civil code took a century to be elaborated, the criminal code was drafted quickly.

Two deputies participated in the drafting of the Criminal Code: José Clemente Pereira and Bernardo Pereira de Vasconcellos, with their respective Criminal Code projects. Each of its drafts had its positive and negative features, and were both analyzed by a committee in the House of Representatives, which, from these two projects, elaborated a third draft, which adopted parts of one of another draft, besides the suggestions of its own committee. During the parliamentary debates, it was found that Representatives were quite familiar with the Bentham's and Beccaria's ideas. As there was little time for discussions due to the closing of the legislative session, the main theme was death penalty, which in principle was not wanted to prevent poor people from being sentenced to death for committing crimes, many of them committed because of poverty and lack of schooling, but allowed its application only for the crimes of insurrection, to avoid rebellions of slaves in Brazil, and homicide. This project was quickly approved by the Senate and enacted in 1830.

Concerning the originality of the 1830 criminal code, Poveda and Filho recognize some influences from the 1810 French criminal code and the 1813 Bavarian code. However, the Brazilian text also has its own originality, resulting from the parliamentary activity, Clemente Pereira's draft and, above all, Bernardo Pereira de Vasconcellos' draft. It was at the time a very modern criminal code, as it reflected some of its institutions: the equalization between crimes and felonies, treated as synonyms; the rejection of the distinction between cruel and infamous punishments from merely cruel punishment; and the declaration of the principle of legality as one of the foundations of criminal law.

Despite the establishment of the death penalty, its regulation was quite different from the one established in other criminal codes of the time—which provided the death penalty for more than thirty circumstances—by setting up milder penalties, granting the proportionality between the legal protected interests and the corresponding penalties. Other important aspects in terms of originality of the 1830 Brazilian Criminal Code lie on the discipline of 'justifiable crimes', on the reparation of damage, as well as on the detailed discipline of mitigating and aggravating circumstances, besides the criminal impunity of minors and insane people, who should be referred to houses intended for them or, also be sent to the family (only insane people had this option). It is precisely these points that were incorporated into the 1848 Spanish Criminal Code, which represented a break of style and arrangement of subjects when compared to the 1822 Spanish Criminal Code.

Chapter 14 explores the codification of criminal law in México. With the title "The Mexican Codification of Criminal Law: Its Foreign Influences," Oscar Cruz Barney (Instituto de Investigaciones Jurídicas, UNAM, México) analyzes the foreign influences on the Mexican codification. In Cruz Barney's view, although the influence of French criminal codification existed in Mexican law, many other sources were used, both legislative and doctrinal in the drafting of the Criminal Code for Mexico City of 1871. In Mexico, the codification task was seen as the organization of "a simple and philosophical legislation at the same time, where without losing sight of the luminous principles of Roman law, those of the natural law are developed." The codification was considered necessary for the purpose of making "quicker, more strong and more effective the action of justice," hence its absence was considered to be one of the great evils that Mexican society suffered in 1862. There was, indeed, an awareness that the codification could not be the work of a year or two, as indeed it happened, "no matter how efficient may be the hands to which they have been entrusted."

Cruz Barney acknowledges the presence of foreign influences, as well as the Mexican, Castilian and *Ius Commune* legal tradition itself reflected on the criminal legislation of the nineteen century. The drafters of the Mexican criminal codes did not intend to do an original work or copy a foreign model, but to collect and reformulate Castilian law, as a part of the national legal tradition.

The chapter shows that the Mexican codification started early in the 19th century (1827) and had its best results in 1871 with the Penal Code of 1871 for Mexico City. Its sources were the *Belgian penal code* of 1867, the *Draft Penal Code of Portugal* of 1864, the Portuguese Penal Code of 1852, the Louisiana Code, the Code of Baviera of 1813, the Code of Prussia of 1851, the Spanish Penal Code of 1848, the (Castilian) Novísima Recopilación of 1805, the Civil Code of Veracruz, the Spanish Civil Code, the ideas of Mittermaïer, Renazzi, Giulio Claro, Joseph Louis E. Ortolan, Rossi, Chauveau and Hélie, Bentham, Edouard Laboulaye, A. de Tocqueville and Gustave de Beaumont, Leon Vidal, Boneville, Philippe Antoine Merlin, and Sourdat. Other sources should be added, namely, the Italian Civil Code of 1865, the Penal Code of Austria of 1803, Nicola Nicolini (*Derecho Penal*), Ferraroti (*Comentario al Código Italiano*), Gregori (*Proyecto de Código Universal*), the Siete Partidas, Fournell, Plaza, Prospero Farinacio, Civil Code of Portugal, Diego de Covarrubias y Leyva, Antonio Gomez, Luis de Molina, Joannes Voet, Pedro Gómez de la Serna y Juan Manuel Montalbán, Robert Joseph Pothier, Jean Jacques Gaspard Foelix, Henry Wheaton, Boneville, Florencio García Goyena and the French Civil Code.

Cruz Barney emphasizes that the most influential authors were Adolphe Chauveau, Faustin Hélie and Joseph Louis Elzéar Ortolan, followed by the Draft Portuguese Penal Code of 1864, the Spanish Penal Code of 1848 and the Criminal Codes of Austria, Italy, Bavaria and finally France.

The last chapter touches upon a subject where foreign influences played an important role in the Western legal tradition: the 19th century Prison Reform. More specifically, Chap. 15 deals with "European and US Influences on the 19th century Prison Reform," written by Isabel Ramos Vázquez (University of Jaén, Spain). In the 19th century, imprisonment became the main penalty of Western societies due to the triumph of Enlightenment movement for humanization of punishments and Rationalist philosophy. Ramos Vázquez explains that philosophy and legal science led a new international culture towards the humanization and rationalization of penalties, and imprisonment was considered the most humane, equal and proportional punishment, able to be individualized for each offender. Thus, this secondary penalty for Absolutist States got to prevail in Liberal States above the ancient corporal, economic or infamous punishments, that were so characteristics of the Ancient Regime.

At that moment, prison reform became an international issue, and Liberal States had to build from nothing a new penalty system, transforming the ancient and obsolete Old Regime's punishments. Changes in the penalty system were used as an engine of social and legal modernization by Liberal States, but they had to decide how to do them without any background, and for this purpose they began an important comparative labour. In this vein, penitentiary laws were commonly inspired by foreign policies and experiences, following common lines of influence in Europe and the United States. The chapter focuses on the American influence in Europe. Two systems inspired the creation of a significant number of prisons in the US and Europe: the *separate system* (e.g. Pennsylvania's prison model) and the *silent system* (the mixed system of Auburn). Ramos Vázquez analyses how the European Penal Colonies and progressive system also had a direct influence on the emergence of American reformatory system and the development of the conditional sentence. She argues that influences were reciprocal and global, although each country developed their own models.

References

Agüero, Alejandro & Lorente, Marta, "Penal enlightenment in Spain: from Beccaria's reception to the first criminal code" (15. Noviembre 2012), *forum historiae iuris*, nn. 36 & 47 *in fine* (available at http://www.forhistiur.de/2012-11-aguero-lorente/; it has also been republished in *The Spanish Enlightenment revisited*, Jesús Astigarraga, ed., Voltaire Foundation–University of Oxford, 2015).

Álvarez García, F. Javier, "Relaciones entre la parte general y la parte especial del Derecho Penal (I)", *Anuario del Derecho Penal y de las Ciencias Penales* 46 (1993), f. III, pp. 1021–1023.

Ancel, Marc, "The Collection of European Penal Codes and the Study of comparative Law," (1957–1958) 106 *U. Pa. L. Rev.* 329, pp. 344–345.

Arnaud, André-Jean, *Origines doctrinelles du code civil francais* (Paris, 1969).

Arnold, Karl, "Erfahrungen aus dem bayerischen *StGB* vom Jahre 1813 und Betrachtungen hierüber", *Archiv des Criminalrechts*, Halle 1843, pp. 96 ff., pp. 240 ff., 377 ff., 512 ff.; 1844, pp. 190 ff.

Ballesteros Llompart, J., "La Historia y la Historicidad del principio jurídico *nulla poena sine lege*", *Estudios en honor al prof. José Corts Grau* (Valencia, 1977), I, pp. 521–537.

Bar, Karl Ludwig von, *A History of Continental Criminal Law* (originally published: Boston: Little, Brown, and Company, 1916; reprinted 1999 by The Lawbook Exchange).

Baumgarten, Edwin, "Das bayerische Strafgesetzbuch von 1813 und Anselm von Feuerbach", *Der Gerichtssaal* 81 (1913), Stuttgart, pp. 98 ff.

Bentley, David, *English Criminal Justice in the Nineteenth Century* (London: Hambledon Press, 1998).

Bermejo Castrillo, Manuel, "Primeras luces de codificación. El Código como concepto y temprana memoria de su advenimiento en España", *Anuario de Historia del Derecho Español* 83 (2013), pp. 9–63.

Binding, Karl, "Zum Hundertjährigen Geburtstage Anselm Feuerbachs", *Strafrechtliche und Strafprozessuale Abhandlungen* I (1915), pp. 507–521.

Blohm, Herbert, *Feuerbach und das Reichsstrafgesetzbuch von 1871* (Breslau, 1935).

Brandt, Christian, *Die Entstehung des Code pénal von 1810 und sein Einfluß auf die Strafgesetzgebung der deutschen Partikularstaaten des 19. Jahrhunderts am Beispiel Bayerns und Preußens* (Frankfurt/Main: Peter Lang, 2002).

Bravo Lira, Bernardino, "Bicentenario del Código penal de Austria. Su proyección desde el Danubio a Filipinas", *Revista de Estudios Histórico-Jurídicos de Valparaíso* (Chile) 26 (2004), pp. 140–145.

Bravo Lira, Bernardino, "Fortuna del Código penal español de 1848. Historia en cuatro actos y tres Continentes: de Mello Freire y Zeiller a Vasconcelos y Seijas Lozano", *AHDE* 74 (2004), pp. 23–58.

Burschmann, Arno, *Textbuch zur Strafrechtsgeschichte der Neuzeit. Die klassischen Gesetze* (München, 1998).

Caenegem, R. C., "Criminal Law in England and Flanders under King Henry II and Count Philip of Alsace", *Actes du Congrès de Naples (1980) de la société italienne d'Histoire du Droit. Studia Historica Gandensia* 253, 1982 (republished in R. C. van Caenegem, ed., *Legal History: a European Perspective*, London, 1991, pp. 37–60).

Caenegem, R. C., *Judges, Legislators and Professors: Chapters in European Legal History* (Cambridge University Press, 1993).
Cairns, David J.A., *Advocacy and the Making of the Adversarial Criminal Trial 1800–1865* (Oxford, 1998).
Camargo Hernández, César, "El Principio de legalidad de los delitos y de las penas", *Revista de la Facultad de Derecho de la Universidad de Madrid*, vol. III, nº5, 1959.
Cañizares-Navarro, Juan B. (with Ramos Vázquez, Isabel), "La influencia francesa en la primera Codificación española: el Código penal francés de 1810 y el Código penal español de 1822", *La Codificación española. Una aproximación doctrinal e historiográfica a sus influencias extranjeras, y a la francesa en particular* (Aniceto Masferrer, ed.) (Pamplona: Aranzadi–Thomson Reuters, 2014), pp. 153–212.
Carbasse, Jean-Marie, "État autoritaire et justice répressive: l'evolution de la législation pénale de 1789 au Code de 1810", *All'ombra dell'Aquila Imperiale. Transformazioni e continuità instituzionali nei territori sabaudi in età napoleonica (1802–1814). Atti del convegno, Torino 15–18 ottobre 1990* (Roma, 1994).
Carbasse, Jean-Marie, "Le droit pénal dans la Déclaration des droits", *Droits: Revue française de théorie juridique* VIII (1988), pp. 123–134.
Carbasse, Jean-Marie, *Introduction historique au droit pénal* (Paris, 1990).
Caroni, Pio, *Lecciones catalanas sobre la historia de la Codificación* (Madrid, 1996).
Cartuyvels, Yves, "Eléments pour une approche généalogique du code penal", *Déviance et Société* 18 (1994), 4, pp. 373–396.
Cartuyvels, Yves, "Le droit pénal entre consolidation étatique et codification absolutiste au XVIIIe siècle", *Le penal dans tous ses Etats. Justice, Etats et Sociétés en Europe (XIIe-Xxe siècles)* (Bruxelles, 1997), pp. 252–278.
Cartuyvels, Yves., *D'où vient le code pénal?: une approche généalogique des premiers codes pénaux absolutistes au XVIIIe siècle* ([Montréal et al.]: Presses de l'Université de Montréal/ Presses de l'Université d'Ottawa/De Boeck Université, 1996).
Castan, Yves, "Les codifications penales d'Ancien Régime", *Le penal dans ses Etats. Justice, Etats et Sociétés en Europe (XIIe-XXe siècles)* (Bruxelles, 1997), pp. 279–286.
Chalmers, M.D., "An Experiment in Codification" (1886) 2 *Law Quarterly Review* 125.
Clavero, Bartolomé, "La idea de Código en la Ilustración jurídica", *Historia. Instituciones Documentos* 6 (1979), pp. 49–88.
Cornish, William Rodolf / Hart, Jenifer / Manchester, A.H. / Stevenson, J., *Crime and Law in Nineteenth Century Britain* (Dublin: Irish University Press, 1978).
D'Aguesseau, Henri F., *Oeuvres complètes du chancelier d'Aguesseau*, 13 vols. (Paris, 1759–1789) (Jean M. Pardessus edited a revised version in 16 vols., Paris, 1819).
Da Passano, Mario, "La codification du droit pénal dans l'Italie jacobine et napoleonienne", *Revolutions et justice en Europe. Modeles français et traditions nationales (1780–1830)* (Paris: L'Harmattan, 1999), pp. 85–99.
Dainow, Joseph, "The Civil Code and the Common Law" (1956–1967) 51 *Nw. U. L. Rev.* 719.
Dedes, Christos, "Sobre el origen del principio «nullum crimen nulla pena sine lege»," *Revista de Derecho Penal y Criminología*, 2ª Época, nº 9 (2002), pp. 141–146.
Delmas-Saint-Hilaire, Jean-Pierre, "1789: un nouveau droit pénal est né...", *Liber Amicorum. Etudes offertes à Pierre Jaubert* (Bourdeaux, 1992), pp. 161–177.
Domat, Jean, *Les lois civiles dans leur ordre natural*, 3 vols. (Paris, 1689–1694).
Emsley, Clive, "Law Reform and Penal Reform in England in the Age of the French Revolution", *Revolutions et justice en Europe. Modeles français et traditions nationales (1780–1830)* (Paris: L'Harmattan, 1999), pp. 319–331.
Espagne, M. & Werner, M., "Deutsch-französischer Kulturtransfer im 18. und 19. Jahrhundert. Zu einem neuen interdiszipliären Forschungsprogramm des C.N.R.S." (1985) 13 *Francia: Forschungen zur westeuropäischen Geschichte*, pp. 502–510.
Espagne, M. & Werner, M., "La construction d'une référence culturelle allemande en France: genèse et histoire (1750–1914)" (1987) 42 *Annales. Économies, Sociétés, Civilisations*, 969–

92; Michel Espagne, *Les transferts culturels francoallemand* (Paris: Presses Universitaires de France, 1999).
Fehrenbach, Elisabeth, *Traditionale Gesellschaft und revolutionäres Recht: Die Einführung des Code Napoleón in den Rheinbundestaaten* (Göttingen, 3 edic., 1983).
Feuerbach, Paul Johann Anselm von, *Lehrbuch des gemeinen in Deutschland gültigen peinlichen Rechts* (Gieβen, 1801).
Feuerbach, Paul Johann Anselm von, *Über die Strafe als Sicherungsmittel vor künftigen Beleidigung des Verbrechers. Nebst einer näheren Prüfung der Kleinischen Strafrechtstheorie* (Chemnitz, 1800).
Finn, Jeremy, "Codification of the Criminal Law: the Australian Parliamentary Experience," B. Godfrey & G. Dunstall (eds.), *Crime and Empire 1840-1940. Criminal Justice in Local and Global Context* (Cullompton: William Publishing, 2005), 224-237 (also available at http://ir.canterbury.ac.nz/bitstream/10092/1828/1/12590980_Codification%20of%20the%20Criminal%20Law.pdf, which I consulted on August 20, 2016).
Garnot, Benoît, "Justice, infrajustice, parajustice et extrajustice dans la France d'Ancien Régime", *Crime, Histoire et Societés* 2000, vol. 4, n. 1, pp. 103–120.
Garnot, Benoît, "L'évolution récente de l'Histoire de la criminalité en France à l'époque moderne", *Histoire de la Justice* 11 (1998), pp. 225–243.
Geisel, Karl, *Der Feuerbachsche Entwurf von 1807: sein Strafsystem und dessen Entwicklung. Ein Beitrag zur Entstehung des Bayerischen Strafgesetzbuches von 1813* (Göttingen, 1929).
Godechot, Jacques, "Les influences étrangères sur le droit pénal de la Révolution française", *La revolution et l'ordre juridique privé. Rationalité ou scandale? Actes du colloque d'Orléans (11-13 septembre 1986)* (Orléans, 1988), I, pp. 47–53.
Gordley, James, "Myths of the French Civil Code," 42 *Am. J. Comp. L.* 459, 488–489 (1994).
Grünhut, Max, "Anselm von Feuerbach und das Problem der strafrechtlichen Zurechnung", *Hamburgische Schriften zur gesamten Strafrechtswissenschaft* (Hamburg, 1922).
Guallart. J./Goicoechea, L. de, "El principio «Nullum crimen, nulla poena sine previa lege» en los Fueros de Aragón," *Homenaje a la memoria de Don Juan Moneva* (Zaragoza, 1954), pp. 659–682.
Hall, Jerome, "Nulla Poena sine Lege," (1937-1938) *Yale L. J.* 168.
Hammond, Anthony, *A Letter to the Members of the Different Circuits* (London, 1826).
Härter, Karl, "Kontinuität und Reform der Strafjustiz zwischen Reichsverfassung und Rheinbund", *Reich oder Nation? Mitteleuropa 1780-1815* (herausgegeben von Heinz Duchhardt und Andreas Kunz). *Veröffentlichungen des Instituts für Europäische Geschichte Mainz*, Abteilung Universalgeschichte, Beiheft 46 (Mainz, 1998), pp. 219–278.
Härter, Karl, "Reichsrecht und Reichsverfassung in der Auflösungsphase des Heiligen Römischen Reichs deutscher Nation: Funktionsfähigkeit, Desintegration und Transfer", *Zeitschrift für Neue Rechtsgeschichte* 28 (2006), Nr. 3/4, pp. 316–337.
Härter, Karl, "Von der «Entstehung des öffentlichen Strafrechts» zur «Fabrikation des Verbrechens». Neuere Forschungen zur Entwicklung von Kriminalität und Strafjustiz im früheneuzeitlichen Europa", *Rechtsgeschichte. Zeitschrift des Max-Planck-Institut für europäische Rechtsgeschichte* 1 (2002), pp. 159–196.
Hartmann, Fritz, *Der Einfluß des französischen Rechts auf das Preußische Strafgesetzbuch von 1851 (Allgemeiner Teil)* (Göttingen, 1923).
Hartung, Fritz, *Deutsche Verfassungsgeschichte vom 15. Jahrhundert bis zur Gegenwart* (Stuttgart: Koehler, 9th ed., 1969).
Herman, Shael, "From Philosophers to Legislators, and Legislators to Gods: The French Civil Code as Secular Scripture," *University of Illinois Law Review* 1984, pp. 597–620.
Hostettler, John, *The Politics of Criminal Law Reform in the Nineteenth Century* (Chichester: Barry Rose, 1992).
Hruschka, Joachim, "Die Unschuldsvemutung in der Rechtsphilosophie der Aufklärung", in *ZStW*, CXII (1990), Heft 2, pp. 285–300.
Huber, Ernst Rudolf (ed.), *Dokumente zur Deutschen Verfassungsgeschichte* (1961. I use the 3rd edition of W. Kohlhammer Verlag, Stuttgard-Berlin-Köln-Mainz, Band 1: *Deutsche*

Verfassungsdokumente 1803-1850 (1978); Band 2: *Deutsche Verfassungsdokumente 1851-1900* (1986); Band 4: *Deutsche Verfassungsdokumente 1919-1933* (1991).

Iñesta-Pastor, Emilia, "La proyección hispanoamericana del Código Penal español de 1848," II, *Estudios, Actas del XIII Congreso del Instituto Internacional de Historia de Derecho Indiano* (González Vale, ed.) (San Juan de Puerto Rico, 2003), pp. 493–521.

Iñesta-Pastor, Emilia, "El Código Penal chileno de 1874," *Revista Chilena de Historia del Derecho*, 19 (Santiago de Chile, 2006), pp. 293–328.

Iñesta-Pastor, Emilia, "Antecedentes histórico-jurídicos del Código penal chileno de 1874", *Derecho, Instituciones y Procesos históricos, XIV Congreso del Instituto Internacional de Historia del Derecho Indiano*, III (José De La Puente Brunke y Armando Guevara Gil, eds.) (Lima: Instituto Riva Agüero, Universidad Pontificia de Lima, 2008), pp. 203–242.

Iñesta-Pastor, Emilia, "La reforma penal del Perú independiente: El Código Penal de 1863," *Actas XV Congreso del Instituto Internacional de Historia del Derecho Indiano*, II, *Córdoba, España, 2005* (Manuel Torres Aguilar, coord.) (Córdoba: Universidad-Diputación, 2008), pp. 1071–1098.

Iñesta-Pastor, Emilia, "The influence of the 1819 criminal code of the Two Sicilies upon the Spanish criminal law codification and the parliament of the nineteenth century", *Culture parlamentari a confronto. Modelli della rappresentanza politica e identità nazionali* (Andrea Romano, ed.) (Bologna: CLUEB, 2016), pp. 245–259.

Iñesta-Pastor, Emilia, "Los delitos contra la propiedad en la codificación penal hispanoamericana: la pervivencia jurídica indiana," *Actas XVIII Congreso del Instituto Internacional de Historia del Derecho Indiano, Córdoba, Argentina, 2012* (Alejando Agüero & Pedro Yanzi Ferreira eds.) (Córdoba, Argentina, 2016), pp. 1287–1327.

Jagermann, Ludwig von, *Das neue Badische Strafgesetzbuch mit systhematischen Übersichten, Competenzbezeichnungen, Parallelstellen, Register u.s.w., zur Erleichterung des Gebrauchs, besonders für Beamte und Geschworne* (Karlsruhe, 1851).

Joaquín Cadafalch y Burguñá, *Discurso sobre el atraso y descuido del Derecho penal hasta el siglo XVIII* (1849).

Jörg Engelbrecht, "The French Model and German Society: the Impact of the Code Penal on the Rhineland", *Revolutions et justice en Europe. Modeles français et traditions nationales (1780-1830)* (Paris: L'Harmattan, 1999), pp. 101–107.

Kenny, R.G., *An Introduction to Criminal Law in Queensland and Western Australia* (LexisNexis Butterworths, 2008), 7th ed.

Kieper, Eberhard, *Johann Paul Anselm Ritter von Feuerbach, sein Leben als Denker, Gesetzgeber und Richter* (Darmstadt, 1969).

Klein, Ernst Ferdinand, *Grundsätze des gemeinen deutschen und preußischen peinlichen Rechts* (Halle, 1796).

Kleinbreuer, Stefan, *Das Rheinische Strafgesetzbuch. Das materielle Strafrecht und sein Einfluß auf die Strafgesetzgebung in Preußen und im Norddeutschen Bund* (Bonn, 1999).

Krey, Volker, *Keine Strafe ohne Gesetz. Eine Einführung in die Dogmengeschichte des Satzes "nullum crimen, nulla poena sine lege"* (Berlin-New York, 1983).

Lalinde Abadía, Jesús, *Iniciación histórica al Derecho español* (1983).

Lascoumes, Pierre/Poncela, Pierrette, "Classer et punir autrement: les incriminations sous l'Ancien Régime et sous la Constituante", *Une autre justice. Contributions à l'histoire de la justice sous la Révolution française* (dir. Robert Badinter) (Fayard, 1989), pp. 73–104.

Lascoumes, Pierre, "Revolution ou reforme juridique? Les codes penaux français de 1791 a 1810", *Revolutions et justice en Europe. Modeles français et traditions nationales (1780-1830)* (Paris: L'Harmattan, 1999), pp. 61–69.

Leca, Antoine, "Les principes de la revolution dans les droits civil et criminel", *Les principes de 1789* (Marseille, 1989), pp. 113–149.

Legrand, Pierre, 'The Impossibility of 'Legal Transplants'' 4 *Maastricht Journal of European and Comparative Law* 1997, 111 ff.

Levasseur, Georges, "Les grands principes de la Déclaration des droits de l'homme et le droit répressif français", *La Déclaration des droits de l'homme et du citoyen de 1789, ses origines – sa pérennité* (Paris, 1990), pp. 233–250.
Limpens, Jean, "Territorial Expansion of the Code," Bernard Schwartz (ed.), *The Code Napoleon and the Common-Law World* (New York, 1956 – I use the The Lawbook Exchange edition, Union-New Jersey, 1998), 93–109.
Lobinger, Charles S., "The Napoleon Centenary's Legal Significance", (1921) 55 *Am. L. Rev.* 665.
Ludi, Regula, *Die Fabrikation des Verbrechens. Zur Geschichte der modernen Kriminalpolitik 1750-1850* (Frühneuzeit-Forschungen 5) (Tübingen, bibliotheca academica, 1999).
Martinage, Renée, "Les innovations des constituants en matière de répression", *Une autre justice. Contributions à l'histoire de la justice sous la Révolution française* (dir. Robert Badinter) (Fayard, 1989), pp. 105–126.
Martinage, Renée, "Les origines de la pénologie dans le code pénal de 1791", *La revolution et l'ordre juridique privé. Rationalité ou scandale? Actes du colloque d'Orléans (11-13 septembre 1986)* (Orléans, 1988), I, pp. 15–29.
Martinage, Renée, *Punir le crime. La repression judiciaire depuis le code pénal* (Villeneuve-d'Ascq, 1989).
Masferrer, Aniceto, "La pena de infamia en la Codificación penal española", *Ius fvgit. Revista interdisciplinar de estudios histórico-jurídicos* 7 (1998), pp. 123–176.
Masferrer, Aniceto, *La pena de infamia en el Derecho histórico español. Contribución al estudio de la tradición penal europea en el marco del ius commune* (Madrid: Dykinson, 2001).
Masferrer, Aniceto, "La dimensión ejemplarizante del Derecho penal municipal catalán en el marco de la tradición jurídica europea. Algunas reflexiones iushistórico-penales de carácter metodológico", *AHDE* 71 (2001), pp. 439–471.
Masferrer, Aniceto, *Tradición y reformismo en la Codificación penal española. Hacia el ocaso de un mito. Materiales, apuntes y reflexiones para un nuevo enfoque metodológico e historiográfico del movimiento codificador penal europeo* (Jaén: Universidad de Jaén, 2003).
Masferrer, Aniceto, "La historiografía penal española del siglo XX. Una aproximación a sus principales líneas temáticas y metodológicas", *Rudimentos Legales* 5 (2003), pp. 29–125.
Masferrer, Aniceto, "Continuismo, reformismo y ruptura en la Codificación penal francesa. Contribución al estudio de una controversia historiográfica actual de alcance europeo", *AHDE* 73 (2003), pp. 403–420.
Masferrer, Aniceto, "El alcance de la prohibición de las *penas inhumanas y degradantes* en el constitucionalismo español y europeo. Una contribución histórico-comparada al contenido penal del constitucionalismo español y alemán", *Presente y futuro de la Constitución española de 1978* (Valencia: tirant lo blanc, 2005), pp. 515–544.
Masferrer, Aniceto, "Codification of Spanish Criminal Law in the Nineteenth Century. A Comparative Legal History Approach", *Journal of Comparative Law* Vol. 4, no. 1 (2009), pp. 96–139.
Masferrer, Aniceto, "Liberal State and Criminal Law Reform in Spain", Sellers, Mortimer & Tomaszewski, Tadeusz (eds.), *The Rule of Law in Comparative Perspective*. Series: *Ius Gentium: Comparative Perspectives on Law and Justice*, vol. 3 (2010), pp. 19–40.
Masferrer, Aniceto, "The Napoleonic *Code pénal* and the Codification of Criminal Law in Spain", *Le Code Pénal. Les Métamorphoses d'un Modèle 1810-2010. Actes du colloque international Lille/Ghent, 16-18 décembre 2010* (Chantal Aboucaya & Renée Martinage, coords.) (Lille: Centre d'Histoire Judiciare, 2012), pp. 65–98.
Masferrer, Aniceto, "The Principle of Legality and Codification in the 19th-century Western Criminal Law Reform", *From the Judge's Arbitrium to the Legality Principle: Legislation as a Source of Law in Criminal Trials* (Georges Martyn, Anthony Musson and Heikki Pihlajamäki, eds.) (Duncker & Humblot, 2013), pp. 253–293.
Masferrer, Aniceto (ed.), *La Codificación española. Una aproximación doctrinal e historiográfica a sus influencias extranjeras, y a la francesa en particular* (Pamplona: Aranzadi–Thomson Reuters, 2014).

Masferrer, Aniceto (ed.), *La Codificación penal española. Tradición e influencias extranjeras: su contribución al proceso codificador*. Parte General (Pamplona: Aranzadi–Thomson Reuters, 2017).

Masferrer, Aniceto (with Sánchez-González, Dolores del Mar), "Tradición e influencias extranjeras en el Código penal de 1848. Aproximación a un mito historiográfico", *La Codificación española. Una aproximación doctrinal e historiográfica a sus influencias extranjeras, y a la francesa en particular* (Aniceto Masferrer, ed.) (Pamplona: Aranzadi–Thomson Reuters, 2014), pp. 213–274.

Masferrer, Aniceto, "Codification as Nationalization or Denationalization of Law: The Spanish Case in Comparative Perspective", *Comparative Legal History* 4.2 (2016), pp. 100–130.

Mirow, Matthew C., "Codification and the Constitution of Cádiz", *Estudios Jurídicos en Homenaje al Professor Alejandro Guzmán Brito* (Patricio-Ignacio Carvajal and Massimo Miglietta, eds.) (Edizioni dell'Orso, 2014), vol. 3, pp. 343–361 (available at http://papers.ssrn.com/sol3/papers.cfm?abstract_id=1844438).

Mirow, Matthew C., "The Legality Principle and the Constitution of Cádiz", *Judges' Arbitrium to the Legality Principle: Legislation as a Source of Law in Criminal Trials* (Anthony Musson / Georges Martyn / Heikki Pihlajamäki, eds.) (Duncker & Humblot, 2013), pp. 189–205 (available at http://papers.ssrn.com/sol3/papers.cfm?abstract_id=1844486).

Mokhtar, Aly, "Nullum Crimen, Nulla Poena Sine Lege: Aspects and Prospects," (2005) *Statute Law Review* 26: 41.

Mousourakis, George, *Roman Law and the Origins of the Civil Law Tradition* (Heidelberg-New York, Dordrecht-London: Springer, 2015).

Pacheco, Joaquín Francisco, *El Código penal concordado y comentado* (1848; I use the 2nd ed.: 1856, in particular, the facsimilar edition with a preliminary study by Abel Téllez Aguilera, Madrid: Edisofer, 2000).

Pauli, Leslau, *Peines corporelles et capitales dans la législation des États européens des années 1751-1903* (Warsawa-Krakow, 1986).

Pifferi, Michele, *Generalia delictorum. Il Tractatus criminalis di Tiberio Deciani e la "parte generale" di diritto penale* (Milano: Giuffrè, 2006).

Pihlajamäki, Heikki, "Private Law Codification, Modernization and Nationalism: A View from Critical Legal History", *Critical Analysis of Law* 1:2 (2015), pp. 135–152 (available at http://cal.library.utoronto.ca/index.php/cal/article/view/22518).

Pino Abad, Miguel., *La pena de confiscación de bienes en el Derecho histórico español* (Córdoba: Universidad de Córdoba, 1999).

Pomorski, Stanislaw, *American Common Law and the Principle Nullum Crimen sine Lege* (Elzbieta Chodakowska trans., 2nd ed., 1975).

Portalis, *Preliminary Address delivered on the occasion of the presentation of the draft of the government commission*, on 1 Pluviôse IX (21 January 1801) (available at http://www.justice.gc.ca/eng/rp-pr/csj-sjc/ilp-pji/code/index.html).

Pothier, Robert Joseph, *Pandectae Iustinianeae in novum ordinem digestae*, 3 vols. (Paris, 1748-1752).

Pothier, Robert Joseph, *Traité des obligations*, 2 vols. (Paris, Orleans, 1761-1764).

Radbruch, Gustav, *Paul Johann Alselm Feuerbach. Ein Juristenleben* (Göttingen, 1969); Mario A. Cattaneo, *Anselm Feuerbach, filosofo e giurista liberale* (Milano, 1970).

Radzinowicz, Sir Leon/Hood, Roger, *A History of English Criminal Law and its Administration from 1750* (London: Stevens & Sons, 1986).

Ramos Vázquez, Isabel "Las reformas borbónicas en el Derecho penal y de Policía criminal de la España dieciochesca" (see http://www.forhistiur.de/zitat/1001ramos.htm).

Ramos Vázquez, Isabel (with Cañizares-Navarro, Juan B.), "La influencia francesa en la primera Codificación española: el Código penal francés de 1810 y el Código penal español de 1822", *La Codificación española. Una aproximación doctrinal e historiográfica a sus influencias extranjeras, y a la francesa en particular* (Aniceto Masferrer, ed.) (Pamplona: Aranzadi–Thomson Reuters, 2014), pp. 153–212.

Rousseau, X./Dupont-Bouchat, M.-S., "Revolutions et justice penale. Modeles français et traditions nationales (1780-1830)", *Revolutions et justice en Europe. Modeles français et traditions nationales (1780-1830)* (Paris: L'Harmattan, 1999), pp. 9–15.

Ruíz Robledo, Agustín, "El principio de legalidad penal en la historia constitucional española", *Revista de Derecho Político* XLII (1997), pp. 137–169.

Russell, Enid, *A History of the Law in Western Australia and its Development from 1829 to 1979* (University of Western Australia Press, 1980).

Sainz Guerra, Juan, *La evolución del Derecho penal en España* (Jaén: Universidad de Jaén, 2004).

Schaffstein, Friedrich, "Tiberius Decianus und seine Bedeutung für die Entstehung des Allgemeinen Teils im Gemeinen deutschen Strafrecht", *Abhandlungen zur Strafrechtsgeschichte und zur Wissenschaftsgeschichte* (Darmstadt: Scientia Verlag Aalen, 1986), pp. 199–226.

Scheickert, Karl, *Das badische Strafedikt von 1803 und das Strafgesetzbuch von 1845. Ein Beitrag zur Geschichte der deutschen Partikularstrafgesetzgebung im 19. Jahrhundert* (Freiburg, 1903).

Schnapper, Bernard, "Les Systemes repressifs français de 1789 a 1815", *Revolutions et justice en Europe. Modeles français et traditions nationales (1780-1830)* (Paris: L'Harmattan, 1999), pp. 17–35.

Schottländer, A., *Die geschichtliche Entwicklung des Satzes: Nulla poena sine lege* (Ruprecht-Karls-Universität Heidelberg, 1911) (*Strafrechtliche Abhandlungen* 1, Heft 132, 1911).

Schubert, Werner, *Der Code pénal des Königreichs Westphalen von 1813 mit dem Code pénal von 1810 im Original und in deutscher Übersetzung* (Frankfurt/Main: Peter Lang, 2001).

Schubert, Werner, *Französisches Recht in Deutschland zu Beginn des 19. Jahrhunderts. Zivilrecht, Gerichtsverfassungsrecht und Zivilprozeßrecht* (Köln, 1977).

Schulze, Reiner, "Rheinisches Recht im Wandel der Forschungsperspektiven", *ZNR* (2002), pp. 65–90.

Sellert, Wolfgang, "Strafrecht und Strafrechtskodifikation im 18. und 19. Jahrhundert in Deutschland", *Rechtsgeschichtliche Abhandlungen. Publikationen des Lehrstuhls für Ungarische Rechtsgeschichte an der Eötvös-Loránd-Universität*, Redakteur Barno Mezey, Band 21 (Budapest, 1997), pp. 131–139.

Sicard, Germain, "Sur la terreur judiciaire a Toulouse (1793-AN II)", *Liber Amicorum. Etudes offertes à Pierre Jaubert* (Bourdeaux, 1992), pp. 679–700.

Silva Forné, Diego, "La Codificación penal y el surgimiento del Estado liberal en España", *Revista de Derecho Penal y Criminología*, 2° época, 7 (2001), pp. 233–309.

Sójka-Zielinska, Katarzyna, "Über den modernen Kodifikationsbegriff", *La codification européene du Moyen-Age au siècle des Lunières. Etudes réunies par Stanislaw Salmonowicz* (Warsawa, 1997), pp. 9–19.

Sprandel, Rolf, "Ivo von Chartres und die moderne Doktrin «nulla poene sine lege»," *Zeitschrift der Savigny-Stiftung für Rechtsgechichte.* Kanonistische Abteilung 47 (1961) pp. 95–108.

Stanislaw Salmonowicz, "Penal codes of the 16th-19th centuries. A discussion of models", *La codification européene du Moyen-Age au siècle des Lunières. Etudes réunies par Stanislaw Salmonowicz* (Warsawa, 1997), pp. 127–141.

Stanković, Emilija, "The influence of Roman law on Napoleon's Code Civil," *'Ex iusta causa traditum': Essays in honour of Eric Pool* (Pretoria: Fundamina, 2005), pp. 310–315.

Stevens, Fred, "La codification penale en Belgique. Heritage français et debats neerlandais (1781-1867)", *Le penal dans tous ses Etats. Justice, Etats et Sociétés en Europe (XIIe-Xxe siècles)* (Bruxelles, 1997), pp. 287–302.

Tarello, Giovanni, *Storia della cultura giuridica moderna*, vol. I: Assolutismo e codificazione del diritto (Bologna, 1976).

Tetley, William, "Mixed jurisdictions: common law v. civil law (codified and uncodified)", *4 Unif. L. Rev.* 591 (1999), pp. 600–601.

Tulkens, Fr./Kerchove, M. van de / Cartuyvels, Y. / Guillain, Ch., *Introduction au droit penal. Aspects juridiques et criminologiques* (Diegem: Kluwer, 2014).

Volk, Klaus, "Napoleon und das deutsche Strafrecht", *JuS* 1991, pp. 281–285.
Von Kräwel, "Über die französischen Elemente im Preußischen Strafgesetzbuch", *Archiv für Preußisches Strafrecht*, Berlin I (1853), pp. 461 ff.
Watson, Alain, "Legal Transplants and European Private Law" *Electronic Journal of Comparative Law* vol. 4.4 (December 2000) (available at http://www.ejcl.org/ejcl/44/44-2.html).
Watson, Alain., *Legal Transplants* (Edinburgh, 1974; Athens, Ga., 1993, 2ª ed.).
Zieschang, Frank, *Das Sanktionensystem in der Reform des französischen Strafrechts im Vergleich mit dem deutschen Strafrecht* (Berlin, 1992).

Professor Aniceto Masferrer teaches legal history and comparative law at the Faculty of Law, University of Valencia, Spain. He is the author of nine books (including his *Spanish Legal Traditions. A Comparative Legal History Outline*, Madrid, 2009; 2012, 2nd ed.) and the editor of ten (including *Post 9/11 and the State of Permanent Legal Emergency: Security and Human Rights in Countering Terrorism*, Springer, 2012; *Counter-Terrorism, Human Rights And The Rule Of Law. Crossing Legal Boundaries in Defence of the State*, Edward Elgar Publishing, 2013; *La Codificación española. Una aproximación doctrinal e historiográfica a sus influencias extranjeras, y a la francesa en particular*, Thomson Reuters-Aranzadi, 2014; and *Human Dignity of the Vulnerable in the Age of Rights: Interdisciplinary Perspectives*, Dordrecht-Heidelberg-London-New York, Springer, 2016), and eighty book chapters/articles published in Spanish, European and American law journals. He has published extensively on criminal law from an historical and comparative perspective, as well as on the codification movement and fundamental rights in the Western legal tradition. He has been a fellow researcher at the Institute Max-Planck for European Legal History (2000–03), Visiting Professor at the University of Cambridge (2005), Visiting Scholar at Harvard Law School (2006–07) and at Melbourne Law School (2008), and Visiting Professor at the University of Tasmania (2010), Visiting Scholar at Louisiana State University—The Paul M. Hebert Law Center—(2013), Visiting Scholar at George Washington University Law School (as the Recipient of the Richard & Diane Cummins Legal History Research Grant for 2014), and Visiting Professor at the École Normale Supérieure—Paris (2015). He has lectured at universities around the world (France, Germany, Belgium, The Netherlands, Malta, Israel, United Kingdom, Sweden, Norway, USA, Canada, Australia and New Zealand). He is a member of the advisory board of several Spanish, European, Anglo-American and Asian Law Journals, and the Chief Editor of *GLOSSAE. European Journal of Legal History* (http://www.glossae.eu). He is member of the *American Society for Legal History*, the current president of the *European Society for Comparative Legal History* (from 2010), and vice-president of the Fundación Universitas. He is also the Director of the *Institute for Social, Political and Legal Studies*, member of the Spanish *Royal Academy of Jurisprudence and Legislation*, and board member of the Valencian Committee for European Affairs.

Part II
Europe

The Influence of the Napoleonic Penal Code on the Development of Criminal Law in Germany: Juridical Discourses, Legal Transfer and Codification

Karl Härter

Abstract The chapter analyzes the transfer and the influences of the Napoleonic penal code (1810) on the development of criminal law in Central Europe and the German States in the first half of the nineteenth century. After the dissolution of the Holy Roman Empire of the German Nation in 1806, the Code pénal influenced the German juridical discourse on criminal law as well as the development of criminal codes and respective reform projects in many German states of the Confederation of the Rhine (1806–1813) and the German Confederation (1815–1866). A systematic survey of these influences shows general aspects of the perception, the transfer and the implementation of the Code pénal in exemplary German states under the conditions of cultural and political diversity, legal pluralism and the need to reform and codify criminal law. The chapter outlines the discussion of the Code pénal in the contemporary German juridical discourse, depicts various modes of its implementation and adoption in some German territories/states (notably Bavaria and Prussia), and analyzes exemplary problems of the legal transfer: the trinity of punishable offences and the integration of police-contraventions, the penalty system and the purposes of punishment, as well as the infeasibility of a strictly codified conformity of offences, penal system, and judiciary. Although many jurists as well as most governments regarded the modernisation of criminal law through the Code pénal as exemplary and helpful to advance reforms of criminal law and justice, an adoption of the French criminal law also created collisions and frictions. The chapter discusses these issues and the principal question of the transfer and adoption of criminal law in nineteenth century Central Europe.

K. Härter (✉)
Max Planck Institute for European Legal History, Frankfurt am Main, Germany
e-mail: haerter@rg.mpg.de

A. Masferrer (ed.), *The Western Codification of Criminal Law*, Studies in the History of Law and Justice 11, https://doi.org/10.1007/978-3-319-71912-2_2

1 Introduction

The Napoleonic Penal Code of 1810 (*Code pénal)* and its companion, the procedural code of 1808 (*Code d'instruction criminelle*), which were partly based on the reform discourses of the Enlightenment and the French revolutionary codes of 1791/1795, had a strong and lasting impact on European criminal law.[1] After the dissolution of the Holy Roman Empire of the German Nation in 1806, the *Code pénal* in particular influenced the German juridical discourse on criminal law as well as the development of criminal codes and respective reform projects in many German states of the Confederation of the Rhine (*Rheinbund*, 1806–1813) and the German Confederation (*Deutscher Bund*, 1815–1866).

Previous research has mostly dealt with the implementation of French criminal law and the Napoleonic codes (mostly the *Code civil* of 1804) in the occupied German territories of the left bank of the Rhine and in the so-called Napoleonic model states, such as the Kingdom of Westphalia, the Grand Duchy of Berg and the Principality of Regensburg/Grand Duchy of Frankfurt.[2] In addition, several studies have dealt with the perception of French criminal law and the attendant discourse in German criminal law jurisprudence from the reform discourses of the Enlightenment and the revolutionary codes of 1791/1795 onwards and the more general implications for reforms of the criminal justice system in various German

[1]Xavier Rousseaux et al. (eds.), *Révolutions et justice pénale en Europe: Modèles français et traditions nationales (1780–1830)* (Paris: L'Harmattan, 1999); Bernard Teyssié (ed.), *Code Pénal et Code d'Instruction Criminelle, livre du bicentenaire* (Paris: Dalloz, 2010); Heike Jung et al. (eds.), *200 Jahre Code d'instruction criminelle - Le Bicentenaire du Code d'instruction criminelle* (Baden-Baden: Nomos, 2010); Chantal Aboucaya & Renée Martinage (eds.), *Le Code pénal. Les métamorphoses d'un modèle 1810–2010: actes du colloque international Lille. Gand 16–18 décembre 2012* (Lille: 2012); Yves Jeanclos (ed.), *La Dimension Historique de la Peine, 1810–2010* (Paris: Economica, 2013); Ulrike Müßig, „Die französischen Strafrechtskodifikationen 1808/1810“, *Feuerbachs Bayerisches Strafgesetzbuch. Die Geburt liberalen, modernen und rationalen Strafrechts* (Arnd Koch et al., eds.) (Tübingen: Mohr Siebeck, 2014), pp. 95–127.

[2]Raimund-Ekkehard Walter, *Die Kriminalpolitik König Jérômes im Königreich Westfalen 1807–1813* (Marburg, Diss., 1971); Stefan Kleinbreuer, *Das rheinische Strafgesetzbuch. Das materielle Strafrecht der Rheinprovinz und sein Einfluß auf die Strafgesetzgebung in Preußen und im Norddeutschen Bund* (Bonn, Diss., 1999); Jörg Engelbrecht, "The French model and German society: The impact of the Code Penal on the Rhineland", *Révolutions et justice pénale en Europe* (Rousseaux, Xavier et al., eds.) (Paris: L'Harmattan, 1999); Christian zur Nedden, *Die Strafrechtspflege im Königreich Westphalen (1807 bis 1813): dargestellt anhand der Praxis westphälischer Gerichte* (Frankfurt a. M. et al.: Lang, 2003); Bettina Severin-Barboutie, *Französische Herrschaftspolitik und Modernisierung – Verwaltungs- und Verfassungsreformen im Großherzogtum Berg (1806–1813)* (München: Oldenbourg, 2008); Thomas Gergen, „Der Einfluss des Code d'instruction criminelle in den deutschen Territorien“, *200 Jahre Code d'instruction criminelle - Le Bicentenaire du Code d'instruction criminelle* (Heike Jung et al., eds.) (Baden-Baden: Nomos, 2010), pp. 40–59.

states.[3] Only one recent case study thoroughly traces the influences of the *Code pénal* on the Bavarian Criminal Code of 1813, which was mainly conceived by Paul Johann Anselm von Feuerbach, and the Prussian Criminal Code of 1851, which appeared much later and became a model for the 1871 Criminal Code of the German Empire.[4]

The following overview cannot comprehensively analyze the wide-range of long-term influences of the *Code pénal* on criminal law, codification projects, and reforms in all German states, nor those of its close companion, the *Code d'instruction criminelle*, and the associated developments of criminal law jurisprudence in Central Europe.[5] Rather, it attempts a more systematic survey that focuses on general aspects of the perception, the transfer and the implementation of the *Code pénal* in exemplary German states under the conditions of cultural and political diversity, legal pluralism and the need to reform and codify criminal law. Hence, I will outline the discussion of the *Code pénal* in the contemporary German juridical discourse, depict various modes of its implementation and adoption in some German territories/states (notably Bavaria and Prussia), and analyze exemplary problems of the legal transfer: the trinity of punishable offences and the integration of police-contraventions (*Polizeidelikte*), the penalty system and the purposes of punishment, as well as the infeasibility of a strictly codified conformity of offences, penal system, and judiciary. I present the results by way of discussing which elements and characteristics of the *Code pénal* impeded or promoted its implementation and impact. Hopefully, this approach will yield some general results for legal comparison in the field of the history of criminal law and crime.

[3]Wolfgang Naucke, „Zur Entwicklung des Strafrechts in der französischen Revolution", *Die Bedeutung der Wörter. Studien zur europäischen Rechtsgeschichte. Festschrift für Sten Gagnér zum 70. Geburtstag* (Michael Stolleis, ed.) (München: 1991), pp. 295–312; Karl Härter, „Kontinuität und Reform der Strafjustiz zwischen Reichsverfassung und Rheinbund", *Reich oder Nation? Mitteleuropa 1780–1815* (Heinz Duchhardt & Andreas Kunz, eds.) (Mainz: von Zabern, 1998), pp. 219–278; Karl Härter, „Die Entwicklung des Strafrechts in Mitteleuropa 1770–1848: Defensive Modernisierung, Kontinuitäten und Wandel der Rahmenbedingungen", *Verbrechen im Blick. Perspektiven der neuzeitlichen Kriminalitätsgeschichte* (Rebekka Habermas & Gerd Schwerhoff, eds.) (Frankfurt am Main/New York: Campus-Verlag, 2009), pp. 71–107.

[4]Christian Brandt, *Die Entstehung des Code pénal von 1810 und sein Einfluß auf die Strafgesetzgebung der deutschen Partikularstaaten des 19. Jahrhunderts am Beispiel Bayerns und Preußens* (Frankfurt a. M. et al.: Lang, 2002). See also the overview by Franz-Stefan Meissel, „Le Code de 1810 et le droit pénal en Europe centrale", *Bicentenaire du Code pénal 1810* (Les Colloques du Sénat, 2011), pp. 125–138.

[5]In particular I have not included Austria, which is covered by the contribution of Martin Paul Schennach to this volume.

2 Penal Law in the Holy Roman Empire Around 1800

In the multi-layered legal system of the Holy Roman Empire the imperial penal code of 1532 (*Constitutio Criminalis Carolina*) was still generally in force, although the particular law of Imperial Estates (*Reichsstände*) and the *ius commune* had altered it in myriad ways.[6] The various imperial estates, which exercised legislative powers within their territorial rule (*Landesherrschaft*), had issued numerous subsidiary penal codes, criminal laws, and police ordinances (*Policeygesetze*) that modified crimes, procedures, punishments, jurisdictions, and the judiciary. The legal diversity of penal law and criminal justice was mainly held together by the writings of the *ius commune* jurists and the rising jurisprudence of public and criminal law. Although many territorial states of the Holy Roman Empire had intensified the centralization of legislative and penal powers at the end of the eighteenth century, the criminal justice system was still characterized by legal pluralism, arbitrariness, and less legal protection. Consequently, it remained in need of reform.[7]

This "state of confusion" was criticized in the juridical-political discourse, which —following the ideas of the Enlightenment (notably Beccaria)—above all demanded a more modern and "enlightened" codification of penal law and yielded several drafts of exemplary criminal codes.[8] Many Imperial Estates discussed or initiated projects to reform the criminal justice system, but only in Tuscany (1786, under Habsburg rule), Austria (the *Josephina* of 1787 and the criminal law of 1803), Bamberg (1796) and in Prussia (*Allgemeines Landrecht* 1794 and *Criminal-Ordnung* 1805) were new penal codes enacted, which were based to some extent on reform ideas of the Enlightenment but also comprised elements of early modern

[6]Karl Härter, "The Early Modern Holy Roman Empire of German Nation (1495–1806): A Multi-layered Legal System", *Law and Empire. Ideas, Practices, Actors* (Jeroen Duindam et al., eds.) (Leiden/Boston: Brill, 2013), pp. 111–131.

[7]Härter, *Strafjustiz*, 1998; Härter, *Entwicklung des Strafrechts*, 2009; Hinrich Rüping & Günter Jerouschek, *Grundriss der Strafrechtsgeschichte* (München: Beck, 2011), pp. 65–80.

[8]Madeleine v. Bellen-Finster, „Die Rezeption Cesare Beccarias im deutschsprachigen Raum um 1800", *Jahrbuch des italienisch-deutschen historischen Instituts in Trient* 11 (1985), pp. 193–219; Eberhard Weis, „Cesare Beccaria und seine Wirkung auf Deutschland, insbesondere auf die Reformen des Strafrechts", *Die Bedeutung der Wörter. Studien zur europäischen Rechtsgeschichte. Festschrift für Sten Gagnér zum 70. Geburtstag* (Michael Stolleis, ed.) (München: Beck, 1991), pp. 535–546. Härter, *Strafjustiz*, 1998; Diethelm Klippel, Martina Henze, Sylvia Kesper-Biermann, „Ideen und Recht. Die Umsetzung strafrechtlicher Ordnungsvorstellungen im Deutschland des 19. Jahrhunderts", *Ideen als gesellschaftliche Gestaltungskraft im Europa der Neuzeit. Beiträge für eine erneuerte Geistesgeschichte* (Lutz Raphael & Heinz-Elmar Tenorth, eds.) (München: Oldenbourg, 2006), pp. 372–394. See, for instance, the draft of Karl Theodor v. Dalberg, *Entwurf eines Gesetzbuchs in Criminalsachen* (Frankfurt/Leipzig: 1792) and Bernd Rehbach, *Der Entwurf eines Kriminalgesetzbuches von Karl Theodor von Dalberg aus dem Jahre 1792* (Berlin: Duncker & Humblot, 1986).

criminal law.[9] All other codification plans failed, particularly on the level of the Empire, which actually obstructed a new imperial penal code as well as legal reforms in the territories of the Imperial Estates.

With the French Revolution and Napoleon the situation radically changed. France not only enacted a new criminal code, but also implemented it in the occupied former territories of the Holy Roman Empire, notably on the left bank of the Rhine from 1798 onwards. After the dissolution of the Holy Roman Empire in 1806, Napoleon forced the now sovereign German states of the Confederation of the Rhine to adopt the Napoleonic codes, among them the *Code d'instruction criminelle* and the *Code pénal.*[10]

The French criminal law (notably the codes of 1791 and 1795) and the Napoleonic penal code together provided a genuine model of a modern, rational, codified law and a corresponding judicial system.[11] They were based on the ideas of the Enlightenment and the principles of strict legality (*nullum crimen, nulla poena sine lege*), the proportionality of crimes and punishments, the humanization of the penalties, and the equity of law. All crimes were entirely and definitely prescribed with the assigned punishments in the three systematically and hierarchically defined categories of crimes, delicts, and contraventions (*crimes, délits, contraventions*—

---

[9]Dirk Blasius, „Strafrechtsreform und Kriminalpolitik in Preußen 1794–1848", *Politischer Wandel, Gesellschaft und Kriminalitätsdiskurse. Beiträge zur interdisziplinären wissenschaftlichen Kriminologie. Festschrift für Fritz Sack zum 65. Geburtstag* (Trutz v. Trotha, ed.) (Baden-Baden: Nomos, 1996), pp. 223–235; Jürgen Regge, „Das Reformprojekt eines "Allgemeinen Criminalrechts für die preußischen Staaten' (1799–1806)", *Das nachfriderizianische Preußen 1786–1806. Rechtshistorisches Kolloquium 11–13. Juni 1987, Christian-Albrechts-Universität zu Kiel* (Hans Hattenhauer & Götz Landwehr, eds.) (Heidelberg: Müller, 1988), pp. 189–223; Gerhard Ammerer, *Das Ende für Schwert und Galgen? Legislativer Prozess und öffentlicher Diskurs zur Reduzierung der Todesstrafe im Ordentlichen Verfahren unter Joseph II. (1781–1787)* (Wien: Studienverlag, 2010); overview: Härter, *Strafjustiz*, 1998, pp. 234–253.

[10]Helmut Berding, *Napoleonische Herrschafts- und Gesellschaftspolitik im Königreich Westfalen 1807–1813* (Göttingen: Vandenhoeck & Ruprecht, 1973); Elisabeth Fehrenbach, *Traditionale Gesellschaft und revolutionäres Recht. Die Einführung des Code Napoleon in den Rheinbundstaaten* (Göttingen: Vandenhoeck & Ruprecht, 1974); Werner Schubert, *Französisches Recht in Deutschland zu Beginn des 19. Jahrhunderts. Zivilrecht, Gerichtsverfassungsrecht und Zivilprozßrecht* (Köln et al.: Böhlau, 1977); Kleinbreuer, *Rheinisches Strafgesetzbuch,* 1999, pp. 10–12; Engelbrecht, *French model*, 1999; Brandt, *Code pénal,* 2002, pp. 251–257; Kathrin Wrobel, *Von Tribunalen, Friedensrichtern und Maires: Gerichtsverfassung, Rechtsprechung und Verwaltungsorganisation des Königreichs Westphalen unter besonderer Berücksichtigung Osnabrücks* (Göttingen: V und R Unipress, 2004); Claudia Schöler, *Deutsche Rechtseinheit. Partikulare und nationale Gesetzgebung (1780–1866)* (Köln et al.: Böhlau, 2004), pp. 73–85.

[11]Jean-Pierre Delmas-Saint-Hilaire, "1789: un nouveau droit pénal est né", *Liber Amicorum. Études offertes a Pierre Jaubert* (Gérard Aubin, ed.) (Bordeaux: Presses Univ. de Bordeaux, 1992), pp. 161–177; A. Leca, "Les principes des la revolution dans les droits civil et criminal", *Principes de 1789* (Jean Imbert, ed.) (Aix-en-Provence: Presses universitaires d'Aix-Marseille, 1989), pp. 113–149; Naucke, *Entwicklung des Strafrechts* 1991, pp. 295–312; Pierre Lascoumes, "Revolution ou reforme juridisque? Les codes penaux français de 1791 à 1810", *Révolutions et justice pénale en Europe* (Rousseaux, Xavier et al., eds.) (Paris: L'Harmattan, 1999), pp. 61–69; Härter, Strafjustiz, 1998, pp. 250–253; Brandt, *Code pénal*, 2002, pp. 26–250 for a detailed survey of the three codes; for a recent overview, see Müßig, *Strafrechtskodifikation*, 2014.

the trinity): "No contravention, delict, or crime can be punished with any penalty not pronounced by the law before the commission thereof".[12] Based on these principles the judiciary was organized into three basic tribunals with commensurate jurisdictions: *le tribunal criminel, le tribunal correctionnel, le tribunal de police*, with a trial by jury for serious crimes that was characterized by the separation of the investigative pretrial, which was still not public and comprised pretrial detention, and the oral public main trial, which included prohibition of torture, defense lawyers, and principles such as *ne bis in idem* and the presumption of innocence. However, the *Code pénal* still threatened capital and other severe punishments, and it was still characterized by inquisitorial and police state elements, notably concerning delicts, contraventions, and the expanded crimes against the state, including internal and external security, public peace, the constitution, and offences of state officials.[13] Especially the orientation of the code towards the state, the nation, and rational utilitarian elements corresponded to reform projects in the German states and the need to establish a public criminal justice system based on the state monopoly of penal power and use of force. On the other hand, the *Code pénal* and French criminal law were regarded as imposed foreign law, tainted by revolutionary principles and Napoleonic power politics.[14]

3 The *Code Pénal* and German Juridical Discourse

These basic conditions shaped the perception of the *Code pénal* in German juridical discourse, which oscillated between appraisal, admiration, and rejection. First, one can discern a growing interest in the development of French criminal law after the enactment of the two revolutionary penal codes in 1791 and 1795 and the inception of the codification process with the first draft of the Napoleonic code in 1802. As many contemporaries believed it impossible to deal with these rapid changes in monographs or books immediately, many German writers of criminal law jurisprudence turned to the evolving journals or even founded their own. In this

---

[12]*Code Penal 1810*, contemporary English translation: Penal code 1819, Art. 4.

[13]Jean-Marie Carbasse, „État autoritaire et justice repressive: l'évolution de la legislation pénale de 1789 au Code de 1810", *All'ombra dell'aquila imperial – trasformazioni e continuità istituzionali nei territori sabaudi in età napoleonica (1802–1814). Atti del convegno, Torino 15–18 ottobre 1990* (Rom, 1994), pp. 313–333; Lascoumes, *codes penaux français*, 1999; Emmanuel Berger, *La justice pénale sous la Révolution. Les enjeux d'un modèle judiciaire liberal* (Rennes: Presses Univ. de Rennes, 2008); André Decocq, "Les crimes et délits contre la sûreté de l'État",*Code Pénal* (Bernard Teyssié, ed.) (Paris: Dalloz, 2010), pp. 426–432.

[14]Kleinbreuer, *Rheinisches Strafgesetzbuch*, 1999; in general and mostly dealing with the *Code civil*: Berding, *Napoleonische Herrschaftspolitik*, 1973; Fehrenbach, *Traditionale Gesellschaft*, 1974; Schubert, *Französisches Recht*, 1977; Christof Dipper et al. (eds.), *Napoleonische Herrschaft in Deutschland und Italien - Verwaltung und Justiz* (Berlin: Duncker & Humblot, 1995); Elmar Wadle, *Französisches Recht in Deutschland. Acht Beiträge zur Geschichte des 19. Jahrhunderts* (Köln: Heymanns, 2002).

regard, French criminal law contributed substantially to the emergence of specific criminal law journals, such as the *Archiv des Criminalrechts* (ACR), founded in 1798 by the Prussian jurist Ernst Ferdinand Klein and the Bavarian jurist Gallus Aloys Kleinschrod. Many of its editors and authors were involved in actual codification and reform projects in Prussia, Bavaria, and other German states and had delivered drafts or extended comments on criminal codes. The *ACR* was published between 1798 and 1807 and again from 1816 to 1857. It was explicitly dedicated to the reform, codification, and comparison of criminal law. Even the first edition of 1798/99 included seven articles by Klein on the usefulness of knowing foreign legal systems (*Nützlichkeit der Kenntniß auswärtiger Justizverfassung*) and the new French criminal law, discussing such issues as the general principles of the codes, the system of the penalties, and the legal conceptualization of violent crimes.[15]

The ACR attentively observed the development of the French criminal justice system (*Französische Criminalverfassung*) and the conceptualization of the *Code pénal*.[16] Klein favorably reviewed the systematic and hierarchical structure of the judiciary, because it was related to the systematization of crimes into the three categories of crimes, delicts, and contraventions. Likewise, he gave an extensive overview of the trial jury, stressing that it was based on the participation of the nation and that public trials would "secure the freedom and the person of the citizen in any and every possible way" (*die Freiheit und Person des Bürgers auf alle nur erdenkliche Weise sicher zu stellen*). But Klein also noted some flaws and contradictions regarding the penal codes of 1791 and 1795, and he criticized the high degree of formality and the opportunities for the government to influence the judiciary.[17] In 1804 he took a more critical view of the jury trial and potential misuse, but he also referred to the first draft of the forthcoming penal code as an appropriate step to further reform the criminal justice system because, among other reasons, the draft would be reviewed in public discourse by jurists and legal scholars.[18]

However, before the new penal code was actually enacted in 1810, the situation in Germany had drastically changed with the Holy Roman Empire's dissolution in

[15]Ernst Ferdinand Klein, „Ueber die Nützlichkeit der Kenntniß auswärtiger Justizverfassung, besonders in Criminalsachen", *Archiv des Criminalrechts* 1/3 (1799), pp. 58–63.

[16]See, in particular, Klein, ACR 1/3, 1799, pp. 58–63; Ernst Ferdinand Klein, „Allgemeine Verordnungen, welche an der Spitze des französischen Gesetzbuches von Strafen und Verbrechen stehen, nebst einigen Bemerkungen darüber", *Archiv des Criminalrechts* 1/3 (1799), pp. 79–89; Ernst Ferdinand Klein, „Von den Strafen, welche in der französischen Republik, zufolge des peinlichen Gesetzbuches vom 25sten Sept. bis 6ten Oct. 1791. und nach dem Anhang zu dem Gesetzbuche von Verbrochen und Strafen vom 3ten Brümär stattfinden", *Archiv des Criminalrechts* 1/3 (1799), pp. 89–96; Ernst Ferdinand Klein, „Ueber den Verwandtenmord, nach französischen Gesetzen, *Archiv des Criminalrechts* 1/3 (1799), pp. 107–110; Ernst Ferdinand Klein, „Französische Criminalverfassung", *Archiv des Criminalrechts* 1/4 (1799), pp. 47–124.

[17]Klein, ACR 1/4, 1799, pp. 47–124, quote 123.

[18]Ernst Ferdinand Klein, „Ueber die Veränderungen, welche der Französischen Criminalgesetzgebung bevorstehen", *Archiv des Criminalrechts* 5/4 (1804), pp. 35–107.

1806 and the formation of the Confederation of the Rhine. Not only did the question arise as to whether or not the former criminal law of the *ius commune* system was still valid or to be immediately substituted by new federal or territorial criminal codes,[19] but Napoleon could now exert pressure on the members of the Confederation to implement French codes. However, the fundamental prerequisite of directly implementing the *Code pénal* and other codes was their translation into German and the concomitant adjustment of some provisions to German legal culture and local circumstances.

Immediately after the *Code pénal* was enacted, two translations by Birnbaum (Straßburg 1810) and Flaxland/Hélie (Trier 1810) appeared in the French Rhineland, and in 1811 an official translation by Blanchard was published in Cologne.[20] In the next two years four other translated and slightly "adjusted" editions and comments were published by Hundrich (Magdeburg 1811), Bourguignon/Zum Bach (Köln 1811), Daniels (Köln 1812), and Rosenthal (Hamburg 1812).[21] Most of the German editions of the code were commissioned by France and were translated and commented upon by lawyers holding an office in the French legal system or in the former German territories in the Rhineland, like Johannes Birnbaum, justice of the peace in Landau, prefect in the Department of the Lower Rhineland and in Luxembourg and vice-presiding judge in Trier, Heinrich Gottfried Wilhelm Daniels, judge at the *cour de cassation*, or Georg Ludwig Friedrich Hundrich, a justice of peace in the Rhenish departments.[22]

Furthermore, the Kingdom of Westphalia, the Grand Duchy of Berg, and the Grand Duchy of Frankfurt, which were not under the direct rule of France but depended heavily on the French emperor as Napoleonic "model states", issued

---

[19]Gallus Aloys Kaspar Kleinschrof, „Ueber den Einfluß der veränderten Staatsverfassung Deutschlands auf das Criminalrecht", *Archiv des Criminalrechts* 7/3 (1807), pp. 355–401.

[20]Johann v. Birnbaum, *Strafgesetzbuch des französischen Reiches. Nach dem offiziellen Texte übersetzt* [...] (Trier: J. J. Lintz, 1810); F. C. Flaxland & F. Hélie (eds.), *Criminal-Gesetzgebung des französischen Reichs 2. Pönal-Codex oder Gesetzbuch der Verbrechen und Strafen* (Straßburg: Treuttel, 1810); Wilhelm Blanchard, *Code pénal. Aus dem Franz. nach der officiellen Ausg. übers.* (Köln: Keil, 1811).

[21]Georg Ludwig Friedrich Hundrich, *Straf-Codex für das französische Reich. Übersetzt und mit Anmerkungen so wie mit einer Übersicht der neuen französichen Criminal-Prozess-Ordnung versehen* (Magdeburg, 1811); Theodor Hartleben, *Napoleons peinliches und Polizey - Strafgesetzbuch. Nach der Original-Ausgabe übersetzt, mit einer Einleitung und Bemerkungen über Frankreichs Justiz- und Polizey-Verfassung, die Motive dieser Gesetzgebung und ihre Verhältnisse zu Oesterreichs und Preußens Gesetzbüchern* (Frankfurt am Main: Varrentrapp, 1811); Claude Sébastien Bourguignon-Dumolard, *Commentar über das Criminal-Gesetzbuch. Manuel d'instruction criminelle. Aus d. Franz. übers. von Carl zum Bach* (Köln: Keil, 1811); Johann Wilhelm August Rosenthal, *Wesentliche Grundzüge des Strafgesetzbuchs Frankreichs; übersichtlich und systematisch darstellt, und mit einem möglichst vollständigen Sachregister versehen, nebst einem, die besondern Gesetze und Decrete in alphabetischer Ordnung enthaltenen Anhange* (Hamburg: Bohn, 1812); Heinrich Gottfried Wilhelm Daniels, *Criminal-Gesetzbuch Frankreichs, Th.1 und 2* (Köln: Keil, 1812).

[22]See Antonio Grilli, *Die französische Justizorganisation am linken Rheinufer 1797–1803* (Frankfurt a. M. et al.: Lang, 1999), pp. 268–287 (with a comprehensive listing of the judges).

translations to facilitate the process of adapting the *Code pénal* to domestic criminal law. The Kingdom of Westphalia, ruled by Napoleon's brother Jérôme from 1807, needed more than two years to conceive and publish a bilingual French and German edition that was slightly modified and set into force in September 1813.[23] The Grand Duke of Frankfurt, Carl Theodor von Dalberg, who supported Napoleon Bonaparte and himself had published a treatise on the reform of the (imperial) criminal code in 1792, immediately commissioned Karl Theodor von Hartleben to translate and adjust the *Code pénal* to the needs of the Grand Duchy and the ongoing reform of its criminal justice system. In 1811 Hartleben published *Napoleons peinliches und Polizey – Strafgesetzbuch*, which was used for subsequent efforts to conceive a criminal code that would also reflect traditional elements of the *ius commune* and the imperial criminal law.[24]

Almost simultaneously German criminal law jurisprudence started to comment on and discuss the French versions of the *Code pénal* as well as the translations.[25] Most jurists and writers appreciated that the *Code pénal* created a homogeneous national criminal law that was based on the sovereign nation-state and, commensurate with its scope of application, abolished the prior legal pluralism and hybridity, applied to every citizen, and established legal equality as well as the principle of *nullum crimen sine lege, nulla poena sine lege*. However, some punishments were perceived as too harsh and humiliating, notably the infamous penalties such as the pillory, banishment, and civic degradation. In this regard, the penalty system of the Napoleonic penal code seemed to resemble the *terreur* of the French Revolution. On the other hand, many authors appreciated general prevention and deterrence as the main purposes of punishment, because they corresponded with the overall purpose of protecting the state, the ruler, and the government. Although the trinity of punishable offences was accepted in general as rational and the most systematic, some authors argued that the distinction was only based on the

---

[23]Modern edition: Werner Schubert (ed.), *Der Code pénal des Königreichs Westphalen von 1813 mit dem Code pénal von 1810 im Original und deutscher Übersetzung* (Frankfurt a.M. et al.: Lang, 2001). See zur Nedden, *Strafrechtspflege*, 2003; Wrobel, *Gerichtsverfassung*, 2004.

[24]Hartleben, *Polizey – Strafgesetzbuch*, 1811; Dalberg, *Entwurf eines Gesetzbuchs*, 1792. See Härter, *Strafjustiz*, 1998, pp. 271–273.

[25]See, for example, Rosenthal, *Grundzüge des Strafgesetzbuchs*, 1812; Eduard Henke, *Beyträge zur Criminalgesetzgebung in einer vergleichenden Uebersicht der neuesten Strafgesetz-Bücher und Entwürfe* (Regensburg: Montag und Weiß, 1813); August Wilhelm Rehberg, *Über den Code Napoleon und dessen Einführung in Deutschland* (Hannover: Hahn, 1814). For an overview, see Carl Joseph Anton Mittermaier, *Die Strafgesetzgebung in ihrer Fortbildung: geprüft nach d. Forderungen d. Wissenschaft u. nach d. Erfahrungen über d. Werth neuer Gesetzgebungen, u. über d. Schwierigkeiten d. Codification, mit vorzüglicher Rücksicht auf d. Gang d. Berathungen von Entwürfen d. Strafgesetzgebung in constitutionellen Staaten* (Heidelberg: Winter, 1st ed., 1841) pp. 1–14; Carl Joseph Anton Mittermaier, *Die Strafgesetzgebung in ihrer Fortbildung: geprüft nach d. Forderungen d. Wissenschaft u. nach d. Erfahrungen über d. Werth neuer Gesetzgebungen, u. über d. Schwierigkeiten d. Codification, mit vorzüglicher Rücksicht auf d. Gang d. Berathungen von Entwürfen d. Strafgesetzgebung in constitutionellen Staaten* (Heidelberg: Winter, 2nd ed., 1843), pp. 244–269; Albert Friedrich Berner, *Die Strafgesetzgebung in Deutschland vom Jahre 1751 bis zur Gegenwart* (Leipzig: Tauchnitz, 1867), pp. 51–78.

degree and form of the penalties. In contrast, the German petty crimes, offences, and police contraventions (*Polizeidelikte*) were often punished with arbitrary penalties not exactly defined in the law. Integrating them into the delicts and contraventions of the *Code pénal* seemed difficult and would have entailed legally fixing the jurisdictions and adjudicative remit of various administrative institutions and police forces or establishing courts and procedures according to the French model and the *Code d'instruction criminelle*.[26] Many authors appreciated the separation of the judiciary and the police, the legal assignment of functions, procedures, and remit of the police and the establishment of the *tribunal correctionnel* and the *tribunal de police* as courts to deal with delicts and contraventions. But this would have implied adopting or enacting a new procedural law that was modeled after the *Code d'instruction criminelle* to establish a new court system with juries and to modify the inquisitorial system, which nearly all German states had retained. These consequences were intensely discussed, and influential jurists such as Paul Johann Anselm Feuerbach or Karl Josef Anton Mittermaier rejected the implementation of the French court system, notably the public jury trial and the juries as well as the justices of the peace to administer the police jurisdiction. Compared to professional jurists, the lay judges were considered inferior, and neither the public jury nor the justices of peace seemed compatible with the traditional and monarchic structure of the administration and the judiciary in Germany.[27]

Although the *Code pénal* seemed to provide a utilitarian model for the reform of penal law in Germany, many jurists of the *Strafrechtswissenschaft* rejected such a "radical cure" and "revolutionary approach".[28] The German states would be ill advised to merely translate or copy the code and hastily set it into force; rather, they should employ the jurisprudence and the legal experts developed in the *Strafrechtswissenschaft* to thoroughly analyze the French law and discern the best principles and provisions to suit German legal culture and traditions as well as the policy needs of the new German states. Both alternatives were investigated.

---

[26]Jung et al., *Code d'instruction*, 2010; Müßig, *Strafrechtskodifikation*, 2014, pp. 119–124.

[27]Paul Johann Anselm v. Feuerbach, *Betrachtungen über das Geschwornen-Gericht* (Landshut: Krüll, 1813); Carl Joseph Anton Mittermaier, *Das deutsche Strafverfahren in der Fortbildung durch Gerichts-Gebrauch und Partikular-Gesetzbücher und in genauer Vergleichung mit dem englischen und französischen Straf-Prozesse* (Heidelberg: Mohr, 1st ed., 1832). See Marie Theres Fögen, *Der Kampf um Gerichtsöffentlichkeit* (Berlin: Duncker & Humblot, 1974); Dirk Blasius, „Der Kampf um die Geschworenengerichte im Vormärz", *Sozialgeschichte heute. Festschrift für Hans Rosenberg zum 70. Geburtstag* (Hans-Ulrich Wehler, ed.) (Göttingen: Vandenhoeck & Ruprecht, 1974), pp. 148–161; Marcel Erkens, *Die französische Friedensgerichtsbarkeit 1789–1814 unter besonderer Berücksichtigung der vier rheinischen Departements* (Köln et al.: Böhlau, 1994); Arnd Koch, "C.J.A. Mittermaier and the 19th century debate about juries and mixed courts", *Revue internationale de droit pénal* 72 (2001), pp. 347–353; Matthias Braun, *Die Entwicklung der Schwurgerichtsfrage in Kurhessen bis zum Jahre 1851* (Berlin: Duncker & Humblot, 2011); Mareike Preisner, „Feuerbach und die Geschworenengerichte", *Feuerbachs Bayerisches Strafgesetzbuch. Die Geburt liberalen, modernen und rationalen Strafrechts* (Arnd Koch et al., eds.) (Tübingen: Mohr Siebeck, 2014), pp. 435–457.

[28]Klein, ACR 1/3, 1799, pp. 58–63, quote: 59 and 63.

4 Transfer and Implementation in the Rhineland and the Napoleonic Model States

After the dissolution of the Holy Roman Empire in 1806, the newly established Confederation of the Rhine never attempted a common penal code for Germany and did not, in fact, pass any law at all. Criminal legislation was left to its now sovereign member states. The remaining German states obtained full sovereignty and, therefore, the opportunity to reform their criminal justice system by enacting a new "modern" penal code. This was all the more urgent because they had gained new territories and citizens, which made homogenization, reform, and uniformity in their legal systems pressing issues. Soon after 1806, many of them proclaimed their intentions to reform the criminal justice system and to enact a new penal code. However, by 1813 almost none of these attempts had produced a comprehensive code, and in some states the imperial criminal code of 1532 and the *ius commune* remained temporarily in force to some extent with many adjustments and additional provisions. The reasons were varied but identifiable: a lack of effective administration and financial resources and adherence to the traditional inquisitorial criminal justice system that provided arbitrary flexible discretionary powers regarding criminal legislation, adjudication, and punishment. A comprehensive modern code would have implied a much higher level of legal bindingness as well as the modification of the inquisitorial procedure concerning public trials and the implementation of a court system and clearly defined jurisdictions to correspond with the classification of crimes in relation to punishments. Reforming the criminal justice system and codifying criminal law according to the model of the *Code pénal* would have implied accepting some measure of "foreign" and "revolutionary" law along with the underlying model of a constitutional state and a civil society, which the majority of the German governments avoided or rejected.[29]

However, a few German states could not elude the *Code pénal* because they were occupied, like the Rhineland, or were ruled as "model states," like Grand Duchy of Frankfurt, the Kingdom of Westphalia, which was ruled by Napoleon's brother Jérôme, and the Grand Duchy of Berg, which was under the rule of Joachim Murat. The Kingdom of Westphalia and the Duchy of Berg enacted translated and somewhat modified versions of the code in 1810, 1811, and 1813. The Grand Duchy of Berg followed the pattern of the French Rhineland and put the original French version of the *Code pénal* and the *Code d'instruction criminelle* into effect. The modification of the French version and its adjustment to the specific legal

[29] Härter, *Strafjustiz*, 1998, pp. 275–278; Karl Härter, „Praxis, Formen, Zwecke und Intentionen des Strafens zwischen Aufklärung und Rheinbundreformen (1770–1815): das Beispiel Kurmainz/ Großherzogtum Frankfurt", *Strafzweck und Strafform zwischen religiöser und weltlicher Wertevermittlung* (Reiner Schulze et al., eds.) (Münster: Rhema, 2008), pp. 213–231. In general and mostly regarding also the *Code civil*, see Schubert, *Französisches Recht*, 1977.

conditions of the Grand Duchy were rejected. Rather, Berg reformed the judiciary in 1812 in accordance to the *Code pénal*.[30]

In Westphalia, conceptualizing a bilingual edition of the *Code pénal* lasted about three years. The Westphalian Minister of Justice Siméon attempted to adjust the code to the specific legal circumstances of the territories and to implement some of his own reform ideas. He modified the systematic order of the crimes, integrated provisions concerning international criminal law and the procedure from the *code d'ìnstruction criminelle*, eliminated the crime of parricide and the harsh penalties of branding and deportation, and enhanced the police contraventions by integrating former police offences. On 17 September 1813, King Jérôme approved the draft, but before the printed edition could be set into force, the kingdom was dissolved.[31]

The Grand Duchy of Frankfurt under the rule of Carl von Dalberg took a somewhat different tack. To avoid pressure from the estates of the Grand Duchy or the criticism of the juridical discourse, Dalberg ordered Karl Theodor von Hartleben to adopt and adjust the translation of the *Code pénal*. This raised a number of problems. Even the title of the translation "*Napoleons peinliches und Polizey – Strafgesetzbuch*" hinted at a crucial problem of the adaptation: the integration of the former German *Criminalverbrechen* (criminal violations) and the *Policeydelikte*, the police contraventions or offences against the good order, into the three categories of punishable offences that the *Code pénal* had established.[32] However, the translation and adjustment largely succeeded in terms of substantive criminal law, with the translated and modified code appearing in February 1812. But concerning the definitive reform of procedure and the judiciary, Dalberg rejected public procedure and jury courts. The system of penalties and the attendant judiciary comprising juries and public trials did not comply with the criminal justice system of the Grand Duchy, which was still based on the traditional inquisitorial procedure that lacked public or jury trials and differentiated between lower local courts and a criminal high court administered by the government. Thus, Dalberg merely renamed existing courts as *Correctionelle Gerichte*, *Specialgerichte*, and *Polizeigerichte* ("correctional courts", "special courts", and "police courts"),

---

[30]Meent W. Francksen, *Staatsrat und Gesetzgebung im Großherzogtum Berg (1806–1813)* (Frankfurt a. M. et al.: Lang, 1982), p. 85; Severin-Barboutie, *Herrschaftspolitik*, 2008.

[31]See Schubert, *Code pénal*, 2001, pp. 10–12 and pp. 253–259 with a concordance of the *code pénal* and the Westphalian version; further: zur Nedden, *Strafrechtspflege*, 2003, pp. 27–33.

[32]Hartleben, *Polizey – Strafgesetzbuch*, 1811; see on the *Policeydelikte*: Sylvia Kesper-Biermann, „Die Grenze des Strafrechts. Zur Abgrenzung von „Criminal-" und „Policeyrecht" in Deutschland und der Schweiz während des 19. und frühen 20. Jahrhunderts", *Kriminalisieren – Entkriminalisieren – Normalisieren* (Claudia Opitz et al., eds.) (Zürich: Chronos, 2006), pp. 173–193; Karl Härter, „Policeygesetzgebung und Strafrecht: Criminalpoliceyliche Ordnungsdiskurse und Strafjustiz in der Frühen Neuzeit", *Kriminalität in Mittelalter und Früher Neuzeit. Soziale, rechtliche, philosophische und literarische Aspekte* (Sylvia Kesper-Biermann & Diethelm Klippel, eds.) (Wiesbaden: Harrassowitz, 2007), pp. 189–210; Härter, *Entwicklung des Strafrechts*, 2009, pp. 74–75, 92–102.

retaining the traditional non-public inquisitorial procedure that partly conformed to the *Code pénal*.[33]

The implementation of the *Code pénal* in Frankfurt, Berg, and Westphalia revealed problems with adapting the new French criminal law to the largely prevailing *ius commune*-based criminal justice system and the legal culture in Germany, but the effect was ephemeral. With the collapse of Napoleonic rule, the three model states were dissolved, integrated into other German states of the German Federation, such as Prussia, Hesse, and Bavaria, and the French codes were abrogated with one exception: the territories on the left bank of the Rhine.

From 1794 France had occupied the German territories on the left bank of the Rhine, which formed four French departments and in which the French law had formally been in force since September 1802. As a result, the *Code pénal* applied directly upon its promulgation, and only a translated version was additionally issued. The judiciary was organized according to the *Code d'instruction criminelle*, and the courts applied the *Code pénal*, which remained in force until 1814.[34] After the defeat of Napoleon and the reintegration of the Rhenish territories into the Kingdom of Prussia (*preußische Rheinprovinz*), the Kingdom of Bavaria (*Rheinpfalz*), and the Grand Duchy of Hessen-Darmstadt (*Rheinhessen*), the *Code pénal* by and large remained in force until the enactment of new national codes. The new rulers hesitated to fully abrogate the French criminal law that had been partly accepted by the population and was considered more modern and rational than the existing criminal law, which remained under the influence of the *ius commune* and required reform and codification. However, the codification process lasted until 1842 in Hessen-Darmstadt and 1851 in Prussia. The juxtaposition of the *Code pénal* in the Rhenish territories and the "indigenous" German criminal law caused many difficulties and collisions, obstructing legal unity.[35] Thus, the *Code pénal* still exerted some influence on the development of criminal law in Germany, notably on the codification process in Prussia that led to the penal code of 1851.[36] Only in Bavaria did the reform of the criminal law produce an earlier code in 1813, which, however, did not derogate from the *Code pénal* in the *Rheinpfalz*.

[33]Härter, *Strafjustiz*, 1998, pp. 271–275.

[34]Kleinbreuer, *Rheinisches Strafgesetzbuch*, 1999, pp. 10–12; Engelbrecht, *French model*, 1999; Grilli, *Französische Justizorganisation*, 1999; Antonio Grilli, „L'organisation judiciaire sur la rive gauche du Rhin et dans l'Italie française de 1800 à 1814", *Révolutions et justice pénale en Europe*, (Xavier Rousseaux et al. eds.) (Paris: L'Harmattan, 1999), pp. 159–176; Barbara Dölemeyer, "L'organisation judiciaire dans les quatre départements rhénans", *Influence du modèle judiciaire français en Europe sous la Révolution et l'Empire. Colloque organisé par le Centre d'Histoire Judiciaire de Lille* (Lille, 1998), pp. 199–206.

[35]Heinrich Christ, *Entstehung und Grundgedanken des Strafgesetzbuchs für das Großherzogtum Hessen vom 1. April 1842* (Marburg, 1968); Kleinbreuer, *Rheinisches Strafgesetzbuch*, 1999, pp. 13–20; Schöler, *Rechtseinheit*, 2004.

[36]Brandt, *Code penal*, 2002, pp. 379–480.

5 The Bavarian Code of 1813 and the *Code Pénal*

Although a member of the Confederation of the Rhine, Bavaria did not initially adopt the *Code pénal*, but rather tried to integrate several principles and provisions via legal experts acquainted with French criminal law, such as Gallus Aloys Kleinschrod, Karl Ludwig Wilhelm von Grolman, and Paul Johann Anselm Feuerbach.[37] The reform of the Bavarian code had already started in 1801, but in 1810 a new legislation commission was established that discussed Feuerbach's draft of 1810, modified it partly with regard to the *Code pénal*, and finally passed the new Bavarian code in 1813.[38] Feuerbach's theory of psychological coercion was in many regards compatible with the *Code pénal*. After all, he had studied the ideas of Enlightenment discourse and recent developments in French criminal law.[39] These included the basic principle of *nulla poena sine lege*, the purposes of punishment (deterrence and general prevention), the penal system with its principal and supplementary penalties (*Haupt- und Nebenstrafen*), the threat of harsh punishments, and the adoption of the infamous penalties, including civic degradation. Moreover, in some cases the Bavarian code heavily relied on French provisions concerning the provisions of attempt, abetment, self-defense, re-offending, and prescription/limitation (*Verjährung*) that had been merely translated.[40]

Although Feuerbach had initially preferred only two categories of punishable offences—crimes and police-contraventions—he finally resorted to the French trinity of crimes, delicts, and contraventions. Approaching them theoretically, he distinguished them not merely in terms of the threatened punishment and the penal powers of the judiciary concerned, but also by the category of the *Rechtsverletzung*: the infringement of legally protected goods. This effectively decriminalized witchcraft, blasphemy, and sexual crimes, such as fornication and adultery, which were transferred to the domain of the police-contraventions. But the code still

---

[37]Erika Schneider, *Gallus Aloys Kleinschrod, sein Leben und Wirken, insbesondere der Entwurf zu einem peinlichen Gesetzbuche für die kurpfalzbaierischen Staaten* (Hamburg, Diss., 1976); Mario A. Cattaneo, *Karl Grolmans strafrechtlicher Humanismus. Aus dem Italienischen von Thomas Vormbaum* (Baden-Baden: Nomos & Berlin: BWV, 1998); Koch et al., *Feuerbachs Bayerisches Strafgesetzbuch*, 2014; Löhnig, *Einfluss napoléonischen Rechts*, 2014, pp. 90–94.

[38]*Strafgesetzbuch für das Königreich Baiern*, 1813; Brandt, *Code penal*, 2002, pp. 258–262; Karl Härter, „Feuerbach, das Bayerische Strafgesetzbuch von 1813 und das Polizeistrafrecht", *Feuerbachs Bayerisches Strafgesetzbuch. Die Geburt liberalen, modernen und rationalen Strafrechts* (Arnd Koch et al., eds.) (Tübingen: Mohr Siebeck, 2014), pp. 129–147, here pp. 135–139; and in general the contributions in: Arnd Koch et al. (eds.), *Feuerbachs Bayerisches Strafgesetzbuch. Die Geburt liberalen, modernen und rationalen Strafrechts* (Tübingen: Mohr Siebeck, 2014).

[39]Wolfgang Naucke, *Kant und die psychologische Zwangstheorie Feuerbachs* (Hamburg: Heitmann, 1962); Wolfgang Naucke, „Feuerbachs Lehre von der Funktionstüchtigkeit des gesetzlichen Strafens", *Der Strafgedanke in seiner historischen Entwicklung Ringvorlesung zur Strafrechtsgeschichte und Strafrechtsphilosophie* (Hilgendorf, Eric & Weitzel, Jürgen, eds.) (Berlin: Duncker & Humblot, 2007), pp. 101–125; Brandt, *Code penal*, 2002, pp. 262–269.

[40]Brandt, *Code penal*, 2002, pp. 301–373.

included fornication and adultery due to infringement of the contract between private parties as *Rechtsverletzung*, and on this basis it classified some former police offences, such as assault, battery, and injuries, as delicts. The delicts, which were called "*Kontraventionen*", and a few police-contraventions were also defined in terms of violation of legal goods, including public order and security, and in the case of some crimes were to be prevented through deterrence or disciplining punishment.[41] In this regard, the Bavarian code generally adopted the French trinity of crimes as well as the harsh penalties and purposes of punishment that characterized the *Code pénal*.

But neither Feuerbach nor the commission managed to develop a codification of the police-contraventions and the respective punishments and sanctions, nor did they consider merely adopting book four of the *Code pénal*, which contained the *contravention de police*. According to the model of the code, they were to be dealt with by correctional courts and police institutions, which could mete out correctional penalties and disciplining sanctions. But this more pragmatic approach diverged from Feuerbach's theoretical model and would have required thoroughly defining the police-contraventions, the respective sanctions, and the penal power of the various administrative and police institutions concerned through the penal code. Such an application of the principle of *nullum crimen sine lege, nulla poena sine lege* to the flexible domain of police-contraventions and police legislation was rejected by the Bavarian government and Feuerbach too, who agreed to exclude them from the criminal code and to conceive a separate code of police-contraventions.[42]

Regarding the German *Policey*, which entailed good order, police, and attendant offences, jurisdictions, and penal powers, neither government policy, Feuerbach's theoretical concepts, nor German *Strafrechtswissenschaft* proved sufficiently compatible with the *Code pénal*.[43] Moreover, the Bavarian government rejected reforming the inquisitorial procedure, the trial, and the judiciary according to the French principles of public oral jury trial (*Schwurgerichtsverfahren*). Feuerbach succeeded in strictly limiting the discretionary powers of the judges to the provisions of the code and in prohibiting all annotations and comments of the code and the sentences.[44] Because of the infeasibility of a strict codified conformity of crimes, penal system, procedure, judiciary, and police, the Bavarian code of 1813, though heavily influenced by French criminal law, fundamentally differed from the *Code pénal*. However, the *Code pénal* remained in force in the Bavarian territory on the left bank of the Rhine. After 1815 the Bavarian government forewent implementing the Bavarian code of 1813 in the regained *Rheinpfalz*. It was

[41]Härter, *Bayerisches Strafgesetzbuch*, 2014; regarding the *contravention de police* in the French penal codes see Brandt, Code penal, 2002, pp. 242–245.

[42]Härter, *Bayerisches Strafgesetzbuch*, 2014, pp. 143–145.

[43]See in general on the relation of *Policey* and criminal law: Kesper-Biermann, *Grenze des Strafrechts*, 2006; Härter, *Policeygesetzgebung*, 2007.

[44]Preisner, *Geschworenengerichte*, 2014.

impossible to align the judiciary and the procedure, especially in relation to jury trials, and the Rhenish citizens insisted on keeping the French judicial system. Moreover, the penal code of 1813 encountered many difficulties concerning the practical application in court, and reforms started immediately. However, a new Bavarian penal code, which also abolished the *Code pénal* in the *Rheinpfalz*, was passed nearly 50 years later in 1861 along with the first police criminal code (*Polizeistrafgesetzbuch*).[45] Thus, in the first half of the nineteenth century the *Code pénal* of 1810 was still applied, without the subsequent French modifications, by the criminal courts of the *Rheinpfalz* as, for instance, in the public jury-trial against German liberals in 1832/33.[46]

6 Conclusion: The Long Term Impact of the *Code Pénal* and the Prussian Penal Code of 1851

The Bavarian code of 1813 demonstrates exemplary problems of the transfer and implementation of the *Code pénal* in Germany through a 'scientific adjustment' by jurists in co-operation with governments. Whereas the former tried in vain to align their philosophical penal theories with the pragmatic utilitarian orientation of the *Code pénal*, the latter only pursued the interests of the state and rejected constitutional achievements, such as the jury and the public oral trial. Moreover, jurists and governments were reluctant to accept the consequences of codifying the police-contraventions (*Polizeidelikte*) and the respective powers of the police and the administration.[47]

After the Confederation of the Rhine disintegrated in 1814, all attempts to transfer or adopt the *Code pénal* into German criminal law were terminated as inappropriate to German legal culture. But with the rejection of "foreign" French criminal law, the reform process to codify criminal law needed more than 25 years to produce new modern penal codes, which were only enacted by Saxony in 1838, Württemberg in 1839, Hessen-Darmstadt in 1842, and Baden in 1845.[48] Without

45Brandt, *Code penal*, 2002, pp. 374–379; Harald Maihold, „Die Diskussion zu Reform und Ablösung des Bayerischen Strafgesetzbuches 1813 bis 1861", *Feuerbachs Bayerisches Strafgesetzbuch. Die Geburt liberalen, modernen und rationalen Strafrechts* (Arnd Koch et al., eds.) (Tübingen: Mohr Siebeck, 2014), pp. 495–523.

46Gergen, *Code d'instruction*, 2010, pp. 46–55.

47See in particular the comprehensive overview and comments in: Mittermaier, *Strafverfahren*, 1832 and Mittermaier, *Strafgesetzgebung*, 1841/1843.

48See the comprehensive study of Sylvia Kesper-Biermann, *Einheit und Recht. Strafgesetzgebung und Kriminalrechtsexperten in Deutschland vom Beginn des 19. Jahrhunderts bis zum Reichsstrafgesetzbuch 1871* (Frankfurt a.M.: Klostermann, 2009); overview: Rainer Schröder, „Die Strafgesetzgebung in Deutschland in der ersten Hälfte des 19. Jahrhunderts", *Die Bedeutung der Wörter. Studien zur europäischen Rechtsgeschichte. Festschrift für Sten Gagnér zum 70. Geburtstag* (Michael Stolleis, ed.) (München: Beck, 1991), pp. 403–420.

the model and the direct push of the *Code pénal*, the broad and intense German codification discourse could not produce concrete legislative results. The German Confederation as a whole never considered enacting a penal code, and its member states defended their particular criminal justice systems as core elements of their sovereignty. Under these conditions, the transfer and implementation of French criminal law seemed to be a renunciation, if not an affront.

By contrast, the influence of French criminal law continued in the former French territories of the Rhineland in which the *Code pénal* as well as elements of the trial and the judiciary remained in force or were still practiced. Most notably the inhabitants of these territories had accepted the French criminal justice system as the more reliable, efficient, and appropriate in comparison to the diverse and hybrid German criminal law that still comprised elements of the former *ius commune*. Besides the Bavarian *Rheinpfalz*, the Rhenish province of Prussia (*preußische Rheinprovinz*) also kept the *Code pénal*. The Prussian government attempted repeatedly to codify the criminal law and produced drafts of a penal code, but it failed to develop them into a comprehensive homogeneous codification. Only after the Ministry of Justice had finally decided in 1848 to substantially integrate the criminal law of the *Rheinprovinz* in 1850—and therefore to follow the model of the *Code pénal*—was an acceptable draft submitted that, after some modification, was finally adopted and enacted in 1851 as the *Strafgesetzbuch für die Preußischen Staaten*. This code then served as the model for the imperial code of 1871.[49]

The Prussian penal code adopted the structure and basic principles of the *Code pénal,* most notably in the general introduction that established the three systematically and hierarchically defined categories of crimes, delicts, and contraventions. Further, its basis in the principle of *nulla poena sine lege* defined the respective punishments as well as the competent courts. The punishments differed somewhat from the French penalties, and the harsher punishments, such as a six-week prison term, were attached to the contraventions. The Prussian code followed the penalty system of the *Code pénal* in its primary and supplementary penalties, a defined range of penalties, a system of mitigating circumstances, and discretionary powers of the judges to decide the range of punishment based on the code.[50]

Only in time did German jurists and governments realize the advantages of the *Code pénal*, which were still intensely discussed within the juridical discourse and justice administrations. The main intent of German governments to implement or partly adopt the *Code pénal* from 1810 onwards was not to humanize criminal justice, nor to establish better legal protection for citizens or their civil rights, because they ultimately rejected a constitutional and a civil society as the political and social base of the code. Rather, modern French criminal law was to serve as a means to rationalize, homogenize, and nationalize criminal law, to establish a monopoly of legislative/jurisdictional power based on sovereignty and the

[49]*Strafgesetzbuch für die Preußischen Staaten* (Berlin, 1851); see Kleinbreuer, *Rheinisches Strafgesetzbuch*, 1999, pp. 16–20, 134–142; Brandt, *Code penal*, 2002, pp-379–397.

[50]Brandt, *Code penal*, 2002, p. 487; Kleinbreuer, *Rheinisches Strafgesetzbuch*, 1999, pp. 145–148.

nation-state, and to make criminal justice more effective in terms of deterrence, prevention, and state security (*Staatsschutz*). As a result, the Napoleonic penal code served as a means of state-building and of "defensive modernization" (Hans-Ulrich Wehler). In this regard, the influence of the *Code pénal* on the development of criminal law in Central Europe underscores the ambiguous nature of the code itself.

References

Aboucaya, Chantal & Martinage, Renée (eds.), *Le Code pénal. Les métamorphoses d'un modèle 1810–2010: actes du colloque international Lille. Gand 16–18 décembre 2012* (Lille: 2012).

Ammerer, Gerhard, *Das Ende für Schwert und Galgen? Legislativer Prozess und öffentlicher Diskurs zur Reduzierung der Todesstrafe im Ordentlichen Verfahren unter Joseph II. (1781–1787)* (Wien: Studienverlag, 2010).

Bellen-Finster, Madeleine v., „Die Rezeption Cesare Beccarias im deutschsprachigen Raum um 1800", *Jahrbuch des italienisch-deutschen historischen Instituts in Trient* 11 (1985), pp. 193–219.

Berding, Helmut, *Napoleonische Herrschafts- und Gesellschaftspolitik im Königreich Westfalen 1807–1813* (Göttingen: Vandenhoeck & Ruprecht, 1973).

Berger, Emmanuel, *La justice pénale sous la Révolution. Les enjeux d'un modèle judiciaire liberal* (Rennes: Presses Univ. de Rennes, 2008).

Berner, Albert Friedrich, *Die Strafgesetzgebung in Deutschland vom Jahre 1751 bis zur Gegenwart* (Leipzig: Tauchnitz, 1867).

Bicentenaire du code pénal 1810–2010, 25–26 novembre 2010 (Paris 2010).

Birnbaum, Johann v., *Strafgesetzbuch des französischen Reiches. Nach dem offiziellen Texte übersetzt* [...] (Trier: J. J. Lintz: 1810).

Blanchard, Wilhelm, *Code pénal. Aus dem Franz. nach der officiellen Ausg. übers.* (Köln: Keil, 1811).

Blasius, Dirk, „Der Kampf um die Geschworenengerichte im Vormärz", *Sozialgeschichte heute. Festschrift für Hans Rosenberg zum 70. Geburtstag* (Hans-Ulrich Wehler, ed.) (Göttingen: Vandenhoeck & Ruprecht, 1974), pp. 148–161.

Blasius, Dirk, „Strafrechtsreform und Kriminalpolitik in Preußen 1794–1848", *Politischer Wandel, Gesellschaft und Kriminalitätsdiskurse. Beiträge zur interdisziplinären wissenschaftlichen Kriminologie. Festschrift für Fritz Sack zum 65. Geburtstag* (Trutz v. Trotha, ed.) (Baden-Baden: Nomos, 1996), pp. 223–235.

Bourguignon-Dumolard, Claude Sébastien, *Commentar über das Criminal-Gesetzbuch. Manuel d'instruction criminelle. Aus d. Franz. übers. von Carl zum Bach* (Köln: Keil, 1811).

Brandt, Christian, *Die Entstehung des Code pénal von 1810 und sein Einfluß auf die Strafgesetzgebung der deutschen Partikularstaaten des 19. Jahrhunderts am Beispiel Bayerns und Preußens* (Frankfurt a. M. et al: Lang, 2002).

Braun, Matthias, *Die Entwicklung der Schwurgerichtsfrage in Kurhessen bis zum Jahre 1851* (Berlin: Duncker & Humblot, 2011).

Carbasse, Jean-Marie, „État autoritaire et justice repressive: l'évolution de la legislation pénale de 1789 au Code de 1810", *All'ombra dell'aquila imperial – trasformazioni e continuità istituzionali nei territori sabaudi in età napoleonica (1802–1814). Atti del convegno, Torino 15–18 ottobre 1990* (Rom, 1994), pp. 313–333.

Cattaneo, Mario A., *Karl Grolmans strafrechtlicher Humanismus. Aus dem Italienischen von Thomas Vormbaum* (Baden-Baden: Nomos & Berlin: BWV, 1998).

Christ, Heinrich, *Entstehung und Grundgedanken des Strafgesetzbuchs für das Großherzogtum Hessen vom 1. April 1842* (Marburg, 1968).

Dalberg, Karl Theodor v., *Entwurf eines Gesetzbuchs in Criminalsachen* (Frankfurt/Leipzig: 1792).

Daniels, Heinrich Gottfried Wilhelm, *Criminal-Gesetzbuch Frankreichs, Th.1 und 2* (Köln: Keil, 1812).

Decocq, André, "Les crimes et délits contre la sûreté de l'État", *Code Pénal* (Bernard Teyssié, ed.) (Paris: Dalloz, 2010), pp. 426–432.

Delmas-Saint-Hilaire, Jean-Pierre, "1789: un nouveau droit pénal est né", *Liber Amicorum. Études offertes a Pierre Jaubert* (Gérard Aubin, ed.) (Bordeaux: Presses Univ. de Bordeaux, 1992), pp. 161–177.

Dipper, Christof, et al. (eds.), *Napoleonische Herrschaft in Deutschland und Italien - Verwaltung und Justiz* (Berlin: Duncker & Humblot, 1995).

Dölemeyer, Barbara, "L'organisation judiciaire dans les quatre départements rhénans", *Influence du modèle judiciaire français en Europe sous la Révolution et l'Empire. Colloque organisé par le Centre d'Histoire Judiciaire de Lille* (Lille, 1998), pp. 199–206.

Engelbrecht, Jörg, "The French model and German society: The impact of the Code Penal on the Rhineland", *Révolutions et justice pénale en Europe* (Rousseaux, Xavier et al., eds.) (Paris: L'Harmattan, 1999).

Erkens, Marcel, *Die französische Friedensgerichtsbarkeit 1789–1814 unter besonderer Berücksichtigung der vier rheinischen Departements* (Köln et al: Böhlau, 1994).

Fehrenbach, Elisabeth, *Traditionale Gesellschaft und revolutionäres Recht. Die Einführung des Code Napoleon in den Rheinbundstaaten* (Göttingen: Vandenhoeck & Ruprecht, 1974).

Feuerbach, Paul Johann Anselm v., *Betrachtungen über das Geschwornen-Gericht* (Landshut: Krüll, 1813).

Flaxland, F.C. & Hélie, F. (eds.), *Criminal-Gesetzgebung des französischen Reichs 2. Pönal-Codex oder Gesetzbuch der Verbrechen und Strafen* (Straßburg: Treuttel, 1810).

Fögen, Marie Theres, *Der Kampf um Gerichtsöffentlichkeit* (Berlin: Duncker & Humblot, 1974).

Francksen, Meent W., *Staatsrat und Gesetzgebung im Großherzogtum Berg (1806–1813)* (Frankfurt a. M. et al: Lang, 1982).

Gergen, Thomas. „Der Einfluss des Code d'instruction criminelle in den deutschen Territorien", *200 Jahre Code d'instruction criminelle - Le Bicentenaire du Code d'instruction criminelle* (Heike Jung et al., eds.) Baden-Baden: Nomos, 2010), pp. 40–59.

Grilli, Antonio, *Die französische Justizorganisation am linken Rheinufer 1797–1803* (Frankfurt a. M. et al: Lang, 1999).

Grilli, Antonio, „L'organisation judiciaire sur la rive gauche du Rhin et dans l'Italie française de 1800 à 1814", *Révolutions et justice pénale en Europe*, (Xavier Rousseaux et al. eds.) (Paris: L'Harmattan, 1999), pp. 159–176.

Härter, Karl, „Kontinuität und Reform der Strafjustiz zwischen Reichsverfassung und Rheinbund", *Reich oder Nation? Mitteleuropa 1780–1815* (Heinz Duchhardt & Andreas Kunz, eds.) (Mainz: von Zabern, 1998), pp. 219–278.

Härter, Karl, „Policeygesetzgebung und Strafrecht: Criminalpoliceyliche Ordnungsdiskurse und Strafjustiz in der Frühen Neuzeit", *Kriminalität in Mittelalter und Früher Neuzeit. Soziale, rechtliche, philosophische und literarische Aspekte* (Sylvia Kesper-Biermann & Diethelm Klippel, eds.) (Wiesbaden: Harrassowitz, 2007), pp. 189–210.

Härter, Karl, „Praxis, Formen, Zwecke und Intentionen des Strafens zwischen Aufklärung und Rheinbundreformen (1770–1815): das Beispiel Kurmainz/Großherzogtum Frankfurt", *Strafzweck und Strafform zwischen religiöser und weltlicher Wertevermittlung* (Reiner Schulze et al., eds.) (Münster: Rhema, 2008), pp. 213–231.

Härter, Karl, „Die Entwicklung des Strafrechts in Mitteleuropa 1770–1848: Defensive Modernisierung, Kontinuitäten und Wandel der Rahmenbedingungen", *Verbrechen im Blick. Perspektiven der neuzeitlichen Kriminalitätsgeschichte* (Rebekka Habermas & Gerd Schwerhoff, eds.) (Frankfurt am Main/New York: Campus-Verlag, 2009), pp. 71–107.

Härter, Karl, "The Early Modern Holy Roman Empire of German Nation (1495–1806): A Multi-layered Legal System", *Law and Empire. Ideas, Practices, Actors* (Jeroen Duindam et al., eds.) (Leiden/Boston: Brill, 2013), pp. 111–131.

Härter, Karl, „Feuerbach, das Bayerische Strafgesetzbuch von 1813 und das Polizeistrafrecht", *Feuerbachs Bayerisches Strafgesetzbuch. Die Geburt liberalen, modernen und rationalen Strafrechts* (Arnd Koch et al., eds.) (Tübingen: Mohr Siebeck, 2014), pp. 129–147.

Hartleben, Theodor, *Napoleons peinliches und Polizey - Strafgesetzbuch. Nach der Original-Ausgabe übersetzt, mit einer Einleitung und Bemerkungen über Frankreichs Justiz- und Polizey-Verfassung, die Motive dieser Gesetzgebung und ihre Verhältnisse zu Oesterreichs und Preußens Gesetzbüchern* (Frankfurt am Main: Varrentrapp, 1811).

Henke, Eduard, *Beyträge zur Criminalgesetzgebung in einer vergleichenden Uebersicht der neuesten Strafgesetz-Bücher und Entwürfe* (Regensburg: Montag und Weiß, 1813).

Hundrich, Georg Ludwig Friedrich, *Straf-Codex für das französische Reich. Übersetzt und mit Anmerkungen so wie mit einer Übersicht der neuen französichen Criminal-Prozess-Ordnung versehen* (Magdeburg, 1811).

Jeanclos, Yves (ed.), *La Dimension Historique de la Peine, 1810–2010* (Paris: Economica, 2013).

Jung, Heike et al. (eds.), *200 Jahre Code d'instruction criminelle - Le Bicentenaire du Code d'instruction criminelle* (Baden-Baden: Nomos, 2010).

Kesper-Biermann, Sylvia, „Die Grenze des Strafrechts. Zur Abgrenzung von „Criminal-" und „Policeyrecht" in Deutschland und der Schweiz während des 19. und frühen 20. Jahrhunderts", *Kriminalisieren – Entkriminalisieren – Normalisieren* (Claudia Opitz et al., eds.) (Zürich: Chronos, 2006), pp. 173–193.

Kesper-Biermann, Sylvia, *Einheit und Recht. Strafgesetzgebung und Kriminalrechtsexperten in Deutschland vom Beginn des 19. Jahrhunderts bis zum Reichsstrafgesetzbuch 1871* (Frankfurt a.M.: Klostermann, 2009).

Klein, Ernst Ferdinand, „Ueber die Nützlichkeit der Kenntniß auswärtiger Justizverfassung, besonders in Criminalsachen", *Archiv des Criminalrechts* 1/3 (1799), pp. 58–63.

Klein, Ernst Ferdinand, „Allgemeine Verordnungen, welche an der Spitze des französischen Gesetzbuches von Strafen und Verbrechen stehen, nebst einigen Bemerkungen darüber", *Archiv des Criminalrechts* 1/3 (1799), pp. 79–89.

Klein, Ernst Ferdinand, „Von den Strafen, welche in der französischen Republik, zufolge des peinlichen Gesetzbuches vom 25sten Sept. bis 6ten Oct. 1791. und nach dem Anhang zu dem Gesetzbuche von Verbrochen und Strafen vom 3ten Brümär stattfinden", *Archiv des Criminalrechts* 1/3 (1799), pp. 89–96.

Klein, Ernst Ferdinand, „Von den Schandstrafen und der Wiedereinsetzung der Verurtheilten in die vorigen Rechte, nach Abtheilung I. T. VII. des französischen Strafcodex", *Archiv des Criminalrechts* 1/3 (1799), 96–99.

Klein, Ernst Ferdinand, „Ueber Mord, Todtschlag und Verwundung, nach französischen Gesetzen", *Archiv des Criminalrechts* 1/3 (1799), pp. 99–107.

Klein, Ernst Ferdinand, „Ueber den Verwandtenmord, nach französischen Gesetzen, *Archiv des Criminalrechts* 1/3 (1799), pp. 107–110.

Klein, Ernst Ferdinand, „Von der Strafe unvollendeter Verbrechen, nach französischen Gesetzen", *Archiv des Criminalrechts* 1/3 (1799), pp. 110–113.

Klein, Ernst Ferdinand, „Beyspiele von Gerechtigkeit und Ungerechtigkeit bey Verwaltung der Rechtspflege in der französischen Republik", *Archiv des Criminalrechts* 1/3 (1799), pp. 119–124.

Klein, Ernst Ferdinand, „Französische Criminalverfassung", *Archiv des Criminalrechts* 1/4 (1799), pp. 47–124.

Klein, Ernst Ferdinand, „Ueber die Veränderungen, welche der Französischen Criminalgesetzgebung bevorstehen", *Archiv des Criminalrechts* 5/4 (1804), pp. 35–107.

Kleinbreuer, Stefan, *Das rheinische Strafgesetzbuch. Das materielle Strafrecht der Rheinprovinz und sein Einfluß auf die Strafgesetzgebung in Preußen und im Norddeutschen Bund* (Bonn, Diss., 1999).

Kleinschrod, Gallus Aloys Kaspar, „Ueber den Einfluß der veränderten Staatsverfassung Deutschlands auf das Criminalrecht", *Archiv des Criminalrechts* 7/3 (1807), pp. 355–401.

Klippel, Diethelm, Henze, Martina, Kesper-Biermann, Sylvia, „Ideen und Recht. Die Umsetzung strafrechtlicher Ordnungsvorstellungen im Deutschland des 19. Jahrhunderts", *Ideen als gesellschaftliche Gestaltungskraft im Europa der Neuzeit. Beiträge für eine erneuerte Geistesgeschichte* (Lutz Raphael & Heinz-Elmar Tenorth, eds.) (München: Oldenbourg, 2006), pp. 372–394.

Koch, Arnd, "C.J.A. Mittermaier and the 19th century debate about juries and mixed courts", *Revue internationale de droit pénal* 72 (2001), pp. 347–353.

Koch, Arnd et al. (eds.), *Feuerbachs Bayerisches Strafgesetzbuch. Die Geburt liberalen, modernen und rationalen Strafrechts* (Tübingen: Mohr Siebeck, 2014).

Lascoumes, Pierre, "Revolution ou reforme juridisque? Les codes penaux français de 1791 à 1810", *Révolutions et justice pénale en Europe* (Rousseaux, Xavier et al., eds.) (Paris: L'Harmattan, 1999), pp. 61–69.

Leca, A., "Les principes des la revolution dans les droits civil et criminal", *Principes de 1789* (Jean Imbert, ed.) (Aix-en-Provence: Presses universitaires d'Aix-Marseille, 1989), pp. 113–149.

Löhnig, Martin, „Wie souverän war das junge Königreich Bayern? Zum Einfluss napoléonischen Rechts auf die bayerische Rechtsreform zu Beginn des 19. Jahrhunderts", *Feuerbachs Bayerisches Strafgesetzbuch. Die Geburt liberalen, modernen und rationalen Strafrechts*, (Arnd Koch et al., eds.) (Tübingen: Mohr Siebeck, 2014), pp. 81–94.

Maihold, Harald, „Die Diskussion zu Reform und Ablösung des Bayerischen Strafgesetzbuches 1813 bis 1861", *Feuerbachs Bayerisches Strafgesetzbuch. Die Geburt liberalen, modernen und rationalen Strafrechts* (Arnd Koch et al., eds.) (Tübingen: Mohr Siebeck, 2014), pp. 495–523.

Meissel, Franz-Stefan, „Le Code de 1810 et le droit pénal en Europe centrale", *Bicentenaire du Code pénal 1810* (Les Colloques du Sénat, 2011), pp. 125–138.

Mittermaier, Carl Joseph Anton, *Das deutsche Strafverfahren in der Fortbildung durch Gerichts-Gebrauch und Partikular-Gesetzbücher und in genauer Vergleichung mit dem englischen und französischen Straf-Prozesse* (Heidelberg: Mohr, 1st ed., 1832).

Mittermaier, Carl Joseph Anton, *Die Strafgesetzgebung in ihrer Fortbildung: geprüft nach d. Forderungen d. Wissenschaft u. nach d. Erfahrungen über d. Werth neuer Gesetzgebungen, u. über d. Schwierigkeiten d. Codification, mit vorzüglicher Rücksicht auf d. Gang d. Berathungen von Entwürfen d. Strafgesetzgebung in constitutionellen Staaten* (Heidelberg: Winter, 1st & 2nd ed., 1841/1843).

Müßig, Ulrike, „Die französischen Strafrechtskodifikationen 1808/1810", *Feuerbachs Bayerisches Strafgesetzbuch. Die Geburt liberalen, modernen und rationalen Strafrechts* (Arnd Koch et al., eds.) (Tübingen: Mohr Siebeck, 2014), pp. 95–127.

Naucke, Wolfgang, *Kant und die psychologische Zwangstheorie Feuerbachs* (Hamburg: Heitmann, 1962).

Naucke, Wolfgang, „Zur Entwicklung des Strafrechts in der französischen Revolution", *Die Bedeutung der Wörter. Studien zur europäischen Rechtsgeschichte. Festschrift für Sten Gagnér zum 70. Geburtstag* (Michael Stolleis, ed.) (München: Beck, 1991), pp. 295–312.

Naucke, Wolfgang, „Feuerbachs Lehre von der Funktionstüchtigkeit des gesetzlichen Strafens", *Der Strafgedanke in seiner historischen Entwicklung Ringvorlesung zur Strafrechtsgeschichte und Strafrechtsphilosophie* (Hilgendorf, Eric & Weitzel, Jürgen, eds.) (Berlin: Duncker & Humblot, 2007), pp. 101–125.

The Penal Code of France, Translated into English with preliminary Dissertation and Notes, London, 1819.

Preisner, Mareike, „Feuerbach und die Geschworenengerichte", *Feuerbachs Bayerisches Strafgesetzbuch. Die Geburt liberalen, modernen und rationalen Strafrechts* (Arnd Koch et al., eds.) (Tübingen: Mohr Siebeck, 2014), pp. 435–457.

Regge, Jürgen, „Das Reformprojekt eines "Allgemeinen Criminalrechts für die preußischen Staaten" (1799–1806)", *Das nachfriderizianische Preußen 1786–1806. Rechtshistorisches Kolloquium 11–13. Juni 1987, Christian-Albrechts-Universität zu Kiel* (Hans Hattenhauer & Götz Landwehr, eds.) (Heidelberg: Müller, 1988), pp. 189–223.

Rehbach, Bernd, *Der Entwurf eines Kriminalgesetzbuches von Karl Theodor von Dalberg aus dem Jahre 1792* (Berlin: Duncker & Humblot, 1986).

Rehberg, August Wilhelm, *Über den Code Napoleon und dessen Einführung in Deutschland* (Hannover: Hahn, 1814).

Rosenthal, Johann Wilhelm August, *Wesentliche Grundzüge des Strafgesetzbuchs Frankreichs; übersichtlich und systematisch darstellt, und mit einem möglichst vollständigen Sachregister versehen, nebst einem, die besondern Gesetze und Decrete in alphabetischer Ordnung enthaltenen Anhange* (Hamburg: Bohn, 1812).

Rousseaux, Xavier et al. (eds.), *Révolutions et justice pénale en Europe: Modèles français et traditions nationales (1780–1830)* (Paris: L'Harmattan, 1999).

Rüping, Hinrich & Jerouschek, Günter, *Grundriss der Strafrechtsgeschichte* (München: Beck, 2011).

Schneider, Erika, *Gallus Aloys Kleinschrod, sein Leben und Wirken, insbesondere der Entwurf zu einem peinlichen Gesetzbuche für die kurpfalzbaierischen Staaten* (Hamburg, Diss., 1976).

Schöler, Claudia, *Deutsche Rechtseinheit. Partikulare und nationale Gesetzgebung (1780–1866)* (Köln et al.: Böhlau, 2004).

Schröder, Rainer, „Die Strafgesetzgebung in Deutschland in der ersten Hälfte des 19. Jahrhunderts", *Die Bedeutung der Wörter. Studien zur europäischen Rechtsgeschichte. Festschrift für Sten Gagnér zum 70. Geburtstag* (Michael Stolleis, ed.) (München: Beck, 1991), pp. 403–420.

Schubert, Werner, *Französisches Recht in Deutschland zu Beginn des 19. Jahrhunderts. Zivilrecht, Gerichtsverfassungsrecht und Zivilprozßrecht* (Köln et al.: Böhlau, 1977).

Schubert, Werner (ed.), *Der Code pénal des Königreichs Westphalen von 1813 mit dem Code pénal von 1810 im Original und deutscher Übersetzung* (Frankfurt a.M. et al: Lang, 2001).

Severin-Barboutie, Bettina, *Französische Herrschaftspolitik und Modernisierung – Verwaltungs- und Verfassungsreformen im Großherzogtum Berg (1806–1813)* (München: Oldenbourg, 2008).

Strafgesetzbuch für die Preußischen Staaten (Berlin, 1851).

Strafgesetzbuch für das Königreich Baiern (München, 1813).

Teyssié, Bernard (ed.), *Code Pénal et Code d'Instruction Criminelle, livre du bicentenaire.* Paris: Dalloz, 2010).

Wadle, Elmar, *Französisches Recht in Deutschland. Acht Beiträge zur Geschichte des 19. Jahrhunderts* (Köln: Heymanns, 2002).

Walter, Raimund-Ekkehard, *Die Kriminalpolitik König Jérômes im Königreich Westfalen 1807–1813* (Marburg, Diss., 1971).

Weis, Eberhard, „Cesare Beccaria und seine Wirkung auf Deutschland, insbesondere auf die Reformen des Strafrechts", *Die Bedeutung der Wörter. Studien zur europäischen Rechtsgeschichte. Festschrift für Sten Gagnér zum 70. Geburtstag* (Michael Stolleis, ed.) (München: Beck, 1991), pp. 535–546.

Wrobel, Kathrin, *Von Tribunalen, Friedensrichtern und Maires: Gerichtsverfassung, Rechtsprechung und Verwaltungsorganisation des Königreichs Westphalen unter besonderer Berücksichtigung Osnabrücks* (Göttingen: V und R Unipress, 2004).

Zur Nedden, Christian, *Die Strafrechtspflege im Königreich Westphalen (1807 bis 1813): dargestellt anhand der Praxis westphälischer Gerichte* (Frankfurt a. M. et al: Lang, 2003).

Professor Dr. Karl Härter is Research Group Leader at the Max Planck Institute for European Legal History, Frankfurt am Main, and teaches Early Modern and Modern History at the University of Darmstadt. His major research interests concern legal history, constitutional history, the history of public (administrative and penal) law and the history of crime/deviance and criminal justice. Current projects are dealing with the history of political crime and the formation of transnational criminal law and security regimes and cultural diversity and criminal justice. In the last years he has edited collected volumes on: Repräsentationen von Kriminalität und öffentlicher Sicherheit (2010), Grazia e giustizia fra tardo medioevo ed età contemporanea (2011), Politische

Kriminalität, Recht, Justiz und Polizei zwischen Früher Neuzeit und 20. Jahrhundert (2012) and Revolts and Political Crime from the 12th to the 19th Century (2013) as well as recently published articles in journals and collected volumes on: Images of dishonoured rebels and infamous revolts: Political crime, shaming punishments and defamation in the early modern pictorial media (Images of Shame, Berlin/Boston 2016); Political crime in early modern Europe: Assassination, legal responses and popular print media (European Journal of Criminology 11, 2014); Security and Cross-border Political Crime: The Formation of Transnational Security Regimes in 18th and 19th Century Europe (Historical Social Research 38, 2013); and Violent Crimes and Retaliation in the European Criminal Justice System between the Seventeenth and Nineteenth Century (http://ssrn.com/abstract=2218350).

Ignoring France? Possible French Influences on the Development of Austrian Penal Law in the 19th Century

Martin P. Schennach

Abstract Since the Austrian criminal code of 1852 was largely based on its precursor, published in 1803, it has been widely accepted that there was no significant French influence. The contribution verifies this assumption and analyses whether the French *Code pénal* played any role in Austrian reform debates in the second half of the 19th century and whether it influenced legal scholarship in Austria.

1 Introduction

The allusion expressed in the title of the article—"ignoring France"—reflects a hypothesis suggested by Austrian legal history[1]: There was no significant influence of French penal law (including the famous Napoleonic *Code pénal* passed in 1810) on the development of Austrian criminal law during the 19th century, at least as far as material law was concerned (whereas French influence on the law of criminal procedure in the middle of the century was evident).[2] The reason can be easily found and seems to be convincing: The Austrian criminal code of 1852 was not a new codification, but only a revision of the codification of Austrian criminal law enacted in 1803[3]; the Austrian

[1]Cf. Franz-Stefan Meissel, "Le Code de 1810 et le droit pénal en Europe centrale", Sénat de France (ed.), Bicentenaire du code pénal (1810–2010) (Paris: Sénat, 2010), pp. 125–137.
[2]Cf. Werner Ogris, "Die Entwicklung von Gerichtsverfassung, Strafrecht und Strafprozeßrecht 1848–1918",Gábor Máthé & Werner Ogris (eds.), *Die Entwicklung der österreichisch-ungarischen Strafrechtskodifikation im XIX–XX. Jahrhundert* (Budapest: UNIÓ, 1996), pp. 55–74, here pp. 61–63; Werner Ogris, *Die Rechtsentwicklung in Österreich. 1848–1918* (Wien: Verlag d. Österreichischen Akademie der Wissenschaften, 1975), pp. 556–562.
[3]Thomas Olechowski, "Zur Entstehung des österreichischen Strafgesetzes 1852", Thomas Olechowski, Christian Neschwara & Alina Lengauer (eds.), *Grundlagen der österreichischen Rechtskultur, Festschrift für Werner Ogris zum 75. Geburtstag*, (Wien/Köln/Weimar: Böhlau, 2010), pp. 319–341.

M. P. Schennach (✉)
University of Innsbruck, Innsbruck, Austria
e-mail: martin.schennach@uibk.ac.at

A. Masferrer (ed.), *The Western Codification of Criminal Law*, Studies in the History of Law and Justice 11, https://doi.org/10.1007/978-3-319-71912-2_3

legislator merely tried to incorporate various ordinances passed in the precedent decades. With regard to the year in which the code was adopted, 1803, it is simply impossible for it to have been influenced by the French Penal Code.

In fact, it would be quite hard to refute this argumentation, and it is not surprising that no standard works on Austrian legal history or on the history of Austrian penal law address wide-ranging foreign (let alone French) impacts on Austrian criminal law.[4] Nevertheless, taking a mere look at the normative framework is too superficial for analysing the role of the French Penal Code on Austrian penal law in the 19th century. We have no idea if and to what extent French role models were used during the various attempts of drafting a completely new codification of penal law in the second half of the century. It is not known yet whether the *Code pénal* and French legal science were taken into account by Austrian jurisprudence when interpreting Austrian penal law. Not only must the normative level be analysed, but also any possible influences of French legal culture on Austrian legal science.

Our limited knowledge of possible French impacts is also due to the poor status of research in this field: The history of (material) criminal law in the Habsburg Monarchy in the 19th century—compared to the history of private law—has basically received only brief treatment in the relevant literature[5]; apart from the codification of 1803 and its revision in 1852, scholars have concentrated on the last decades of the 18th century, with its fundamental reforms in the field of criminal and especially procedural law inspired by natural law and rationalism and realised

---

[4]Cf. for example Hugo Hoegel, *Geschichte des österreichischen Strafrechts in Verbindung mit einer Erläuterung seiner grundsätzlichen Bestimmungen* (Wien: Manz, 1904); Arbeitsgemeinschaft österreichische Rechtsgeschichte (ed.), *Rechts-und Verfassungsgeschichte* (Wien: Facultas, [4]2016); Hermann Baltl & Gernot Kocher, *Österreichische Rechtsgeschichte. Unter Einschluß sozial- und wirtschaftsgeschichtlicher Grundzüge. Von den Anfängen bis zur Gegenwart* (Graz: Leykam, [12]2009).

[5]Cf. Gábor Máthé & Werner Ogris (eds.), *Die Entwicklung der österreichisch-ungarischen Strafrechtskodifikation im XIX–XX. Jahrhundert* (Budapest: UNIÓ, 1996); Hinrich Rüping, *Grundriss der Strafrechtsgeschichte* (Schriftenreihe der Juristischen Schulung 73) (München: Beck, [6]2011); Markus Steppan, *Die österreichische Strafrechtsentwicklung im mitteleuropäischen Konnex* (Graz: Habil. Univ. Graz, 2002); Sergo Vinciguerra & Sergio Ambrosio (eds.), *Codice Penale Universale Austriaco (1803)* (Casi, fonti e studi per il diritto penale Serie 2, Le fonti 18) (Padova: CEDAM, 2001); Friedrich Hartl, *Das Wiener Kriminalgericht. Strafrechtspflege vom Zeitalter der Aufklärung bis zur österreichischen Revolution* (Wiener Rechtsgeschichtliche Arbeiten 10) (Wien et al.: Böhlau, 1973); Hugo Hoegel, *Freiheitsstrafe und Gefängniswesen in Österreich von der Theresiana bis zur Gegenwart* (Graz: Moser, 1916). Günter Jerouschek, Hinrich Rüping & Barna Mezey (eds.), *Strafverfolgung und Staatsraison. Deutsch-ungarische Beiträge zur Strafrechtsgeschichte* (Rothenburger Gespräche zur Strafrechtsgeschichte 6) (Gießen: Psychosozial-Verlag, 2009); Reinhard Moos, *Der Verbrechensbegriff in Österreich im 18. und 19. Jahrhundert. Sinn- und Strukturwandel* (Rechtsvergleichende Untersuchungen zur gesamten Strafrechtswissenschaft N.F. 39) (Bonn: Röhrscheid, 1968).

by enlightened absolutism.[6] Given the current inadequate status of research, an extensive examination of the development of Austrian penal law in the 19th century (including various reform projects) and especially of scientific legal literature on criminal law would be a major desideratum for Austrian legal history—and by the way, not only as far as the role of the French Penal Code on Austria is concerned.

It is evident that these research gaps cannot be filled in by this paper, particularly regarding the considerable and substantially untapped archival funds in the Austrian National Archives. The poor status of research becomes even more obvious if we compare it to the enormous efforts made by legal historians since the 19th century in the field of the history of the Austrian General Civil Code (*Allgemeines Bürgerliches Gesetzbuch*) and the history of private law.

2 A Survey on the History of Austrian Penal Law

Realising "unification by codification"—id est, creating a uniform civil and penal law for all Austrian hereditary lands—was one of the main objectives of both legislative commissions initiated by Maria Theresa in 1753.[7] Although the monarch rejected the civil code's first draft submitted in 1766, the Constitutio Criminalis Theresiana was issued in 1768 and remained valid until 1786.[8] It was deeply rooted in early modern tradition, maintaining the death penalty in its various forms (by hanging, decapitating, quartering etc.) as well as mutilations and delicts such as witchcraft and blasphemy, which were already heavily disputed in legal theory. Torture was only abolished in 1776, due to the efforts of Joseph von Sonnenfels.[9] The Josephine Penal Code of 1787 (*General Code on crimes and their punishment/*

[6]Cf. the recent publication of Gerhard Ammerer, *Das Ende für Schwert und Galgen? Legislativer Prozess und öffentlicher Diskurs zur Reduzierung der Todesstrafe im Ordentlichen Verfahren unter Joseph II. (1781–1787)* (Mitteilungen des Österreichischen Staatsarchiv, Sonderbd. 11) (Innsbruck et al.: Studienverlag, 2010) (with many further literature suggestions).

[7]Cf. Leopold Pfaff & Leopold Hofmann, *Commentar zum österreichischen allgemeinen bürgerlichen Gesetzbuche, Bd. 1, Abt.1* (Wien: Manz, 1877), pp. 8–11; Philipp Harras von Harrasowsky, *Der Codex Theresianus und seine Umarbeitungen, vol. I: Codex Theresianus* (Wien: Gerold, 1883), pp. 2–23; Wilhelm Brauneder, *Österreichs Allgemeines Bürgerliches Gesetzbuch (ABGB), vol. 1: Entstehung und Entwicklung des ABGB bis 1900* (Schriften zur europäischen Rechts- und Verfassungsgeschichte 60) (Berlin: Duncker & Humblot, 2014), p. 27.

[8]Cf. Ernst Carl Hellbling, *Grundlegende Strafrechtsquellen der österreichischen Erbländer vom Beginn der Neuzeit bis zur Theresiana. Ein Beitrag zur Geschichte des Strafrechts in Österreich* (Wien et al.: Böhlau, 1996), pp. 22–23; Friedrich Hartl, "Grundlinien der österreichischen Strafrechtsgeschichte bis zur Revolution von 1848", Gábor Máthé & Werner Ogris (eds.), *Die Entwicklung der österreichisch-ungarischen Strafrechtskodifikation im XIX–XX. Jahrhundert* (Budapest: UNIÓ, 1996), pp. 13–54, here pp. 16–22; Hoegel, *Geschichte des österreichischen Strafrechts*, vol. 1, pp. 65–72.

[9]Cf. Werner Ogris, "Joseph von Sonnenfels als Rechtsreformer", Helmut Reinalter (ed.), *Joseph von Sonnenfels* (Veröffentlichungen der Kommission für die Geschichte Österreichs 13) (Wien: Verlag d. Österreichischen Akademie der Wissenschaften, 1988), pp. 11–95, here pp. 63–65.

Allgemeines Gesetzbuch über Verbrechen und deren Bestrafung)[10]—valid until 1803—did not regulate procedural law. It fixed the principle of legality in Austrian penal law for the first time, made no more distinctions between noblemen on the one hand and commoners (peasants and burghers) on the other, and replaced the death penalty in all non-military criminal proceedings. It could only be proscribed once martial law had been imposed. Instead, the convicted person was condemned to heavy labour—that is, generally pulling boats up the Danube River. As this punishment took place under miserable conditions, it usually led to the death of the delinquent within a few years, but it was in accordance with the utilitarian idea of taking advantage for as long as possible of a culprit's ability to work.[11] Some crimes regularly punished by the death penalty in early modern times were decriminalised (e.g. attempted suicide, blasphemy); for others, the sanctions were considerably mitigated (e.g. male homosexuality). Mutilations as sanctions were abolished, but the Josephine Penal Code still foresaw public humiliation in pillories as well as corporal punishment (flogging with rods or whips). As early as 1795, when a supposed "Jacobine conspiracy" had been revealed in Vienna, the death penalty was reintroduced—even without the imposition of martial law.[12]

Reform debates started in the early 1790s, and in 1797, a new Penal Code was enacted in the western parts of Galicia, which had been incorporated a few years earlier by the Habsburg Monarchy and where the need for a modernised criminal law seemed to be particularly urgent.[13] The legislative commission charged with the revision of this statute law was led by Franz von Zeiller, and it elaborated a new codification of criminal law put into force in 1803 by Emperor Francis II (*Criminal Code on crimes and police contraventions/Strafgesetz über Verbrechen und schwere Polizey-Übertretungen*).[14] In contrast to its precursor, it contains

---

[10]Cf. with further literature suggestions Ammerer, *Ende für Schwert und Galgen*; Hartl, *Grundlinien*, pp. 25–31; Yves Cartuyvels, *D'où vient le code pénal? Une approche généalogique des premiers codes pénaux absolutistes au XVIIIe siècle. Préface de Françoise Tulkens* (Paris/ Bruxelles: De Boeck-Wesmael et al., 1996), pp. 247–300; Hoegel, *Geschichte des österreichischen Strafrechts*, pp. 78–85; Werner Ogris, "Joseph II.: Staats- und Rechtsreformen", Werner Ogris, *Elemente europäischer Rechtskultur. Rechtshistorische Aufsätze aus den Jahren 1961–2003*, ed. by Thomas Olechowski (Wien et al.: Böhlau, 2003), pp. 125–164, here pp. 150–153 (first published in 1990).

[11]This punishment replacing death penalty was also discussed (and criticised) in France, cf. Stefano Solimano, "Les précédents européens au XVIIIe siècle du code pénal de 1810", Sénat de France (ed.), *Bicentenaire du code pénal (1810–2010)* (Paris: Sénat, 2010), pp. 45–61, here pp. 50–51.

[12]Ammerer, *Ende für Schwert und Galgen*, pp. 409–414; Stephan Tschigg, "La formazione del codice penale austriaco del 1803", Sergio Vinciguerra & Sergio Ambrosio (eds.), *Codice Penale Universale Austriaco (1803)* (Casi, fonti e studi per il diritto penale Serie 2, Le fonti 18) (Padova: CEDAM, 2001), pp. 51–67, here pp. 56–57.

[13]Cf. Hoegel, *Geschichte des österreichischen Strafrechts*, vol. 1, pp. 85–89; Christian Neschwara, "Franz von Zeiller und das Strafrecht", *Journal on European History of Law* 1: pp. 4–15, 2010, here p. 5.

[14]Cf. Vinciguerra & Ambrosio, *Codice Penale Universale Austriaco*; Hartl, *Das Wiener Kriminalgericht*, pp. 25–27.

substantive and procedural law (the latter adheres to the inquisitorial system of the Ancien Régime). The number of crimes which were sanctioned by the death penalty rose to six (high treason, insurrection, producing counterfeit money, arson, manslaughter and murder), and punishments remained very severe. For instance, the code distinguished three ways of imprisonment: The most draconic one consisted of putting the convicted into chains, forcing him to perform hard labour and feeding him only bread and water. Even contemporary legal scholars harshly criticised the rigour of the Austrian penal code,[15] although this characteristic was in accordance with the criminal theory of Anselm von Feuerbach and his idea of "psychological coercion": In order to prevent the individual from committing crimes, the damage imposed by criminal courts (by passing a sentence) must be more severe than the benefits taken from the offence.[16] Nevertheless, the practice of criminal law significantly mitigated the severe sanctions fixed in the penal code by consequently imposing the mildest punishment possible.[17]

During the following decades, the statute law was specified, clarified and developed by dozens of single ordinances and decrees.[18] The consequence was a growing complexity of criminal law which became harder and harder to handle by juridical practice. Therefore, as early as 1817, attempts were made to elaborate a new codification. Once again, Franz von Zeiller was involved.[19] This rapid revision

---

[15]Cf. Franz von Zeiller, "Recensionen des Strafgesetzes Franz I. über Verbrechen und schwere Polizey-Uebertretungen. Schriften über inländische Gesetzgebung. Anzeiger neuer, im Auslande bekannt gemachter Gesetzbücher oder Entwürfe", Franz von Zeiller (ed.), *Jährlicher Beytrag zur Gesetzeskunde und Rechtswissenschaft in den Oesterreichischen Erbstaaten, vol. 1* (Wien: Hof- und Staatsdruckerey, 1806), pp. 201–232, here pp. 208, 211, 214–222.

[16]Cf. Thomas Vormbaum, *Einführung in die moderne Strafrechtsgeschichte* (Berlin: Springer, ³2015), pp. 37 38 and pp. 43–51

[17]Cf. Loredana Garlati, "Das Gericht als Interpret der Gerechtigkeit. Die Anwendung des Strafgesetzbuchs von 1803 im Königreich Lombardo-Venetien", Ettore Dezza & Loredana Garlati (eds.), *Beiträge zur Geschichte der habsburgischen Strafgesetzgebung in Italien. Mit einem Anhang: Cesare Beccarias Gutachten zum Allgemeinen Gesetzbuch über Verbrechen und Strafen aus dem Jahre 1791* (Rechtsgeschichte und Rechtsgeschehen, Kleine Schriften 24) (Berlin et al.: LIT-Verlag, 2010), pp. 89–102, here pp. 93, 96; Francesca Brunet, *Pena di morti e grazia sovrana nel Regno Lombardo-Veneto (1816–1848)* (PhD Thesis, Innsbruck, 2013).

[18]Vgl. Hartl, *Grundlinien*, pp. 43 and 47; Ogris, *Die Entwicklung von Gerichtsverfassung*, p. 64; Hoegel, *Geschichte des österreichischen Strafrechts*, vol. 1, pp. 91–94; in his edition of the penal code, Stephan Blumentritt, *Das österreichische Strafgesetz über schwere Polizei-Uebertretungen vom 3. September 1803. Teil 1/2* (Wien: Braumüller, ²1846) indicates and cites all decrees referring to paragraphs of the codification; cf. also Ignaz Maucher, *Das österreichische Strafgesetz über Verbrechen sammt den auf dasselbe sich beziehenden Gesetzen und Verordnungen, sistematisch bearbeitet als Hilfsbuch beim Studium desselben* (Wien: Braumüller, 1847) (every paragraph is commented on, and respective decrees and ordinances are at least mentioned).

[19]Cf. Hoegel, *Geschichte des österreichischen Strafrechts*, vol. 1, pp. 95–96; Neschwara, *Franz von Zeiller*, pp. 6–10; Christian Neschwara, "Pratobevera – Zeiller – Jenull: Eine 'herrliche Trias …unserer Gesetzgebung'. Ein Beitrag zur Gesetzgebungsgeschichte des österreichischen Strafrechts im Vormärz", Ulrike Aichhorn & Alfred Rinnerthaler (eds.), *Scientia iuris et historia. Festschrift für Peter Putzer, vol. I* (Egling: Kovar, 2004), pp. 579–612; Hartl, *Das Wiener Kriminalgericht*, p. 27.

of the penal code was not due to its (inferior) quality—on the contrary, contemporary (also foreign) legal scholars praised the precision of legal definitions and the strict distinction between crimes and contraventions.[20] Nevertheless, Zeiller himself was convinced that criminal law—in contrast to civil law—constantly had to be adapted to "the progress of an era, to the level of a society's civilisation, to new institutions in other branches of government and to changing circumstances."[21] Zeiller pointed out that new developments in the penal law of other countries should also be taken into account.[22] After Zeiller's death in 1828, revisions were carried out by Sebastian Jenull, professor of criminal law at the University of Vienna, but these led to no results—until the Revolution of 1848. Regarding substantive law, the revolution led to some innovations, which concerned above all the system of sanctions: Branding, corporal punishment, public labour and public humiliation were abolished.[23] Procedural law underwent considerable changes: From 1850 to 1873, three codes of criminal procedure were passed.[24]

In 1848, revisionary work to the penal code was intensified, and Anton Hye, professor of criminal law at the University of Vienna, was put in its charge by the Ministry of Justice.[25] However, it took almost four years for the revised penal code to be put into force (in 1852). In contrast to the code passed in 1803,[26] the new codification was valid not only in the Austrian hereditary lands (respectively in the Austrian Empire), but also (until 1861) in the Kingdom of Hungary and in its *partes adnexae* like Croatia, Slavonia and Transylvania.[27] The penal code of 1852 primarily incorporated the numerous decrees and ordinances enacted in the decades

[20]Cf. Zeiller, *Recensionen*, esp. pp. 202, 210, 213; Moos, *Verbrechensbegriff*, p. 312.

[21]Franz von Zeiller, "Zweck und Prinzipien der Criminal-Gesetzgebung. Grundzüge der Geschichte des österreichischen Criminal-Rechts. Darstellung der durch das neue Criminal-Gesetzbuch bewirkten Veränderungen, sammt ihren Gründen", Franz von Zeiller (ed.), *Jährlicher Beytrag zur Gesetzeskunde und Rechtswissenschaft in den Oesterreichischen Erbstaaten, vol. 1* (Wien: Hof- und Staatsdruckerey, 1806), pp. 71–185, here p. 95; cf. also Neschwara, *Pratobevera*, p. 584.

[22]Neschwara, *Franz von Zeiller*, p. 7.

[23]Olechowski, *Entstehung des österreichischen Strafgesetzes 1852*, p. 326; Ogris, *Rechtsentwicklung*, p. 565.

[24]Hartl, *Das Wiener Kriminalgericht*, pp. 28–29; Ogris, *Entwicklung von Gerichtsverfassung*, pp. 61–63; Ogris, *Rechtsentwicklung*, pp. 555–563.

[25]Olechowski, *Entstehung des österreichischen Strafgesetzes 1852*, p. 327.

[26]Cf. Szilvia Bató, "Österreichische Wirkungen in der ungarischen Strafrechtswissenschaft vor 1848 am Beispiel der Straftaten gegen das Leben", Attila Badó et al. (eds.), *Internationale Konferenz zum zehnjährigen Bestehens des Instituts für Rechtsvergleichung der Universität Szeged* (Acta Iuridica Universitatis Potsdamiensis 1) (Potsdam: Universitätsverlag Potsdam, 2014), pp. 71–90, here pp. 73 and 75; Szilvia Bató, "Ein Überblick über die ungarische Strafrechtsentwicklung bis zum Jahre 1948", Arndt Sinn, Walter Gropp & Ferenc Nagy (eds.), *Grenzen der Vorverlagerung in einem Tatstrafrecht. Eine rechtsvergleichende Analyse am Beispiel des deutschen und ungarischen Strafrechts* (Schriften des Zentrums für Europäische und Internationale Strafrechtsstudien 1) (Göttingen: V&R unipress, 2011), pp. 41–52.

[27]Cf. Olechowski, *Entstehung des österreichischen Strafgesetzes 1852*, p. 336; Ogris, *Rechtsentwicklung*, p. 566.

before and thus re-established a coherent and logic system of criminal law. However, it also contained a series of innovations and improvements,[28] for instance by reducing the punishments for many delicts and specifying others, and by defining some legal terms or by taking into account technical progress, such as the telegraph. Special attention was paid to crimes against the state: With regard to the restoration of absolutism in Austria by Emperor Francis Joseph, high treason was defined more broadly.

Due to its character as a revision of the code of 1803, the codification of criminal law passed in 1852 was not a modern one. Contemporary critics at first pointed out that developments in the field of criminal theory were completely ignored by Austrian penal law; they later identified that the findings of criminal statistics and criminal sociology were equally ignored[29]: for instance, the discussions between Karl Binding and Franz von Liszt on the objective of sanctions or the appropriate age of criminal responsibility.[30] In addition, the wide range of crimes against the state and the severe sanctions imposed for these offences were increasingly considered inadequate.[31] From the 1860s onwards, there were regular debates as to whether a completely new codification should be elaborated. These plans led to several drafts of penal codes submitted to the *Reichsrat* in 1867, 1870 and 1874—the latter was discussed until the mid 90s—and finally 1912.[32]

3 French Influences on Austria and on Austrian Legislation in the 19th Century

With regard to the respective date of entry into force, it is evidently impossible that the Napoleonic Penal Code of 1810 could have influenced its Austrian equivalent, which had already been passed in 1803. Nevertheless, an impact of the French

[28]Briefly Olechowski, *Entstehung des österreichischen Strafgesetzes 1852*, pp. 337–338; Ogris, *Entwicklung von Gerichtsverfassung*, pp. 64–65. Changes and innovation in comparison to the code of 1803 are described in a very detailed way by an anonymous legal scholar: *Das Oesterreichische Strafgesetz vom 27. Mai 1852 und die Verordnungen über die Gerichts-Competenz. Erläutert zur Darstellung der in den bisherigen Gesetzen eingetretenen Veränderungen. Von einem praktischen Juristen […]* (Wien: Tendler, 1852); a survey of all changes is delivered by Anton Hye, *Das österreichische Strafgesetz über Verbrechen, Vergehen und Uebertretungen und die Preßordnung vom 27. Mai 1852* (Wien: Manz, 1855), pp. 10–22.

[29]Cf. Österreichisches Staatsarchiv (Wien), Allgemeines Verwaltungsarchiv, Legislative Angelegenheiten, Karton 1059 (from 1881), Karton 1066 (from 1899 until 1917).

[30]Cf. Vormbaum, *Einführung*, pp. 125–136.

[31]Cf. Philip Czech, *Der Kaiser ist ein Lump und Spitzbube: Majestätsbeleidigung unter Kaiser Franz Joseph* (Wien et al.: Böhlau, 2010), p. 87.

[32]Cf. Hoegel, *Geschichte des österreichischen Strafrechts*, vol. 1, p. 100; August Finger, *Das Strafrecht. Mit Berücksichtigung des Vor-Entwurfs zu einem österr. Strafgesetzbuch, vol. 1* (Berlin: Heymanns, [3]1912), pp. 123–125; Friedrich, Nowakowski, *Probleme der österreichischen Strafrechtsreform* (Opladen: Westdeutscher Verlag, 1972), p. 8.

Penal Code of 1791/1795[33] is imaginable, especially if we take into account that a comparative perspective on foreign statute laws was not unusual during the process of the codification of the Austrian civil code enacted in 1811. During its preparation, the legislative committee—which consisted to some extent of the same persons involved in the drafting of the penal code (e.g. Franz von Zeiller)—regularly perused the French civil code.[34] Nevertheless, we have no indication that a similar procedure occurred during the preparation of the penal code of 1803.[35] Various reasons may explain this phenomenon[36]: Without any doubt, the Josephine code of 1787 was considered a modern and adequate foundation, so there was no need to search for foreign prototypes. Incidentally, if there had been such a desideratum, the *Leopoldina* of the Grand Duchy of Tuscany passed in 1786 by the Habsburg ruler Pietro Leopoldo (later on Leopold II, as Emperor of the Holy Roman Empire)[37] would have been a more obvious choice—but we have no evidence that the *Leopoldina* was taken into account, in spite of the fact that the legislative commission was installed during the reign of Leopold II. Possibly it would also have been inadequate to consider the penal codes enacted in revolutionary France,[38] but with regard to the process of codification of civil law, this explanation does not appear convincing.

Therefore, it is not surprising that none of the commentaries on the Austrian penal code published in the decades after 1803 mentions any French influences.[39] That does not mean that Austrian legal scholars were unfamiliar with the works of

---

[33]Cf. Jean-Marie Carbasse, *Histoire du droit pénal et de la justice criminelle,* avec la collaboration de Pascal Vielfaure (Paris: Presses Universitaires de France, [3]2014), pp. 439–442 (code of 1791) and pp. 447–448 (code of 1795 which essentially repeated, as far as substantive law is concerned, the provisions passed in 1791).

[34]Cf. Franz Stephan Meissel, "De l'esprit de modération–Zeiller, das ABGB und der Code Civil", Thomas Olechowski, Christian Neschware & Alina Lengauer (eds.), *Grundlagen der österreichischen Rechtskultur, Festschrift für Werner Ogris zum 75. Geburtstag* (Wien/Köln/ Weimar: Böhlau, 2010), pp. 265–292; Johannes Michael Rainer, "Franz von Zeiller und der Code civil", Constanze Fischer-Czermak et al. (eds.), *Festschrift 200 Jahre ABGB, vol. 1* (Wien: Manz, 2011), pp. 45–57; Helmut Heiss, "Der Einfluß des Code civil auf die österreichische Privatrechtskodifikation", Heinz Barta, Rudolf Palme & Wolfgang Ingenhaeff (eds.), *Naturrecht und Privatrechtskodifikation. Tagungsband des Martini-Colloquiums 1998* (Wien: Manz, 1999), pp. 515–542.

[35]Cf. Tschigg, *La formazione*; Adriano Cavanna, "Ragioni del diritto e ragioni del potere nel Codice penale austriaco del 1803", Sergio Vinciguerra & Sergio Ambrosio (eds.), *Codice Penale Universale Austriaco (1803)* (Casi, fonti e studi per il diritto penale Serie 2, Le fonti 18) (Padova: CEDAM, 2001), pp. 219–265, here pp. 230–231.

[36]Cf. Moos, *Verbrechensbegriff*, p. 189: "Ein unmittelbarere Einfluß des französischen *Code pénal* kann aus verschiedenen Gründen außer Betracht bleiben [...]."

[37]Cf. recently Hans Schlosser, *Die „Leopoldina". Toskanisches Strafgesetzbuch vom 30. November 1786. Originaltext, deutsche Übersetzung und Kommentierung* (Strafrechtswissenschaft und Strafrechtspolitik 23) (Berlin/New York: de Gruyter, 2010).

[38]These reasons are already listed by Moos, *Verbrechensbegriff*, p. 189.

[39]Cf. for instance Franz von Egger, *Kurze Erklärung des Österreichischen Gesetzbuches über Verbrechen und schwere Polizey-Uebertretungen, vol. 1* (Wien/Triest: Geistinger, 1816); Blumentritt, *Das österreichische Strafgesetz*; Maucher, *Das österreichische Strafgesetz*.

their French colleagues, but that these only played a minor role. The work by Sebastian Jenull on Austrian criminal law is a good example. In its introduction—dealing with the characteristics, history, sources and interpretation of criminal law—he points out that the knowledge of foreign penal codes could be helpful for interpreting the Austrian codification; yet he stresses that particularly the criminal law of German states would be instructive and he omits other countries.[40] When explaining which other knowledge is advantageous for scholars of criminal law, Jenull also mentions—besides forensic medicine, psychology and logics—criminal policy in general. In this context, he cites renowned European works on criminal law and its theory,[41] above all, Cesare Beccaria's "Dei delitti e delle pene". He also mentions three French authors whose works were translated into German, in particular (besides scholars like Antoine Nicolas Servin and Claude-Emmanuel de Pastoret) Jacques Pierre Brissot and his "Théorie des lois criminelles".[42]

When it came to the first attempts to revise the code in 1817, Zeiller, as the scholar in charge, named some reasons why a modernisation seemed to be necessary. Among others, he emphasised that new codifications had been enacted in France and in the Duchy of Oldenburg and that he had used them when working on the revision of the penal code.[43] However, as these efforts were unsuccessful, the only explicit mentioning of the French Penal Code as a potential role model remains an exception, and we do not know to what extent Zeiller used it as a source for his revisions.

When Anton Hye was charged with modernising the Austrian codification in 1848, we again have no indication of any French impact, which would naturally have been improbable, since the penal code of 1852 mainly incorporated previous ordinances and decrees without changing the system and structure of its precursor. Even some superficial similarities cannot be taken as hints of a French influence. Whereas the code of 1803 only distinguishes between crimes (*Verbrechen*) and delicts (*Vergehen*), the new codification of 1852 introduces a third category ("contraventions"/*Übertretungen*)[44]; however, contraventions are neither regulated by the penal code nor sanctioned by criminal courts; they are however fixed in administrative law and sanctioned by administrative authorities.[45] The distinction between the three categories is not due to an impact from the Napoleonic code

[40]Cf. Sebastian Jenull, *Das Oesterreichische Kriminal-Recht. Erster Theil* (Graz: Ferstl, 1808).

[41]Cf. Jenull, *Das Oesterreichische Kriminal-Recht*, p. 28.

[42]Antoine Nicolas Servin, *De la législation criminelle. Mémoire fini en 1778 […]. Avec des considérations générales sur les loix et sur les tribunaux de judicature* (Basle: Schweighauser, 1782); Claude-Emmanuel Pastoret, *Des loix pénales. 2 vol.* (Paris: Buisson, 1790); Jacques Pierre Brissot de Warville, *Théorie des loix criminelles* (Neuchâtel/Paris: Desauges, 1781).

[43]Neschwara, *Franz von Zeiller*, p. 7.

[44]Cf. Hye, *Das österreichische Strafgesetz*, pp. 50–51.

[45]Cf. Gerald Kohl, *Die Anfänge der modernen Gerichtsorganisation in Niederösterreich. Verlauf und Bedeutung der Organisierungsarbeiten 1849–1854* (Studien und Forschungen aus dem niederösterreichischen Institut für Landeskunde 33) (St. Pölten: Selbstverl. d. NÖ Inst. für Landeskunde, 2000), p. 110.

(or from the Prussian code of 1851),[46] but it clarifies the difference between administrative and criminal justice and brings no fundamental change to the 1803 code.[47] Moreover, there is a statement by Anton Hye that foreign codifications definitely were not relevant to the revision of the Austrian codification. Parenthetically, it is not the French code that he refers to but the Prussian code, which had entered into force one year earlier.[48]

Ten years later, it was once again Anton Hye who submitted the draft; this time it was a draft of a completely new codification. In a (printed) report to the Minister of Justice, Franz Klein, Hye pointed out that in preparation he had thoroughly reviewed "all foreign laws" (without explicitly mentioning the French code) and recent developments of legal science; however, he continued, despite the intensive study of the "recent codifications and drafts in all other European states and even of North America, in particular of other German states", he stressed that he had chosen "none as a dominant or preferred model", but that he had followed his own ideas in forging ahead on a new code appropriate to the special needs and circumstances of the Austrian monarchy.[49] When Hye mentioned foreign norms in the explanation of his draft, he referred to regulations in Prussia, England and Baden—but not in France.

---

[46]Cf. Robert von Hippel, *Deutsches Strafrecht, vol. 2: Das Verbrechen. Allgemeine Lehren* (Berlin/Heidelberg/New York: Springer, 1971), pp. 94–95; unclear and superficial Moos, *Verbrechensbegriff*, p. 313.

[47]Cf. Karl Hiller, "Österreich", Franz von Liszt (ed.), *Das Strafrecht der Staaten Europas. Im Auftrag der internationalen kriminalistischen Vereinigung* (Berlin: Liebmann, 1894), pp. 114–161, here p. 130: "Mit der gleichlautenden Dreiteilung der strafbaren Handlungen der modernen Strafgesetzgebung (preuss. StGB. von 1851, bayerisches StGB. von 1861, deutsches RStGB. [...]), welche dem auf die Strafsätze der einzelnen Delikte gebauten System des Code pénal folgt, hat die Einteilung des österreichischen Gesetzbuchs jedoch nichts als die Wortbezeichnung gemein. Die Erklärung der Gesamteinteilung kann deshalb nur aus dem Gesetzbuche von 1803 entnommen werden."

[48]Cf. Hye, *Das österreichische Strafgesetz*, pp. 8–9.

[49]Österreichisches Staatsarchiv (Wien), Allgemeines Verwaltungsarchiv, Legislative Angelegenheiten, Karton 1053, Zl. 1292/1863: "Allein so sorgfältig und allseitig ich auch auf die neueren in den übrigen Staaten Europa's und selbst Nordamerika's, und insbesondere auf die in den anderen deutschen Landen bestehenden Strafgesetze und vorliegenden Gesetz-Entwürfe Bedacht nahm, so habe ich mir dennoch kein einziges derselben bei meiner Arbeit, so es nun in Beziehung auf die Anlage, Gliederung und Eintheilung im allgemeinen, oder in Ansehung der Art der Strafen oder des Strafensystems überhaupt, oder in Betreff der Definitionen und Strafbestimmungen bei den einzelnen strafbaren Handlungen, zum vorherrschenden oder auch nur vorzugsweisen Musterbilde oder Anhaltspuncte genommen, sondern ich bin in den mehresten Puncten meinen eigenen Gang gegangen, nicht nur deßhalb, weil ich ebenfalls die schon mehrfach von sehr competenten Stimmführern ausgesprochene Ansicht theile, daß selbst die jüngsten deutschen oder überhaupt europäischen Strafgesetzbücher und Strafgesetz-Entwürfe nicht überall mit dem Höhepuncte der Strafrechtswissenschaft der Jetztzeit gleichen Schritt halten, - sondern insbesondere auch darum, weil mein Hauptaugenmerk doch zunächst darauf gerichtet sein mußte, ein den speciellen Verhältnissen Oesterreich's nach seiner heutigen politischen und socialen Gestaltung entsprechendes Strafgesetz zu Stande zu bringen."

The same is true for all attempts to achieve a new penal code in the following decades, where also archival sources deliver no hint of any influence of the French legislation.[50] The drafts submitted from 1874 onwards followed to some extent the German penal code (*Reichsstrafgesetzbuch*) passed in 1871.[51] When the legal scholars Heinrich Lammasch, Hugo Hoegel and Carl Stooss discussed a new draft from 1899 to 1902, frequent references were made to the German *Reichsstrafgesetzbuch*, to criminal codes in Swiss cantons and to the existing draft of a universal Swiss criminal code[52]—the latter was evidently due to the participation of Stooss.[53] In extremely rare cases, enquiries were made of the French legal situation: for instance, with regard to the experiences of other European countries, including France, in the suspension of a sentence.[54] No French influence, however, even during preparatory works, can be detected in the draft of the new penal code submitted in 1912.[55]

The complete lack of any impact of the Napoleonic codification of criminal law on Austrian discussions and plans in the second half of the 19th century is more than comprehensible. At that time, the *Code pénal* was no longer perceived as a modern codification which could serve as a role model to other states (by the way, as the Austrian code itself, which was increasingly criticised in the latter decades of the 19th century).[56] Indeed, Franz-Stefan Meissel pointed out some similarities between the French and the Austrian codes,[57] for instance, concerning the severe repertoire of sanctions enforced in both France and Austria and the high importance attributed therein to crimes against the state. Both codifications followed the principle of legality. In a few aspects, the slightly older Austrian code appears to be even more modern: It no longer recognised property confiscation, which was considered a sanction imposed not only on the convicted but also on his or her

[50]Cf. Österreichisches Staatsarchiv (Wien), Allgemeines Verwaltungsarchiv, Legislative Angelegenheiten, Karton 1059.

[51]Cf. Hiller, *Österreich*, pp. 158–161.

[52]Cf. Österreichisches Staatsarchiv (Wien), Allgemeines Verwaltungsarchiv, Legislative Angelegenheiten, Karton 1071.

[53]Cf. recently (with further literature suggestions) Martino Mona, "Strafrechtstheoretische Grundlagen der Vereinheitlichung des Schweizer Strafrechts unter Carl Stooss: Die Wurzeln des Präventionsmus", *Zeitschrift für Neuere Rechtsgeschichte 35*, pp. 21–32 (2013).

[54]Zl. Cf. Österreichisches Staatsarchiv (Wien), Allgemeines Verwaltungsarchiv, Legislative Angelegenheiten, Karton 1066, Zl. 124757/8.

[55]Indeed, the commission regularly adopted a comparative view and took into consideration the codes of foreign countries, but the French Penal Code seems to be never mentioned (although further research has to be done on the archival material), cf. for instance Österreichisches Staatsarchiv (Wien), Allgemeines Verwaltungsarchiv, Legislative Angelegenheiten, Karton 1067B, 1073.

[56]In the first half of the 19th century, even French legal scholars adopted a positive attitude towards the Austrian code of 1803: With a few exceptions, such as corporal punishment, it is appreciated by Victor Foucher, *Code pénal général de l'Empire d'Autriche avec des appendices contenant les règlements généraux les plus récents* (Paris: Impr. Royale, 1833), pp. IV–X.

[57]Cf. Meissel, *Le code de 1810*, 131–133.

family. Moreover, due to the legal regulation of aggravating and extenuating circumstances, the margin of discretion left to Austrian criminal courts was much wider than in France, where the code stipulated strict sanctions.

4 Summary and Conclusions

As we have seen, there was no significant reciprocal influence between French and Austrian penal law during the 19th century. The timeline makes any substantial impact of the French code on its Austrian equivalent impossible: The Austrian codification dates from 1803, and the French was passed several years later. During the process of codification which led to the code of 1803, there was also no need to take into account the French penal code of 1791, since the older Austrian codification passed in 1787 offered a modern basis for reform debates. When the Austrian code was revised in 1852, Anton Hye did not use foreign templates—and even if he had done so, the French statute would already have been outdated by the middle of the 19th century.

Nevertheless, the similarities between both codifications are considerable—as Franz-Stefan Meissel has demonstrated[58]—, although it is due to common roots in rational law and Enlightenment rather than reciprocal impacts. As far as legal science is concerned, Austrian scholars referred to the French code only rarely.[59] When they adopted a comparative view, they regularly preferred to consult codifications in other German-speaking countries.

Even though the Austrian penal code was not influenced by the Napoleonic codification, it served as a model in other countries. As can be observed in private law,[60] the German-speaking Swiss cantons used the Austrian codification as a source of inspiration, whereas in the western part of Switzerland, the French code set an example for cantonal legislators ("Basel-City", "Basel-Country", St. Gallen). Moreover, the Austrian code seems to have influenced the codification of penal law

[58]Cf. Meissel, *Le code de 1810*, 131–133.

[59]Cf. Joseph Kitka,"Gegenbemerkung über die Behauptung, daß das Verbrechen des Mißbrauchs der Amtsgewalt nur von solchen Beamten, denen eine executive Gewalt anvertraut ist, begangen werden könne", *Zeitschrift für österreichische Rechtsgelehrsamkeit und politische Gesetzkunde* 9, pp. 93–130, 1833, here p. 113.

[60]Barbara Dölemeyer, "Der Einfluss des ABGB auf die Schweiz", Elisabeth Berger (ed.), *Österreichs Allgemeines Bürgerliches Gesetzbuch (ABGB). Eine europäische Privatrechtskodifikation, vol. III: Das ABGB außerhalb Österreichs* (Schriften zur Europäischen Rechts- und Verfassungsgeschichte 57) (Berlin: Duncker & Humblot, 2010), pp. 319–338.

in Brazil in 1830[61]; and the Brazilian codification was a model for later codifications in many Spanish- und Portuguese-speaking countries in the 19th century (Spain, Portugal, Mexico, Philippines and Chile). The penal code for the Kingdom of Poland enacted in 1818 was influenced by the Austrian and by the French codification.[62]

One completely neglected impact by the French Penal Code on Austria has to be mentioned for the sake of completeness. After all, the Napoleonic codification had been put into force in the Illyrian provinces (which constituted a part of the French Empire) and in the Kingdom of Italy, as a French satellite state. When the Illyrian provinces (including parts of Carinthia, Crain and the Tyrol) and the northern parts of the Kingdom of Italy were re-integrated into the Austrian Empire according to the Treaty of Vienna, Austrian penal law was also re-introduced.[63] But due to the fact that Austrian courts had to apply French penal law in all cases of French and Italian domination, it was necessary to impose some adaptations: For instance, since the sanction of "civil degradation" (civil death)—implying among other things that the culprit no longer had the right to dispose of his property and had lost all political rights—was unknown in Austrian law, it was stated in 1817 that if this punishment was imposed during French rule, it ought to be replaced by imprisonment.[64]

---

[61]Cf. Meissel, *Le code de 1810*, 134; Bernardino Bravo Lira, "La fortuna del código penal español de 1848. Historia en cuatro actos y tres continentes: de Mello Freire y Zeiller a Vasconcelos y Seijas Lozano", *Anuario de historia del derecho español* 74, pp. 23–58, 2004; Bernardino Bravo Lira, "Bicentenario del Código Penal de Austria: Su proyección desde el Danubio a Filipinas", *Revista de estudios histórico-jurídicos* 26, pp. 115–155, 2004; Bernardino Bravo Lira, "El código penal de Austria (1803). Epicentro de la codification penal en tres continentes", *Anuario de Filosofía Jurídica y Social* 21, pp. 299–344, 2003. Recent research seems to contest Bravo Lira's thesis citing a significant Austrian influence on the Brazilian codification of penal law (cf. the contribution of Diego Nunes in this volume).

[62]Lesław, Pauli, "Die Bedeutung Zeillers für die Kodifikation des Strafrechtes unter besonderer Berücksichtigung der polnischen Strafrechtsgeschichte", Walter Selb & Herbert Hofmeister (eds.), *Forschungsband Franz von Zeiller (1751–1828). Beiträge zur Gesetzgebungs- und Wissenschaftsgeschichte* (Wiener rechtsgeschichtliche Arbeiten 13) (Wien et al.: Böhlau, 1980), pp. 180–191, here pp. 189–190.

[63]Whereas there are numerous works dealing with the introduction of the Austrian General Civil Code in these territories (e.g. recently Jürgen Busch & Alexander Besenböck, "Von Mailand bis Czernowitz. Die Einführung des österreichischen ABGB, Gesamtstaatsidee und nationaler Partikularismus", Andreas Bauer & Karl H. L. Welker (eds.), *Europa und seine Regionen. 2000 Jahre Rechtsgeschichte* (Wien et al.: Böhlau, 2007), pp. 535–597), the introduction of Austrian penal law has not been paid attention to by legal history. Cf. JGS (Justizgesetzsammlung/ Collection of civil and criminal laws) 1148/1815; 1267/1816; Provinzial-Gesetzsammlung für Tyrol und Vorarlberg/Collection of provincial laws for the Tyrol and the Vorarlberg XI/1814; Martin P. Schennach, "'Kein Volk österreichischer Staaten kömmt einer ähnlichen Mannigfaltigkeit einheimischer Rechte und Gewohnheiten gleich.' Von der Rechtsvielfalt zur Rechtseinheit. Der lange Weg Tirols zum ABGB", *Tiroler Heimat* 72, pp. 249–279, 2008, here p. 269.

[64]Cf. Maucher, *Das österreichische Strafgesetz*, pp. 29–30.

References

Ammerer, Gerhard, *Das Ende für Schwert und Galgen? Legislativer Prozess und öffentlicher Diskurs zur Reduzierung der Todesstrafe im Ordentlichen Verfahren unter Joseph II. (1781–1787)* (Mitteilungen des Österreichischen Staatsarchiv, Sonderbd. 11) (Innsbruck et al.: Studienverlag, 2010).

Anonymous, *Das Oesterreichische Strafgesetz vom 27. Mai 1852 und die Verordnungen über die Gerichts-Competenz. Erläutert zur Darstellung der in den bisherigen Gesetzen eingetretenen Veränderungen. Von einem praktischen Juristen [...]* (Wien: Tendler, 1852).

Arbeitsgemeinschaft österreichische Rechtsgeschichte (ed.), *Rechts-und Verfassungsgeschichte* (Wien: Facultas, [4]2016).

Baltl, Hermann & Kocher, Gernot, *Österreichische Rechtsgeschichte. Unter Einschluß sozial- und wirtschaftsgeschichtlicher Grundzüge. Von den Anfängen bis zur Gegenwart* (Graz: Leykam, [12]2009).

Bató, Szilvia, "Ein Überblick über die ungarische Strafrechtsentwicklung bis zum Jahre 1948", Arndt Sinn, Walter Gropp & Ferenc Nagy (eds.), *Grenzen der Vorverlagerung in einem Tatstrafrecht. Eine rechtsvergleichende Analyse am Beispiel des deutschen und ungarischen Strafrechts* (Schriften des Zentrums für Europäische und Internationale Strafrechtsstudien 1) (Göttingen: V&R unipress, 2011), pp. 41–52.

Bató, Szilvia, "Österreichische Wirkungen in der ungarischen Strafrechtswissenschaft vor 1848 am Beispiel der Straftaten gegen das Leben", Attila Badó et al. (eds.), *Internationale Konferenz zum zehnjährigen Bestehens des Instituts für Rechtsvergleichung der Universität Szeged* (Acta Iuridica Universitatis Potsdamiensis 1) (Potsdam: Universitätsverlag Potsdam, 2014), pp. 71–90.

Blumentritt, Stephan, *Das österreichische Strafgesetz über schwere Polizei-Uebertretungen vom 3. September 1803. Teil 1/2* (Wien: Braumüller, [2]1846).

Brauneder, Wilhelm, *Österreichs Allgemeines Bürgerliches Gesetzbuch (ABGB), vol. 1: Entstehung und Entwicklung des ABGB bis 1900* (Schriften zur europäischen Rechts- und Verfassungsgeschichte 60) (Berlin: Duncker & Humblot, 2014).

Bravo Lira, Bernardino, "El código penal de Austria (1803). Epicentro de la codification penal en tres continentes", *Anuario de Filosofía Jurídica y Social* 21, pp. 299–344, 2003.

Bravo Lira, Bernardino, "Bicentenario del Código Penal de Austria: Su proyección desde el Danubio a Filipinas", *Revista de estudios histórico-jurídicos* 26, pp. 115–155, 2004.

Bravo Lira, Bernardino, "La fortuna del código penal español de 1848. Historia en cuatro actos y tres continentes: de Mello Freire y Zeiller a Vasconcelos y Seijas Lozano", *Anuario de historia del derecho español* 74, pp. 23–58, 2004.

Brissot de Warville, Jacques Pierre, *Théorie des loix criminelles* (Neuchâtel/Paris: Desauges, 1781).

Brunet, Francesca, *Pena di morti e grazia sovrana nel Regno Lombardo-Veneto (1816–1848)* (PhD thesis, Innsbruck, 2013).

Busch, Jürgen & Besenböck, Alexander, "Von Mailand bis Czernowitz. Die Einführung des österreichischen ABGB. Gesamtstaatsidee und nationaler Partikularismus", Andreas Bauer & Karl H. L. Welker (eds.), *Europa und seine Regionen. 2000 Jahre Rechtsgeschichte* (Wien et al.: Böhlau, 2007), pp. 535–597.

Carbasse, Jean-Marie, *Histoire du droit pénal et de la justice criminelle,* avec la collaboration de Pascal Vielfaure (Paris: Presses Universitaires de France, [3]2014).

Cartuyvels, Yves, *D'où vient le code pénal? Une approche généalogique des premiers codes pénaux absolutistes au XVIIIe siècle. Préface de Françoise Tulkens* (Paris/Bruxelles: De Boeck-Wesmael et al., 1996).

Cavanna, Adriano, "Ragioni del diritto e ragioni del potere nel Codice penale austriaco del 1803, Sergio Vinciguerra & Sergio Ambrosio (eds.), *Codice Penale Universale Austriaco (1803)* (Casi, fonti e studi per il diritto penale Serie 2, Le fonti 18) (Padova: CEDAM, 2001), pp. 219–265.

Czech, Philip, *Der Kaiser ist ein Lump und Spitzbube: Majestätsbeleidigung unter Kaiser Franz Joseph* (Wien et al.: Böhlau, 2010).

Dölemeyer, Barbara, "Der Einfluss des ABGB auf die Schweiz", Elisabeth Berger (ed.), *Österreichs Allgemeines Bürgerliches Gesetzbuch (ABGB). Eine europäische Privatrechtskodifikation, vol. III: Das ABGB außerhalb Österreichs* (Schriften zur Europäischen Rechts- und Verfassungsgeschichte 57) (Berlin: Duncker & Humblot, 2010), pp. 319–338.

Egger, Franz von, *Kurze Erklärung des Österreichischen Gesetzbuches über Verbrechen und schwere Polizey-Uebertretungen, vol. 1* (Wien/Triest: Geistinger, 1816).

Finger, August, *Das Strafrecht. Mit Berücksichtigung des Vor-Entwurfs zu einem österr. Strafgesetzbuch, vol. 1* (Berlin: Heymanns, [3]1912).

Foucher, Victor, *Code pénal général de l'Empire d'Autriche avec des appendices contenant les règlements généraux les plus récents* (Paris: Impr. Royale, 1833).

Gábor Máthé & Werner Ogris (eds.), *Die Entwicklung der österreichisch-ungarischen Strafrechtskodifikation im XIX–XX. Jahrhundert* (Budapest: UNIÓ, 1996).

Garlati, Loredana, "Das Gericht als Interpret der Gerechtigkeit. Die Anwendung des Strafgesetzbuchs von 1803 im Königreich Lombardo-Venetien", Ettore Dezza & Loredana Garlati (eds.), *Beiträge zur Geschichte der habsburgischen Strafgesetzgebung in Italien. Mit einem Anhang: Cesare Beccarias Gutachten zum Allgemeinen Gesetzbuch über Verbrechen und Strafen aus dem Jahre 1791* (Rechtsgeschichte und Rechtsgeschehen, Kleine Schriften 24) (Berlin et al.: LIT-Verlag, 2010), pp. 89–102.

Harrasowsky, Philipp Harras von, *Der Codex Theresianus und seine Umarbeitungen, vol. I: Codex Theresianus* (Wien: Gerold, 1883).

Hartl, Friedrich, Grundlinien der österreichischen Strafrechtsgeschichte bis zur Revolution von 1848, Gábor Máthé & Werner Ogris (eds.), *Die Entwicklung der österreichisch-ungarischen Strafrechtskodifikation im XIX–XX. Jahrhundert* (Budapest: UNIÓ, 1996), pp. 13–54.

Hartl, Friedrich, *"Das Wiener Kriminalgericht. Strafrechtspflege vom Zeitalter der Aufklärung bis zur österreichischen Revolution* (Wiener Rechtsgeschichtliche Arbeiten 10) (Wien et al.: Böhlau, 1973).

Heiss, Helmut, Der Einfluß des Code civil auf die österreichische Privatrechtskodifikation, Heinz Barta, Rudolf Palme & Wolfgang Ingenhaeff (eds.), *Naturrecht und Privatrechtskodifikation. Tagungsband des Martini-Colloquiums 1998* (Wien: Manz, 1999), pp. 515–542.

Hellbling, Ernst Carl, *Grundlegende Strafrechtsquellen der österreichischen Erbländer vom Beginn der Neuzeit bis zur Theresiana. Ein Beitrag zur Geschichte des Strafrechts in Österreich* (Wien et al.: Böhlau, 1996).

Hiller, Karl, "Österreich", Franz von Liszt (ed.), *Das Strafrecht der Staaten Europas. Im Auftrag der internationalen kriminalistischen Vereinigung* (Berlin: Liebmann, 1894), pp. 114–161.

Hippel, Robert von, *Deutsches Strafrecht, vol. 2: Das Verbrechen. Allgemeine Lehren* (Berlin/Heidelberg/New York: Springer, 1971).

Hoegel, Hugo, *Freiheitsstrafe und Gefängniswesen in Österreich von der Theresiana bis zur Gegenwart* (Graz: Moser, 1916).

Hoegel, Hugo, *Geschichte des österreichischen Strafrechts in Verbindung mit einer Erläuterung seiner grundsätzlichen Bestimmungen* (Wien: Manz, 1904).

Hye, Anton, *Das österreichische Strafgesetz über Verbrechen, Vergehen und Uebertretungen und die Preßordnung vom 27. Mai 1852* (Wien: Manz, 1855).

Jenull, Sebastian, *Das Oesterreichische Kriminal-Recht. Erster Theil* (Graz: Ferstl, 1808).

Jerouschek, Günter, Hinrich Rüping & Barna Mezey (eds.), *Strafverfolgung und Staatsraison. Deutsch-ungarische Beiträge zur Strafrechtsgeschichte* (Rothenburger Gespräche zur Strafrechtsgeschichte 6) (Gießen: Psychosozial-Verlag, 2009).

Kitka, Joseph, "Gegenbemerkung über die Behauptung, daß das Verbrechen des Mißbrauchs der Amtsgewalt nur von solchen Beamten, denen eine executive Gewalt anvertraut ist, begangen werden könne", *Zeitschrift für österreichische Rechtsgelehrsamkeit und politische Gesetzkunde 9*, pp. 93–130, 1833

Kohl, Gerald, *Die Anfänge der modernen Gerichtsorganisation in Niederösterreich. Verlauf und Bedeutung der Organisierungsarbeiten 1849–1854* (Studien und Forschungen aus dem niederösterreichischen Institut für Landeskunde 33) (St. Pölten: Selbstverl. d. NÖ Inst. für Landeskunde, 2000).

Maucher, Ignaz, *Das österreichische Strafgesetz über Verbrechen sammt den auf dasselbe sich beziehenden Gesetzen und Verordnungen, sistematisch bearbeitet als Hilfsbuch beim Studium desselben* (Wien: Braumüller, 1847).

Meissel, Franz Stephan, "De l'esprit de modération – Zeiller, das ABGB und der Code Civil", Thomas Olechowski, Christian Neschwara & Alina Lengauer (eds.), *Grundlagen der österreichischen Rechtskultur. Festschrift für Werner Ogris zum 75. Geburtstag* (Wien/Köln/Weimar: Böhlau, 2010), pp. 265–292.

Meissel, Franz-Stefan, "Le Code de 1810 et le droit pénal en Europe centrale", Sénat de France (ed.), *Bicentenaire du code pénal (1810–2010)* (Paris: Sénat, 2010), pp. 125–137.

Mona, Martino, "Strafrechtstheoretische Grundlagen der Vereinheitlichung des Schweizer Strafrechts unter Carl Stooss: Die Wurzeln des Präventionsmus", *Zeitschrift für Neuere Rechtsgeschichte 35*, pp. 21–32, 2013.

Moos, Reinhard, *Der Verbrechensbegriff in Österreich im 18. und 19. Jahrhundert. Sinn- und Strukturwandel* (Rechtsvergleichende Untersuchungen zur gesamten Strafrechtswissenschaft N.F. 39) (Bonn: Röhrscheid, 1968).

Neschwara, Christian, "Franz von Zeiller und das Strafrecht", *Journal on European History of Law* 1, pp. 4–15, 2010.

Neschwara, Christian, "Pratobevera – Zeiller – Jenull: Eine 'herrliche Trias ... unserer Gesetzgebung'. Ein Beitrag zur Gesetzgebungsgeschichte des österreichischen Strafrechts im Vormärz", Ulrike Aichhorn & Alfred Rinnerthaler (eds.), *Scientia iuris et historia. Festschrift für Peter Putzer, vol. I* (Egling: Kovar, 2004), pp. 579–612.

Nowakowski, Friedrich, *Probleme der österreichischen Strafrechtsreform* (Opladen: Westdeutscher Verlag, 1972).

Ogris, Werner, *Die Rechtsentwicklung in Österreich. 1848–1918* (Wien: Verlag d. Österreichischen Akademie der Wissenschaften, 1975).

Ogris, Werner, "Joseph von Sonnenfels als Rechtsreformer", Helmut Reinalter (ed.), *Joseph von Sonnenfels* (Veröffentlichungen der Kommission für die Geschichte Österreichs 13) (Wien: Verlag d. Österreichischen Akademie der Wissenschaften, 1988), pp. 11–95.

Ogris, Werner, "Joseph II.: Staats-und Rechtsreformen", Werner Ogris, *Elemente europäischer Rechtskultur. Rechtshistorische Aufsätze aus den Jahren 1961–2003*, ed. by Thomas Olechowski (Wien et al.: Böhlau, 2003), pp. 125–164 (first published in 1990).

Ogris, Werner, "Die Entwicklung von Gerichtsverfassung, Strafrecht und Strafprozeßrecht 1848–1918", Gábor Máthé & Werner Ogris (eds.), *Die Entwicklung der ósterreichisch-ungarischen Strafrechtskodifikation im XIX–XX. Jahrhundert* (Budapest: UNIÓ, 1996), pp. 55–74.

Olechowski, Thomas, "Zur Entstehung des österreichischen Strafgesetzes 1852", Thomas Olechowski, Christian Neschwara & Alina Lengauer (eds.), *Grundlagen der österreichischen Rechtskultur, Festschrift für Werner Ogris zum 75. Geburtstag* (Wien/Köln/Weimar: Böhlau, 2010), pp. 319–341.

Pastoret, Claude-Emmanuel, *Des loix pénales. 2 vol.* (Paris: Buisson, 1790).

Pauli, Lesław, "Die Bedeutung Zeillers für die Kodifikation des Strafrechtes unter besonderer Berücksichtigung der polnischen Strafrechtsgeschichte", Walter Selb & Herbert Hofmeister (eds.), *Forschungsband Franz von Zeiller (1751–1828). Beiträge zur Gesetzgebungs- und Wissenschaftsgeschichte* (Wiener rechtsgeschichtliche Arbeiten 13) (Wien et al.: Böhlau, 1980), pp. 180–191.

Pfaff, Leopold & Hofmann, Leopold, *Commentar zum österreichischen allgemeinen bürgerlichen Gesetzbuche, Bd. 1, Abt.1* (Wien: Manz, 1877).

Rainer, Johannes Michael, "Franz von Zeiller und der Code civil", Constanze Fischer-Czermak et al. (eds.), *Festschrift 200 Jahre ABGB, vol. 1* (Wien: Manz, 2011), pp. 45–57.

Rüping, Hinrich, *Grundriss der Strafrechtsgeschichte* (Schriftenreihe der Juristischen Schulung 73) (München: Beck, [6]2011).

Schennach, Martin P. "'Kein Volk österreichischer Staaten kömmt einer ähnlichen Mannigfaltigkeit einheimischer Rechte und Gewohnheiten gleich.' Von der Rechtsvielfalt zur Rechtseinheit. Der lange Weg Tirols zum ABGB", *Tiroler Heimat* 72, pp. 249–279, 2008.

Schlosser, Hans, *Die „Leopoldina". Toskanisches Strafgesetzbuch vom 30. November 1786. Originaltext, deutsche Übersetzung und Kommentierung* (Strafrechtswissenschaft und Strafrechtspolitik 23) (Berlin/New York: de Gruyter, 2010).

Servin, Antoine Nicolas, *De la législation criminelle. Mémoire fini en 1778 [...]. Avec des considérations générales sur les loix et sur les tribunaux de judicature* (Basle: Schweighauser, 1782).

Solimano, Stefano, "Les précèdents européens au XVIIIe siècle du code pénal de 1810", Sénat de France (ed.), *Bicentenaire du code pénal (1810–2010)* (Paris: Sénat, 2010), pp. 45–61.

Steppan, Markus, *Die österreichische Strafrechtsentwicklung im mitteleuropäischen Konnex* (Graz: Habil. Univ. Graz, 2002).

Tschigg, Stephan, "La formazione del codice penale austriaco del 1803", Sergio Vinciguerra & Sergio Ambrosio (eds.), *Codice Penale Universale Austriaco (1803)* (Casi, fonti e studi per il diritto penale Serie 2, Le fonti 18) (Padova: CEDAM, 2001), pp. 51–67.

Vinciguerra, Sergio & Sergio Ambrosio (eds.), *Codice Penale Universale Austriaco (1803)* (Casi, fonti e studi per il diritto penale Serie 2, Le fonti 18) (Padova: CEDAM, 2001).

Vormbaum, Thomas, *Einführung in die moderne Strafrechtsgeschichte* (Berlin: Springer, [3]2015).

Zeiller, Franz von, "Recensionen des Strafgesetzes Franz I. über Verbrechen und schwere Polizey-Uebertretungen. Schriften über inländische Gesetzgebung. Anzeiger neuer, im Auslande bekannt gemachter Gesetzbücher oder Entwürfe", Franz von Zeiller (ed.), *Jährlicher Beytrag zur Gesetzeskunde und Rechtswissenschaft in den Oesterreichischen Erbstaaten, vol. 1* (Wien: Hof- und Staatsdruckerey, 1806), pp. 201–232.

Zeiller, Franz von, "Zweck und Prinzipien der Criminal-Gesetzgebung. Grundzüge der Geschichte des österreichischen Criminal-Rechts. Darstellung der durch das neue Criminal-Gesetzbuch bewirkten Veränderungen, sammt ihren Gründen", Franz von Zeiller (ed.), *Jährlicher Beytrag zur Gesetzeskunde und Rechtswissenschaft in den Oesterreichischen Erbstaaten, vol. 1* (Wien: Hof- und Staatsdruckerey, 1806), pp. 71–185.

Dr. Martin P. Schennach professor for legal history at the University of Innsbruck (since 2012), born in 1975, studies of both history and law in Innsbruck and Vienna (both completed with a Ph. D.); post graduate studies in Vienna ("Master of advanced studies for historical and archival science"), member of the Institut für Österreichische Geschichtsforschung in Vienna; habilitation for "legal history" (2008) and "Austrian history" (2011); head of department of the Institute for Roman law and legal history (since 2013); co-editor of the journal "Zeitschrift für Neuere Rechtsgeschichte" and "Beiträge zur Rechtsgeschichte Österreichs"; main areas of research: history of legislation and codification, constitutional history (especially statebuilding in early modern times, assemblies of estates of the realm, early constitutionalism), historical implementation of the law, history of criminal law, research on early modern revolts, history of science (especially the history of public law in Austria).

The Influence of the French Penal Code of 1810 on the Belgian Penal Code of 1867: Between Continuity and Innovation

Yves Cartuyvels

Abstract As soon as Belgium became independent, a will to reform the Napoleon Penal Code of 1810 emerged. In 1848, a reform commission initiated the reform process that will lead to the new Penal Code of 1867. Under the impetus of J.J. Haus, a penalist from the Ghent University, the revision process took a rather abstract and technical direction. Influenced by the dominating neoclassical penal thought, the new Penal Code of 1867 does not mark a clear rupture with the imperial Code of 1810. The text oscillates between reform and continuity, with a specific wish to correct the punitive excesses of the earlier text.

1 Introduction

Still a young European State today, Belgium was founded in 1830. Before the revolution, the Belgian provinces, previously under French dominion, were incorporated into the Dutch provinces between 1814 and 1830. Over the course of that period, the Dutch authorities attempted to reform the French Imperial Code of 1810. The "*Project of criminal code for the united Netherlands*" was met with resistance by the Belgian provinces, where it was viewed as a manifestation of the authoritarian power of the House of Orange. As soon as Belgium became independent, however, a will to reform the 1810 Penal Code resurfaced. Following the failure of the *Lebeau project* in 1834, a reform commission was constituted in 1848, under the direction of Jacques Joseph Haus, a penalist from Ghent University. Strongly influenced by the evolution of the French doctrine, the commission produced a text that would match the liberal spirit of the times and that was eventually promulgated in 1867. Deeply marked by the neoclassical penal thought, this Penal Code of 1867 is first and foremost a technical work, centered around general principles of penal Law and concerned with promoting a penology that would be

Y. Cartuyvels (✉)
University of Saint-Louis, Brussels, Belgium
e-mail: yves.cartuyvels@usaintlouis.be

A. Masferrer (ed.), *The Western Codification of Criminal Law*, Studies in the History of Law and Justice 11, https://doi.org/10.1007/978-3-319-71912-2_4

more humane than that of 1810. Thus oscillating between continuity and change, the new penal code clearly retains traces of the Napoleonic Code, striving mostly to soften its punitive excesses, and to weather its overarching utilitarianism.

2 The Premises of the 1810 Penal Code's Reform During the Dutch Period

Following the battle of Fleurus of 1794, France had annexed the Belgian provinces and imposed there its police and penal system.[1] The Penal Code of 1810 came into effect in the Belgian provinces from that point on, and would remain in effect there for the next twenty years or so. Upon the fall of the French Empire in 1814, the Belgian departments were incorporated into the Dutch departments to form the "United Provinces", placed under the Sovereignty of the Prince of Orange. The 1815 Vienna Treaty implicitly acknowledged the application, in Belgium, of laws in effect in the Netherlands.[2] Among these laws, we find the Penal Code of 1810, whose application had been maintained in the Netherlands by a provisional decree of 11 December, 1813.

Very shortly thereafter, the fundamental law of the new Kingdom of the Netherlands of 24 August 1815 provided, however, the drafting of new codes, including a penal code.[3] The function assigned to the proposed new General Code was, in accordance with the codifying tradition,[4] directly political: its purpose is, thanks to "the introduction of a uniform national legislation … to establish the new kingdom on solid grounds," with the belief that a new Dutch-inspired code would be "a powerful link between the various provinces" of the North and South of the country.[5]

As part of this unifying project, a *criminal code project for the United Netherlands* was filed in 1815 (Stevens 1997, 295). This text, which included criminal law as well as criminal proceedings, ended up being a failure, mainly because of differences of opinion between Belgian and Dutch specialists. In the North, people were anxious to get rid of the French Penal Code of 1810, which was by and large rejected. In these provinces, the Imperial Code "reminded foreign domination that at home, more than elsewhere, was burdensome and unfriendly to

[1]L. Van Outrive, Y. Cartuyvels, P. Ponsaers, *Les polices en Belgique. Histoire socio-politique du système policier de 1794 à nous jours* (Bruxelles: Vie Ouvrière, 1992, pp. 7–16).

[2]*Pasinomie* (Bruxelles: Moniteur, 1814–1815), p. 199.

[3]*Pasinomie*, (1815), p. 333.

[4]Y. Cartuyvels, *D'où vient le code pénal? Une approche généalogique des premiers codes pénaux absolutistes* (Bruxelles, Montréal, Ottawa: PUM, PUO, De Boeck Université, 1996).

[5]J.S.C. Nypels, *Législation criminelle de la Belgique ou Commentaire et complément du Code pénal belge*, T.I., Bruxelles, Bruylant-Christophe, 1867, Introduction, II–III.

the nation".[6] In addition, the French codes had recently been introduced there and had not truly left their mark on the legal level. In the Belgian provinces, the French legislation was better assimilated. The 1810 Penal Code thus aroused less resistance there, and its useful elements were acknowledged. Moreover, the focus of the study of the new texts was their Dutch language version, "whereas a French translation … would be too time consuming".[7] The language barrier was not likely met with benevolence in the Southern Provinces, where the dominant language was French. Belgian lawyers were also critical of a text that included the reintroduction of incriminations and penalties of the Old Regime, whose "inhuman and arbitrary" character they denounced,[8] or which still caused some confusion between a substantive criminal law and criminal procedure.

The text did not only produce controversy among the specialists in charge of examining over a hundred of its articles.[9] It was also rejected by the general public opinion as well as by certain Belgian reformers, who would later play an important role in the country's legislation. These include, for instance, the future promoter of solitary confinement in Belgium, Edouard Ducpétiaux.[10] Moreover, the bottom line of the criticism—a denunciation of a set of "atrocious, vague, absurd, unintelligible laws, written in an arch, scholastic style"[11]—was backed by the increasing hostility of the Belgian provinces to the authoritarian political evolution of the Dutch regime.[12] Described as "hideous",[13] the definitive draft of the criminal code for the United Netherland[14] filed in 1827 by the Dutch government, would be abandoned a year later, in 1828.

[6]J.S.G. Nypels, *Législation criminelle de la Belgique ou Commentaire et complément du Code pénal belge*, T.I., III.

[7]J. Beltjens, *Encyclopédie du droit criminel belge, 1ere partie. Le Code pénal et les lois spéciales* (Bruxelles-Paris: Bruylant-Christophe et Marescq, 1901), col. 1491J.

[8]J. Gilissen, "Codifications et projets de codification en Belgique au XIXe siècle (1804–1914)", *Revue belge d'histoire contemporaine*, (1983) p. 225.

[9]F. Stevens, La codification pénale en Belgique. Héritage français et débats néerlandais (1781–1867), in X. ROUSSEAUX, R. LEVY (dir.), *Le pénal dans tous ses états. Justice, Etats et sociétés en Europe (XIIe-XXe siècles)*, (Bruxelles: FUSL, 1997), p. 296.

[10]E. Rubbens, *Edouard Ducpétiaux*, 1804–1868 (Bruxelles: Louvain, Société d'études morales, sociales et juridiques, vol. I. et II, 1922), pp. 35–49; J. Gilissen, "Codifications et projets de codification en Belgique au XIXe siècle (1804–1914), (1983), pp. 226–227.

[11]J. Savart, 1826, quoted in F. Stevens, *La codification pénale en Belgique. Héritage français et débats néerlandais (1781–1867)*, p. 298.

[12]E. Berger, D. Heirbaut, H. Leuwers, X. Rousseaux, "La justice avant la Belgique: tentatives autrichiennes, influences françaises et expériences néérlandaises (1780–1830)", in M. De Koster, D. Heirbaut, X. Rousseaux (dir.), *Twee honderd jaar Justitie. Historische encyclopedie van de Belgische justitie. Deux siècles de Justice. Encyclopédie historique de la justice belge* (Brugge: Die Keure-La Charte, 2015), p. 44.

[13]J.S.G. Nypels, *Législation criminelle de la Belgique ou Commentaire et complément du Code pénal belge*, T.I.1867, introduction, p. III.

[14]*Ontwerp-Wetboek van strafrecht. Verslag der handelingen van de tweede kamer der Staten-Generaal gedurende de zitting van 1826–1827, gehouden te Brussel, van 16 oktober 1826 tot 8 mei 1827, 1ste deel, n° XXIII.*

The Belgian revolution of 1830 finally put an end to the reform process of the 1810 Penal Code under the Dutch governance. Three additional factors may explain the failure of the reform attempt. First, the Dutch criminal code project does not reflect the reformist ideology looming at the time in Europe. The text appears at odds with the new trends of the time.[15] It remains, paradoxically, overly faithful to the legacy of the Napoleonic codes of 1809 and 1810. Leaving an important place to corporeal punishment (whipping, branding, public execution), it is still largely based on theories of intimidation and retribution that were increasingly questioned at the time.[16] Secondly, from a political perspective, the text is too closely tied to an authoritarian state power, which the Belgian southern provinces were seeking to overcome. A consensus between North and South over the promulgation of a new penal code was a perilous political undertaking at a time when independence fever was taking hold in the South. Finally, in the southern provinces, the proximity of language and acculturation to technical legislative drafting of the Penal Code of 1810 made this text a difficult monument to overcome: if plans to reform the text to fit the ideas of the time were envisioned, it was out of the question to outright eliminate it, at least not immediately.

3 The Reform of the Criminal Code Between 1830 and 1867 in Belgium Between French Influence and New Ideas Being Circulated in Europe

3.1 The Lasting Influence of France at the Heart of a European Movement

In France, the severity of the 1810 Penal Code was regularly questioned over the course of the following years.[17] The highlight of this development, *the 28 April 1832 Act amending the Penal Code*, carried two types of reforms that focused on punishment and reflected a new mindset: on the one hand, this law "humanized" sentences, removing punishment (stocks, branding, etc.) and decreasing the severity of punishment for certain offenses. On the other hand, it 'correctionalized' certain indictable offences (in matters of theft and larceny) and extended the system of mitigating circumstances to all offences.[18] This law was actually a partial reform of

[15] N. Hennequin, *Observations sur le projet du Code pénal du Royaume des Pays-Bas* (Liège: ed. Lebeau-Ouwerx, 1827).

[16] J. Constant, "A propos d'un centenaire", *Revue de droit pénal et de criminologie*, 2 (1967), p. 92.

[17] A. Chauveau, F. Helie, *Théorie du Code pénal*, T.I (Paris: Legrand, 1845), p. 25.

[18] A. Chauveau, *Code pénal progressif. Commentaires sur la loi modificative du Code penal* (Paris: rue Coquellière, 1832).

the Penal Code of 1810, pending a more general reform of the latter.[19] It developed a movement of individualization of punishment that broke with the objectivism of the Penal Code of 1810. As Michel Foucault points out, "under the label of crime, what is judged are not only the legal objects defined by the code, but also, at one and the same time, passions, instincts, anomalies".[20] From behind the crime, the criminal individual emerges to seek a more just sentence, taking into account the guilt and moral responsibility of the author. The utilitarianism of the 1810 Penal Code is enhanced here by a moral principle, which takes into account the subjectivity of the author. As we will see below, the French reforms would often serve as a guideline for the early penal reforms and penal reform projects of the new Belgian state.

This evolution in France was the result of a neoclassical doctrinal current, borne in that country by authors like Guizot,[21] Rossi[22] or Ortolan.[23] Critical of the excessive severity of the Penal Code of 1810, the neoclassical doctrine sought a compromise between Benthamian utilitarianism, which dominates the imperial text, and Kantian moral retributivism. The logic of intimidation of the 1810 Penal Code was denounced on the grounds that it sometimes led to the setting of excessive sentences and, accordingly, to occasional excessive indulgence on the part of juries.[24] The neoclassical school advocated therefore a first form of individualization of punishment which resulted in a reduction of sentences within existing criminal categories, both for reasons of justice and to favor effectiveness of sentences.[25] This neoclassical thought found a wide resonance in Belgium, with Jacques Joseph Haus, the father of the Belgian Penal Code of 1867 and J.S.G. Nypels, one of the code's most enlightened commentators.[26] Rossi's *Traité de droit penal* (Treaty of criminal law), published in 1829, would become an important reference for the Belgian criminal neoclassical school. Moreover, in the 1830s, if the prison had definitely established itself as the ultimate form of punishment, it was the subject in France of heated debates that would also have an impact in Belgium.

---

[19]J.S.G. Nypels, *Législation criminelle de la Belgique ou Commentaire et complément du Code pénal belge*, T.I., 1867, T. I, p. 19.

[20]M. Foucault, *Surveiller et punir. Naissance de la prison* (Paris: Gallimard, 1975), pp. 22–23.

[21]Fr. Guizot, *Des conspirations et de la justice politique. De la peine de mort en matièrepolitique*, (Paris: Sautelet-Alexandre Mesnier-J. Barbezat, 1822), (ed. Paris: Fayard, 1984).

[22]P. Rossi, *Traité de droit penal*, (Bruxelles: Louis Hauman et Cie, 1829).

[23]J. Ortolan, *Cours de législation pénale comparée*, T. II, (Paris: Joubert, 1841).

[24]H. Donnedieu de Vabres, *Traité de droit criminel et de législation compare* (Paris: Sirey, 1947, 32).

[25]Y. Cartuyvels, "Légalité pénale, délégation au juge et habilitation de l'exécutif: le jeu pluriel des sources en droit penal", in I. Hachez, Y. Cartuyvels, H. Dumont, Ph. Gerard, F. Ost, M. van de Kerchove (dir.), *Les sources du droit revisitées. Vol. II., Normes internes infraconstitutionnelles* (Bruxelles: Anthemis-USL, 2012), pp. 66–67.

[26]J.J. Haus, *Les principes généraux du droit pénal belge*, 2 T. (Gand-Paris: Hoste-Thorain 1869); J.S.G. Nijpels, *Législation criminelle de la Belgique ou Commentaire et complément du Code pénal belge*, T.I. (Bruxelles; Bruylant-Christophe), 1867.

In France, Alexis de Tocqueville and Charles Lucas clashed on the pros and cons of the cellular model.[27] Echoing the debate in Belgium, Edouard Ducpétiaux introduced the generalization of solitary confinement, arguing for its advantages in terms of atonement and moral reformation for the inmate.[28] This new approach would also bear on the reform of the system of penalties in the Penal Code of 1867.

Lastly, the neoclassical period was also characterized by the development, in France and elsewhere in Europe, of the *legal technique* which influenced the numerous codifications carried out on the old continent.[29] In Belgium, this will to "improve the criminal legislative technique"[30] would clearly be present behind the Penal Code of 1867. This explains the decision to entrust the management of the reform to a top-flight technician, Jacques Joseph Haus. Haus chose to remain faithful to the main categories of the Penal Code of 1810, considered clearer and more concise than its legislative rival, the Bavarian Penal Code of 1813, inspired by Feuerbach. But the wish to produce a technical masterpiece in light of the Penal Code of 1810 would favor a refinement of various penal concepts, such as the principle of legality, offence attempt, concurrence of offenses or recidivism.[31]

The penal reform process in Belgium thus took place in a vibrant intellectual environment. On the one hand, it remained heavily influenced by developments of penality in France, a country with which Belgium shares both a language and a penal tradition. On the other hand, it was clearly inspired by another "discourse of truth" on penality,[32] carried by the neoclassical school that was also implanting itself across Europe at the time. The neoclassical discourse pushed indeed to reform the penal code in various European countries and to adapt penality to the level of civilizational advancement of their respective countries. At that time, as Rossi points out, "everywhere work is conducted on penal laws; the luxury of codification is all over [us]".[33] And as Haus explained, the country should not stay behind in terms of the institutional and intellectual changes of the time: "It matters a great deal to Belgium, which has the most liberal political institutions of Europe, to

---

[27]See F. Digneffe, "Problèmes sociaux et représentations du crime et du criminel. De Howard (1777- à Engels (1845)", in Ch. Debuyst, Fr. Dgneffe, J.M. Labadie, A.P. Pires, *Histoire des savoirs sur le crime & la peine*, vol. I (Montréal, Ottawa: De Boeck Université, 1995), pp. 185–190.

[28]L. Ducpétiaux, *Réforme des prisons. Système cellulaire* (Bruxelles: Victor Devaux et C°, 1865).

[29]Including in Russia (1845); Portugal (1852); Austria (1852); 'Germany' (1870); Spain (1870): the Netherlands (1881) or in Italy (1899).

[30]M. Ancel, Réflexions d'un pénaliste étranger sur le Code pénal de 1867, *Revue de Droit Pénal et de Criminologie,* 1967, n°2, p. 121.

[31]M. Ancel, Réflexions d'un pénaliste étranger sur le Code pénal de 1867, *Revue de Droit Pénal et de Criminologie,* 1967, pp. 123–124.

[32]M. Foucault, *L'ordre du discours*, Paris, Gallimard, 1971, p. 20.

[33]P. Rossi, *Traité de droit pénal*, 3e ed., Paris, Libraire de Guillaumin, 1863, p. 23.

follow the general movement (to) put into practice the theories that have been confirmed by the experience of other people."[34]

In Belgium, the penal reform was thus marked by multiple influences. The French heritage was analyzed and discussed against the background of legislative changes at work there, but also with the desire to give place to home-grown liberal political thought and to new ideas regarding criminal law, which were blowing across Europe at the time. The influence of France remained important but was also diluted in a movement of broader ideas at the European level, something which was underlined by the call made by Haus regarding comparative law as inspiration for reform.[35] This eclecticism of influences explains in great part the future orientations of the 1867 Penal Code, which oscillated between continuity and change regarding the Napoleon Penal Code of 1810.

3.2 *The Political Reform Process: A Doctrinal Work in Accordance with the Spirit of the Times*

From the establishment of Belgium in 1830, the Belgian government considered, as did the Kingdom of the Netherlands in 1815, the revision of the existing codes. A few months after the revolution, the Constitution of 7 February 1831 foresaw, in its Article 139, 12°, the revision of the codes "as soon as possible". The process was conventional and emphasized once again the importance of the codifying instrument in asserting the political power of the State. Without waiting for the promulgation of a new code, a reform movement was quickly initiated in the field of criminal law, in order to respond to the proposed liberal society model of the new Belgian state. The Constitution thus reminded the cardinal principle of legality of crime and punishment (Art. 9), canceled general confiscation as penalty (Article 12), and abolished civil death (Article 13), seen as an "equally heinous and useless" punishment,[36] or even as an absurd leftover fantasy from another time.[37] A few months earlier, a decree of the provisional government of 16 October 1830 had

[34]"Rapport de la Commission chargée de la révision du Code pénal", *Annales parlementaires*, Chambre, session 1849–1850, p. 325.

[35]One should "Take advantage of the experience of others and take from it all that is good and useful." (First report, corresponding to chapters I, II and III of the project comprised of the penal system, made in the name of the government commission by Mr. J.J. Haus, and addressed to the Minister of Justice/Premier rapport correspondant aux chapitres I, II, et III du projet comprenant le système pénal, fait au nom de la commission du gouvernement par M. J. J. HAUS et adressé à M. le ministre de la Justice, in J. S. G. Nypels, *Législation criminelle de la Belgique ou Commentaire et complément du Code penal belge*, T.I, (Bruxelles: Bruylant, 1867) p. 22.

[36]See E. Huyttens, *Discussions du Congrès national de Belgique*, 5 vol. (Bruxelles: Société typographique belge, 1844), pp. 668–669.

[37]J.J. Haus, *Observations sur le projet de révision du Code pénal présenté aux chambres belges, suivies d'un nouveau projet*, 3 vol. (Gand: De Buscher-Braeckman, 1835), p. 34.

decriminalized violations of the right of association, invoking respect for "the sacred rights of the individual and political freedom",[38] while another decree of October 22, 1830 repealed the "surveillance de haute police" (high police surveillance) of the 1810 Penal Code, to control the convicts after their release. Revoked on the grounds that it favored an unduly security-oriented logic and undermined the reintegration of prisoners into society, high police surveillance would however be partially restored by a law of December 3, 1836, in view of the high numbers of recidivism.[39]

From early on, thus, the liberal spirit inspired partial changes facing the authoritarian system of the Penal Code of 1810. In the spirit of previous change and inspired by the French legislation, a Belgian law of 29 February 1832 introduced the "correctionalization" of certain indictable offences for which the "Cour d'Assises" had the power to impose correctional penalties.[40] The law was criticized by some commentators because it did not correctionalize enough crimes and was insufficiently liberal or progressive. In fact, its purpose was more pragmatic than philosophical, aiming mainly to unburden the Cour d'Assises from cases deemed unworthy of its time and intervention.[41] Two years later, in 1834, a more ambitious reform bill was filed in the House, by the Minister of Justice Joseph Lebeau.[42] Inspired by the French reform of 1832, the *Draft Penal Code of 1834* corrected the most glaring excesses of the 1810 Penal Code, such as banishment, deportation and stocks. But the text also intended to innovate by removing the death penalty for political crimes.[43] Furthermore, it proposed the introduction of mitigating circumstances, with the twofold aim of finding a better balance between punishment and crime, and to optimize the effectiveness of the sentencing.[44] Behind a more humanitarian discourse, the project remained true to the spirit of the Penal Code of 1810, retaining the latter's general structure as well as its sequence of articles.[45] The text was abandoned a few years later, as a result of which a number of punishments (stocks, branding, mutilation) were officially still in effect, even if they were hardly ever enforced any more.[46]

---

[38] *Pasinomie* (1830), p. 35.

[39] J. Vanderlinden, "Le Code pénal belge entre 1830 et 1867", in *Mélanges offerts à Robert Legros*, (Bruxelles: U.L.B., 1985), pp. 709–714.

[40] *Pasinomie* (1832), p. 272.

[41] J. Vanderlinden, "Le Code pénal belge entre 1830 et 1867", in *Mélanges offerts à Robert Legros*, (Bruxelles: U.L.B., 1985), p. 712.

[42] J. De Brouwer, Jacques-Joseph Hauss et l'esprit de la réforme du Code penal de 1810, *Journal des Tribunaux*, 2010, n°6413, p. 646.

[43] "If France preceded Belgium, in removing the death penalty for all crimes against property, Belgium shall outperform all of Europe, in proposing the deletion of the deah penalty in all political crimes" (*Moniteur Belge* (9 October 1834).

[44] J. De Brouwer, Jacques-Joseph Hauss et l'esprit de la réforme du Code penal de 1810, *Journal des Tribunaux*, 2010, n°6413, p. 646.

[45] J. Constant, "A propos d'un centenaire", *Revue de droit pénal et de criminologie*, (1967), p. 95.

[46] F. Muller, X. Rousseaux, 2016, "Politiques et pratiques pénales à l'aune des transformations de l'Etat belge (1830–2012)", in M. De Koster, D. Herbaut, X. Rousseaux (dir.), *Twee honderd jaar*

Faced with the reluctance of the judiciary, the draft Penal Code received scathing criticism, primarily from Haus. Published in 1835, his *Observations on the draft revision of the Penal Code presented to the Belgian Chambers, with a new project* was to play a key role in the reform process.[47] Behind his criticism of the Lebeau project, Haus indeed drew the pillars of the penal reform to come, as he conceived of and emphasized the new direction to be taken by a penal law in line with the progress of society in its fight against crime. Building on Rossi and his *Traité de droit pénal* published in 1829, Haus strongly criticized Bentham's utilitarianism and its dominance in the Penal Code of 1810, as well as its philosophy basing the legitimacy of the sentence only on the need to defend society against crime. Haus used harsh words in his critique of the Napoleon Code: "It is the basis on which the Penal Code rests which is vicious. This basis is utility, the only utility; as far as justice itself is concerned, it is trampled underfoot".[48] Anxious to limit the influence of the utilitarian function of punishment with a retributive function, and eager to reconnect "the just" and "the useful", Haus was also critical of the sentence's intimidation function, and sensitive to the principles of expiation and amendment at the heart of neoclassical criminal science.[49] The text is essential because, through these observations made in 1835, Haus actually devised "the matrix of the Explanatory Memorandum of the 1867 Penal Code".[50]

While referring to the progress of the "science of criminal law," a Royal Decree of 1 May 1848, commissioned the examination of the 1834 draft. The aim was to "identify gaps revealed through the experience of recent years" (Article 1) in the *Projet Lebeau* and to propose a new project on this basis. In the minds of the authorities, the reform of the Penal Code of 1810 was still a priority, but one which took into account both the new neoclassical spirit that dominated criminal science in Europe and the lessons of case law that had developed in Belgium since 1830. Theory and empirical practice had to nurture the spirit of the reform in equal part. In fact, the central role given, within the Committee, to J.J. Haus[51] would guide the

Justitie. Historische encyclopedie van de Belgische justitie. Deux siècles de Justice. Encyclopédie historique de la justice belge (Brugge: Die Keure-La Charte), 2015, p. 194.

[47]J.J. Haus, *Observations sur le projet de révision du Code pénal présenté aux chambres belges, suivies d'un nouveau projet*, 3 volumes (Gand: De Buscher-Braeckman, 1835).

[48]J.J. Haus, *Observations sur le projet de révision du Code pénal présenté aux chambres belges, suivies d'un nouveau projet*, p. 25.

[49]J.J. Haus, *Discours prononcé par M. J.J. Haus, recteur de l'Université de Gand, à la réouverture des cours, le 10 octobre 1865. Du principe de l'expiation considéré comme base de la loi pénale*, (Gand: C. Annoot-Braeckman, 1865).

[50]J. De Brouwer, Jacques-Joseph Hauss et l'esprit de la réforme du Code penal de 1810, *Journal des Tribunaux*, 2010, n°6413, p. 646., p. 647.

[51]J.Y. Dautricourt, "Les auteurs du Code Pénal belge de 1867? Jacques Joseph Haus (1796–1881), Jean-Servais-Guillaume Nypels (1804–1886), *Revue de droit penal et de criminologie*, 1967, n°2, pp. 79–85.

work of the commission towards an essentially scientific approach. In 1867, the new text that some also called the "*Haus Code*" at the time[52] would leave very little room to the teachings of Belgian case law. To such an extent that some evoked the hypothesis of a "divorce" between the essentially doctrinal work of Haus (supported by Nypels, another brilliant academic partner in the reform process) and the Belgian case law, especially that of the "Cour de Cassation", de highest jurisdiction in Belgium, often more repressive or even at odds with the "spirit of time" that inspired the drafters of the new code.[53] What is significant in any case is "the almost total absence of reference to case law and, more broadly, to judicial practice" in the project.[54]

Under the impetus of Haus, the revision process of the 1810 Penal Code took a rather abstract direction. The work is mostly devoted to technical issues on various general principles of criminal law, leaving little room for discussion of political and social issues, conflicts of interests and values that are usually to be seen behind a Penal Code's set of offences and penalties. Prepared by a committee of experts, the Book I project, dealing with general principles of criminal law, was presented in two parts to the House of Representatives, on 14 December 1848 and 20 March 1850. Subject to discussion, the draft was forwarded to the Senate and then returned to the House, before being definitively adopted by the Senate on 11 March 1853. Overall, the political discussion did not significantly change the draft of the commission, largely designed by Haus. At most, one can discern a marginally more progressive tendency in the House of deputies, where some members tried to increase the liberal nature of the project on technical points, while the Senate adopted a somewhat more conservative approach.[55] Book II, entitled *Des infractions et de leur répression en particulier* (*On offences and their punishment in particular*) was presented to the House on 20 January 1858. Dedicated to special criminal law, or the incriminations and their penalties, Book II was also the subject of a long process of discussion in the House and Senate before being definitively adopted in the Senate on 17 May 1867. Initiated with the critical reaction of Haus to the draft proposed by Lebeau in 1835, the reform process had been in the making for 32 years.

---

[52]*La Belgique judiciaire*, 1881.

[53]J. Vanderlinden, Le Code pénal belge entre 1830 et 1867, in *Mélanges offerts à Robert Legros*, Bruxelles, U.L.B., 1985, 1985, p. 724.

[54]Fr. Tulkens, M. van de Kerchove, Y. Cartuyvels, Ch. Guillain, *Introduction au droit pénal. Aspects juridiques et criminologiques*, (Diegem: Kluwer, 2014), p. 108.

[55]J. De Brouwer, Jacques-Joseph Hauss et l'esprit de la réforme du Code penal de 1810, *Journal des Tribunaux*, 2010, n° 6413, p. 650.

4 The Belgian Penal Code of 1867 and the Imperial Code 1810: Between Continuity and Change

4.1 A Technical Work, Centered on the General Principles of Criminal Law

From the outset, the Penal Code draft proposed by Haus wavered between revision and reform. Anxious to mark the importance of the break with the past, Haus first stated that the 1810 Criminal Code needed to be "completely overhauled" and that the adaptation of Belgian criminal law in the new liberal political project implied "a complete reform of our criminal law" whose mindset must clearly distance itself from the "excessive severity" of the Napoleonic Code.[56] But this clear position was immediately tempered by the assertion whereby the Commission draft was not intended as a "review of our criminal laws" and that Haus did not claim to create "an entirely new code." It would indeed be "foolish to topple the substantive criminal code from top to bottom and replace it with an entirely different system, for the sake of creating national legislation only." It was therefore no longer a question of replacing the 1810 Penal Code system by an entirely new one, but merely "to correct its defective parts and to fill in its gaps."[57]

Haus took over the reformist philosophy from its inception in Belgium—the Lebeau project—while developing the project further. If we look at the structure of the Code and its general principles, elements of continuity with the Imperial Code are clearly preserved. Thus, the 1867 Penal Code maintains the tripartite structure of incriminations from the Penal Code of 1810, although it inverts the order of presentation. Admittedly, this tripartite division (crime, delict, contravention) was rejected by some foreign codes[58] and questioned at the time in Belgium on behalf of its "strictly formal" relevance.[59] But Haus stressed the fact that this structure, which governed the hierarchy of incriminations based on the applicable penalty, was found in various European codes of the time (in France, Italy, Germany or even the Netherlands). He also emphasized that, on a scientific level, one could not formulate "any serious objection" to this "practical division, so intimately related to our

[56]"First report, corresponding to chapters I, II and III of the project comprised of the penal system, made in the name of the government commission by Mr. J.J. Haus, and addressed to the Minister of Justice", in J. S. G. Nypels, *Législation criminelle de la Belgique ou Commentaire et complément du Code penal belge*, T.I, (Bruxelles: Bruylant, 1867) pp. 18–21.

[57]Ibidem, 23.

[58]M. Ancel, Réflexions d'un pénaliste étranger sur le Code pénal de 1867, *Revue de Droit Pénal et de Criminologie,* 1967, n°2, 1967, p. 117.

[59]A. Prins, 1889, *Science pénale et droit positif*, (Bruxelles-Paris: Bruylant-Marescq, 1889), no. 145.

judicial institutions that it can't be erased from our criminal laws."[60] Similarly, various general principles of repression were derived in straight line from the Napoleonic system, such as the system of aggravating circumstances in case of criminal participation, or Article 71 of the Penal Code with respect to criminal responsibility, the latter article being directly modeled on the famous Article 64 of the Code of 1810. Finally, with regard to incriminations, qualifications were regularly maintained.[61]

However, a number of inflections are noticeable, which clearly mark a formal evolution compared to the 1810 Penal Code. Thus, the 1867 Code was structured in two parts and not four, as had been the case for the 1810 Code, or the Lebeau project from 1834, which had remained faithful to the imperial code in this respect. In so doing, the Penal Code of 1867 revived the tradition of some traditional criminal codes of the absolutist period[62] and the mathematical spirit of a qualitative ideal of codification carried by the Natural Law School from the late seventeenth century.[63] Reviving the thread of a project inaugurated by Leibniz in the German Empire,[64] Haus considered the Code as a logico-deductive whole, with a strong articulation between the general principles of Book I and the incriminations and penalties of Book II. In this perspective, the importance of Book I, dedicated to general principles, becomes essential, since its construction would determine the application of incriminations and penalties *in concreto*. Also, where the 1810 Penal Code was mainly devoted to the question of specific incriminations and penalties, the Code of 1867 "would reverse the order of priorities",[65] demonstrating a central interest to the technical discussion of the general principles of criminal law contained in Book I. The rules relative to criminal participation, to the causes of justification, to excuses, to concurrence of offences or even still to recidivism, are also the subject of much further development than in the Code of 1810, without falling into the traps of an overly complex criminal casuistry. In this regard, the Code of 1867 is a true manifestation of neoclassical thought, featuring both its advantages and disadvantages: while the text is distinguished by a concern for

[60]"Explanatory Memorandum made in the name of the government commission by M. J.J. Haus and to the attention of M. the minister of Justice", in J.S.G. Nypels, *Législation criminelle de la Belgique ou Commentaire et complément du Code penal belge*, 1867, II, 26. On this issue, see F. Bartholeyns, Ch. Guillain, "La division tripartie des infractions", *Journal des Tribunaux*, 6413, (2010), pp. 654–658.

[61]M. van de Kerchove, "La peine, de 1810 à 1867, entre continuité et changement", *Journal des Tribunaux*, 6413, (2010), p. 678.

[62]Y. Cartuyvels, *D'où vient le code pénal? Une approche généalogique des premiers codes pénaux absolutistes*, (Bruxelles, Montréal, Ottawa: PUM, PUO, De Boeck Université, 1996), pp. 135–296.

[63]C. Varga, "Utopias of rationality in the development of the idea of codification", *Rivista internazionale di filosofia del diritto*, 1, (1978), 21–38.

[64]Y. Cartuyvels, "Entre la règle et le cas: réflexions sur les raisons et les impasses d'un modèle géométrique du droit", *Revue Interdisciplinaire d'Etudes Juridiques*, 76, (2016), pp. 191–194.

[65]Fr. Tulkens, M. van de Kerchove, Y. Cartuyvels, Ch. Guillain, *Introduction au droit penal. Aspects juridiques et criminologiques*, (Diegem: Kluwer, 2014), p. 98.

technical perfection, the focus on the question of "how to punish" is sometimes overly deployed to the detriment of the political question of "why" and "wherefore" punish.

4.2 A Humanist Penology, Faithful to the Neoclassical Spirit

Some twenty years after the enactment of the Criminal Code of 1867, A. Prins, one of the founders, alongside Dutchman Von Hammel and German von Litz, of the *International Union of Penal Law*, emphasized its anthropological matrix. This Code, Prins said, is "a work of optimism and humanity, hope and faith in the perfectibility of man".[66] In so doing, the 1867 Code contrasted with the spirit of the Penal Code of 1810. But—as Prins implicitly highlights—the text is also out of step with the new security-oriented scientism embodied by the Italian positivistic school and the movement for social defense emerging in the late nineteenth century in Belgium and Europe.[67]

This humanistic optimism, which aroused both the respect and distrust of Adolphe Prins, is reflected in the fate of certain general principles on temporal/motivational concurrence, causes of justification, attempted offence, or criminal participation, for which the new Code introduced rules that refined and generally softened repression. Furthermore, in terms of incrimination, a large number of indictable offences saw themselves downgraded to summary offences, resulting in mitigation of punishment by the judges *in concreto*.[68] So that, while retaining the architecture of the Criminal Code of 1810, the 1867 text modified the items that "bore the stamp of excessive severity."[69] But it is particularly with respect to the level of punishment that the evolution is the sharpest. Succeeding the 1810 Penal Code, the 1867 Code deleted the term "afflictive and defamatory punishment", replacing it by "criminal penalty". Following once more the French penal reform of 1832, the 1867 Code officially abolished several "afflictive" corporal penalties.[70] This is the case of amputation of the hand in case of parricide, deportation, or general confiscation, deemed "unfortunate legacies of barbarous times, many of these sentences imbued with cruelty, which our milder manners have forever

---

[66]A. Prins, *Science pénale et droit positif*, (Bruxelles-Paris: Bruylant-Marescq), 1889, p. 98.

[67]F. Tulkens, (dir.), *Généalogie de la défense sociale en Belgique (1880–1914)*, (Bruxelles: Ed. Story-Scientia, 1988).

[68]J. Constant, A propos d'un centenaire, *Revue de droit pénal et de criminologie*, 2, (1967), p. 112.

[69]Explanatory Memorandum made in the name of the government commission by M. J.J. Haus and to the attention of M. the minister of Justice, in J.S.G. Nypels, *Législation criminelle de la Belgique ou Commentaire et complément du Code penal belge*, T.I, (Bruxelles: Bruylant, 1867) T. II, p. 18.

[70]M. van de Kerchove, "La peine, de 1810 à 1867, entre continuité et changement", *Journal des Tribunaux*, 6413, 2010), p. 679.

postponed."[71] As for the death penalty, even if it was not formally abolished in political matters, the will for its more general abolition made progress. First, the 1867 Code restricted its application "within limits that had not been admitted by the Code's revision in France in 1832".[72] And secondly, the reform commission, true to the vision of Haus on this point,[73] expressed the hope that it "will be applied increasingly scarcely, so that the future generations may complete the abolition of this repressive means."[74] As for "defamatory" penalties, many of them were deleted, because of their stigmatizing character, and their counter-productive nature in terms of reintegration of the convict after he/she had finished to serve the sentence. Again, the weight of the French doctrine played a significant role[75] and compelled the authors of the Criminal Code of 1867 to eliminate altogether branding, civic degradation, public exhibition or stocks.[76]

In general, the softer penology of the 1867 Penal Code is marked by a double influence. On the one hand, thinking about the foundations and purposes of punishment had changed dramatically. Punishment was no longer conceived for its sole function of intimidation, as in the Penal Code of 1810. It now included a concern for the criminal's atonement, but also "a new principle, namely the amendment of the condemned," which "now dominates the making of the criminal laws of all civilized nations." This new corrective perspective "required a radical change in the penal system of the 1810 Code"[77] and explains the elimination of various "cruel" and "defamatory" forms of punishment, which were incompatible with the latter objective. On the other hand, the debate over the prison issue, which dealt with the execution of the sentence, changed the way to conceive sentencing. By the mid-nineteenth century, the American debate on imprisonment, pitting supporters of the "Pensylvanian model" and those of the "Auburnian model", burst onto the

[71]Report made in the name of the commission by M. Adolphe Roussel, *Parliamentary Documents Chamber* 2 of July, 1851, n°245, p. 12. One will note that, while most of these penalties were abolished in France in 1832, the expression "afflictive penalty" was maintained up until 1992 (M. van de Kerchove, 2010, 679).

[72]L. Thésard, De la revision du Code pénal en Belgique (Paris: 1867), p. 15.

[73]see J.J. Haus, *La peine de mort - Son passé, son présent, son avenir*, (Gand: Hoste, 1867), p. 139.

[74]Report made in the name of the commission by M. Adolphe Roussel, *Documents Parlementaires, Chambre*, n°245, 13.

[75]M. van de Kerchove, "La peine, de 1810 à 1867, entre continuité et changement, *Journal des Tribunaux*, 6413, (2010), p. 679.

[76]Idem, 12. Note that the proposed Dutch Penal Code, presented to the House of Representatives in 1827, provided, in Article 66, a specific sentence of "declaration of infamy" (eerloosverklaring) for certain crimes "worthy of this moral blight" (Wetboek van Ontwerp van Strafregt 1827 in Noordziek, 1883 39).

[77]J.S.G. Nypels, *Le Code pénal belge interprété*, (Bruxelles: Bruylant-Christophe), 1867: pp. 31–32.

European scene.[78] Introduced in France by Beaumont and Tocqueville,[79] this debate discussed the pros and cons of collective imprisonment versus solitary confinement (the cellular model). In Belgium, collective confinement, still favored by the *projet Lebeau* of 1834, was gradually dismissed, notably under the impetus of Edouard Ducpétiaux, the Kingdom's inspector general of prisons, who was largely favorable to the cellular model. For Ducpétiaux, solitary confinement, which revived the tradition of a religious ideal of penitence and moral reformation, met the new ideals of atonement and moral reformation brought about by the prison sentence.[80] Haus and the Penal Code reform committee thereafter clearly opted for Ducpétiaux's proposal,[81] favoring a strict solitary confinement, day and night, so as to also prevent 'contagion' among inmates. This isolating perspective, which makes the sentence more painful, then explains a change in the scale and length of punishments, generally softened. Similarly, this would become the basis for a discussion on the possible abolition of life sentences. Haus and the Reform Commission were indeed favorable to the removal of these life sentences, which they considered incompatible with the strict regime of complete isolation.[82] Their proposal was rejected, however, by political actors in the Senate. The latter deemed that while one must avoid punitive excesses, one should also "be wary of this cruel philanthropy that seems to protect the crime against innocence, and commiserate more with the fate of the guilty parties than with the victims."[83]

Finally, the abolition of the death penalty for political crimes and the removal of other political penalties under the Criminal Code of 1810 (deportation, exile, loss of civil rights) led the legislator of 1867 to introduce a specific sentence of "detention" for political crimes. True to a romantic conception of the political crime, associated more with a noble ideal or passion than with the perversity or antisocial character of its author, the detention sentence implied preferential treatment on various levels. In this respect, the reversal witnessed in our early 21st century is obviously striking: in a context dominated by the issue of terrorism, the political dimension of crime is less and less recognized. And when it is invoked, this political dimension appears increasingly as an aggravating factor and no longer a mitigating one.

---

[78]F. Digneffe, "Problèmes sociaux et représentations du crime et du criminel. De Howard (1777)- à Engels (1845), in Ch. Debuyst, Fr. Digneffe, J.M. Labadie, A.P. Pires, *Histoire des savoirs sur le crime & la peine*, vol. I, (Bruxelles,: De Boeck Université, 1995), pp. 180–183.

[79]G. de Beaumont, A. de Tocqueville (1833), *On the Penitentiary System in the United States and Its Application in France* (Carbondale & Edwards ville, Southern Illinois University Press, 1979).

[80]L. Ducpétiaux, *Réforme des prisons. Système cellulaire*, (Bruxelles: Victor Devaux et C°, 1865).

[81]"Rapport de la Commission chargée de la révision du Code pénal", *Annales parlementaires*, Chambre, (session 1849–1850), p. 327.

[82]Haus report in the name of the government commission, in J.S.C. Nypels, *Législation criminelle de la Belgique ou Commentaire et complément du Code pénal belge*, T.I. (Bruxelles: Bruylant-Christophe 1867), p. 31.

[83]Baron d'Anethan's report to the Senate session, 24 March 1852, in J.S.C. Nypels, 1867, *Législation criminelle de la Belgique ou Commentaire et complément du Code pénal belge*, T.I. (Bruxelles: Bruylant-Christophe 1867), p. 283.

5 Conclusion

Although the Belgian Penal Code of 1867 was the result of a political initiative that dates back to the aftermath of the Belgian revolution, its political character was relatively weak. Significantly less than other codes, it was promoted as the nationalization law instrument meant to assert symbolically the power and authority of the new state. A technical work, the Criminal Code of 1867 primarily reflected the desire to not stay behind the various, liberally-inflected developments in criminal law that were spreading across Europe at the time. More than a political project, the text therefore bore the seal of neoclassical thought that dominated the legal debate in France and other European countries at the time. A work of revision, the text does not mark a clear break with the imperial Code of 1810. In this regard, the text fits between reform and continuity, with a particular care to correct the punitive excesses of the earlier text, following the movement initiated by the French neighbors through different partial reforms. It is therefore important for the legislator to re-inject, next to the principle of utility, an ideal of justice and equity, overly sacrificed by the Code of 1810 to the Reason of State and to the concern of public order alone.

Paradoxically, once promulgated the text appeared out of step with its time. Like the Zanardelli Code of 1889 in Italy,[84] the editors of the Belgian Penal Code of 1867 did not take the measure of the emergence of a new reading of crime, borne by criminal anthropology and the social defense movement in the last part of the century. If the principle of individualization of the penalty, so dear to the neoclassical school, was preserved, it now was resting on new assumptions in a world that had changed. As part of an emerging "insurance society"[85] driven by the concepts of risk, insurance and guarantee, in which the state is now summoned to protect individuals against risks of any kind, the notions of fault, moral responsibility and fair compensation were challenged by new concepts such as determinism, social responsibility and dangerousness. As a result of a proper compromise in the spirit of "penal welfarism"[86] that developed in Europe at the time, the 1867 Penal Code underwent however no fundamental changes: it remained in effect but would be completed very quickly on its margins by "social defense laws" for various categories of dangerous individuals. "Guilt" and "dangerousness" then complement each other to refine the mesh of a penal net whose basic architecture is still marked today by the 1867 text.

---

[84]L. Lacche, Un code pénal pour l'Unité italienne, le Code Zanardelli (1889). La genèse, le débat, le projet juridique, in X. ROUSSEAUX, R. LEVY (dir.), *Le pénal dans tous ses états. Justice, Etats et sociétés en Europe (XIIe-XXe siècles)* (Bruxelles: FUSL, 1997), pp. 316–317.

[85]See F. Ewald, *L'Etat providence*, Paris, Grasset, 1986.

[86]D. Garland, *Punishment and Welfare. A History of Penal Strategies* (Brookfield: Gower Publishing, 1985).

Bibliography

Ancel, Marc, “Réflexions d'un pénaliste étranger sur le Code pénal de 1867”, Revue de Droit Pénal et de Criminologie, 2 (1967), 115–129.

Belgique judiciaire, t. 39, 13 mars 1881.

Bartholeyns, Frédérique, “La codification en droit pénal: une voie sans issue?”, in *Actualités du droit pénal - Droit belge et européen, Revue de la Faculté de droit de l'U.L.B.*, 2003, n°2, 166–171.

Bartoleyns, Frédérique, Guillain Christine, “La division tripartie des infractions”, Journal des Tribunaux, 6413 (2010), 654–658.

Belgique Judiciaire, 1881.

Beltjens, Georges, *Encyclopédie du droit criminel belge, 1ere partie. Le Code pénal et les lois spéciales* (Bruxelles-Paris: Bruylant-Christophe et Marescq, 1901).

Berger, Emmanuel, Heirbaut Dirk, Luwers Hervé, Rousseaux Xavier, «La justice avant la Belgique: tentatives autrichiennes, influences françaises et expériences néérlandaises (1780–1830)», in, *Twee honderd jaar Justitie. Historische encyclopedie van de Belgische justitie. Deux siècles de Justice. Encyclopédie historique de la justice belge*, (De Koster, Margaux, Heirbaut, Dirk, Rousseaux, Xavier (eds.), (Brugge: Die Keure-La Charte, 2015), 27–46.

Cartuyvels, Yves, “Légalité pénale, délégation au juge et habilitation de l'exécutif: le jeu pluriel des sources en droit penal”, in I. HACHEZ, Y. CARTUYVELS, H. DUMONT, Ph. GERARD, F. OST, M. van de KERCHOVE (dir.), *Les sources du droit revisitées. Vol. II., Normes internes infraconstitutionnelles*, (Hachez, Isabelle, Cartuyvels, Yves, Dumont, Hugues, Gerard, Philippe, Ost, François, van de Kerchove, Michel (eds.), (Bruxelles: Anthemis-FUSL., 2012), 55–104.

Cartuyvels, Yves, *D'où vient le code pénal ? Une approche généalogique des premiers codes pénaux absolutistes*, Bruxelles (Montréal, Ottawa, Bruxelles: PUM, PUO, De Boeck Université, 1996).

Cartuyvels, Yves, “Entre la règle et le cas: réflexions sur les raisons et les impasses d'un modèle géométrique du droit”, Revue Interdisciplinaire d'Etudes Juridiques, 76 (2016), 177–209.

Chaveau Adolphe, *Code pénal progressif. Commentaires sur la loi modificative du Code penal* (Paris: rue Coquellière, 1832).

Chauveau, Adolphe, Hélie, Faustin, *Théorie du Code pénal*, T.I, Paris, Legrand, 1845.

Constant, Jean, “A propos d'un centenaire”, *Revue de droit pénal et de criminologie*, 2 (1967), 87–113.

Dautricourt, Jean-Yves, “Les auteurs du Code Pénal belge de 1867? Jacques Joseph Haus (1796–1881), Jean-Servais-Guillaume Nypels (1804–1886), *Revue de droit penal et de criminologie*, 1967, n°2, pp. 79–85.

de Beaumont, Gustave, de Tocqueville, Alexis, *Système pénitentiaire aux Etats-Unis et de son application en France. Suivi d'un appendice sur les colonies pénales* (Paris: Librairie Charles Gosselin, 1845).

de Beaumont, Gustave, de Tocqueville, Alexis, (1833), *On the Penitentiary System in the United States and Its Application in France* (Carbondale & Edwards ville: Southern Illinois University Press, 1979).

De Brouwer, Jérôme, “Jacques-Joseph Hauss et l'esprit de la réforme du Code penal de 1810”, Journal des Tribunaux, 6413 (2010), 646–650.

Donnedieu de Vabres, Henry, *Traité de droit criminel et de législation compare* (Paris: Sirey, 1947).

Ducpétiaux, Edouard, *Réforme des prisons. Système cellulaire* (Bruxelles: Victor Devaux et C°, 1865).

Digneffe, Françoise, “Problèmes sociaux et représentations du crime et du criminel. De Howard (1777- à Engels (1845)”, in *Histoire des savoirs sur le crime & la peine*, vol. I (Debuyst, Christian, Digneffe, Françoise, Labadie, Pires, Alvaro (eds.), (Montréal, Ottawa, Bruxelles: PUM, PUO, De Boeck Université, 1995), 139–212.

Foucault, Michel, L'ordre du discours (Paris: Gallimard, 1971).
Foucault, Michel, *Surveiller et punir. Naissance de la prison* (Paris: Gallimard, 1975).
Garland, David, *Punishment and Welfare. A History of Penal Strategies* (Brookfield: Gower Publishing, 1985).
Gilissen, Jean, "Codifications et projets de codification en Belgique au XIXe siècle (1804–1914)", Revue belge d'histoire contemporaine, 1983, 203–285.
Guizot, François, *Des conspirations et de la justice politique. De la peine de mort en matière politique (*Paris: Sautelet-Alexandre Mesnier-J. Barbezat, 1822, rep. Paris, Fayard, 1984).
Haus, Jean-Jacques, *Observations sur le projet de révision du Code pénal présenté aux chambres belges, suivies d'un nouveau projet*, 3 volumes (Gand: De Buscher-Braeckman, 1835).
Haus, Jean-Jacques, *Discours prononcé par M. J.J. Haus, recteur de l'Université de Gand, à la réouverture des cours, le 10 octobre 1865. Du principe de l'expiation considéré comme base de la loi pénale* (Gand: C. Annoot-Braeckman, 1865).
Haus, Jean-Jacques, *La peine de mort - Son passé, son présent, son avenir*, Gand, Hoste, 1867.
Haus, Jean-Jacques. *Les principes généraux du droit pénal belge*, 2 Vol. (Gand-Paris: Hoste-Thorain, 1869).
Hennequin, Nicolas, *Observations sur le projet du Code pénal du Royaume des Pays-Bas* (Liège: ed. Lebeau-Ouwerx, 1827).
Huyttens, Emile, *Discussions du Congrès national de Belgique*, 5 vol. (Bruxelles: Société typographique belge, 1844).
Lacchè Luiggi, "Un code pénal pour l'Unité italienne, le Code Zanardelli (1889). La genèse, le débat, le projet juridique, in *Le pénal dans tous ses états. Justice, Etats et sociétés en Europe (XIIe-XXe siècles)* (Rousseaux, Xavier, Levy, René, eds.) (Bruxelles: FUSL, 1997), 303–319.
Muller, Françoise, Rousseaux, Xavier, Politiques et pratiques pénales à l'aune des transformations de l'Etat belge (1830–2012), in, *Twee honderd jaar Justitie. Historische encyclopedie van de Belgische justitie. Deux siècles de Justice. Encyclopédie historique de la justice belge*, (De Koster, Margaux, Heirbaut, Dirk, Rousseaux, Xavier (eds.), (Brugge: Die Keure-La Charte, 2015) 191–197.
Noordziek, Jan-Jacobus Frederik, *Geschiedenies der beraadslagingen gevoerd in de tweede kamer der Staten-generaal over het ontwerp Wetboek van strafregt*, eerste deel, (s'Gravenhage: Martinus Nijhof, 1883).
Nypels, Jean Servais Guillaume, *Législation criminelle de la Belgique ou Commentaire et complément du Code pénal belge*, T.I. (Bruxelles: Bruylant-Christophe, 1867).
Nypels, Jean Servais Guillaume, *Le Code pénal belge interprété* (Bruxelles: Bruylant-Christophe, 1867).
Ontwerp-Wetboek van strafrecht. Verslag der handelingen van de tweede kamer der Staten-Generaal gedurende de zitting van 1826–1827, gehouden te Brussel, van 16 oktober 1826 tot 8 mei 1827, 1ste deel.
Ortolan, Joseph Louis Elzéar, *Cours de législation pénale comparée*, T. II (Paris: Joubert, 1841).
Prins Adolphe, *Science pénale et droit positif* (Bruxelles-Paris: Bruylant-Marescq, 1889).
Rossi Pelegrino, *Traité de droit pénal*, (Bruxelles: Louis Hauman et Cie, 1829).
Rubbens, Edmond, *Edouard Ducpétiaux*, 1804–1868, Bruxelles, vol. I. et II (Louvain: Société d'études morales, sociales et juridiques, 1922).
Saleilles, Raymond, L'individualisation de la peine (1898), in *L'individualisation de la peine. De Saleilles à aujourd'hui* (Ottenhof, Raymond, eds.) (Toulouse: Eres, 2001).
Stevens, Frédéric, "La codification pénale en Belgique. Héritage français et débats néerlandais (1781–1867"), in *Le pénal dans tous ses états. Justice, Etats et sociétés en Europe (XIIe-XXe siècles)* (Rousseaux, Xavier, Lévy, René, eds.), (Bruxelles: FUSL, 1997), 287–302.
Thésard, Louis, *De la revision du Code pénal en Belgique* (Paris: 1867).
Tulkens, Françoise (eds.), *Généalogie de la défense sociale en Belgique (1880–1914)*, (Bruxelles: Ed. Story-Scientia, 1988).
van de Kerchove, Michel, "La peine, de 1810 à 1867, entre continuité et changement", Journal des Tribunaux, 6413, (2010) 677–680.

Vanderlinden, Jean, "Le Code pénal belge entre 1830 et 1867", in *Mélanges offerts à Robert Legros* (Bruxelles: U.L.B., 1985), 707–731.

Van Outrive, Lode, Cartuyvels, Yves, Ponsaers, Paul, *Les polices en Belgique. Histoire socio-politique du système policier de 1794 à nous jours* (Bruxelles: Vie Ouvrière, 1992).

Varga, Csaba, "Utopias of rationality in the development of the idea of codification", Rivista internazionale di filosofia del diritto, 1, (1978), 21–38.

Yves Cartuyvels is Ordinary Professor at the Faculty of Law of the Université Saint-Louis-Brussels (USL-B, Belgium) where he teaches Penal Law, Introduction to the History of Criminology and Theory of Law. As co-director of the Interdisciplinary Seminar of Legal Studies (SIEJ), vice-Director of the Sociological Studies Center (CES) and member of the Research Group on Penal and Criminal Questions (GREPEC) at the USL-B, he has directed and is conducting numerous national and international researches on crime and deviance in an interdisciplinary perspective. Besides socio-legal and empirical researches on Penal Law, Juvenile Justice, Sentencing and Internment, he always kept a main interest for legal history, with the publication of books on The Socio-Political History of Police in Belgium (1991), The Genealogy of Penal codification in Europe (1996) and Juvenile Justice In Europe and its evolutions (2002); articles on "Elements for a genealogical approach of the Penal Code" (1994), "Prevention in the Prussian Landrecht of 1794" (1999), "The Reforms of Penality in a genealogical perspective" (2014), "The uses of biologisation of crime at the end of the 19th century" (2015), "Moral Responsibility and dangerousness, two conflictual versions of the Individualisation of the Sentences in Belgium at the end of the XIXe Century" (2015) or "The Punishment of Mentally ill Offenders in Belgium" (2016).

The Influence of the French Penal Code of 1810 Over the "General Part" of the Portuguese Penal Code of 1852: The Visible and the Invisible

Frederico de Lacerda da Costa Pinto and Pedro Caeiro

Abstract This chapter aims at assessing whether or not the Code Pénal of 1810 (the *Code*) bore any influence on the "general part" of the Portuguese Penal Code of 1852 (PC1852)—and, if so, to what extent. To that effect, it is necessary to understand how the reform of the penal laws developed in Portugal from the late 18th century to 1852, the first milestone being the Draft Penal Code authored by Mello Freire and submitted to Queen Maria I in 1786. It is also important to analyse the process in the context of the political and military strife that ravaged the country during the first half of the 19th century, namely the Napoleonic invasions and the constitutional reforms that resulted from the civil war between liberals and absolutists. The general conclusion of our study is that the *Code* was one of the references that has been taken into account in the reform of the Portuguese criminal law that led to the enactment of the PC1852, along with other foreign laws and the Portuguese legal tradition, and its influence was more felt in the sanctions system than on the other sections of the new code.

1 The Context of the Portuguese Penal Code of 1852

Although the first (modern) Portuguese Penal Code did not come into force until 1852,[1] the attempts to reform the penal legislation had started a long time before.

[1]The general laws of the Kingdom (*Ordenações*), including the criminal law, were compiled for the first time in the *Ordenações Afonsinas* (1446–47), which were later repealed by the *Ordenações Manuelinas* (1512–21). In 1603, under the rule of King Filipe II of Spain, a third compilation came into force, the *Ordenações Filipinas* (1603); the criminal law contained therein (Book 5) was in force until as late as 1852.

F. de Lacerda da Costa Pinto (✉)
NOVA University of Lisbon, Lisboa, Portugal
e-mail: fcostapinto@fd.unl.pt

P. Caeiro
University of Coimbra, Coimbra, Portugal
e-mail: pcaeiro@fd.uc.pt

A. Masferrer (ed.), *The Western Codification of Criminal Law*, Studies in the History of Law and Justice 11, https://doi.org/10.1007/978-3-319-71912-2_5

As a matter of fact, the movement for legal reform that swept across Europe at the end of the *Ancien Régime* led Queen Maria I to charge a commission, in 1778, with the assessment and overall review of all the existing legislation, much of which dated back to the 14th and 15th centuries. To the Queen's view, the reform was necessary because "the happiness of the people depends much on the rendering of prompt and full justice, which in turn cannot be achieved without a clear, precise and undoubtful intelligence of the laws", and such understanding "is more difficult today, due to the multiplicity of the laws and also to some of them having become outdated and impracticable with the course of time".[2]

The Commission's task was to identify: (i) the laws that should be deemed "old-fashioned and, due to changing things, useless for the present and for the future"; (ii) those that had already been officially repealed; (iii) those that gave rise to divergent interpretation/application by the courts; and (iv) those that "required innovation, for the benefit of the public". According to the Royal Decree, the conclusions of such exercise were to be brought to the Queen, who should then decide whether a "new code" (*sic*) was needed and which contents it should bear.

Apparently, the Commission's work did not progress much in the following years and, in 1783, the Queen appointed a new member, the scholar Paschoal José de Mello Freire, who was a Professor at the University of Coimbra, with the specific task of drafting a penal code as well as a public law code. The drafts were finished five years later and are highly praised by the legal literature, not only for their technical accuracy, but also for being the first official Portuguese materials on criminal law where the ideals of the Enlightenment enjoy moderate reflection, in particular through the admitted influence of Beccaria, Filangieri and Blackstone.[3]

However, the drafts never entered into force, due to a series of factors: in the first place, the Portuguese sovereigns were certainly wary of the liberal principles that underpinned the political convulsions at the end of the 18th century, in particular the French revolution; in the second place, the perspective of the coming wars with Spain and France overshadowed national politics and legal reform. In any case,

---

[2]Decree 31 March 1778.

[3]Mello Freire's project was a compromise between the legal structures of the *Ancien Régime* and the new spirit of the (Italian and French) Enlightenment, whereby the (new) principle of equal treatment and the abolition of torture as a method of obtaining evidence coexisted with the cruelty of the execution of the death penalty in the case of, e.g., high treason: in more detail, see Eduardo Correia, *Estudos sobre a Evolução das Penas no Direito Português*, vol. I, separata do vol. LIII do Boletim da Faculdade de Direito da Universidade de Coimbra, s/d, p. 67 f.; Maria João Antunes/Pedro Caeiro, "Portugal", in *International Encyclopedia of Laws. Criminal Law, Suppl. 6 (May 1995)*, Kluwer Law International, The Hague, etc., 1995, p. 24 f. On the relevance of Mello Freire's project, see also António Hespanha, "Da «Iustitia» à «Disciplina». Textos, Poder e Política Penal no Antigo Regime" in *Justiça e Litigiosidade: História e Prospectivas*, Lisboa: Gulbenkian, 1993, p. 323 f.; and Frederico de Lacerda da Costa Pinto, *A Categoria da Punibilidade na Teoria do Crime*, vol I, Coimbra: Almedina, 2013, p. 228 f.

some of the proposals contained in the drafts were singled out and passed as separate laws in the early 19th century, under the rule of King João VI (e.g., the limitation of the application of the death penalty[4]).

After the occupation by the Napoleonic army (1807–1815), the Kingdom of Portugal became a British protectorate until 1820. The *Cortes* (Parliament) in charge after the liberal revolution of 1820 refused to pass, the following year, a draft criminal code offered to them by Jeremy Bentham and appointed a commission charged with the drafting of a new one, which however did not deliver.

In the very first months of their mandate, the *Cortes* passed a number of laws carrying some of the liberal principles that had inspired the Revolution. The Holy Tribunal of the Inquisition was abolished, as well as the privilege of forum (or benefit) of the clergy.[5] The fundamental principles of the Enlightenment concerning criminal matters made their way into the written Portuguese law for the first time with the Constitution of 1822, which enshrined the principles of necessity and proportionality of the criminal law, as well as the intransmissibility of punishment and the formal abolition of torture,[6] confiscation, infamy, flogging, branding, shameful exposure and parading, and "all other cruel and opprobrious punishment".[7] Four years later, the Constitutional Charter of 1826 reaffirmed these principles (which were upheld again in the Constitution of 1838) and laid down the promise of "drafting a Criminal Code, grounded on the solid bases of justice and equity".[8]

In 1837, a draft criminal code authored by José Manuel da Veiga was passed under the dictatorial regime of Passos Manuel,[9] but did not come into force because it was eventually not included in the "bill of indemnity" that ratified, later that year, several acts passed during the dictatorship.[10] And, in the words of Eduardo Correia, "monstrously, the old *Ordenações* persisted in force".[11]

---

[4]See the Decree of 11 January 1802 and Eduardo Correia, *Estudos*, p. 64.

[5]See José António Barreiros, "As instituições criminais em Portugal no século XIX: subsídios para a sua história", *Análise Social* 63-3 (1980), p. 589; Paulo Pinto de Albuquerque, *A Reforma da Justiça Criminal em Portugal e na Europa*, Coimbra: Almedina, 2003, p. 81 f.; and Pedro Caeiro, *Fundamento, Conteúdo e Limites da Jurisdição Penal do Estado. O Caso Português*, Coimbra: Wolters Kluwer/Coimbra Editora, 2010, p. 180 f.

[6]As a matter of fact, the judicial *praxis* had already restricted the use of torture to the most serious offences since the mid-17th century: see Levy Maria Jordão, *Commentario ao Codigo Penal Portuguez*, vol. I, Lisboa: Typograhia de José Baptista Morando, 1853, p. XV.

[7]Articles 10.º and 11.º of the Constitution 1822.

[8]Article 145.º, § 17, of the Constitutional Charter 1826.

[9]Decree of 4 January 1837.

[10]Charter (*Carta de Lei*) of 27 April 1837.

[11]See also Teresa Pizarro Beleza, *Direito Penal*, vol. 1, 2. ed., Lisboa: AAFDL, 1984, pp. 371–373. The abhorrent nature of the situation was first acknowledged by the Decree 18 August 1832, which created yet another commission to draft a new penal code that might replace "that monstrous penal codification of the *Ordenações* (…)". The civil war that ensued prevented the commission from delivering: see Francisco Silva Ferrão, *Theoria do Direito Penal Applicada ao Codigo Penal Portuguez*, vol. I, Lisboa; Typographia Universal, 1853, p. LIV.

It was not until 1852 that a Penal Code was passed, thus repealing, at last, the Fifth Book of the *Ordenações*. Notwithstanding, as soon as it was published, it was doomed by the literature as "having been born old", and Queen Maria II immediately appointed a commission to revise it (1853). The work of this commission was eventually used at a later moment, in the drafting of the Penal Code of 1886.

The legal and political context described so far suggests already that, in the middle of the 19th century and unlike what might have happened with the codifications in other countries, the *Code* could hardly be taken as *the* essential reference for the Portuguese penal reform.

In the first place, because the legislative process had already begun a long time before, having materialised, by the end of the 18th century, in the draft code Mello Freire (1786). Although the draft was not passed, many aspects of the new proposals were explained and further developed in the handbook authored by the same scholar,[12] which was the fundamental reference in the university teaching until the mid-19th century. Hence, the draft code informally started to influence the interpretation and application of the *Ordenações*: together with the handbook, they formed a relevant *corpus* of materials and solutions for the penal reform in several countries of Latin America[13]—and, eventually, for the Portuguese legislature.[14]

In the second place, at a political level, it would arguably not have been appropriate to explicitly adopt the *Code* as a model for the Portuguese law a few years after having fought the French troops in terrible battles, especially if we bear in mind the symbolic value of the criminal law as an expression of the sovereign power. Moreover, the resistance to the French has generated an ambiance of growing nationalism and "patriotic fervour"[15] hardly compatible with a straightforward acknowledgment of the *Code*'s value. Finally, the severance of relations that followed the French invasion of Spain (1823)[16] has deepened the estrangement between the two countries.

Some of the works published in the 19th century and the analysis of the evolution of the legislative process concur with the preceding considerations.

In one of the first Portuguese books on the criminal law to be published after the *Code* was passed,[17] the prevailing subjects are the need for proportionality between

[12]*Institutiones Juris Criminalis Lusitani*, Liber singularis, Olisipone, Ex Typographia Regalis Academiae, 1794.

[13]On this influence, see Zaffaroni, "La influencia del pensamento de Cesare Beccaria sobre la politica criminal en el mundo", *ADPCP* 1989, p. 529 f., who stresses the relevance of the works of Mello Freire for the expansion of the Enlightenment in Latin America.

[14]Almost seventy years after its publication, Levy Maria Jordão wrote that the draft code Mello Freire was "of great merit for his time and still has much that can be used today": Levy Maria Jordão, *Commentario*, T. I, p. XVII. See also Francisco Silva Ferrão, *Theoria*, vol. I, p. LII; and Victor Faveiro, "Melo Freire e a formação do Direito Público nacional", *Ciência e Técnica Fiscal* 110 (1968), pp. 89–92.

[15]Rui Ramos *et al.*, *História de Portugal*, Lisboa: Esfera dos Livros, 2009, p. 450.

[16]*Ibidem*, p. 473.

[17]Francisco Freire de Mello, *Discurso sobre Delictos e Penas*, London: T.C. Hansard, 1816.

the offences and the penalties, the abolition of the cruel/inhumane penalties and the need to adjust the penal sanctions to the political and social goals of the Republic.

Two interesting details might reveal the way in which this Author thought the penal reform should be achieved.

In the first place, the book bears a dedication that embodies the anti-French political formula of the time, which, by transforming the Portuguese Empire in a unity of several parts, allowed for maintaining the legitimacy of the Crown even when a part of the territory was occupied by a foreign army: "[Dedicated to] His Highness and Most Powerful Prince Regent of the United Kingdom of Portugal, and of the Brazil and the Algarve, Father of the Homeland".[18]

In the second place, the Author makes no reference to the French Penal Code: instead, he repeatedly mentions the draft code Mello Freire (1786) as a basis for a future penal reform. In other words, to the Author's mind, it was urgent to resume the reform of the criminal law, but building on what had been done at the end of the previous century, by assessing the proposals for new solutions in the light of the lessons of the best scholars (Filangieri, Renazzi, Lardizabal, Blackstone), among which he included (his uncle) Paschoal de Mello Freire.[19]

As a matter of fact, the thought and the works of Mello Freire published in the end of the 18th century bore a strong impact on the scholarly elaboration on the criminal law throughout the first half of the 19th century. At the University level, the several editions of the Lectures (*Lições*) published by Basílio Alberto de Sousa Pinto[20] establish a permanent dialogue with Mello Freire's handbook and his proposals, together with other historical and doctrinal elements and with the new penal codifications published in the first decades of the 19th century.

It is clear that, by 1850, the *Code* was no longer the most modern and decisive reference. One year after the publication of the Portuguese Code of 1852, the prominent lawyer Levy Maria Jordão did not hesitate in identifying the Prussian Code (published also in 1852) as the example of modern law: "arguably the most complete work of this kind to date".[21]

The general confrontation between French and English influence was also felt in the field of the criminal law reform, especially after the liberal revolution of 1820, from which the Constitution of 1822 emerged.

As a matter of fact, the revolution triggered the will, by the British, to intervene in the legislative process, which is documented in the intense exchange of letters between Jeremy Bentham and the liberal members of Parliament[22]; in the offer of a

---

[18]"Ao Mui Alto e Mui Poderoso Príncipe Regente do Reino Unido de Portugal, e do Brazil e Algarves, Pai da Patria".

[19]See Francisco Freire de Mello, *Discurso*, pp. 34 f. and 58.

[20]*Lições de Direito Criminal*, Coimbra: Imprensa da Universidade, 1845; *Lições de Direito Criminal*, Lisboa: Imprensa União-Typographica, 1857, and *Lições de Direito Criminal Portuguez*, Coimbra: Imprensa da Universidade, 1861.

[21]Levy Maria Jordão, *Commentario*, T. I, p. XXI.

[22]See Catherine Fuller, "«Primeiro e mais antigo Constitucional da Europa»: Bentham's contact with Portuguese liberals 1820–23", *Journal of Bentham Studies*, vol. 3 (2000), pp. 1–12.

draft penal code by the former to Parliament[23]; and in the decision taken by the latter to publish, in Portuguese, Jeremy Bentham's works. Eventually, the draft penal code was not adopted and fell into oblivion, but the works were actually published.[24]

The long timespan in which the reform of Portuguese criminal law took place contributed to the blurring of the *Code*'s relevance, because many of its solutions had been challenged by other foreign codifications passed in the meantime, especially the Bavarian Penal Code (1813).[25] Hence, the authors identify a plurality of sources and influences in the making of the PC1852: along with the *Code*, there are references to the Austrian Code (1803), the Neapolitan Code (1819), the Brazilian Code (1830) and the Spanish Code (1848). Such heterogeneity was criticized as the most important flaw of the new Portuguese Code, because it made it particularly hard to ascertain the legislator's perspective on the fundament of the *ius puniendi*: in some cases, the law paid homage to the utilitarian/sensualist school, in other cases it came closer to the ideas propounded by the spiritualist theories.[26]

Indeed, the legal literature that has elaborated on the *Code*—especially Chauveau/Hélie and Rossi—was in many cases deemed to be more relevant than the *Code* itself.[27]

In this context, it is not surprising that the solutions brought by the *Code* are sometimes followed and other times deliberately set aside by the PC1852, as the next section of this study purports to illustrate.

[23]Henriques Sêcco, "Da historia do direito criminal portuguez desde os mais remotos tempos", *Revista de Legislação e Jurisprudência* IV (1871/1872), p. 582; Manuel Cavaleiro de Ferreira, *Direito Penal Português*, Parte Geral, vol. I, Lisboa: Verbo, 1982, p. 71.

[24]*Tradução das Obras Políticas do Sábio Jurisconsulto Jeremias Bentham, Vertidas do Inglez na língua Portugueza por Mandado do Soberano Congresso das Cortes Gerais, Extraordinarias e Constituintes da Mesma Nação*, Tomos I e II, Lisboa: Na Imprensa Nacional, Anno 1822.

[25]On the contrast between the two laws, see the report of the Commission for the Reform of the Code of 1852, authored by Levy Maria Jordão, in *Código Penal Portuguez*, Tomo I, Relatório da Commissão, Lisboa: Imprensa Nacional, 1861, pp. 7–8.

[26]See Levy Maria Jordão *Commentario*, T. I, p. XVIII. See also Peter Hünerfeld, *Strafrechtsdogmatik in Deutschland und Portugal*, Nomos, 1981, pp. 42–43, and Manuel Cavaleiro de Ferreira, *Direito Penal*, pp. 71–72.

In a slightly different direction, Francisco Silva Ferrão, *Theoria*, vol. I, p. LXII, wrote that "the drafters [of the PC1852] bore always in mind the French and the Spanish Codes, which are easily acknowledgeable as predominant both at a doctrinal and at a literal level".

[27]Levy Maria Jordão, *Commentario*, Tomo I, p. XVIII; in the same direction, Francisco Silva Ferrão, *Theoria*, vol. I, p. LXII, who deems the opinion of those French scholars to be "abundantly" reflected in the PC1852; Eduardo Correia, *Direito Criminal (com a colaboração de J. Figueiredo Dias)*, Coimbra, 1963, vol I. pp. 106–107; and Manuel Cavaleiro de Ferreira, *Direito Penal*, p. 72.

2 The Portuguese Penal Code of 1852

2.1 Classification of the Offences

One of the *Code*'s most distinctive features was the *tripartite classification* of the offences (*crimes, délits et contraventions*), based on the severity of the sanctions and on the applicable procedural regime (article 1 of the *Code*). Such classification was deliberately rejected by the Portuguese legislator, who, following the Portuguese tradition, has not distinguished between crimes and delicts, but only between *crimes* and *contraventions*.[28]

The reasons underpinning that option were twofold. In the first place, the French literature had criticised the distinction between crimes and delicts, especially because it did not spring from the gravity of the acts, but rather from the severity of the applicable penalties[29]; in the second place, that distinction had also been rejected by the new legislation passed in other countries, such as the German states and Spain.[30]

Moreover, the establishment of crimes and contraventions as separate categories in the PC1852 relied on a substantive definition of the type of conduct[31] rather than on the formal criterion of the applicable penalties.

Nevertheless, and in spite of not being entirely followed by the Portuguese law, the *Code* still exerted some influence on the reform in this matter. Indeed, the inclusion of contraventions as *criminal* offences, under the competence of the judiciary,[32] meant a deliberate departure from Mello Freire's draft, which kept those violations within the realm of administrative police law ("*infracções de polícia*").[33]

---

[28]Levy Maria Jordão, *Commentario*, T. I, pp. 3–4. The concept of *delito* had a different nature in the Portuguese tradition: according to Joaquim José Cateano Pereira e Sousa, *Classes dos Crimes por Ordem Systematica, com as Penas correspondentes, segundo a Lei actual*, Lisboa, Regia Officina Typografica, 1803, p. 3 (fn. 6), "crime differs from delict ["*delicto*"] as species from gender. Delict means any violation of the order. There are three sources of delicts: sins, crimes and vices. The violation of the divine order is called a sin. The violation of the civil order, which tends to the detriment of another, is properly called crime. If it concerns ourselves, it is understood as vice".

[29]In more detail, Henriques da Silva, "Crimes, delictos e contravenções", *Estudos Juridicos* 5 (1903), p. 402 f. But see, in a different direction and upholding the French system, Francisco Silva Ferrão, *Theoria*, vol. I, p. 3 f.

[30]See Levy Maria Jordão, *Commentario*, T. I, p. 402 f., *maxime* p. 404 f.

[31]According to article 1.° of the PC1852, "crime, or delict, is the voluntary act punished by the law", whereas article 3.° defined contravention as "the voluntary, punishable act, which consists exclusively of the violation or inobservance of the preventative provisions contained in the laws and regulations, irrespective of any maleficent intention".

[32]José de Faria Costa, "A importância da recorrência no pensamento jurídico. Um exemplo: a distinção entre o ilícito penal e o ilícito de mera ordenação social", in IDPEE (org.), *Direito Penal Económico e Europeu*, Vol. I, Coimbra: Coimbra Editora, 1998, p. 123 and p. 112 f.

[33]See Basílio Alberto Sousa Pinto, *Lições de Direito Criminal*, Coimbra: Imprensa da Universidade, 1845, p. 373 f.

2.2 Structure

The *structure* of the two Codes also presents significant differences.

The "general part" of the *Code* basically concerns the penalties and their effects, with few norms on the criminal act,[34] whereas the PC1852, following the rich regulation contained in Mello Freire's draft, deals *first* with the criminal act and the requirements for its imputation (Title I, with three chapters "on offences in general and on criminals") and *then* with the penalties and their effects (Title II).[35]

This normative structure—which has been kept in the following Portuguese codes—allows for a more accurate and logical presentation of the exercise of punitive power, by laying down the conditions under which a person might be held responsible for an offence and, as a consequence, subject to the application of a sanction.

In a nutshell, the *Code*'s regulation of the criminal act is limited to the classification of the offences and the definition of attempt, liability and complicity—which led Levy Maria Jordão to comment that "arguably, the French Code has no general part"[36]—, whereas the PC1852 rules extensively on the conditions for the allocation of criminal responsibility, including the establishment and definition of several defences. For instance: while the *Code* restricts the scope of self-defence to the justification of homicide and battery (articles 328 and 329),[37] the PC1852 endows self-defence with a general scope in article 14.°, n.° 3, rendering it potentially applicable to the justification of any act.

---

[34]The first articles establish the classification of the offences, the definition of attempt and the prohibition of retroactive application of the criminal law.

[35]This type of structure was deemed to be so "natural" that Levy Maria Jordão, *Commentario*, T. I, p. 112, produced the following comment: "this system is so natural that the [Portuguese] Code, despite the many flaws in its method, could not but adopt it". In the same direction, Victor Faveiro, "Melo Freire e a formação do Direito Público nacional", p. 90. On the relevance, within Mello Freire's system, of a specific regulation of the criminal act preceding the establishment of the penalties, see Frederico de Lacerda da Costa Pinto, *A Categoria da Punibilidade*, p. 230 f.

[36]Levy Maria Jordão, *Commentario*, T. I, p. 47; the comment is made in the context of more concrete criticism regarding the fact that the Portuguese Code established premeditation as a general aggravating circumstance (article 19.°) but did not provide for its definition *in general*. Instead, it followed the *Code* in this instance and defined premeditation only in relation to murder, in article 352.° (this provision was, in fact, an *ipsis verbis* translation of article 297.° of the *Code*, which also attracted Jordão's criticism).

[37]On this restriction see Chauveau/Hélie, *Théorie du Code Pénal*, 3. ed., T. I, Paris: Cosse, 1852, p. 447: "(...) de la provocation et de la légitime défense, causes d'excuse ou de justification spéciales aussi pour le meurtre et les coups et blessures, *et dont le code ne s'est lui-même occupé qu'a raison de ces crimes*"; Id., *ibid.*, T. IV, p. 102: "De ce nombre sont la provocation et la légitime défense, causes d'excuse ou de justification de l'homicide volontaire et des coups ou blessures, *et qui n'ont été admises par la loi qu'en ce qui concerne ces deux crimes*" (emphasis added).

2.3 Principles

The different weight given to the regulation of the criminal act and of the penalties is replicated in the way the two codes enunciate the *principles of legality* and *retroactive application* favor rei.

The *Code* seems to conceive the principle of legality as a prohibition of applying penalties that are not provided for in a prior law.[38] Indeed, the French literature read the provision as encompassing not only the penalties but also the criminal acts.[39] However, the direct reference of the principle to the offences themselves was clearer in the PC1852. Additionally to the legality of the penalties (*nulla poena sine lege*), provided for in article 68. in terms similar to the French law, the Portuguese Code inserted the need for a legal prohibition in the very notion of offence,[40] in the prohibition of retroactive application of the penal law[41] and in the prohibition of analogy as a tool to qualify the act as an offence.[42]

Those provisions—which had no parallel in the *Code* and were justified by the literature with the citizens' security before the executive and the judicial power[43]—furthered the Portuguese tradition. Under the old *Ordenações*, the judges already respected the legal definitions of the offences and, as a rule, the literature did not accept incriminations by analogy or extensions of the legal texts.[44] Criminal laws were "*odiosa*" (Francisco Suárez) and, thus, their scope might be restricted, but not expanded. Moreover, the draft Mello Freire already included the need for a legal provision in the general notion of offence: "whomever by his own will commits an act prohibited by the law, or abstains from doing what it commands, perpetrates an offence".[45] In the same vein, § 9 of the draft provided that "the citizen may, freely and with impunity, act in any way that is not contrary to the laws".

The persistent attention paid to the criminal act also reflected on the way the PC1852 dealt with the retroactive application of the law *in melius*. The first part of

---

[38]Article 4 of the *Code*: "*Nulle contravention, nul délit, nul crime, ne peuvent être punis de peines qui n'étaient pas prononcées par la loi avant qu'ils fussent commis*".

[39]See Chauveau/Hélie, *Théorie*, p. 33 f.; R. Garraud, *Précis de Droit Criminel*, 3. ed., Paris: L. Larose et Forcel, 1888, p. 82.

[40]Article 1.º: "Crime, or delict, is the voluntary act *punished by the law*" (emphasis added).

[41]Article 5.º: "No act or omission can be deemed an offence if it is not qualified as such by a prior law".

[42]Article 18.º: "It is not permissible to resort to analogy, induction by parity or *a fortiori* reasoning with a view to qualify an act as an offence; it is always necessary that the essential elements of the offence, as explicitly defined by the law, materialise".

[43]On this subject, see Levy Maria Jordão, *Commentario*, T. I, pp. 8, 43–45, 169. The judge had the duty to examine whether or not the act imputed to the defendant contained "the features that constitute the offence as described by the law" (Francisco Silva Ferrão, *Theoria*, vol. I, p. 24).

[44]In more detail, collecting several examples, see Frederico de Lacerda da Costa Pinto, *A Categoria da Punibilidade*, pp. 150–153.

[45]The Author of the draft used the same definition of the offence, at a purely doctrinal level, in his handbook: see Mello Freire, *Institutiones Juris Criminalis Lusitani*, Titulo I, § II.

article 70.º adopts, under a more general and abstract wording, the solution brought by the *Décret du 25 juillet 1810*, concerning the publication of the penal codes[46]: "if, after the perpetration of the offence, the law modifies the penalty, the more lenient penalty will always be applied, even if the penalty provided for at the time of the sentence is more severe".

Interestingly, the second part of article 70.º (§ único) read: "if the act is not an offence under the law in force at the time of the sentence, no penalty shall be applied, even if such act was an offence when it was committed". Hence, the PC1852 was, in this realm, closer to the French Code of 1791—which entailed, apparently for the first time ever, a similar norm[47] –, as the *Code* did not provide for a specific rule on *decriminalisation*.

2.4 Rules on Participation

The Portuguese legislator has also deliberately departed from the *Code*'s rules on *participation*.

The *Code* established a distinction between principals and accessories, but, as a principle and unless a particular provision ruled otherwise, both categories were punished with the same penalties (article 59 of the *Code*).[48]

Such solution was explicitly criticised by Basílio Alberto de Sousa Pinto, Professor of Criminal Law at the University of Coimbra, who deemed more just and appropriate the differentiation of punishment according to the individual's role in the perpetration of the offence, as established, e.g., in the penal codes of Prussia, Brazil and Louisiana.[49] As a matter of fact, the PC1852 chose to follow the latter approach and punished the accomplices with the penalties established for mitigating circumstances (article 88.º).

---

[46]"If the penalty provided for in our new penal code is more lenient than the penalty stated in the current code, the courts and tribunals will apply the penalties of the new code".

[47]See the last provision at the end of the Code 1791: "Pour tout fait antérieur à la publication du présent code, si le fait est qualifié crime par les lois actuellement existantes, et qu'il ne le soit pas par le présent décret; ou si le fait est qualifié crime par le présent, code, et qu'il ne le soit pas par les.lois existantes, l'accusé sera acquitté, sauf à être correctionnellement puni, s'il y échoit".

[48]On the historical-normative meaning of this solution, see António M. Almeida Costa, *Ilícito pessoal, Imputação Objectiva e Comparticipação em Direito Penal,* Coimbra: Almedina, 2014, p. 157 e ss.

[49]Basílio Alberto Sousa Pinto, *Lições de Direito Criminal*, pp. 47–51. The solution adopted by the *Code* was even considered to be "barbaric and inflexible" (Levy Maria Jordão, *Commentario*, T. I, p. 204).

2.5 Penalties

As far as *penalties* are concerned, there are some differences, but also important similarities, between the two codes.

In the first place, as Figueiredo Dias points out, the way in which the PC1852 regulates punishment shows that the Portuguese legislator did not simply import the conception of general deterrence embodied in the fixed penalties established by the *Code*. In fact, due to the influence of the Brazilian and Spanish Codes, not only most of the penalties varied, in the abstract, between a minimum and a maximum level, but also their concrete application by the courts should take into due consideration the lists of aggravating and mitigating circumstances and their influence on the "guilt of the offender" (articles 20.º-11 and 80.º). Hence, it has aptly been argued that the PC1852 adopted a model of punishment based on general deterrence, limited by a strict principle of proportionality, *rectius*, in its "most perfect form, by the idea of *guilt*".[50]

In the second place, it is no surprise that the PC1852 did not provide for many of the penalties present in the original version of the *Code*. By 1852, the *Code* itself had already been significantly modified: in the meantime, general confiscation and the most gruesome penalties[51] had been abolished, respectively, by the Constitutional Charter of 1814 (article 66) and Law of 28 April 1832.

Moreover, a parallel movement for the humanisation of the criminal sanctions had developed in Portugal[52] and the legislator of 1852 could not adopt penalties that had been proscribed by the Constitutional Charter of 1826 (in force at the time[53]) either because they had a cruel or opprobrious nature[54] or because their effects were deemed to affect third parties (like, e.g., infamy or general confiscation[55]).

In the third place, the classification of the sanctions did not quite follow the *Code*'s scheme (*peines afflictives et infamantes, peines infamantes, peines correctionnelles*). They were divided in common and special penalties; the latter applied only to public officials (dismissal, suspension of office and reproach) and the former were further sub-divided in two categories: major penalties and correctional penalties (*penas maiores e penas correccionais*). However, and unlike the

---

[50]Jorge de Figueiredo Dias, *Direito Penal. Parte Geral. Tomo I*, 2. ed., Coimbra, Coimbra Editora, 2007, p. 68 f.

[51]The branding with a hot iron, the amputation of the right hand of parricides before the execution of the death penalty, the straightjacket (but not the public exhibition of the criminals convicted to certain penalties: see article 22 of the *Code*, even after 1832), etc.

[52]See supra, I., 2.

[53]As a matter of fact, the abolition of these sanctions was already provided for by the liberal Constitution of 1822 (article 11).

[54]Article 145.º, § 18, of the Charter: "Flogging, torture, branding with hot iron and all the other cruel penalties are abolished".

[55]Article 145.º, § 19, of the Charter: "No penalty shall affect people other than the convict. Hence, there shall be in no case confiscation of property, nor shall the infamy of the Defendant be transmitted to his relatives, irrespective of the degree". On "special confiscation", see *infra*.

Code, such distinction lacked proper criterion and purpose (and was therefore criticised by the literature[56]), as there was no straight correspondence between the category of the penalty and the type of the offence (crime/contravention), nor was it related to a particular form of criminal procedure.

A fourth aspect where the Portuguese Code apparently departed from the *Code*'s sanctioning system—adopting instead a regime closer to the Brazilian and German codes—was the establishment of the fines. According to article 41.º, the amount of the fine should be "proportional to the convict's income of up to three years, not less than 100 *reis* nor exceeding 2000 *reis*, except where the law provides for a fixed amount".[57] Nevertheless, it might be argued that the two laws were not that different, at least if the French law was interpreted in the sense that the judge, while determining the concrete amount of the fine within the framework set by the law for each offence, should take into consideration not only the circumstances of the offence, but also the social position and the economic condition of the convict.[58]

Finally, article 42.º of the PC1852 provided for the sanction of reprimand ("*repreensão*"), which had a general scope and should not be confused with the reproach ("*censura*") applicable only to public officials. This penalty was not known to the *Code*, and was drawn from the Spanish and German legislation.[59]

In any case, and notwithstanding the strong criticism voiced by some of the most authoritative Portuguese commentators regarding the *Code*'s sanctions system,[60] Portuguese law has adopted many of the solutions found therein.

It copied, in some instances, the very wording of the *Code*, even when the penalty itself existed already in the old national law. This was clearly the case of article 33.º (forced labour), which translated article 15 of the *Code*[61]; of article 36.º (expulsion), which apparently "imported" article 32 of the *Code*,[62] although the ban

[56]See Levy Maria Jordão, *Commentario*, T. I, p. 114 f., who deemed the distinction "unjustifiable"; and Jorge de Figueiredo Dias, *Direito Penal Português. As Consequências Jurídicas do Crime* (Aequitas, 1993), p. 99.

[57]The need to differentiate between the "rich and the poor" in the application of fines was already present in the draft Mello Freire (*Título* III, § 13).

[58]In this direction, see Chauveau/Hélie, *Théorie*, T. I, p. 182.

[59]See Francisco Silva Ferrão, *Theoria*, vol. II, p. 178 f., who questioned the usefulness of this penalty and advocated its abolition.

[60]According to Francisco Silva Ferrão, *Theoria*, vol. I, p. XXXV, "the French revolution and the Codes it produced made the criminal law progress with giant steps; but these results have been mitigated by the Code of 1810, still in force in France, notwithstanding the many modifications introduced by the law of 28 April 1832 and many other laws, and judicial and penitentiary institutions, which make that Code one of the most lapsed, and almost barren, in Europe, in relation to the enforcement of the penalties it provides for, which have already been solemnly declared, by M. Dumon, as *vicious*".

[61]Levy Maria Jordão, *Commentario*, T. I, p. 117 f.; and Francisco Silva Ferrão, *Theoria*, vol. II, p. 131.

[62]However, unlike the *Code*, the PC1852 did not restrict the scope of expulsion to political offences or set a maximum limit to its duration: see Francisco Silva Ferrão, *Theoria*, vol. II, p. 156.

(*banimento*) was already known to the ancient Portuguese law; and of article 64.º, which ordered the confiscation of the proceeds and instrumentalities of crime in a similar fashion to article 11 of the *Code*,[63] although this "special confiscation" was also known to old Portuguese law.[64]

In other cases, the Portuguese legislator merged and reshaped some of the *Code*'s penal provisions, establishing solutions largely inspired by the French legislation, especially the laws of 1824 and 1832. However, in doing so, the Portuguese drafters sometimes overlooked part of the legal regime they were drawing upon, leading to inconsistencies or unnecessary anachronisms. For instance: article 34.º, which regulated "major imprisonment" (*prisão maior*, the equivalent to the French "*réclusion*") by merging articles 21 and 20 of the *Code* (in the version after 1832), adopted also the possibility of applying the product of the convict's work for his own profit. This solution ignored article 41 of the *Code*, which, regulating the product of the work by *detainees* (viz., criminals convicted to "*emprisonnement*" as a "*peine correctionnelle*"), allocated such income in a way that had a more appropriate penological purpose.[65]

The *Code*'s strong influence is to be found also in the following articles of the PC1852: article 20.º (mitigating circumstances)[66]; articles 52.º ff., on the strength of which the convict to certain penalties lost his political and civil rights ("quasi civil death") or had them suspended (in case of temporary penalties),[67] and articles 59.º–61.º, which regulated the measure of "special surveillance by the police", to be applied during the enforcement of "*desterro*"[68] or after the execution of the penalties of forced labour, imprisonment or expulsion from the Kingdom.[69]

[63]See Levy Maria Jordão, *Commentario*, T. I, p. 164.

[64]Eg., in *Alvará* of 4 June 1825, concerning the confiscation of instrumentalities and proceeds of tax offences (smuggling): see also João Conde Correia, *Da Proibição do Confisco à Perda Alargada*, Lisboa: INCM, 2012, p. 35 f.

[65]Hence, contrary to the suggestion of Levy Maria Jordão, *Commentario*, T. I, p. 121, who rightly criticised the Portuguese law for not adopting it, this was not an innovation brought by the Spanish Code. It should be noted that "correctional imprisonment" ("*prisão correccional*") in the PC1852 did not include mandatory work, which might explain why article 41 of the *Code* was not transposed into Portuguese law.

[66]Levy Maria Jordão, *Commentario*, T. I, p. 64 f.

[67]Cfr. articles 18 and 28 f. of the Code. This penalty was criticised by the French and Portuguese literature for lacking proportionality and a significant link to the offences that could prompt its application: see Chauveau/Hélie, *Théorie*, pp. 124–133 and Levy Maria Jordão, *Commentario*, T. I, pp. 147–157; Francisco Silva Ferrão, *Theoria*, vol. II, p. 237 f.

[68]The penalty of "*desterro*", unknown to French law, was a sort of intrastate banishment, where the convict was obliged to (or prevented from) residing or staying in certain parts of the country.

[69]This measure replicated the "*renvoi sous la surveillance de la haute police*" (articles 44 f. of the *Code*).

The rules on the replacement of the harshest penalties in the case where the convict is a minor (articles 71.º–72.º of the PC1852), a woman or an elderly person were also largely inspired—albeit with small differences in the details[70]—by articles 70–72 of the *Code*.

In this field, there is an interesting difference between the two Codes concerning the treatment dispensed to minors (under 16 years in the *Code*, under 14 years in the PC1852) who have committed a crime without discernment.[71] Both Codes provided for the acquittal of those minors[72] and, at the same time, conferred upon the judge the power to send them to a correction house (*maison de correction*, *casa de educação*) for a number of years. Although this measure was unequivocally *not penal* in nature,[73] the French code explicitly set an absolute limit to its duration (the twentieth anniversary of the internee), whereas Portuguese law apparently conferred upon the judge total discretion in determining the length of the measure.[74]

3 Conclusion

The comparison between the *Code* and the PC1852 with a view to analyzing the influence of the former over the latter's "general part" produces a mixed picture.

On the one hand, the sections of the general part of the PC1852 that regulate the criminal act itself and the requirements for its imputation proceed clearly from other sources (namely, the works of Mello Freire). On the other hand, the punitive system adopted by the PC1852 bears a significant influence of the *Code*, especially in the version in force after 1832, as well as its critique by Chauveau/Hélie, even if, in some cases, the regime of the *Code* was deemed to be already outdated or plainly inappropriate in the eyes of the Portuguese literature.

It is likely that the same mixed picture emerges from the analysis of the "special part" (the offences), as suggested by the preliminary view of the normative structure of that section and the contents of some of the paradigmatic offences (eg., crimes against the State and against society, and murder).

---

[70]Eg, the age threshold below which the death penalty could not be applied (16 years in the *Code*, 17 in the PC1852) and the penalty chosen for its replacement (imprisonment for 10–20 years in a correctional facility in the Code, life imprisonment with work in the PC1852—a departure much criticised by the Portuguese literature); the age threshold above which forced labour could not be applied or should cease and be replaced by imprisonment (70 years in the *Code*, 60 in the PC1852); the inclusion of disabilities, together with age and gender, as a ground for replacement of forced labour; etc.

[71]Article 66 of the *Code*, article 73.º of the PC1852.

[72]In the Portuguese case, this consequence was not spelt out in article 73.º: it rather followed from the fact that article 23.º, n.º 3, which had no parallel in the *Code*, excluded the criminal liability of this category of minors.

[73]See Chauveau/Hélie, *Théorie*, T. I, p. 220; Levy Maria Jordão, *Commentario*, T. I, p. 174.

[74]Which met harsh criticism from Francisco Silva Ferrão, *Theoria*, vol. III, p. 29.

References

Albuquerque, Paulo Pinto de, *A Reforma da Justiça Criminal em Portugal e na Europa* (Coimbra: Almedina, 2003).

Antunes, Maria João / Caeiro, Pedro, "Portugal", in *International Encyclopedia of Laws. Criminal Law*, Suppl. 6 (May 1995) (The Hague, etc.: Kluwer Law International, 1995).

Barreiros, José António, "As instituições criminais em Portugal no século XIX: subsídios para a sua história", *Análise Social* 63-3 (1980).

Beleza, Teresa Pizarro, *Direito Penal*, vol. 1, 2. ed. (Lisboa: AAFDL, 1984).

Caeiro, Pedro, *Fundamento, Conteúdo e Limites da Jurisdição Penal do Estado. O Caso Português* (Coimbra: Coimbra Editora, 2010).

Chauveau, Adolphe / Hélie, Faustin, *Théorie du Code Pénal*, 3. ed., vol. I (Paris: Cosse, 1852).

Correia, Eduardo, *Direito Criminal (com a colaboração de J. Figueiredo Dias)*, vol. I (Coimbra: Almedina, 1963).

Correia, Eduardo, *Estudos sobre a Evolução das Penas no Direito Português, vol. I, separata do vol. LIII do Boletim da Faculdade de Direito da Universidade de Coimbra,* s/d.

Correia, João Conde, *Da Proibição do Confisco à Perda Alargada*, Lisboa: INCM, 2012.

Costa, António M. Almeida, *Ilícito pessoal, Imputação Objectiva e Comparticipação em Direito Penal* (Coimbra: Almedina, 2014).

Costa, José de Faria, "A importância da recorrência no pensamento jurídico. Um exemplo: a distinção entre o ilícito penal e o ilícito de mera ordenação social", in IDPEE (org.), *Direito Penal Económico e Europeu,* vol. I, p. 109 f. (Coimbra: Coimbra Editora, 1998).

Dias, Jorge de Figueiredo, *Direito Penal Português. As Consequências Jurídicas do Crime* (Lisboa: Aequitas, 1993).

Dias, Jorge de Figueiredo, *Direito Penal. Parte Geral. Tomo I*, 2. ed. (Coimbra: Coimbra Editora, 2007).

Faveiro, Victor, "Melo Freire e a formação do Direito Público nacional", *Ciência e Técnica Fiscal* 110 (1968), p. 71 f.

Ferrão, Francisco Silva, *Theoria do Direito Penal Applicada ao Codigo Penal Portuguez*, vol. I (Lisboa: Typographia Universal, 1853).

Ferreira, Manuel Cavaleiro de, *Direito Penal Português, Parte Geral*, vol. I, (Lisboa: Verbo, 1982).

Freire, Pascoal José de Mello, *Ensaio do Codigo Criminal a que mandou proceder a rainha D. Maria I (...), oferece e dedica Miguel Setáro* (Lisboa: Typ. Maigrense: 1823); the second edition was published in the same year under the title *Codigo Criminal intentado pela Rainha D. Maria I. Autor Pascoal José de Mello Freire*, 2. ed. (Lisboa: Typ. Simão Thaddeo Ferreira, 1823).

Freire, Pascoal José de Mello, *Institutiones Juris Criminalis Lusitani, Liber singularis* (Olisipone: Ex Typographia Regalis Academiae, 1794).

Fuller, Catherine, "«Primeiro e mais antigo Constitucional da Europa»: Bentham´s contact with Portuguese liberals 1820–23", *Journal of Bentham Studies*, vol. 3 (2000), p. 1 f.

Garraud, R., *Précis de Droit Criminel*, 3. ed. (Paris: L. Larose et Forcel, 1888).

Hespanha, António, "Da «Iustitia» à «Disciplina». Textos, Poder e Política Penal no Antigo Regime" in *Justiça e Litigiosidade: História e Prospectivas* (Lisboa: Gulbenkian 1993).

Hünerfeld, Peter, *Strafrechtsdogmatik in Deutschland und Portugal* (Baden-Baden: Nomos, 1981).

Jordão, Levy Maria, *Commentario ao Codigo Penal Portuguez*, vol. I (Lisboa: Typograhia de José Baptista Morando, 1853).

Jordão, Levy Maria, [Report of the Commission for the Reform of the Code of 1852], in *Código Penal Portuguez.* Vol I, Relatório da Commissão (Lisboa: Imprensa Nacional, 1861).

Mello, Francisco Freire de, *Discurso sobre Delictos e Penas* (London: T.C. Hansard, 1816).

Pinto, Basílio Alberto de Sousa, *Lições de Direito Criminal* (Coimbra: Imprensa da Universidade, 1845); *Lições de Direito Criminal* (Lisboa: Imprensa União-Typographica, 1857); *Lições de Direito Criminal Portuguez* (Coimbra: Imprensa da Universidade, 1861).

Pinto, Frederico de Lacerda da Costa, *A Categoria da Punibilidade na Teoria do Crime*, vol I (Coimbra: Almedina, 2013).
Ramos, Rui, *et al.*, *História de Portugal* (Lisboa: Esfera dos Livros, 2009).
Sêcco, Henriques, "Da historia do direito criminal portuguez desde os mais remotos tempos", *Revista de Legislação e Jurisprudência* 4 (1871/1872).
Silva, Henriques da, "Crimes, delictos e contravenções", *Estudos Juridicos* 5 (1903).
Sousa, Joaquim José Cateano Pereira e, *Classes dos Crimes por Ordem Systematica, com as Penas correspondentes, segundo a Lei actual* (Lisboa: Regia Officina Typografica, 1803).
Zaffaroni, Eugenio Raúl, "La influencia del pensamento de Cesare Beccaria sobre la politica criminal en el mundo", *ADPCP* 1989, p. 521 f.

Frederico de Lacerda da Costa Pinto is Professor of Criminal Law, Economic Criminal Law and Criminal Procedure at the Faculty of Law of the NOVA University of Lisbon (www.fd.unl.pt); Researcher at Centro de Investigação e Desenvolvimento sobre Direito e Sociedade/Research Center on Law and Society of the Faculty of Law of the NOVA University of Lisbon (CEDIS—FDUNL); Legal Adviser to the Board of the Portuguese Securities Market Commission (CMVM: Comissão do Mercado de Valores Mobiliários). He published several works about Criminal Law, Criminal Procedure, Rules of Evidence and Defendants Rights, Economic Criminality, Administrative offenses and History of Criminal Law, in Portugal, Spain, Italy, Germany, Brazil and Peru.

Pedro Caeiro studied law at the University of Coimbra (Portugal) where he received his LL.L (1990) and his LL.M in criminal law (1995) with a thesis on bankruptcy crimes. In 2008, he received his Ph.D. degree at the same University with a thesis on the Fundament, Contents and Limits of State Jurisdiction in Criminal Matters. He teaches criminal law at the University of Coimbra since 1990. He is a founding member, contact point for Portugal and member of the management committee of the European Criminal Law Academic Network (ECLAN). He is a member of the European Commission's Expert Group on Criminal Policy. Since 2015, he is also a member of the European Criminal Policy Initiative (ECPI). Currently, he is an Assistant Professor with tenure at the Faculty of Law and a researcher at the University of Coimbra Institute for Legal Research (UCILeR). He has participated as an expert in several international academic research projects and has authored and co-authored over sixty titles, most of them on jurisdiction and European and international criminal law.

An Autonomous Path for the Italian Penal Code of 1889: The Constructing Process and the First Case Law Applications

Stefano Vinci

La nazionalità è il più grande bisogno, cui la legislazione deve soddisfare (Nationality is the greatest need that legislation is obliged to satisfy).
Francesco Alemagna

Abstract The essay, through the close examination of parliamentary acts and doctrinal works, aims at pointing out the "national path" followed by the Italian penal science in the process of drafting the Criminal Code which came to light in 1889, after a long debate lasted about 30 years. It examines the main stages of the criminal codification process and highlights the effort of Italian criminal science to abandon the 1810 Napoleonic example. It focuses also on the practical application difficulties of the new Code in the Courts, as it is possible to evince by reading the first judgments of the Courts and the lectures of the general attorneys of the Court of Cassation in Rome, had been referred to the jurisdiction of the criminal cases all over the Kingdom of Italy.

1 Searching for a "National Pattern" of Penal Code

Giuseppe Zanardelli in his speech, delivered on 14 March 1889 on the occasion of laying the foundation stone of the Palace of Justice in Rome, pointed out how the autonomy of the Italian legal traditions had made it possible to build the commercial law, the early outlines of the civil law and the penal code. In fact, "till today Italy is pointed out as the real home of the Criminal Law by the most eminent scholars".[1] The Minister extolled publicly and proudly the glories of the Italian

[1]Giuseppe Zanardelli, *Pel collocamento della prima pietra del Palazzo di Giustizia in Roma. Discorso pronunziato dal ministro guardasigilli G. Zanardelli il XIV marzo MDCCCLXXXIX* (Roma, 1889), p. XIV.

S. Vinci (✉)
University of Bari Aldo Moro, Bari, Italy
e-mail: stefano.vinci@uniba.it

A. Masferrer (ed.), *The Western Codification of Criminal Law*, Studies in the History of Law and Justice 11, https://doi.org/10.1007/978-3-319-71912-2_6

criminal science since on these days, the Parliament brought an end to the difficult task of realizing a unique penal code Italy had been expecting since 1861.[2]

The obstacles to the Italian criminal codification (lasted about thirty years[3]) depended "not only on the different legal schools which prevailed in the different provinces of the Kingdom, not only on the diversity of customs which had been purified, more or less, by the effects of the civil and religious despotism; but, in a more particular manner, owing to the traditions of the previous criminal laws which the respective rulers had imposed on the several provinces, as fundamental tenets of the civil living".[4]

In fact, the criminal codification process had passed through the inheritance of several different criminal laws which, after the Napoleonic rule, had caught on with the States preceding the unification of Italy the day after the Congress of Vienna. The pre-unification Italian governments had introduced different criminal laws mostly modeled after the 1810 Napoleonic Code.[5] They were also conformed to the

[2]The problem of the genesis of the Italian criminal code of 1889 was the subject of well-established studies by legal historiography that has highlighted its original characters in comparison with the models beyond the Alps, which rules penetrated into the criminal legislation of the preunitary states. Among the many studies on the subject see especially Mario Sbriccoli, "Il diritto penale liberale. La Rivista penale di Luigi Lucchini (1874–1900)", *Quaderni fiorentini per la storia del pensiero giuridico*, 16 (1987); Luigi Lacchè, "Un code penal pour l'Unite italienne, le code Zanardelli (1889) la genese, le debat, le project juridique", X. Rousseaux y R. Lévy, (eds), *Le pénal dans tous ses Etats. Justice, Etats et sociétés en Europe (XII–XX siécles)* (Bruxelles, 1997), pp. 303–319; Tullio Padovani, "La tradizione toscana nel codice Zanardelli", Sergio Vinciguerra (ed.), *Diritto penale dell'ottocento. I codici preunitari e il codice Zanardelli* (Padova, 1999); Laurent Mayali, Antonio Padoa Schioppa yDieter Simon, *Officium advocati* (Frankfurt amMain, 2000); Angela Santangelo Cordani, *Alla vigilia del Codice Zanardelli: Antonio Buccellati e la riforma penale nell'Italia postunitaria* (Milano, 2008); Mario Sbriccoli, "La penalistica civile. Teorie e ideologie del diritto penale nell'Italia Unita", Id. (ed.), *Storia del diritto penale e della giustizia: scritti editi e inediti (1972–2007)* (Milano, 2009); Michele Pifferi, M., Alla ricerca del «genio italico». Tradizione e progetti nella penalistica postunitaria", G. Cazzetta (ed.), *Retoriche dei giuristi e costruzione dell'identità nazionale*, (Bologna, 2013); Floriana Colao, "Profili di federalismo penale in Italia dall'Unità al codice Zanardelli", L. Lacchè y M. Stronati (eds.), *Questione criminale e identità nazionale in Italia tra Otto e Novecento* (Macerata, 2014).

[3]Colao, "Profili di federalismo penale in Italia dall'Unità al codice Zanardelli", pp. 141 ss.

[4]Francesco Carrara, "Codicizzazione (Studi legislativi)" (1869), *Opuscoli di diritto criminale* (Lucca, 1870), vol. II, p. 227. On the contribution of Francesco Carrara in the criminal codification process see Marco Paolo Geri, *La metamorfosi che la politica voleva fare a danno della giustizia: Francesco Carrara e l'unità del "giure penale"* (Bologna, 2005); Paolo Cappellini, "Francesco Carrara e il problema della codificazione del diritto", *Criminalia* (2007), pp. 305–323; Luigi Lacchè, "La penalistica costituzionale e il 'liberalismo giuridico'. Problemi e immagini della legalità nella riflessione di Francesco Carrara", *Quaderni fiorentini per la storia del pensiero giuridico moderno*, 36 (2007), Tomo I, pp. 663–695.

[5]On *Code pénal* of 1810 see Jean-Marie Carbasse, *Histoire du droit pénale et de la justice criminelle* (Paris 2000); Bernard schnapper, "Compression et répression sous le Consulat et l'Empire", *Revue historique de droit français et étranger*, 69 (1991), pp. 17–40; Andrè Laingui, "Il diritto penale della Rivoluzione francese e dell'Impero", S. Vinciguerra (ed.), *Diritto penale dell'Ottocento. I codici preunitari e il codice Zanardelli* (Padova, 1999), pp. 49–52; Mario Da Passano, *Emendare o intimidire. La codificazione del diritto penale in Francia e in Italia durante*

distinctive local legal traditions which lightened the harshness of the capital punishment provided for more than thirty criminal cases, the forfeiture of his own estates, the brand, the *infamia iuris* and the pillory.[6] They also overcame the equivalence between the attempt and the perpetration of the crime and between the complicity and the primary responsibility.[7]

The Italian criminal science, on the basis of the "Progetto di un codice penale pel Regno italico" of 1806, important for the originality of its content and its independence on the transalpine patterns,[8] and the Neapolitan law "Sui delitti e sulle pene" (May 20, 1808)[9] laid the foundation for an original and independent criminal code model. It is sufficient to have a look through the Code promulgated in Naples in 1819. It brought changes which bettered the theory of criminal responsibility, fixed a gradation of punishment between the attempted crime and the perpetrated one and the necessary cooperation and the unnecessary one, provided in the French code of 1810.[10] In addition to all that, it abolished the brand, the infamy, the confiscation and the pillory, which were still present in the Napoleonic code. Similar changes were also introduced into the codes promulgated in the Duchy of Parma and in the Kingdom of Sardinia. In 1853, the Grand Duchy of Tuscany, on the contrary, after an initial return to the criminal law by Pietro Leopoldo, achieved a code drawing its inspiration from the Grand Duchy of Baden of 1845. It was more

la Rivoluzione e l'Impero (Torino, 2000), pp. 87–157; Adriano Cavanna, *Storia del diritto moderno in Europa. 2. Le fonti e il pensiero giuridico* (Milano, 2005), p. 592 ss.

[6]Enrico Pessina, *Il diritto penale in Italia da Cesare Beccaria sino alla promulgazione del codice penale vigente (1764–1890)* (Milano, 1906), p. 35.

[7]*Ibid.*, p. 37.

[8]The project was an important example on subsequent codification thanks to the dissemination of the preparatory work published in six volumes in the *Collezione dei Travagli sul Codice Penale pel Regno d'Italia* published in Brescia in 1807, which made the text known throughout Italy until it became the "Italian model of code". See Adriano Cavanna, *La codificazione penale in Italia. Le origini lombarde* (Milano, 1975); Mario Sbriccoli, "Caratteri originari e tratti permanenti del sistema penale italiano", L. Violante (ed.), *Legge, diritto, giustizia* (Torino, 1998); Ettore Dezza, "Appunti sulla codificazione penale nel primo Regno d'Italia: il progetto del 1809", Vinciguerra, *Diritto penale dell'Ottocento*; Alberto Cadoppi, *Introduzione allo studio del diritto penale comparato* (Padova, 2004).

[9]Praised by Gaspare Capone, *Discorso sopra la storia delle leggi patrie* (Napoli, 1844), t. 2, p. 53, as "*uno dei migliori lavori che si son fatti dai nostri in materia legislativa*", the law was also the result of a long debate that was a remarkable achievement, considering that Rambaud, J., *Naples sous Joseph Bonaparte*, Paris 1911, p. 414 praised what had seemed to him "*un'adoption interessante, oeuvre de justice et de science, qu'animel'esprit des Filangieri, des Pagano, des Briganti*". See Francesco Mastroberti, *Codificazione e giustizia penale nelle Sicilie dal 1808 al 1820* (Napoli, 2001), pp. 133–146.

[10]Pessina, *Il diritto penale in Italia*, p. 42. See on this Francesco Mastroberti, *Codificazione e giustizia penale nelle Sicilie dal 1808 al 1820* (Napoli, 2001).

innovative than the French code of 1810 and the other Italian codes of Restoration.[11]

All these different traditions became immediately apparent that it would have been necessary to construct a code having Italian characteristics rather than "the foreign ones imported and badly adjusted to our customs and tendencies".[12] It was necessary to trace the criminal laws of the new state back to "a symmetrical unit" in order to get "a national pattern" instead of "a copy of the foreigner ones", but such an operation was obstructed just in the ignorance of the local customs and the criminal traditions in force for the different provinces.[13] So, it would be necessary to adopt a special "governmental prudence" in the employment of "the coding penal method".[14] That is why Francesco Carrara expressed his great disappointment against the proposal to widen the Sardinian code (by Napoleonic inspiration) out of the Tuscan provinces. He was absolutely sure public opinion would poorly digest this proposal and all that would have created serious "complaints and disaffections".[15] It would have been advisable to work on an original penal code which found its roots in the "Italian glories of the criminal law" ("scienza del giure penale"), which had been growing and prospering for five centuries thanks to the work of an "uninterrupted series of lawyers, philosophers and publicists whose names have already gained undying fame".[16]

---

[11]The example followed by the Grand Duke Leopold II was that of *Codice penale del Granducato di Baden* of 1845, translated by Francesco Mori in *Scritti germanici di diritto criminale*, published in 1847. See on this Mario Da Passano, *Il diritto penale toscano dai Lorena ai Borboni (1786–1807)* (Milano, 1988); Id., "Il primo progetto di codice penale toscano (1824)", *Materiali per una storia della cultura giuridica*, 1 (1992), pp. 41–64; Id., "La storia esterna del codice penale toscano (1814–1859)", *Istituzioni e società in Toscana nell'età moderna. Atti delle giornate di studio dedicate a Giuseppe Pansini* (Roma, 1994), pp. 564–589; Sergio Vinciguerra (ed.), *Codice penale per il Granducato di Toscana (1853)* (Padova, 1995); Tullio Padovani, "La tradizione toscana nel codice Zanardelli", Vinciguerra, *Diritto penale dell'Ottocento*; Riccardo Ferrante, "Il problema della codificazione", *Enciclopedia italiana. Il Contributo italiano alla storia del pensiero – Diritto* (Roma, 2012).

[12]Francesco Carrara, "La cessata procedura lucchese (Discorso letto alla R. Accademia Lucchese il 3 maggio 1862)", *Opuscoli di diritto criminale* (Lucca, 1870), vol. II, p. 43: "*E questo desiderio e questa aspirazione si manifesta, più che in ogni altro argomento, vivace e razionale nella materia della giustizia punitiva; in cui facile è persuadersi che né i divieti, né le repressioni, né i metodi giudiziari, possono avere un'attitudine cosmopolita. Le vestigia dell'antico nostro municipalismo fanno sì che in mezzo a tanta mania d'imitare o Francia o Germania, si aborra dal formare neppure soggetto di fugace studio le istituzioni degli Stati minori, nelle quali pur potria darsi che si trovasse qualche cosa di buono; perché Dio nella sua giustizia non diede, no, ai grandi stati soltanto il monopolio di generare ingegni veloci*".

[13]Francesco Carrara still remarked: "Opera difficilissima adunque; e specialmente tra noi Italiani, che siamo in generale più edotti, dicasi pur francamente, nelle leggi di Francia e Brittannia, di quello forse noi siamo negli usi e regolamenti di una contigua provincia". *Ibidem.*

[14]Francesco Carrara, "Sulla crisi legislativa in Italia (Considerazioni)", *Opuscoli di diritto criminale*, p. 176.

[15]Carrara, "Sulla crisi legislativa", p. 212.

[16]Francesco Carrara, *Pensieri sul progetto di codice penale italiano del 1874* (Firenze, 1974), p. 7.

The Syracusan lawyer, Francesco Alemagna, wrote, on 20 January 1863, in the legal journal "Monitore dei Tribunali": "The anxiety of breaking with the chains still binding our separated brothers", had not to lead them to the slavish imitation of French codes. All that would have represented a serious mistake, or even a "poison" to the legal life of the Country.[17]

So, the attempt by the Piedmontese government to introduce its Code (promulgated in 1859) in the annexed provinces[18] provoked a strong opposition everywhere. It was caused—as Mittermaier pointed out in 1863—because the lawyers of the new provinces, on comparing their particular legislation with the one that had to take its place, highlighted that their old laws had to be preferred to the new ones, so that in Lombardy "it was no good at pretending that the Austrian code had greater value in many respects".[19] But, it met with the strongest opposition in Naples and Tuscany, where the different laws on the death penalty would have done less tolerable than ex abrupto imposition of a different code.[20] The need of getting down to an Italiancriminallaw considering the different provinces of the Kingdom, led the Government to convince itself it would have been necessary to choose a better moment to consult with local forces. That is why the Government chose to leave temporarily and use different criminal laws, such as the Sardinian-Piedmontese penal code of 1859, which was granted to most of the Italian regions[21] (with some amendments adopted for the territories of the former Kingdom of the Two Sicilies.[22] The same went for the Tuscan criminal code of 1853, operative in the Tuscan provinces[24] and the exceptional police laws issued to

[17]Francesco Alemagna, "L'Italia e i suoi codici", *Monitore dei Tribunali. Giornale di legislazione e giurisprudenza civile e penale e del contenzioso amministrativo*, anno IV, n. 3 (20 gennaio 1863), p. 44.

[18]The Sardinian Code of 1859 confirmed, in its general part, the most common conquests of the Enlightenment century: the principle of strict legality, non-retroactivity of criminal law, a more precise definition of the attempt, the lowering of the level of penalties and the provision of mitigating circumstances. The principle of legality suffered, however, important exceptions in special part of code: for example, on the subject of political offences and offences against public tranquillity. See on this Lacchè, *Un code penal*, p. 306.

[19]Karl Joeph AntonMittermaier, "Il progetto di revisione del Codice 1859 pel regno d'Italia, presentato al Senato in Torino nel 9 gennaio 1862", *Monitore dei Tribunali. Giornale di legislazione e giurisprudenza civile e penale e del contenzioso amministrativo*, anno IV, n. 3 (20 gennaio 1863), p. 50.

[20]Carlo Ghisalberti, "Legislazione e codificazione", *Enciclopedia italiana. L'unificazione* (Roma, 2011).

[21]See on this Vinciguerra, *Diritto penale dell'Ottocento*; Mayali, Padoa Schioppa y Simon, *Officium advocati*; Santangelo Cordani, *Alla vigilia del Codice Zanardelli.*

[22]*Collezione celerifera delle leggi, decreti, istruzioni e circolari*, Torino 1862, decreto luogotenenziale 17 febbraio 1861. See Alberto Aquarone, *L'unificazione legislativa e i codici del 1865* (Milano, 1960), pp. 89–97 and Marco Nicola Miletti, "Piemontizzare le contrade italiane. L'adeguamento del codice penale sardo alle province meridionali", Sergio Vinciguerra (ed.), *Il codice penale per gli stati del Re di Sardegna e per l'Italia Unita (1859)* (Padova, 2008), pp. CV–CXXXIII.

manage the state of emergency caused by the insurrection of the peasant people in Southern Italy.[23]

2 The Texture of the "tela di Penelope" Towards the Final Version of a Criminal Code

The choice of leaving Italy divided into geographically different criminal laws could not satisfy the requirements of a unified Country, which would needed a consolidated code of law for all regions. During the parliamentary debate on consolidated laws given at the Chamber of Deputies on 12 February 1865 Deputy Sebastiano Tecchio pointed out that the diversities existing among the Neapolitan, the Tuscan, and the Sardinian penal codes impeded enforcement of some of them because they had fallen into disuse. This made room for the free will of the judges and conflicting interpretations in rulings by several courts. That caused an "incessant and flagrant" violation of the Albertine Statute, sanctioning the principle that the law has to be equal for everyone.[24] Therefore, it was impossible to admit the political union of the country, aside from the sameness of its public law, of which the penal law had to be considered its integral part. That is why Minister Vacca pointed out that the unification of penal code was urgent and necessary both, politically and nationally.[25]

This started off an intense season of research and propositions which absorbed the efforts of Italian academies and lawyers. In the parliamentary seats and through the pages of the most accredited journals, they meant to contribute to draw up a penal code bearing consolidated and distinctive hallmarks.[26]

---

[23]This emergency situation strongly influenced the Italian penal system in view of the massive recourse to exceptional legislation, which basic principles persisted even after the overcome political emergency. See Santangelo Cordani, *Alla vigilia del codice Zanardelli*, pp. 6–7.

[24]Atti Parlamentari, *Camera dei Deputati*, Discussioni, Tornata del 15 febbraio 1865, p. 8253. *Seguito della discussione del disegno di legge con cui è fatta facoltà al Governo di promulgare alcune leggi per l'unificazione.*

[25]*Ibid.*, p. 8257.

[26]See, for example, the project of the Sicilian lawyer Emanuele Rapisardi: *Saggio d'un progetto del codice penale italiano* published in Catania in 1862 *Saggio d'uno progetto del Codice penale italiano corredato d'osservazioni dell'avvocato Emanuele Rapisardi,* Catania, 1862, p. 4. This essay was mentioned by Francesco Carrara in his *Programma*, in which he observed: "*Il Signor Rapisardi ha testè pubblicato un suo disegno di codice penale italiano: e quantunque egli abbia preso a tipo i soli due codici Sardo e Napoletano, dimenticando che in Italia vi era pure una qualche cosa, come il codice penale Toscano, che avendo richiamato gli elogi dei dotti delle più remote parti di Europa, meritava di non essere dimenticato da un italiano, pure il suo libro è meritevole in qualche parte di elogio*". Francesco Carrara, *Programma del corso di diritto criminale dettato nella Regia Università di Pisa dal professore Francesco Carrara. Parte generale* (Lucca, 1860), p. 409.

We can have a summarized account of a long debate in two macro-periods which, according to the schematic lines followed by Enrico Pessina, go from 1860 to 1875 and from 1874 to 1887. The years from 1860 to 1875 were characterized by works criticizing the current Italian Codes and their comparison with the foreign criminal laws, such as the *Programma del corso di diritto criminale* by Francesco Carrara. This scholar stressed the differences between the Italian and French criminal law on the most serious penal questions (such as the questions of attempt and complicity), and defined the French code of 1810 a "living anachronism".[27] These studies were followed by doctrinal works resulting in the reflections of famous jurists, such as Buccellati, Tolomei, Canonico, and Paoli who marked an important milestone in the progress of the Italian penal science. In fact, as Mario Sbriccoli highlighted, in front of the issues such as criminality and public order,[28] the Italian jurists, had to face with the foreign experiences and new sciences such as the emerging criminology, statistics, prison regulations, legal medicine, anthropology and criminal sociology. These horizons would have made up a very important scope for the scientific reflection from the criminal lawyers, divided by the unresolved conflict between the positive school[29] (grounded on the anthropological sociology) and the classical school (exponent of the liberal criminal culture).[30]

In contrast, the second period (1874–1887) brought to light details of the early projects of the penal code that the Parliament had closely examined and were the fruits of the work carried out by the various ministerial Committees in which participated eminent jurists who centred their debates on the problems of abrogation

[27]Carrara, *Programma del corso di diritto criminale*, p. 276.

[28]Mario Sbriccoli, "La penalistica civile. Teorie e ideologie del diritto penale nell'Italia Unita", Id., *Storia del diritto penale e della giustizia*, p. 534: "*Il codice [...] è un punto di approdo. Ma è anche la magna quaestio che per trent'anni tiene impegnati giuristi e legislatori in un confronto altamente significativo. Nella sua lunghissima gestazione si trova la chiave per comprendere e valutare insieme i problemi che l'Italia si trovava davanti in termini di criminalità, ordine pubblico o scontro sociale, e i travagli della scienza giuridica, che doveva dare loro una risposta legislativa capace di conciliare repressione e garanzie, efficacia e civiltà*".

[29]*Ibid.*, p. 535. See on this Floriana Colao, *Il delitto politico tra Ottocento e Novecento. Da «delitto fittizio» a «nemico dello Stato»* (Milano, 1986); Luigi Lacchè, *La giustizia per i galantuomini. Ordine e libertà nell'Italia liberale. Il dibattito sul carcere preventivo (1865–1913)* (Milano, 1990); Ettore Dezza, *Saggi di storia del diritto penale moderno* (Milano, 1992); Carlo Federico Grosso, "Le grandi correnti del pensiero penalistico italiano tra Ottocento e Novecento", *Storia d'Italia, Annali 12* (Torino 1997), pp. 7–34; Paolo Grossi, *Scienza giuridica italiana. Unprofilostorico (1860–1950)* (Milano, 2000).

[30]The paradigm of criminal schools kicks off by the battle waged by Enrico Ferriat the beginning of the Eighties of the Nineteenth century against criminologists of different backgrounds, which he called "classical school" and adjusted their cultural and historical boundaries. The term "classical school" appears in the opening lecture of Siena of 1882, November 18, Enrico Ferri, *La scuola positiva di diritto criminale* (Siena, 1883), p. 11 and then in the conference Enrico Ferri, "Le ragioni storiche della Scuola positiva di diritto criminale", *Rivista di filosofia scientifica* II (1882–83), p. 5. See on this Sbriccoli, "Il diritto penale liberale", pp. 105–83.

of death penalty, the regulations of political crimes[31] and the individuation of the tripartite structure (crimes, delicts, contraventions) or bipartisan (delicts and contraventions).[32] Many projects were developed (De Falco in 1866, Pironti in 1868 and again De Falco in 1873), but the first one to overcome the close examination by the Senate was the text of 1874, produced under the Paolo Onorato Vigliani government.[33]

In the explanatory memorandum to the proposals for the Senate (24 February 1874), it was pointed out the necessity of overcoming the differences and contradictions among the penal laws in force in the Italian provinces.[34] Thanks to the fruits of the previous commissions' work and the maturity achieved by the science of the Italian criminal law, the project had solved the most serious and difficult problems concerning the criminal subject by choosing the opinions that conformed to the local traditions and the practical needs of the dispensation of justice.[35] On the basis of those conditions, the wording of the project reduced the harshness of sentences by reducing the cases of application of the death penalty and the quashing of hard labor which were replaced with imprisonment and confinement; it accepted the rules concerning the criminal responsibility provided by the Tuscan Code and the matter concerning the complicity of the people provided by the Neapolitan Code; it provided for the reduction of punishment for the attempted crime and the committed one. It also granted the reduction of the sentence by two or three degrees for the attempted crime. From the Sardinian Code of 1859, it resumed the rules regarding concurrent offences, while it preserved crimes classified into three categories, even though it recognized the greatest scientific value of the bipartisan system.[36]

---

[31]Michele Pifferi, "Difendere i confini, superare le frontiere. Le 'zone grigie' della legalità penale tra Otto e Novecento", *Quaderni fiorentini*, 36 (2007), *Principio di legalità e diritto penale (per Mario Sbriccoli)*, I, pp. 743–799.

[32]The main problem that was debated in doctrine was closely related to the criminalization of illegal contravention, because the extension of the threshold of punishment even to actions of mere danger to public safety or common prosperity resulted from good governance choices in civil society. See Carlo Ghisalberti, *La codificazione del diritto in Italia 1865–1942* (Roma, 1994), pp. 167–173; Lacchè, "Un code pénal pour l'Unité italienne", pp. 309 ss.; Santangelo Cordani, *Alla vigilia del Codice Zanardelli*, pp. 71–2.

[33]Pessina, *Il diritto penale in Italia*, p. 145.

[34]*Progetto del codice penale del regno d'Italia preceduto dalla relazione ministeriale presentata al Senato del Regno nella tornata del 24 febbraio 1874 dal ministro di Grazia e Giustizia (Vigliani)* (Roma, 1874), p. 1: "*Tre codici penali imperano simultaneamente nelle nostre provincie: il subalpino del 20 novembre 1859 nelle province dell'Alta Italia e nelle romane; il toscano del 20 giugno 1853 nelle province toscane; e lo stesso codice subalpino, ma essenzialmente modificato da decreti delle Luogotenenze generali del Re, nelle province meridionali*".

[35]*Ibid.*, p. 6.

[36]The choice was justified on the will to not deviate too much from the existing criminal law in most Italian regions. On this point, it should be noted that a first draft Code of 1868 was more innovative than later, because it abandoned the criterion of the tripartite division. Santangelo Cordani, *Alla vigilia del Codice Zanardelli*, p. 75.

These rules, briefly summarized, made the text particularly innovative compared to the previous ones. Francesco Carrara stressed its originality faced with the Napoleonic penal code.[37] Giovanni Carmignani defined the French penal Code: "funesta importazione delle bajonette straniere". According to this Author, the Napoleonic code had constituted a serious disaster for our Peninsula. For these reasons, it would have been necessary to drive the Napoleonic Code back "beyond the Alps", once and for all.[38]

There were many observations by Italian jurists to improve the project given to the revision of a senatorial commission,[39] the results of which were summarized by Lugi Lucchini in the critical essay *Intorno al progetto Vigliani*. In this text, he pointed out the widespread will of science and modern legislation to abandon the model of the French Code.[40] The parliamentary process reached a deadlock because of the fall of the government in 1876. But the work on that project was not lost. In fact, the new Ministry of Justice Pasquale Stanislao Mancini entrusted a commission of experts with the job of revising the text. Their job would have been fulfilled with the greatest care by collecting the opinions and documents drawn up by the magistrates, the legal faculties and professional associations Mancini had expressly requested to collaborate.[41] The result of this study brought to submit the *First book* of the new penal code project into the Chamber of Deputies on 20 November 1876. It suggested a new scheme of penal code which appeared to be particularly original with reference to the harshness of a sentence since it provided for the total abolition of death penalty and the introduction of life sentence as life imprisonment.[42] The

[37]Carrara, *Pensieri sul progetto di codice penale italiano del 1874*, p. 5: "*Se il progetto di codice penale presentato al Senato dallo illustre Guardasigilli Vigliani, fosse uno di quei tanti progetti che fecondati all'uggia del codice penale francese e nati senza vertebra non hanno diritto a vivere, né speranza di vita, sarebbe vanità formarne argomento di studii. Ma il progetto Vigliani è un progetto serio, è il riassunto dei tentativi fatti in Italia negli ultimi dieci anni, è ricco di alcune bellissime idee; moltissime cose eccellenti contiene; e molte che, quantunque altri potesse desiderarle migliori, pur sono accettabili*".

[38]*Ibid.*, p. 10. Overall, the opinion of Carrara was negative. In fact, he again emphasized certain defects, that would be necessary to amend, with regard to norms on premeditation, failed crime and attempt, prescription, pimping and rape. *Ibid.*, pp. 180–183.

[39]See *Osservazioni e proposte della Facoltà di giurisprudenza nella R. Università di Torino intorno al nuovo progetto di Codice penale pel Regno d'Italia* (Torino, Contributi di T. Canonico, E. Pasquali, P.C. Gariazzo, G. Delvitto, B. Gianolio); *Osservazioni sul progetto del Codice penale presentato dal Ministro Vigliani al Senato nella tornata del 24 febbraio 1874: lette al Circolo giuridico da Giovanni Gorritte* (Palermo, 1875); *Intorno lo schema di Codice penale italiano presentato dal Ministro Guardasigilli al Senato del Regno nella tornata del 24 febbraio 1874: osservazioni e proposte del prof. Enrico Pessina accolte dalla Facoltà giuridica della R. Università di Napoli* (Napoli, 1875); *Le fonti del Codice penale italiano. 1. Relazioni, progetti, emendamenti, discussioni avanti il Senato del Regno* (Roma, 1875).

[40]*Intorno al progetto Vigliani 24 febbraio 1874 di un nuovo codice penale per l'Italia riveduto dalla commissione senatoria. Rassegna critica di Luigi Lucchini* (Padova, 1875), p. 9.

[41]Ghisalberti, *La codificazione del diritto in Italia*, p. 170.

[42]On the characters of Mancini project, I refer again to the excellent synthesis of Pessina, *Il dirittopenale in Italia*, pp. 158–162.

Chamber of Deputies approved the text towards the end 1877, but the works (which had started also on the second book) came back to the "parliamentary limbo" because of Mancini's resignation.

The fate of the "never-ending job"—done and undone because of the different principles and doctrinal studies discussed in departmental and parliamentary rooms by the representatives of the different schools[43]—was reconstructed in short in 1885 by Luigi Lucchini in the pages of the first issue of *Seconda Serie* of *Rivista Penale* complained *To the readers* that in spite of all efforts, the text of the penal code was still at the planning stage.[44]

Indeed, Lucchini referred to the latest project written in 1883 under the pressure of minister Giuseppe Zanardelli and that, owing to the sudden changes at the Ministry of Justice (where succeeded one another Bernardino Giannuzzi Savelli, Enrico Pessina, Diego Tajani and Zanardelli till 1887), had to be faced with a very difficult process would come to a close with its final passage in 1889. The obtained code was the result of the Italian liberal criminal law tradition, the postulate of which allowed the passing of a modern and balanced text arising from the remains of the Sardinian penal code inspired by Napoleonic penal Code and the Tuscan one inspired by Code of Grand Duchy of Baden. The new text was, therefore, in search of a meticulous clarity and brevity of concepts and it also got important results as regards its definitions, meticulous and concise, on realizing a satisfactory proportion of parts and homogeneity of formulas, and avoiding any arid case records.[45] Zanardelli himself, in his *Report to the King*, admitted he had proceeded to make a decomposition of the articles of the earlier project with the intention of regulating and ordering better the matter and explaining the legislative text.[46]

The system followed would not have given, then, problems of interpretation, particularly considering that in the text of the code it was not made use of locutions to be so abstract to give even the unlearned men to be enabled to understand all that the code forbidden, by themselves and without any need for them to have interpreters.[47]

As for its structure and contents, the code resulted to be "really modern"—as pointed out by Carlo Ghisalberti[48]—not only for the abolition of death penalty was

---

[43]Luigi Lucchini, "Ai Lettori", *Rivista penale di dottrina legislazione e giurisprudenza*, XXI (1885), p. 5. The "Journa" was founded by Lucchini in 1874, year of the presentation in the Senate of Vigliani project, just to provide a forum that would serve as an aid to the criminal codification process.

[44]*Ibid.*, p. 6.

[45]Mario Da Passano, "Le definizioni nella storia del diritto penale italiano contemporaneo", A. Cadoppi (ed.), *Omnis definitio in iure periculosa? Il problema delle definizioni legali nel diritto penale* (Padova, 1966), p. 95.

[46]*Relazione a S.M. IL Re del Ministro Guardasigilli (Zanardelli) nell'udienza del 30 giugno 1889 per l'approvazione del testo definitivo del codice penale* (Roma, 1889), p. 9.

[47]*Ibid.*, p. 10.

[48]Ghisalberti, *La codificazione del diritto in Italia,* p. 171. An efficient synthesis of the Zanardelli code characters is in Guido Neppi Modona y Luciano Violante, *Poteri dello Stato e sistema penale. Corso di lezioni universitarie*, Torino 1978, p. 175 and in Sbriccoli, *Caratteri originari e tratti permanenti*, p. 509.

replaced by life imprisonment,[49] but also for the solutions it proposed with regard to the most controversial questions concerning the penal law such as the acceptance of the bipartite subdivision of offences into delicts and contraventions, which had been inherited from the Tuscan code,[50] the resolution of the complex question concerning the criminal responsibility by taking into account the wilfulness of the action defined as a crime,[51] the prediction of a low-grade penalty to be imposed on the attempted crime compared to the perpetrated one,[52] the distinction between the main executors and the accomplices to the crime[53] and the establishment of minimum and maximum penalties by assigning the judge a certain discretion in its right determination according to the principle of the offender rehabilitation.[54]

---

[49]Regarding the punitive system, the new system provided, at the top of the criminal scale for the crimes perpetual imprisonment, which was followed by the two parallel penalties of imprisonment provided for intentional crimes "*arising from inherently evil impulse*" and detention for the culpable crimes "*committed with a state of mind that recalls the benign regard of the legislator*". Followed the penalty of confinement, fine and exclusion from public office. For the contraventions, however, the "criminal scale" consisted in arrest, fines and suspension from the exercise of a profession or art. *Relazione a S.M. il Re del Ministro Guardasigilli*, p. 21.

[50]The tripartite system had its origins in the French revolutionary law, then incorporated in the Napoleonic Penal Code of 1810, and subsequently in pre-unification Italian codes of the Two Sicilies, Parma and Sardinia, while the Tuscan Code followed bipartite scheme of crimes and transgressions and the code of Duchy of Modena was articulated in crimes and contraventions. After a long debate, that had gone through the different projects alternated in different solutions, it was finally abandoned the old tripartite division which also includes the crimes, namely the violation of the criminal law considered most serious and brutal, continued to be followed especially in France and abroad. See Tullio Padovani, "Il binomio irriducibile. La distinzione dei reati in delitti e contravvenzioni fra storia e politica criminale", G. Marinucci y E. Dolcini (eds.), *Diritto penale in trasformazione* (Milano, 1985), pp. 421–464; Santangelo Cordani, *Alla vigilia del Codice Zanardelli*, pp. 69–77.

[51]As regards the theme of criminal responsibility, the Zanardelli code followed the example of the Tuscan code, which differed from other previous Italian codes that had transposed the principle of the *Code pénal* of 1810, which excluded the existence of a crime when the defendant was in state of insanity or when he had been forced by an irresistible force. This formula—taken by almost all the preunitary penal codes in the desire to make very clear the discipline of criminal responsibility and culpability—did not offer a definition of imputability, limiting it only to predict the causes of its exclusion. Ettore Dezza, "Imputabilità e infermità mentale: la genesi dell'art. 46 del Codice Zanardelli", Id., *Saggi di storia del diritto penale moderno*, pp. 283 ss.

[52]The final formulation of the Zanardelli project adopted the choice of a significant simplification compared to the many provisions reserved to the attempt in preunitary codifications, inputting only two rules governing the attempted offense and failed crime, except for any hypotheses concerning attempted contraventions. Stefano Del Corso, "Il tentativo nel codice Zanardelli", Vinciguerra, *Diritto penale dell'Ottocento*, p. 554.

[53]In the wake of the most modern science of criminal law, Zanardelli Code distinguished between main agents and accomplices of the crime, by adopting a system that provided, between the physical accomplices, not only the executors, but also the immediate collaborators of the act. Among the moral accomplices, it envisaged the participants in an offense which determined the executor to commit it. Santangelo Cordani, *Alla vigilia del codice Zanardelli*, pp. 166 ss.

[54]The original features of the Italian criminal code are derived mainly from the role played by the "correctional component", which refused the sanctioning rigour that characterized the different criminal codifications, since the time of the revolutionary codifications. See Sergio Moccia, "Ideologia e diritto nelle sanzioni del codice Zanardelli", Vinciguerra, *Diritto penale dell'Ottocento*, p. 566.

3 The *mise en Place* of the Penal Code "Seal and Crown of the Unity the Homeland"

The text of the new penal code was accepted very enthusiastically by the followers of the classical School who claimed its authorship.[55] It was opposed by the conflicting rumours of the positivists whose spokesman Lombroso criticized: "having tried the same dress on people having different sizes".[56] As a matter of fact, it was the product of the followers of the Classical School. It was representative—as Franz von Listz would point out in 1894—of a sort of compromise between the past and the future on joining the already inappropriate old theories and the still questionable new ones[57]:

> Les antropologue l'ont traité "d'éclectique", oubliant que l'écletisme etait nécessaire au moment de sa confection. Pour eux il est trop arriéré, pour certains jurists il est trop progressiste. C'est dire que pour le juger sainement, il ne faut pas se placer au point de vue exclusif d'une école.[58]

Apart from agreeing to the one or the other school, the code was welcome by a great many of the Italian lawyers who had been waiting for the issuing of a new text for a long time. But, let the new text really abandon the old one which had been welcome by the courtrooms up to then? The answer will obviously be negative: in fact, failing a case law in the making and works commenting on the Zanardelli code, legal practitioners happened to enforce the new penal laws in compliance with the Italian and French old case law and doctrinal apparatus. In fact, we are not in lacking in examples of forensic productions in which lawyers went on referring to the doctrinal quotations by Sante Roberti's, Niccola Nicolini's and Francesco Carrara's works based on the codes preceding the unification of Italy[59] or the

[55]Sbriccoli, "Il diritto penale liberale", p. 931.

[56]Cesare Lombroso in an essay entitled *Troppo presto. Appunti al nuovo Progetto di Codice penale* (Torino, 1888) claimed the fact that the code was launched while the 'new school' was changing the direction of the country in the field of criminal policies. It was not given the time to assert its new ideas in the field of criminal law codification, which meant that the code was born full of numerous errors including the uniqueness of the code for the 'four Italies' (north, south, centre and islands), the abolition of death penalty, the conditional release, an excessive mildness of the penalties, the impracticality of prison sentences. See Sbriccoli, "Il diritto penale liberale", p. 950.

[57]Franz Von Listz, *La législation pénale comparée, Ier volume, Le droit criminel des États européens* (Berlin. 1894), p. 120.

[58]*Ibid.*

[59]Alessandro Criscuolo, *Per G. Palma notaio. Falso per supposizione di qualità personale* (Taranto, 1894), p. 3: "*Assai elegante quistione della quale dissero Sante Roberti nel libro della falsità, le leggi penale del regno delle due Sicilie, interpretando, Nicola Nicolini, nel volume di quelle del Rito, di ogni altra italica dottrina sul falso di qualità personale, il dottissimo Carrara al titolo:dei Criteri essenziali del falso in documento pubblico*".

quotations of the French case law originated from the *Répertoire général et raisonné du droit criminel* byAchille Morin[60] and the *Répertoire de législation, de doctrine et de jurisprudence* by Victor Alexis Désiré Dalloz,[61] the *Recueil alphabetique de questions de droit* by Philippe Antoine Merlin[62] as well as the *Commentaire sur le Code penal* by Joseph-François-Claude Carnot[63] and the *Traité du droit criminal* by Achille Francois Le Sellyer.[64]

The above mentioned examples—to which we have to add the considerable references to the ante 1889 Italian previous cases of law[65] and comparisons between the Neapolitan and Sardinian legal regulations and the ones by Zanardelli[66]—let us highlight the difficulties perceived by the Italian lawyers in the employment of the last text, the fortune of which "was handed up" the Italian judiciary so it might give a diligent definition and interpretation of the new case law courses. The General

---

[60]Achille Morin, *Répertoire général et raisonné du droit criminel ou sont méthodiquement exposées la législation, la docrtine et la jurisprudence sur tout ce qui constitue le grand et le petit criminel en toutes matières et dans toutes les jurisdictions*, 2 voll. (Paris, 1850–1).

[61]Victor Alexis Désiré Dalloz, *Jurisprudence générale, repertoire metodique et alphabetique de législation et de doctrine et de jurisprudence en matière de droit civil, commercial, criminel et administratif, de droit des gens et de droit public, nouvelle edition considrablement augmentée et précédé d'une essai sur l'histoire générale du droit françois*, 44 voll (Paris, 1844–74).

[62]Philippe-Antoine Merlin, *Recueil alphabetique des questions de droit qui se presentent le plus frequemment dans les tribunaux; ouvrage dans lequel sont fondus et classes la plupart des plaidoyers et requisitoires de l'Auteur, avec le texte de jugemens du tribunal de Cassation, qui s'en sont ensuivis* (Porthmann, 1802–1805).

[63]Joseph François Claude Carnot, *Commentaire sur le Code pénal contenant: la manière d'en faire une juste application, l'indicazion des améliorations dont il est susceptible, et des dissertations sur les questions les plus importantes qui peuvent s'y rattacher*, 2 voll. (Bruxelles, 1823–4).

[64]Achille-François Le Sellyer, *Traité du droit criminel appliqué aux actions publique et privée qui naissent des contraventions, des délits et des crimes: ouvrage contenant l'explication de la plus partie des matières les plus importantes du droit criminel*, 6 voll. (Paris, 1844).

[65]Criscuolo, *In difesa di G. Palma*, p. 24: "*Dunque è l'antica dottrina che si ripete, dalla quale nasce la illazione che non costituendo il falso, ma la frode del pubblico ufficiale, notaio, è mestieri provare in costui: 1° la volontà di carpire l'altrui; 2° l'uso dei mezzi idonei; 3° il pregiudizio; gli elementi insomma tutti della frode. Così ebbe a giudicare la Corte di Appello di Trani, a 13 Gennaio 1879, De Martino e Pirro; così pure la Cassazione di Torino, a 23 maggio 1867, nella causa Marani*".

[66]*Ibid.*, p. 25: "*È invero, delle falsità avvenute per negligenza o inavvertenza, non si preoccupò il Codice del 1819. È una disposizione che trovavasi soltanto nel Codice Sardo del 1859 e riguardava il caso del rilascio delle copie. Il Codice Napoletano non aveva alcuna sanzione punitiva pel notaio che stipulasse un atto senza conoscere le parti. L'ebbe il Codice Sardo nell'articolo 348, che puniva di carcere tale trasgressione. Il Codice attuale invece ha una sanzione nuova ed è nell'articolo 279 la quale rivela questo pensiero del legislatore: il notaio può essere tratto in inganno, tale fatto è punibile per colui che lo commette, ma della negligenza, il notaio risponde alla legge notarile. Questo è il pensiero del 279, pensiero che chiaramente si rileva dalla sua dizione*".

Attorney Francesco Auriti shared the same views[67] so much that in his speech addressed to the general assembly on 4 January 1890 in front of Court of Cassation in Rome (the only one body legitimated to pronounce judgement with full acknowledge of all the criminal legal cases in the Italian Kingdom[68]), he expressed approval for "the audacious and generous initiative" of the new Italian penal Code.[69] The Senator, besides the abolition of death penalty all over Italy, stressed the scrapping of the tripartite division of offences borrowed from the French Code which had added a generic classification based not on the quality but on the quantity of penalty, up to the specific causes of the fact.[70]

The new Code followed the bipartite trend in expectation of two categories of crimes which were distinct and parallel in their terms (imprisonment and detention), and which is why it was possible to distinguish the crimes "arisen from wicked intentions and animal instincts" from the ones provoked by political, passion reasons or great provocations. it established the "cornerstones necessary to the individuation of the greatest categories of crimes, and specified the elements making up each type of crime and the procedural methods which could be functionally formulated",[71] Attorney Auriti identified the room that the Code had provided for the activity of judges who were competent in the concrete implementation of generic concepts such as the extent of the damage (limited or considerable) which had been previously fixed by rough, arbitrary and inadequate criteria and the possibility of imposing a considerable latitude of penalties to be adapted to the indeterminable variety of the individual cases.[72]

By these words, the General Attorney pointed out the highly responsible task of the Courts in carrying out the new Criminal Code which "within well-defined borders, but not within cramped spaces" would assure a fair judgement of the individual cases. That is why the General Attorney believed to trust the chance of the new Code to the Italian Court.[73] In fact, if the High Court was highly responsible for capturing the spirit of the new provisions of the law, connecting the

[67]Descended from a noble family, Francesco Auriti (Guardiagrele, February 24, 1822 - Rome, April 3, 1896) graduated in Law in Naples; in 1845 he beganto practice as a lawyer in Chieti. In 1861 he was appointed judge of the High Civil Court in L'Aquila, then Deputy Prosecutor General in Naplesand Director of Cassation in Palermoand in 1874 the first President of the Court of Appeal of Trani. In 1875 he became President of the Chamber of the Supreme Court and Attorney General in 1886. Many of his speeches and indictments pronounced before the Court of Cassation in Rome are kept in the Senate. See Senato del Regno, *Attiparlamentari. Discussioni,* 4 maggio 1896.

[68]The Law December 6, 1888 n. 5825 had, in fact, referred to the Court of Cassation in Rome the cognition of all criminal cases of the Kingdom of Italy (Gazz. Uff. 10 dicembre 1888 n. 289).

[69]Francesco Auriti, *Discorso pronunziato dal Senatore Francesco Auriti Procuratore Generale del Re presso la Corte di Cassazione di Roma nella assemblea generale del 4 gennaio 1890* (Roma, 1890), p. 6.

[70]*Ibid.*

[71]*Ibid.*, p. 7.

[72]*Ibid.*, p. 7.

[73]*Ibid.*, p. 8.

principles, defining the specific elements of each crime, the court was due the task of making good use of the large latitude of choice it was allowed in the application of penalty, even for the cases which had been verified by the verdict of jury.[74]

Beginning from one year since the first opening address, on 3 January 1891 Francesco Auriti reported on the application of the Criminal Code and the difficulties concerning mainly the temporary and coordination laws with regard to the nature of their balanced arrangements, the need to change a whole system formerly based on the tripartite division of crimes and the difficulties to define the boundaries established for the retroactivity of the most indulgent criminal provisions.[75] In fact, the courts of the Kingdom happened to have to coordinate and harmonize the old and new provisions to enforce the principle of retroactivity which was granted within certain limits only for the rules in favour of an offender within the limits of awaiting judgements of first and second instance in the days of the promulgation of the new Penal Code.[76] And as for the judgements already pending in the Supreme Court, although the principle of retroactivity was not enforceable, the Supreme Court would have had to try at the solution of several questions with regard to the application of the new law in the event the criminal proceedings were still kept on the Court of Cassation judgement. Only in a few cases—Auriti reported—the Cassation case law had recognized the new Code the retroactive effects of the previous convictions, and in particular, in the event of life imprisonment for the acts which had been punished with temporary punishment.[77]

This example represented the criterion used by the Supreme Court which chose to interpret and to integrate the conception of a partial disposition by coordinating it with all the others similar provisions it had to be. In this way, the application of the coexistence and coordination principles would have had to be prevalent over the misleading sentence of the text and the fragmentary and often uncertain and in embryo concepts discussed during the preliminary works of the Code itself.[78] In support of this principle, the General Attorney called to mind the article 39 of the

[74]*Ibid.*, pp. 8–9.

[75]Francesco Auriti, *Discorso pronunziato dal Senatore Francesco Auriti Procuratore Generale del Re presso la Corte di Cassazione di Roma nella assemblea generale del 3 gennaio 1891* (Roma, 1891), pp. 7–8.

[76]*Ibid.*: "*Ma dov'è propriamente questo confine? Ecco il primo problema. Fino a che dura il giudizio di merito, ha risposto la nostra Corte, vi è luogo ad applicare la pena più mite della legge sopravvenuta, ossia anche in grado di appello, ma non nello stadio in Corte di Cassazione, la quale, rivedendo il giudicato alla stregua delle leggi che lo reggevano, non può di regola, altrimenti che per violazione di quelle pronunziare l'annullamento. Annullare con la sentenza di dibattimento e il fatto con esso accertato, sarebbe legittimare un effetto senza causa, crescendo ingombro al corso spedito della giustizia; annullare la sola applicazione della pena, ritenuto il fatto della sentenza, sarebbe voler porre in equazione termini non corrispondenti tra loro. Imperocchè il fatto della sentenza rileva le sole circostanze influenti secondo la legge del tempo, ed è muta su quelle che pur potrebbero aggravare la pena per disposizione della nuova legge, sotto altri riguardi più mite*".

[77]*Ibid.*, p. 11.

[78]*Ibid.*, p. 12.

implementing provisions of the Criminal Code[79] the interpretation of which allowed defining which the choice to make for a life sentence the new code had punished it by a temporary punishment: in that case it would have been necessary to inquiry into the verdict of guilty the substantive fact "which is defined in the specific title of the offense, excluding the minor modalities".[80]

The question concerning the practical application of the penalty was entrusted to the magistrates, whose "latitude to arbitration" had never been free from criticism, so much so that the Substitute Attorney General Isidoro Broggi in his inaugural speech, made in 1892, devoted some of his observations to that question, and declared the large powers given to the judges had to be limited by the responsibility of the magistrates who had been called to operate within the limits set by the criminal code, which met the proportion between the fact and the penalty much better than the 1859 code.[81]

This comparison highlighted why the censorship claimed the new code marked by "excessive mildness" had no basis, just as had no basis the censorship claiming the new code let a judge have a wide discretionary power in the application of penalties by the marked narrow boundaries which would not allow him to go too far. In fact, by comparing the Neapolitan code with the Zanardelli one, the Substitute Attorney mentioned the case of the wilful murder which in the Southern provinces was punished with 20 years hard labour. In fact, the sentence might have a 10 year reduction only for the general extenuating circumstances which were often granted by the jury without any criteria and about if they would grant a grace. By the new code, on the contrary, a judge might not have had the possibility of sentencing less than 15 years' reclusion, since it had been decreed that the penalty might have a one sixth reduction thanks to the extenuating circumstances.[82] Then, the fact the legislator had provided for the abolition of the reduction or increase of the degree system instead of the quotient system had assured to make the punishment fit the crime.

4 Early Case Law Applications Between the Old and the New Criminal Law

The earlier case law interventions by the Court of Cassation were basic to steer the lawyers and the lower courts towards the application of the new Code which was soon followed by commentary works which sorted out the most relevant legitimacy

[79]On this topic, Auriti had already dedicated a specific study, printed in 1890, on the pages of the journal *La legge*. Francesco Auriti, "Sunto di requisitoria sull'interpretazione dell'art. 39 delle disposizioni per l'attuazione del nuovo Codice penale e sentenza della Corte di Cassazione", *La legge* 1, n. 2 (1890).

[80]Auriti, *Discorso* ... 1891, p. 12.

[81]Isidoro Broggi, "Discorso pronunciato dal sostituto proc. generale commendatore Isidoro Broggi presso la Corte di Cassazione di Roma", *Inaugurazione dell'anno giudiziario 1892 alla Corte di Cassazione di Roma il di 4 gennaio* (Roma 1892), p. 13.

[82]*Ibid.*, p. 14.

rulings,[83] many of which were summarized and noted in the main sector journals which were increasing just in those years.[84] They, primarily in the first years, never lacked in referring to the pre-existing codes the comparison proving to be necessary to remove any doubt and uncertainty resulting from the several pre-existing Codes which often led the lower courts into error. A few examples are sufficient to proof all said. By the judgement of 26 May 1891 the Court of Cassation of Rome was called to give a statement on the appeal filed by the defendants Viggiano Agostino, D'Addio Antonio and Buro Elpidio, sentenced on 21 March 1891 by the Assize Court of Santa Maria Capua Vetere for murder to the respective penalty of 8 years imprisonment for the first two and 5 years and 10 months for the third. The main pleas were related to the alleged violation of articles 368 and 378 of penal code[85] "for having applied the hypothesis of article 378 also to the 368 one".[86] In order to declare the inadmissibility to appeal against the grounds for a judgement, the Court

[83]Among the first case law comments addressed to the practice, see: Luigi Bozzo, *Codice penale italiano e la sua genesi: con note di giurisprudenza ed altre utili per la pratica* (Roma, 1890); Giulio Crivellari, *Il codice penale per il Regno d'Italia interpretato sulla scorta della dottrina, delle fonti, della legislazione comparata e della giurisprudenza* (Torino, 1890–1898); Luigi Majno, *Commento al codice penale italiano* (Verona, 1890–1894); Angiolo Coen, *Manuale di giurisprudenza sul Codice penale italiano e sulle disposizioni per l'attuazione del codice penale* (Livorno, 1891); Giovanni Suman, *Manuale pei giudici ed avvocati penali, ufficiali ed agenti di polizia giudiziaria: contenente esposte in ordine alfabetico le disposizioni dei Codici penale e di procedura penale, legge e regolamento di pubblica sicurezza: con illustrazioni, casi pratici e giurisprudenza* (Torino, 1891); Luigi Manzitti, *Giurisprudenza sul codice penale del regno d'Italia: anni 1890, 1891, 1892. Prima appendice al codice penale annotato per Giambattista conte Milano* (Napoli, 1893).

[84]In addition to the already existing journals—as well as *Il foro italiano* by Enrico Scialoja and *Rivista penale* by Luigi Lucchini -were born *Cassazione unica* in 1889, *La Scuola Positiva* in 1891 (renamed, in 1893, *La Scuola Positiva nella Giurisprudenza penale*), *Il foro penale. Rivista critica di diritto e giurisprudenza penale e di discipline carcerarie* in 1892 and *La Giustizia penale. Rivista critica settimanale di dottrina, giurisprudenza, legislazione*in 1895. See Floriana Colao, "«Consorelle» tra «vincoli indissolubili», «scuole», «indirizzi» del penale", Luigi Lacche y Monica Stronati (eds.), *Una tribuna per le scienza criminali. La 'cultura' delle Riviste nel dibattito penalistico tra Otto e Novecento* (Macerata, 2012), p. 42.

[85]Art. 368 p.c.: "*Chiunque, con atti diretti a commettere una lesione personale, cagiona la morte di alcuno è punito con la reclusione da dodici a diciotto anni, nel caso dell'articolo 364; da quindici a venti anni, nei casi dell'articolo 365; e non minore di venti anni, nei casi dell'articolo 366. Se la morte non sarebbe avvenuta senza il concorso di condizioni preesistenti ignote al colpevole, o di cause sopravvenute e indipendenti dal suo fatto, la pena è della reclusione da otto a quattordici anni, nel caso dell'articolo 364; da undici a sedici anni nei casi dell'articolo 365; e da quindici a venti anni nei casi dell'articolo 366*". Art. 378 p.c.: "*Quando più persone prendano parte alla esecuzione di alcuno dei delitti preveduti negli articoli 364, 365, 366, 372 e 373 e non si conosca l'autore dell'omicidio o della lesione, esse soggiacciono tutte alle pene ivi rispettivamente stabilite diminuite da un terzo alla metà, e all'ergastolo è sostituita la reclusione non inferiore ai quindici anni. Questa diminuzione di pena non si applica al cooperatore immediato del fatto*".

[86]Corte di Cassazione, Sezione I, udienza 25 maggio 1891, Pres. Ghiglieri, Rel. Miraglia, PM. Broggi, Ric. Viggiano Agostino ed altri, *Il foro penale. Rivista critica di diritto e giurisprudenza penale e di discipline carcerarie*, anno I, vol. I, parte seconda, p. 17.

started off a long motivational path referring to the case law formed in the Southern provinces. Here, in fact, it was formed a wide course of study concerning the enforcement of the criminal laws of 1819 by criteria of responsibility defined as "complicitàcorrespettiva" which happened when even if many people had committed murder or injury, the real culprit of death or injury was unknown. This principle was also transposed in articles 101 and 102 of the Sardinian Code. The applicants still argued this principle had to be applied only to wilful murders and not also to the manslaughters in virtue of the assumption upholding the article 378 of the new code referred only to wilful murders. By finding the groundlessness of the demur defect, the judges of the Court pointed out that art. 378 p.c. also referred to art. 372–373 which were attendant only the physical injuries, according to the criterion indicating only the objective part of the offense consisting in the death provoked by harms to body or health. In fact, it would have been inconceivable—pointed out the judges—the law had recognized a connivance among the ones who had taken part in the action which had caused the weakening of an organ and that it had ruled this connivance out for the ones who had taken part in the action provoking the death:

> Neppure all'epoca del Codice Sardo si dubitò mai nelle province meridionali che la complicità corrispettiva esistesse pure nelle ferite produttive di morte (Not even at the time of the then-existing Sardinian Code of Law, there was any doubt in the Southern Provinces that the connivance among the ones who had taken part in the action existed as well when the wounds had caused death).[87]

The proof of the frequent comparison with the previous codification in order to clarify the meaning and the importance of the new rules, is mainly evicted by a different new judgement of the Supreme Court in Rome dated 7 December 1891. It was called to resolve a question of interpretation about art. 426 p.c. punishing the abusive grazing someone else's farm or the damage caused by letting the animals go free to someone's else farm.[88] The question examined by the supreme judges arose owing to a conflict of jurisdiction originated with the doubt whether it was enforceable the first or the second part of the art. 426 p.c. when damage to the farm had been provoked by leaving the cattle free to pasture. The close examination of the problem, apparently of no importance, allowed setting out the terms of the problem involving the wilfulness of conduct regulated by art. 45 p.c.[89] In fact, starting from the abolished Penal Code, which in the sections concerning "guasti e distruzioni" provided in the articles 672 and 674, formulated two different

---

[87] *Ibid.*, p. 18.

[88] Art. 468 p.c.: "*Chiunque arreca danno al fondo altrui, introducendovi senza diritto o abbandonandovi animali, è punito secondo le disposizioni dell'articolo 424. Per il solo fatto di averveli introdotti o abbandonati abusivamente per farveli pascolare, il colpevole è punito, a querela di parte, con la detenzione sino a tre mesi o con la multa sino a lire cinquecento*".

[89] Art. 45 p.c.: "*Nessuno può essere punito per un delitto, se non abbia voluto il fatto che costituisce, tranne che la legge lo ponga altrimenti a suo carico, come conseguenza della sua azione od omissione. Nelle contravvenzioni ciascuno risponde della propria azione od omissione, ancorchè non si dimostri che egli abbia voluto commettere un fatto contrario alla legge*".

hypotheses of damages in the others' farm and the abusive grazing. The judges recognized the new code had taken steps to put together the two provisions in a single rule, so it was possible for them to think no innovation had been introduced to that fact as regards the system of the previous code. It had, therefore, to be believed incorrect the identification of the difference between the two crimes from the existence or not of a damage which would make more or less serious the criminal act.[90] It had to be considered that the introduction of animals in the other people's grazing lands always provoked a damage (even if it might be less) and so the difference between the two crimes could not be considered "quantitative", but "qualitative" for the matter it was not anchored to "the material and exterior element of the crime", but on "the moral and interior element" or on the essence itself of the crime. So the claimed quantitative utilization had to be considered as "incomplete, vain, inorganic" in the place of the different qualitative criterion "organic, productive, complete" which referred to the "historical antecedents of the Roman Law and Modern Codes".[91] On the basis of these reasons, the Supreme Court regarded the abusive grazing offence committed without any injury against property subject to be punishable up to three months' imprisonment and fined up to 500 lire (following a complaint).

In this way, the Court recognized the jurisdiction of the *Pretore* who, vacated his warrant of incompetency, stayed proceedings. The decision was noted down "Il foropenale" by its editorial staff who applauded the interpretation given to the beginning paragraph of art. 426 p.c. by the Court of Cassation since they considered the different views to include an evident mistake, "result of the unpardonable negligence in the fundamental principles of the punitive law".[92] In fact, without the will of the fact or the specific intent, there might be no crime, but for express or exceptional provision of the law, such as culpable manslaughters or bodily harm or apparent danger. This principle had drawn a boundary line as regards the criminal system adopted by the previous laws, where this moral element of the offence was repeated each time in every provision by the words "intentionally, wilfully, knowingly, and other equivalent similar expressions". On the contrary, the Italian legislator had made up, by art. 45 p.c., a criminal responsibility general principle, which influenced the whole Criminal Code. The result was that putting out to pasture their own animals in someone's else farm, just to let them grazing, never completed the crime provided for that case by art. 426 p.c., even if a real damage had really been caused. So much because the *damnum injuria datum* (the damage), without any will to injury and damage, had to considered as a legal absurdity.[93]

As it is evicted from the mentioned judgement, the most innovative rules were the ones that gave more enforcing difficulties: it is an effective example the criminal

---

[90]Corte di Cassazione, sezione I, udienza 7 dicembre 1891. Pres. Ghiglieri, Est. Spera, PM Broggi. Risoluzione di conflitto in causa Lenzotti Luigi, *Il foro penale*, a. I (1892), vol. I, pp. 203–206.

[91]*Ibid.*, p. 206.

[92]*Ibid.*, p. 205.

[93]*Ibid.*

association mentioned in art. 248 p.c.,[94] the interpretative doubts of which were the object of a judgement passed by the Roman Cassation on 24 November 1892 in the action brought against the so called "anarchists". The question of law, brought to the Court's attention, concerned the question of the enforceability of the association offence joined to the episodes of rebellion committed by 62 defendants in Piazza Santa Croce in Jerusalem (Rome) on May 1891. The question had already been broached widely by the Court of first appeal in Rome, which—through a close examination of the subject already tackled in the remote French and Sardinian Codes and in the parliamentary debate which had promoted the passing of art. 248 p.c.—had thought that, in this particular case, it could concern neither the criminal association nor of associations constituted to attack the national security, but that the facts ascertained in the trial debate incurred the penalties provided for by art. 247 and 251 p.c. penalizing, as a common crime against the public order, the incitement to civil rebellion and the class hatred.[95] That decision had been reversed by the Court of Appeal in Rome which had differently shown as among all the defendants had been a mutual criminal intention consisting in destroying the right of ownership and the State. A few people condemned by criminal association rose up that decision and appealed the Supreme Court by demurring at the infringement of art. 248 p.c. since the Cassation had believed sufficient a momentary and accidental binding force of law rather than a stable and permanent one to have ruled the Roman anarchistic association delinquent purposes rather than political purposes.

The close examination of the first question moved from the assumption the Court of Appeal in Rome had not verified whether that association had or had not tried to have the accurate organization which marked legally collective bodies. This omission, however, was justified because the new penal code differed from the provisions laid down by the Sardinian code and the Tuscan one, which provided special rules as regards the scheme of the internal organization or the benefit sharing, since the previous doctrine and case law had asserted a concept similar to

[94]Art. 248 p.c.: "*Quando cinque o più persone si associano per commettere delitti contro l'amministrazione della giustizia, o la fede pubblica, o l'incolumità pubblica, o il buon costume e l'ordine delle famiglie, o contro la persona o la proprietà, ciascuna di esse è punita, per il solo fatto dell'associazione, con la reclusione da uno a cinque anni. Se gli associati scorrano le campagne o le pubbliche vie, e se due o più di essi portino armi o le tengano in luogo di deposito, la pena è della reclusione da tre a dieci anni. Se vi siano promotori o capi dell'associazione, la pena per essi è della reclusione da tre a otto anni, nel caso indicato nella prima parte del presente articolo, e da cinque a dodici anni, nel caso indicato nel precedente capoverso. Alle pene stabilite nel presente articolo è sempre aggiunta la sottoposizione alla vigilanza speciale dell'Autorità di pubblica sicurezza*".

[95]Tribunale penale di Roma, sezione VIII, udienza del 24 marzo 1892. Pres. ed Est. Osterman; P.M. Vico. Causa Cipriani Amilcare ed altri, *Il foro penale*, a. I (1892), vol. I, pp. 302–308. The editors of "Il foro penale" dedicated a wide commentary on the judgement, pointing out that the parliamentary debate (on the wording of article 248 p.c.) excluded any doubt about the possibility that this provision could be applied to political associations, as also made cleared in France after the promulgation of the Napoleonic penal code.

the one advocated by the appellants. To tell the truth, the Italian legislator had rejected the previous formulation of association crime and he had preferred to keep the peace regardless of the organizational rules existing inside a criminal organization formed by mutual consent to commit crimes. With regard to the other complaint, the Supreme Court considered to be proper the decision of the trial court which had recognized a program of "destruction by violence against people, property and the public power instituted to protect either thing" and not only the one proposing to set up the social order on new bases.[96] The appeal was turned down since it was considered to be proper the enforcement of art. 248 p.c. by the court of appeal.

The several references to the Italian codes pre-existing in the judgements of the Supreme Court highlight the necessity to offer as the grounds for a judgement some means to foster which might promote a renewed criminal awareness from the forensic people who were still clung, for training and experience, to the above codes, whose rules were often mentioned in the appeals to the Court of Cassation. That's why the judges of the Supreme Court were careful to explain the similarities and differences between the old and new law. So, in the judgement pronounced by the Supreme Court on 21 December 1892 concerning bodily harms, the grounds for the judgement proved to be exclusively founded on the comparison with the Sardinian code in order to state the principle that "the justification of the excess in the end, as in art. 374 of the current code, does not cease owing to the easy predictability of the event, unlike the abrogated criminal code".[97] In the specific instance, the Supreme Court, by a close explanation, believed to be wrong (and not in line with the current penal code) the grounds advanced by the lower Court to exclude the justification circumstance consisting having used the principle asserted in art. 569 p.c. of 1859,[98] denying any mitigation of a sentence to the one who had merely meant to hit or to injure, had committed a crime more serious than the one foreseen at the beginning.

On the contrary, art. 374 of the current penal code decreed that if the fact had gone beyond the offender's intent, the penalties should have been shortened from one third to the half. For a better interpretation of the rule, the latest one had to be read in conjunction with art. 45 of the same Code which provided the principle of the wilfulness of the conduct, according to which:

---

[96]*Ibid.*, c. 15.

[97]Corte di Cassazione di Roma, udienza 21 dicembre 1892. Pres. De Cesare, Est. Onnis, Ric. Masciari, *Il foro italiano*, a. XVIII (1893), vol. XVIII, c. 126. Art. 374 p.c. provided: "*Quando, nei casi preveduti negli articoli precedenti, il fatto ecceda nelle conseguenze il fine propostosi dal colpevole, le pene ivi stabilite sono diminuite da un terzo alla metà*".

[98]Art. 569 Sardinian penal code: "*Colui che nell'intenzione soltanto di percuotere o ferire commette un reato più grave, e che sorpassa nelle sue conseguenze l' avuto disegno, sarà punito colla pena stabilita pel reato più grave diminuita di uno o di due gradi. Questa diminuzione non avrà luogo quando il delinquente avesse potuto facilmente prevedere le conseguenze del proprio fatto*".

> Nessuno poteva essere punito per un delitto, se non avesse voluto il fatto che lo costituisce, tranne che la legge lo ponesse altrimenti a suo carico, come conseguenza della sua azione od omissione (Nobody could have been punished for a crime, in absence of the willfulness of the conduct, unless the Law charged him of the crime, as a consequence of his action or omission).[99]

By comparing these two articles it clearly emerged that the inquiries made by the lower Court, in similar cases, should have been addressed to ascertain the defendant's aim and the crime he wanted to commit rather than the possible predictability of the consequences deriving from the crime itself. Then, the mistake made by the Court was originated with the fact they had considered only "the fallacious criterion" of the predictability, the legislator had rejected in the new code, which did not agree to accept this element as the only one which might be considered sufficient to understand the willingness to commit the offence.[100]

5 The Consolidation of the New Penal System Between Doctrine and Case Law

The setting-in period of the new penal code may be said completed only after the initial years of its application, when the references to the previous codifications by the Court of Cassation started becoming less frequent. In fact, the judges started to concentrate their motivational efforts on the principles of law based on the new rules, many of which might be said already consolidated in the Supreme Court's case law. Except for the offences committed under the rule of the previous Sardinian code of 1859 (for which it would have been necessary an examination of the milder rule between the old and new law[101]) the judges of the Supreme Court in Rome believed to be unnecessary to go on making comparisons with obsolete provisions or references to preliminary works or parliamentary reports, however, continued to be present in the notes accompanying the most relevant and innovative pronunciations, in order to explain better the principle enunciated or disagree with it.

In this regard, it is appropriate to mention the judgement of 25 May 1894 concerning the matter of receiving of stolen goods, where the Supreme Court affirmed the principle of the individuality of this crime:

> È indubitato che la ricettazione assume una individualità sua propria, il cui elemento morale consiste unicamente nella scienza del colpevole che si tratti di ricettazione di cose provenienti da un delitto qualsiasi, senza che sia necessario che egli conosca altresì tutte quelle altre circostanze che possono avere la efficacia di aumentare la pena degli autori o correi del reato principale, dal quale esso si origina (It is out of doubt that the Receiving of Stolen

---

[99]Corte di Cassazione di Roma, udienza 21 dicembre 1892, c. 127.

[100]*Ibid.*

[101]Corte di Cassazione di Roma, udienza 12 ottobre 1893. Pres. De Cesare, Est. Onnis, Rc. PM e Forcellino, *Il foro italiano*, a. XIX (1894), vol. XIX, cc. 64–66; Corte di Cassazione di Roma, udienza 28 dicembre 1893. Pres. De Cesare, Est. Lucchini, Ric. Porzio, *ibid.*, cc. 99–100; Corte di Cassazione di Roma, udienza 21 gennaio 1895. Pres. Canonico, Est. Basile, Ric. Carnevali y Menghini, *Il foro italiano*, a. XX (1895), vol XX, cc. 75–82.

Goods acquires its own individuality, in which the moral element is given uniquely by the consciousness of the guilty that he is receiving stolen goods coming from a general crime, without the knowledge of all those circumstances which may increase the punishment of the authors or accomplices of the main crime, that originates the Receiving of Stolen Goods).[102]

This supposition, which was well-established on the strength of the previous legitimacy pronunciation, allowed the judges of the Supreme Court to believe wrong the appealed judgement passed by the Court of Assizes in Catania and to uphold the appeal by the Prosecutor's Office who had believed to be proper the application of art. 421 p.c.,[103] referred to the penalty to be applied to the specific case.[104]

The question resolved by the Supreme Court, although it was nothing new in the history of the criminal doctrine and case law, drew the editors' attention of *Rivista di giurisprudenza penale* who added a rich comment signed by lawyer Gennaro Escobedo to the publication of the judgement. Lawyer Gennaro Escobedo, by referring to the preparatory and doctrinal works of the new penal code, argued strongly against the principle passed by the Supreme Court who asserted the stolen goods' liability had to be regulated only by greater or lesser penalty threatened to the principal offense and, so, by its greater or lesser gravity. This thesis—which reminded, among the others, a previous study by the same author published in the journal *Cassazione unica*—was also argued on the basis of a comparison with the equivalent provisions of the Sardinian code and on the previous judgements of the same Roman Cassation, from which this latter appeared to diverge. On this basis, Escobedo came to the conclusion that the responsibility of the receiver of

[102]Corte di Cassazione di Roma, udienza 25 maggio 1894. Pres. Canonico, Est. Basile, Ric. PM c. D'Agata y Cristaldi, *Il foro italiano*, a. XIX (1894), vol. XIX, cc. 458–465.

[103]Art. 421 p.c.: "*Chiunque, fuori del caso preveduto nell'articolo 225, acquista, riceve o nasconde danato o cose provenienti da un delitto, o si intromette in qualsiasi modo nel farle acquistare, ricevere o nascondere, senza essere concorso nel delitto medesimo, è punito con la reclusione sino a due anni e con la multa sino a lire mille. Se il danaro o le cose provengano da un delitto che importi pena restrittiva della libertà personale per un tempo maggiore dei cinque anni, il colpevole è punito con la reclusione da uno a quattro anni e con la multa da lire cento a tremila. In ambedue i casi preveduti nelle precedenti disposizioni, la reclusione non può superare la metà della pena stabilita per il delitto da cui le cose provengano: ed ove si tratti di pena pecuniaria, per determinare tale misura si fa il ragguaglio secondo le norme stabilite nell'articolo 19. Se il colpevole sia ricettatore abituale, la reclusione è da tre a sette anni, nel caso preveduto nella prima parte del presente articolo, e da cinque a dieci anni, nel caso preveduto nel primo capoverso: e si aggiunge sempre la multa da lire trecento a tremila*".

[104]Corte di Cassazione di Roma, udienza 25 maggio 1894, c. 465: "*La Corte d'assise di Catania errò dunque quando dominata da un opposto concetto di diritto ed indusse ad accogliere l'istanza della difesa a proporre ai giurati la questione: se gli accusati conoscessero che le fedi di credito da essi ricettate provenivano da una rapina commessa da più persone con minacce nella vita: e, trascinata dalla risposta negativa da essi data a siffatta questione, applicò agli accusati la minor pena comminata dalla prima parte dell'art. 421 cod. pen., mentre avrebbe dovuto invece applicare quella stabilita dal primo capoverso dello stesso articolo; laonde, dovendo in questa parte accogliersi il ricorso del p.m., deve ritenersi come sovrabbondante ed improduttiva di effetti giuridici la risposta data dai giurati alla questione suddetta, e lasciata ferma la dichiarazione da essi già fatta, si annulla soltanto la sentenza impugnata, onde da altra Corte d'assise si proceda a nuova e più corretta applicazione di pena*".

stolen goods had to be considered as independent from the main offence's author and that the Supreme Court had refused such a principle.

The above mentioned example proves the fluidity of the relationship between the theory and the case law in the years when we were having the consolidation of the new penal system, in which the settlement of the court decisions encouraged the authoritative debate based on specific themes, to which the practice had just drawn its attention. The commentators' notes on the judgements set as a goal to highlight any diversity of course as to the following tradition or the legitimacy judgement or to fill any possible gap in the asserted principles, by following the goal—that some journals as "Il foropenale" had upheld in their programs—"to remind the judges their offices is not to crystallize the written law or to give it the brute force of a steel rolling-mill, but to soften the harshness and the dissonances of the law and to provoke the slow, but it still ever-growing evolution".[105] In this way, the old law went on being present in the debate started off the judgements themselves which referred to no longer.

For example, the judgement of the Supreme Court in Rome on 11 June 1895 offered points of reflection and analysis about the forgery of a judicial deed.[106] It had affirmed the principle according to which the defendant who commits perjury to identify himself under interrogation in the instructor's presence, has to be considered as responsible for the offence under art. 279 p.c.[107] and not for a mere contravention under art. 436 p.c.[108] The differences between the two criminal hypotheses were because it was necessary to have the perjury committed or in a public act, or in a register act or in an act of the judicial authority and that this false declaration had to result from a private or public harm.

On the contrary, as concerns the contravention under art. 436 p.c., it was sufficient for a citizen to provide the public official with a piece of false information

[105]*Programma*, *Il foro penale*, a. I (1892), vol. 1, p. III.

[106]Corte di Cassazione di Roma, udienza 11 giugno 1895. Pres. Risi, Est. Toraldo, Ric. PM e Filippini, *Il foro italiano*, a. XX (1895), vol. XX., cc. 313–325. The judgement annulled the decision of the Court of Appeal of Rome, which had held the applicability of article 279 p.c. and not of art. 436 p.c. to defendant Filippini, guilty of having declared false personal information to the law enforcement agents and in particular of having hired the identity of his maternal uncle Romeo Cardellini, "*non già con l'intendimento e coldisegno di recare a costuinocumento, ma unicamentealloscopo di render minore la propriaresponsabilità per furto, facendosicredere un individuoimpregiudicato quale era ilCardellini*".

[107]Art. 279 p.c.: "*Chiunque attesta falsamente al pubblico ufficiale, in un atto pubblico, l'identità o lo stato della propria o dell'altrui persona, o altri fatti dei quali l'atto sia destinato a provare la verità, ove ne possa derivare pubblico o privato nocumento è punito la reclusione da tre mesi ad un anno; e da nove a trenta mesi, se trattasi di un atto dello stato civile o dell'Autorità giudiziaria. È punito con la reclusione da tre mesi ad un anno chi in titoli o effetti di commercio attesta falsamente l'identità della propria o dell'altrui persona*".

[108]Art. 436 p.c.: "*Chiunque rifiuta d'indicare ad un pubblico ufficiale nell'esercizio delle sue funzioni il proprio nome, cognome, stato o professione, luogo di nascita o di domicilio, o altre qualità personali, è punito con l'ammenda sino a lire cinquanta; e, se dia indicazioni mendaci, con l'ammenda da lire cinquanta a trecento*".

about his personal qualities, without being in need of a public act in which to insert the false declaration, and any private or public harm.

In the present case, it might be considered as integrated the offence under art. 279 p.c. owing to the recurrence of the two above-mentioned qualifications concerning the forgery of a public deed and the prospective damage might be exposed the one whose personal data had been provided by the offender.[109] The solution offered by the Supreme Court was accompanied by a wide comment appeared in *Rivista di giurisprudenza penale*, in which the commentator rebuilt the ranks of the debate which presented doctrinal (which had already highlighted on the journals *Rivistapenale* and *Foro penale*)[110] and law case conflicts either about the merit and the legitimacy. It made use of extensive references to the previous rules of the Sardinian code and the legislative works of the new penal code to highlight the vagueness and the "serious doubts" arising from the above examined pronunciation.[111]

6 Conclusions

The Italian criminal codification process had passed through the inheritance of the several and different criminal laws which, aftermath the Napoleonic rule, had caught on the States preceding the unification of Italy the day after the Congress of Vienna.

The Italian preunitary governments had introduced different criminal laws mostly modelled after the 1810 Napoleonic Code. The coexistence of those different laws in the various Italian provinces represented, therefore, the basic question producing a sort of delay in the uniform codification process which met serious obstacles to contemplate the different legal traditions into a consolidation one.

In any case it became immediately apparent it would have been necessary to construct a code having Italian characteristics rather than the foreign ones imported and badly adjusted to our customs and tendencies. It started off, therefore, an intensive season of studies and propositions which absorbed legitimately the Italian academies and lawyers who in the parliamentary seats and through the pages of the

[109]Corte di Cassazione di Roma, udienza 11 giugno 1895, c. 325: "*se la menzogna di Filippini non fosse stata scoverta; se lo errore in cui egli trasse l'autorità giudiziaria non fosse stato provvidenzialmente messo in chiaro; se non si fosse venuto a conoscere che l'individuo condannato con la sentenza del 25 luglio 1894 chiamavasi Oreste Filippini, e non Cardellini Romeo, costui oltre l'onta di sapersi un giorno imputato di furto, avrebbe indubbiamente sofferto il danno di vedere macchiata la sua fedina penale, ed inserito il suo nome nel casellario giudiziario. Questi ed altri danni avrebbe egli potuto soffrire per* via *della falsa indicazione del Filippini, il cui fatto pertanto ricade sotto alla sanzione dell'art. 279 cod. pen.*"

[110]The reference is, particularly, to "Rivista penale", vol. XXXIII, III serie, 1891, p. 553 and to "Il foro penale", a. II (1893), parte II, p. 221.

[111]Corte di Cassazione di Roma, udienza 11 giugno 1895, c. 324.

most accredited journals and drafts printed freely, meant to contribute to draw up a penal code bearing consolidated and distinctive hallmarks.

The obtained code was the result of the Italian liberal criminal law tradition, the postulate of which allowed the passing of a modern and balanced text arising from the remains of the Sardinian penal code inspired by Napoleonic penal Code and the Tuscan one inspired by Code of Grand Duchy of Baden. The new text was, therefore, in search of a meticulous clarity and brevity of concepts and it also got important results as regards its definitions, meticulous and concise, on realizing a satisfactory proportion of parts and homogeneity of formulas, and avoiding any arid case records.

The new penal code was welcome by a great many of the Italian lawyers who had been waiting for the issuing of a new text for a long time. But, the new text didn't allow to really abandon the old one which had been welcome by the courtrooms up to then. In fact, failing a case law in the making and works commenting on the Zanardelli code, legal practitioners happened to enforce the new penal laws in compliance with the Italian and French old case law and doctrinal apparatus.

These difficulties perceived by the Italian lawyers in the employment of the new Code, needed an important intervention of the Italian judiciary to give a diligent definition and interpretation of the new case law courses. The earlier case law interventions by the Court of Cassation were basic to steer the lawyers and the lower courts towards the application of the new Code which was soon followed by commentary works which sorted out the most relevant legitimacy rulings, many of which were summarized and noted in the main sector journals which were increasing just in those years. They, primarily in the first years, never lacked in referring to the pre-existing codes the comparison proving to be necessary to remove any doubt and uncertainty resulting from the several pre-exiting Codes which often led the lower courts into error.

The setting-in period of the new penal code may be said completed only after the initial years of its application, when the references to the previous codifications by the Court of Cassation started becoming less frequent. In fact, the judges started to concentrate their motivational efforts on the principles of law based on the new rules, many of which might be said already consolidated in the Supreme Court's case law.

Except for the offences committed under the rule of the previous Sardinian code of 1859 (for which it would have been necessary an examination of the milder rule between the old and new law[112]) the judges of the Supreme Court in Rome believed to be unnecessary to go on making comparisons with obsolete provisions or references to preliminary works or parliamentary reports, however, continued to be

[112]Corte di Cassazione di Roma, udienza 12 ottobre 1893. *Pres. De Cesare, Est. Onnis, Rc. PM e Forcellino*, "Il foro italiano", a. XIX (1894), vol. XIX, cc. 64–66; Corte di Cassazione di Roma, udienza 28 dicembre 1893. *Pres. De Cesare, Est. Lucchini, Ric. Porzio*, ivi, cc. 99–100; Corte di Cassazione di Roma, udienza 21 gennaio 1895. *Pres. Canonico, Est. Basile, Ric. Carnevali e Menghini*, "Il foro italiano", a. XX (1895), vol XX, cc. 75–82.

present in the notes accompanying the most relevant and innovative pronunciations, in order to explain better the principle enunciated or disagree with it.

On this way, the new penal code went to his consolidation, though, soon, it would have started a new debate that would lead to the adoption of a new penal code under the fascist regime.

References

Alemagna, Francesco, "L'Italia e i suoi codici", *Monitore dei Tribunali. Giornale di legislazione e giurisprudenza civile e penale e del contenzioso amministrativo*, anno IV, n. 3 (20 gennaio 1863).

Aquarone, Alberto, *L'unificazione legislativa e i codici del 1865* (Milano, 1960).

Auriti, Francesco "Sunto di requisitoria sull'interpretazione dell'art. 39 delle disposizioni per l'attuazione del nuovo Codice penale e sentenza della Corte di Cassazione", *La legge*, n. 2 (1890).

Auriti, Francesco *Discorso pronunziato dal Senatore Francesco Auriti Procuratore Generale del Re presso la Corte di Cassazione di Roma nella assemblea generale del 4 gennaio 1890* (Roma, 1890).

Auriti, Francesco *Discorso pronunziato dal Senatore Francesco Auriti Procuratore Generale del Re presso la Corte di Cassazione di Roma nella assemblea generale del 3 gennaio 1891* (Roma, 1891).

Bozzo, Luigi, *Codice penale italiano e la sua genesi: con note di giurisprudenza ed altre utili per la pratica* (Roma, 1890).

Broggi, Isidoro, "Discorso pronunciato dal sostituto proc. generale commendatore Isidoro Broggi presso la Corte di Cassazione di Roma", *Inaugurazione dell'anno giudiziario 1892 alla Corte di Cassazione di Roma il dì 4 gennaio* (Roma, 1892).

Cadoppi, Alberto, *Introduzione allo studio del diritto penale comparato* (Padova, 2004).

Capone, Gaspare, *Discorso sopra la storia delle leggi patrie*, t. 2 (Napoli, 1844).

Cappellini, Paolo, "Francesco Carrara e il problema della codificazione del diritto", *Criminalia. Annuario di scienze penalistiche* (2007).

Carbasse, Jean-Marie, *Histoire du droit pénale et de la justice criminelle* (Paris, 2000).

Carnot, Joseph François Claude, *Commentaire sur le Code pénal contenant: la manière d'en faire une juste application, l'indicazion des améliorations dont il est susceptible, et des dissertations sur les questions les plus importantes qui peuvent s'y rattacher*, 2 voll. (Bruxelles, 1823–4).

Carrara, Francesco "Codicizzazione (Studi legislativi)" (1869), *Opuscoli di diritto criminale*, Lucca 1870, vol. II, p. 227.

Carrara, Francesco *Pensieri sul progetto di codice penale italiano del 1874* (Firenze, 1974).

Carrara, Francesco *Programma del corso di diritto criminale dettato nella Regia Università di Pisa dal professore Francesco Carrara. Parte generale* (Lucca, 1860).

Cavanna, Adriano *La codificazione penale in Italia. Le origini lombarde* (Milano, 1975).

Cavanna, Adriano *Storia del diritto moderno in Europa. 2. Le fonti e il pensiero giuridico*, (Milano, 2005).

Coen, Angiolo, *Manuale di giurisprudenza sul Codice penale italiano e sulle disposizioni per l'attuazione del codice penale* (Livorno, 1891).

Colao, Floriana "Profili di federalismo penale in Italia dall'Unità al codice Zanardelli", *Questione criminale e identità nazionale in Italia tra Otto e Novecento*, (Lacchè, L., Stronati, M., eds), Macerata, 2014.

Colao, Floriana "«Consorelle» tra «vincoli indissolubili», «scuole», «indirizzi» del penale", *Una tribuna per le scienza criminali. La 'cultura' delle Riviste nel dibattito penalistico tra Otto e Novecento* (Lacchè, L., Stronati, M., eds.), Macerata 2012.

Colao, Floriana *Il delitto politico tra Ottocento e Novecento. Da «delitto fittizio» a «nemico dello Stato»* (Milano, 1986).

Colao, Floriana *Collezione celerifera delle leggi, decreti, istruzioni e circolari* (Torino, 1862).

Colao, Floriana Corte di Cassazione di Roma, udeinza 28 dicembre 1893. Pres. De Cesare, Est. Lucchini, Ric. Porzio, *Il foro italiano*, a. XIX (1894), vol. XIX.

Corte di Cassazione di Roma, udienza 11 giugno 1895. Pres. Risi, Est. Toraldo, Ric. PM e Filippini, *Il foro italiano*, a. XX (1895), vol. XX.

Corte di Cassazione di Roma, udienza 12 ottobre 1893. Pres. De Cesare, Est. Onnis, Rc. PM e Forcellino, *Il foro italiano*, a. XIX (1894), vol. XIX.

Corte di Cassazione di Roma, udienza 21 dicembre 1892. Pres. De Cesare, Est. Onnis, Ric. Masciari, *Il foro italiano*, anno XVIII (1893), vol. XVIII.

Corte di Cassazione di Roma, udienza 21 gennaio 1895. Pres. Canonico, Est. Basile, Ric. Carnevali e Menghini, *Il foro italiano*, a. XX (1895), vol XX.

Corte di Cassazione di Roma, udienza 24 novembre 1892. Pres. Canonico, Est. Ferro-Luzzi, Ric. Bardi ed altri, *Il foro italiano*, anno XVIII (1893), vol. XVIII.

Corte di Cassazione di Roma, udienza 25 maggio 1894. Pres. Canonico, Est. Basile, Ric. PM c. D'Agata e Cristaldi, *Il foro italiano*, a. XIX (1894), vol. XIX.

Corte di Cassazione, Sezione I, udienza 25 maggio 1891, Pres. Ghiglieri, Rel. Miraglia, PM. Broggi, Ric. Viggiano Agostino ed altri, *Il foro penale. Rivista critica di diritto e giurisprudenza penale e di discipline carcerarie*, anno I, vol. I, parte seconda.

Corte di Cassazione, sezione I, udienza 7 dicembre 1891. Pres. Ghiglieri, Est. Spera, PM Broggi. "Risoluzione di conflitto in causa Lenzotti Luigi", *Il foro penale*, a. I (1892), vol. I.

Criscuolo, Alessandro, *Per G. Palma notaio. Falso per supposizione di qualità personale* (Taranto, 1894).

Crivellari, Giulio, *Il codice penale per il Regno d'Italia interpretato sulla scorta della dottrina, delle fonti, della legislazione comparata e della giurisprudenza* (Torino, 1890–1898).

Da Passano, Mario "Le definizioni nella storia del diritto penale italiano contemporaneo", *Omnis definitio in iure periculosa? Il problema delle definizioni legali nel diritto penale* (Cadoppi, A. ed.) (Padova, 1966).

Da Passano, Mario "Il primo progetto di codice penale toscano (1824)", *Materiali per una storia della cultura giuridica*, 1 (1992), pp. 41–64.

Da Passano, Mario *Emendare o intimidire. La codificazione del diritto penale in Francia e in Italia durante la Rivoluzione e l'Impero* (Torino, 2000), pp. 87–157.

Da Passano, Mario *Il diritto penale toscano dai Lorena ai Borboni (1786–1807)* (Milano, 1988).

Da Passano, Mario "La storia esterna del codice penale toscano (1814–1859)", *Istituzioni e società in Toscana nell'età moderna. Atti delle giornate di studio dedicate a Giuseppe Pansini* (Roma, 1994), pp. 564–589.

Dalloz, Victor Alexis Désiré, *Jurisprudence générale, repertoiremetodique et alphabetique de législation et de doctrine et de jurisprudence en matière de droit civil, commercial, criminel et administratif, de droit des gens et de droit public, nouvelle editionconsidrablement augmentée et précédé d'une essai sur l'histoire générale du droit françois*, 44 voll (Paris, 1844–74).

Del Corso, Stefano, "Il tentativo nel codice Zanardelli", *Diritto penale dell'Ottocento. I codici preunitari e il codice Zanardelli*, Vinciguerra, S. (ed.) (Padova, 1999).

Dezza, Ettore "Appunti sulla codificazione penale nel primo Regno d'Italia: il progetto del 1809", *Diritto penale dell'Ottocento. I codici preunitari e il codice Zanardelli* (Padova, 1999).

Dezza, Ettore "Imputabilità e infermità mentale: la genesi dell'art. 46 del Codice Zanardelli", *Saggi di storia del diritto penale moderno* (Milano, 1992).

Ferrante, Riccardo, "Il problema della codificazione", *Enciclopedia italiana. Il Contributo italiano alla storia del pensiero – Diritto* (Roma, 2012).

Ferri, Enrico "Le ragioni storiche della Scuola positiva di diritto criminale", *Rivista di filosofia scientifica* II (1882–83).

Ferri, Enrico *I nuovi orizzonti del diritto e della procedura penale* (Bologna, 1881).

Ferri, Enrico *La scuola positiva di diritto criminale* (Siena, 1883).

Geri, Marco Paolo, *La metamorfosi che la politica voleva fare a danno della giustizia: Francesco Carrara e l'unità del "giure penale"* (Bologna, 2005).

Ghisalberti, Carlo "Legislazione e codificazione", *Enciclopedia italiana. L'unificazione* (Roma, 2011).

Ghisalberti, Carlo *La codificazione del diritto in Italia 1865–1942* (Roma, 1994).

Grossi, Paolo, *Scienza giuridica italiana. Un profilo storico (1860–1950)* (Milano, 2000).

Grosso, Carlo Federico, "Le grandi correnti del pensiero penalistico italiano tra Ottocento e Novecento", *Storia d'Italia, Annali 12* (Torino, 1997), pp. 7–34.

Intorno al progetto Vigliani 24 febbraio 1874 di un nuovo codice penale per l'Italia riveduto dalla commissione senatoria. Rassegna critica di Luigi Lucchini (Padova, 1875).

Intorno lo schema di Codice penale italiano presentato dal Ministro Guardasigilli al Senato del Regno nella tornata del 24 febbraio 1874: osservazioni e proposte del prof. Enrico Pessina accolte dalla Facoltà giuridica della R. Università di Napoli (Napoli, 1875).

Lacchè, Luigi "La penalistica costituzionale e il 'liberalismo giuridico'. Problemi e immagini della legalità nella riflessione di Francesco Carrara", *Quaderni fiorentini per la storia del pensiero giuridico moderno*, 36 (2007), t. I, pp. 663–695.

Lacchè, Luigi *La giustizia per i galantuomini. Ordine e libertà nell'Italia liberale. Il dibattito sul carcere preventivo (1865–1913)* (Milano, 1990).

Lacchè, Luigi Un code penal pour l'Unite italienne, le code Zanardelli (1889) la genese, le debat, le project juridique, "Le pénal dans tous ses Etats. Justice, Etats et sociétés en Europe (XII–XX siécles)" (Rousseaux, X., Lévy R., eds) (Bruxelles, 1997), pp. 303–319.

Laingui, André, "Il diritto penale della Rivoluzione francese e dell'Impero", *Diritto penale dell'Ottocento. I codici preunitari e il codice Zanardelli*, Vinciguerra, S. (ed.) (Padova, 1999).

Moccia, Sergio, "Ideologie e diritto nel sistema sanzionatorio del codice Zanardelli", *Diritto penale dell'Ottocento. I codici preunitari e il codice Zanardelli*, Vinciguerra, S. (ed.) (Padova, 1999).

Le fonti del Codice penale italiano. 1. Relazioni, progetti, emendamenti, discussioni avanti il Senato del Regno (Roma, 1875).

Le Sellyer, Achille-François, *Traité du droit criminel appliqué aux actions publique et privée qui naissent des contraventions, des délits et des crimes: ouvrage contenant l'explication de la plus partie des matières les plus importantes du droit criminel*, 6 voll. (Paris 1844).

Lombroso, Cesare, *Troppo presto. Appunti al nuovo Progetto di Codice penale* (Torino, 1888).

Lucchini, Luigi, "Ai Lettori", *Rivista penale di dottrina legislazione e giurisprudenza*, XXI (1885).

Majno, Luigi, *Commento al codice penale italiano* (Verona, 1890–1894).

Mangoni, Luisa, "Introduzione alla sezione: Eziologia di una nazione", "Delitto, genio, follia. Scritti scelti di C. Lombroso" (Frigessi, D., Giacanelli, F., Mangoni, L. eds.) (Torino, 1995), pp. 685–709.

Manzitti, Luigi, *Giurisprudenza sul codice penale del regno d'Italia: anni 1890, 1891, 1892. Prima appendice al codice penale annotato per Giambattista conte Milano* (Napoli, 1893).

Mastroberti, Francesco, *Codificazione e giustizia penale nelle Sicilie dal 1808 al 1820* (Napoli, 2001).

Mayali Laurent, PadoaSchioppa, Antonio, Simon Dieter, *Officiumadvocati* (Frankfurt am Main, 2000).

Merlin, Philippe-Antoine, *Recueil alphabetique des questions de droit qui se presentent le plus frequemment dans les tribunaux; ouvrage dans lequel sont fondus et classes la plupart des plaidoyers et requisitoires de l'Auteur, avec le texte de jugemens du tribunal de Cassation, qui s'en sont ensuivis* (Porthmann, 1802–1805).

Miletti, Marco Nicola, "Piemontizzare le contrade italiane. L'adeguamento del codice penale sardo alle province meridionali", *Il codice penale per gli stati del Re di Sardegna e per l'Italia Unita (1859)*, Vinciguerra, S. (ed.) (Padova, 2008).

Mittermaier, Karl Joseph Anton, "Il progetto di revisione del Codice 1859 pel regno d'Italia, presentato al Senato in Torino nel 9 gennaio 1862", *Monitore dei Tribunali. Giornale di legislazione e giurisprudenza civile e penale e del contenzioso amministrativo*, anno IV, n. 3 (20 gennaio 1863).

Morin, Achille, *Répertoire général et raisonné du droit criminel ou sont méthodiquement exposées la législation, la docrtine et la jurisprudence sur tout ce qui constitue le grand et le petit criminel en toutes matières et dans toutes les jurisdictions*, 2 voll. (Paris, 1850–1).

Neppi Modona, Guido, "Una 'scuola' dimenticata: il socialismo giuridico nel diritto penale", *Giustizia e Costituzione* II (1971), n. 4.

Neppi Modona, Guido, Violante, Luciano, *Poteri dello Stato e sistema penale. Corso di lezioni universitarie* (Torino, 1978).

Osservazioni e proposte della Facoltà di giurisprudenza nella R. Università di Torino intorno al nuovo progetto di Codice penale pel Regno d'Italia (Torino, 1874).

Osservazioni sul progetto del Codice penale presentato dal Ministro Vigliani al Senato nella tornata del 24 febbraio 1874: lette al Circolo giuridico da Giovanni Gorritte (Palermo, 1875).

Padovani, Tullio "Il binomio irriducibile. La distinzione dei reati in delitti e contravvenzioni fra storia e politica criminale", *Diritto penale in trasformazione* (Marinucci, G., Dolcini, E. eds.) (Milano, 1985).

Padovani, Tullio "La tradizione toscana nel codice Zanardelli", *Diritto penale dell'Ottocento.I codici preunitari e il codice Zanardelli* (Vinciguerra, S., ed.) (Padova, 1999).

Pessina, Enrico, *Il diritto penale in Italia da Cesare Beccaria sino alla promulgazione del codice penale vigente (1764–1890)* (Milano, 1906).

Pifferi, Michele "Alla ricerca del «genio italico». Tradizione e progetti nella penalistica postunitaria", *Retoriche dei giuristi e costruzione dell'identità nazionale*, (Cazzetta, G., ed.) (Bologna, 2013).

Pifferi, Michele "Difendere i confini, superare le frontiere. Le 'zone grigie' della legalità penale tra Otto e Novecento", *Quaderni fiorentini*, 36 (2007), *Principio di legalità e diritto penale (per Mario Sbriccoli)*, I, pp. 743–799.

Progetto del codice penale del regno d'Italia preceduto dalla relazione ministeriale presentata al Senato del Regno nella tornata del 24 febbraio 1874 dal ministro di Grazia e Giustizia (Vigliani) (Roma, 1874).

"Programma", *Il foro penale*, anno I (1892), vol. 1, p. III.

Rambaud, Jacques, *Naples sous Joseph Bonaparte* (Paris, 1911).

Relazione a S.M. IL Re del Ministro Guardasigilli (Zanardelli) nell'udienza del 30 giugno 1889 per l'approvazione del testo definitivo del codice penale, (Roma, 1889).

Saggio d'uno progetto del Codice penale italiano corredato d'osservazioni dell'avvocato Emanuele Rapisardi (Catania, 1862).

Santangelo Cordani, Angela, *Alla vigilia del Codice Zanardelli: Antonio Buccellati e la riforma penale nell'Italia postunitaria* (Milano, 2008).

Sbriccoli, Mario "Caratteri originari e tratti permanenti del sistema penale italiano", *Legge, diritto, giustizia* (Violante, L., ed.) (Torino, 1998).

Sbriccoli, Mario "Il diritto penale liberale. La Rivista penale di Luigi Lucchini (1874–1900)", *Quaderni fiorentini per la storia del pensiero giuridico*, 16 (1987).

Sbriccoli, Mario "La penalistica civile. Teorie e ideologie del diritto penale nell'Italia Unita", *Storia del diritto penale e della giustizia: scritti editi e inediti (1972–2007)*, (Sbriccoli, M., ed.) (Milano, 2009).

Schnapper, Bernard, "Compression et répression sous le Consulat et l'Empire", *Revue historique de sdroit françaisetétranger* 69 (1991), pp. 17–40.

Senato del Regno, *Atti parlamentari. Discussioni,* 4 maggio 1896.

Suman, Giovanni, *Manuale pei giudici ed avvocati penali, ufficiali ed agenti di polizia giudiziaria: contenente esposte in ordine alfabetico le disposizioni dei Codici penale e di procedura penale, legge e regolamento di pubblica sicurezza: con illustrazioni, casi pratici e giurisprudenza* (Torino, 1891).

Tribunale penale di Roma, sezione VIII, udienza del 24 marzo 1892. Pres. Ed Est. Osterman; P.M. Vico. Causa Cipriani Amilcareedaltri, *Il foropenale*, anno I, vol. I (1892).

Vinciguerra, Sergio (ed.), *Codice penale per il Granducato di Toscana (1853)* (Padova, 1995).

Vinciguerra, Sergio (ed.), *Diritto penale dell'Ottocento. I codici preunitari e il codice Zanardelli* (Padova, 1999).
Von Listz, Franz, *La législation pénale comparée, Ier volume, Le droit criminel des États européens* (Berlin, 1894).
Zanardelli, Giuseppe, *Pel collocamento della prima pietra del Palazzo di Giustizia in Roma. Discorso pronunziato dal ministro guardasigilli G. Zanardelli il XIV marzo MDCCCLXXXIX* (Roma, 1889).

Stefano Vinci is assistant professor in History of Medieval and Modern Law at the University of Bari Aldo Moro, where he teaches History of Italian law. Graduated magna cum laude in Jurisprudence, M.A.A. at the Faculty of Law of the University of Bari in 1999, he achieved the Ph.D. in "History of Law" at the University of Macerata (Italy) in 2007. He had fellowships in Max-Planck-Institut-für-europäische-Rechtsgeschichte of Frankfurt am Main and he was visiting professor in several universities as Madrid, Freiburg and Bonn. He is a member of the European society for comparative legal history (ESCLH), Italian Society of History of Law (SISD) and Società di Storia Patria per la Puglia (SSPP). He has been part in national and international research projects funded by University of Bari Aldo Moro and by Italian and Spanish Government. Rapporteur in national and international conferences and author of many publications, his fields of legal history research regards reforms in the Kingdom of Naples between XVIII and XIX centuries, history of advocacy during Italian fascism, history of justice between medieval, modern and contemporary law. In particular, he has published more than 50 publications. His monograph researches are: Genuzio Bentini. La deontologia dell'avvocato penalista, Taranto 2007; Regimento et guberno. Amministrazione e finanza nei comuni del Mezzogiorno tra antico e nuovo regime, Bari, Cacucci 2013; Il dibattito sul giudice unico in Italia tra Ottocento e Novecento, Napoli 2016. He published books with co-autors: Tribunali e giurisprudenza nel Mezzogiorno. I. Le Gran Corti di Napoli e Trani, Napoli 2010; Il Liber Belial e il processo romano-canonico in Europa tra XV e XVI secolo, Bari 2014. He edited also the following books: Alessandro Criscuolo. Un avvocato tra età liberale e fascism, Napoli 2013; Il Mediterraneo e la Grande Guerra: diritto, politica e istituzioni, Taranto 2016; Le Supreme Corti di Giustizia nella storia giuridica del Mezzogiorno, Napoli 2016.

The Roots of Italian Penal Codification: Nation Building and the Claim for a Peculiar Identity in Criminal Law

Michele Pifferi

Abstract The chapter analyses the discourses used by Italian pre- and post-unitarian jurisprudence to corroborate the existence of a national genius of criminal law. After the political unity jurists were committed to penal codification, which, however, should not be based on foreign models and in particular on the Napoleonic Code (imposed to the Kingdom of Italy from 1811 to 1814), but had to correspond to the Italian most sophisticated and most shining ancient tradition of criminal law. In order to create rather than simply recognize such unitarian and independent tradition, some scholars emphasised the pivotal role of a national legal history as a cultural means to pave the way to a prompt codification. Other scholars, yet, more realistically recognized the considerable differences between criminal law approaches as well as the lack of a theoretical identity. Following the Savignyan method, they suggested to postpone the national codification until the gradual formation of a truly national criminal law doctrine, influenced neither by the French jurisprudence nor by the German doctrine. The Zanardelli code of 1889 was the final outcome of this hybrid past- and future-oriented attitude.

M. Pifferi (✉)
University of Ferrara, Via Ercole I D'Este, 37, 44121 Ferrara, Italy
e-mail: m.pifferi@unife.it

A. Masferrer (ed.), *The Western Codification of Criminal Law*, Studies in the History of Law and Justice 11, https://doi.org/10.1007/978-3-319-71912-2_7

1 Introduction

The French Penal Code of 1810 was imposed by Napoleon on the Kingdom of Italy in 1811 and extended with a few amendments to the Kingdom of Naples in 1812, despite efforts made by Italian jurists to enact different, autonomous penal codes.[1] Following the Congress of Vienna and the restoration of previous sovereigns in 1814, the Italian pre-Unitarian states abolished the French code and enacted their own penal codes, some of which were primarily based on or somehow inspired by the French model (e.g., the Penal Codes of the Kingdom of the Two Sicilies in 1919, of the Dukedom of Parma in 1820,[2] of the Papal State in 1832, and of the Kingdom of Sardinia in 1839 and 1859[3]), while others were influenced by the Austrian Penal Code of 1803, the Bavarian Penal Code of 1813 or the Baden Penal Code of 1845[4] (the Penal Code of the Grand Duchy of Tuscany of 1853).[5] In past decades, legal historians and criminal law scholars have analytically scrutinized these pieces of legislation, their drafts, and the vicissitudes of their enactment, and they have stressed the French imprint,[6] the peculiarities and the Austro-German inspiration.[7]

---

[1]For extended details see Mario Da Passano, *Emendare o intimidire? La codificazione del diritto penale in Francia e in Italia durante la Rivoluzione e l'Impero* (Torino: Giappichelli, 2000), pp. 170–189; Mario Da Passano, "La codification du droit pénal dans l'Italie "jacobine" et napoléonienne", *Révolution et justice pénale en Europe. Modèles français et traditions nationales (1780-1830)* (Xavier Rousseaux, Marie-Sylvie Dupont-Bouchat, Claude Vael, eds.) (Paris: L'Harmattan, 1999), pp. 85–99; see also the contributions in *Le leggi penali di Giuseppe Bonaparte per il Regno di Napoli (1808)* (Padova: Cedam, 1998), and, with specific reference to Giuseppe Bonaparte's penal laws for the Kingdom of Naples, see Francesco Mastroberti, *Codificazione e giustizia penale nelle Sicilie dal 1808 al 1820* (Napoli: Jovene, 2001), especially pp. 133–146.

[2]Alberto Cadoppi, "Il codice penale parmense del 1820", *I Codici preunitari e il Codice Zanardelli. Diritto penale dell'Ottocento* (Sergio Vinciguerra, ed.) (Padova: Cedam, 1999), pp. 196–272, in particular pp. 222–233.

[3]See Sergio Vinciguerra, "I codici penali sardo-piemontesi del 1839 e del 1859", *I Codici pre-unitari e il Codice Zanardelli. Diritto penale dell'Ottocento* (Sergio Vinciguerra, ed.) (Padova: Cedam, 1999), pp. 350–393.

[4]Regarding the characteristics of these criminal codes, see H.S. Sanford, *The Different Systems of Penal Codes in Europe* (Washington: Beverley Tucker Senate Printer, 1854), pp. 83–87 and 90–92; Geoffrey Drage, *The Criminal Code of the German Empire* (London: Chapman and Hall, 1885), pp. 14 ff.; Giuseppe Panattoni, "Opinioni del Prof. Mittermaier sullo stato della scienza, e della legislazione penale in Germania, e in Italia", *La Temi. Giornale di legislazione e giurisprudenza*, 4/37 (1853) 47–53, 111–119; Thomas Vormbaum, Michael Bohlander (eds.), *A Modern History of German Criminal Law* (Berlin – Heidelberg: Springer, 2014), pp. 65 ff.

[5]See Alberto Cadoppi, "Il 'modello italiano' di codice penale. Dalle 'origini lombarde' ai progetti di un nuovo codice penale", *L'Indice Penale*, 1(2003a), 19–74.

[6]See, e.g., Sergio Vinciguerra, "L'influence du Code de 1810 en Italie", *Les colloques du Sénat. Les actes. Bicentenaire du code pénal (1810-2010)*, (Paris: Sénat de France, 2010), pp. 110–121.

[7]See *I Codici preunitari e il Codice Zanardelli. Diritto penale dell'Ottocento* (Sergio Vinciguerra, ed.), (Padova: Cedam, 1999).

The Zanardelli Code of 1889, which was the first penal code of the unified nation, was the outcome of a thirty-year theoretical discussion dominated primarily by liberal scholars, adherents to what would be later labelled the classical school.[8] The delay of this piece of legislation in relation to the prompt enactment in 1865 of the civil code, soon after the political unification, can be explained by radical differences on crucial issues of criminal law, such as support for or opposition to the death penalty, by the breaking out of brigandage in southern regions and by the choice to fight such crime by means of exceptional and illiberal laws, and by the conflicting views on how to address political crimes.[9] However, there is another reason for this long delay that can be interpreted in terms of the gradual formation of a cohesive, unitary criminal-law doctrine upon which a national code, consistent with the ancient and sophisticated Italian cultural tradition of criminal law, could be built. This contribution addresses specifically the relationship between nation building and the codification of penal law in Italy during the pre- and post-unification era and focuses on how Italian jurists and politicians emphasized, discovered, or invented an Italian genius of criminal law on which the new penal code should be based as a peculiar creation influenced by neither the Napoleonic code nor the German model.

2 The Janus-Faced Genius of Italian Criminal Law

In the decades before and after Italian unification, legal projects and policy plans were strictly and necessarily intertwined and mutually upheld. Moreover, the nation-building process rested on the exaltation of rediscovered common cultural roots, among which the fictitious national characterization of legal tradition also played a key role in contraposition to the passing laws imposed by foreign sovereigns. This type of 'Italianness' of law and legal culture was part of a twofold approach. Although there was a focus on the future to plan the legal order of the new state, there was also an examination of the past to find in long-established practices and principles those signs of continuity in which the Italian character could be identified, despite the transitory political fragmentations and regional difference.[10] Jurists drew on multiple discourses, not without apparent

[8]Marco Nicola Miletti, "L'ultima pietra. Il contributo di Enrico Pessina alla formazione del codice Zanardelli", *Diritto penale XXI secolo*, IX/2 (2010) 393–411; L. Lacchè, "Un code pénal pour l'Unité italienne: le code Zanardelli (1889). La genèse, le débat, le projet juridique", *Le pénal dans tous ses états. Justice, Etats et Sociétés en Europe (XIIe–XXe siècles)* (R. Levy and X. Rousseaux, eds.) (Bruxelles: Publications de l'Université Saint-Louis), pp. 303–319.

[9]See M. Sbriccoli, *La penalistica civile: teorie e ideologie del diritto penale nell'Italia unita* (1990), now in Id., *Storia del diritto penale e della giustizia. Scritti editi e inediti (1972–2007)*, (Milano, Giuffrè, 2009) pp. 493–590.

[10]See Pietro Costa, "Un diritto italiano? Il discorso giuridico nella formazione dello Stato italiano", *Retoriche dei giuristi e costruzione dell'identità nazionale* (Giovanni Cazzetta, ed.) (Bologna: Il

contradictions, to support political unification by having recourse to legislative means of unification as well as doctrinal standardization. The *invention* or creation of an *Italian* legal identity was bolstered, at the same time, by a historical appeal to the national tradition and by an emphasis on the novelty of the Risorgimento.[11] In private law, post-Unitarian jurists were forced to rhetorical efforts to differentiate the Civil Code of 1865 from both the Napoleonic Code of 1804 and the pre-Unitarian codifications, relying on the rich legacy of common Roman law.

In criminal law, on the contrary, they had a claim to a cultural primacy, referring to their own "stars" whose brightness was original and not reflected by others.[12] It could be legitimately considered as typically Italian not only the creative time of medieval criminal law doctrine, but also the imprint on European penal enlightenment symbolized by Beccaria's book, the reform of Leopold II in Tuscany in 1786 (the so called "Leopoldina"), the draft of an autonomous penal code for the Lombardy in 1791–92,[13] the philosophical reflection on the fundamentals of the right to punish by Carmignani and Romagnosi, the Luosi's project of 1801-02 for the Lombardy,[14] the project of a penal code for the Kingdom of Italy in 1809[15] that was later defined as «a legislative monument entirely indigenous»,[16] and the Romagnosi's code of criminal procedure of 1807.[17] However, such a richness of available scientific and normative heritage did not correspond after the Unification to a faster process of penal codification; to the contrary, rooted regional cultural

Mulino, 2013) pp. 163–200; Adriano Cavanna, "Mito e destini del Code Napoléon in Italia", *Europa e diritto privato* (2001) 85–129.

[11]See Giovanni Cazzetta, *Codice civile e identità giuridica nazionale. Percorsi e appunti per una storia delle codificazioni moderne* (Torino: Giappichelli, 2011), especially chs. I–IV, pp. 1–161; see also Riccardo Ferrante, *Un secolo sì legislativo. La genesi del modello otto-novecentesco di codificazione e la cultura giuridica* (Torino, Giappichelli, 2015), chs. III–IV, pp. 117 ss.

[12]See Adriano Cavanna, *Storia del diritto moderno in Europa. Le fonti e il pensiero giuridico*, II (Milano: Giuffrè, 2005) pp. 190 ss., with specific reference to Beccaria.

[13]Regarding this project, drafted by a criminal committee whose members included Beccaria, see Adriano Cavanna, *La codificazione penale in Italia. Le origini lombarde* (Milano: Giuffrè, 975).

[14]See Adriano Cavanna, "Codificazione del diritto italiano e imperialismo giuridico francese nella Milano napoleonica. Giuseppe Luosi e il diritto penale", *Ius Mediolani. Studi di storia del diritto milanese offerti dagli allievi a Giulio Vismara* (Milano: Giuffrè, 1996), pp. 659–760, and Adriano Cavanna, Gianfrancesco Vanzelli, *Il primo progetto di codice penale per la Lombardia napoleonica (1801-1802)* (Padova: Cedam, 2000).

[15]Regarding this draft bill, elaborated by a committee formed by, among others, distinguished scholars such as Giandomenico Romagnosi, Tommaso Nani, Giacomo Giuliani and Giuseppe Compagnoni, and which somehow became a issue of national interest, see Ettore Dezza, "Appunti sulla codificazione penale nel primo Regno d'Italia: il progetto del 1809", *Saggi di storia del diritto penale moderno* (Ettore Dezza) (Milano: LED, 1992), pp. 199–280.

[16]Angelo Recchia, *Discorso per la inaugurazione della cattedra universitaria di Diritto penale accresciuta al Real Liceo delle Puglie* (Bari: Tip. Gissi, 1865) p. 23.

[17]Being the only code of the Napoleonic era not to be imposed by French government and with significant traits of originality, it deeply marked the character of following criminal procedure laws, both pre- and post-Unitarian; see Ettore Dezza, *Il Codice di procedura penale del Regno Italico (1807). Storia di un decennio di elaborazione legislativa* (Padova: Cedam, 1983).

differences and varied doctrinal and judicial attitudes led to a version of «penal federalism» that lasted until 1889.[18]

Therefore, the undisputed value of the Italian tradition of criminal law during the unifying process played a double role. On the one hand, its proud evocation was a key argument used by legal culture to avoid the fast imposition of the Sardinian penal code of 1859 on the entire country, as that code was considered too heavily influenced by the French model and to not correspond to the most progressive national penal thought. On the other hand, the reference to the founding fathers of Italian criminalistics was exploited as a political strategy to make the differences uniform. Thus, the reference implied that a long commitment was necessary to form a criminal law scholar community that was truly consistent with and driven by shared values within a highly diversified country and to draft a feasible penal code that embodied the *new* national legal tendency.

Mario Sbriccoli defined "penalistica civile"[19] as a culture of criminal law committed to civilize the entire society by means of a more civilized criminal law system, characterised by this Janus-faced approach. Jurists undertook the task of encouraging the legal and social progress of the country by planning a new order that, however, was based on an understanding of the past forced into a unitary tradition. By so doing, the history of Italian criminal law was interpreted taking into consideration a philosophy of history that combined Vico's historicism with the principles of tradition and progress, both of which were used to legitimize the image of an Italian school of criminal law that, due to its continuity with its own past, could build a better future. During the period between Italian unification and WWI, i.e., between the onset of the debate about *national* characteristics of criminal law and the apex of the struggle between the Positivist School and the Classical School, the purpose herein is to analyse the rhetoric used by jurists to design, shape, and implement the Italian penal code as the peculiar product of the national genius, unaffected by the Napoleonic Code and other foreign schemes.

Until the Zanardelli Code, the unity of criminal law was certainly one of the main concerns of jurists.[20] More specifically, this problem refers to the conflicting views with respect to the right pace of codification, debates regarding the model of codification to be followed, historical studies on the Italian peculiarities, and a general rethinking about the foundations of the right to punish, a concept upon which the new code should be based. After 1889, with conflicting views between adherents to the Positivist School and the Classical School of thought, the primary

[18]Floriana Colao, "Profili di federalismo penale in Italia dall'Unità al Codice Zanardelli", *Rivista di storia del diritto italiano*, 84 (2011), 103–117.

[19]I refer to his seminal essay: Mario Sbriccoli, "La penalistica civile: teorie e ideologie del diritto penale nell'Italia unita", *Storia del diritto penale e della giustizia. Scritti editi e inediti (1972–2007)* (M. Sbriccoli) (Milano: Giuffrè, 2009), in particular pp. 502–509.

[20]See, e.g., the 'call to arms' of Emanuele Rapisardi, *Saggio d'un Progetto del Codice penale italiano corredato d'osservazioni* (Catania: Pietro Giuntini, 1862) in particular pp. 3–5.

legal issue concerned the core of criminal law, namely, the themes of liability, free will, and purpose of punishment. As a consequence, even the history of the Italian tradition of criminal law was rethought from a different perspective, whereas the constitutional dimension of the discipline was deeply reshaped.

2.1 In Search of a National Legal History of Criminal Law: Enrico Pessina

In 1861, Enrico Pessina concludes his inaugural lecture at the University of Naples by evoking the «ancient symbol of our Italy, two-faced Janus» where the one turns to the past of great glories and great misfortunes and the other faces the future.[21] This image perfectly epitomizes the task of post-Unitarian criminalistics, namely, the cultural duty of a discipline whose authoritativeness to design the nation's legal future had to be founded on its continuity with tradition.

The enthusiasm about the new political regime and a renewed national life that, being based on free institution and having removed all of the political hindrances to a full scientific development, is embedded in a programmatic civic engagement such that «now the national doctrine will have to formulate a penal legislation whose roots will certainly not lie in the interests of absolute governments of which we are now rid, but rather in the moral and legal conscience of the Italian people».[22] Soon after the victory of the Risorgimento, Pessina predicts both the method and the problems that will characterize the work of the jurist in the coming years and recognizes, beyond the transformations caused by the new political scenario, the need to be rooted in the past. If today, as the Neapolitan professor explains, «the problem of criminal law is eminently philosophical» and is determined by principles and theories aiming to define the relationship between the individual and authority, another distinctive feature of penal science should be «the assessment of past institutions and legal history».[23]

By suggesting a valorization of legal history, both universal and national, Pessina remarks on the need for a methodological divide that includes «a denial of the past and a disregard for history» as imposed by the French Revolution, as well

---

[21]Enrico Pessina, "Discorso inaugurale alle lezioni di Diritto penale letto nella Regia Università di Napoli il dì 5 dicembre 1861", *Discorsi varii* (E. Pessina) (Napoli: Casa ed. Napoletana, 1915) vol. VI, p. 57.

[22]Enrico Pessina, "Discorso inaugurale alle lezioni di Diritto penale letto nella Regia Università di Napoli il dì 5 dicembre 1861", *Discorsi varii* (E. Pessina) (Napoli: Casa ed. Napoletana, 1915) vol. VI, p. 56.

[23]Enrico Pessina, "Discorso inaugurale alle lezioni di Diritto penale letto nella Regia Università di Napoli il dì 5 dicembre 1861", *Discorsi varii* (E. Pessina) (Napoli: Casa ed. Napoletana, 1915) vol. VI, p. 51.

as «an idolatry of the past» that was adopted by historical schools and the clerical power of the Middle Ages through «the hypocritical or superstitious adoration of old institutions».[24] Pessina's philosophy of history distinguishes among the peculiarities of each historical period and between the elements destined to be abandoned and those fated to lead to progress that are handed down to subsequent generations according to an evolutionary process. If applied to the study of criminal law of mankind (*Diritto penale dell'Umanità*) from a universal perspective, this approach implies an investigation into how punitive law has been regulated throughout history as well as its changes, perceived progress, social functions within different civilizations, and achieved truths. By so doing, «each era of criminal law gains its own significance», indicating that the historical progress of criminal law and its rules are recognized and that mankind can find, «in the past, the key of the future».[25]

However, in addition to the philosophy of universal history leading to the interpretation of punitive experiences regarding the constant progress of civilization and the move from the law of retaliation and private vengeance to the modern retributive and reformative social function of punishment,[26] in the 19th century, the historical discourse necessarily had to assume a national connotation as national history. There is a manifest shift from the «universal history of penality» to national history.[27] That is, there is a clear argumentative leap from the general level to the national one, from preconditions to the celebration of the thread linking Italian criminal law jurists from the medieval judge Gandino to Mario Pagano and passing through Giulio Claro, Tiberio Deciani, Filippo Maria Renazzi, Cesare Beccaria, Gaetano Filangieri, Giovanni Carmiganni, Gaindomenico Romagnosi, and Pellegrino Rossi.

---

[24]Enrico Pessina, "Discorso inaugurale alle lezioni di Diritto penale letto nella Regia Università di Napoli il dì 5 dicembre 1861", *Discorsi varii* (E. Pessina) (Napoli: Casa ed. Napoletana, 1915) vol. VI, pp. 51–52.

[25]Enrico Pessina, "Discorso inaugurale alle lezioni di Diritto penale letto nella Regia Università di Napoli il dì 5 dicembre 1861", *Discorsi varii* (E. Pessina) (Napoli: Casa ed. Napoletana, 1915) vol. VI, p. 53. Pessina takes up again a reasoning developed by Niccola Nicolini in a speech given on December 1st, 1831, at the University of Naples, where he stressed the study of the universal history of criminal law as «an essential part of my teaching»; see N. Nicolini, "Dell'indole e del corso del diritto penale", *Quistioni di diritto trattate nelle conclusioni, ne' discorsi ed in altri scritti legali* (N. Nicolini) (Livorno: V. Mansi, 1844) pp. 177–178.

[26]A corroboration of this methodological approach is given by Pietro Ellero's inaugural lecture at the University of Bologna, entitled "Delle origini storiche del diritto di punire" ("On the historical origins of the right to punish"), published in *Giornale per l'abolizione della pena di morte* 3 (1862) 218–262.

[27]See Enrico Pessina, *Propedeutica al diritto penale delle Due Sicilie* (Napoli: Stabilimento tipografico dei classici italiani, 1858) pp. 7–8.

2.2 Scientific Unity in Spite of Political Divisions

Pessina's methodology, however, was not entirely original, as Emerico Amari had suggested something similar twenty years earlier. In a lecture on criminal law history given in 1840, the Sicilian professor makes extensive use of historical comparison by encompassing a broad temporal and geographical space (from Blackstone to Bentham, from the United States to France and Spain).[28] However, he then focuses on Italy and exalts a typical characteristic that will later became a standard feature in the post-Unitarian search for the *Italian genius*, viz. the primacy of scientific dimension as the central role of legal thought that has always been extremely vital despite «a lack of political life».[29] In a country politically divided and at times forced to undergo laws imposed by foreign powers,[30] the future and progress of criminal law, in the Kingdom of Naples as well as in other Italian regions, rested exclusively on the theoretical capacity and on the design of legal science. Another anticipation of legal discourses that is exploited later in the Risorgimento is provided by Pietro Calà Ulloa, who, depicting an historical reconstruction of the Italian criminal law from Roman law to the 1840s doctrine, considers criminal law a field in which «the plant of the Italian civilization has always stood out».[31]

After 1861, Pessina resumes the rhetorical topos of the contrast between the constant progress achieved by the Italian doctrine of criminal law and the more unfortunate political vicissitudes of different legislations to depict a cultural unity and a ceaseless national tradition upon which the law of the new state can be built.[32]

---

[28]Emerico Amari, "Quadro storico dei progressi della Scienza, e delle Legislazioni criminali da Beccaria insino a Noi", *Filosofia civile e diritto comparato in Emerico Amari* (G. Bentivegna, ed.) (Napoli: Guida, 2003), pp. 167–218. Amari draws on the same historical method in his following lectures "Degli elementi che costituiscono la scienza del Diritto Penale. Tentativo di una teoria del progresso"; "Delle vicende del Diritto penale nel Medio Evo. Parte prima"; and "Delle vicende del Diritto penale nel Medio Evo. Parte seconda", *Filosofia civile e diritto comparato in Emerico Amari* (G. Bentivegna, ed.) (Napoli: Guida, 2003), pp. 246–270; 303–330 and 331–365.

[29]Emerico Amari, "Quadro storico dei progressi della Scienza, e delle Legislazioni criminali da Beccaria insino a Noi", *Filosofia civile e diritto comparato in Emerico Amari* (G. Bentivegna, ed.) (Napoli: Guida, 2003), p. 188.

[30]According to Emerico Amari, "Quadro storico dei progressi della Scienza, e delle Legislazioni criminali da Beccaria insino a Noi", *Filosofia civile e diritto comparato in Emerico Amari* (G. Bentivegna, ed.) (Napoli: Guida, 2003), p. 199, Napoleon's dynasty put down any reform movement in the Kingdom of Naples, and Naples itself became «the miniature of all of the less beautiful French institutions».

[31]Pietro Calà Ulloa, "Delle vicissitudini e de' progressi del diritto penale in Italia dal risorgimento delle lettere sin oggi", *Il Progresso delle scienze, delle lettere e delle arti*, 16 (1837), n. 31 pp. 30–57; n. 32, pp. 193–222; 17 (1837), n. 33, pp. 28–46; later published as a monograph in Napoli by Flautina in 1837, and in Palermo by Lao in 1842. On the importance of the philosophy of history as a nation-building means in the 19th century, see Pietro Rossi, *Il senso della storia. Dal Settecento al Duemila* (Bologna: Il Mulino, 2012), in particular pp. 271–296.

[32]For a general depiction of this historical Italian primacy in legal culture, see, e.g., Benedetto Crisafulli Zappalà, "Autorità degli italiani nella scienza del diritto", *La Temi. Giornale di legislazione e giurisprudenza*, 6 (1857) 365 ff., 484 ff., 596 ff., 726 ff.; 7 (1859) 30 ff., 103 ff., 171 ff., 238 ff., 287 ff., 336 ff., 401 ff.: for a brief synthesis see, in particular, his conclusions pp. 406–408.

Thus, the historical reconstruction of a national criminal law becomes one of his key concerns, the more so when difficulties enacting the new code emerge. In 1863, he notes the arguments that will be used by post-Unitarian jurists to identify themselves within the concept, i.e., the *invention*, of a cultural identity rooted in a nation's past, a peculiar expression of «its distinctive historical vocation» that not only was developed despite the lack of political unity but was also apt to become a prophetic means to strengthen the new patriotism of the Risorgimento.[33]

In the crucial time of the construction of an Italian legal order, the reclamation of those elements (mostly scientific but also normative) that can serve as national symbolic monuments and consolidate the national identity becomes a key factor in legitimizing all the jurists who are engaged, either in law schools or in Parliament, in designing the new penal code of the unified Italy. References to Beccaria, who was the purest and most enviable glory of Italy, Romagnosi, the Leopoldina that represented «the result of indigenous Italian progress»,[34] and the Penal Code of the Kingdom of the Two Sicilies of 1819 were all directed towards the same identifying target.

2.3 *The Great Differences with the French Penal Code*

The more sensitive political issue after unity was how to mark the difference and independence between the Italian and the French criminal law. Even before debating the scheme of codification to be adopted, it was essential to overthrow the notion that legal unification had been anticipated by the Napoleonic imposition of the French code and its influence on the pre-Unitarian penal codes. The discourse, for both civil and criminal law, depended on two crucial sets of arguments. According to the first reasoning, just as the novelties of the French Revolution in the penal field had their origins in Beccaria's *On Crimes and Punishments*, so, too, the French codes were nothing less than a continuation of the Roman law tradition «upon which the genius of the Latin race had imprinted indelible vestiges». Only because of this were the French codes «accepted in Italy as a great progress

[33]Enrico Pessina, "Introduzione al diritto penale in Italia al 1847 (1863)", *Discorsi varii* (E. Pessina) vol. VII (Napoli: Casa ed. Napoletana, 1916) pp. 3–4: «The lack of national life and the subjection to foreign powers for many centuries did not prevent the Italian people from formulating into a common legislation its own legal conscience; and the national tradition of criminal law could only partly be preserved in school teaching and forensic experience, due to the dissipation of Italian life in many small states».

[34]Angelo Recchia, *Discorso per la inaugurazione della cattedra universitaria di Diritto penale accresciuta al Real Liceo delle Puglie* (Bari: Tip. Gissi, 1865), pp. 18 and 22. See also Enrico Pessina, *La riforma del diritto penale in Italia nella seconda metà del secolo decimottavo* (Napoli: Tessitore, 1905), pp. 3–4, where Beccaria and the Grand Duchy Peter Leopold are considered «two great benefactors of mankind».

compared to previous legislations and received as a conquest of modern civilization».[35]

Therefore, not only was there no imposition of entirely foreign codes because they were inspired by Roman, and thus Italian, wisdom,[36] but even when they were in force, they were «subjected in Italy to transformations made by the Italian scientific doctrine; and this was a healthy remedy, as there were in them many points extraneous to national traditions because they were foreign laws».[37] The legal doctrine, thus, had the merit of preserving the *Italianness* of the penal system by interpreting and amending the more evident distortion of French laws from national tradition.

The second anti-French reasoning claimed that pre-Unitarian codes, by sanctioning the end of political dependency, brought back to criminal law the spirit and institutions proper of the Italian original legal culture. In fact, if they were based on French laws, such as the Neapolitan Code of 1819, they «were only of use to Italian lawmakers as a starting point for further progress».[38] In other cases, «the vigorous scientific tradition withstood the reactionary movement and forced the same despotic government» such that, just as in ancient Rome, the firmness of jurists

---

[35]Enrico Pessina, "Introduzione al diritto penale in Italia al 1847 (1863)", *Discorsi varii* (E. Pessina) vol. VII (Napoli: Casa ed. Napoletana, 1916), p. 4. Similarly, Gabriele Napodano, *Posto che occupa il codice italiano del 1859 in mezzo alle legislazioni odierne e di fronte alla scienza del giure penale* (Napoli: Gennaro De Angelis, 1888) p. 6, argued that the French legislation from the Revolution to the Penal Code of 1810 «on the one side, was linked to Roman law traditions and, on the other side, it maintained the reform movement inaugurated in Italy by the eloquent word of Cesare Beccaria».

[36]Gabriele Napodano, *Il diritto penale romano nelle sue attenenze col diritto penale moderno* (Napoli: G. de Angelis e Figlio, 1878), p. X, notes that the reference to Roman roots of the legal institution was not aimed at historicizing ancient sources, but rather at exploiting those notions and principles in which it was possible to read a continuity with the present.

[37]Enrico Pessina, "Introduzione al diritto penale in Italia al 1847 (1863)", *Discorsi varii* (E. Pessina) vol. VII (Napoli: Casa ed. Napoletana, 1916), p. 6. Similarly see also Pietro Calà Ulloa, "Delle vicissitudini e de' progressi del diritto penale in Italia dal risorgimento delle lettere sin oggi", *Il Progresso delle scienze, delle lettere e delle arti*, 16 (1837), n. 32, p. 219, and Gabriele Napodano, *Posto che occupa il codice italiano del 1859 in mezzo alle legislazioni odierne e di fronte alla scienza del giure penale* (Napoli: Gennaro De Angelis, 1888) p. 9.

[38]Enrico Pessina, "Introduzione al diritto penale in Italia al 1847 (1863)", *Discorsi varii* (E. Pessina) vol. VII (Napoli: Casa ed. Napoletana, 1916) p. 10; according to Gabriele Napodano, *Posto che occupa il codice italiano del 1859 in mezzo alle legislazioni odierne e di fronte alla scienza del giure penale* (Napoli: Gennaro De Angelis, 1888), p. 8, the code of 1819 «by accepting the good things of French legislation, revived the Italian traditions, not without taking into account the last scientific progresses». Regarding the Penal Code of 1819 and the autonomism of the Neapolitan legal culture, see Aldo Mazzacane, "Una scienza per due regni: la penalistica napoletana della restaurazione", *Codice per lo Regno delle Due Sicilie (1819). Parte seconda. Leggi penali* (Padova: Cedam, 1996), pp. XXVII–XLIV, and Alfonso Maria Stile, "Il Codice penale del 1819 per lo Regno delle Due Sicilie", *I Codici preunitari e il Codice Zanardelli. Diritto penale dell'Ottocento* (Sergio Vinciguerra, ed.) (Padova: Cedam, 1999), pp. 183–195; Francesco Mastroberti, *Codificazione e giustizia penale nelle Sicilie dal 1808 al 1820* (Napoli: Jovene, 2001), especially pp. 256–267.

tempered the ruinous despotism of the emperors.[39] The purpose of depicting a historiographical picture that emphasizes the unity of Italian legal culture, its autonomy, the continuity of theories, the progressive development of institutions and principles, the tradition constantly oriented to more civilized penal laws and the leniency of punishments is evident.

In 1812, Nicolini, Advocate General of the Supreme Court of Justice in Naples, with the aim of fiercely upholding local historical-legal heritage, censured the «servile method» of courts constantly referring to the authority of French jurisprudence and law because, «before the enactment of new [French] laws, they were certainly neither without laws nor jurisprudence». It was necessary, he went on, to regain a sense of «improvement and continuity» between the novelty introduced by the Napoleonic codification and the past legal system. As Nicolini further stated, they have blood ties, common roots, and analogies consisting of their Roman law imprint, and «it should not be omitted that our legislation and the French one had both, before the new laws, a common foundation in an Italian code, namely, the Roman law».[40]

After the Risorgimento, the history of Italian criminal law assumed a clear public purpose that had «the noble aim of reawakening among Italian people an awareness of a national legal tradition despite the most varied laws applied in different regions of the peninsula».[41] By means of its celebrating narration regarding the magnificence of the Italian genius in contraposition to French jurisprudence, it becomes part of the nation-building effort and demands that jurists overcome their regional differences and find solidarity in their unitary belonging to the Italian tradition and their commitment to draft the new penal code.[42] It is perceived as a *duty* for the legal culture «to be tied to the ancient Italian tradition and maintain a national legal

[39]Enrico Pessina, "Introduzione al diritto penale in Italia al 1847 (1863)", *Discorsi varii* (E. Pessina) vol. VII (Napoli: Casa ed. Napoletana, 1916), p. 7. Pessina's interpretation voluntarily omits or minimizes the not slight doctrinal and legislative differences among the pre-unitarian states; a more realistic view is provided by Pietro Calà Ulloa, "Delle vicissitudini e de' progressi del diritto penale in Italia dal risorgimento delle lettere sin oggi", *Il Progresso delle scienze, delle lettere e delle arti*, 16 (1837), n. 32, p. 221.

[40]Niccola Nicolini, "Delle attribuzioni della Corte suprema di giustizia. Discorso (Prima parte delle conclusioni nella causa Tobia Lepore, 2 giugno 1812)", *Quistioni di diritto trattate nelle conclusioni, ne' discorsi ed in altri scritti legali* (N. Nicolini) (Livorno: V. Mansi, 1844), pp. 10–11. Similar arguments, stressing the need of autonomous codification process and style for Tuscany, different from both the French and German models, are used, e.g., by Ludovico Bosellini, "Lettera sulla Codificazione, specialmente in Italia, e sul Codice civile già progettato in Toscana", *La Temi. Giornale di legislazione e giurisprudenza*, 4/37 (1853) 393–396, on which see Alberto Spinosa, "«L'economia dei codici moderni». Legislazione e giurisprudenza nella dottrina italiana dell'Ottocento, *Quaderni fiorentini per la storia del pensiero giuridico moderno*, 40 (2011) 747–780, in particular 766–774.

[41]With these words, Pessina ("Introduzione al diritto penale in Italia al 1847 (1863)", *Discorsi varii* (E. Pessina) vol. VII (Napoli: Casa ed. Napoletana, 1916), p. 25) praises Ulloa's pioneering work that he himself seeks to carry on and consolidate.

[42]See Enrico Pessina, *Dei progressi del diritto penale nel secolo XIX* (Firenze: Civelli, 1868), pp. VI–VII.

conscience, which, notwithstanding the dismemberment of Italy into many small states for centuries, was never defeated».[43] Therefore, it is essential that legal history operate at the service of political unity by corroborating and spreading the discourse of Italian primacy in criminal law.

Pessina, who is the main storyteller,[44] even in 1868, complained about the dearth of historiographical studies on criminal law and praised those studies focused on medieval criminal law because they formed «a valuable collection of materials for a normative history of Italian criminal law (...) and thanks to them it will be easier to find the origins of many institutions and recognize the national tradition that, together with the *jus commune*, contributed to the formation of the *communis opinio doctorum* and later the modern Italian legislations».[45] This is the spirit underlying the first two volumes of the dell'*Enciclopedia del diritto penale italiano* edited by Pessina, which is a scientific enterprise to represent the entire progressive development, the cultural peculiarity, and the theoretical richness of the history of national criminal law.[46] Jurists were well aware that a legal comparison was crucial

---

[43]E. Pessina, "Del diritto penale nel Regno d'Italia dal 1859 sino al 1867", *Discorsi varii* (E. Pessina), vol. VII, (Napoli: Casa ed. Napoletana, 1916), p. 168.

[44]After his two contributions of 1863 ("Introduzione al diritto penale in Italia al 1847", and "Movimento legislativo e scientifico del diritto penale negli stati italiani dal 1848 al 1859 (1863)", *Discorsi varii* (E. Pessina), vol. VII (Napoli: Casa ed. Napoletana, 1916), pp. 33–85), Pessina carried on historical studies, first, in 1868 with "Del diritto penale nel Regno d'Italia dal 1859 sino al 1867" (in the same volume pp. 87–169. These three essays were then merged into the work *Dei progressi del diritto penale nel secolo XIX* (Firenze: Civelli, 1868). Secondly, in 1874 with "Cenni sul movimento del diritto penale in Italia dal 1868 al 1874", *Discorsi varii* (E. Pessina), vol. VII (Napoli: Casa ed. Napoletana, 1916), pp. 171–191), and, thirdly, in 1906 with the publication of "Movimento legislativo del diritto penale in Italia dal 1874 al 1887" (same volume, pp. 193–225). In these writings he took into account every draft bill and constantly updated the bibliography. In 1905 he wrote *La riforma del diritto penale in Italia nella seconda metà del secolo decimottavo* (Napoli: Tessitore, 1905). All of these works, with the addition of the last headings on "Movimento scientifico nell'ultimo trentennio del secolo decimonono" and the Zanardelli Code, were then merged into the long essay "Il diritto penale in Italia da Cesare Beccaria sino alla promulgazione del codice penale vigente (1764-1890)", *Enciclopedia del diritto penale italiano* (E. Pessina, ed.), vol. II (Milano: Società Editrice Libraria, 1906), pp. 539–768. Regarding his in-progress narration, see "La penalistica civile: teorie e ideologie del diritto penale nell'Italia unita", *Storia del diritto penale e della giustizia. Scritti editi e inediti (1972–2007)* (Milano: Giuffrè, 2009), p. 506; Floriana Colao, "Profili di federalismo penale in Italia dall'Unità al Codice Zanardelli", *Rivista di storia del diritto italiano*, 84 (2011), p. 110; Marco Nicola Miletti, "Enrico Pessina", *Dizionario Biografico degli Italiani*, vol. 82 (Roma: Istituto della Enciclopedia Italiana, 2015).

[45]Enrico Pessina, "Del diritto penale nel Regno d'Italia dal 1859 sino al 1867", *Discorsi varii* (E. Pessina), vol. VII (Napoli: Casa ed. Napoletana, 1916), p. 148.

[46]In the first volume (Milano: Società Editrice Libraria, 1905) the essays are written by Contardo Ferrini, "Esposizione storica e dottrinale del diritto penale romano", pp. 1–428; Pasquale Del Giudice, "Diritto penale germanico rispetto all'Italia", pp. 429–609; and Domenico Schiappoli, "Diritto penale canonico", pp. 611–967. They show the three roots of Italian legal tradition, that is, Roman law, German law and Canon law. In the second volume of 1906, there two contributions by Carlo Calisse "Svolgimento storico del diritto penale in Italia dalle invasioni barbariche alle riforme del secolo XVIII", pp. 1–538, and by Pessina "Il diritto penale in Italia da Cesare Beccaria sino alla promulgazione del codice penale vigente (1764-1890)".

to design the system of a modern code,[47] but never in terms of «fawning imitation», as the purpose was always to find something useful within foreign laws and «make it consistent with our tendencies, traditions, and national character».[48]

3 A Doctrinal Unity Still to Be Built

The formation of a strong idea of historical continuity in the penal culture as a way to promote the perception of belonging to a common scientific movement represents a difficult process of identity conquest, notwithstanding Pessina's effort to celebrate the 'natural' Italianness of criminal law. Indeed, although it is true that during the years of unification, jurists recognized that within the penal reasoning brilliant brains had made the Italian name illustrious, even abroad, due to figures such as Beccaria and Rossi; it is likewise true that «this was the last victory of Italian civilization» and that penal studies should resume with renewed ambition «because the field is not yet free from weeds», and therefore, it surely must be improved.[49] Although political unification paves the way to legal unification, the issues at stake are not few and are relatively difficult to solve. Not only do the three penal codes simultaneously testify to the persistent legal fragmentation, but the enthusiasm for the building of the new state is accompanied by a realistic acknowledgement of the great differences in the legal culture among the different regions and an awareness of the lack of a unique school upon whose theories the penal code could be built.

In 1860, Filippo Ambrosoli stated that «the new legislation, for debt of gratitude and national necessity, had to be neither Sardinian nor Lombard but Italian». Therefore, the new penal code could not be based on any previous model but rather that «within Italian laws and traditions, it was necessary to find the congenital law of the Italian people», and that if it was not possible to raise this «legal flag» in a short space of time, it would be better to adopt merely provisional laws and allow scholars and practitioners with the aim of studying the country and its real needs the time to formulate the elements of new Italian law. In so doing, the penal code would have been «not created but deducted, not imposed but desired and accepted».[50] In 1866, Luigi Borsari, writing on penal action and seeking to give his work a new and unusual direction for Italian ideas, types, and shapes, proclaimed his «desire for a noble and salutary reaction of the Italian genius». He desired theoretical autonomy

[47]See Angelo Recchia, *Discorso per la inaugurazione della cattedra universitaria di Diritto penale accresciuta al Real Liceo delle Puglie* (Bari: Tip. Gissi, 1865), pp. 43–46.

[48]Enrico Pessina, "Del diritto penale nel Regno d'Italia dal 1859 sino al 1867", *Discorsi varii* (E. Pessina), vol. VII (Napoli: Casa ed. Napoletana, 1916), p. 169.

[49]So wrote Pietro Ellero on June 12th, 1860, "Della critica criminale", *Trattati criminali* (P. Ellero) (Bologna: Fava e Garagnani 1875), pp. 93–94.

[50]Filippo Ambrosoli, *Sulla nuova codificazione nei regj stati. Osservazioni* (Pavia: Tipografia dei Fratelli Fusi, 1860), pp. 26–28.

of national jurisprudence in such a way that «our bibliographical poverty can be resolved and the absolute and tyrannical need of French books, despite the differences in character, methods, customs and even laws and principles, can be stopped».[51] In 1890, immediately following the enactment of the Zanardelli Code, Federico Benevolo, reminded of Borsari's goal, noted that «at that time, for a scientist to think in an Italian way was something quite unusual».[52] In his inaugural lecture in Turin, Benevolo, after recognizing the progress achieved by penal studies from the Risorgimento to the Zanardelli, restated that the Piedmont legal culture in the 1860s was dominated by French doctrine and case law,[53] and that it was only due to the influence and authority of Carrara's *Programma* that criminal law returned to the pure sources of Italian classical science and assumed a national form.[54]

Under the surface of a celebrated Italian tradition, there was a criminalistic diversified world, which, beyond rhetorical reference to the common founding fathers, was culturally divided, largely dependent on foreign doctrine, and without any shared legislation or case law. The principle of equality, as argued by Lucchini in 1878, is in favour of a «harmonious deal» between political unity and peno-legislative unity, though the target is not yet achieved due to the lack of a national legal conscience, the country's indolence, and the varied doctrinal positions.[55] While the Sardinian-Piedmont Kingdom was affected by a strong French influence, even though the penal code of 1859 was claimed to be more autonomous,[56] in the South, the doctrinal and legislative differences of the French penal code were so strong that the government amended the Piedmont Code (Law of 17 February 1861) before applying it in those regions.[57] In Tuscany, the Penal Code of 1853, the «outcome of a judicious and wise eclecticism»,[58] was deeply influenced

---

[51]Luigi Borsari, *Della azione penale* (Torino: Unione Tipografico-Editrice, 1866), p. 10.

[52]Federico Benevolo, *L'unificazione della legislazione penale e la pena suprema* (Torino: Unione Tipografico-Editrice, 1890), p. 6.

[53]Federico Benevolo, *L'unificazione della legislazione penale e la pena suprema* (Torino: Unione Tipografico-Editrice, 1890), p. 5: «here, in Piedmont, criminal law issues were solved by means of arguments based on the repertoires of Merlin, Morin and Dalloz, as well as on the treaties of Rossi, Chauveau and Hélie, Ortolan, Trébutien, Legraverend, and with the authority of decisions taken by the Court of Cassation in Paris».

[54]Federico Benevolo, *L'unificazione della legislazione penale e la pena suprema* (Torino: Unione Tipografico-Editrice, 1890), p. 7.

[55]Luigi Lucchini, *Della dignità politica del diritto penale* (Siena: Lazzeri, 1878), p. 19.

[56]See Gabriele Napodano, *Posto che occupa il codice italiano del* 1859 *in mezzo alle legislazioni odierne e di fronte alla scienza del giure penale* (Napoli: Gennaro De Angelis, 1888).

[57]Marco Nicola Miletti, "«Piemontesizzare le contrade italiane». L'adeguamento del codice penale sardo alle provincie meridionali", *Il Codice Penale per gli Stati del Re di Sardegna e per l'Italia unita (1859)* (Padova: Cedam, 2008), pp. CV–CXXXIII; Ettore Dezza, "Il «colpo di stato legislativo » del 1859 e la nascita del codice Rattazzi", *Il Codice Penale per gli Stati del Re di Sardegna e per l'Italia unita (1859)* (Padova: Cedam, 2008), pp. XI–XX.

[58]Filippo Ambrosoli, *Studi sul Codice penale toscano confrontato specialmente coll'austriaco* (Mantova: Negretti e Comp., 1857), p. 6.

by the Baden Code and the German jurisprudence spread by Mori's translations, though the usual rhetoric insisted on fidelity to the Italian school and the heritage of Leopold's reform.[59]

4 Carrara and the Savigyan Approach to Penal Codification

While Pessina, through his historical discourse, was seeking to emphasize the consistency and uniformity of the penal culture as a way to respond to the legislative urgencies, different opinions about the timing and method of codification were growing. It was not just a matter of choice from among different models, namely, the French model of 1810, the German codes or a third Italian model yet to be discovered,[60] but the very opportunity to enact a code and, above all, to do it quickly, was contested. Carrara's well-known and harsh words against the «rush to codify»[61] appeased the enthusiasm for a rapid legal unification and amplified a widespread view among post-Unitarian jurists that was cautious because of the fear of a dull standardization rather than an optimistic view about the project of a legal unity. The choice between looking forward towards Germany or looking backward towards France took on the political-constitutional significance of a «matter of civilization».[62] If, indeed, as according to Carrara, the core principle of criminal law, namely, that of legal protection (*tutela giuridica*), is based on absolute principles that should be universally applied, there are, nonetheless, conditions of time and place, customs, and individual peculiarities that justify the variety in the concrete application of that same principle. With reference to the Italian political conditions, Carrara rejects the need of a quick codification by accusing the recurring

---

[59]On the formation of the Tuscan penal code of 1853, see Mario Da Passano, "La storia esterna del codice penale toscano (1814b-1859)", *Istituzioni e società in Toscana nell'età moderna. Atti delle giornate di studio dedicate a Giuseppe Pansini: Firenze 4-5 dicembre 1992*, vol. 2 (Roma: Ministero per i beni culturali e ambientali, 1994), pp. 564–589; Mario Da Passano, "La codificazione penale nel Granducato di Toscana (1814-1860)", *Codice Penale pel Granducato di Toscana (1853)* (rist. anastatica, Padova: Cedam, 1995), pp. VII–XLVII; Sergio Vinciguerra, "Fonti culturali ed eredità del codice penale toscano", in the same volume, pp. CLIX–CLXXX; Tullio Padovani, "La tradizione penalistica toscana nel codice Zanardelli", in *I Codici preunitari e il Codice Zanardelli. Diritto penale dell'Ottocento* (Sergio Vinciguerra, ed.) (Padova: Cedam, 1999), in particular pp. 402–405.

[60]See Alberto Cadoppi, "Il 'modello italiano' di codice penale. Dalle 'origini lombarde' ai progetti di un nuovo codice penale", *L'Indice Penale*, 1(2003), 19–74.

[61]Francesco Carrara, "Codicizzazione (Studi legislativi)", *Opuscoli di diritto criminale* (F. Carrara), II (Lucca: Giusti, 1870), p. 225.

[62]Francesco Carrara, "Codicizzazione (Studi legislativi)", *Opuscoli di diritto criminale* (F. Carrara), II (Lucca: Giusti, 1870), p. 230.

call for unity to be «a *mystical formula* rather than a demonstration».[63] If legal unification implies the imposition on a more civilized Tuscany of the Piedmont law, which provides for the death penalty, it is much better to maintain the legal fragmentation, which corresponds to a cultural and legal divide as well as to different *moral conditions* that could be made uniform only over time.[64]

Carrara, by reinterpreting the reasons of German historicism as a «type of Italian Savigny»,[65] uses his scientific authoritativeness in favour of anti-codification views and suggests instead to enact special laws because the time is not ripe for a universal code that is shared and well thought out by the doctrine. If the code is unable to regulate all the problems according to the criteria of «supreme justice», it is better to postpone the code, wait, and build the bases for shared and enduring reforms because «a lacuna is more valuable than the apostolate of a false doctrine».[66] «To wait and to hope», stressed Carrara in 1862, is the motto that summarizes the attitude of criminal law scholars after the unification. That is, «to wait and to hope that punitive law will purge itself of any relics of ancient rust» and that academic teaching will have an impact on every-day law; «to wait and to hope that proper moderation in punishment will stimulate people to fraternal love»; «to wait and to hope that, by abolishing the death penalty, sovereigns will teach citizens a respect for human life». Now that Italy has regained political independence, Carrara goes on, Italy should be able to restart its «holy mission» for the regeneration of penal science.[67] As Sbriccoli said, it was neither an appeal to the civic lack of commitment nor a recognition of the subjection of jurists to lawmakers, but rather an admonition of the long way to go.[68]

Carrara's opinion was not at all unconditionally opposed to codification. In an article published in 1877, he clarified that he was absolutely in favour of the unification of substantial criminal law via codification, so crimes would be

---

[63]Francesco Carrara, "Se la unità sia condizione del giure penale (Prolusione al corso accademico dell'anno 1865-66)", *Opuscoli di diritto criminale* (F. Carrara), II (Lucca: Giusti, 1870), p. 31.

[64]Francesco Carrara, "Se la unità sia condizione del giure penale (Prolusione al corso accademico dell'anno 1865-66)", *Opuscoli di diritto criminale* (F. Carrara), II (Lucca: Giusti, 1870), p. 39: «the progress is a barbaric regress, if those who are in advance in the holy pilgrimage of universal civilization are pushed backwards».

[65]The definition is given by Paolo Cappellini, "Francesco Carrara e il problema della codificazione del diritto", *Criminalia*, 2 (2007), 305–323.

[66]Francesco Carrara, "Codicizzazione (Studi legislativi)", *Opuscoli di diritto criminale* (F. Carrara), II (Lucca: Giusti, 1870), p. 235; see also p. 240. On Carrara's position about legal unification see Marco Paolo Geri, "'La metamorfosi che la politica voleva fare a danno della giustizia'. Francesco Carrara e l'unità del 'giure penale'", *Materiali per la storia della cultura giuridica moderna*, 35/2 (2005) 333–359; Floriana Colao, "Profili di federalismo penale in Italia dall'Unità al Codice Zanardelli", *Rivista di storia del diritto italiano*, 84 (2011), pp. 107–110.

[67]Francesco Carrara, "Varietà della idea fondamentale del giure punitivo (Prolusione al corso accademico dell'anno 1862-63)", *Opuscoli di diritto criminale* (F. Carrara), I (Lucca: Giusti, 1870), pp. 187–188.

[68]See Mario Sbriccoli, "Politica e giustizia in Francesco Carrara", *Storia del diritto penale e della giustizia. Scritti editi e inediti (1972–2007)* (M. Sbriccoli) (Milano: Giuffrè, 2009), I, pp. 485–492.

perceived equally throughout the entire country, but he opposed the need to standardize penalties. In contrast, he considered this step to be «premature, as it lacked foresight and could be dangerous».[69] While equality with respect to incriminations and liability criteria was regarded as a positive achievement in the process of national codification, the choice of applying to all the regions the sanctions provided by the Piedmont Penal Code was considered a great injustice. Carrara criticized the «fanatic Unitarian tendency» of Italian jurists regarding unification as well as the premise, spread by the French Revolution, according to which legal unity was a necessary consequence of a political unity. He emphasized that, from his perspective, it was «a matter of *justice*, not of *politics*».[70] What was at stake, in his opinion, was not just the reintroduction of the death penalty in Tuscany, but a more general distinction between absolute philosophical principles and reasons for political expediency, because if the death penalty was still conceivable in some regions due to exceptional reasons, it could become a general rule.

4.1 Hindrances to Penal Unification

The abolition of capital punishment, especially, but not exclusively, for Tuscan jurists (Pietro Ellero and Pasquale Stanislao Mancini, e.g., were keen abolitionists even though not Tuscan) represented one of the more effective arguments against the quick enactment of a penal code based on the French model.[71] Pessina's enthusiasm for a prompt codification was oppressed by a contrasting historicist view, which, by considering codification as the construction of an unshakable monument, asked for patience, the identity of doctrines, and harmony with original popular feelings. These were all things that, in the young Italian nation, were not yet available. Writing to the Minister of Justice Pisanelli in 1863, Pietro Ellero

[69]Francesco Carrara, "Scienza criminale e scienza penale", *Opuscoli di diritto criminale* (F. Carrara), VII (Prato: Giachetti, 1887), p. 11.

[70]Francesco Carrara, "Scienza criminale e scienza penale", *Opuscoli di diritto criminale* (F. Carrara), VII (Prato: Giachetti, 1887) ("Nota"), p. 19. See Luigi Lacchè, "La penalistica costituzionale e il 'liberalismo giuridico'. Problemi e immagini della legalità nella riflessione di Francesco Carrara", *Quaderni fiorentini per la storia del pensiero giuridico moderno*, 36 (2007b), in particular pp. 674–680; and Giovannangelo De Francesco, "Funzioni della pena e limiti della coercizione: caratteri ed eredità del classicismo penale", *Quaderni fiorentini per la storia del pensiero giuridico moderno*, 36 (2007a), 660–661.

[71]Regarding the problem of abolitionism and its opponents, see Elio Tavilla, "Guerra contro il crimine. Pena di morte e abolizionismo nella cultura giuridica italiana", *Il diritto come forza la forza del diritto. Le fonti in azione nel diritto europeo tra medioevo ed età contemporanea* (Alberto Sciumè, ed.) (Torino: Giappichelli, 2012), pp. 151–185; Ettore Dezza, "Il problema della pena di morte", *Enciclopedia Italiana di scienze, lettere ed arti. Il contributo italiano alla storia del pensiero. Ottava appendice. Diritto* (Roma: Istituto dell'Enciclopedia Treccani, 2012), pp. 223–231; Mario Da Passano, "La pena di morte nel Regno d'Italia (1859-1889), *I Codici preunitari e il Codice Zanardelli. Diritto penale dell'Ottocento* (Sergio Vinciguerra, ed.) (Padova: Cedam, 1999), pp. 579–651.

deployed the Savignyan model as a means to design an autonomous Italian path to penal codification such that the code could not be created suddenly because, after 1861, there were too many political concerns, difficulties and conflicting interests in the path of unity and order. National legislation, Ellero stated, «should be *original* and peculiar to a people, as is its language», and the fact that it cannot be quickly enacted does not mean that it is not one of the main targets of legal science.[72] The condition that was lacking for codification is exactly what Pessina sought to *invent* through historical analysis, namely, a common and shared Italian penal jurisprudence capable of giving *Italian* content to the code.

Ellero, similar to Ambrosoli and Carrara, suggests adopting provisional laws and, at the same time, initiating a long cultural enterprise. It was not a task to be delegated to a few jurists who were not representative of all the varieties of national legal and political thought, but rather a task to be based on the «broad, patient, and serious cooperation» of the best jurists and judges who, after careful study, could elaborate laws that were «truly Italian».[73] According to Ellero, a legislative reform cannot be modelled on exotic copies, in particular, that of the French, but it is also unthinkable to enact, in a short time, a penal code that is «the work of the volition and customs of all of the Italian provinces» and that truly warrants the title of «*national legislation*».[74] The definition of a national legal identity requires the slow process of discussion regarding different schools and traditions and a gradual refinement of institutions through a comparison of different doctrines and decisions of the courts. It is not, therefore, the starting point for elaborating a penal code already available, but rather, it is a target to be achieved, a cultural enterprise to be pursued. The tradition of the Italian criminal law doctrine is remarkable, but the characteristics of its identity should be rediscovered to regain theoretical autonomy after so many years of foreign influence. Ellero criticizes the draft code presented at the Senate in January 1862, which was a hybrid Sardinian-Lombard model, because it was essentially an improved reproduction of the French Code and thus could «not overcome all the defects that abounded in the incorrigible type on which it was modelled».[75] Rather, Ellero prefers the Tuscan Penal Code of 1853, an imitation of the German model, because it was «more systematic, shorter, clearer, more accurate, more harmonious, more lenient, and more rational» than the codes based on

---

[72]Pietro Ellero, "Sulla revisione delle leggi penali del Regno d'Italia", *Opuscoli criminali* (P. Ellero), (Bologna: Fava e Garagnani, 1874), pp. 201. Regarding Ellero's thought and political role, see Cristina Vano, "Ellero, Pietro", *Dizionario biografico degli italiani*, vol. XLII (Roma: Istituto della Enciclopedia Italiana, 1993), pp. 512–520.

[73]Pietro Ellero, "Sulla revisione delle leggi penali del Regno d'Italia", *Opuscoli criminali* (P. Ellero), (Bologna: Fava e Garagnani, 1874), p. 202.

[74]Pietro Ellero, "Sulla revisione delle leggi penali del Regno d'Italia", *Opuscoli criminali* (P. Ellero), (Bologna: Fava e Garagnani, 1874), p. 203.

[75]Pietro Ellero, "Sulla revisione delle leggi penali del Regno d'Italia", *Opuscoli criminali* (P. Ellero), (Bologna: Fava e Garagnani, 1874), p. 208. Similarly, see Pietro Ellero, "Note critiche al primo libro del Codice penale italiano", *Opuscoli criminali* (P. Ellero), (Bologna: Fava e Garagnani, 1874), p. 318.

the Napoleonic type. Nonetheless, he contends that neither the Sardinian-Lombard penal code nor the Tuscan one suits the new Italian state.[76]

The new country, politically independent, deserves a codification that is autonomous and completely rethought on the basis of the characteristics and spirit of the new state. It is not a matter of taking a certain quality from a pre-Unitarian code and using it to create a new penal code, nor is it possible to merge the codes of 1853–1859, which are founded on different systems; «one that is doctrinal, conceptual and spiritualistic and another that is analytical, pragmatic, and utilitarian». Similarly, it is not possible to create a hybrid model by correcting the German codes, i.e., Bavaria's Code of 1813 and Baden's Code of 1845, or the 'incorrigible' codifications modelled on the French Code, e.g., the Sardinian-Lombard Code, the Belgian Code and the Dutch Code.[77] Rather than amendments or makeshift solutions, the ambitious target of Italian criminalistics should be the well-thought preparation of an autonomous legislation that takes into consideration the theoretical progress and the specific criminal singularities of the country, such as camorra, brigandage, clerical betrayal and duels. Even Ellero, in the founding phase of the Unitarian state, expresses a principle or a desire that is burning in the heart of every citizen, namely, «*that Italy establish laws that are truly Italian*».[78]

4.2 *The Prevailing Historicist Argument*

The historicist argument seems to prevail in post-Unitarian jurisprudence and yields a positive delay in the codification process, due to what Baldassare Paoli, following a usual Savignyan cliché, called «the advantages of long waiting».[79] The stream of draft codes[80] and the lively debate with respect to the content and language of the

[76]Pietro Ellero, "Sulla revisione delle leggi penali del Regno d'Italia", *Opuscoli criminali* (P. Ellero), (Bologna: Fava e Garagnani, 1874), p. 209. Among the good qualities of the Tuscan code, Ellero considers the formulation of offences in terms of conceptual types rather than analytical cases; the well-articulated doctrine of criminal intent, attempt, complicity; the quite lenient and proportionate penalties; and a general unity and harmony that reveal «a very scientific spirit». Its worst defect, legacy of the hypocrisy and fear of previous domination, «consists of the cruel punishments for religious and political crimes» (p. 209).

[77]Pietro Ellero, "Sulla revisione delle leggi penali del Regno d'Italia", *Opuscoli criminali* (P. Ellero), (Bologna: Fava e Garagnani, 1874), pp. 208–209.

[78]Pietro Ellero, "Note critiche al primo libro del Codice penale italiano", *Opuscoli criminali* (P. Ellero), (Bologna: Fava e Garagnani, 1874), p. 324.

[79]Baldassare Paoli, "Della necessità di mantenere nelle nostre leggi penali il linguaggio giuridico italiano (Saggio di studio)", *Rivista penale* 1 (1874), p. 12.

[80]Regarding the different draft codes and the long process of codification, see Mario Da Passano, "Il problema dell'unificazione legislativa e l'abrogazione del codice napoletano", *Codice per lo Regno delle Due Sicilie (1819). Parte seconda. Leggi penali* (Padova: Cedam, 1996), pp. LXIX–CXLII; Franca Mele, *Un codice unico per un'Italia nuova. Il progetto di codice penale di Pasquale Stanislao Mancini* (Roma: Carocci, 2002); Anna Santangelo Cordani, *Alla vigilia del Codice Zanardelli. Antonio Buccellati e la riforma penale nell'Italia postunitaria* (Milano: Giuffrè, 2008).

text are proof of the work-in-progress of penal jurisprudence. Necessarily, national traditions should be gradually rediscovered to the detriment of foreign imprints to create a codification «with entirely national features»,[81] that is, an authentic outcome of the study of past legal orders, customs, and jurisprudence of different parts of the country. The advantages of such waiting are remarkable from both political and cultural perspectives.

The characteristics of the time, as Emilio Brusa says, are those of «instability and temporariness, respectively, the daughter and sister of uncertainty», and accordingly, these conditions are impediments to a firm, future-oriented codification; instead, they encourage the violence of prompt provisions as well as an unjustified and fruitless hatred for the past. Brusa further argues that there is no common legal culture as yet, and thinking that there is already a «fully developed, clear, precise, and determined legal consciousness is risky and completely inconsequent».[82] The existence of an Italian school of criminal law cannot be considered an undisputed fact that is in continuity with national tradition, but it is rather a target to be achieved in full awareness of the differences among the *multiple* Italian legal cultures. Following Carrara's opinion, Brusa criticizes the need for legal uniformity as a consequence of the political unity, arguing that because «civic and legal feelings» have been perceived as a reflection of different traditions for a long time, it is now difficult to merge them into a unique and consistent framework.[83] Both *methods* and *forms* of criminal justice are diversified within the state, and thus trying to force them into a unitary scheme represents a «wishful thinking» that risks becoming a «violation of civil liberty».[84] Similarly, Arabia, analysing the faults of the many draft codes and commenting on the difficult process of legislative unification, censures the notion that penal reform is urgently needed at all cost without considering what can be retained from the past. He posits that «the words 'amending', 'reforming', 'modifying' and even 'unifying' are conceived as synonyms of 'destroying everything' and 'redoing the entire thing' and that, as such, this is bad».[85] Referring to Vico's concept, Arabia warns against the rush to delete or ignore legal institutions of the past, because often what seems to be just a veneer of the past is, instead, its essence, and therefore, throwing away the historical value of institutions and laws is certainly a wrong choice.[86]

The repercussions in terms of civic conscience, the struggles against a reductive legal unification, and the waiting for a more lenient penal law with more safeguards as a consequence of social progress are all conditions that justify the decision to not

[81]Baldassare Paoli, "Della necessità di mantenere nelle nostre leggi penali il linguaggio giuridico italiano (Saggio di studio)", *Rivista penale* 1 (1874), p. 11.

[82]Emilio Brusa, "L'unificazione penale e la politica", *Rivista penale*, 1 (1874), p. 25.

[83]Emilio Brusa, "L'unificazione penale e la politica", *Rivista penale*, 1 (1874), p. 30.

[84]Emilio Brusa, "L'unificazione penale e la politica", *Rivista penale*, 1 (1874), p. 30.

[85]Francesco Saverio Arabia, *Del Codice penale italiano* (Napoli: Tip. della Regia Università, 1887), p. 31.

[86]Francesco Saverio Arabia, *Del Codice penale italiano* (Napoli: Tip. della Regia Università, 1887), p. 31.

enact a penal code based on foreign models, as occurred with the Civil Code of 1865, and that explain, instead, the waiting for the scientific maturation of a genuine Italian penal code.

5 The Zanardelli Code and New Challenges for the Italian School

In the thirty years between unification and the enactment of the Zanardelli Penal Code in 1889, Italian criminal law scholars regrouped and discovered in the *Rivista Penale*, founded and directed by Luigi Lucchini, the cultural space to build their disciplinary identity.[87] They were proceeding towards the three goals identified by Mario Sbriccoli, namely, the unification of penal legislation, the (re)building of the system of administration of criminal justice, and the need for research and scientific knowledge connected to academic teaching.[88] The enactment of the Zanardelli code was celebrated as the achievement of the coveted legislative goal, and its technical features and systematic consistency were highly praised.[89] The Italian school claims credit for the slow but important theoretical debate that resulted in the international recognition of the Zanardelli, an original code, and it confirms its commitments to further penal reforms even after the codification. As Lucchini clarifies, the penal code, rather than being the end of a process, represents the beginning of a new experience, and it does not put an end to the golden trend of the Italian legal school, which, on the contrary, will continue to operate to create a more civilized society.[90] The new event of codification, which surely represents significant progress and «marks new horizons for the doctrine»,[91] cannot live within the society without the contributions of the jurists, and it is not limited to an exegetic explanation of the text but rather requires a more active interpretation and application. In other words,

---

[87]Mario Sbriccoli, "Il diritto penale liberale. La "Rivista Penale" di Luigi Lucchini 1874-1900", *Storia del diritto penale e della giustizia. Scritti editi e inediti (1972–2007)* (M. Sbriccoli) (Milano: Giuffrè, 2009), II, pp. 903–979.

[88]Mario Sbriccoli, "La penalistica civile: teorie e ideologie del diritto penale nell'Italia unita", *Storia del diritto penale e della giustizia. Scritti editi e inediti (1972–2007)* (M. Sbriccoli) (Milano: Giuffrè, 2009).

[89]See, e.g., Francesco De Cola Proto, *L'unificazione legislativa e le riforme procedurali* (Messina: Tipogr. Dell'Epoca - Sava e Anastasi, 1891), p. 5, who considers the code as «loyal to the traditions of the good Italian doctrine»; Federico Benevolo, *L'unificazione della legislazione penale e la pena suprema* (Torino: Unione Tipografico-Editrice, 1890); Mario De Mauro, "L'ufficio della pena e il nuovo codice penale italiano", *Antologia Giuridica*, 4/1 (1890) 22–42.

[90]Luigi Lucchini, "La Terza Serie della Rivista penale", *Rivista penale*, 31 (1890), p. 8.

[91]Luigi Lucchini, "La Terza Serie della Rivista penale", *Rivista penale*, 31 (1890), pp. 7–8. Similarly see also Federico Benevolo, *L'unificazione della legislazione penale e la pena suprema* (Torino: Unione Tipografico-Editrice, 1890), pp. 38–39 and Francesco Saverio Arabia, *Sull'applicazione del codice penale italiano* (Napoli: Tip. della Regia Università, 1893).

the penal code should not be merely a monument of past theories but a text that is always open to new improvements.

With respect to its contents, the Zanardelli code has some peculiarities that differentiate it from the French penal code and that are proudly considered to be distinctive characteristics of the Italian jurists. First, the offenses are divided into two categories, namely, crimes and contraventions (*delitti* and *contravvenzioni*), rather than into three categories, as is the case in France (*crimes*, *délits* and *contraventions*), and this distinction is based on conceptual and substantial differences rather than on reasons of jurisdiction.[92] Second, the attempted crime is punished not such as a perpetrated crime, but rather with a different and more lenient penalty, based on objective criteria related to the suitability of the deed to cause harm and/or danger to the protected legal good.[93] Third, complicity in a crime is subjected to different penalties according to the role played by the accomplice as typified by the law, rather than punishing accomplices and offenders in the same way. Fourth, judges are given some discretion in sentencing by means of aggravating and mitigating circumstances to ensure that the punishment fit the specific case (e.g., the French code of 1810 provided for circumstances in extremely limited cases and was modified in 1832 to extend the court's power to apply mitigating circumstances[94]), and the scales of punishment were well calibrated according to the seriousness of the offence.[95] The death penalty, after long debate, was abolished.[96]

While the Zanardelli code represented the product of the liberal school, which, after three decades of theoretical debate, had reached shared opinions on the fundamentals of criminal law, the 1881 inaugural lecture of Enrico Ferri at the

---

[92]See Michele Pifferi, "Difendere i confini, superare le frontiere. Le 'zone grigie' della legalità penale tra Otto e Novecento", in *Quaderni fiorentini per la storia del pensiero giuridico moderno*, 36 (2007) 743–799; Tullio Padovani, "Il binomio irriducibile. La distinzione dei reati in delitti e contravvenzioni, fra storia e politica criminale", *Diritto penale in trasformazione* (Giorgio Marinucci and Emilio Dolcini, eds.) (Milano: Giuffrè, 1985), pp. 421–464.

[93]See Roberto Isotton, Crimen in itinere. *Profili della disciplina del tentativo dal diritto comune alle codificazioni penali* (Napoli: Jovene, 2006), pp. 345 ff.; Sergio Seminara, *Il delitto tentato* (Milano: Giuffrè, 2012), chs I-III; Stefano Del Corso, "Il tentativo nel Codice Zanardelli", *I Codici preunitari e il Codice Zanardelli. Diritto penale dell'Ottocento* (Sergio Vinciguerra, ed.) (Padova: Cedam, 1999), pp. 512–561; Giovanni Chiodi, "Il tentativo e la penalistica europea dal XIX al XXI secolo: una riflessione storica per il giurista contemporaneo", *Quaderni fiorentini per la storia del pensiero giuridico moderno*, 42 (2013) 601–637.

[94]See Floriana Colao, "Il problema delle circostanze del reato. Dall'*arbitrium* al 'potere discrezionale del giudice' nell'individualizzazione della pena. Un percorso italiano tra Otto e Novecento", *Attualità e storia delle circostanze del reato. Un istituto al bivio tra legalità e discrezionalità* (Roberto Bartoli and Michele Pifferi, eds.) (Milano: Giuffrè, 2016), pp. 79–99.

[95]Regarding the peculiar and more lenient system of penalties, different from the French one, elaborated by the Italian school see Annamaria Monti, "L'influence du Code Pénal français de 1810 sur les conceptions de la peine en Italie", *La Dimension Historique de la Peine 1810-2010*, (Yves Jeanclos, ed.) (Paris: Economica, 2013), pp. 277–292.

[96]See Floriana Colao, "'Il dolente regno delle pene'. Storie della 'varietà della idea fondamentale del giure punitivo' tra Ottocento e Novecento", in *Materiali per una storia della cultura giuridica*, 40/1 (2010), 129–156.

University of Bologna paved the way for another thirty years of strong contraposition between the positivist school and the classical school. The struggle, both methodological and theoretical, concerned all the tenets of criminal law, and among the most controversial issues were the notions of free will, criminal liability, determinism, and the individualization of punishment.[97] Thus, it is not surprising that even the adherents to these conflicting schools considered themselves to be followers of the Italian tradition of criminal law, which was under progressive transformation. Moreover, even during the fascist regime, criminal law scholars committed to prevent the criminal justice system from totalitarian degeneration by defending liberal principles and insisting on the need to maintain the legal tradition and avoid Nazi influences.[98]

Although the problem of the influence of the French (or other foreign) penal code was overcome, the use of rhetorical arguments referring to the Italian genius of criminal law and the national traditional identity at the roots of the criminal justice system proved to remain effective.

6 Conclusions

The influence of the French Penal Code of 1810 on Italian penal codifications can be analysed from three different viewpoints.

Firstly, the idea (or ideal) of a penal code as symbol of the unified nation and of centralized sovereignty was strongly influenced by the Napoleonic model. Despite draft codes were elaborated in Italy even before 1810, and some codes were also enacted, the myth of the Napoleonic Code as a sign of modernity, namely of

[97]See Mario Sbriccoli, *La penalistica civile*; Floriana Colao, "Le scuole penalistiche", in *Enciclopedia Italiana di scienze, lettere ed arti. Il contributo italiano alla storia del pensiero. Ottava appendice. Diritto* (Roma: Istituto della Enciclopedia Italiana, 2012), pp. 349–356; Michele Pifferi, *Reinventing Punishment. A Comparative History of Criminology and Penology in the 19th and 20th Century* (Oxford, Oxford University Press, 2016), ch. 2; Michele Pifferi, "Alla ricerca del «genio italico»: tradizione e progetti nella penalistica postunitaria", *Retoriche dei giuristi e costruzione dell'identità nazionale* (G. Cazzetta, ed.), (Bologna: Il Mulino, 2013), pp. 285–295.

[98]See Giorgio Marinucci, "Giuseppe Bettiol e la crisi del diritto penale negli anni Trenta", *Quaderni fiorentini per la storia del pensiero giuridico moderno*, 37 (2008), 325–347. On the role played by criminal law scholars soon after the fall of the fascist regime and during the period of transition towards the Republic, see Remo Pannain, "Notizie e spunti sulla riforma dei codici penali", *Archivio penale*, 1/1-2 (1945) 56–61; Luigi Lacchè, "«Sistemare il terreno e sgombrare le macerie». Gli anni della 'costituzione provvisoria': alle origini del discorso sulla riforma della legislazione e del codice di procedura penale (1943-1947)", *L'inconscio inquisitorio. L'eredità del Codice Rocco nella cultura processualpenalistica italiana* (Loredana Garlati, ed.) (Milano: Giuffrè, 2010), pp. 271–304; Massimo Donini, "La gestione penale del passaggio dal fascismo alla democrazia in Italia. Appunti sulla memoria storica e l'elaborazione del passato 'mediante il diritto penale'", *Materiali per una storia della cultura giuridica*, 39/1 (2009) 183–216.

centralization, systematization, rationalization and simplification of legal sources, is undeniable.

Secondly, in terms of their contents, there are similarities but also substantial differences between pre-Unitarian codes as well as the Zanardelli Code and the French Code of 1810. The choice for bipartition (rather than tripartition) of offences, a general inclination to leniency, and the great attention to the principle of proportionality are some characteristic features. Many rules or articles, rather than being the imprint of the Napoleonic model, were the reflection of a long doctrinal elaboration well rooted into the Italian tradition.

There is, finally, the rhetorical viewpoint. Political discourses on national identity and tradition led to emphasize the Italian genius of criminal law and the Italianness of penal code(s). A forced continuity of legal doctrines and institutions from Roman law to the 19th century is emphasised. Despite transitory political fragmentations and regional difference, a consistent and unitary matrix of the Italian criminal law is rediscovered (and partially invented) through historical studies. According to this interpretation grounded on national legal history there is no room for any influence of the French invader's penal code.

References

Amari, Emerico, "Degli elementi che costituiscono la scienza del Diritto Penale. Tentativo di una teoria del progresso", *Filosofia civile e diritto comparato in Emerico Amari* (G. Bentivegna, ed.) (Napoli: Guida, 2003), pp. 246–270.

Amari, Emerico, "Delle vicende del Diritto penale nel Medio Evo. Parte prima", *Filosofia civile e diritto comparato in Emerico Amari* (G. Bentivegna, ed.) (Napoli: Guida, 2003), pp. 303–330.

Amari, Emerico, "Delle vicende del Diritto penale nel Medio Evo. Parte seconda", *Filosofia civile e diritto comparato in Emerico Amari* (G. Bentivegna, ed.) (Napoli: Guida, 2003), pp. 331–365.

Amari, Emerico, "Quadro storico dei progressi della Scienza, e delle Legislazioni criminali da Beccaria insino a Noi", *Filosofia civile e diritto comparato in Emerico Amari* (G. Bentivegna, ed.) (Napoli: Guida, 2003), pp. 167–218.

Ambrosoli, Filippo, *Studi sul Codice penale toscano confrontato specialmente coll'austriaco* (Mantova: Negretti e Comp., 1857).

Ambrosoli, Filippo, *Sulla nuova codificazione nei regj stati. Osservazioni* (Pavia: Tipografia dei Fratelli Fusi, 1860).

Arabia, Francesco Saverio, *Del Codice penale italiano* (Napoli: Tip. della Regia Università, 1887).

Arabia, Francesco Saverio, *Sull'applicazione del codice penale italiano* (Napoli: Tip. della Regia Università, 1893).

Benevolo, Federico, *L'unificazione della legislazione penale e la pena suprema* (Torino: Unione Tipografico-Editrice, 1890).

Borsari, Luigi, *Della azione penale* (Torino: Unione Tipografico-Editrice, 1866).

Bosellini, Ludovico, "Lettera sulla Codificazione, specialmente in Italia, e sul Codice civile già progettato in Toscana", *La Temi. Giornale di legislazione e giurisprudenza*, 4/37 (1853) 393–396.

Brusa, Emilio, "L'unificazione penale e la politica", *Rivista penale*, 1 (1874), pp. 24–37.

Cadoppi Alberto, "Il 'modello italiano' di codice penale. Dalle 'origini lombarde' ai progetti di un nuovo codice penale", *L'Indice Penale*, 1(2003), 19–74.

Cadoppi Alberto, "Il codice penale parmense del 1820", *I Codici preunitari e il Codice Zanardelli. Diritto penale dell'Ottocento* (Sergio Vinciguerra, ed.) (Padova: Cedam, 1999), pp. 196–272.
Calà Ulloa, Pietro, "Delle vicissitudini e de' progressi del diritto penale in Italia dal risorgimento delle lettere sin oggi", *Il Progresso delle scienze, delle lettere e delle arti*, 16 (1837), n. 31 pp. 30–57; n. 32, pp. 193-222; 17 (1837), n. 33, pp. 28–46.
Calisse, Carlo, "Svolgimento storico del diritto penale in Italia dalle invasioni barbariche alle riforme del secolo XVIII", *Enciclopedia del diritto penale italiano* (E. Pessina, ed.), vol. II (Milano: Società Editrice Libraria, 1906), pp. 1–538.
Cappellini, Paolo, "Francesco Carrara e il problema della codificazione del diritto", *Criminalia*, 2 (2007), 305–323.
Carrara, Francesco "Se la unità sia condizione del giure penale (Prolusione al corso accademico dell'anno 1865-66)", *Opuscoli di diritto criminale* (F. Carrara), II (Lucca: Giusti, 1870), p. 6–39.
Carrara, Francesco, "Codicizzazione (Studi legislativi)", *Opuscoli di diritto criminale* (F. Carrara), II (Lucca: Giusti, 1870), p. 217–230.
Carrara, Francesco, "Scienza criminale e scienza penale", *Opuscoli di diritto criminale* (F. Carrara), VII (Prato: Giachetti, 1887), pp. 5–22.
Carrara, Francesco, "Varietà della idea fondamentale del giure punitivo (Prolusione al corso accademico dell'anno 1862-63)", *Opuscoli di diritto criminale* (F. Carrara), I (Lucca: Giusti, 1870), pp. 153–188.
Cavanna Adriano, "Codificazione del diritto italiano e imperialismo giuridico francese nella Milano napoleonica. Giuseppe Luosi e il diritto penale", *Ius Mediolani. Studi di storia del diritto milanese offerti dagli allievi a Giulio Vismara* (Milano: Giuffrè, 1996), pp. 659–760.
Cavanna Adriano, "Mito e destini del Code Napoléon in Italia", *Europa e diritto privato* (2001) 85–129.
Cavanna Adriano, *La codificazione penale in Italia. Le origini lombarde* (Milano: Giuffrè, 1975).
Cavanna Adriano, *Storia del diritto moderno in Europa. Le fonti e il pensiero giuridico*, II (Milano: Giuffrè, 2005).
Cavanna Adriano, Vanzelli Gianfrancesco, *Il primo progetto di codice penale per la Lombardia napoleonica (1801-1802)* (Padova: Cedam, 2000).
Cazzetta Giovanni, *Codice civile e identità giuridica nazionale. Percorsi e appunti per una storia delle codificazioni moderne* (Torino: Giappichelli, 2011).
Chiodi, Giovanni, "Il tentativo e la penalistica europea dal XIX al XXI secolo: una riflessione storica per il giurista contemporaneo", *Quaderni fiorentini per la storia del pensiero giuridico moderno*, 42 (2013) 601–637.
Colao, Floriana, "'Il dolente regno delle pene'. Storie della 'varietà della idea fondamentale del giure punitivo' tra Ottocento e Novecento", in *Materiali per una storia della cultura giuridica*, 40/1 (2010), 129–156.
Colao, Floriana, "Il problema delle circostanze del reato. Dall'*arbitrium* al 'potere discrezionale del giudice' nell'individualizzazione della pena. Un percorso italiano tra Otto e Novecento", *Attualità e storia delle circostanze del reato. Un istituto al bivio tra legalità e discrezionalità* (Roberto Bartoli and Michele Pifferi, eds.) (Milano: Giuffrè, 2016), pp. 79–108.
Colao, Floriana, "Le scuole penalistiche", in *Enciclopedia Italiana di scienze, lettere ed arti. Il contributo italiano alla storia del pensiero. Ottava appendice. Diritto* (Roma: Istituto della Enciclopedia Italiana, 2012), pp. 349–356.
Colao, Floriana, "Profili di federalismo penale in Italia dall'Unità al Codice Zanardelli", *Rivista di storia del diritto italiano*, 84 (2011), 103–117.
Costa Pietro, "Un diritto italiano? Il discorso giuridico nella formazione dello Stato italiano", *Retoriche dei giuristi e costruzione dell'identità nazionale* (Giovanni Cazzetta, ed.) (Bologna: Il Mulino, 2013) pp. 163–200.
Crisafulli Zappalà, Benedetto, "Autorità degli italiani nella scienza del diritto", *La Temi. Giornale di legislazione e giurisprudenza*, 6 (1857) 365 ff., 484 ff., 596 ff., 726 ff.; 7 (1859) 30 ff., 103 ff., 171 ff., 238 ff., 287 ff., 336 ff., 401 ff.

Da Passano Mario, "La codification du droit pénal dans l'Italie "jacobine" et napoléonienne", *Révolution et justice pénale en Europe. Modèles français et traditions nationales (1780-1830)* (X. Rousseaux, M.-S. Dupont-Bouchat, C. Vael., eds.) (Paris: L'Harmattan, 1999), pp. 85–99.

Da Passano Mario, *Emendare o intimidire? La codificazione del diritto penale in Francia e in Italia durante la Rivoluzione e l'Impero* (Torino: Giappichelli, 2000).

Da Passano, Mario, "Il problema dell'unificazione legislativa e l'abrogazione del codice napoletano", *Codice per lo Regno delle Due Sicilie (1819). Parte seconda. Leggi penali* (Padova: Cedam, 1996), pp. LXIX–CXLII.

Da Passano, Mario, "La codificazione penale nel Granducato di Toscana (1814-1860)", *Codice Penale pel Granducato di Toscana (1853)* (rist. anastatica, Padova: Cedam, 1995), pp. VII–XLVII.

Da Passano, Mario, "La pena di morte nel Regno d'Italia (1859-1889)", *I Codici preunitari e il Codice Zanardelli. Diritto penale dell'Ottocento* (Sergio Vinciguerra, ed.) (Padova: Cedam, 1999), pp. 579–651.

Da Passano, Mario, "La storia esterna del codice penale toscano (1814-1859)", *Istituzioni e società in Toscana nell'età moderna. Atti delle giornate di studio dedicate a Giuseppe Pansini: Firenze 4-5 dicembre 1992*, vol. 2 (Roma: Ministero per i beni culturali e ambientali, 1994), pp. 564–589.

De Cola Proto, Francesco, *L'unificazione legislativa e le riforme procedurali* (Messina: Tipogr. Dell'Epoca - Sava e Anastasi, 1891).

De Francesco, Giovannangelo, "Funzioni della pena e limiti della coercizione: caratteri ed eredità del classicismo penale", *Quaderni fiorentini per la storia del pensiero giuridico moderno*, 36 (2007), 611–662.

De Mauro, Mario, "L'ufficio della pena e il nuovo codice penale italiano", *Antologia Giuridica*, 4/1 (1890) 22–42.

Del Corso, Stefano, "Il tentativo nel Codice Zanardelli", *I Codici preunitari e il Codice Zanardelli. Diritto penale dell'Ottocento* (Sergio Vinciguerra, ed.) (Padova: Cedam, 1999), pp. 512–561.

Del Giudice, Pasquale, "Diritto penale germanico rispetto all'Italia", *Enciclopedia del diritto penale italiano* (E. Pessina, ed.), vol I (Milano: Società Editrice Libraria, 1905), pp. 429–609.

Dezza Ettore, "Appunti sulla codificazione penale nel primo Regno d'Italia: il progetto del 1809", *Saggi di storia del diritto penale moderno* (Ettore Dezza) (Milano: LED, 1992), pp. 199–280.

Dezza, Ettore, "Il « colpo di stato legislativo » del 1859 e la nascita del codice Rattazzi, *Il Codice Penale per gli Stati del Re di Sardegna e per l'Italia unita (1859)*, (Sergio Vinciguerra, ed.) (Padova: Cedam, 2008), pp. XI–XX.

Dezza, Ettore, "Il problema della pena di morte", *Enciclopedia Italiana di scienze, lettere ed arti. Il contributo italiano alla storia del pensiero. Ottava appendice. Diritto* (Roma: Istituto dell'Enciclopedia Treccani, 2012), pp. 223–231.

Dezza, Ettore, *Il Codice di procedura penale del Regno Italico (1807). Storia di un decennio di elaborazione legislativa* (Padova: Cedam, 1983).

Donini, Massimo, "La gestione penale del passaggio dal fascismo alla democrazia in Italia. Appunti sulla memoria storica e l'elaborazione del passato 'mediante il diritto penale'", *Materiali per una storia della cultura giuridica*, 39/1 (2009) 183–216.

Drage Geoffrey, *The Criminal Code of the German Empire* (London: Chapman and Hall, 1885).

Ellero, Pietro, "Della critica criminale", *Trattati criminali* (P. Ellero) (Bologna: Fava e Garagnani 1875), pp. 93–94.

Ellero, Pietro, "Delle origini storiche del diritto di punire", *Giornale per l'abolizione della pena di morte* 3 (1862) 218–262.

Ellero, Pietro, "Note critiche al primo libro del Codice penale italiano", *Opuscoli criminali* (P. Ellero), (Bologna: Fava e Garagnani, 1874), p. 318–324.

Ellero, Pietro, "Sulla revisione delle leggi penali del Regno d'Italia", Giornale per l'abolizione della pena di morte, X (1865), pp. 200–221.

Ferrante, Riccardo, *Un secolo sì legislativo. La genesi del modello otto-novecentesco di codificazione e la cultura giuridica* (Torino, Giappichelli, 2015).

Ferrini, Contardo, "Esposizione storica e dottrinale del diritto penale romano", *Enciclopedia del diritto penale italiano* (E. Pessina, ed.), vol I (Milano: Società Editrice Libraria, 1905), pp. 1–428.

Geri, Marco Paolo, "'La metamorfosi che la politica voleva fare a danno della giustizia'. Francesco Carrara e l'unità del 'giure penale'", *Materiali per la storia della cultura giuridica moderna*, 35/2 (2005) 333–359.

Isotton, Roberto, Crimen in itinere. *Profili della disciplina del tentativo dal diritto comune alle codificazioni penali* (Napoli: Jovene, 2006).

Lacchè, Luigi, "«Sistemare il terreno e sgombrare le macerie ». Gli anni della 'costituzione provvisoria': alle origini del discorso sulla riforma della legislazione e del codice di procedura penale (1943-1947)", *L'inconscio inquisitorio. L'eredità del Codice Rocco nella cultura processualpenalistica italiana* (Loredana Garlati, ed.) (Milano: Giuffrè, 2010), pp. 271–304.

Lacchè, Luigi, "La penalistica costituzionale e il 'liberalismo giuridico'. Problemi e immagini della legalità nella riflessione di Francesco Carrara", *Quaderni fiorentini per la storia del pensiero giuridico moderno*, 36 (2007), 663–695.

Lacchè, Luigi, "Un code pénal pour l'Unité italienne: le code Zanardelli (1889). La genèse, le débat, le projet juridique", *Le pénal dans tous ses états. Justice, Etats et Sociétés en Europe (XIIe–XXe siècles)* (R. Levy and X. Rousseaux, eds.) (Bruxelles: Publications de l'Université Saint-Louis), pp. 303–319.

Le leggi penali di Giuseppe Bonaparte per il Regno di Napoli (1808) (Padova: Cedam, 1998).

Lucchini, Luigi, "La Terza Serie della Rivista penale", *Rivista penale*, 31 (1890), pp. 5–9.

Lucchini, Luigi, *Della dignità politica del diritto penale* (Siena: Lazzeri, 1878).

Marinucci, Giorgio, "Giuseppe Bettiol e la crisi del diritto penale negli anni Trenta", *Quaderni fiorentini per la storia del pensiero giuridico moderno*, 37 (2008), 325–347.

Mastroberti, Francesco, *Codificazione e giustizia penale nelle Sicilie dal 1808 al 1820* (Napoli: Jovene, 2001).

Mazzacane, Aldo, "Una scienza per due regni: la penalistica napoletana della restaurazione", *Codice per lo Regno delle Due Sicilie (1819). Parte seconda. Leggi penali* (Padova: Cedam, 1996), pp. XXVII–XLIV.

Mele, Franca, *Un codice unico per un'Italia nuova. Il progetto di codice penale di Pasquale Stanislao Mancini* (Roma: Carocci, 2002).

Miletti, Marco Nicola, "«Piemontesizzare le contrade italiane ». L'adeguamento del codice penale sardo alle provincie meridionali", *Il Codice Penale per gli Stati del Re di Sardegna e per l'Italia unita (1859)*, (Sergio Vinciguerra, ed.) (Padova: Cedam, 2008), pp. CV–CXXXIII.

Miletti, Marco Nicola, "Enrico Pessina", *Dizionario Biografico degli Italiani*, vol. 82 (Roma: Istituto della Enciclopedia Italiana, 2015).

Miletti, Marco Nicola, "L'ultima pietra. Il contributo di Enrico Pessina alla formazione del codice Zanardelli", *Diritto penale XXI secolo*, IX/2 (2010) 393–411.

Monti, Annamaria, "L'influence du Code Pénal français de 1810 sur les conceptions de la peine en Italie", *La Dimension Historique de la Peine 1810-2010*, (Yves Jeanclos, ed.) (Paris: Economica, 2013), pp. 277–292.

Napodano, Gabriele, *Il diritto penale romano nelle sue attenenze col diritto penale moderno* (Napoli: G. de Angelis e Figlio, 1878).

Napodano, Gabriele, *Posto che occupa il codice italiano del 1859 in mezzo alle legislazioni odierne e di fronte alla scienza del giure penale* (Napoli: Gennaro De Angelis, 1888).

Nicolini, Niccola, "Dell'indole e del corso del diritto penale", *Quistioni di diritto trattate nelle conclusioni, ne' discorsi ed in altri scritti legali* (N. Nicolini) (Livorno: V. Mansi, 1844) pp. 171–180.

Nicolini, Niccola, "Delle attribuzioni della Corte suprema di giustizia. Discorso (Prima parte delle conclusioni nella causa Tobia Lepore, 2 giugno 1812)", *Quistioni di diritto trattate nelle conclusioni, ne' discorsi ed in altri scritti legali* (N. Nicolini) (Livorno: V. Mansi, 1844), pp. 9–29.

Padovani, Tullio, "Il binomio irriducibile. La distinzione dei reati in delitti e contravvenzioni, fra storia e politica criminale", *Diritto penale in trasformazione* (Giorgio Marinucci and Emilio Dolcini, eds.) (Milano: Giuffrè, 1985), pp. 421–464.
Padovani, Tullio, "La tradizione penalistica toscana nel codice Zanardelli", in *I Codici preunitari e il Codice Zanardelli. Diritto penale dell'Ottocento* (Sergio Vinciguerra, ed.) (Padova: Cedam, 1999), pp. 397–408.
Panattoni, Giuseppe, "Opinioni del Prof. Mittermaier sullo stato della scienza, e della legislazione penale in Germania, e in Italia", *La Temi. Giornale di legislazione e giurisprudenza*, 4/37 (1853) 47–53, 111–119.
Pannain, Remo, "Notizie e spunti sulla riforma dei codici penali", *Archivio penale*, 1/1–2 (1945) 56–61.
Paoli, Baldassare, "Della necessità di mantenere nelle nostre leggi penali il linguaggio giuridico italiano (Saggio di studio)", *Rivista penale* 1 (1874), p. 11–23.
Pessina, Enrico, "Cenni sul movimento del diritto penale in Italia dal 1868 al 1874", *Discorsi varii* (E. Pessina), vol. VII (Napoli: Casa ed. Napoletana, 1916), pp. 171–191.
Pessina, Enrico, "Del diritto penale nel Regno d'Italia dal 1859 sino al 1867", *Discorsi varii* (E. Pessina), vol. VII (Napoli: Casa ed. Napoletana, 1916), pp. 87–169.
Pessina, Enrico, "Discorso inaugurale alle lezioni di Diritto penale letto nella Regia Università di Napoli il dì 5 dicembre 1861", *Discorsi varii* (E. Pessina) (Napoli: Casa ed. Napoletana, 1915) vol. VI, pp. 35–57.
Pessina, Enrico, "Il diritto penale in Italia da Cesare Beccaria sino alla promulgazione del codice penale vigente (1764-1890)", *Enciclopedia del diritto penale italiano* (E. Pessina, ed.), vol. II (Milano: Società Editrice Libraria, 1906), pp. 539–768.
Pessina, Enrico, "Introduzione al diritto penale in Italia al 1847 (1863)", *Discorsi varii* (E. Pessina) vol. VII (Napoli: Casa ed. Napoletana, 1916) pp. 1–31.
Pessina, Enrico, "Movimento legislativo del diritto penale in Italia dal 1874 al 1887", *Discorsi varii* (E. Pessina), vol. VII (Napoli: Casa ed. Napoletana, 1916), pp. 193–225.
Pessina, Enrico, "Movimento legislativo e scientifico del diritto penale negli stati italiani dal 1848 al 1859 (1863)", *Discorsi varii* (E. Pessina), vol. VII (Napoli: Casa ed. Napoletana, 1916), pp. 33–85.
Pessina, Enrico, *Dei progressi del diritto penale nel secolo XIX* (Firenze: Civelli, 1868).
Pessina, Enrico, *La riforma del diritto penale in Italia nella seconda metà del secolo decimottavo* (Napoli: Tessitore, 1905).
Pessina, Enrico, *Propedeutica al diritto penale delle Due Sicilie* (Napoli: Stabilimento tipografico dei classici italiani, 1858).
Pifferi, Michele, "Alla ricerca del « genio italico »: tradizione e progetti nella penalistica postunitaria", *Retoriche dei giuristi e costruzione dell'identità nazionale* (G. Cazzetta, ed.), (Bologna: Il Mulino, 2013), pp. 257–295.
Pifferi, Michele, "Difendere i confini, superare le frontiere. Le 'zone grigie' della legalità penale tra Otto e Novecento", in *Quaderni fiorentini per la storia del pensiero giuridico moderno*, 36 (2007), 743–799.
Pifferi, Michele, *Reinventing Punishment. A Comparative History of Criminology and Penology in the 19th and 20th Century* (Oxford, Oxford University Press, 2016).
Rapisardi, Emanuele, *Saggio d'un Progetto del Codice penale italiano corredato d'osservazioni* (Catania: Pietro Giuntini, 1862).
Recchia Angelo, *Discorso per la inaugurazione della cattedra universitaria di Diritto penale accresciuta al Real Liceo delle Puglie* (Bari: Tip. Gissi, 1865).
Rossi, Pietro, *Il senso della storia. Dal Settecento al Duemila* (Bologna: Il Mulino, 2012).
Sanford H.S., *The Different Systems of Penal Codes in Europe* (Washington: Beverley Tucker Senate Printer, 1854).
Santangelo Cordani, Anna, *Alla vigilia del Codice Zanardelli. Antonio Buccellati e la riforma penale nell'Italia postunitaria* (Milano: Giuffrè, 2008).

Sbriccoli Mario, "La penalistica civile: teorie e ideologie del diritto penale nell'Italia unita" (1990), *Storia del diritto penale e della giustizia. Scritti editi e inediti (1972– 2007)* (M. Sbriccoli) (Milano, Giuffrè, 2009) pp. 493–590.
Sbriccoli, Mario, "Il diritto penale liberale. La "Rivista Penale" di Luigi Lucchini 1874-1900", *Storia del diritto penale e della giustizia. Scritti editi e inediti (1972– 2007)* (M. Sbriccoli) (Milano: Giuffrè, 2009), II, pp. 903–979.
Sbriccoli, Mario, "Politica e giustizia in Francesco Carrara", *Storia del diritto penale e della giustizia. Scritti editi e inediti (1972– 2007)* (M. Sbriccoli) (Milano: Giuffrè, 2009), I, pp. 485–492.
Schiappoli, Domenico, "Diritto penale canonico", *Enciclopedia del diritto penale italiano* (E. Pessina, ed.), vol I (Milano: Società Editrice Libraria, 1905), pp. 611–967.
Seminara, Sergio, *Il delitto tentato* (Milano: Giuffrè, 2012).
Spinosa, Alberto, "«L'economia dei codici moderni ». Legislazione e giurisprudenza nella dottrina italiana dell'Ottocento, *Quaderni fiorentini per la storia del pensiero giuridico moderno*, 40 (2011) 747–780.
Stile, Alfonso Maria, "Il Codice penale del 1819 per lo Regno delle Due Sicilie", *I Codici preunitari e il Codice Zanardelli. Diritto penale dell'Ottocento* (Sergio Vinciguerra, ed.) (Padova: Cedam, 1999), pp. 183–195.
Tavilla, Elio, "Guerra contro il crimine. Pena di morte e abolizionismo nella cultura giuridica italiana", *Il diritto come forza la forza del diritto. Le fonti in azione nel diritto europeo tra medioevo ed età contemporanea* (Alberto Sciumè, ed.) (Torino: Giappichelli, 2012), pp. 151–185.
Vano, Cristina, "Ellero, Pietro", *Dizionario biografico degli italiani*, vol. XLII (Roma: Istituto della Enciclopedia Italiana, 1993), pp. 512–520.
Vinciguerra Sergio (ed.), *I Codici preunitari e il Codice Zanardelli. Diritto penale dell'Ottocento*, (Padova: Cedam, 1999).
Vinciguerra Sergio, "I codici penali sardo-piemontesi del 1839 e del 1859", *I Codici preunitari e il Codice Zanardelli. Diritto penale dell'Ottocento* (Sergio Vinciguerra, ed.) (Padova: Cedam, 1999), pp. 350–393.
Vinciguerra Sergio, "L'influence du Code de 1810 en Italie", *Les colloques du Sénat. Les actes. Bicentenaire du code pénal (1810-2010)*, (Paris: Sénat de France, 2010), pp. 110–121.
Vinciguerra, Sergio, "Fonti culturali ed eredità del codice penale toscano", *Codice Penale pel Granducato di Toscana (1853)* (rist. anastatica, Padova: Cedam, 1995), pp. CLIX–CLXXX.
Vormbaum Thomas, Bohlander Michael (eds.), *A Modern History of German Criminal Law* (Berlin – Heidelberg: Springer, 2014).

Michele Pifferi Law degree (cum laude) at the University of Ferrara (1999), Ph.D. at the University of Macerata (2004). From September to December 2002 visiting researcher at the Max-Planck-Institut für europäische Rechtsgeschichte in Frankfurt am Main. From 2003 to 2010 research fellow in Legal History at the University of Ferrara. From October 2010 to November 2017 Associate Professor of Legal History and from December 2017 Full Professor of Legal History at the University of Ferrara, Law Department. Emil Noël Fellow (Fall Semester 2009) at the Jean Monnet Center for International & Regional Economic Law and Justice, New York University School of Law. Robbins Fellow (September-October 2012) at Berkeley UC - School of Law. Academic Visitor at the Oxford Centre for Criminology, University of Oxford, from January to March 2014 and from September to October 2016. From November 2012 to December 2016 scientific coordinator of a research unit working on a national project (FIR) on "Migration Policies and Legal Transplant in the Mediterranean Area: Control Strategies between Colonialism and Post-Colonialism". From July 2015 to February 2017 Alexander von Humboldt Research Fellow at the University of Hamburg, Faculty of Law. From 2011 member of the Editorial Board of the series Rechtsgeschichte und Rechtsgeschehen—Italien (LIT Verlag), directed by Thomas

Vormbaum. His research interests focus on comparative legal history of criminal law and criminology and history of immigration law. He has written three monographs: Reinventing Punishment. A Comparative History of Criminology and Penology in the 19th and 20th Century (Oxford: OUP, 2016); L'individualizzazione della pena. Difesa sociale e crisi della legalità penale tra Otto e Novecento (Milano, 2013); Generalia delictorum. Il Tractatus criminalis di Tiberio Deciani e la "parte generale" di diritto penale (Milano, 2006). He has co-edited the books: Il controllo dello straniero. I "campi" dall'Ottocento ad oggi (Roma, 2017); Attualità e storia delle circostanze del reato. Un istituto al bivio tra legalità e discrezionalità (Milano, 2016); Diritti individuali e processo penale nell'Italia repubblicana (Milano, 2011); Diritto contro. Meccanismi giuridici di esclusione dello straniero (Torino, 2009). Among his articles: Global Criminology and National Tradition: The Impact of Reform Movements on Criminal Systems at the Beginning of the 20th Century, in T. Duve (ed), Entanglements in Legal History: Conceptual Approaches, Global Perspectives on Legal History (Frankfurt a. M., 2014); Individualization of Punishment and the Rule of Law: Reshaping Legality in the United States and Europe between the 19th and the 20th Century, in «The American Journal of Legal History», 52/3 (2012). Full publications on: http://docente.unife.it/michele.pifferi.

The Myth of French Influence Over Spanish Codification: The General Part of the Criminal Codes of 1822 and 1848

Aniceto Masferrer

Abstract The chapter aims to explore the scope of the foreign influences, that of the French in particular, in the criminal codes of 1822 and 1848/50. In doing so, the author departs from the views of some 19th century criminal lawyers who, like J. F. Pacheco, stated that in the old criminal laws "nothing was worthy of respect, or conservation" and "there was only one legitimate and viable system, the system of codification, the system of absolute change," and recognizing that drafters were fully acquainted with the case of France, a jurisdiction that managed to turn its old laws—including the criminal ones—into modern codes (1804–1811). The author briefly presents the *status quaestionis* of the dichotomy between tradition and foreign influences in the 19th century codification of criminal law, then focuses on the scope of French influence in the criminal codes of 1822 and 1848/50, and concludes with some final considerations.

1 Introduction: The Long Shadow of French Codification Over Spain

In 19th century Europe, French codes were familiar to all lawyers and politicians who were even remotely involved in drafting or approving laws. The long shadow of French codification was also present in Spain. In this chapter I will restrict myself to the domain of criminal law.

This work was undertaken in the context of two research projects entitled "La influencia de la Codificación francesa en la tradición penal española: su concreto alcance en la Parte General de los Códigos decimonónicos" (ref. DER2012-38469), and "Las influencias extranjeras en la Codificación penal española: su concreto alcance en la Parte Especial de los Códigos decimonónicos" (ref. DER2016-78388-P), both financed by the Spanish 'Ministerio de Economía y Competitividad.'

A. Masferrer (✉)
University of Valencia, Valencia, Spain
e-mail: aniceto.masferrer@uv.es

A. Masferrer (ed.), *The Western Codification of Criminal Law*, Studies in the History of Law and Justice 11, https://doi.org/10.1007/978-3-319-71912-2_8

Referring to the first Spanish criminal code (CP 1822), Federico García Goyena, a prestigious lawyer and famous politician of the 19th century, stated that "it could be said in general terms that it was a copy of the French one."[1]

Five years later, Joaquín Francisco Pacheco, a member of the committee in charge of drafting the criminal code of 1848 (CP 1848) and its main commentator,[2] giving a more balanced view of the CP 1822, affirmed that "it was composed of the *Fuero Juzgo* and *Partidas*, mixed with the character of the Code of Napoleon."[3] Explaining the variety of sources he used in his concordances with the CP 1848—both antecedent (*Fuero Juzgo*, *Fuero Real*, *Partidas*, *Novísima Recopilación*) and contemporary (the criminal codes of France, Austria, Naples and Brazil)—, he featured the French source as "the model of all present ones."[4]

Benito Gutiérrez Fernández, a Spanish lawyer who wrote a book on the historical development of criminal law, compared the CP 1848 and its French counterpart and pointed out that the former was in many respects superior to the latter, although it should have emulated more faithfully the preciseness and clarity of its French model."[5]

If in the old criminal laws, as Pacheco affirmed, "nothing was worthy of respect, or conservation" and "there was only one legitimate and viable system, the system of codification, the system of absolute change,"[6] the fixation on France,

---

[1]Florencio García Goyena, *Código criminal español, según las leyes vigentes, comentado y comparado con el penal de 1822, el francés y el inglés*, t. I (Madrid, 1843), p. 12: "...en general puede decirse que está calcado sobre el francés de 1810." Unless otherwise indicated, all translations are the author's.

[2]On this matter, see Eugenio Cuello Calón, "Centenario del Código de 1848: Pacheco, penalista y legislador", *Información Jurídica* (Madrid, 1948), pp. 5–8; Luis Jiménez de Asúa, "Pacheco, en el centenario del Código penal español", *El Criminalista* (Buenos Aires) 9 (1951), pp. 20–22; José Antón Oneca, "El Código penal de 1848 y D. Joaquín Francisco Pacheco", *Anuario de Derecho Penal y de las Ciencia Penales* 18 (1965), pp. 473–495; Francisco Candil Jiménez, "Observaciones sobre la intervención de D. Joaquín Francisco Pacheco en la colaboración del Código Penal de 1848", *ADPCP* 28 (1975), pp. 405–441; M. Magdalena Rodríguez Gil, "Joaquín Francisco Pacheco, un penalista en el marco constitucional", *Revista de la Facultad de derecho de la Universidad Complutense* 83 (1993–1994), pp. 259–294; R. Revuelta Benito, "El Código penal de 1848 y su gran comentarista don Joaquín Francisco Pacheco", *Revista de Estudios Penales* 6 (1945), p. 31 ff.; Pacheco also wrote his *Estudios de Derecho Penal* (lectures given at the *Ateneo* of Madrid) (Madrid, 1868).

[3]Joaquín Francisco Pacheco, *Código penal concordado y comentado* (Madrid, 1856), 2nd ed., t. I, p. 54: "*...en él algo del Fuero Juzgo y de las Partidas, envuelto con el carácter del código de Napo-león*".

[4]Pacheco, *El Código penal concordado y comentado*, LXII: "...el francés, modelo de todos los del día".

[5]Benito Gutiérrez Fernández, *Examen histórico del Derecho penal* (Madrid, 1866), p. 245: "*...un poco severo, menos preciso y claro de lo que convenía imitar, aunque me-jorándose en muchos puntos al Código francés*".

[6]Pacheco, *El Código penal concordado y comentado*, LII: "... [A] rule in which nothing was worthy of respect, or conservation: no part could be saved for the ordering of future society. All of it, entirely all, needed to be left behind (...) The cart of destruction and reform had to pass through the ruined building, because in it there was scarcely an arch, scarcely a column, that could nor should be saved ... In Spanish criminal law there was only one legitimate and viable system, the system of codification, the system of absolute change".

a jurisdiction that managed to turn its old laws—including the criminal ones—into modern codes (1804–1811), is understandable. Whereas the 18th century idea of the code[7] could not entirely solve the "criminal problem,"[8] the French Revolution and the introduction of the liberal system provided a model of how to undertake criminal law reform in line with Enlightenment thought. The advent of constitutional liberalism eclipsed 18th century resistance to the rationalist method,[9] and it marked the beginning of a modern conception of code.[10] In other words, the constitutional system constituted a precondition (*conditio sine qua non*) for the codification process.[11]

In Spain—as in other European jurisdictions—18th century criminal law was in need of reform.[12] The introduction of a liberal system paved the way for criminal law reform, which was noticeable from its inception at the beginning of the 19th century in the parliament of Cádiz[13] and in its constitution

---

[7]Bartolomé Clavero, "Idea de Código en la Ilustración Jurídica", *Historia. Instituciones. Documentos (HID)* 6 (1979), pp. 49–88.

[8]Giovanni Tarello, *Storia della cultura giuridica moderna.* Vol. I: Assolutismo e codificazione del diritto (Bologna, 1976), p. 383; for an interesting treatment of Enlightenement thought and criminal law, see pp. 383–483.

[9]Manuel Bermejo Castrillo, "Primeras luces de codificación. El Código como concepto y temprana memoria de su advenimiento en España", *AHDE* 83 (2013), pp. 9–64, particularly pp. 23–34, where he shows how the rationalist method encountered the resistance of tradition.

[10]Bermejo Castrillo, "Primeras luces de codificación…," pp. 34–48, 55 ff.; see also Bartolomé Clavero, "La disputa del método en las postrimerías de una sociedad, 1789–1808", *AHDE* 48 (1978), pp. 307–334; Carlos Petit, "El código inexistente (I). Por una historia conceptual de la cultura jurídica en la España del siglo XIX", *Anuario de Derecho Civil*, t. XLVIII, fasc. IV (octubre-diciembre 1995), pp. 1429–1465, pp. 1432–1444.

[11]Francisco Tomás y Valiente, "La codificación de utopía a técnica vulgarizada", *Códigos y Constituciones (1808–1978)* (Madrid: Alianza, 1989), pp. 11–124; Bartolomé Clavero, "Origen constitucional de la codificación civil en España (entre Francia y Norteamérica)", C. Petit (coord.), *Derecho privado y revolución burguesa* (Madrid: Marcial Pons, 1990), pp. 53–85; see also Juan Baró Pazos, "El proceso de la codificación del Derecho en el marco del constitucionalismo español", E. Martínez Ruiz, M. Torres Aguilar y M. de Pazzis Pi Corrales (eds.), *Codificación y constitucionalismo: Actas del IX Encuentro España-Suecia* (Córdoba: Diputación de Córdoba, 2003), pp. 22–40.

[12]A description of the Spanish criminal law in the 18th century can be found in Isabel Ramos Vázquez, "Las reformas borbónicas en el Derecho penal y de Policía criminal de la España dieciochesca", *forum historiae iuris* (available at http://www.forhistiur.de/zitat/1001ramos.htm); an 18th century view of that period of criminal-law can be found in Joaquín Cadafalch y Burguñá, *Discurso sobre el atraso y descuido del Derecho penal hasta el siglo XVIII* (Madrid, 1849); for a comparative analysis, see also Isabel Ramos Vázquez, "Criminal Law Reform in the Eighteenth Century Europe. A comparative study: England, France, Spain", *International Journal of Humanities and Social Science*, vol. 2, n 4 (special issue- February 2012), pp. 26–37.

[13]J. Babiano Mora / A. Fernández Asperilla, "Justicia y delito en el Discurso liberal de las Cortes de Cádiz", *Antiguo Régimen y Liberalismo. Homenaje a Miguel* Artola, vol. 2, Economía y Sociedad (Madrid, 1995), pp. 387–399; see also Mª Paz Alonso Romero, *Orden procesal y garantías entre Antiguo Régimen y constitucionalismo gaditano* (Madrid: Centro de Estudios Constitucionales, 2008); Isabel Ramos Vázquez, "La Comisión de Justicia y el Proyecto de Reglamento para causas criminales de 1811", *Revista de la Facultad de Ciencias Sociales y Jurídicas de la Universidad Miguel Hernández* 5 (2009), pp. 93–112; sobre la regulación del delito

(1812).[14] The absolutist period (1814–1820) impeded the promulgation of any code. The codification process resumed in the Liberal Triennium (*Trienio liberal*, 1820–1823), when the parliament discussed and approved the first modern Spanish code: the criminal code of 1822 (CP 1822).[15] Unfortunately, it was hardly in force (from January to early April 1823)[16] before the return of Fernando VII (1823), who, aided by the 'Hundred Thousand Sons of Saint Louis' (the popular name for a

de traición en las Cortes de Cádiz, véase el estudio de Aniceto Masferrer, "The Crime of *infidencia* in the Cortes of Cádiz: An Approach to the Crime of Treason during the Early Spanish Constitutionalism (1808–1814)," *Revolten und politische Verbrechen zwischen dem 12. und 19. Jahrhundert. Rechtliche Reaktionen und juristisch-politische Diskurse / Revolts and Political Crime from the 12th to the 19th Century. Legal Responses and Juridical-Political Discourses*, herausgegeben von Angela De Benedictis und Karl Härter unter redaktioneller Mitarbeit von Tina Hannappel und Thomas Walter (Studien zur europäischen Rechtsgeschichte 285) (Frankfurt am Main: Klostermann 2013), pp. 447–473.

[14]On this matter, see Juan Sainz Guerra, "La Constitución de 1812: de las reformas penales y procesales a la abolición de la tortura", *Cortes y Constitución de Cádiz. 200 años* (Escudero López, J. A., dir.), tomo II (Madrid, 2011), pp. 247–276; David Torres Sanz, "El liberalismo gaditano ante el Derecho penal", *Cortes y Constitución de Cádiz. 200 años* (Escudero López, J. A., dir.), tomo II (Madrid, 2011), pp. 277–284; Blanca Sáenz de Santa María Gómez Mampaso, "Codificación y formación de los Códigos civil, criminal y mercantil", *Cortes y Constitución de Cádiz. 200 años* (Escudero López, J. A., dir.), tomo II (Madrid, 2011), pp. 467–481; Isabel Ramos Vázquez, "Principios procesales en la Constitución de Cádiz. De la administración de Justicia en lo civil y en lo criminal", *Sobre un hito jurídico. La Constitución de 1812. Reflexiones actuales, estado de la cuestión, debates historiográficos* (Chamocho Cantudo, M.A., Lozano Miralles, J., edit.) (Jaén: Universidad de Jaén, 2012), pp. 469–482; I.F. Benítez Ortúzar, "El principio de legalidad penal en la Constitución española de 1812. Su proyección en el Código Penal de 1822", *Sobre un hito jurídico. La Constitución de 1812. Reflexiones actuales, estado de la cuestión, debates historiográficos* (Chamocho Cantudo, M. A., Lozano Miralles, J., edit.) (Jaén: Universidad de Jaén, 2012), pp. 195–209.

[15]Manuel Torres Aguilar, *Génesis parlamentaria del Código penal de 1822* (Sicania University Press, 2008); see also Manuel Torres Aguilar, "El proceso de la primera codificación penal y la Constitución de Cádiz", *Cortes y Constitución de Cádiz. 200 años* (Escudero López, J. A., dir.), tomo II (Madrid, 2011), pp. 442–468; José R. Casabó Ruíz, *El Código penal de 1822* (Valencia, 1968, Doctoral thesis unpublished); see also J.F. Lasso Gaite, *Crónica de la Codificación española. Codi-ficación penal* (Madrid, 1970), vol. 5-I, pp. 142–144.

[16]On the validity of the CP 1822, see J.M. Alonso y Alonso, "De la vigencia y aplicación del Código Penal de 1822", *Revista de Estudios penitenciarios* 11 (1946), pp. 2–15, José Antón Oneca, "Historia del Código Penal de 1822", *Anuario de Derecho Penal y Ciencias Penales* 18 (1965), pp. 263 ss.; F. Javier Álvarez García, "Contribución al estudio sobre la aplicación del Código Penal de 1822", *Cuadernos de Política criminal,* (1978), p. 229 ss.; Alicia Fiestas Loza, "Algo más sobre la vigencia del Código penal de 1822", *Revista de Historia del Derecho*, Universidad de Granada, (1977–1978), II-l, p. 57 ss.; José R. Casabó Ruíz, "La aplicación del Código penal de 1822", *Anuario de Derecho penal y Ciencias penales,* fasc. II (1979), pp. 333–344; José Luis Bermejo Cabrero, "Sobre la entrada en vigor del Código Penal de 1822", *Anuario de Historia del Derecho Español*, 66 (1996), pp. 967–972; E. de, Benito Fraile, "Nuevas aportaciones al estudio sobre la aplicación práctica del Código Penal de 1822", *Foro. Nueva época* 8 (2008), pp. 41–68.

French army of Louis XVIII), reestablished royal absolutism. This absolute power abrogated all laws approved by the liberal government, including the CP 1822, and simultaneously reenacted and revalidated the previously existing criminal laws.[17] This situation lasted until the promulgation of the CP 1848,[18] five years after the creation of the General Commission of Codification.[19] Although two other criminal codes were approved during the 19th century (in 1850[20] and 1870[21]), these more accurately regarded as reforms of the CP 1848 rather than new codes. Moreover, the

[17]Juan Baró Pazos, "El derecho penal español en el vacío entre dos códigos (1822–1848)", *AHDE* 83 (2013), pp. 105–138.

[18]Mª Dolores del Mar Sánchez González, *Los Códigos Penales de 1848 y 1850* (Madrid, 2003); Emilia Iñesta-Pastor, *El Código penal de 1848* (Valencia: tirant lo blanc, 2010); see also F. Castejón, "Apuntes de historia política y legislativa del Código penal de 1848", *Revista General de Legislación y Jurisprudencia* (Madrid, 1953), pp. 105–113.

[19]Emilia Iñesta-Pastor, "La Comisión General de Codificación (1843–1997). De la codificación moderna a la descodificación contemporánea", *AHDE* 83 (2013), pp. 65–103; see also Gabriela Cobo del Rosal, *Las Actas de la Comisión General de Codificación* (Madrid: Dykinson, 2013); Gabriela Cobo del Rosal, *La creación Legislativa en materia penal en los Siglos de la Codificación XIX-XX* (Madrid: Dykinson, 2013).

[20]Sánchez González, *Los Códigos Penales de 1848 y 1850*, cited in fn n. 19.

[21]Ruperto Núñez Barbero, *La reforma penal de 1870* (Salamanca, 1969); José Antón Oneca, "El Código Penal de 1870", *Anuario del Derecho Penal y de las Ciencias Penales* 23 (1970), pp. 229–251; Jacobo López Barja de Quiroga, "El Código penal de 1870 y su contexto histórico", *Centenario del Código civil* (coord. E. Tierno Galván) (Madrid, 1989), vol. II, pp. 477–491; José Manuel Pérez-Prendes y Muñoz de Arraco, "La prensa y el Código penal de 1870", *Hispania* 31 (1971), pp. 551–579; Alicia Fiestas Loza, "La libertad de imprenta en las dos primeras etapas del liberalismo español", *Anuario de Historia del Derecho Español* 59 (1989), pp. 351–490; F. Castejón, "Las ideas penales en la época del Código penal de 1870", *Conmemoración del centenario de la Ley provisional sobre organización del Poder Judicial y del Código penal de 1870* (Madrid: Real Academia de Jurisprudencia y Legislación, 1970); Manuel Cobo del Rosal, "El sistema de penas y el arbitrio judicial en el Código penal de 1870", en conmemoración del centenario de la Ley provisional sobre organización del Poder Judicial y del Código penal de 1870 (Madrid: Real Academia de Jurisprudencia y Legislación, 1970), pp. 69–89; Juan del Rosal, "La palabra y la expresión en el Código penal de 1870", *Conmemoración del centenario de la Ley provisional sobre organización del Poder Judicial y del Código penal de 1870* (Madrid: Academia de Jurisprudencia y Legislación, 1970) (republished later, with the same title in *Cosas de Derecho penal* (Madrid, 1973), pp. 67–132.

20th century criminal codes (1928,[22] 1932,[23] 1944[24] and 1995) also drew heavily from the CP 1848.

Although the CP 1870 was valid for the longest period, the Spanish criminal codes of 1822 and 1848 are, in my view, more relevant from a historical perspective. Whereas the content and structure of latter two remained largely untouched throughout the time and outlasted the subsequent codes (1870, 1928, 1932, 1944 and 1995), the former was the first modern code in Spain.

This chapter aims to explore the scope of the foreign influences, that of the French in particular, in the criminal codes of 1822 and 1848/50. After the introduction (1), I will briefly present the *status quaestionis* of the dichotomy between tradition and foreign influences in the 19th century codification of criminal law (2). I then will focus on the scope of French influence (3) in the criminal codes of 1822 (3.1) and 1848/50 (3.2). I conclude with some final considerations (4).

When analyzing the extent of French influence in the Spanish codes of 1822 and 1848, I distinguish three different levels: (1) the inspiration arising out of the "modern idea of Code," an area in which French codes enjoyed indisputable—and

---

[22]Luis Jiménez de Asúa / José Antón Oneca, *Derecho penal conforme al Código penal de 1928. Parte general* (Madrid, 1929); José Antón Oneca, "Los antecedentes del nuevo Código penal", *Revista General de Legislación y Jurisprudencia* 154 (1929), pp. 30–61; F. Castejón, *Derecho penal, Criminología general y especial ajustada a la legislación española vigente hasta fin de 1930,* vol. I (Madrid, 1931); Eugenio Cuello Calón, *El nuevo Código penal español* (Barcelona, 1929); Eugenio Cuello Calón, *Código penal de 8 de septiembre de 1928* (Barcelona, 1929); J.M. Fabregas del Pilar, "El nuevo Código penal y el discurso del Señor Ministro de Gracia y Justicia en la apertura de los Tribunales", *Revista General de Legislación y Jurisprudencia*, 1928, p. 282 ff.; A. Jaramillo García, *Novísimo Código penal, comentado y cotejado con el de 1870* (Salamanca: Imprenta de Silvestre Ferreira, 1928); A. Pessini Pulido, "El nuevo Código penal", *Revista General de Legislación y Jurisprudencia* 154 (1929), pp. 314–322; Gabriela Cobo del Rosal, "Codificación en un periodo de alteración de los Derechos Fundamentales: el Código penal de 1928", *Estado de Derecho y derechos fundamentales en la lucha contra el terrorismo. Una aproximación multidisciplinar (histórica, jurídico-comparada, filosófica y económica* (Aniceto Masferrer, ed.) (Madrid, Aranzadi-Thomson Reuters, 2011).

[23]Eugenio Cuello Calón, *Exposición del Código penal reformado de 1932* (Barcelona, 1933); F. Castejón, *Derecho penal, Criminología general y especial*, t. I (Madrid, 1935); Luis Jiménez de Asúa, *La Legislación penal de la República española,* vol. LI (Madrid, 1932); Luis Jiménez de Asúa, "El Derecho penal vigente en la República española", *Revista de Derecho Público,* year I, vol. I (February 1932), pp. 39–48; Luis Jiménez de Asúa, *Código penal reformado de 27 de octubre de 1932 y disposiciones penales de la República*, vol. LV (Madrid, 1934); F. Puig Peña, *Código penal reformado* (Madrid, 1934); M. López-Rey y Arrojo / F. Álvarez Valdés, *El nuevo Código penal* (Madrid, 1933).

[24]F. Castejón, "Génesis y breve comentario del Código penal de 23 de diciembre de 1944", *Revista General de Legislación y Jurisprudencia* 9 (1945), pp. 170 ff., 327 ff., 457 ff., and 634 ff.; Eugenio Cuello Calón, "Reformas introducidas en el Código penal y en las Leyes penales especiales por la Legislación del nuevo Estado", *Revista de la Facultad de Derecho,* Madrid, 6–7 (July-December 1941), pp. 37–51; Eugenio Cuello Calón, *Derecho penal conforme al Código penal, Texto Refundido de 1944. Parte general* (Madrid, 1946); Eugenio Cuello Calón, *Manual de Derecho penal español conforme al nuevo Código penal. Parte general* (Barcelona, 1945); Juan del Rosal, "Ideas histórico-dogmáticas del Código penal de 1944", *Información jurídica*, Madrid 54 (1947), pp. 3–38; A. Ferrer Sama, *Comentarios al Código penal*. Murcia, 1946 (vol. I) and 1947 (vol. II); I. Sánchez Tejerina, *Derecho penal español* (Madrid, 1945).

undisputed—authority up to the mid-19th century; (2) the "formal/structural influence," which other European codes (including the Spanish one) could have followed to a greater or lesser extent; and (3) a "substantive influence" in the strictest sense, which allows determination of the extent to which notions, principles, and institutions from Spanish codes were inspired by the French model, whether they constituted an autochthonous legacy (or genuinely French), or were rather the product of the development of institutions derived from transnationally valid *ius commune* and integrated into the *iura propria* of several European territories.

An exhaustive analysis of the subject would exceed the limits of this chapter, but I hope this contribution might at least shed some light on whether the Spanish codification contributed to the nationalization or denationalization of criminal law.[25]

2 Tradition and Foreign Influences in the 19th Century Codification of Criminal Law: A Brief Historiographical Overview

The codification movement has been productively explored by Spanish scholars.[26] In the last decade Spanish historiography has shown the weight of tradition in the codification of criminal law,[27] but the scope of foreign influences had hardly been explored until more recently.

In 2014 an edited volume appeared with the aim of analyzing the doctrine and historiography of foreign influences, particularly that of the French,[28] and touching

[25]On this matter, see Aniceto Masferrer, "Codification as Nationalization or Denationalization of Law: The Spanish Case in Comparative Perspective", *Comparative Legal History* 4.2 (2016), pp. 100–130; see also Aniceto Masferrer, "La Codificación española y sus influencias extranjeras. Una revisión en torno al alcance del influjo francés", *La Codificación española. Una aproximación doctrinal e historiográfica a sus influencias extranjeras, y a la francesa en particular* (Aniceto Masferrer, ed.) (Pamplona: Aranzadi–Thomson Reuters, 2014), pp. 19–43.

[26]See, for example, Carlos García Valdés, "La Codificación penal y las primeras recopilaciones legislativas complementarias", *AHDE* 82 (2012), pp. 37–66. However, a book on the whole process would be welcome to complement J. González Miranda y Pizarro, *Historia de la Codificación penal española y crítica del Código vigente* (doctoral Thesis, unpublished) (Madrid, 1906).

[27]For an overview on the codification of criminal law in Spain, see Aniceto Masferrer, *Tradición y reformismo en la Codificación penal española. Hacia el ocaso de un mito. Materiales, apuntes y reflexiones para un nuevo enfoque metodológico e historiográfico del movimiento codificador penal europeo* (Jaén: University of Jaén, 2003); Aniceto Masferrer, "Codification of Spanish Criminal Law in the Nineteenth Century. A Comparative Legal History Approach", *Journal of Comparative Law* Vol. 4, no. 1 (2009), pp. 96–139; Aniceto Masferrer, "Liberal State and Criminal Law Reform in Spain", Sellers, Mortimer and Tomaszewski, Tadeusz (Eds.), *The Rule of Law in Comparative Perspective* (Springer, Series: *Ius Gentium: Comparative Perspectives on Law and Justice*, vol. 3, 2010), pp. 19–40.

[28]Aniceto Masferrer (ed.), *La Codificación española. Una aproximación doctrinal e historiográfica a sus influencias extranjeras, y a la francesa en particular* (Pamplona: Aranzadi–Thomson Reuters, 2014).

upon a variety of legal domains: civil law,[29] civil law procedure,[30] criminal law (CP 1822[31] and CP 1848[32]), criminal law procedure,[33] commercial law,[34] and mortgage law[35]). This book was the first autonomous and roughly comprehensive study of foreign influences on Spanish codification. However, prior works on this subject exist both in the civil law and criminal law domains.

From 2005 onwards works dealing with French influence on the Spanish codification of civil law have started to appear.[36]

---

[29]Juan Baró Pazos, "La influencia del Código civil francés (1804) en el Código civil español (1889)", *La Codificación española. Una aproximación doctrinal e historiográfica a sus influencias extranjeras, y a la francesa en particular* (Aniceto Masferrer, ed.) (Pamplona: Aranzadi–Thomson Reuters, 2014), pp. 53–128.

[30]Miguel Pino Abad, "Las leyes de enjuiciamiento civil de 1855 y 1881. Apuntes sobre las influencias recibidas y aportadas", *La Codificación española. Una aproximación doctrinal e historiográfica a sus influencias extranjeras, y a la francesa en particular* (Aniceto Masferrer, ed.) (Pamplona: Aranzadi–Thomson Reuters, 2014), pp. 429–447.

[31]Isabel Ramos Vázquez / Juan B. Cañizares, "La influencia francesa en la primera Codificación española: el Código penal francés de 1810 y el Código penal español de 1822", *La Codificación española. Una aproximación doctrinal e historiográfica a sus influencias extranjeras, y a la francesa en particular* (Aniceto Masferrer, ed.) (Pamplona: Aranzadi–Thomson Reuters, 2014), pp. 193–270.

[32]Aniceto Masferrer / Mª Dolores del Mar Sánchez-González, "Tradición e influencias extranjeras en el Código penal de 1848. Aproximación a un mito historiográfico" (con D. del M. Sánchez-González), *La Codificación española. Una aproximación doctrinal e historiográfica a sus influencias extranjeras, y a la francesa en particular* (Aniceto Masferrer, ed.) (Pamplona: Aranzadi–Thomson Reuters, 2014), pp. 271–349.

[33]Antonio Bádenas Zamora, "Influjos de la codificación en el proceso penal español", *La Codificación española. Una aproximación doctrinal e historiográfica a sus influencias extranjeras, y a la francesa en particular* (Aniceto Masferrer, ed.) (Pamplona: Aranzadi–Thomson Reuters, 2014), pp. 449–496.

[34]Dionisio A. Perona Tomás, "La influencia francesa en la codificación mercantil española del siglo XIX", *La Codificación española. Una aproximación doctrinal e historiográfica a sus influencias extranjeras, y a la francesa en particular* (Aniceto Masferrer, ed.) (Pamplona: Aranzadi–Thomson Reuters, 2014), pp. 351–427; see also Perona Tomás, Dionisio A., *Notas sobre el proceso de la Codificación mercantil en la España del siglo XIX* (Madrid: Dykinson, 2015).

[35]Margarita Serna Vallejo, "La influencia del derecho europeo, en particular del derecho francés, en la reforma hipotecaria española del siglo XIX a partir del análisis de la doctrina", *La Codificación española. Una aproximación doctrinal e historiográfica a sus influencias extranjeras, y a la francesa en particular* (Aniceto Masferrer, ed.) (Pamplona: Aranzadi–Thomson Reuters, 2014), pp. 129–191.

[36]Manuel J. Peláez Albendea, "Le *Code* de 1804, le *Code* civil espagnol de 1889 et le principe de la liberté (Réception particulière a l'Espagne)", *Le Code civil et les droits de l'homme* (Jean-Luc Chabot, Jean L., Ph. Didier, Ph., J. Ferrand, J., eds.), Actes du Colloque international de Grenoble (Paris, 2005), pp. 309–317; Carlos Petit, "España y el *Code* Napoleon", *Anuario de Derecho Civil* 41.4 (October 2008), pp. 1774–1840; Aniceto Masferrer / Juan B. Cañizares-Navarro, "Should Legal Uniqueness Be Compared? The Spanish Civil Code: Its Subsidiary Character", *Comparative law and... / Droit Comparé et...* (A. Albarian, O. Moréteau eds.) (Presses universitaires d'Aix-Marseille, 2015), pp. 85–96; see also Masferrer, "Codification as Nationalization or Denationalization of Law: The Spanish Case in Comparative Perspective", cited in fn n. 26.

With regards to criminal law, in the last few years scholars have explored French and other foreign influences on the Spanish codification. Some works present a general overview of French influence on the codification of criminal law in Spain,[37] whereas others take a historiographical approach to examine foreign influences in specific criminal codes, particularly those of 1822[38] and 1848–1850.[39] Some works have reconstructed the particular extent of foreign influences in depth in the codification of particular criminal law institutions. In this vein, the legacy of tradition and foreign influences on the legality principle have been carefully analyzed[40] as well as the principle's relation to judicial discretion.[41] Moreover, some scholars have treated mutual influences among criminal codes. Javier Alvarado carefully analyzed the influence of the Brazilian code (1830) on the Spanish CP 1848[42]; Bernardino Bravo Lira studied the diverse influences and impacts of the criminal

---

[37]Masferrer, Aniceto, "The Napoleonic Code pénal and the Codification of Criminal Law in Spain", *Le Code pénal. Les metamorphoses d'un modèle 1810-1820. Actes du colloque international Lille / Gand 16–18 décembre 2012*. Textes réunis et présentés par Chantal Aboucaya et Renée Martinage (Centre d'Histoire Judiciaire, 2012), pp. 65–98.

[38]Juan B. Cañizares-Navarro, "El Código Penal de 1822: sus fuentes inspiradoras. Balance historiográfico (desde el s. XX)", *GLOSSAE. European Journal of Legal History* 10 (2013), pp. 108–136 (available at http://www.glossae.eu); Ramos Vázquez / Cañizares-Navarro, "La influencia francesa en la primera Codificación española: el Código penal francés de 1810 y el Código penal español de 1822", cited in fn n. 32.; Alejandro Agüero / Marta Lorente, "Penal enlightenment in Spain: from Beccaria's reception to the first criminal code", *Forum Historiae Iuris*, http://www.forhistiur.de/zitat/1211aguero-lorente.htm, November, 2012 (it has also been republished in *The Spanish Enlightenment revisited* (Jesús Astigarraga, ed.), Voltaire Foundation–University of Oxford, 2015).

[39]Masferrer / Sánchez González, "Tradición e influencias extranjeras en el Código penal de 1848. Aproximación a un mito historiográfico", cited in fn n. 33.

[40]Clara Álvarez Alonso, "¿Neoclásicos o prerrománticos? La Ilustración penal española entre la 'barroca prohibición' de interpretar las leyes y el principio de legalidad revolucionario", *Quaderni Fiorentini per la storia del pensiero giuridico moderno* 36 (2007), pp. 81–130; Marta Lorente (ed.), *De justicia de jueces a justicia de leyes. Hacia la España de 1870* (Madrid, 2007); Aniceto Masferrer, "The Principle of Legality and Codification in the 19th century Western Criminal Law Reform", *From the Judge's Arbitrium to the Legality Principle: Legislation as a Source of Law in Criminal Trials* (Georges Martyn, Anthony Musson and Heikki Pihlajamäki, eds.) (*Duncker and Humblot*, 2013), pp. 253–293.

[41]Isabel Ramos Vázquez, "La individualización judicial de la pena en la primera codificación francesa y española", *Anuario de Historia del Derecho Español* 84 (2014), pp. 315–351; for an overview of the judicial discretion in the early-modern-age Castile, see Benjamín González Alonso, "Jueces, justicia, arbitrio judicial (Algunas reflexiones sobre la posición de los jueces ante el Derecho en la Castilla moderna)", *Vivir el Siglo de Oro. Poder, cultura e historia en la Época Moderna. Estudios en homenaje al profesor Ángel Rodríguez Sánchez* (Salamanca, 2003), pp. 223–241; for a broader geographical context, see Michele Pifferi, *Reinventing Punishment. A Comparative History of Criminology and Penology in the 19th and 20th Century* (Oxford: Oxford University Press, 2016); Michele Pifferi, *L'individualizzazione della pena. Difesa sociale e crisi della legalità penale tra Otto e Novecento* (Milano: Giuffrè, 2013).

[42]Javier Alvarado Planas, "La codificación penal en la España isabelina: la influencia del Código penal del Brasil en el Código penal español de 1848", *España en la época de la Fundación de la Guardia Civil* (V Seminario Duque de Ahumada: 18, 19 y 20 May 1993) (Madrid: Ministerio del Interior, 1994), pp. 43–82.

codes of Spain (1848) and Austria (1803) in Europe as well as Latin America[43]; and Emilia Iñesta-Pastor assessed the effect of the criminal code of the Two Sicilies on the Spanish parliament in the mid-19th century,[44] the Latin-American impact of the Spanish CP 1848[45] and Spanish influence on the criminal code of Perú (1863).[46]

It is evident that the Spanish criminal code of 1848 has drawn more scholarly attention than others and not just by legal historians, but also by criminal lawyers.[47] This is due to the fact that, as mentioned above, many of the current criminal law institutions originated in that code. Lawyers have even discovered that seemingly new criminal law institutions had been in force in medieval and early modern Spain and that the CP 1848 faithfully preserved this legacy.[48]

Moreover, some extensive monographs on the criminal code of 1848/50 have contributed to the recognition of its influence.[49] All these scholarly works represent but starting point for a line of ongoing research.[50] There is still much to be done.[51]

---

[43]Bernardino Bravo Lira, "Fortuna del Código penal español de 1848. Historia en cuatro actos y tres Continentes: de Mello Freire y Zeiller a Vasconcelos y Seijas Lozano", *AHDE* 74 (2004), pp. 23–58; Bernardino Bravo Lira, "Bicentenario del Código penal de Austria. Su proyección desde el Danubio a Filipinas", *Revista de Estudios Histórico-Jurídicos de Valparaíso* (Chile) 26 (2004), pp. 140–145).

[44]Emilia Iñesta-Pastor, "The influence of the 1819 criminal code of the Two Sicilies upon the Spanish criminal law codification and the parliament of the nineteenth century", *Culture parlamentari a confronto. Modelli della rappresentanza politica e identità nazionali* (Andrea Romano, ed.) (Bologna: CLUEB, 2016), pp. 245–259.

[45]Emilia Iñesta-Pastor, "La proyección hispanoamericana del Código Penal Español de 1848", *XIII Congreso del Instituto Internacional de Historia del Derecho Indiano: San Juan, 21 al 25 de mayo de 2000* (Luis E. González Vale, coord.) (San Juan, Puerto Rico: Instituto Internacional de Historia del Derecho Indiano; Oficina del Historiador Nacional de Puerto Rico, 2003), vol. II, Estudios, pp. 493–520.

[46]Emilia Iñesta-Pastor, "La reforma penal del Perú independiente: el código penal de 1863", *Actas del XV Congreso del Instituto Internacional de Historia del Derecho Indiano* (Córdoba, septiembre 2005) (Córdoba: Diputación de Córdoba; Universidad de Córdoba, 2008), pp. 1071–1098.

[47]M.J. Virto Larruscain, *El caso fortuito y la construcción del sistema de culpabilidad en el Código penal de 1848* (Bilbao, 1984).

[48]Miguel Cuerdo Mir / Mª Dolores del Mar Sánchez González, "Tradiciones penales en la maquinación para alterar el precio de las cosas del Código Penal de 1848", *AHDE* 84 (2014), pp. 301–326.

[49]Iñesta-Pastor, *El Código penal de 1848*, cited in fn n. 19; Sánchez González, *Los Códigos Penales de 1848 y 1850*, cited in fn n. 19.

[50]Aniceto Masferrer (ed.), *La Codificación penal española. Tradición e influencias extranjeras: su contribución al proceso codificador* (Pamplona: Aranzadi–Thomson Reuters, 2017), that came out when this chapter was already in print.

[51]This volume on French influence on Western criminal law codification is part of a research project involving several Spanish, European and American legal scholars (in progress). The first project, entitled 'La influencia de la Codificación francesa en la tradición penal española: su concreto alcance en la Parte General de los Códigos decimonónicos' (ref. DER2012-38469), was followed by a second one with the title 'Las influencias extranjeras en la Codificación penal española: su concreto alcance en la Parte Especial de los Códigos decimonónicos' (ref. DER2016-78388-P); they are both funded by the Spanish 'Ministerio de Economía y Competitividad.'.

Nonetheless, these preliminary results are already comparable to those of the criminal historiography of other European jurisdictions, like Italy[52] and Germany.[53]

3 Between Myth and Reality: The Scope of French Influence on the Spanish Codes of 1822 and 1848/50

As indicated already, several scholars have recently devoted themselves to the study of the dichotomy between tradition and reform in the codification criminal law[54] and the balance between tradition and foreign influences in drafting the

---

[52]A. Cavanna, "Codificazione del diritto italiano e imperialismo giuridico francese nella Milano napoleonica. Giuseppe Luosi e il diritto penale", *Ius Mediolani. Studi di Storia del diritto milanese offerti dagli allievi a Giulio Vismara* (Milano, 1996), pp. 659–760; A. Cavanna, *La codificazione penale in Italia. Le origine lombade* (Milano, 1975); M. da Passano, "La codification du droit pénal dans l'Italie jacobine et napoleonienne", *Revolutions et justice en Europe. Modeles francais et traditions nationales (1780–1830)* (L'Harmattan, 1999), pp. 85–99; E. Dezza, "Un critico milanese della codificazione penale napoleonica. Pietro Mantegazza e le Osservazione criminaledel cessato Regno d'Italia (1814)", *Ius Mediolani. Studi di Storia del diritto milanese offerti dagli allievi a Giulio Vismara* (Milano, 1996), pp. 909–977.

[53]Christian Brandt, *Die Entstehung des Code pénal von 1810 und sein Einfluß auf die Strafgesetzgebung der deutschen Partikularstaaten des 19. Jahrhunderts am Beispiel Bayerns und Preußens* (Frankfurt/Main: Peter Lang, 2002); J. Engelbrecht, "The French model and German society: the impact of the code pénal on the Rhineland", *Revolutions et justice en Europe. Modeles francais et traditions nationales (1780–1830)* (L'Harmattan, 1999), pp. 101–107; E. Feherenbach, *Traditionale Gesellschaft und revolutionäres Recht: Die Einführung des Code Napoleón in den Rheinbundestaaten* (Göttingen, 3 ed., 1983); K. Häfner, *Die Strafen des französischen Rechtes und ihr Vollzug, ein Grundriss* (Gieβen, 1936); Karl Härter, "Kontinuität und Reform der Strafjustiz zwischen Reichsverfassung und Rheinbund", *Reich oder Nation? Mitteleuropa 1780–1815* (herausgegeben von Heinz Duchhardt und Andreas Kunz), *Veröffentlichungen des Instituts für Europäische Geschichte Mainz*, Abteilung Universalgeschichte, Beiheft 46 (Mainz, 1998), pp. 219–278; Karl Härter, "Von der «Entstehung des öffentlichen Strafrechts » zur « Fabrikation des Verbrechens». Neuere Forschungen zur Entwicklung von Kriminalität und Strafjustiz im früheneuzeitlichen Europa", *Rechtsgeschichte. Zeitschrift des Max Planck-Institut für europäische Rechtsgeschichte 1* (2002), pp. 159–196; F. Hartmann, *Der Einfluß des französischen Rechts auf das Preußische Strafgesetzbuch von 1851 (Allgemeiner Teil)* (Göttingen, 1923); S. Kleinbreuer, *Das Rheinische Strafgesetzbuch. Das materielle Strafrecht und sein Einfluß auf die Strafgesetzgebung in Preußen und im Norddeutschen Bund* (Bonn, 1999); K.J.A. Mittermaier, "Blicke auf den Zustand der Ausbildung des Kriminalrechts in Frankreich", *Kritische Zeitschrift für Rechtswissenschaft* III (20), pp. 416 ff.; K.J.A. Mittermaier, "Über den neusten Zustand der Gefängnisse in England und Frankreich", *Neues Archiv des Criminalrechts* 40 (1820), I, pp. 571 ff.; E.J. Paraquin, *Die französische Gesetzgebung. Das Strafgesetzbuch*, vol. V (München 1861); W. Schubert, *Französisches Recht in Deutschland zu Beginn des 19. Jahrhunderts. Zivilrecht, Gerichtsverfassungsrecht und Zivilprozeßrecht* (Köln, 1977); W. Schubert, *Der Code pénal des Königreichs Westphalen von 1813 mit dem Code pénal von 1810 im Original und in deutscher Übersetzung* (Frankfurt/Main: Peter Lang, 2001); L. von Stein, *Geschichte des französischen Strafrechts und des Prozesses* (Basel, 1875; Aalen Verlag, 1968); K. Volk, "Napoleon und das deutsche Strafrecht", *JuS* (1991), pp. 281 ff.

[54]See, for example, fn nn. 28 y 52.

criminal codes.[55] The results obtained have already dispelled part of the mythologized view of French influence on the Spanish codification of criminal law.

In my view, the two best ways to analyze French influence on the codification of the Spanish criminal law are:

(1) The exploration of the materials and sources used by those who drafted the codes as well as their corresponding parliamentary debates, paying particular attention to the codification's committees (*Comisiones de Codificación*) and parliamentary debates (*Diario de Sesiones de las Cortes*).
(2) The study of commentary literature, or *Comentarios a los códigos*, referring to the Spanish criminal codes (since all Spanish criminal codes were studied and commented upon, sometimes even article by article, by lawyers and experts in criminal law). The commentaries of the codes of 1848–1850[56] and 1870[57] are, among others,[58] particularly relevant.

---

[55]See fn nn. 29 ff.

[56]In addition to the Pacheco's *Código penal concordado y comentado*, cited in fn n. 4, see also José de Castro Orozco / Manuel Ortiz de Zúñiga, *Código penal explicado para la común inteligencia y fácil explicación de sus disposiciones*. 3 vols. (Granada: Manuel Sanz, 1848); Tomás María de Vizmanos / Cirilo Álvarez Martínez, *Comentarios al Nuevo Código Penal* (Madrid: Establecimiento Tipográfico de J. González y A. Vicente, 1848); D. J. S. / D. A., de B., *Código penal de España comentado* (Barcelona: Imprenta de Tomás Gorchs, 1949); on this matter, see Sánchez González, *Los Códigos Penales de 1848 y 1850*, pp. 198–203; several manuals dealt with the 1848 Criminal Code, being one of them that of Gómez de la Pedro Serna / Juan Manuel Montalbán, *Elementos del Derecho Penal de España*. 2 vols. (Madrid, 1849); on the manuals dealing with that code, see Sánchez González, *Los Códigos Penales de 1848 y 1850*, pp. 205–208.

[57]Alejandro Groizard y Gómez de la Serna, *El Código penal de 1870 concordado y comentado*, 8 vols. (Burgos, 1870–1899); Narciso Buenaventura Selva, *Comentarios al Código penal reformado y planteado provisionalmente por Ley de 3 de junio de 1870* (Madrid, 1870); José González y Serrano, *Apéndice á los Comentarios del Código Penal de Don Joaquín Francisco Pacheco* (Madrid: Imprenta y Fundación de Manuel Tello, 1876); Pedro Gómez de la Serna / Juan Manuel Montalván, *Elementos del Derecho Civil y Penal de España* (Madrid: Librería de Gabriel Sánchez, 1881); on the 1870 criminal Code, see also Luis Silvela, *El Derecho penal estudiado en principios y en la legislación vigente en España* (Madrid, 2nd ed., 1903); M. Azcutia, *La Ley penal. Estudios prácticos sobre la interpretación, inteligencia y aplicación del Código de 1870, en su relación con los de 1848 y 1850, con nuestras antiguas Leyes patrias y con las principales legislaciones extranjeras* (Madrid, 1876); Quintiliano Saldaña, *Comentarios científico-prácticos al Código penal de 1870. Infracción y responsabilidad*, vol. I, t. I (Madrid, 1920); S. Viada y Vilaseca, *El Código penal reformado de 1870*. 3 vols. (Madrid, 1894); J.A. Hidalgo y García, *El Código penal conforme a la doctrina del Tribunal Supremo* (Madrid, 1908); J. Álvarez Cid / T. Álvarez Cid, *El Código penal de 1870* (Córdoba, 1908).

[58]On the Spanish criminal code of 1928, compared to that of 1870, see Jaramillo García, *Novísimo Código Penal comentado y cotejado con el de 1870*, cited in fn n. 22; Luis San Martín Losada, *El Código penal de 1928. Su estudio y comparación con el de 1870* (Madrid, 1928).

The study of the concordances published by Pacheco in 1848[59] and Groizard y Gómez de la Serna in 1870[60] are further sources useful in analyzing the French criminal code's influence in Spain. However, their approach lacks accuracy because the concordances do not really prove any particular influence in the drafting of the code. They may be a useful starting point for a comprehensive comparative study, article by article, between the French criminal code and the Spanish codes.

Since an exhaustive exploration of the French influence would exceed the limits of this chapter, I examine what drafters and lawyers thought about the French influence on the CPs of 1822 and 1848/50. To do so, I will use the parliamentary debates, which represent drafters' views, and the commentary literature (or *Comentarios a los códigos*), which contains criminal lawyers' views, supplemented by insights from recent literature. Both historical sources are linked, particularly when those who published the commentaries had been members of the committee in charge of drafting the code.[61]

It is true that deputies' and lawyers' opinions on the French influence of the codes might not always be fully reliable. Deputies did not always say what they really thought. Lawyers might also have been biased in relation to a specific subject, or they could have just been misled out of ignorance. However, the analysis of various voices, including those of radicals as well as antagonists and dissenters, offers the most accurate picture of the thought of the deputies and lawyers who discussed, approved, and commented upon the criminal codes of 1822 and 1848.

In describing deputies' and lawyers' views on the French influence on the codes, I will distinguish the three types of influence mentioned above: (1) the idea of the code itself; (2) formal/structural influence; and (3) substantive influence.

3.1 The Idea of the Code Itself in the Parliamentary Debates

The influence of the *Code pénal* of Napoleon over Spain and other European countries was primarily due to it being the first modern criminal code in Europe. Several codes had been enacted in Europe during the 18th century and the beginning of the 19th century, but the Napoleonic criminal code was the first that can be regarded as 'modern.'[62] Hence, European drafters fixed their eyes on the

---

[59]Pacheco, *El Código penal concordado y comentado*, cited in fn n. 4; Pacheco is one of the most remarkable 19th century Criminal law scholar and the main commentator of the Spanish Criminal Codes of 1848 and 1850.

[60]Groizard y Gómez de la Serna, *El Código penal de 1870 concordado y comentado*, cited in fn n. 58.

[61]That was the case, for example, with Joaquín Francisco Pacheco, or Tomás María de Vizmanos, and Cirilo Álvarez Martínez; see in fn n. 57.

[62]This expression refers to its promulgation in the context of a politically liberal system. More specifically: (a) it was approved by a parliament, not a king; (b) the recognition of national sovereignty had replaced royal absolutism; and (c) liberal principles like legality and equality had already been introduced.

French model. The publication of many translations of the French text into various other languages shows the prestige of the Napoleonic code and reveals that French was the most well-known European language at the time, particularly among intellectuals, as was explicitly recognized by Conde de Toreno, a member of the 1822 Spanish parliament.[63] This explains why the Napoleonic code was taken as a model, cited so frequently in the concordances of other codes and parliamentary debates, as well as its use as a reference for comparative law. Another question is whether the French institutions and categories were adopted, and if so, how.

3.1.1 The Code as a Tool for Legal Reform

In Spain, whereas the approval of the CP 1822 did not trigger much parliamentary debate about the propriety of reforming criminal law through the codification scheme, the enactment of the 1848 criminal code was very different. Moreover, the parliamentarians in 1848 did not feel the same urgency to codify criminal law[64] that motivated their predecessors in 1822.[65]

Some of them strongly defended the cause of codification, presenting it as an urgent task and an important parliamentary duty.[66] Hence, there was no need to discuss the whole draft, following—according to some parliamentarians,[67] but not all[68]—in French footsteps. Others were not convinced about the propriety of codifying criminal law for other reasons: some thought it would be much better to enact particular statutes rather than a general code[69]; some held that such a drastic legislative measure required exigent reasons to justify it[70]; some argued that there was no need to approve the code hurriedly (remembering how the previous criminal

[63]On this matter, see chapter 1 of this volume; (Conde de Toreno) "La situación de la Francia con respecto á este asunto es diferente de la nuestra. Su idioma es general en toda la Europa, al paso que el nuestro es muy poco usado. Si allí se escribiese un periódico en lengua española, solo circularía aquí, y poco daño podría hacer a otras potencias, pero escrito en lengua francesa circularía por toda la Europa…" (DSC, Congreso, 24 January 1822, p. 1984).

[64]On this matter, see Sánchez González, *Los Códigos Penales de 1848 y 1850*, pp. 93–96.

[65]DSC, Congreso, 22 April 1821, p. 1156.

[66](Seijas) "No hay nada más apremiante, señores, que la necesidad del Código penal" (DSC, Congreso, 13 March 1848, p. 1757).

[67]Pardo Montenegro, DSC, Congreso, 10 March 1848, p. 1706; Fernández Baeza, DSC, Congreso, 11 March 1848, pp. 1732–1733; see also Seijas, DSC, Congreso, 15 March 1848, p. 1792.

[68]Mayans, DSC, Congreso, 16 March 1848, pp. 1809–1810.

[69]Fernández Baeza, DSC, Congreso, 11 March 1848, p. 1734.

[70]Pidal, DSC, Congreso, 14 March 1848, pp. 1772–1775; see Sánchez González, *Los Códigos Penales de 1848 y 1850*, pp. 94–95.

code had been promulgated)[71]; other deputies simply opposed codifying criminal law,[72] although not very strongly or coherently.[73]

Leaving aside whether the code was the proper way to reform criminal law, there remains the question of whether the Napoleonic *Code pénal* (1810) arose when the deputies discussed promulgating a modern code.

3.1.2 Explicit References to the Napoleonic Criminal Code

The parliamentary debates show that, although the French criminal code was well known and mentioned as a legal text that had been consulted by the codes' drafters, it was never regarded or recognized as a model. However, the deputies who wanted to criticize the draft or the bill presented for approval in parliament, either on particular points or over the impropriety of accepting a foreign legal source as a model for Spain, were an exception.[74] Perhaps this was due to the relatively recent War of Independence (1808–1814) that occurred in Spain as a consequence of the French invasion.[75] This may apply to the 1822 criminal code, but it was not the case

[71]Corzo, DSC, Congreso, 15 March 1848, p. 1789.

[72]Gómez Laserna, DSC, Congreso, 14 March 1848, pp. 1764–1768; on this matter, see Sánchez González, *Los Códigos Penales de 1848 y 1850*, pp. 93–94.

[73]Gómez Laserna, DSC, Congreso, 14 March 1848, p. 1772.

[74]That was precisely the point made by Calatrava in discussing a specific matter concerning the freedom of the press, arguing that the French regulation could not work in Spain. On this matter, see DSC, Congreso, 5 February 1822, p. 2169.

[75]The wartime parliamentary debates reveal feelings of suspicion and hatred toward the French; see, for example: DSC, Congreso, 9 December 1810, p. 153: "…infernal política de Bonaparte"; DSC, Congreso, 16 December 1810, p. 168: "…el despotismo francés en los reinos de España"; DSC, Congreso, 17 December 1810, p. 182: "…excluidos los hijos de franceses…monstruos…"; DSC, Congreso, 17 December 1810, p. 183: "…hijos, nietos y biznietos de los franceses"; DSC, Congreso, 17 December 1810, p. 183: "…indignación contra los franceses"; DSC, Congreso, 17 December 1810, p. 183: "…sangre francesa"; DSC, Congreso, 17 December 1810, p. 183: "…los franceses son los mayores enemigos del género humano, y especialmente de España"; DSC, Congreso, 18 December 1810, p. 185: "…resistir al furioso ímpetu de los franceses…"; DSC, Congreso, 19 December 1810, p. 191: "…franceses, peores que los moros…"; DSC, Congreso, 19 December 1810, p. 191: "…aun los mismos muertos le [a Napoleón] hacen la guerra…"; DSC, Congreso, 19 December 1810, p. 193: "…infelices españoles que están en Francia"; DSC, Congreso, 20 December 1810, p. 197: "…dar la propiedad de todo lo que quitasen a los franceses"; DSC, Congreso, 21 December 1810, p. 204: "…que no imitemos a los franceses en este denominación de Poder ejecutivo, y creo sería más conveniente que continuase el nombre de Consejo de Regencia"; DSC, Congreso, 24 December 1810, p. 223: "…perfidia francesa…"; DSC, Congreso, 28 December 1810, p. 240: "…indulto a los afrancesados…"; DSC, Congreso, 29 December 1810, p. 247: "…nación francesa"; DSC, Congreso, 29 December 1810, p. 248: "… aborrecimiento a la tiranía y dominación extranjera"; DSC, Congreso, 29 December 1810, p. 248: "…que no quede un solo francés en la Península"; DSC, Congreso, 29 December 1810, p. 248: "…convertida la Península en Colonia francesa"; DSC, Congreso, 29 December 1810, p. 250: "En España, por desgracia, hay algunos que siguen el partido de los franceses"; DSC, Congreso, 29 December 1810, p. 250: "…formar un partido con los españoles franceses"; DSC, Congreso, 29

for the 1848 code. Yet, it is surprising that the code's drafters and supporters were more reluctant to accept the influence of the French criminal code in 1848 than in 1822.

Positive views: France among the 'learned nations'

Deputies' opinions concerning France as a nation were sometimes confusing because they held such a wide variety of them. In presenting and discussing the criminal codes, some praised and regarded France as an enlightened and civilized nation. The speech given by José Maria Calatrava, the main drafter of the 1822

December 1810, p. 252: "Temo mucha la perfidia de los franceses, la seducción de los afrancesados, el frío desaliento de los egoístas, y las instigaciones sordas de los que, atendiendo a sus intereses particulares, los hallan en contradicción con el nuevo orden de cosas que las Cortes han de introducir en el Estado"; DSC, Congreso, 29 December 1810, p. 252: "...trata de sembrar la división en el Reino la perfidia francesa"; DSC, Congreso, 29 December 1810, p. 252: "Que nada se trate con los franceses sin que primero evacuen la Península"; DSC, Congreso, 29 December 1810, p. 252: "...una guerra eterna, no ya sólo al pérfido Napoleón y su raza, sino a toda la Francia misma y sus cobardes aliados..."; DSC, Congreso, 29 December 1810, p. 253: "...esa serpiente de Francia derramó la ponzoña de la discordia en el seno de la familia reinante"; DSC, Congreso, 29 December 1810, p. 254: "...inmensas usurpaciones de la embrutecida y ensangrentada Francia"; DSC, Congreso, 29 December 1810, p. 254: "¡La Francia amiga de España! ¡Qué caprichoso delirio! Desde que las dos naciones existen, han sido siempre rivales..."; DSC, Congreso, 29 December 1810, p. 254: "¡Guerra eterna, guerra de sangre y muerte contra la pérfida Francia!: antes perecer mil veces que capitular con ella"; DSC, Congreso, 29 December 1810, p. 254: "... ahogar la perfidia y altanería francesa"; DSC, Congreso, 29 December 1810, p. 255: "...caigamos al fin, y sin poder remediarlo, en las [manos] impuras de los franceses, todavía empapadas de la inocente sangre de nuestros padres y hermanos"; DSC, Congreso, 29 December 1810, p. 255: "... declarar eterna guerra a la Francia..."; DSC, Congreso, 29 December 1810, p. 257: "...que no hará la paz con Francia, y no cederá en esta santa guerra mientras no esté restablecido en España con entera libertad nuestro amado monarca..."; DSC, Congreso, 29 December 1810, p. 257: "...han introducido en España las preocupaciones y los errores, y ahora intentan sujetarla al despotismo"; DSC, Congreso, 29 December 1810, p. 257: "El pueblo español no quiso ser francés: el pueblo conoció bien la intención de Napoleón"; DSC, Congreso, 29 December 1810, p. 258: "...del ave de rapiña de la Francia"; DSC, Congreso, 29 December 1810, p. 258: "...aquellos dignos españoles, como nosotros, no quieren ser esclavos de los franceses"; DSC, Congreso, 29 December 1810, p. 258: "...el pueblo español..., perecerá antes que ser francés"; DSC, Congreso, 29 December 1810, p. 260: "...no se excederá nunca V.M. en tomar medidas de cautela contra los franceses. Es malísima gente, Señor, abominable, diabólica"; DSC, Congreso, 29 December 1810, p. 260: "...el carácter fraudulento y doloso de los franceses, acreditada por la experiencia de todos los siglos..."; DSC, Congreso, 29 December 1810, p. 261: "...para que vea ese monstruo que el pueblo español nunca será amigo de Francia"; DSC, Congreso, 29 December 1810, p. 261: "Yo pido se declare que primero moriremos que dejarnos subyugar por ese infame [Napoleón]"; DSC, Congreso, 30 December 1810, p. 264: "...nosotros peleamos con vándalos franceses, mucho más bárbaros que aquéllos"; DSC, Congreso, 30 December 1810, p. 267: "...yugo francés"; DSC, Congreso, 30 December 1810, p. 268: "...la idea de guerra eterna a la Francia, y alianza eterna con la Inglaterra"; DSC, Congreso, 30 December 1810, p. 268: "...jamás debiera hacerse la paz con Francia", advertencia de ministro Pitt a un monarca inglés; DSC, Congreso, 30 December 1810, p. 270: "...los intereses de Francia han sido y serán eternamente que la España sea una provincia suya"; DSC, Congreso, 31 December 1810, p. 272: "...debilitada (la Fe) con la corrupción de las costumbres y máximas francesas".

criminal code,[76] to present his project was a paramount example. He criticized that Spain was overdue in following the good example of its neighbor nations.[77] For him, it was time to follow the path of the nations that had codified their criminal laws,[78] referring to the "learned nations of Europe,"[79] "the political societies of Europe,"[80] or just the "nations of Europe,"[81] and to draft a criminal code that could be counted among the most learned in Europe.[82] He did not mention France, but it was understood that that neighbor was counted among the "learned nations of Europe."

Other parliamentarians of 1822 explicitly referred to France, sometimes along with England, as "the two most learned nations of the Universe."[83] Some institutions also praised the 1822 criminal code for having adopted some principles from the best criminal codes, not always mentioning the French code.[84]

Something similar occurred in 1848 when deputies gazed with great interest on the European legal landscape.[85] They regarded France and England as important nations[86] and once labeled France as "one of the greatest legislators of the world."[87] Some seemed to think that an institution's absence in any European code was an authoritative indicator of its superfluity.[88] There were some exceptions, such as

[76]Juan Sainz Guerra, "José María Calatrava o la Codificación penal a comienzos del siglo XIX", *Estudios de Historia de las Ciencias Criminales en España* (J. Alvarado y A. Serrano Maíllo, eds.) (Madrid: Dykinson, 2007), pp. 351–384.

[77]*Discurso de Presentación del Título preliminar*, CP 1822, in DSC, Congreso, 22 April 1821, p. 1155.

[78]*Discurso de Presentación del Título preliminar*, CP 1822, in DSC, Congreso, 22 April 1821, p. 1157).

[79]*Discurso de Presentación del Título preliminar*, CP 1822: "La primera se halla adoptada por varias naciones cultas de Europa…" (DSC, Congreso, 22 April 1821, p. 1157).

[80]*Discurso de Presentación del Título preliminar*, CP 1822, in DSC, Congreso, 22 April 1821, p. 1158.

[81]*Discurso de Presentación del Título preliminar*, CP 1822: "…las naciones de Europa, es un resto de los siglos bárbaros…" (DSC, Congreso, 22 April 1821, p. 1158).

[82]*Discurso de Presentación del Título preliminar*, CP 1822, in DSC, Congreso, 22 April 1821, p. 1159.

[83]Álvarez de Sotomayor, DSC, Congreso, 17 December 1821, p. 1332.

[84]*Observaciones previas ó generales que hacen en pró y en contra algunos de los informantes*: "La Audiencia de Valladolid opina que se ha adoptado en el proyecto los principios luminosos de los mejores Códigos criminales…" (DSC, Congreso, 23 November 1821, p. 922).

[85]DSC, Congreso, 10 March 1848, p. 1712 (referring to the nations of Europe); DSC, Congreso, 10 March 1848, p. 1718 (referring to the Austrian criminal code); DSC, Congreso, 11 March 1848, p. 1734 (referring to some foreign criminal codes, the French and Brazilian ones among them).

[86]DSC, Congreso, 10 March 1848, p. 1709.

[87](Pardo Montenegro) "Napoleón, por ejemplo, encargó al Consejo de Estado la formación de los Códigos que dio á la Francia y que le elevaron á la altura de unos de los grandes legisladores del mundo…" (DSC, Congreso, 10 March 1848, p. 1706).

[88]Seijas, DSC, Congreso, 10 March 1848, p. 1718.

Fernández Baeza. He denounced the practice of looking too much to other legal systems while neglecting a deeper analysis of the nature and principles that govern all territories regardless of their specific circumstances.[89]

General references to the tradition of France—even just concerning specific matters—were neither frequent nor uncommon.[90] Sometimes they even recognized the French system as a model for administrative matters[91] other than criminal law.

Negative views: the French 'despotic exercise of government' or 'tyranny' There were also less positive references to France. Some parliamentarians' statements show a different view about France and its codes, including the criminal code, namely that it was neither a free nation nor a free people.[92] Moreover, it was said that the French criminal code was approved to ensure despotic government[93] or tyranny.[94] Similar criticisms were voiced in the United States of America by those who opposed the codification scheme at the end of the 19th century.[95]

The argument that the French code restricted freedom much more than the Spanish one was used even when the Spanish code substantially constrained the scope of citizens' liberties. In discussing the right to association, for example, Borrego opposed the idea that any private association of 20 members required express authorization before being allowed to gather.[96] Manuel de Seijas, the main drafter of the CP 1848,[97] replied by noting that this was not an oversight. He based his counterargument on principles and authority. Focusing on the latter, he argued

---

[89]Fernández Baeza, DSC, Congreso, 11 March 1848, p. 1734.

[90]DSC, Congreso, 19 December 1821, p. 1364; DSC, Congreso, 3 December 1821, p. 1084; Calatrava, on art. 791, DSC, Congreso, 1 February 1822, p. 2102); Rey, on art. 791, DSC, Congreso, 1 February 1822, p. 2102, related to that, see also DSC, Congreso, 1 February 1822, p. 2103; DSC, Congreso, 13 March 1848, p. 1742; Corzo, DSC, Congreso, 13 March 1848, p. 1751; Pidal, DSC, Congreso, 14 March 1848, pp. 1776 y 1777; Seijas, DSC, Congreso, 15 March 1848, p. 1792.

[91]DSC, Congreso, 19 May 1821, p. 1699.

[92]Calatrava, discussing art. 526, DSC, Congreso, 22 January 1822, p. 1959; Calatrava, discussing art. 302, DSC, Congreso, 16 January 1822, p. 1832.

[93]Gil de Linares, DSC, Congreso, 10 December 1821, p. 1173.

[94]DSC, Congreso, 23 November 1821, p. 923 (from the *Colegio de abogados* of Madrid).

[95]On this matter, see Aniceto Masferrer, "The Passionate Discussion among Common Lawyers about postbellum American Codification: An approach to its Legal Argumentation" *Arizona State Law Journal* 40, 1 (2008), pp. 173–256, particularly, pp. 198–199 and 233–238; see also Aniceto Masferrer, "Defense of the Common Law against postbellum American Codification: Reasonable and Fallacious Argumentation", *American Journal for Legal History* 50.4 (2008–2010), pp. 355–430.

[96]Borrego, DSC, Congreso, 16 March 1848, p. 1824.

[97]On this matter, see N. Antonio Fernández, *Manuel de Seijas Lozano. Tras las huellas de un liberal olvidado* (Madrid: Colegio de Registradores de la Propiedad y Mercantiles de España, 2007); A. Martínez Dhier, *Manuel de Seijas (Hernández) Lozano. Precursor de la codificación en España* (Córdoba, 2009).

that permitting associations without authorization would impair public order and social security. To bolster this claim, he dared mention the French code, whose regulation had not changed since the 1830 revolution despite several intervening reforms.[98] Later on, though, he added that the Spanish regulation was less strict than the French one, so "Spaniards will enjoy more liberty than the French".[99] Borrego recognized and lauded that the Spanish regulation granted citizens more freedom than the French code. He lamented, though, that the commission did not refer to other European models, whose legal regimes on the matter were much better, nor to Spanish traditions and jurisprudence, which contained useful precedents on how to regulate the right of association in a spirit of greater liberty (since he maintained that the moral, political and economic progress of the society depend on the exercise of that right).[100]

The rejection of the Napoleonic criminal code as a model for Spain

The efforts of the codes' drafters to make clear that they had not used the *Code pénal* as a model are surprising indeed. There are traces of this in the 1822 code,[101] but they are more pronounced in the 1848 text. Only in a few cases was it recognized that a specific article came from the French code.[102] Although some observers reported that a group of articles, a title or even whole book had been adopted from the *Code pénal*,[103] the codes' drafters never affirmed the link.[104] Still, some institutions, like the Bar Association of Madrid (*Colegio de abogados*), criticized the 1822 project for being drafted on the model of the French code,[105]

[98](Seijas) "...y el Código francés, que ha sufrido tantas reformas después de la revolución de 1830, está intacto en este punto" (DSC, Congreso, 16 March 1848, p. 1825).

[99]Seijas, DSC, Congreso, 16 March 1848, p. 1826.

[100]Borrego, DSC, Congreso, 16 March 1848, p. 1827.

[101]Calatrava, DSC, Congreso, 23 November 1821, p. 924.

[102](Rey, discussing art. 789) "Yo por fin solo añadiré, ya que se ha hecho á la comisión la inculpación de haber modelado su Código por el Código francés, que aunque en general no es verdad, es exactísimo en cuanto á haberse tomado este artículo de él, porque los franceses son buenos economistas, y están más adelantados que nosotros en este ramo. Los ingleses también lo tienen, y así la comparación es exacta" (DSC, Congreso, 1 February 1822, p. 2101).

[103](*Observaciones previas ó generales que hacen en pró y en contra algunos de los informantes*) "La [Audiencia] de Castilla La Nueva dice que el proyecto del Código (...) comprende disposiciones y capítulos enteros, pertenecientes á otro Código, como lo de acusaciones, rebeldías, ejecución de las sentencias etc., y particularmente lo relativo al Jurado, que no se debe anticipar hasta que las Cortes resuelvan silo há de haber, á cuyo fin cita la ley anterior que se proyectó para la sustanciación de causas criminales" (DSC, Congreso, 23 November 1821, p. 921); DSC, Congreso, 23 November 1821, p. 923; see also DSC, Congreso, 23 November 1821, p. 923 (*Colegio de Abogados* of Madrid).

[104]See, for example, DSC, Congreso, 23 November 1821, p. 924; DSC, Congreso, 1 February 1822, p. 2101.

[105]DSC, Congreso, 23 November 1821, p. 923.

even though that very *Colegio* proposed to follow that model on a few occasions.[106]

The main drafter of the 1822 criminal code, José María Calatrava, dared to acknowledge that "many things were taken from the French code",[107] which, however, did not mean that the *Code pénal* had been the model for the whole 1822 project. He tried to assert that the project was truly Spanish and considered the specific circumstances of Spain as a particular nation.[108] He took pains to distinguish himself from the French system at every opportunity.[109] Other deputies made a similar point, denying that the French code had been used as a model but accepting that some specific articles of it had been used.[110] This position was in line with the view of Dueñas, a deputy of the Cortes of Cádiz who had been member of commission ('*Comisión de Justicia General*') in charge of drafting criminal law reforms a decade earlier.[111] He stated that a tenth of the project was not original and derived from the older criminal legislation.[112]

[106]See, for example, Calatrava' reproach of that Colegio in discussing art. 526 of the 1822 project: "El Colegio de Madrid dice que el artículo le parece durísimo con los superiores, que dará lugar a multitud de causas, y que el Gobierno debe velar y remover á los ineptos (...). Con este motivo elogia la disposición del Código francés sobre que los proveedores no puedan ser perseguidos en justicia sino por denuncia ó acusación del Gobierno. Yo no alcanzo ciertamente cómo el Colegio de Madrid recomienda una disposición que en mi concepto es uno de los mayores lunares que tiene aquel Código. Eso se inventó en tiempo de Bonaparte para que los asentistas y proveedores, en complaciendo al Gobierno, aunque sacrificasen a todos los demás, estuviesen á cubierto de esta pena, y aun de que se examinase su conducta en juicio; y yo creo que no es esto lo que conviene en España ni en ningún pueblo libre" (DSC, Congreso, 22 January 1822, p. 1959); see also fn nn. 162–162.

[107]DSC, Congreso, 23 November 1821, p. 924 (see fn n. 103).

[108]Calatrava, DSC, Congreso, 23 November 1821, p. 924; see also Calatrava, discussing art. 16, DSC, Congreso, 3 December 1821, p. 1089; Calatrava, discussing art. 59, DSC, Congreso, 22 December 1821, p. 1410; Calatrava, discussing the death penalty, DSC, Congreso, 22 December 1821, pp. 1414–1415; Calatrava, DSC, Congreso, 3 January 1822, p. 1610; Calatrava, discussing art. 255, DSC, Congreso, 14 January 1822, p. 1807; Calatrava, discussing art. 261, DSC, Congreso, 14 January 1822, pp. 1807–1808.

[109]Calatrava, discussing art. 59, DSC, Congreso, 22 December 1821, p. 1411.

[110]DSC, Congreso, 1 February 1822, p. 2101 (see fn n. 104).

[111]Requested by Agustín de Argüelles, the *Comisión de Justicia General* was created on 30 March 1811. It was composed of five deputies: Dueñas, Luján, Moragues, Navarro and Goyanes. The *Proyecto de Reglamento para las causas criminales* was read in the session on 19 April 1811 (DSCGE, n. 200, 19 April 1811, p. 894); on the *Comisión de Justicia General*, see Ramos Vázquez, "La Comisión de Justicia y el Proyecto de Reglamento para causas criminales de 1811", cited in fn n. 14; se also Ramos Vázquez / Cañizares-Navarro, "La influencia francesa en la primera Codificación española: el Código penal francés de 1810 y el Código penal español de 1822", p. 212.

[112]"...la comisión no presume haber dicho nada nuevo, porque apenas tendrá una décima parte que no esté prevenido por las leyes. Pero como la comisión habla á V.M delante de la Nación entera, ha querido instruir al pueblo de los derechos que tiene, y que V.M. sanciona, y quiere que se guarden, porque no hay duda que se disminuirá el atrevimiento de los malos jueces á proporción del conocimiento que tengan los súbditos de sus derechos" (DSCGE, n. 200, 19 April 1811, p. 896; the text has been drawn from also Ramos Vázquez / Cañizares-Navarro, "La influencia francesa en la primera Codificación española: el Código penal francés de 1810 y el Código penal español de 1822", p. 213).

As mentioned above, the efforts of the 1848 criminal code's drafters to disclaim that the *Code pénal* had been used as a model were particularly strong. Seijas ventured to state that, although it was generally true that all of Europe was governed by the French criminal code, that code was, in his view, "the worst code of France", so his committee rather resorted to the Brazilian code.[113] Regardless, the 1848 project was "a purely Spanish code", and "it won't be said it is French because it has no contact at all with it [referring to the *Code pénal*]; it won't be said it belongs to another European country: not at all, the code we present [before the parliament] is purely Spanish."[114] In so doing, he disregarded the 1822 criminal code in particular.[115]

The deputy Alonso disagreed with Seijas on this matter, stating that many articles came from the French code, which Seijas denied by saying that there were many differences between the articles of the two codes. Alonso accepted Seijas's point, but he added that he had detected at least twelve articles contained in the book of *faltas* that were very similar to those contained in the Napoleonic code.[116] Seijas, in replying to Alonso's argument that the book of *faltas* had adopted the French code as a model, rendering it a purely French product, argued demagogically that Alonso was right inasmuch as no code could avoid the regulation of some standard criminal acts like homicide, parricide, theft, etc., which had already been regulated by the French code.[117] Alonso finally asserted that he just wanted to state that some articles had been copied from the French code, but it seemed—he continued—that there was no will to acknowledge it.[118] Other deputies lamented that some aspects had not been regulated in line with national jurisprudence, referring to the customs and legal tradition in Spain.[119]

[113]On the influence of the Brazilian code over the CP 1848, see Alvarado, "La codificación penal en la España isabelina: la influencia del Código penal del Brasil en el Código penal español de 1848", cited in fn n. 43; Iñesta-Pastor, *El Código penal de 1848*, pp. 295–298.

[114]Seijas, DSC, Congreso, 10 March 1848, pp. 1714–1715; Seijas, DSC, Congreso, 13 March 1848, p. 1758; see also Iñesta-Pastor, *El Código penal de 1848*, pp. 79–80, 294–298, and 300–302.

[115](Seijas) "El Código penal que se discutió en España en 1822 después de oír a todo el mundo lo que quiso decir, después de largos y detenidos debates, hubo que abandonarle porque era muy malo." (DSC, Congreso, 13 March 1848, p. 1758); it has been said that although deputies strove to downplay the influence of the 1822 code in the elaboration of the 1848 law, some articles of the Special Part show revealing similarities (Iñesta-Pastor, *El Código penal de 1848*, pp. 299–300).

[116](Alonso) "Nos ha dicho el Sr. Seijas que el Código es todo español, que es puramente español, que no tiene contacto ninguno con el Código francés. Yo no quiero sino que se coteje el título francés 'De las faltas' con el título 'De las faltas' también de nuestro Código, y se verá que éste no es más que un traslado de aquel...

El Sr. Seijas: hay mucha diferencias...

El Sr. Alonso: Hay diferencias, es cierto; ...lo menos 12 artículos conformes" (DSC, Congreso, 15 March 1848, p. 1791); on this matter, see also (Alonso) (DSC, Congreso, 15 March 1848, p. 1789).

[117]Seijas, DSC, Congreso, 15 March 1848, p. 1798.

[118]Alonso, DSC, Congreso, 15 March 1848, p. 1799.

[119]On this matter, see the view of the parliamentarian Borrego (DSC, Congreso, 16 March 1848, p. 1827).

3.1.3 Explicit References to the Spanish Legal Tradition (Legal Sources and Doctrine)

Parliamentary debates also contained explicit references to legal and doctrinal sources of the Spanish tradition, not necessarily to show that codes were genuinely Spanish rather than French or from some other foreign nation. More specifically, the 1822 project contained passages from modern authors, like Filangieri and Bexon, but also from 17th century lawyers, like Matheu i Sanz and Antonio Gómez.[120] José María Calatrava mentioned some sources of the Spanish legal tradition, emphasizing the importance of the *Partidas*,[121] sometimes to argue against alternative ways of regulating particular matters.[122] In doing so, the deputy Gareli asked Calatrava whether there was any other Spanish legal source supporting what the *Partidas* prescribed, citing also the *Fuero Real* and other *Pragmáticas* promulgated by Philip II, Philip V and Charles III.[123] Beyond that, few 1822 parliamentarians made references to historical legal sources.[124]

Seijas, the main drafter of the 1848 penal code, included few references and criticized those who cited the text of the *Partidas* excessively without realizing that it was not really applied by the tribunals.[125] In Seijas view, the *Partidas* should not be taken as a reference unless case law (or the 'jurisprudencia' of the Spanish tribunals) might have invoked and applied its specific texts.[126] Other deputies, like Maldonado and Pardo Montenegro, seemed more attached to legal sources of the Spanish tradition.[127]

[120]*Observaciones previas ó generales que hacen en pró y en contra algunos de los informantes*: "...y que entre las máximas de Filangieri y Bexon se han salpicado locuciones como las de Matheu y Antonio Gómez" (DSC, Congreso, 23 November 1821, p. 922).

[121]"...las Partidas usan de estas mismas palabras" (DSC, Congreso, 25 November 1821, p. 964); Calatrava, DSC, Congreso, 27 November 1821, p. 1001; (Calatrava) "La distinción del delito y de la culpa es mucho más antigua que nuestras leyes: todos saben cuán conocida es en el Derecho romano, del cual la tomaron los autores de nuestras Partidas" (DSC, Congreso, 27 November 1821, p. 1001).

[122](Calatrava) "Las Leyes de Partida previenen que se les disminuya el castigo, reconociendo que no merecen tanto como los adultos. ¿Y nosotros iríamos ahora á imponer la pena de muerte á muchachos de esa edad? No podré convenir nunca en esto" (DSC, Congreso, 22 December 1821, pp. 1414–1415).

[123]DSC, Congreso, 22 December 1821, p. 1415.

[124]In addition to Calatrava and Gareli, see also Cepero's discourse in DSC, Congreso, 27 November 1821, p. 1002.

[125]Seijas, DSC, Congreso, 10 March 1848, p. 1717.

[126]Seijas, DSC, Congreso, 10 March 1848, p. 1717.

[127]DSC, Congreso, 10 March 1848, p. 1706.

3.2 *Formal/Structural Influence*

The second level of influence of the French Napoleonic code concerns its contribution from a formal/structural point of view. In my view, the greatest legacy of the modern codification was more formal than substantive, for which the division between the General Part and the Special Part is a paramount example.

It should be noted that the division of these two parts was not original to the French criminal code. In fact, Tiberio Decianus (1509–1582), in his posthumous *Tractatus criminalis* (1590), developed the general principles of criminal law, going beyond the treatment of individual crimes and stages of procedure. For example, he formulated the concepts of the objective and subjective constituent elements of a criminal act.[128] The French criminal code, however, contributed greatly to the elaboration of this distinction in successive European codes.

3.2.1 Parliamentary Debates

The parliamentary debates showed deputies' general conformity with this distinction. Deputies as well as the drafters were aware of most of the particular notions, concepts, categories and institutions of the General Part. The fact that they became a pertinent reference for the Spanish drafters does not imply, however, their endorsement. On the contrary, Spanish drafters often departed markedly from the French model.

Types of criminal offences

In distinguishing the different kinds of crimes, the Napoleonic code—following the 1791 criminal code[129]—introduced the distinction, depending upon the gravity of crimes and procedural diversity, between *crimes*, *délits* and *contraventions*.[130]

[128]On this matter, see Ernst Holthöfer, "Deciani, Tiberio", *Juristen: ein biographisches Lexikon; von der Antike bis zum 20. Jahrhundert* (Michael Stolleis, ed.) (München: Beck, 2nd ed., 2001), p. 170; see also Michele Pifferi, *Generalia delictorum. Il Tractatus criminalis di Tiberio Deciani e la "parte generale" di diritto penale* (Milano: Giuffrè, 2006); see also Friedrich Schaffstein, "Tiberius Decianus und seine Bedeutung für die Entstehung des Allgemeinen Teils im Gemeinen deutschen Strafrecht", *Abhandlungen zur Strafrechtsgeschichte und zur Wissenschaftsgeschichte* (Darmstadt: Scientia Verlag Aalen, 1986), pp. 199–226; see also F. Javier Álvarez García, "Relaciones entre la parte general y la parte especial del Derecho Penal (I)", *Anuario del Derecho Penal y de las Ciencias Penales* 46 (1993), f. III, pp. 1021–1023; Masferrer, *Tradición y reformismo en la Codificación penal española…*, pp. 114–117.

[129]The classification into *crimes*, *délits* and *contraventions* was incorporated into the French Code in 1791 with the aim of capturing not only the different gravity of the crimes, but also their procedural diversity: crimes were province of the *cours d'assies*; offences were the domain of *tribunaux correctionnels*, and breaches were province of *tribunaux de police*, with progressively simplified procedures.

[130]Art. 1 FPC 1810: The offence which the laws punish with penalties of *police* is called a CONTRAVENTION (*contravention*). The offence which the laws punish with *correctional* penalties is called a DELICT (*délit*). The offense which the laws punish with *afflictive* or *infamous* penalty is called a CRIME (*crime*).

Spanish codes, by contrast, distinguished between *delito* and *culpa* (CP 1822), or *delitos* and *faltas* (CP 1848).[131]

The parliamentary debates contain some comments on these matters. The deputy Vadillo, for example, extolled that French 'correctional penalties' had not been adopted in the Spanish code.[132] Calatrava criticized the erroneous criticism made by Conde de Toreno, who lamented the fact that the 1822 Spanish project had imitated the French code in distinguishing '*delito*' and '*culpa*'.[133] In trying to define the notion of *delito*, parliamentarians discussed first of all the appropriateness of defining crime in the code, bringing the French model into the discussion. Some maintained that the Napoleonic code made an effort to define crime. Others asserted that the French code did not contain a proper definition of criminal behavior in its different forms (*crimes*, *délits* and *contraventions*), instead just describing them depending on the kind of punishment they would carry.[134] Considering the fact that the Napoleonic code did not provide a true definition of crime, some maintained that there was no real need for a code to do so.[135] Other parliamentarians argued that the commission should be free to deviate from the French distinction between *crime* and *délit*.[136]

Calatrava took advantage of this discussion to emphasize that the distinction between *delito* and *culpa* did not come from France but from Spanish legal sources, like the *Partidas*, which in turn originated in Roman law.[137] He was convinced,

[131]Spanish deputies were fully aware that their code had willingly departed from the Napoleonic code, having rejected in general terms the French classification of crimes and punishments, and some of them seemed to be very proud of it (on this matter, see, for example, DSC, Congreso, 24 November 1821, p. 938; the roots of this classification date back to the Roman tradition and later to the *ius commune* (*delicta atrocissima, gravia et levia*). From the *ius commune* comes the distinction between *delicta atrocissima, delicta gravia et delicta levia*. The first, also known as *atrociora*, were those to which the gravest punishment (more than simple death) was attached; *gravia* (or *atrocia*), were those carrying the natural or civil death penalty; and *levia*, the ones carrying the remaining punishments. Both the French and Spanish codes departed then from this *ius commune* model; Masferrer, *Tradición y reformismo en la Codificación penal española*..., p. 121; on the 'atrocious crimes' in the Castilian legal tradition, see Isabel Ramos Vázquez, "La represión de los delitos atroces en el Derecho castellano de la Edad Moderna", *Revista de Estudios Histórico-Jurídicos* [Sección Historia del Derecho Europeo] XXVI (Valparaíso, Chile, 2004), pp. 255–299.

[132]Vadillo, DSC, Congreso, 24 November 1821, p. 938.

[133]Calatrava, DSC, Congreso, 27 November 1821, p. 1001.

[134]Gil de Linares, DSC, Congreso, 25 November 1821, p. 964; Ramonet, DSC, Congreso, 25 November 1821, p. 971; (La-Santa) "El Código francés, que se ha citado, no da definiciones de esta clase, porque decir que el crimen es aquel que se castiga con pena infamante ó corporal, no es dar definición alguna" (DSC, Congreso, 27 November 1821, p. 1003); see also DSC, Congreso, 24 November 1821, p. 938 (see fn n. 134).

[135]Conde de Toreno, DSC, Congreso, 27 November 1821, p. 1001.

[136]See, for example, Victorica, DSC, Congreso, 25 November 1821, p. 971.

[137](Calatrava) "La distinción del delito y de la culpa es mucho más antigua que nuestras leyes: todos saben cuán conocida es en el Derecho romano, del cual la tomaron los autores de nuestras Partidas" (DSC, Congreso, 27 November 1821, p. 1001).

however, that it was entirely proper for the code to give a minimal idea of *delito*, even though its definition may not have been very precise, as had happened with the *Code pénal*, whose notion of *délit* was 'not exact at all".[138] Cepero maintained the opposite opinion, namely, that it was much better not to define crime rather than to formulate an improper one.[139] He might have agreed with Gil de Linares' assertion that a definition's wording could become a matter of life or death for those governed by a criminal code.[140]

Types of punishments

As far as punishments are concerned, whereas the French code distinguished between the 'punishments of police' for contraventions, 'correctional penalties' for delicts, 'infamous punishments' and 'afflictive and infamous punishments' for crimes,[141] Spanish codes distinguished between corporeal punishments (*penas corporales*), non-corporeal punishments (*penas no corporales*), and pecuniary punishments (CP 1822, art. 28), or between corporeal punishments (*penas aflictivas*), correctional punishments (*penas correccionales*), and minor punishments (*penas leves*) (CP 1848, art. 24).

3.2.2 The Doctrinal Roots of Codifiers' Systematization Efforts: The Case of Self-defense

It may be said that Spanish codes generally adopted the structure of the Napoleonic code, as did many other European codes. It should be noted, however, that such structure resulted from the doctrinal approach to criminal law taken by *ius commune* lawyers before the French Revolution. Moreover, many aspects of the formal/structural model of the French code had appeared in previous criminal codes, which were generally accurate and formally developed.

In this sense, the systematization of criminal law, which contributed to the codification movement, was derivative and rooted in doctrinal sources. The distinction between the General Part and the Special Part, the classifications of crimes and punishments, the circumstances of criminal responsibility and the like located in the General Part had been carefully and systematically analyzed in the doctrine, although they hardly appeared in legislation prior to codes. So systematization constituted a great—but not original—contribution of the codification scheme to modern criminal law.[142] The originality consisted sometimes in translating the

[138]Calatrava, DSC, Congreso, 27 November 1821, p. 1002.

[139]Cepero, DSC, Congreso, 27 November 1821, p. 1002.

[140]Gil de Linares, DSC, Congreso, 25 November 1821, p. 964.

[141]See fn n. 132.

[142]On this matter, see Masferrer, *Tradición y reformismo en la Codificación penal española*, pp. 109 ff.; Masferrer, "Codification of Spanish Criminal Law in the Nineteenth Century…", pp. 111 ff.; see also Ramos Vázquez, "La individualización judicial de la pena en la primera codificación francesa y española", p. 130.

Latin expressions of developed institutions into modern, vernacular language. That is the case of '*moderamen inculpatae tutelae*', which the 1791 and 1810 codes called 'self-defense', a term all subsequent European codes adopted.

The *Code pénal* of 1791 was the first to substitute the old expression '*moderamen inculpatae tutelae*' with 'self-defense', which continued into the Napoleonic code (1810), although both codes curiously placed the institution in the Special Part and not in the General Part. The most important aspects were the requirements prescribed for necessary defense, which were structured around the generic expression '*cum moderamine inculpatae tutelae*,' introduced by Innocence III in the *Decretales* (*De Homicidio c.18, X*): (i) the illegal aggression in question; (ii) the *moderamen inculpatae tutelae*, that is, the *modus defensionis*, which constituted 'the true innovation' introduced by canon law in self-defense, and (iii) the defense of valuable goods.[143] The ethical implications of self-defense in canon law logically ceased with the Enlightenment, but canon law strongly contributed to its later evolution.[144]

3.3 Substantive Influences

The question remains to what extent the Napoleonic Code influenced the 19th century codification of Spanish criminal law from a substantive point of view, or to what extent the Spanish criminal codes of 1822 and 1848/50 adopted the substantive criminal law of the French code.

Whereas French influence is quite evident concerning the *Code pénal* as a legal tool and from its formal point of view, the influence was substantively much weaker for three reasons:

(1) Spanish criminal law had a long and strong tradition both legally and doctrinally. This is evident in particular institutions of criminal law whose regulation differed from that contained in the French code, such as the classification of crimes and punishments as well as the specific legal regime of some punishments that reveal their historical descent rather than the adoption of the French model.
(2) Sources depict the reluctance of some lawyers to resort to the French model when the Spanish tradition provided its own institutions, as described above. This reluctance is evident either in deputies' opinions or in the commentators'

[143]On the scholarly development of this *ius-commune* notion, see Kenneth Pennington, "*Moderamen Inculpatae Tutelae*: The Jurisprudence of a Justifiable Defense", 24 *Rivista Internazionale de Diritto Comune* 27 (2014), pp. 27–55.

[144]On the origins and development of self-defense, see Pennington, "*Moderamen Inculpatae Tutelae*: The Jurisprudence of a Justifiable Defense", cited above; from a comparative perspective, see Miguel Ángel Iglesias Río, *Perspectiva histórico-cultural y comparada de la legítima defensa* (Burgos: Universidad de Burgos, 1999); see also Masferrer, *Tradición y reformismo en la Codificación penal española…*, pp. 132–137; Masferrer, "Codification of Spanish Criminal Law in the Nineteenth Century…", pp. 122–124.

works, where lawyers emphasized cases in which Spanish provisions differed or deviated from the French model.[145]

(3) As is well known, several criminal codes were promulgated in Spain (1822,[146] 1848–1850,[147] 1870,[148] 1928,[149] 1932,[150] 1944[151] and 1995). However, the most important was that of 1848, which was the main model and reference for those that followed. While the 1822 code contained many institutions coming from the Spanish legal tradition, with the 1810 French code the main foreign influence, the code of 1848 shows much richer and diverse foreign influences, particularly the 1830 Brazilian code,[152] and resorts frequently to the Spanish legal tradition. This does not mean that French influence was totally absent. It remained, but it was much weaker than it may seem and had usually been maintained by some Spanish scholars.

Since a complete analysis of the influence of the French penal code over the Spanish would exceed the limits of this chapter, I will give a broad overview, distinguishing between the CP 1822 and the CP 1848/50. I will mainly use three sources: the parliamentary debates, particularly in the discussion of the CP 1822; the contemporary legal literature, in particular the commentaries of the CP 1848/50; and recent historiography. The overall picture will hopefully dispel the common myth about the French influence on the Spanish codes.

3.3.1 The Criminal Code of 1822

The parliamentary debates

In addition to parliamentarians' references to the French code made in 1822 and 1848 mentioned above, a few others compared specific criminal institutions that were more or less similar to the *Code pénal.*[153] The majority of the parliamentarians' comments comparing the Spanish project and the Napoleonic code dealt with

[145]See, for example, Groizard y Gómez de la Serna, *El Código penal de 1870 concordado y comentado,* vol. II, pp. 236–237.

[146]See fn n. 16.

[147]See fn n. 19.

[148]See fn n. 22.

[149]See fn n. 23.

[150]See fn n. 24.

[151]See fn n. 25.

[152]On the influence of the Brazilian code over the CP 1848, see the bibliography cited in fn nn. 43, 44 and 115.

[153]Parliamentarians strove to compare the French code in light of the Spanish social and legal background, although not always succeeding, as one reproached another in discussing article 41 of the 1822 project: Pidal, DSC, Congreso, 14 March 1848, p. 1778.

punishments rather than either the description of the crime or procedural matters. Whereas some deputies appeared satisfied that the Spanish project departed from the French text, others seemed to prefer the French regulation. Some statements even betray mixed feelings.[154]

In justifying the regulation of the punishment of '*marca*' in the Discourse of the Preliminary Title, France was mentioned, where the 1791 code abrogated that penalty only to have the 1810 code reintroduce it to deal with recidivism. So punishment was not reintroduced to humiliate or degrade the convicted, but just as a measure to assess whether the accused had been previously convicted. The 1822 commission, which first doubted the propriety of introducing this kind of punishment into the project,[155] decided to do so with the same purpose, that is, as a measure to deal effectively with recidivism.[156] Although, as the *Colegio de abogados* of Madrid noted, it was imposed less frequently than in France.[157]

In debating the death penalty, comparisons with France and England arose, either to analyze the propriety of introducing it into the code,[158] or just with the clear purpose of justifying its introduction into the penalty system.[159] Referring to specific articles, the *Colegio de abogados* of Madrid lamented that art. 347 of the 1822 project did not include the death penalty, as did the French code for the same crime.[160] Calatrava took advantage of this to criticize the *Colegio*'s incoherence, since it had initially criticized the excessive imposition of the death penalty, but became more amenable to it later.[161] The same *Colegio* requested the death penalty

---

[154]This is evident, for example, in the discussion of art. 18 of the General Part, where Gil de Linares affirmed: "Cité el Código francés, no porque deba servir de modelo para el nuestro, sino porque siendo un Código formado para afianzar el despotismo, se vé en él, no obstante, que no se impone la misma pena á todos los receptadores, sino á aquellos que lo son por hábito o profesión, y ni siquiera se hace mención de los que proporcionaban la fuga de un criminal…" (DSC, Congreso, 10 December 1821, p. 1173).

[155](*Discurso de Presentación del Título preliminar*, CP 1822) "Dudó al principio la Comisión sobre la pena de deportación y sobre la marca. La primera se halla adoptada por varias naciones cultas de Europa…" (DSC, Congreso, 22 April 1821, p. 1157); *Discurso de Presentación del Título preliminar*, CP 1822) "Pero la Asamblea Constituyente de Francia, siguiendo los pasos del gran Duque de Toscana, desterró la marca del código publicado en 1791. Pero se volvió á restablecer en el de 1810 con varias modificaciones" (DSC, Congreso, 22 April 1821, p. 1158).

[156]*Discurso de Presentación del Título preliminar*, CP 1822, DSC, Congreso, 22 April 1821, p. 1158.

[157]Calatrava, discussing art. 401 of the 1822 Project, DSC, Congreso, 21 January 1822, p. 1934; the *Colegio de abogados* of Madrid seemed to be very acquainted with the French code, as its report contained many references to it, at least compared to those given by other institutions which also sent their reports about the 1822 Project.

[158]DSC, Congreso, 10 March 1848, p. 1709.

[159]DSC, Congreso, 17 December 1821, p. 1332.

[160]The 1822 Project can be seen in DSC, Congreso, 22 April 1821, pp. 1155–1226.

[161]Calatrava, discussing art. 347 of the 1822 Project, DSC, Congreso, 20 January 1822, p. 1915.

for arson, even when no homicide resulted from it, as the Napoleonic code provided. Calatrava, talking on behalf of the commission over which he presided, rejected this proposal as overly severe.[162] Calatrava did the same with other proposals whose supporters' arguments were mainly based on the French code.[163]

The *Code pénal* particular severity was widely acknowledged. This explains why exceptional cases, for which the French code's punishments seemed softer than usual, attracted more comment from the deputies.[164] The *Colegio de abogados* of Madrid did not consistently favor severe punishments, as with art. 401 of the 1822 project, in which case—as Calatrava reported—the *Colegio* applauded that the Spanish text had departed from the severity of the French code.[165] José María Calatrava made good use of every opportunity available to emphasize the leniency of his project compared with the severity of the *Code pénal*. In replying those who wanted to impose the death penalty on 17-year-old convicts, he commented: "Are we going to be more severe in our code than the French one?"[166]

Calatrava was responsible for replying to all the criticisms made by legal institutions that had sent their reports to the parliament.[167] Sometimes, the institutions mentioned the French code when they found it more accurate or consistent. This is what the *Audiencia* (a tribunal) of Madrid did, complaining that the 1822 Project was too long (around 800 articles), whereas the *Code pénal* had only 400 articles. Calatrava made good use of these comparisons to show his acuity, responding, "if what matters is to draft an incomplete code, then I could follow the French model, feeling myself able to draft it even shorter than the French one."[168]

There were also references to the French model in discussing matters of procedural law. The procedure had to minimize the risk of convicting and executing the innocent in order to avoid repeating tragic French episodes, in which some tribunals posthumously exonerated some convicts who had already been

---

[162](Calatrava, discussing art. 800 of the 1822 Project) "El Colegio de Madrid dice que tiene por más justa la pena de muerte que impone el Código francés al incendiario aunque no resulte homicidio. En esto no puede convenir la comisión, como ya lo dije en el art. 641" (DSC, Congreso, 1 February 1822, p. 2103).

[163]See, for example, DSC, Congreso, 23 November 1821, p. 923; DSC, Congreso, 22 December 1821, p. 1409; DSC, Congreso, 16 January 1822, p. 1832; DSC, Congreso, 20 January 1822, p. 1915; DSC, Congreso, 22 January 1822, p. 1959; DSC, Congreso, 1 February 1822, p. 2103; DSC, Congreso, 5 February 1822, p. 2169.

[164](Calatrava, referring to art. 742) "El Colegio de Madrid observó que el artículo, según se presentó al principio, que faltaban algunas excepciones a favor de los hijos, mujeres, etc., añadiendo que era más benigno en esta parte el Código francés" (DSC, Congreso, 31 January 1822, p. 2086); see also DSC, Congreso, 3 January 1822, p. 1610.

[165]Calatrava, discussing art. 401 of the 1822 Project, DSC, Congreso, 24 January 1822, p. 2085.

[166]Calatrava, DSC, Congreso, 22 December 1821, pp. 1414–1415.

[167]These reports can be seen in DSC, Congreso, 23 November 1821, pp. 921 ff.

[168]Calatrava, DSC, Congreso, 23 November 1821, p. 925.

executed.[169] Another procedural matter whose debate led parliamentarians to mention the French code was the cases of '*retractación*', that is, pardons in capital cases.[170]

The question as to whether fugitives should be judged by a popular tribunal called a '*Jurado*' or by an 'extraordinary tribunal' was particularly controversial. Martínez de la Rosa maintained that fugitives should be judged by the *Jurado* rather than a special tribunal, as the French code prescribed.[171] Calatrava recognized that the commission took the *Code pénal* into consideration in this respect, although—as he said—the *Code* was not generally well regarded by its members. Eventually the commission decided that fugitives should not be judged by a *Jurado* because they did not deserve it, and the 'public good' required that these accused submit to an extraordinary procedure.[172] Romero Alpuente criticized the commission's decision because, after departing from the extraordinary tribunal foreseen in the French model, it was just stipulated that these accused go through an 'extraordinary and short procedure' that did not seem to safeguard the usual guarantees.[173] Calatrava replied to Romero Alpuente's objections by admonishing the incoherence of criticizing a commission's preference for an 'extraordinary procedure', which was similar to the solution in the French code that Romero Alpuente esteemed so much.[174]

Parliamentary debates hardly contain references to the influence of French code concerning specific criminal behaviors, leaving aside the controversy I already referred to about the book of *faltas*.[175]

An isolated reference to the French code appears in the discussion of article 302 of the 1822 project concerning the crime of rebellion or sedition ('*motín*' in

[169]"...y nos expondríamos, con escándalo de la humanidad, á ver lo que ha sucedido en Francia y en otras partes, cuando los tribunales han tenido que declarar inocentes á personas que habían hecho morir en un suplicio por falsas pruebas ó por la precipitación con que fueron juzgadas" (DSC, Congreso, 19 December 1821, p. 1364).

[170]Romero Alpuente, discussing art. 35 of the 1822 Project, DSC, Congreso, 19 December 1821, p. 1364.

[171](Martínez de la Rosa, discussing art. 59 of the 1822 Project) "Más diré: si la mente de la comisión, según han explicado sus individuos, es admitir la disposición del Código francés, y no someter al juicio de jurados estos delincuentes, también me opongo, porque la calidad de ser prófugo el acusado no debe privar á un español de la ventaja de este juicio" (DSC, Congreso, 22 December 1821, p. 1410).

[172](Calatrava, discussing art. 59 of the 1822 Project) "...nos ha citado como respetable el ejemplo del Código francés. Aunque no lo es mucho para la comisión, esta lo ha tenido presente, y ha creido que no solo porque tales reos no merecen otra cosa, sino porque el bien público lo exige, conviene que sean juzgados de una manera extraordinaria" (DSC, Congreso, 22 December 1821, p. 1410).

[173]Romero Alpuente, discussing art. 59 of the 1822 Project, DSC, Congreso, 22 December 1821, p. 1409.

[174](Calatrava, discussing art. 59 of the 1822 Project) "...y si no me equivoco, al decir que debíamos respetar el ejemplo que nos dan los franceses señalando un juicio extraordinario para estos casos, parece que lejos de impugnar la idea de la comisión, la apoya" (DSC, Congreso, 22 December 1821, p. 1409).

[175]See fn nn. 119 ff., and their main texts.

Spanish). Lagrava commented that requiring 40 people as a constitutive element of rebellion was excessive—20 were more than enough, corresponding to the *Code pénal*.[176] Calatrava's answer was drastic: since the French code did not distinguish between *motín* (rebellion or sedition) and *asonada* (violent protest), the *Code* should not have more authority than the *Cortes*, which had decided that 40 people were required for *sedición*.[177]

The discussion of art. 589 of the 1822 project contain further references to the *Code pénal*. This article defined the criminal behavior of those who refused to bear witness or give testimony. Sánchez Salvador asserted that following the French code would improve the article in terms of compensating those who forfeited their regular income to testify in a criminal trial.[178] Calatrava accepted the reasoning and added that this aspect would be introduced in the procedural code.[179]

A brief historiographical overview

Spanish historiography has carefully analyzed the sources and general influences of the CP 1822.[180] It is enough to note that (i) drafters viewed the French code as one source to examine, though it was neither the only one, nor even the most predominant[181]; and (ii) that the foreign influence in the CP 1822 was much more doctrinal than normative.[182] In this vein, along with the undeniable influence of foreign authors like Montesquieu, Voltaire, Beccaria, Bentham, Bexon and Filangieri, Spanish authors like Matheu i Sanz, Antonio Gómez and Lardizábal also had a considerable impact on the first Spanish criminal code.[183]

[176](Lagrava, discussing art. 302 of the 1822 Project) "Pero como son diferentes las penas de uno y otro delito, quisiera se pusiera el número de 20 personas como en Francia, para que siendo mayor la pena, se retrajesen de estos movimientos" (DSC, Congreso, 16 January 1822, p. 1832).

[177](Calatrava, discussing art. 302 of the 1822 Project) "El Código de Francia no distingue motines de asonada, y no debe ser autoridad para nosotros superior á la de estas Cortes, que señalaron el número de 40 personas para la sedición" (DSC, Congreso, 16 January 1822, p. 1832).

[178](Sánchez Salvador, discussing art. 589 of the 1822 Project) "…pero quisiera que así como en la legislación francesa se dice que á los que tengan que declarar separándoles de su trabajo, se les abone una gratificación, se hiciese aquí lo mismo" (DSC, Congreso, 24 January 1822, p. 1983).

[179]Calatrava (discussing art. 589 of the 1822 Project), DSC, Congreso, 24 January 1822, p. 1983.

[180]See the references in fn n. 39.

[181]Ramos Vázquez / Cañizares-Navarro, "La influencia francesa en la primera Codificación española: el Código penal francés de 1810 y el Código penal español de 1822", p. 182.

[182]According to Ramos Vázquez and Cañizares-Navarro, in their work entitled "La influencia francesa en la primera Codificación española: el Código penal francés de 1810 y el Código penal español de 1822", pp. 255–259, historiography had traditionally shown that the main sources of the CP 1822 were: (1) Encyclopedism and Cesare Beccaria; (2) the French codification movement; (3) Benthamian thought; and (4) the Spanish legal tradition. However, more recent literature shows that foreign influences were more doctrinal (Filangieri and Bexon) than normative (with the French code among others).

[183]Ramos Vázquez / Cañizares-Navarro, "La influencia francesa en la primera Codificación española: el Código penal francés de 1810 y el Código penal español de 1822", pp. 224–225.

José Ramon Casabó Ruiz, a criminal lawyer, carefully studied what inspired the CP 1822 in 1968,[184] as did a few legal historians, particularly Juan Cañizares-Navarro and Isabel Ramos Vázquez.[185]

They have shown how the drafters of CP 1822, departing from the French classification of crimes (*crimes*, *délits* and *contraventions*), opted for the simple division between *public crimes* and *private crimes*.[186]

The regulation of the principle of legality was indebted more to legal doctrine than to the French code. Whereas Filangieri and Bexon notably influenced the legality of the crime,[187] art. 3 of the CP 1822 concerning the legality of punishments was influenced by both Bexon project (art. 138 and 365) and by art. 4 of the *Code pénal*.[188] Substantively speaking, however, the introduction of some political criminal law principles that originated at the constitutional level into the European codes was not due to French influence, such as the principle of legality, concerning both the crime and its punishment, among others.[189] This principle was not new, and its 'constitutionalization' was a precondition for its 'legalization' (or 'positivization'), that is, for its introduction into the codes. From this perspective, the modern constitutions (starting with that France promulgated in 1791) and *Déclarations* (particularly of 1789) exerted more influence over the principle of legality in other European jurisdictions—Spain, among them—than the French code. However, it is also true that, once this principle was adopted in the French code, it did play a role as a legal source in its dissemination among other jurisdictions.[190]

[184]Casabó Ruiz, *El Código penal de 1822*, cited in fn n. 15.

[185]Cañizares-Navarro, "El Código Penal de 1822: sus fuentes inspiradoras. Balance historiográfico (desde el s. XX)", pp. 118–133; Ramos Vázquez / Cañizares-Navarro, "La influencia francesa en la primera Codificación española: el Código penal francés de 1810 y el Código penal español de 1822", pp. 221 ss.; see also Torres Aguilar, "El proceso de la primera codificación penal y la Constitución de Cádiz", pp. 462–464.

[186]See fn nn. 131–133; Ramos Vázquez / Cañizares-Navarro, "La influencia francesa en la primera Codificación española: el Código penal francés de 1810 y el Código penal español de 1822", p. 231; Cañizares-Navarro, "El Código Penal de 1822: sus fuentes inspiradoras. Balance historiográfico (desde el s. XX)", pp. 115–116; see also Joaquín Cuello Contreras, "Análisis de un informe anónimo aparecido en Sevilla sobre el proyecto de Código penal de 1822", *Anuario de Derecho Penal y Ciencias Penales* 30.1 (1977), pp. 83–110, particularly 99–100.

[187]Casabó Ruiz, *El Código penal de 1822*, p. 215; see also Cañizares-Navarro, *ibid.*, pp. 118–119; Ramos Vázquez / Cañizares-Navarro, *Ibid.*, pp. 234–235.

[188]Casabó Ruiz, *El Código penal de 1822*, p. 220; see also Cañizares-Navarro, *ibid.*, pp. 118–119; Ramos Vázquez / Cañizares-Navarro, *Ibid.*, pp. 234–235.

[189]Other political criminal law principles could be added, namely, the proportionality between crime and punishment, the individuality of punishment, favorable decision, favorable interpretation, and the presumption of innocence.

[190]On this matter, see the first chapter of this volume; see also Masferrer, "The Principle of Legality and Codification in the 19th century Western Criminal Law Reform", cited in the fn n. 41.

The CP 1822 distinguished crime and guilt (‘*crimen*’ and ‘*culpa*’), which was derived from the Spanish legal tradition rather than from the French code, as described above.[191] Whereas the definition of crime was indebted to the medieval texts of the *Siete Partidas* and to Filangieri,[192] both Bexon and Filangieri influenced the notion of guilt.[193]

The doctrine of commission by omission, which is contained in the CP 1822, originated in the Spanish criminal law tradition.[194]

Most of the institutions revolving around the *iter criminis* bear the mark of Bexon and Filangieri,[195] although the institution of attempt could also have been derived from the Napoleonic code.[196]

The origins of the institutions concerning those who committed or participated in the commission of crimes are not entirely clear. They might have come from neither foreign legal sources nor from the Spanish legal tradition.[197] Whereas the definition of authors or perpetrators of criminal offences might have partly originated in the doctrine of Bexon,[198] the regulation of the accomplice (‘*cómplice*’), the person concealing the act (‘*encubridor*’ or abettor), and the accessory (‘*receptador*’) could derive from both Bexon and the French code.[199]

The punishment’s purpose of both general and specific prevention (read: deterrence) in the CP 1822 was highly influenced by Jeremy Bentham and Scipion Bexon.[200]

---

[191]See fn nn. 133–135; Casabó Ruiz, *El Código penal de 1822*, pp. 282–283; see also Cañizares-Navarro, *ibid.*, p. 119; Ramos Vázquez / Cañizares-Navarro, *Ibid.*, pp. 235–236.

[192]Casabó Ruiz, *El Código penal de 1822*, pp. 247–248; José Antón Oneca, “Historia del Código penal de 1822”, *Anuario de Derecho Penal y Ciencias Penales* 18.2 (1965), pp. 263–278, particularly 272–273; see also Cañizares-Navarro, *ibid.*, p. 120; Ramos Vázquez / Cañizares-Navarro, *Ibid.*, pp. 236–237.

[193]Casabó Ruiz, *El Código penal de 1822*, pp. 248–249; see also Cañizares-Navarro, *ibid.*, pp. 120–121; Ramos Vázquez / Cañizares-Navarro, *Ibid.*, p. 237.

[194]Casabó Ruiz, *El Código penal de 1822*, pp. 266–269; see also Cañizares-Navarro, *ibid.*, p. 122; Ramos Vázquez / Cañizares-Navarro, *Ibid.*, p. 238.

[195]Casabó Ruiz, *El Código penal de 1822*, pp. 292–307; see also Cañizares-Navarro, *ibid.*, pp. 123–124; Ramos Vázquez / Cañizares-Navarro, *Ibid.*, pp. 239–240.

[196]Casabó Ruiz, *El Código penal de 1822*, pp. 310–311; see also Cañizares-Navarro, *ibid.*, p. 124; Ramos Vázquez / Cañizares-Navarro, *Ibid.*, p. 240.

[197]Casabó Ruiz, *El Código penal de 1822*, pp. 321–323, 328–331; see also Cañizares-Navarro, *ibid.*, pp. 124–125; Ramos Vázquez / Cañizares-Navarro, *Ibid.*, pp. 241–242.

[198]Casabó Ruiz, *El Código penal de 1822*, pp. 333–334; see also Cañizares-Navarro, *ibid.*, p. 125; Ramos Vázquez / Cañizares-Navarro, *Ibid.*, p. 242.

[199]Casabó Ruiz, *El Código penal de 1822*, pp. 339–346, 355; see also Cañizares-Navarro, *ibid.*, p. 125; Ramos Vázquez / Cañizares-Navarro, *Ibid.*, pp. 243–244.

[200]Casabó Ruiz, *El Código penal de 1822*, pp. 361–371; see also Cañizares-Navarro, *ibid.*, p. 127; Ramos Vázquez / Cañizares-Navarro, *Ibid.*, p. 246.

Concerning the extinction of criminal responsibility, Bexon also influenced the regulation of the deprivation of burial in public cemeteries, as well as marking the graves of those who had been convicted and executed for the crime of treason or parricide.[201]

The legal regime regarding the pardon applications of those who had been convicted or were serving their sentence was based upon Filangieri's theory of limited cases.[202]

The regulation of the rehabilitation—or *restitution in integrum*—of the convicted was required by the Constitution of Cádiz, in which all convicts whose punishment included the loss of citizenship and the attendant rights needed to be rehabilitated and regain that legal status. This constitutional provision was directly imported from the French constitution of 1793.[203]

3.3.2 The Criminal Code of 1848/50

The parliamentary debates

It is revealing that parliamentary debates rarely contain references to the French model when discussing provisions concerning substantive matters of criminal law. Unlike in 1821 and 1822, deputies did not seem to feel the need to mirror the *Code pénal* when debating the CP 1848. The two available references touch upon punishments.

Arguing in 1848 about capital punishment for political crimes, Gómez Laserna stated that, before that penalty was abrogated in France, he had already opposed its imposition for such crimes.[204]

It was also Gómez Laserna who, criticizing the severity of the '*interdicción civil*' in the 1848 Project, asserted that this punishment was somehow worse than the 'civil death' foreseen in the French code.[205]

[201]Casabó Ruiz, *El Código penal de 1822*, pp. 382–386; see also Cañizares-Navarro, *ibid.*, pp. 128–129; Ramos Vázquez / Cañizares-Navarro, *Ibid.*, pp. 248–249.

[202]Casabó Ruiz, *El Código penal de 1822*, p. 393; see also Cañizares-Navarro, *ibid.*, p. 129; Ramos Vázquez / Cañizares-Navarro, *Ibid.*, p. 249.

[203]Casabó Ruiz, *El Código penal de 1822*, pp. 401–402; see also Cañizares-Navarro, *ibid.*, p. 130; Ramos Vázquez / Cañizares-Navarro, *Ibid.*, pp. 249–250; on this matter, see also Aniceto Masferrer, "La pena de infamia en la Codificación penal española", *Ius fugit. Revista Interdisciplinar de Estudios Histórico-Jurídicos* 7 (1998), pp. 123–176, particularly pp. 160–163; Aniceto Masferrer, *La pena de infamia en el Derecho histórico español. Contribución al estudio de la tradición penal europea en el marco del ius commune* (Madrid: Dykinson, 2001), pp. 380–385.

[204]Gómez Laserna, discussing the propriety of imposing the death penalty on the convicts for political crimes, DSC, Congreso, 13 March 1848, p. 1742.

[205]Gómez Laserna, DSC, Congreso, 14 March 1848, p. 1769.

Recent historiography and legal doctrine: the commentaries of the CP 1848/50

In exploring the foreign influences of the CP 1848/50, scholars have carefully analyzed the parliamentary debates and the commentaries written by criminal lawyers, at least some of whom were members of its drafting committees. This work has revealed that only few commentators discussed the inspirations for and influences on the CP provisions. Specifically, only two commentaries of the CP 1848/50 contain relevant references, namely, Pacheco's *Código penal concordado y comentado*[206] and Vizmanos and Álvarez Martínez's *Comentarios al Nuevo Código penal*,[207] both published in 1848.[208] Moreover, these commentators were all drafters of the CP 1848.

Just as the CP 1822 diverged from the classification of criminal offences of the French code (*crimes, délits and contraventions*),[209] so too did the CP 1848, distinguishing between crime (or '*delito*') and misdemeanor (or '*falta*').[210]

Concerning the institutions relating to the iter criminis,[211] the CP 1848 followed neither the Spanish legal tradition nor foreign influences. Along with the consummation of the offence (or '*delito consumado*'), drafters made an unprecedented distinction between 'complete attempts' ('*delito fustrado*'), in which the perpetrator accomplished all plans to achieve the desired result but without success, and 'incomplete attempts' (or '*tentativa*' [de delito]), in which the perpetrator failed to complete the acts needed to achieve the crime's result successfully. Pacheco underlined the unprecedented character of this distinction, which was not foreseen by "either by the French code, the Austrian code or the Brazilian one."[212]

Dealing with the offenders (perpetrators and accomplices)[213] with a more explicit focus on the diverse types of participation and after rejecting the old laws on the matter, Vizmanos and Álvarez Martínez also emphasized the originality of the Spanish text, which did not follow the foreign models (France, Austria, the Two Sicilies and Brazil) and whose final outcome was "not comparable to other European models."[214] Pacheco, commenting on the accomplices, particularly on

---

[206]See fn n. 4.

[207]See fn n. 57.

[208]On this matter, see Masferrer / Sánchez-González, "Tradición e influencias extranjeras en el Código penal de 1848…", pp. 281–296 (Joaquín Francisco Pacheco), 297–322 (Tomás María de Vizmanos and Cirilo Álvarez Martínez), 322–331 (concerning other lawyers who made no references at all on the foreign influences of the CP 1848).

[209]See fn n. 188.

[210]Pacheco, *Código penal concordado y comentado*, pp. 70–72; Masferrer / Sánchez-González, "Tradición e influencias extranjeras en el Código penal de 1848…", pp. 288–289.

[211]On the CP 1822, see fn nn. 197 and 198.

[212]Pacheco, *Código penal concordado y comentado*, p. 98; Masferrer / Sánchez-González, "Tradición e influencias extranjeras en el Código penal de 1848…", p. 290.

[213]Vizmanos / Álvarez Martínez, *Comentarios al Nuevo Código Penal*, pp. 239–240.

[214]Vizmanos / Álvarez Martínez, *Comentarios al Nuevo Código Penal*, pp. 158–161, particularly p. 161; Masferrer / Sánchez-González, "Tradición e influencias extranjeras en el Código penal de 1848…", pp. 304–307.

those who conspire and incite the perpetration of a crime (art. 4 CP 1848), pointed out that such regulation might have derived from CP 1822, which was indirectly indebted to the French code.[215]

According to Pacheco, the regulation of madness or insanity ('locura' or 'demencia') as grounds to eliminate culpability (or non-accountability; art. 8.1 CP 1848) originated both in the Spanish legal tradition and in the code of Brazil.[216] He pointed out the same concerning the self-defense.[217]

Vizmanos and Álvarez Martínez maintained that the legal regime of the CP 1848 concerning circumstances mitigating criminal responsibility was unique, combining elements of the Spanish legal tradition (*Siete Partidas*) and the *Code pénal* of 1791.[218] They also stated that the evaluation of convicts' economic circumstances for pecuniary punishments derived from the medieval text of the *Siete Partidas* (P. VII, 31, 8).[219]

Judicial discretion and circumstances of crimes were drafted in accordance with the Brazilian code, rejecting both the Spanish legal tradition and the French model.[220]

The provisions concerning the enforcement of criminal sanctions did not come from any foreign model. The CP 1848 drafters, after having rejected the legal regimes contained in the codes of France, Brazil, the Two Sicilies and Austria, opted for a different legal regime.[221]

According to Vizmanos and Álvarez Martínez, the regulation of the gradation of punishment partly adopted the Brazilian model.[222] They also pointed out that the

---

[215]Pacheco, *Código penal concordado y comentado*, pp. 107–108; Masferrer / Sánchez-González, "Tradición e influencias extranjeras en el Código penal de 1848...", p. 291.

[216]Pacheco, *Código penal concordado y comentado*, pp. 130–131; Masferrer / Sánchez-González, "Tradición e influencias extranjeras en el Código penal de 1848...", p. 292.

[217]Pacheco, *Código penal concordado y comentado*, pp. 149–150; Masferrer / Sánchez-González, "Tradición e influencias extranjeras en el Código penal de 1848...", p. 292.

[218]Vizmanos / Álvarez Martínez, *Comentarios al Nuevo Código Penal*, p. 101; Masferrer / Sánchez-González, "Tradición e influencias extranjeras en el Código penal de 1848...", pp. 297–298.

[219]Vizmanos / Álvarez Martínez, *Comentarios al Nuevo Código Penal*, pp. 307–308; Masferrer / Sánchez-González, "Tradición e influencias extranjeras en el Código penal de 1848...", p. 298.

[220]Vizmanos / Álvarez Martínez, *Comentarios al Nuevo Código Penal*, pp. 103–110, 129–130; Masferrer / Sánchez-González, "Tradición e influencias extranjeras en el Código penal de 1848...", pp. 299–302.

[221]Vizmanos / Álvarez Martínez, *Comentarios al Nuevo Código Penal*, pp. 279–280; Masferrer / Sánchez-González, "Tradición e influencias extranjeras en el Código penal de 1848...", pp. 307–308.

[222]Vizmanos / Álvarez Martínez, *Comentarios al Nuevo Código Penal*, pp. 302–305; Masferrer / Sánchez-González, "Tradición e influencias extranjeras en el Código penal de 1848...", pp. 310–311.

drafters, in writing the provisions concerning the age of criminal responsibility, adopted a variety of elements from different foreign codes.[223]

The sources also divulge information about the commentators' attitudes toward foreign influences in general and the French in particular. Pacheco explicitly acknowledged that the Spanish CP 1848 was particularly influenced by the code of Brazil.[224] He thought that the regulation of some matters was already obsolete in the mid-19th century. That was the case, for example, of the regulation of the gradation of punishments (art. 79 CP 1848), where it would have been senseless to resort to the French code when the codes of Brazil and the Two Sicilies were much more advanced.[225] However, he did not seem to have any aversion to the French code. In fact, he sometimes lamented that some provisions (for example, art. 42 and 70 of the CP 1848) had not been drafted in accordance with the French model.[226]

Vizmanos and Álvarez Martínez severely disdained the French code and were not shy in expressing it. Comparing the models of Brazil and France, they praised the former and criticized the latter.[227] Such criticism was particularly strong when dealing with particular institutions, like the punishments of infamy, civil interdiction, civil death or the perpetual penalties, which reflected the inhumanity of the French code compared to other foreign models.[228] There were exceptions, in which they praised French regulation, when looking at the legal regime of pardons for example, because they would have preferred the models of France and Naples, where it was regulated in the criminal procedure code rather than in the criminal code.[229] But these were just exceptions to the rule of criticizing the French code.

---

[223]Vizmanos / Álvarez Martínez, *Comentarios al Nuevo Código Penal*, pp. 297–298, 70–71; Masferrer / Sánchez-González, "Tradición e influencias extranjeras en el Código penal de 1848…", pp. 315–316.

[224]Pacheco, *Código penal concordado y comentado*, pp. 66–67: "Un solo código ha seguido el mismo método que el nuestro; ó por decirlo mas bien, somos nosotros los que hemos copiado el suyo. Hablamos del código de Brasil. En esa ley fue en la que encontró nuestra comisión el modelo artístico, el boceto, si así puede decirse, de su obra. Parecióle filosófico y oportuno; y lo aceptó sin vacilar, salvo el extender sus proporciones, y el mejorarlo ó completarlo en sus detalles. Hizo bien; y nadie la culpará por ser imitadora, si lo que imitaba era digno de ser seguido. La exactitud y el acierto en estas materias no son únicamente propiedad de quien las halla: son propiedad común, pertenecen el mundo todo. La razón y la filosofía son como el sol, patrimonio de la humanidad"; Masferrer / Sánchez-González, "Tradición e influencias extranjeras en el Código penal de 1848…", p. 282; see also fn nn. 43 and 44.

[225]Pacheco, *Código penal concordado y comentado*, p. 427; Masferrer / Sánchez-González, "Tradición e influencias extranjeras en el Código penal de 1848…", pp. 295–296.

[226]Pacheco, *Código penal concordado y comentado*, p. 347 (art. 42) and 401 (art. 70); Masferrer / Sánchez-González, "Tradición e influencias extranjeras en el Código penal de 1848…", p. 294.

[227]Masferrer / Sánchez-González, "Tradición e influencias extranjeras en el Código penal de 1848…", pp. 307–308.

[228]Vizmanos / Álvarez Martínez, *Comentarios al Nuevo Código Penal*, pp. 219, 257–259; Masferrer / Sánchez-González, "Tradición e influencias extranjeras en el Código penal de 1848…", pp. 313–314; on the punishment of infamy, see the bibliography of the fn n. 205.

[229]Vizmanos / Álvarez Martínez, *Comentarios al Nuevo Código Penal*, p. 265; Masferrer / Sánchez-González, "Tradición e influencias extranjeras en el Código penal de 1848…", p. 315.

Along with the references to the French code (1810), Vizmanos and Álvarez Martínez frequently mentioned other foreign codes, particularly the codes of Brazil (1830), Austria (1803),[230] Naples (1819)[231] and the Two Sicilies (1819).[232] The code of Brazil was undoubtedly the most cited,[233] and it also seems to be the most favored by the drafters of the CP 1848.[234]

Particular institutions: an on-going research project

Punishments are a particularly informative group of criminal law institutions with regard to the influence of the French codes over the codification of criminal law in Spain. A historical analysis of the French tradition reveals that the codification's punitive system was relatively similar to that in force in France in the 18th century. Describing the variety of punishments, Muyart de Vouglans, a famous French lawyer,[235] mentioned the following typology of punishments: capital,[236] corporeal,[237] afflictive,[238] infamous,[239] and pecuniary.[240]

[230]Vizmanos and Álvarez Martínez, in their *Comentarios al Nuevo Código Penal*, repeatedly mentioned the code of Austria when dealing with: the aggravating circumstance of recidivism (pp. 147–148), judicial discretion in the gradation of punishments (pp. 302–303), age of criminal responsibility (pp. 70–71), prescription of punishments (pp. 405, 407–408), order of pecuniary responsibilities of crimes committed by the perpetrator and several accomplices (pp. 269–271).

[231]Vizmanos and Álvarez Martínez, in their *Comentarios al Nuevo Código Penal*, mentioned several times the code of Naples, when dealing with the pardon (p. 383) and the gradation of punishments (pp. 407–408).

[232]Vizmanos and Álvarez Martínez, in their *Comentarios al Nuevo Código Penal*, mentioned several times the code of Two Sicilies, when dealing with the following matters: minority or age of criminal responsibility (pp. 70–71, 269, 279), mitigating circumstances of criminal responsibility (pp. 146–147, 265, 383, 408), and the order of pecuniary responsibilities of crimes committed by the perpetrator and several accomplices (p. 269).

[233]Vizmanos and Álvarez Martínez, *Comentarios al Nuevo Código Penal*, pp. 129, 146, 188, 279, 297, 305, 307, 309, 323, 383, 399, etc.; Masferrer / Sánchez-González, "Tradición e influencias extranjeras en el Código penal de 1848…", pp. 297 ff., particularly 317–319.

[234]Masferrer / Sánchez-González, "Tradición e influencias extranjeras en el Código penal de 1848…", pp. 316–319; see also the references contained in fn n. 115.

[235]Pierre-Francois Muyart de Vouglans, *Les lois criminelles de France, dans leus ordre naturel* (Paris, 1780), pp. 53–88; for an overview of the French criminal law in the 18th century, see also his *Institutes au droit criminel, ou principes généraux sur ces matières, suivant le droit civil, canonique, et la jurisprudence du Royaume; avec un traité particulier des crimes*. Paris, 1768.

[236]Muyart de Vouglans, *Les lois criminelles de France…*, pp. 53–59.

[237]Muyart de Vouglans, *Les lois criminelles de France…*, pp. 59–67.

[238]Muyart de Vouglans, *Les lois criminelles de France…*, pp. 68–73.

[239]Muyart de Vouglans, *Les lois criminelles de France…*, pp. 74–81; among the infamous punishments, he distinguished the *infamia iuris* from the *infamia facti*. He regarded as *infamia iuris* the civil death, *la condamnation de la memoire*, the *blâme*, the nobility's degradation, and the perpetual interdiction or the disqualification—privation—from holding an office (Muyart de Vouglans, *Les lois criminelles de France…*, pp. 75–77). He considered as *infamia facti* the punishment of admonition, *l'abstention des lieux*, and the temporary interdiction (Muyart de Vouglans, *Les lois criminelles de France…*, pp. 80–81).

[240]Muyart de Vouglans, *Les lois criminelles de France…*, pp. 81–88.

Bérenguer distinguished between capital punishments (death penalty,[241] galleys, perpetual exile or banishment), afflictive punishments (any kind of corporeal punishment), and infamous punishments (*l'amende*, temporary exile, *le blame*, and the criminal *amende*).[242] In addition to these, he showed that the distinction between principal penalties and accessory penalties existed at least from the Criminal Ordinances of 1670 promulgated by Louis XIV.[243]

It may be that some punishments included in the French criminal code were partly adopted by other European codes, but this requires careful analysis. For Spain, as in France, many punishments in the codes originated in the domestic criminal law tradition.[244] The question is to what extent these punishments were influenced by the *Code pénal*. I will briefly a few some examples.

The French model scarcely influenced the punishment of infamy in the 1822 criminal code,[245] and it was abolished in 1848,[246] even though France continued to enforce it until 1994.[247] The disqualification from holding public office as a consequence of a criminal conviction reflects a certain degree of influence from the Napoleonic code,[248] but much less than from other European jurisdictions, such as Germany.[249] The same applies to civil interdiction. Whereas in Spain this

---

[241]Civil death was regulated in France for the first time with this expression ('*morte civil*') in the Criminal Ordinances of 1670; on this matter, see Achille Renaud, *La mort civile en France. Par suite de condamnations judiciaires, son origine et développement* (Paris, 1843), p. 10.

[242]Alphonse-Marie-Marcellin-Thomas Bérenger, *De la répression pénale, de ses formes et de ses effets* (Paris, 1855), pp. 410–411.

[243]Bérenger, *De la répression pénale…*, p. 412; see also Daniel Jousse, *Nouveau commentaire sur l'Ordennance criminelle du mois d'Aout 1670* (Paris, 1763).

[244]For a general view on that matter, see Masferrer, *Tradición y reformismo en la Codificación penal española…*, pp. 159 ff.; Masferrer, "Codification of Spanish Criminal Law in the Nineteenth Century…", pp. 132–136.

[245]On the punishment of infamy in the Spanish criminal-law tradition, see Masferrer, *La pena de infamia en el Derecho histórico español…*, cited in fn n. 205; Masferrer, "La pena de infamia en la Codificación penal española", also cited in fn n. 205.

[246]Art. 23 CP 1848: "La ley no reconoce pena infamante alguna" ['Law does not recognize any penalty of infamy']; on the abolition of this punishment in Spain, see Masferrer, *La pena de infamia en el Derecho histórico español…*, pp. 385–389; Masferrer, "La pena de infamia en la Codificación penal española", pp. 170–175; Masferrer, "Codification of Spanish Criminal Law in the Nineteenth Century…", pp. 131–132.

[247]On the punishment of infamy in the French criminal-law tradition, see Bernard Beignier, *L'honneur et le droit* (Paris, 1995); see also Pierre Louis de Lacretelle, *Discours sur le préjugé des peines infamantes* (Paris, 1784).

[248]Aniceto Masferrer, *La inhabilitación y suspensión del ejercicio de la función pública en la tradición penal europea y anglosajona. Especial consideración a los Derechos francés, alemán, español, inglés y norteamericano* (Madrid: Servicio de Publicaciones del Ministerio del Interior, 2009), pp. 185–316.

[249]For the development of this punishment in Germany, see Masferrer, *La inhabilitación y suspensión del ejercicio de la función pública en la tradición penal europea y anglosajona*, pp. 101–183.

punishment affected only private law,[250] in other European countries (Prussia, Portugal, Italy and Belgium, among others) its legal consequences affected both private law and public law because of the French model's influence.[251]

More examples could be added. In fact, this is the subject of on-going research involving a group of scholars from various jurisdictions, Spain among them.[252] This volume presents some of its results, and the present chapter hardly encapsulates what Spanish historiography has achieved in recent years. Moreover, a group of Spanish legal historians are working on a book that will notably advance the current state of the field.[253]

4 Conclusions

Nineteenth century criminal law reform was carried out through codification. The weight of legal tradition and foreign influences in the codification process is inextricably linked to the dichotomy between tradition and reform. The traditional historiography, which presents the criminal codes as breaking with the past, has contributed to overestimations of French influence over European codes in general and the Spanish ones in particular, creating a myth of French influence over the Spanish codification of criminal law.

The present chapter aimed to dispel this myth. Without denying French influence, the sources, particularly the parliamentary debates, legal doctrine and historiography, enable a more balanced view that shows the specific scope of French influence. I have distinguished three levels or types of influence: (1) the idea of the code itself; (2) the formal/structural influence; and (3) the substantive influence.

(1) The French influence on *the idea of the code itself* is undeniable. The influence of the *Code pénal* of Napoleon on Spain and other European countries was primarily due to its being the first modern criminal code in Europe. The Napoleonic codes were the first 'modern' codes, which is why European drafters focused on them. The Spanish parliamentary debates neatly reflect this kind of influence.

---

[250]José Luis Manzanares Samaniego, "La pena de interdicción civil", *Anuario del Derecho Penal y de las Ciencias Penales*, 1979, II pp. 345–380; Juan José González Rus, "La supresión de la pena de interdicción civil", *La Ley. Revista jurídica española de doctrina, jurisprudencia y bibliografía* 4 (1984), pp. 1088–1094; Fermín Morales Prats, "Fundamento político-criminal de la supresión de la pena de interdicción civil", *Revista Jurídica de Catalunya* 85, I (1986), pp. 155–180.

[251]Groizard y Gómez de la Serna, *El Código penal de 1870 concordado y comentado,* vol. II, pp. 236–237; see also Masferrer, *La inhabilitación y suspensión del ejercicio de la función pública en la tradición penal europea y anglosajona*, pp. 254–255.

[252]See fn n. 52.

[253]Masferrer, *La Codificación penal española…*, cited in fn n. 50.

(2) The second level of influence of the French Napoleonic code, that is, *the formal or structural one*, was also present, although perhaps slightly weaker than the first one. The greatest legacy of the modern codification was the division between the General Part and the Special Part. This division was not original to the French criminal code, but the French text highly contributed to its propagation among European codes. The Spanish criminal codes generally adopted the structure of the Napoleonic code, as did many other European codes, but (i) this structure was the result of the doctrinal approach to criminal law undertaken by *ius commune* lawyers before the French Revolution, and (ii) many aspects of the formal/structural model of the French code had been introduced in more recent criminal codes (e.g. Brazil), which were considerably well structured or formally developed.

I emphasized that most of the criminal law institutions contained in the General Part (the classification of crimes and punishments, the circumstances of criminal responsibility, etc.) had been carefully and systematically analyzed with reference to doctrine, although they hardly appeared in legislation prior to the codes. Systematization was one of the main contributions of the codification scheme to modern criminal law, but it was not original. Decianus's late 16th century *Tractatus criminalis* shows the progressive, systematic approach to the criminal law by lawyers in the *ius-commune* tradition. The origin and development of the expression '*moderamen inculpatae tutelae*', which was introduced as 'self-defense' in the French codes of 1791 and 1810, and later adopted by all subsequent European codes, also shows the gradual process of systematization over the centuries.

(3) If the greatest legacy of the modern codification was more formal than substantive, the division between the General Part and the Special Part being paramount, it is understandable *the substantive influence* of the Napoleonic Code over 19th century Spanish criminal codes was weaker. Whereas the formal influence of the *Code pénal* and as a legal tool is evident, it was much weaker substantively for three reasons:

(i) Spanish criminal law had a long and strong tradition both legally and doctrinally, which was reflected in the divergence of some criminal law institutions from the French model.
(ii) The sources document the reluctance of many lawyers to resort to the French model when the Spanish tradition had comparable institutions of its own. Such reluctance came either from deputies or commentators, where lawyers emphasized the cases in which the Spanish provisions differed or deviated from the French model.
(iii) Although several criminal codes were promulgated in Spain (1822, 1848–1850, 1870, 1928, 1932, 1944 and 1995), CP 1848 was the most important as the main model and reference for those that followed. Though the code of 1822 contained many institutions coming from the Spanish legal tradition, the 1810 French code being the main foreign influence, the code of 1848 shows much richer and diverse foreign influences, particularly the 1830

Brazilian code, as well as a considerable debt to the Spanish legal tradition. This does not mean that French influence was totally absent substantively. It was present, but it was much weaker than it may seem, and weaker than usually maintained in Spanish historiography.

References

Agüero, Alejandro / Lorente, Marta, "Penal enlightenment in Spain: from Beccaria's reception to the first criminal code", *Forum Historiae Iuris*, http://www.forhistiur.de/zitat/1211aguero-lorente.htm, November, 2012 (it has also been republished in *The Spanish Enlightenment revisited*, Jesús Astigarraga, ed., Voltaire Foundation–University of Oxford, 2015).

Alonso Romero, Mª Paz, *Orden procesal y garantías entre Antiguo Régimen y constitucionalismo gaditano* (Madrid: Centro de Estudios Constitucionales, 2008).

Alonso y Alonso, J. M., "De la vigencia y aplica-ción del Código Penal de 1822", *Revista de Estudios penitenciarios* 11 (1946), pp. 2–15.

Alvarado Planas, Javier, "La codificación penal en la España isabelina: la influencia del Código penal del Brasil en el Código penal español de 1848", *España en la época de la Fundación de la Guardia Civil* (V Seminario Duque de Ahumada: 18, 19 y 20 May 1993) (Madrid: Ministerio del Interior, 1994), pp. 43–82.

Álvarez Alonso, Clara, "¿Neoclásicos o prerrománticos? La Ilustración penal española entre la 'barroca prohibición' de interpretar las leyes y el principio de legalidad revolucionario", *Quaderni Fiorentini per la storia del pensiero giuridico moderno* 36 (2007), pp. 81–130.

Álvarez Cid, J. / Álvarez Cid, T., *El Código penal de 1870* (Córdoba, 1908).

Álvarez García, F. Javier, "Contribución al estudio sobre la aplicación del Código Penal de 1822", *Cuadernos de Política criminal,* (1978), pp. 229 ss.

Álvarez García, F. Javier, Relaciones entre la parte general y la parte especial del Derecho Penal (I)", *Anuario del Derecho Penal y de las Ciencias Penales* 46 (1993), f. III, pp. 1021–1023.

Antón Oneca, José, "Los antecedentes del nuevo Código penal", *Revista General de Legislación y Jurisprudencia* 154 (1929), pp. 30–61.

Antón Oneca, José, "El Código penal de 1848 y D. Joaquín Francisco Pacheco", *Anuario de Derecho Penal y de las Ciencia Penales* 18 (1965), pp. 473–495.

Antón Oneca, José, "El Código Penal de 1870", *Anuario del Derecho Penal y de las Ciencias Penales* 23 (1970), pp. 229–251.

Antón Oneca, José, "Historia del Código Penal de 1822", *Anuario de Derecho Penal y Ciencias Penales* 18 (1965), pp. 263 ss.

Antonio Fernández, N., *Manuel de Seijas Lozano. Tras las huellas de un liberal olvidado* (Madrid: Colegio de Registradores de la Propiedad y Mercantiles de España, 2007).

Azcutia, M., *La Ley penal. Estudios prácticos sobre la interpretación, inteligencia y aplicación del Código de 1870, en su relación con los de 1848 y 1850, con nuestras antiguas Leyes patrias y con las principales legislaciones extranjeras* (Madrid, 1876).

Babiano Mora, J., y Fer-nández Asperilla, A., "Justicia y delito en el Discurso liberal de las Cortes de Cádiz", *Antiguo Régimen y Liberalismo. Homenaje a Miguel* Artola, vol. 2, Econo-mía y Sociedad (Madrid, 1995), pp. 387–399.

Bádenas Zamora, Antonio, "Influjos de la codificación en el proceso penal español", *La Codificación española. Una aproximación doctrinal e historiográfica a sus influencias extranjeras, y a la francesa en particular* (Aniceto Masferrer, ed.) (Pamplona: Aranzadi–Thomson Reuters, 2014), pp. 449–496.

Baró Pazos, Juan, "El derecho penal español en el vacío entre dos códigos (1822–1848)", *AHDE* 83 (2013), pp. 105–138.

Baró Pazos, Juan, "El proceso de la codificación del Derecho en el marco del constitucionalismo español", E. Martínez Ruiz, M. Torres Aguilar y M. de Pazzis Pi Corrales (eds.), *Codificación y constitucionalismo: Actas del IX Encuentro España-Suecia* (Córdoba: Diputación de Córdoba, 2003), pp. 22–40.

Baró Pazos, Juan, "La influencia del Código civil francés (1804) en el Código civil español (1889)", *La Codificación española. Una aproximación doctrinal e historiográfica a sus influencias extranjeras, y a la francesa en particular* (Aniceto Masferrer, ed.) (Pamplona: Aranzadi–Thomson Reuters, 2014), pp. 53–128.

Beignier, Bernard, *L'honneur et le droit* (Paris, 1995).

Benítez Ortúzar, I. F., "El principio de legalidad penal en la Constitución española de 1812. Su proyección en el Código Penal de 1822", *Sobre un hito jurídico. La Constitución de 1812. Reflexiones actuales, estado de la cuestión, debates historiográficos* (Chamocho Cantudo, M. A., Lozano Miralles, J., edit.) (Jaén: Universidad de Jaén, 2012), pp. 195–209.

Benito Fraile, E. de, "Nuevas aportaciones al estudio sobre la aplicación práctica del Código Penal de 1822", *Foro. Nueva época* 8 (2008), pp. 41–68.

Bérenger, Alphonse-Marie-Marcellin-Thomas, *De la répression pénale, de ses formes et de ses effets* (Paris, 1855).

Bermejo Cabrero, José Luis, "Sobre la entrada en vigor del Código Penal de 1822", *Anuario de Historia del Derecho Español*, 66 (1996), pp. 967–972.

Bermejo Castrillo, Manuel, "Primeras luces de codificación. El Código como concepto y temprana memoria de su advenimiento en España", *AHDE* 83 (2013), pp. 9–64.

Brandt, Christian, *Die Entstehung des Code pénal von 1810 und sein Einfluß auf die Strafgesetzgebung der deutschen Partikularstaaten des 19. Jahrhunderts am Beispiel Bayerns und Preußens* (Frankfurt / Main: Peter Lang, 2002).

Bravo Lira, Bernardino, "Bicentenario del Código penal de Austria. Su proyección desde el Danubio a Filipinas", *Revista de Estudios Histórico-Jurídicos de Valparaíso* (Chile) 26 (2004), pp. 140–145).

Bravo Lira, Bernardino, "Fortuna del Código penal español de 1848. Historia en cuatro actos y tres Continentes: de Mello Freire y Zeiller a Vasconcelos y Seijas Lozano", *AHDE* 74 (2004), pp. 23–58.

Buenaventura Selva, Narciso, *Comentarios al Código penal reformado y planteado provisionalmente por Ley de 3 de junio de 1870* (Madrid, 1870).

Cadafalch y Burguñá, Joaquín, *Discurso sobre el atraso y descuido del Derecho penal hasta el siglo XVIII* (Madrid, 1849).

Candil Jiménez, Francisco, "Observaciones sobre la intervención de D. Joaquín Francisco Pacheco en la colaboración del Código Penal de 1848", *ADPCP* 28 (1975), pp. 405–441.

Casabó Ruiz, José R., "La aplicación del Código penal de 1822", *Anuario de Derecho penal y Ciencias penales,* fasc. II (1979), pp. 333–344.

Casabó Ruiz, José R., *El Código penal de 1822* (Valencia, 1968, Doctoral thesis unpublished).

Castejón, F., "Apuntes de historia política y legislativa del Código penal de 1848", *Revista General de Legislación y Jurisprudencia* (Madrid, 1953), pp. 105–113.

Castejón, F., "Génesis y breve comentario del Código penal de 23 de diciembre de 1944", *Revista General de Legislación y Jurisprudencia* 9 (1945), pp. 170 ff., 327 ff., 457 ff., and 634 ff.

Castejón, F., "Las ideas penales en la época del Código penal de 1870", *Conmemoración del centenario de la Ley provisional sobre organización del Poder Judicial y del Código penal de 1870,* Real Academia de Jurisprudencia y Legislación (Madrid, 1970).

Castejón, F., *Derecho penal, Criminología general y especial ajustada a la legislación española vigente hasta fin de 1930,* vol. I (Madrid, 1931).

Castejón, F., *Derecho penal, Criminología general y especial*, t. I (Madrid, 1935).

Castro Orozco, José de / Ortiz de Zúñiga, Manuel, *Código penal explicado para la común inteligencia y fácil explicación de sus disposiciones*. 3 vols. (Granada: Manuel Sanz, 1848).

Cavanna, A., "Codificazione del diritto italiano e imperialismo giuridico francese nella Milano napoleonica. Giuseppe Luosi e il diritto penale", *Ius Mediolani. Studi di Storia del diritto milanese offerti dagli allievi a Giulio Vismara* (Milano, 1996), pp. 659–760.

Cavanna, A., *La codificazione penale in Italia. Le origine lombade* (Milano, 1975).
Clavero, Bartolomé, "Idea de Código en la Ilustración Jurídica", *Historia. Instituciones. Documentos (HID)* 6 (1979), pp. 49–88.
Clavero, Bartolomé, "La disputa del método en las postrimerías de una sociedad, 1789–1808", *AHDE* 48 (1978), pp. 307–334.
Clavero, Bartolomé, "Origen constitucional de la codificación civil en España (entre Francia y Norteamérica)", C. Petit (coord.), *Derecho privado y revolución burguesa* (Madrid: Marcial Pons, 1990), pp. 53–85.
Cobo del Rosal, Gabriela, "Codificación en un periodo de alteración de los Derechos Fundamentales: el Código penal de 1928", *Estado de Derecho y derechos fundamentales en la lucha contra el terrorismo. Una aproximación multidisciplinar (histórica, jurídico-comparada, filosófica y económica* (Aniceto Masferrer, ed.) (Pamplona: Aranzadi-Thomson Reuters, 2011).
Cobo del Rosal, Gabriela, *La creación Legislativa en materia penal en los Siglos de la Codificación XIX-XX* (Madrid: Dykinson, 2013).
Cobo del Rosal, Gabriela, *Las Actas de la Comisión General de Codificación* (Madrid: Dykinson, 2013).
Cobo del Rosal, M., "El sistema de penas y el arbitrio judicial en el Código penal de 1870", en conmemoración del centenario de la Ley provisional sobre organización del Poder Judicial y del Código penal de 1870, *Real Academia de Jurisprudencia y Legislación* (Madrid, 1970), pp. 69–89.
Cuello Calón, E., "Reformas introducidas en el Código penal y en las Leyes penales especiales por la Legislación del nuevo Estado", *Revista de la Facultad de Derecho,* Madrid, 6–7 (July-December 1941), pp. 37–51.
Cuello Calón, Eugenio, *Código penal de 8 de septiembre de 1928* (Barcelona, 1929).
Cuello Calón, Eugenio, *Derecho penal conforme al Código penal, Texto Refundido de 1944. Parte general* (Madrid, 1946).
Cuello Calón, Eugenio, *El nuevo Código penal español* (Barcelona, 1929).
Cuello Calón, Eugenio, *Exposición del Código penal reformado de 1932* (Barcelona, 1933).
Cuello Calón, Eugenio, *Manual de Derecho penal español conforme al nuevo Código penal. Parte general* (Barcelona, 1945).
Cuello Calón, Eugenio, "Centenario del Código de 1848: Pacheco, penalista y legislador", *Información Jurídica.* Madrid, 1948, pp. 5–8.
Cuello Contreras, Joaquín, "Análisis de un informe anónimo aparecido en Se-villa sobre el proyecto de Código penal de 1822", *Anuario de Derecho Penal y Ciencias Penales* 30.1 (1977), pp. 83–110.
Cuerdo Mir, Miguel / Sánchez González, Mª Dolores del Mar, "Tradiciones penales en la maquinación para alterar el precio de las cosas del Código Penal de 1848", *AHDE* 84 (2014), pp. 301–326.
D. J. S. / D. A., de B., *Código penal de España comentado* (Barcelona: Imprenta de Tomás Gorchs, 1949).
De Lacretelle, Pierre Louis, *Discours sur le préjugé des peines infamantes* (Paris, 1784).
Del Rosal, Juan, "Ideas histórico-dogmáticas del Código penal de 1944", *Información jurídica*, Madrid 54 (1947), pp. 3–38.
Del Rosal, Juan, "La palabra y la expresión en el Código penal de 1870", *Conmemoración del centenario de la Ley provisional sobre organización del Poder Judicial y del Código penal de 1870.* Academia de Jurisprudencia y Legislación, Madrid, 1970 (republished later, with the same title in *Cosas de Derecho penal* (Madrid, 1973), pp. 67–132.
Dezza, E., "Un critico milanese della codificazione penale napoleonica. Pietro Mantegazza e le Osservazione criminaledel cessato Regno d'Italia (1814)", *Ius Mediolani. Studi di Storia del diritto milanese offerti dagli allievi a Giulio Vismara* (Milano, 1996), pp. 909–977.
Engelbrecht, J., "The French model and German society: the impact of the code pénal on the Rhineland", *Revolutions et justice en Europe. Modeles francais et traditions nationales (1780–1830)* (L'Harmattan, 1999), pp. 101–107.

Fabregas del Pilar, J.M., "El nuevo Código penal y el discurso del Señor Ministro de Gracia y Justicia en la apertura de los Tribunales", *Revista General de Legislación y Jurisprudencia*, 1928, pp. 282 ff.
Feherenbach, E., *Traditionale Gesellschaft und revolutionäres Recht: Die Einführung des Code Napoleón in den Rheinbundestaaten* (Göttingen, 3rd ed., 1983).
Ferrer Sama, A., *Comentarios al Código penal*. Murcia, 1946 (vol. I) and 1947 (vol. II).
Fiestas Loza, Alicia, "Algo más sobre la vigencia del Código penal de 1822", *Revista de Historia del Derecho*, Universidad de Granada, (1977- 1978), II-1, pp. 57 ss.
Fiestas Loza, Alicia, "La libertad de imprenta en las dos primeras etapas del liberalismo español", *Anuario de Historia del Derecho Español* 59 (1989), pp. 351–490.
García Goyena, F., *Código criminal español, según las leyes vigentes, comentado y comparado con el penal de 1822, el francés y el inglés*, t. I (Madrid, 1843).
García Valdés, C., "La Codificación penal y las primeras recopilaciones legislativas complementarias", *AHDE* 82 (2012), pp. 37–66.
Gómez de la Serna, Pedro / Montalbán, Juan Manuel, *Elementos del Derecho Penal de España*, 2 vols. (Madrid, 1849).
Gómez de la Serna, Pedro / Montalván, Juan Manuel, *Elementos del Derecho Civil y Penal de España* (Madrid: Librería de Gabriel Sánchez, 1881).
González Alonso, B., "Jueces, justicia, arbitrio judicial (Algunas reflexiones sobre la posición de los jueces ante el Derecho en la Castilla moderna)", *Vivir el Siglo de Oro. Poder, cultura e historia en la Época Moderna. Estudios en homenaje al profesor Ángel Rodríguez Sánchez* (Salamanca, 2003), pp. 223–241.
González Miranda y Pizarro, J., *Historia de la Codificación penal española y crítica del Código vigente* (doctoral Thesis, unpublished) (Madrid, 1906).
González Rus, Juan José, "La supresión de la pena de interdicción civil", *La Ley. Revista jurídica española de doctrina, jurisprudencia y bibliografía* 4 (1984), pp. 1088–1094.
González y Serrano, José, *Apéndice á los Comentarios del Código Penal de Don Joaquín Francisco Pacheco* (Madrid: Imprenta y Fundación de Manuel Tello, 1876).
Groizard y Gómez de la Serna, Alejandro, *El Código penal de 1870 concordado y comentado*. Burgos, 1870–1899 (8 vols.).
Gutiérrez Fernández, B., *Examen histórico del Derecho penal* (Madrid, 1866).
Häfner, K., *Die Strafen des französischen Rechtes und ihr Vollzug, ein Grundriss* (Gießen, 1936)
Härter, Karl, "Kontinuität und Reform der Strafjustiz zwischen Reichsverfassung und Rheinbund", *Reich oder Nation? Mitteleuropa 1780–1815* (herausgegeben von Heinz Duchhardt und Andreas Kunz), *Veröffentlichungen des Instituts für Europäische Geschichte Mainz*, Abteilung Universalgeschichte, Beiheft 46 (Mainz 1998), pp. 219–278.
Härter, Karl, "Von der « Entstehung des öffentlichen Strafrechts » zur « Fabrikation des Verbrechens » . Neuere Forschungen zur Entwicklung von Kriminalität und Strafjustiz im früheneuzeitlichen Europa", *Rechtsgeschichte. Zeitschrift des Max Planck-Institut für europäische Rechtsgeschichte 1* (2002), pp. 159–196.
Hartmann, F., *Der Einfluß des französischen Rechts auf das Preußische Strafgesetzbuch von 1851 (Allgemeiner Teil)* (Göttingen, 1923).
Hidalgo y García, J. A., *El Código penal conforme a la doctrina del Tribunal Supremo* (Madrid, 1908).
Holthöfer, Ernst, "Deciani, Tiberio", *Juristen: ein biographisches Lexikon; von der Antike bis zum 20. Jahrhundert* (Michael Stolleis, ed.) (München: Beck, 2001, 2nd ed.)
Iglesias Río, Miguel Ángel, *Perspectiva histórico-cultural y comparada de la legítima defensa* (Burgos: Universidad de Burgos, 1999).
Institutes au droit criminel, ou principes généraux sur ces matières, suivant le droit civil, canonique, et la jurisprudence du Royaume; avec un traité particulier des crimes (Paris, 1768).
Iñesta-Pastor, Emilia, "La Comisión General de Codificación (1843–1997). De la codificación moderna a la descodificación contemporánea", *AHDE* 83 (2013), pp. 65–103.
Iñesta-Pastor, Emilia, "La proyección hispanoamericana del Código Penal Español de 1848", *XIII Congreso del Instituto Internacional de Historia del Derecho Indiano: San Juan, 21 al 25 de*

mayo de 2000 (Luis E. González Vale, coord.), San Juan, Puerto Rico: Instituto Internacional de Historia del Derecho Indiano; Oficina del Historiador Nacional de Puerto Rico, 2003, vol. II, Estudios, pp. 493–520.

Iñesta-Pastor, Emilia, "La reforma penal del Perú independiente: el código penal de 1863", *Actas del XV Congreso del Instituto Internacional de Historia del Derecho Indiano* (Córdoba, septiembre 2005) (Córdoba: Diputación de Córdoba; Universidad de Córdoba, 2008), pp. 1071–1098.

Iñesta-Pastor, Emilia, "The influence of the 1819 criminal code of the Two Sicilies upon the Spanish criminal law codification and the parliament of the nineteenth century", *Culture parlamentari a confronto. Modelli della rappresentanza politica e identità nazionali* (Andrea Romano, ed.) (Bologna: CLUEB, 2016), pp. 245–259.

Iñesta-Pastor, Emilia*El Código penal de 1848* (Valencia, tirant lo blanc, 2010).

Jaramillo García, A., *Novísimo Código Penal comentado y cotejado con el de 1870* (Salamanca, Imprenta de Silvestre Ferreira, 1928).

Jiménez de Asúa, L. / Antón Oneca, J., *Derecho penal conforme al Código penal de 1928. Parte general* (Madrid, 1929).

Jiménez de Asúa, Luis, "El Derecho penal vigente en la República española", *Revista de Derecho Público,* year I, vol. I (February 1932), pp. 39–48.

Jiménez de Asúa, Luis, *Código penal reformado de 27 de octubre de 1932 y disposiciones penales de la República*, vol. LV (Madrid, 1934).

Jiménez de Asúa, Luis, *La Legislación penal de la República española,* vol. LI (Madrid, 1932).

Jiménez de Asúa, Luis, "Pacheco, en el centenario del Código penal español", *El Criminalista* (Buenos Aires) 9 (1951), pp. 20–22.

Jousse, Daniel, *Nouveau commentaire sur l'Ordennance criminelle du mois d'Aout 1670* (Paris, 1763).

Kleinbreuer, S., *Das Rheinische Strafgesetzbuch. Das materielle Strafrecht und sein Einfluß auf die Strafgesetzgebung in Preußen und im Norddeutschen Bund* (Bonn, 1999).

Lasso Gaite, J. F., *Crónica de la Codificación española. Codi-ficación penal*, vol. 5-I (Madrid, 1970).

López Barja de Quiroga, Jacobo, "El Código penal de 1870 y su contexto histórico", *Centenario del Código civil* (coord. E. Tierno Galván). Madrid, 1989, vol. II, pp. 477–491.

López-Rey y Arrojo, M. / Álvarez Valdés, F., *El nuevo Código penal* (Madrid, 1933).

Lorente, Marta (ed.), *De justicia de jueces a justicia de leyes. Hacia la España de 1870* (Madrid, 2007).

Manzanares Samaniego, José Luis, "La pena de interdicción civil", *Anuario del Derecho Penal y de las Ciencias Penales*, 1979, II pp. 345–380.

Martínez Dhier, A., *Manuel de Seijas (Hernández) Lozano. Precursor de la codificación en España* (Córdoba, 2009).

Masferrer, Aniceto, "La pena de infamia en la Codificación penal española", *Ius fugit. Revista Interdisciplinar de Estudios Histórico-Jurídicos* 7 (1998), pp. 123–176.

Masferrer, Aniceto, *La pena de infamia en el Derecho histórico español. Contribución al estudio de la tradición penal europea en el marco del ius commune* (Madrid: Dykinson, 2001).

Masferrer, Aniceto, (ed.), *La Codificación española. Una aproximación doctrinal e historiográfica a sus influencias extranjeras, y a la francesa en particular* (Pamplona: Aranzadi–Thomson Reuters, 2014).

Masferrer, Aniceto, (ed.), *La Codificación penal española. Tradición e influencias extranjeras: su contribución al proceso codificador* , Pamplona: Aranzadi–Thomson Reuters, 2017.

Masferrer, Aniceto, "Codification as Nationalization or Denationalization of Law: The Spanish Case in Comparative Perspective", *Comparative Legal History* 4.2 (2016), pp. 100–130.

Masferrer, Aniceto, "Codification of Spanish Criminal Law in the Nineteenth Century. A Comparative Legal History Approach", *Journal of Comparative Law* Vol. 4, no. 1 (2009), pp. 96–139.

Masferrer, Aniceto, "Defense of the Common Law against postbellum American Codification: Reasonable and Fallacious Argumentation", *American Journal for Legal History* 50.4 (2008–2010), pp. 355–430.

Masferrer, Aniceto, "La Codificación española y sus influencias extranjeras. Una revisión en torno al alcance del influjo francés", *La Codificación española. Una aproximación doctrinal e historiográfica a sus influencias extranjeras, y a la francesa en particular* (Aniceto Masferrer, ed.) (Pamplona: Aranzadi–Thomson Reuters, 2014), pp. 19–43.

Masferrer, Aniceto, "Liberal State and Criminal Law Reform in Spain", Sellers, Mortimer & Tomaszewski, Tadeusz (Eds.), *The Rule of Law in Comparative Perspective*. Series: *Ius Gentium: Comparative Perspectives on Law and Justice*, vol. 3 (2010), pp. 19–40.

Masferrer, Aniceto, "The Crime of *infidencia* in the Cortes of Cádiz: An Approach to the Crime of Treason during the Early Spanish Constitutionalism (1808–1814)," *Revolten und politische Verbrechen zwischen dem 12. und 19. Jahrhundert. Rechtliche Reaktionen und juristisch-politische Diskurse / Revolts and Political Crime from the 12th to the 19th Century. Legal Responses and Juridical-Political Discourses*, herausgegeben von Angela De Benedictis und Karl Härter unter redaktioneller Mitarbeit von Tina Hannappel und Thomas Walter (Studien zur europäischen Rechtsgeschichte 285) (Frankfurt am Main: Klostermann, 2013), pp. 447–473.

Masferrer, Aniceto, "The Napoleonic Code pénal and the Codification of Criminal Law in Spain", *Le Code pénal. Les metamorphoses d'un modèle 1810–1820. Actes du colloque international Lille / Gand 16–18 décembre 2012*. Textes réunis et présentés par Chantal Aboucaya et Renée Martinage (Centre d'Histoire Judiciaire, 2012), pp. 65–98.

Masferrer, Aniceto, "The Passionate Discussion among Common Lawyers about postbellum American Codification: An approach to its Legal Argumentation" *Arizona State Law Journal* 40, 1 (2008), pp. 173–256, particularly, pp. 198–199 and 233–238.

Masferrer, Aniceto, "The Principle of Legality and Codification in the 19th-century Western Criminal Law Reform", *From the Judge's Arbitrium to the Legality Principle: Legislation as a Source of Law in Criminal Trials* (Georges Martyn, Anthony Musson and Heikki Pihlajamäki, eds.) (*Duncker & Humblot*, 2013), pp. 253–293.

Masferrer, Aniceto, *La inhabilitación y suspensión del ejercicio de la función pública en la tradición penal europea y anglosajona. Especial consideración a los Derechos francés, alemán, español, inglés y norteamericano* (Madrid: Servicio de Publicaciones del Ministerio del Interior, 2009).

Masferrer, Aniceto, *Tradición y reformismo en la Codificación penal española. Hacia el ocaso de un mito. Materiales, apuntes y reflexiones para un nuevo enfoque metodológico e historiográfico del movimiento codificador penal europeo* (Jaén: Universidad de Jaén, 2003).

Masferrer, Aniceto / Cañizares-Navarro, Juan B., "Should Legal Uniqueness Be Compared? The Spanish Civil Code: Its Subsidiary Character", *Comparative law and... / Droit Comparé et...* (A. Albarian, O. Moréteau eds.) (Presses universitaires d'Aix-Marseille, 2015), pp. 85–96.

Masferrer, Aniceto / Sánchez-González, Mª Dolores del Mar, "Tradición e influencias extranjeras en el Código penal de 1848. Aproximación a un mito historiográfico" (con D. del M. Sánchez-González), *La Codificación española. Una aproximación doctrinal e historiográfica a sus influencias extranjeras, y a la francesa en particular* (Aniceto Masferrer, ed.) (Pamplona: Aranzadi–Thomson Reuters, 2014), pp. 271–349.

Mittermaier, K.J.A., "Blicke auf den Zustand der Ausbildung des Kriminalrechts in Frankreich", *Kritische Zeitschrift für Rechtswissenschaft* III (20), pp. 416 ff.

Mittermaier, K.J.A., "Über den neusten Zustand der Gefängnisse in England und Frankreich", *Neues Archiv des Criminalrechts* 40 (1820), I, pp. 571 ff.

Morales Prats, Fermín, "Fundamento político-criminal de la supresión de la pena de interdicción civil", *Revista Jurídica de Catalunya* 85, I (1986), pp. 155–180.

Muyart de Vouglans, Pierre-Francois, *Les lois criminelles de France, dans leus ordre naturel* (Paris, 1780), pp. 53–88.

Núñez Barbero, Ruperto, *La reforma penal de 1870* (Salamanca, 1969).

Pacheco, Joaquín Francisco, *Código penal concordado y comentado* (Madrid, 1856, 2nd ed.).

Pacheco, Joaquín Francisco, *Estudios de Derecho Penal* (lectures given at the *Ateneo* of Madrid) (Madrid, 1868).

Paraquin, E.J., *Die französische Gesetzgebung. Das Strafgesetzbuch*, vol. V (München, 1861).

Passano, M. da, "La codification du droit pénal dans l'Italie jacobine et napoleonienne", *Revolutions et justice en Europe. Modeles francais et traditions nationales (1780–1830)* (L'Harmattan, 1999), pp. 85–99.

Peláez Albendea, Manuel J., "Le *Code* de 1804, le *Code* civil espagnol de 1889 et le principe de la liberté (Réception particulière a l'Espagne)", *Le Code civil et les droits de l'homme* (Jean-Luc Chabot, Jean L., Ph. Didier, Ph., J. Ferrand, J., eds.), Actes du Colloque international de Grenoble (Paris, 2005), pp. 309–317.

Pennington, Kenneth, "*Moderamen Inculpatae Tutelae*: The Jurisprudence of a Justifiable Defense", 24 *Rivista Internazionale de Diritto Comune* 27 (2014), pp. 27–55.

Pérez-Prendes y Muñoz de Arraco, José Manuel, "La prensa y el Código penal de 1870", *Hispania* 31 (1971), pp. 551–579.

Perona Tomás, Dionisio A., "La influencia francesa en la codificación mercantil española del siglo XIX", *La Codificación española. Una aproximación doctrinal e historiográfica a sus influencias extranjeras, y a la francesa en particular* (Aniceto Masferrer, ed.), Pamplona: Aranzadi–Thomson Reuters, 2014, pp. 351–427.

Perona Tomás, Dionisio A., *Notas sobre el proceso de la Codificación mercantil en la España del siglo XIX* (Madrid: Dykinson, 2015).

Pessini Pulido, A., "El nuevo Código penal", *Revista General de Legislación y Jurisprudencia* 154 (1929), pp. 314–322.

Petit, Carlos, "El código inexistente (I). Por una historia conceptual de la cultura jurídica en la España del siglo XIX", *Anuario de Derecho Civil*, t. XLVIII, fasc. IV (octubre-diciembre 1995), pp. 1429–1465.

Petit, Carlos, "España y el *Code* Napoleon", *Anuario de Derecho Civil* 41.4 (October 2008), pp. 1774–1840.

Pifferi, Michele, *Generalia delictorum. Il Tractatus criminalis di Tiberio Deciani e la "parte generale" di diritto penale* (Milano, Giuffrè, 2006).

Pifferi, Michele, *L'individualizzazione della pena. Difesa sociale e crisi della legalità penale tra Otto e Novecento* (Milano: Giuffrè, 2013).

Pifferi, Michele, *Reinventing Punishment. A Comparative History of Criminology and Penology in the 19th and 20th Century* (Oxford: Oxford University Press, 2016).

Pino Abad, Miguel, "Las leyes de enjuiciamiento civil de 1855 y 1881. Apuntes sobre las influencias recibidas y aportadas", *La Codificación española. Una aproximación doctrinal e historiográfica a sus influencias extranjeras, y a la francesa en particular* (Aniceto Masferrer, ed.), Pamplona: Aranzadi–Thomson Reuters, 2014, pp. 429–447.

Puig Peña, F., *Código penal reformado* (Madrid, 1934).

Ramos Vázquez, Isabel / Cañizares, Juan B., "La influencia francesa en la primera Codificación española: el Código penal francés de 1810 y el Código penal español de 1822", *La Codificación española. Una aproximación doctrinal e historiográfica a sus influencias extranjeras, y a la francesa en particular* (Aniceto Masferrer, ed.), Pamplona: Aranzadi–Thomson Reuters, 2014, pp. 193–270.

Ramos Vázquez, Isabel, "Criminal Law Reform in the Eighteenth Century Europe. A comparative study: England, France, Spain", *International Journal of Humanities and Social Science*, vol. 2, n 4 (special issue- February 2012), pp. 26–37.

Ramos Vázquez, Isabel, "La Comisión de Justicia y el Proyecto de Reglamento para causas criminales de 1811", *Revista de la Facultad de Ciencias Sociales y Jurídicas de la Universidad Miguel Hernández* 5 (2009), pp. 93–112.

Ramos Vázquez, Isabel, "La individualización judicial de la pena en la primera codificación francesa y española", *Anuario de Historia del Derecho Español* 84 (2014), pp. 315–351.

Ramos Vázquez, Isabel, "La represión de los delitos atroces en el Derecho castellano de la Edad Moderna", *Revista de Estudios Histórico-Jurídicos* [Sección Historia del Derecho Europeo] XXVI (Valparaíso, Chile, 2004), pp. 255–299.

Ramos Vázquez, Isabel, "Las reformas borbónicas en el Derecho penal y de Policía criminal de la España dieciochesca", *forum historiae iuris* (http://www.forhistiur.de/zitat/1001ramos.htm).

Ramos Vázquez, Isabel, "Principios procesales en la Constitución de Cádiz. De la administración de Justicia en lo civil y en lo criminal", *Sobre un hito jurídico. La Constitución de 1812. Reflexiones actuales, estado de la cuestión, debates historiográficos* (Chamocho Cantudo, M. A., Lozano Miralles, J., edit.) (Jaén: Universidad de Jaén, 2012), pp. 469–482.

Renaud, Achille, *La mort civile en France. Par suite de condamnations judiciaires, son origine et développement* (Paris, 1843).

Revuelta Benito, R., "El Código penal de 1848 y su gran comentarista don Joaquín Francisco Pacheco", *Revista de Estudios Penales* 6 (1945), pp. 31 ff.

Rodríguez Gil, M. Magdalena, "Joaquín Francisco Pacheco, un penalista en el marco constitucional", *Revista de la Facultad de derecho de la Universidad Complutense* 83 (1993–1994), pp. 259–294.

Sáenz de Santa María Gómez Mampaso, Blanca, "Codificación y formación de los Códigos civil, criminal y mercantil", *Cortes y Constitución de Cádiz. 200 años* (Escudero López, J. A., dir.), tomo II (Madrid, 2011), pp. 467–481.

Sainz Guerra, Juan, "José María Calatrava o la Codificación penal a comienzos del siglo XIX", *Estudios de Historia de las Ciencias Criminales en España* (J. Alvarado y A. Serrano Maíllo, eds.) (Madrid, Dykinson, 2007), pp. 351–384.

Sainz Guerra, Juan, "La Constitución de 1812: de las reformas penales y procesales a la abolición de la tortura", *Cortes y Constitución de Cádiz. 200 años* (Escudero López, J. A., dir.), tomo II (Madrid, 2011), pp. 247–276.

Saldaña, Q., *Comentarios científico-prácticos al Código penal de 1870. Infracción y responsabilidad*, vol. I, t. I (Madrid, 1920).

San Martín Losada, Luis, *El Código penal de 1928. Su estudio y comparación con el de 1870* (Madrid, 1928).

Sánchez González, Mª Dolores del Mar, *Los Códigos Penales de 1848 y 1850* (Madrid, 2003).

Sánchez Tejerina, I., *Derecho penal español* (Madrid, 1945).

Schaffstein, Friedrich, "Tiberius Decianus und seine Bedeutung für die Entstehung des Allgemeinen Teils im Gemeinen deutschen Strafrecht", *Abhandlungen zur Strafrechtsgeschichte und zur Wissenschaftsgeschichte* (Darmstadt: Scientia Verlag Aalen, 1986), pp. 199–226.

Schubert, W., *Der Code pénal des Königreichs Westphalen von 1813 mit dem Code pénal von 1810 im Original und in deutscher Übersetzung* (Frankfurt / Main: Peter Lang, 2001).

Schubert, W., *Französisches Recht in Deutschland zu Beginn des 19. Jahrhunderts. Zivilrecht, Gerichtsverfassungsrecht und Zivilprozeßrecht* (Köln, 1977).

Serna Vallejo, Margarita, "La influencia del derecho europeo, en particular del derecho francés, en la reforma hipotecaria española del siglo XIX a partir del análisis de la doctrina", *La Codificación española. Una aproximación doctrinal e historiográfica a sus influencias extranjeras, y a la francesa en particular* (Aniceto Masferrer, ed.), Pamplona: Aranzadi–Thomson Reuters, 2014, pp. 129–191.

Silvela, Luis, *El Derecho penal estudiado en principios y en la legislación vigente en España* (Madrid, 2nd ed., 1903)

Stein, L. von, *Geschichte des französischen Strafrechts und des Prozesses* (Basel 1875; Aalen Verlag, 1968).

Tarello, Giovanni, *Storia della cultura giuridica moderna*. Vol. I: Assolutismo e codificazione del diritto. Bologna, 1976.

Tomás y Valiente, Francisco, "La codificación de utopía a técnica vulgarizada", *Códigos y Constituciones (1808–1978)* (Madrid: Alianza, 1989), pp. 11–124.

Torres Aguilar, Manuel, "El proceso de la primera codificación penal y la Constitución de Cádiz", *Cortes y Constitución de Cádiz. 200 años* (Escudero López, J. A., dir.), tomo II (Madrid, 2011), pp. 442–468.

Torres Aguilar, Manuel, *Génesis parlamentaria del Código penal de 1822* (Sicania University Press, 2008).

Torres Sanz, David, "El liberalismo gaditano ante el Derecho penal", *Cortes y Constitución de Cádiz. 200 años* (Escudero López, J. A., dir.), tomo II, Madrid, 2011, pp. 277–284.
Viada y Vilaseca, S., *El Código penal reformado de 1870*. 3 vols. (Madrid, 1894).
Virto Larruscain, M. J., *El caso fortuito y la construcción del sistema de culpabilidad en el Código penal de 1848* (Bilbao, 1984).
Vizmanos, Tomás María de / Álvarez Martínez, Cirilo, *Comentarios al Nuevo Código Penal* (Madrid: Establecimiento Tipográfico de J. González y A. Vicente, 1848).
Volk, K., "Napoleon und das deutsche Strafrecht", *JuS* (1991), pp. 281 ff.

Professor Aniceto Masferrer teaches legal history and comparative law at the Faculty of Law, University of Valencia, Spain. He is the author of nine books (including his *Spanish Legal Traditions. A Comparative Legal History Outline*, Madrid, 2009; 2012, 2nd ed.) and the editor of ten (including *Post 9/11 and the State of Permanent Legal Emergency: Security and Human Rights in Countering Terrorism*, Springer, 2012; *Counter-Terrorism, Human Rights and the Rule of Law. Crossing Legal Boundaries in Defence of the State*, Edward Elgar Publishing, 2013; *La Codificación española. Una aproximación doctrinal e historiográfica a sus influencias extranjeras, y a la francesa en particular*, Thomson Reuters-Aranzadi, 2014; and *Human Dignity of the Vulnerable in the Age of Rights: Interdisciplinary Perspectives*, Dordrecht-Heidelberg-London-New York, Springer, 2016), and eighty book chapters/articles published in Spanish, European and American law journals. He has published extensively on criminal law from an historical and comparative perspective, as well as on the codification movement and fundamental rights in the Western legal tradition. He has been a fellow researcher at the Institute Max-Planck for European Legal History (2000–03), Visiting Professor at the University of Cambridge (2005), Visiting Scholar at Harvard Law School (2006–07) and at Melbourne Law School (2008), and Visiting Professor at the University of Tasmania (2010), Visiting Scholar at Louisiana State University—The Paul M. Hebert Law Center—(2013), Visiting Scholar at George Washington University Law School (as the Recipient of the Richard and Diane Cummins Legal History Research Grant for 2014), and Visiting Professor at the École Normale Supérieure—Paris (2015). He has lectured at universities around the world (France, Germany, Belgium, The Netherlands, Malta, Israel, United Kingdom, Sweden, Norway, USA, Canada, Australia and New Zealand). He is a member of the advisory board of several Spanish, European, Anglo-American and Asian Law Journals, and the Chief Editor of *GLOSSAE. European Journal of Legal History* (http://www.glossae.eu). He is member of the *American Society for Legal History*, the current president of the *European Society for Comparative Legal History* (from 2010), and vice-president of the Fundación Universitas. He is also the Director of the *Institute for Social, Political and Legal Studies*, member of the Spanish *Royal Academy of Jurisprudence and Legislation*, and board member of the Valencian Committee for European Affairs.

The Influence Exerted by the 1819 Criminal Code of the Two Sicilies upon Nineteenth-Century Spanish Criminal Law Codification and Its Projection in Latin America

Emilia Iñesta-Pastor

Abstract Nineteenth-century Spanish criminal law codification was inspired by foreign code models. One of the least known models is the 1819 Criminal Code of the Kingdom of the Two Sicilies. Its influence on the 1848 Criminal Code, considered the Spanish criminal code par excellence of the 19th century, becomes clearly visible both in the General Part and in the Special Part. As reasons for the projection of this Code of the Two Sicilies stands out the progress that it represents with regard to the 1810 French Criminal Code, as a result of the influence exerted by the advanced Italian criminal law doctrine. It is these advances that will determine its adoption as a model by the 1848 legislators and that will later arrive in Latin America either directly or through the projection of the 1848 Spanish Criminal Code, giving rise to an important succession of Codes as the expression of a set of "travelling codes".

The present study was carried out within the framework of the Project: "Las influencias extranjeras en la Codificación penal española: su concreto alcance en la Parte Especial de los Códigos decimonónicos [Foreign influences on Spanish criminal law codification: their specific scope in the Special Part of nineteenth-century Codes]" (ref. DER2016-78388-P), financed by the Ministry of Economy and Competitiveness. This work has drawn on some of the materials used in Emilia Iñesta-Pastor, "The influence of the 1819 criminal code of the Two Sicilies upon the Spanish criminal law codification and the parliament of the nineteenth century," Culture parlamentari a confronto. Modelli della rappresentanza politica e identità nazionali (Andrea Romano, ed.) (Bolonia: Clueb, 2016), pp. 245–259.

E. Iñesta-Pastor (✉)
Law Faculty, University of Alicante, Alicante, Spain
e-mail: emilia.inesta@ua.es

A. Masferrer (ed.), *The Western Codification of Criminal Law*, Studies in the History of Law and Justice 11, https://doi.org/10.1007/978-3-319-71912-2_9

1 The Criminal Code of the Two Sicilies Within the Framework of Foreign Influences on Nineteenth-Century Spanish Criminal Law Codification

Scholarship generally admits the influence exerted by the 1810 French Criminal Code upon the nineteenth-century liberal codifying process in a large number of European countries because of its unquestionable technical superiority.[1] Spanish was no exception in that context. Historiography has acknowledged the influence exerted by the French criminal code upon nineteenth-century Spanish criminal codes: 1822, 1848 and, through the latter, on its 1850 and 1870 reforms.[2]

Nevertheless, recent studies have highlighted the difference existing between the statement of that influence in doctrine or in code commentators; or in the references to foreign codes made in the actual codification commissions, or even in parliament debates during the discussion of Codes; and the effective and specific influence exerted by foreign codes upon codified texts.[3]

Foreign influences were explicitly recognized by the drafting Commission of the 1822 Spanish Criminal Code in the debates held during the discussion of the Draft at the *Cortes* [Parliament]. It was thus done by the Drafting Commission's spokesman, José María Calatrava. Taking as his starting point that it was not based

[1]Bartolomé Clavero, *Manual de Historia Constitucional de España* (Madrid: Alianza ed. 1989), p. 22; Luis Jiménez de Asúa, *Tratado de Derecho Penal, I*, (Buenos Aires: Editorial Losada, 1964), pp. 317–318; recent studies on the influence exerted by the French Code on European codification, see Sergio Vinciguerra, "L' influence du code de 1810 en Italie," *Bicentenaire du Code Pénal. 1810–2010, Les colloques du Sénat, 25–26 novembre 2010* (Paris: Sénat, 2010), pp. 113–124, p. 113 (avalable at https://www.senat.fr/colloques/actes_bicentenaire_code_penal/actes_bicentenaire_code_penal.pdf); Franz-Stefan Meissel, "Le code de 1810 et le droit pénal en Europe Centrale," *Bicentenaire du Code Pénal. 1810–2010,* pp. 125–138, p. 130 and ff. Mario Da Passano, "La codification du droit pénal dans l'Italie jacobine et napoleonienne," *Revolutions et justice en Europe. Modeles français et traditions nationales (1780–1830)* (X. Rousseaux, M.-S. Dupont-Bouchat, C. Vael, dirs.) (Paris: L'Harmattan, 1999), pp. 85–100; Fred Stevens, "La codification pénale en Belgique. Heritage français et debats neerlandais (1781–1867)", *Le pénal dans tous ses Etats. Justice, Etats et Sociétés en Europe (XIIe XXe siècles)* (Rousseaux, X. Levy, R., dirs.) (Bruxelles: Facultés Universitaires Saint-Louis, 1997), pp. 287–302.

[2]Quintiliano Saldaña, *Historia del Derecho Penal en España*, Adiciones al *Tratado de Derecho Penal* de Von Listz (Madrid: Instituto editorial Reus, 3ª ed., s.f.), pp. 473–474; Jiménez de Asúa, *Tratado de Derecho Penal*, I, p. 757; José Antón Oneca, *Derecho penal. Parte General* (Madrid: Akal, 2ª ed., 1986), p. 73; José Ramón Casabó Ruiz, *El Código penal de 1822*, Unpublished Doctoral Thesis (Valencia, 1968), p. 119.

[3]A study about the specific foreign influences on the articles of the 1848 Spanish Criminal Code and on the doctrinal assessments thereof can be found in Emilia Iñesta-Pastor, *El Código penal español de 1848* (Valencia: Tirant lo Blanch, 2011), also, Aniceto Masferrer, "la codificación española y sus influencias extranjeras. Una revisión en torno al alcance del influjo francés", *La codificación española. Una aproximación doctrinal e historiográfica a sus influencias extranjeras, y a la francesa en particular* (Aniceto Masferrer, ed.) (Pamplona: Thomson-Aranzadi), 2014), pp. 21-52, p. 21.

on a single foreign code, Calatrava admits the inspiration in "the Codes with a greater prestige and reputation in Europe." However, he insists on the originality of the drawn-up Code, which came as a result of the new political situation in Spain as well as of the need to reform the existing criminal legislation which had become obsolete for its time. His intervention stressed the Commission's special reluctance to admit the 1810 French Code as an exclusive model, perhaps for political reasons, for the fear of being described as "Frenchified."[4]

Nevertheless, the first Spanish Criminal Code promulgated in 1822 actually allows us to check the influence of criminal law doctrine, especially of Bentham and Filangieri in the first place, and of Beccaria to a lesser extent. It is also worth highlighting the projection of Bexon's Draft Criminal Code, of Spanish legal tradition, and of the 1810 French Criminal Code to a lesser extent.[5]

It must additionally be stressed that the Napoleonic criminal code was not the only foreign code used as a model by Spanish legislators. This can be verified in the most important Spanish criminal code of the 19th century, the 1848 Criminal Code. The codes are recognised as models which inspired the authors of the 1848 Spanish text: the 1803 Austrian Criminal Code, the 1810 French one, the 1819 Neapolitan Code or Code of the Two Sicilies, the 1822 Spanish Criminal Code, and the 1830 Brazilian one, the last three being clearly indebted to the French code.[6]

The overall influence exerted by foreign codes was admitted during the sessions held at the General Commission for Codes in the discussion of the Draft for the 1848 Code, sometimes directly and, on other occasions, in an indirect way. It was made clear that foreign codes not only from Europe but also from America were

---

[4]Eugenio Raúl Zaffaroni, "La influencia del pensamiento de Cesare Beccaria sobre la política criminal en el mundo," *Anuario de Derecho Penal y Ciencias Penales (ADPCP)* 42 (1989), pp. 135–149, p. 138.

[5]See for all of them, Joaquín Francisco Pacheco, *El Código penal concordado y comentado*, I (Madrid: Imprenta de Santiago Saunaque, 1848), pp. LVII–LVIII; Benito Gutiérrez Fernández, *Examen histórico del Derecho Penal* (Madrid: Imprenta de Antonio Peñuelas, 1866), p. 245; Casabó Ruiz, *El Código penal de 1822*, pp. 111–126; Juan Francisco Lasso Gaite, *Codificación Penal. Crónica de la Codificación Española*, V, I, (Madrid: Ministerio de Justicia, 1970), pp. 50–53, 144–153; Juan Sainz Guerra, "José María Calatrava o la Codificación penal a comienzos del siglo XIX," *Estudios de Historia de las Ciencias Criminales en España* (J. Alvarado y A. Serrano Maíllo, eds.) (Madrid: Dykinson 2007), pp. 351–384, p. 357; José Antón Oneca, "Historia del Código penal de 1822," *ADPCP* 17 (1965), pp. 262–278, pp. 268–272; Manuel Torres Aguilar, *Génesis parlamentaria del Código penal de 1822*, (Messina, Sicania-University Press, 2008), pp. 70 and ff; Juan Baró Pazos, "Historiografía sobre la Codificación del Derecho Penal en el siglo XIX," (Germán Rueda (ed.), *Doce Estudios de Historiografía contemporánea*, (Santander: Universidad de Santander, 1991), pp. 1–40, pp. 25–26; recently, Juan Benito Cañizares-Navarro, "El Código penal de 1822: sus fuentes inspiradoras. Balance historiográfico (desde el s. XX)," *Glossae, European Journal of Legal History* 10 (2013), pp. 109–136, p. 133 (http://www.glossae.eu); Isabel Ramos Vazquez & Juan Benito Cañizares-Navarro, "La influencia francesa en la primera codificación penal española: el Código penal francés de 1810 y el Código penal español de 1822," *La codificación española. Una aproximación doctrinal e historiográfica a sus influencias extranjeras y a la francesa en particular* (Aniceto Masferrer, ed.) (Pamplona: Thomson-Aranzadi, 2014), pp. 193–270, pp. 224–225.

[6]About the foreign code models, see Iñesta-Pastor, *El Código penal español de 1848*, pp. 294–303.

known, though. However, it was the 1819 Neapolitan Code or Code of the Two Sicilies and the 1830 Brazilian one—among all the aforementioned codes—that exerted the strongest influence. This was pointed out by Seijas Lozano:

> The first thing that I did was to consult the various models that Europe and America offer us… I deduced that the dominant idea in all of them was to ensure simplicity and that some of them had admirably succeeded in achieving it. I honestly declare that I loved the structure of the Brazilian code, the accuracy of the Neapolitan one… I thought that I had to study them in detail and follow them as models." Nevertheless, he points out that it was not a copy, insofar as they "did not blindly follow the rules of those two codes.[7]

In turn, Domingo María Vila specified the existence of different influences on each one of the books, which implied the existence of various criminal law orientations:

> The first Book… was taken from the principle of the Brazil Code and that of Mr. Claròs (Book II) by that of the Sicilian one, these two Codes differing in how they were agreed.[8]

Drawing a comparison between the 1830 Brazilian code and the Spanish code of 1848 allows us to see how the influence exerted by the 1830 Brazilian Code becomes visible in the Code's Book I, in the General Part, in Titles I and II. That influence is less strong in the Special Part. Even though attention must be paid to the influence exerted by the 1822 Spanish Criminal Code upon the Brazilian text, since many of the innovations contained in the latter improved what had already been regulated by the Spanish on.[9]

To this must be added that the Code of the Two Sicilies—as will be shown below—was going to influence both the General and the Special Parts of the 1848 Spanish Code.

The preference for the Brazilian text and the Neapolitan one (also known as the Code of the Two Sicilies) did not prevent the recognition of the preeminence that the 1810 French Criminal Code had at a European level, albeit in critical terms and

---

[7]*Actas de las sesiones de la Comisión General de Codificación, 1828–1994* (Madrid: Ministerio de Justicia, 2007). *Archivo Comisión General de Codificación del Ministerio de Justicia* (hereinafter ACGC). *Actas Código Pena*l (hereinafter ACP), session, October 2nd 1844, leg. 6, fol. 2r; Iñesta-Pastor, *El Código penal español de 1848*, p. 79, fn n. 71.

[8]ACGC. ACP, session, April 24th 1844, leg. 6, fol. 85v; *ibid,* p. 73.

[9]It is necessary to highlight the influence exerted by the 1822 Spanish criminal Code, the fact that it arose during the Liberal Triennium caused it to be silenced by doctrine, as well as by the drafters of the 1848 Code, who preferred to resort to the Brazilian Criminal Code when, in fact, some of its contributions had been collected by the Brazilian text from the 1822 Spanish Code; Antonio Quintano Ripollés, *La influencia del Derecho español en las legislaciones hispanoamericanas* (Madrid: Ediciones de Cultura Hispánica, 1953), pp. 21–22, 96; Javier Alvarado Planas, "La Codificación penal en la España Isabelina: la influencia del Código penal del Brasil en el Código penal español de 1848," *España en la época de la Fundación de la Guardia Civil. V. Seminario Duque de Ahumada*, Madrid (Madrid: UNED, 1994), pp. 43–82, p. 48; Iñesta-Pastor, *El Código penal español de 1848*, pp. 295–300; V. Chieregati Costa, *Codificaçao e formaçao do Estado-nacional brasileiro: o Código Criminal de 1830 e a positiaçao das leis na pós-Independência.* (Dissertaçao de mestrado, Universidade de Sao Paulo, Istituto de Estudos Brasileiros: Sao Paulo, 2013), pp. 101 ff, 241 ff.

underrating its impact on the Spanish one, perhaps for the purpose of justifying the preference for the Brazilian and Neapolitan codes. This was pointed out by Manuel Seijas Lozano during the discussion of the Draft for the 1848 Code at Parliament:

> (The) Europe..., is governed by no other than the French Code... the worst Code considering how it was worst drawn up, worst combined and worst calculated...[10]

Collating both codes makes it possible to identify the influence of the French Code on the Special Part, and on Book III, *On offences*, too. Nevertheless, the 1848 Spanish text turns out to be more complete and systematic than the French one in the General Part. This could be explained by the time elapsed since its promulgation, despite its reform in 1832.[11] It must not be forgotten either that French influence could also indirectly reach Spain through the Brazilian Code and the Code of the Two Sicilies.[12]

However, as highlighted by some scholars, most of the commentators of the 1848 Code hardly bother to assess the specific influences exerted by foreign legislation "even though they are so frequently cited in the concordances of commentaries."[13] The Brazilian Code and that of the Two Sicilies will be the most-oft cited by the most prestigious commentators: Joaquin Francisco Pacheco, Tomás María de Vizmanos and Cirilo Álvarez[14] which does not mean that the two codes mentioned above had an effective influence on the institutions mentioned by these two commentators.[15]

---

[10]Manuel Seijas Lozano, drafter of Books I and III at the Congress, Diario de Sesiones de las Cortes, Congreso de los Diputados (Diary of Sessions of the Cortes [Parliament], Congress of Deputies), (hereinafter DSC. Congreso), legislature 1847–48, No. 79, March 10th 1848, pp. 1715–1716; Iñesta-Pastor, *El Código penal español de 1848*, p. 80.

[11]*Ibid.*, pp. 295–298.

[12]Vinciguerra, "L'influence du code de 1810 en Italie," p. 121.

[13]Domingo Teruel Carralero, "El Código del 48 en su Centenario," *Revista de la Escuela de Estudios Penitenciarios (REEP)* 40 (1948), pp. 8–13, p. 12.

[14]Pacheco, *El Código penal concordado y comentado*, 3 t. Tomás María de Vizmanos & Cirilo Álvarez Martínez, *Comentarios al Nuevo Código Penal* (Madrid: Establecimiento tipográfico de J. González y A. Vicente, 1848), 3 t.

[15]Alvarado Planas, "La Codificación penal en la España Isabelina: la influencia del Código penal del Brasil," p. 46; Iñesta-Pastor, *El Código penal español de 1848*, p. 294 and ff. Aniceto Masferrer & María del Mar Sánchez González, "Tradición e influencias extranjeras en el Código penal de 1848," *La codificación española. Una aproximación doctrinal e historiográfica a sus influencias extranjeras y a la francesa en particular* (Aniceto Masferrer, ed.) (Pamplona: Thomson-Aranzadi, 2014), pp. 271–349.

2 The Influence Exerted by Italian Doctrine upon Nineteenth-Century Spanish Criminal Law Codification

The deep transformation operated within the context of criminal law in the late 18th century and early 19th century as a result of the influence exerted by the philosophy of the Enlightenment and by the social contract theory, as well as its effective implementation derived from the social and political change entailed by the French Revolution, would have an impact on Spain at the same time that the Liberal State became consolidated.[16]

Spain was going to know the work of Beccaria, *De Los Delitos y las Penas* [Of offences and penalties], its translation and printing being allowed in 1774.[17] It would influence the Spanish doctrine of its time in authors such as Alfonso María de Acevedo and Manuel de Lardizábal.[18] According to

[16]Manuel Gallego Díaz, *El sistema español de determinación legal de la pena, Estudio de las reglas de aplicación de penas del Código penal* (Madrid: ICAI, 1985), p. 41; Jean Marie Carbasse, *Introduction historique au droit pènal* (Paris: PUF, 1990), pp. 301–314; by the same author, "État autoritaire et justice répressive. L'évolution de la législation penale de 1789 au Code Pénal de 1810," *All'ombra dell'Aquila Imperiale. Transformazioni e continuità instituzionali nei territorio sabaudi in età napoleónica (1802–1814). Atti del Convegno, Torino 15–18 ottobre 1990* (Roma: Ministero per i beni culturali e ambientali, Ufficio centrale per i beni archivistici, 1994), I, pp. 313–333, p. 314; Jean Pierre Delmas Saint-Hilaire, "1789: un nouveau droit pénal est né...," *Liber Amicorum. Etudes offertes à Pierre Jaubert* (Gérard Aubin, ed.) (Bourdeaux: Presses Universitaires de Bordeaux, 1992), pp. 161–162, 170–177.

[17]Beccaria's work was translated into Spanish by Juan Antonio de las Casas in 1774, accompanied by a long prologue where its context was toned down as much as possible; Cesare Beccaria, *De los delitos y las penas*, translation of Juan Antonio de las Casas, introduction, appendix and notes by Juan Antonio del Val, (Madrid: Alianza ed., 1968).

[18]Antonio Risco, "Présence de Beccaria dans l'Espagne des Lumières," *Becccaria et la culture juridique des Lumières. Actes du colloque européen de Genève, 25–26 novembre 1995* (Michel Porret, ed.) (Genève: Droz, 1997), pp. 149–167, pp. 150–154; G. Calabro, "Beccaria e la Spagna," *Atti del Convegno Internazionale sul Cesare Beccaria, Torino 2–6 ottobre 1964 (Torino: Accademia delle Scienze,* serie 4, No. 9, 1966) pp. 101–120, p. 103 and ff; Juan Antonio Delval, Introducción a la edición de *Los delitos y las penas*, p. 166; see for all of them Adela Asúa Batarrita, "Reivindicación o superación del programa de Beccaria," *El Pensamiento penal de Beccaria: su actualidad* (Adela Asúa Batarrita coord.) (Bilbao: Universidad de Deusto, 1990); José Antón Oneca, Estudio preliminar al *Discurso sobre las penas* de Manuel de Lardizábal, *Revista de Estudios Penitenciarios* 174 (1966), pp. 597–626; Manuel de Rivacoba y Rivacoba, "Lardizábal, un penalista ilustrado," *Anuario del Instituto de Investigaciones Históricas de la Universidad Nacional del Litoral*, 7 (1964), pp. 210–248; Luis Prieto Sanchís, "*La filosofía penal de la Ilustración española*," *Homenaje a Dr. Barbero Santos, in memoriam* (L., Fuente Arroyo Zapatero & I. Berdugo de la Torre, drs.) (Cuenca: Universidad de Castilla la Mancha, Universidad de Salamanca, 2001), pp. 489–510; Iñesta-Pastor, *El Código penal español de 1848*, pp. 37–38, amongst others.

recent doctrine, it had a very limited influence on the 1822 Spanish Criminal Code.[19]

Gaetano Filangieri's work will come to be known as well in Spain.[20] The close analogy between the system proposed by Filangieri and the first Draft Criminal Codes in Spain—more precisely the 1787 Draft Criminal Code—is unanimously recognised in Spain. It has the same analogy with the degree system for the application of penalties which was going to be adopted by the 1822 Spanish Criminal Code, the different Draft Criminal Codes prior to 1848, and the 1848 Criminal Code itself.[21]

Finally, an author of recognised influence both on doctrine and on nineteenth-century criminal law codification was Pellegrino Rossi. Rossi's eclecticism regarding criminal law, which becomes visible in his work *Traité de Droit*

---

[19]Saldaña, *Historia del Derecho Penal en España. Adiciones al Tratado de Derecho Penal* de Franz Von Liszt, p. 474; Casabó Ruiz, *El Código penal de 1822*, p. 228–229; Torres Aguilar, *Génesis parlamentaria del Código penal de 1822*, p. 87; Alejandro Agüero & Marta Lorente, "Penal enlightenment in Spain: from Beccaria's reception to the first criminal code," *Forum Historiae Iuris*, (15 November 2012) (http://www.forhistiur.de/2012-11-aguero-lorente/); Isabel Ramos Vazquez & Juan Benito Cañizares-Navarro, "La influencia francesa en la primera codificación penal española: el Código penal francés de 1810 y el Código penal español de 1822," *La codificación española. Una aproximación doctrinal e historiográfica a sus influencias extranjeras*, p. 258.

[20]Gaetano Filangieri, *Scienzia della legislazione*, Nápoles, 1780–1785, translation of J. Rubio, Madrid, 1822. His influence is regarded as unquestionable by: José Sánchez Osés, "Gaetano Filangieri," *ADPCP* 19, (1966), pp. 413–438; José Antón Oneca, "Historia del Código penal de 1822," *ADPCP* 17 (1965), pp. 262–278, p. 271; Fernando Galindo Ayuda, "La Scienza della legislazione en España," *Gaetano Filangieri e l'Illuminismo Europeo, Atti del Convengo «Gaetano Filangieri e l'Illuminismo Europeo»* (Nápoles: Guida ed. 1991), pp. 375–401, pp. 388–395. The opposite expression/view is reflected in: Jesús Lalinde Abadía, "El eco de Gaetano Filangieri en España," *Gaetano Filangieri e l'Illuminismo Europeo, Atti del Convengo «Gaetano Filangieri e l'Illuminismo Europeo,»* (Nápoles: Guida ed. 1991), pp. 453–506; Francisco Sanchez Blanco, *Europa y el pensamiento español del siglo XVIII* (Madrid: Alianza ed. 1991); José Antonio Sainz Cantero, "El informe de la Universidad de Granada sobre el Proyecto que dio lugar al Código penal de 1822," *ADPCP* 20 (1967), pp. 509–538, pp. 512–513; Juan Baró Pazos, "Historiografía sobre la Codificación del Derecho Penal en el siglo XIX," *Doce Estudios de Historiografía contemporánea* (Germán Rueda, ed.) (Santander: Universidad de Santander, 1991), pp. 1–40, pp. 25–26; María Dolores del Mar Sánchez González, "Historiografía penal española (1808–1870): La Escuela Clásica", *Estudios de Historia de las Ciencias criminales*, (J. Alvarado y A. Serrano Maíllo, eds.) (Madrid: Dykinson, 2007), p. 70; Marta Lorente Sariñena, "De la suerte normativa de la ciencia de la legislación: Filangieri y la codificación moderna en la España decimonónica," *Nuevo Mundo Mundos Nuevos* (online), Colloques, 28 janvier, 2007 (http://nuevomundo.revues.org/3510); Jesús Astigarraga, "La ilustración napolitana imputada. Críticas y censuras a la Scienza della legislazione de G. Filangieri en la España de finales del siglo XVIII," *Nuevo Mundo Mundos Nuevos* (online), Colloques, 18 juin 2007 (http://nuevomundo.revues.org/6911).

[21]José Ramón Casabó Ruiz, "Los orígenes de la Codificación penal en España: el plan de Código Criminal de 1787," *ADPCP* 22 (1969), pp. 313–342, p. 313; Iñesta-Pastor, *El Código penal español de 1848*, pp. 33–34.

Pénal [*Treatise on Criminal Law*],[22] decisively influenced Spanish criminal law doctrine. Spanish legal experts already knew about Rossi's ideas even before the translation of his *Treatise on Criminal Law* in 1839,[23] but it was Joaquín Francisco Pacheco that disseminated all this information to a greater extent.[24] Likewise, the principles of eclecticism inspired the 1848 Spanish criminal code, even though the latter still keeps reminiscences of the previous utilitarianism,[25] an orientation which remained in the 1850 reform[26] and the 1870 Criminal Code.[27]

[22]Pellegrino Rossi, *Tratado de Derecho Penal*, translation of Cayetano Cortés, 2 vols. (Madrid: Imprenta de D. José María Repullés), 1839); Faustin Hélie, *Traité de Droit Pénal* of Pellegrino Rossi, *Introduction* (Paris: Librairie de Guillaumin et Cie, 1863). Various aspects of Rossi's work can be consulted, *Des libertés et des peines. Actes du Colloque Pellegrino Rossi organisé à Genève, 23–24 novembre de 1979* (Genève: Université de Genève, 1980); also, *Un Liberale europeo: Pellegrino Rossi (1787–1848)* (a cura de Luigi Lachè) (Milano: 2001); Mario Sbriccoli, "*Pellegrino Rossi et la Science Juridique," Des libertés et des peines. Actes du Colloque Pellegrino Rossi organisé à Genève*, 23–24 novembre de 1979 (Genève, Librairie de l' Université, 1980), pp. 179–184, p. 184. Rossi's influence upon Spanish criminal doctrine and criminal law in Emilia Iñesta-Pastor, "La interpretación del eclecticismo en la doctrina y en la legislación penal de la España del siglo XIX," *Ius Fugit* 19 (2016), pp. 209–230, pp. 212–214; by the same author, *El Código penal español de 1848,* pp. 262–290.

[23]Eugenio Cuello Calón, "Centenario del Código penal de 1848. Pacheco penalista y Legislador. Su influjo en este cuerpo legal," *Información Jurídica* (1948), pp. 5–15. p. 12. Marino Barbero Santos, *Política y Derecho penal en España* (Madrid: Tucar, 1977), p. 31.

[24]Joaquín Francisco Pacheco, *Estudios de Derecho Penal* (3ª ed.), 2 vols. (Madrid: Viuda de Jordán e Hijos, 1868). An assessment about the work of Joaquin Francisco Pacheco and his interpretation of Eclecticism and Rossi's influence can be found in Iñesta-Pastor, "La interpretación del eclecticismo en la doctrina y en la legislación penal de la España del siglo XIX," pp. 215–219.

[25]Luís Jiménez de Asúa, "Don Joaquín Francisco Pacheco en el Centenario del Código Penal español", *El Criminalista* 9 (1951), pp. 13–33, pp. 29–30; José María Rodríguez Devesa, *Derecho Penal Parte General* (Madrid: 1976), p. 90; Barbero Santos, *Política y Derecho penal en España*, p. 31; Iñesta-Pastor, *El Código penal español de 1848*, pp. 273–290.

[26]María Dolores del Mar Sánchez González, *La Codificación penal española: los Códigos de 1848 y 1850* (Madrid: Boletín Oficial del Estado, Centro de Estudios Políticos y Constitucionales, 2004), pp. 237–330; Iñesta-Pastor, *El Código penal español de 1848*, pp. 763–894.

[27]Luis Silvela, *El Derecho español estudiado en principios y en la legislación vigente en España*, (2nd ed), II (Madrid: Establecimiento Tipográfico de Ricardo Fe, 1903), p. 172; Federico Castejón, "Las ideas penales en la época del Código penal de 1870," *Conmemoración del centenario de la Ley provisional sobre organización del Poder Judicial y del Código penal de 1870* (Madrid: Real Academia de Legislación y jurisprudencia, 1970), p. 63; Alejandro Groizard, *El Código penal de 1870, concordado y comentado*, II (Burgos: Esteban hermanos impresores, 1870), pp. 79–88, 254–255; Iñesta-Pastor, "La interpretación del eclecticismo en la doctrina y en la legislación penal de la España del siglo XIX,", pp. 225–226.

3 The 1819 Criminal Code of the Kingdom of the Two Sicilies

3.1 Political-Doctrinal Orientation

As is well known, the kingdom of the Two Sicilies arose in 1815 after the union of the kingdoms of Naples and Sicily, with Ferdinand I of Bourbon after the Bourbon Restoration. At the time when it was formed, this kingdom was characterised by a number of significant cultural and legal-institutional differences which resulted in a complex political situation.[28]

Ferdinand I was going to use codification as a political organisation tool which also served to consolidate his power. A twofold aim was thus achieved: an absolute, centralised, confessional monarchy—and also modern from an administrative point of view—was strengthened; and, above all, legal unity was achieved without any concessions whatsoever to constitutionalism.[29]

This marks the beginning for a policy of successive reforms that will lead to the creation of a single Code in order to put an end to the situation of disparity regarding criminal law that existed in the territories which made up the Kingdom of the Two Sicilies. Thus, the criminal legislation enacted during the French domination initially remained in force in Naples. It is worth highlighting the law of 20 March 1808, "about offences and penalties", promulgated by José Bonaparte[30] and the 1810 Napoleonic criminal Code, in force since 1812 with some modifications introduced by Neapolitan jurists during Joaquín Murat's administration; thus highlighting how Napoleonic Codes were introduced in Italy without any problems whatsoever.[31] Nevertheless, doctrine highlights that the introduction of the 1810 Criminal Code was going to generate an important resistance in the Kingdom of Naples. In that respect, Murat's Government constitutes a unique example in the

[28]Guido Landi, *Istituzioni di diritto pubblico del Regno delle Due Sicilie (1815–1861)* (Milano: A. Giuffrè, 1977), p. 83. Despite the drawing-up of several draft codes, Sicily did not eventually succeed in having its own codes; Daniela Novarese, *Costituzione e codificazione nella Sicilia dell'Ottocento. Il progetto di códice penale del 1813* (Milano: A. Giuffrè 2000), pp. 40–41, 52–56; Enza Pelleriti, 1812–1848. *La Sicilia fra due costituzioni* (Milano: A. Giuffrè 2000).

[29]Andrea Romano, *Difesa dei diritti e diritto alla difesa nell'esperienza del "Codice per lo Regno delle Due Sicilie," De la Ilustración al liberalismo. Symposium en honor al profesor Paolo Grossi* (Madrid: Centro de Estudios Constitucionales, 1995), p. 333; Gian Savino Pene Vidari, "La Codificazione e i codici: Genni", *Storia del Diritto contemporáneo* (Enrico Genta and G. S. Pene Vidari, ed.) (Torino: Giappichelli ed. 2005), pp. 22–23.

[30]Mario Da Passano, *Emendare o intimidare. La codificazione del Diritto penale in Francia e in Italia durante la Rivoluzione e l'Impero* (Torino: Giappichelli ed. 2000), pp. 176–182.

[31]Alfonso M. Stile, "Il codice penale del 1819 per lo Regno delle due Sicilie", *Diritto penale del Ottocento. Il codici preunitari e il códice Zanardelli* (S. Vinciguerra coord.) (Milano: Cedam, 1993), pp. 183–195, p. 186; Da Passano, *Emendare o intimidare*, pp. 182–183.

Napoleon-ruled peninsula.[32] Instead, Sicily maintained a set of ancestral criminal law provisions of a different nature.[33]

Seeking to face the legal inequality which prevailed in the kingdom, to put an end to the Ancien Regime's institutions and, especially, to guarantee the security of individuals as well as the property of the new bourgeois society,[34] Ferdinand I appointed a codification commission in 1815 entrusted with preparing a national body of law for the whole Kingdom. The codifying commission was formed by Neapolitan jurists and magistrates, all of them Murat's collaborators, in a clear example of the moderate—and not break-oriented—policy followed by Ferdinand I and his ministers.[35]

The Code of the Two Sicilies came into force on 1 September 1819.[36] It was a single Code which consisted of five books,[37] the second of them dedicated to criminal law.[38] The criminal code, "Parte Seconda, Leggi penali," was structured in three books: the first one devoted to penalties and the overall rules for their application; the second one to offences and crimes; and the third, to misdemeanours.[39]

The drafting commission resorted to foreign criminal codes to draw up the criminal law text, in particular the 1810 French model and, to a lesser extent, the

[32]Francesco Mastroberti, *Codificazione e Giusticia Penale nelle Sicilie dal 1808 al 1820*, (Napoli: Jovene editore, 2001), pp. 13–14.

[33]Art. 3 Decree for the promulgation of the criminal Code, May 21st 1819.

[34]Armando De Martino, *Illuminismo e codificazione, La codificazione del diritto dall'atlantico al moderno* (Napoli: Scientifica ed., 1998), pp. 339–376, p. 375.

[35]Raffaele Feola, *Dall'Illuminismo alla Restaurazione, Donnato Tommasi e la legislazione delle Sicilie* (Napoli: Jovene editore, 1977), p. 197.

[36]*Códice per lo Regno delle Due Sicilie. Parte Seconda, Leggi Penali,* Prima edizione originale e uffiziale (Napoli: Dalla Real Tipografia del Ministero di Reato della Cancelleria Generale, 1819); recent edition, *Codice per lo Regno delle Due Sicilie (1819), Parte seconda, Leggi Penali* (Presentazione di Mario da Passano, Aldo Mazzacane, Vicenzo Patalano & Sergio Vinciguerra) (Padova: Cedam, 1996). Spanish translation, *Código Penal de las Dos Sicilias (1819). Colección de Códigos penales de los Estados Modernos,* Madrid, 1848. Doctrine interchangeably adopted the name of Code of the Two Sicilies or Neapolitan Code.

[37]Following the model of the five French Codes: civil; criminal; criminal procedural; civil procedural; and commercial.

[38]The criminal Section was formed by: Francesco Canofari, Nicola Nicolini, Nicola Libetta, Giovanni Vittorio Englen, Giuseppe Raffeli and Rafele Di Giorgio –the first four, Murat's collaborators. About the relationship of Neapolitan jurists with the government and the administration, see De Martino, *Iluminismo e codificazione*, p. 348 and ff; Aldo Mazzacane, "Una Sciencia per due Regni", *Codice per lo Regno delle Due Sicilie (1819),* Parte Seconda, *Leggi penali* (Presentazione di Mario da Passano, Aldo Mazzacane, Vicenzo Patalano & Sergio Vinciguerra) (Padova, Cedam, 1996), pp. XXVII–XLIV, pp. XXXVIII and ff. The absence of Sicilian jurists has been recently studied by Daniela Novarese through the analysis of the 1819 Draft Criminal Code belonging to the Sicilian legal expert Francesco Pasqualino. Daniela Novarese, *Istituzioni e proceso di codificazione nel Regno delle Due Sicilie* (Milano: Giuffré, 2000), pp. 35–47 and 51 and ff.

[39]The authorship of the first two books corresponds to Nicola Nicolini, and that of the third one to Vittorio Englen.

1803 Austrian criminal code and the 1806 Draft Criminal Code for the Italian Kingdom.[40] Nevertheless, the Code of the Two Sicilies constitutes the final outcome of an evolution which began with the French revolutionary legislation received through the 1808 Law *about offences and penalties* and, subsequently, in the amendments to the French Code made by Murat in 1812. To all this must be added the influence of Italian experts in criminal law.[41]

Some scholars have highlighted how the 1808 Law about offences and penalties made it possible to incorporate aspects from the 1791 French revolutionary legislation such as penalty mitigation and the principle of legality for offences and penalties into the code of the Two Sicilies. These innovations turned out to be highly valuable insofar as they triggered the subsequent evolution towards a more rigorous criminal law that eventually culminated in the Napoleonic codification, with regard to which the 1819 Neapolitan codification represents an undeniable—though partial—improvement.[42] Moreover, that law of 20 May 1808 was also going to collect the contributions of Neapolitan illuminists such as Filangieri and Pagano—to which Romagnosi's innovations should be added. They all developed Roman and Italian legal science in an original fashion, paying special attention to the doctrine of wilful misconduct, of guilt, of imputability, as well as of failed attempts and concurrent offences, which would be received in the 1819 text—hence its categorisation as a "monument of Italian Science and Jurisprudence."[43] As stated by doctrine, the implementation of the French Criminal Code in Italy had to confront a specific tradition in criminal law matters which was very alive in the 19th century.[44]

Everything that has been explained above shows that, although the Neapolitan Criminal Code did not constitute an absolute innovation, its national character and its originality are recognised, as well as the unquestionable improvement of its model: the 1810 French code.[45]

---

[40]See introductory studies about the *Codice per lo Regno delle Due Sicilie (1819)*, Parte Seconda, Leggi penali.

[41]Ugo Spiritto, *Storia del Diritto penale italiano* (Firenze: Sansoni, 1974), p. 65.

[42]Vicenzo Patalano, "Sulle leggi penali contenute nella parte seconda del Códice pero lo Regno delle Due Sicilie", *Codice per lo Regno delle Due Sicilie (1819)*, Parte Seconda, *Leggi penali*, Presentazione di Mario da Passano, Aldo Mazzacane, Vicenzo Patalano & Sergio Vinciguerra) (Padova: Cedam, 1996), pp. XLVII.

[43]Bernardino Alimena, "Derecho penal de Italia", Franz Von Liszt, *La legislación penal comparada*, I. *El Derecho criminal de los Estados europeos* (translation Alberto Posada) (Madrid-Berlín, 1896), pp. 500–531, p. 501; Enrico Pessina, *Elementos de Derecho Penal*, (translation of Hilarión González), (Barcelona, ed. Reus, 1919), pp. 283–284.

[44]Enrico Pessina, "Il diritto penale in Italia da Cesare Beccaria sino alla promulgazione del códice penale vigente (164–1890)," *Enciclopedia del Diritto penale italiano* (Enrico Pessina, dir.), (Milano, 1906), p. 593 and ff.

[45]Sergio Vinciguerra, *Diritto penale italiano*, I (Milano: Padova, 1999), p. 245. Da Passano, *Emendare o intimidare*, p. 189.

3.2 Innovations in the Criminal Code of the Two Sicilies in Relation to the 1810 French Criminal Code

The advances in criminal law are mostly found in the General Part, much more detailed than the French Codes of 1791 and 1810[46], in Book I, Chapter I.

From a systematic point of view, the Criminal Code of the Two Sicilies follows the French model and begins with the rules meant to regulate Penalties. However, the Code of the Two Sicilies acquires its own personality in this respect by placing the emphasis on the humanisation of the penalty, linked to Neapolitan legal illuminism, when it states the following in Article 1, 2nd: "no penalty is infamous," albeit with a limited scope, since the penalty of banishment and ban on holding public office was maintained in Article 8. Doctrine has highlighted the influence exerted by Beccaria's doctrine at this point.[47] The civil death of the French Criminal Code does not exist either. However, despite this statement, such infamous penalties as banishment—under the name of exile—and interdiction, instead of the civil degradation of the French Code, are kept.

French influence results in the consolidation of the principle of personality for the penalty (Article 1 3rd) as well as the principle of non-retroactivity for criminal law (Article 60), that were both foreseen in the French text.

As for penalties, the concern for the adaptation of the penalty to the offence within the broad catalogue of penalties stands out. And as a distinctive sign, a system of scales and degrees is adopted for their determination, in accordance with the purpose of the penalties, which pursue retribution, general prevention and the rehabilitation of the offender (Article 46).[48]

In this regard, the Code of the Two Sicilies moved away from the flexibility awarded to the judge in the 1810 criminal code, which, except for the most serious crimes, punished with fixed penalties, had established a maximum and minimum limit where the judge enjoyed a discretional power to individualise penalties, which sometimes resulted in sacrificing their proportionality.[49]

The division of the penalty into grades stands out as one of the most original features in the Code of the Two Sicilies. The Draft Criminal Code prepared by Giuseppe Luosi in Milan in 1806 was followed this time. Together with a

---

[46]José Luis Guzmán Dálbora, "«Código Penal francés de 1791», Traducción y nota introductoria," *Revista de Derecho Penal y Criminologia* (RDPCrim.) 3ª época nº 1 (2009), pp. 481–517; *Código Penal del Imperio Francés*. (Traslation Don Benito Redondo de Toledo) (Paris: Imprenta de P.N. Rougeron, 1810).

[47]Sergio Vinciguerra, "Una técnica giuridica raffinata al servizio dell'assolutismo regio: «le leggi penale» delle Due Sicilie," *Codice per lo Regno delle Due Sicilie (1819)*, Parte Seconda, *Leggi penali*, Presentazione di Mario da Passano, Aldo Mazzacane, Vicenzo Patalano & Sergio Vinciguerra) (Padova: Cedam, 1996), pp. XIX–XX; also, "L'influence du code de 1810 en Italie," p. 122.

[48]Pantalano, "Sulle leggi penali contenute nella parte seconda del Códice pero lo Regno delle Due Sicilie," p. LV.

[49]Vinciguerra, "L'influence du code de 1810 en Italie," p. 121.

subsequent Draft of 1809, jointly prepared by Luosi and Gian Domenico Romagnosi. The technical superiority of the latter deserves to be highlighted. It contains the ideas that Romagnosi—considered the modern theorist of general prevention, towards which the 1809 Draft Code is oriented[50]—had about penalties. It clearly represents an example of the strength that Italian criminal law doctrine had, since they were drawn up while Italy found itself under foreign domination. Amongst other issues, both Drafts were going to improve the penalty prediction system adopted by the Italian Republic on 25 February 1804.[51] Both Drafts are regarded as the link between Italian criminal law tradition, eighteenth-century Austria House's codifications and French imperial codification. This makes it clear that Italy already had a certain codifying experience when the French Criminal Code was imposed.[52]

The system consisted in the existence of intermediate degrees between the aforementioned maximum and minimum degrees foreseen for each penalty. The law suggests to the judge which penalty must be applied, as well as its degree, according to the circumstances modifying criminal responsibility. Such circumstances will permit to increase or reduce the penalty amount within a single interval and even, the passage from one type of penalty to another in specific cases.[53]

As highlighted by doctrine with the degree system, the Italian school had learnt to understand the difference between the degree of the offence and that of the penalty—a necessary distinction when it comes to accurately determining the sanction.[54]

The scales and degrees in penalties have been maintained in every Italian code and they also exerted an influence upon Spain from the 1848 Criminal Code up to the 1995 Code currently in force.[55]

Another of the innovations in the Two Sicilies text is undoubtedly the consideration of circumstances modifying criminal responsibility. The 1810 French Criminal Code only admits extenuating circumstances in correctional matters, and it was not until the reform undertaken in 1832 that extenuating circumstances began to be applied to all crimes. A special mention needs to be made of the regulation

---

[50]Annamaría Monti, "L'influence du Code Pénal français de 1810 sur les conceptions de la peine en Italie", *La dimensión historique de la peine* (1810–2010), *Bicentenaire du Code Pénal de 1810, Colloque International de Strasbourg, 27–28 mai 2010* (Ives Jeanclos, dir.) (Paris: editeur Economica, 2011), pp. 277–292, pp. 280–281.

[51]Vinciguerra, "L'influence du code de 1810 en Italie," p. 121.

[52]Monti, "L'influence du Code Pénal français de 1810 sur les conceptions de la peine en Italie," p. 282; Adriano Cavanna, *Le leggi penali di Giuseppe Bonaparte per il Regno di Napoli (1808)*, facsimile edition with comments by S. Vinciguerra, (Padova: Cedam, 1988), pp. CCCXC–CCCXCIII.

[53]Vinciguerra, "L'influence du code de 1810 en Italie," p. 121; Monti, "L'influence du Code Pénal français de 1810 sur les conceptions de la peine en Italie," pp. 287–288.

[54]*Ibid.*, p. 288.

[55]Vinciguerra, *Diritto penale italiano,* I, pp. 251–252.

concerning the adoption of madness or dementia as grounds for acquittal, and irresistible force, with some variants with respect to the French one.[56]

Great relevance corresponds to the treatment of minority, where an exclusion of the penalty was distinguished for children below 9 years of age, establishing a reduction of punishability according to several age groups which continued the Roman tradition—unlike the French text, where a distinction was made according to whether the minor acted with or without discernment.[57] A more lenient treatment will also be given to pregnant women condemned to death.[58] Reasons for acquittal were equally going to appear in the treatment of blood offences, legitimate defence or due obedience being contemplated.[59]

With regard to kinds of penalties, the difference between both codes cannot be denied. The application of death penalty decreases, the fist amputation imposed upon parricides disappears,[60] together with the confiscation of property penalty, the mark in forced labour and the ring.[61]

Without a doubt, one of its main contributions is the distinction between attempted offence and failed attempt. Following Romagnosi's doctrine, there will be an attempted offence when all the acts needed to produce the criminal action had been performed but, for reasons alien to the actor's will, the offence was not committed. And there will be a failed attempt when the action was not completed. A penalty reduction was foreseen in both cases—higher in the second case.[62]

As for the parties involved in the offence, the 1819 code was going to draw a distinction between author and accomplice, defining the latter as the person who had supplied means for the commission of the offence, had given instructions, provided help or assistance thereto; penalties were reduced in the first two cases.[63]

The regulation of recidivism and repetition is also of great interest. Maximum extension was given to recidivism, punishing it with a higher-degree penalty—having life imprisonment as the limit and excluding death penalty.[64] Repetition was envisaged when the person accused of an offence, crime or misdemeanour for which he had not been legally condemned yet committed another one. In order to

---

[56]*Codice per lo Regno delle Due Sicilie (1819)* (hereinafter CPDS 1819), Articles 61–62; *Código penal del Imperio francés* (1810) (hereinafter, CPF 1810). Article 64.

[57]CPDS 1819, Articles 64–65.

[58]CPDS 1819, Article 68.

[59]Patalano, "Sulle leggi penali contenute nella parte seconda del Códice pero lo Regno delle Due Sicilie," p. LIX.

[60]CPF 1810, Article 13.

[61]CPF 1810, Articles 7, 77, 87, 92 and 97.

[62]CPDS 1819, Articles 69 and 70. The influence of Italian doctrine and the 1808 laws, Pantalano, "Sulle leggi penali contenute nella parte seconda del Códice pero lo Regno delle Due Sicilie," p. LX and **ff.;** Sergio Vinciguerra, "L'influence du code de 1810 en Italie," p. 119.

[63]CPDS 1819, Articles 74–76.

[64]CPDS 1819, Articles 78–84.

achieve penalty proportionality, the punishment will be determined depending on whether repetition exists (in which case the penalty for the most serious offence would be applied in an augmented degree); or when there are concurrent offences other than repetition (in which case the higher degree of the penalty established for the most serious offence would be applied—always with the limit of death penalty).[65]

As for the *Special Part,* offences in particular, the Second Book starts with offences against the State followed by offences against religion. It is worth highlighting the rigour in their punishment, the same as the harshness in offences against property, which is indicative of the special protection given to owners and to the ruling class. This clearly revealed the political-criminal orientation of a Code which was an instrument of an absolute, monarchic and confessional State where, as opposed to the technical solutions provided in the General Part…

> the civil and political rights, the individual and collective liberties were considered enemies to be chased rather that assets to be protected… in open contradiction with the principles stated in the Code.[66]

In short, Italian historiography and legal doctrine regard the 1819 criminal law text of the Two Sicilies as "the first pre-unitary Italian criminal law where its nature as a code cannot be questioned."[67] Special value is equally acknowledged to this text because it served as a model in those other pre-unitary Italian states.[68]

Also foreign doctrine recognised the advances made in the Code of the Two Sicilies. Ortolan highlights the superiority of the General Part of this Neapolitan text. This is also done by Lavergne and Mittermaier.[69] Its projection as a model for the 1848 Spanish criminal Code and in a number of aspects that have been maintained up to the 1995 code currently in force is acknowledged as well.[70]

[65]CPDS 1819, Articles 85–86.

[66]Vinciguerra, *Diritto penale italiano,* I, p. 253.

[67]Some pre-unitary Italian states which rejected anything coming from France were inspired by the Neapolitan code, Vinciguerra, "Una técnica giuridica raffinata al servizio dell'assolutismo regio: «le leggi penale» delle Due Sicilie," pp. IX–X.

[68]Gian Savino Pene Vidari, *Constitutzioni e Codici* (Torino: Giappichelli, ed. 1996), p. 90.

[69]Mazzacane, "Una Sciencia per due Regni," p. XXI.

[70]Vinciguerra, *Diritto penale italiano*, I, p. 245; Iñesta-Pastor, *El Código penal español de 1848*, p. 298; Antón Oneca, *Derecho Penal. Parte General*, p. 76.

4 The Specific Influence Exerted by the 1819 Criminal Code of the Two Sicilies upon the 1848 Spanish Criminal Code

4.1 The 1848 Spanish Criminal Code

One of the legal texts of greatest significance during the reign of Isabella II, in the course of the Moderate Decade,[71] was the 1848 Criminal Code.[72] Drawn up by the General Codification Commission created in 1843,[73] it was going to put an end to a long period characterised by the lack of a systematised criminal legislation –with the only exception of the short period during which the 1822 criminal code was in force.[74] The structure and scientific orientation of the 1848 text would have a recognised influence not only on the subsequent Spanish codes up to that of 1995 currently in force but also on Latin America.[75]

The 1848 criminal law text ensured the defence of the legal values created by the organisation of the Moderate State, although it must be underlined that the criminal Code meant a reform of a technical nature, the need for which was felt by all the representatives of liberalism.[76]

With regard to its doctrinal orientation, the 1848 Spanish criminal code constitutes a clear example of the influence exerted by Italian criminal law doctrine,

---

[71]José Luis Comellas, *Los Moderados en el poder (1844–1854)* (Madrid: Consejo Superior de Investigaciones Científicas, 1979), p. 243.

[72]*Código Penal de España*, Madrid, Imprenta Nacional, 1848 (hereinafter CPE 1848); Jacobo López Barja de Quiroga, Luis Rodríguez Ramos y Lourdes Ruiz de Gordezuela López, *Códigos penales españoles, 1822, 1848, 1850, 1928, 1932, 1944. Recopilación y concordancias* (Madrid: Akal, 1988); see for all of them José Antón Oneca, "El Código penal de 1848 y D. Joaquín Francisco Pacheco," *ADPCP* 18 (1965), pp. 473–495; recent studies, Sánchez González, *La Codificación penal española: los Códigos de 1848 y 1850;* Iñesta-Pastor, *El Código Penal español de 1848.*

[73]Emilia Iñesta-Pastor, "La Comisión General de codificación (1843–1976). De la codificación moderna a la descodificación contemporánea," *Anuario de Historia del Derecho Español (AHDE)* 83 (Madrid, 2013), pp. 65–103.

[74]See for all of them Casabó Ruiz, *El Código penal de 1822*; José Antón Oneca, "Historia del Código penal de 1822," *ADPCP* 17 (1965), pp. 262–278; Torres Aguilar, *Génesis parlamentaria del Código penal de 1822.*

[75]Iñesta-Pastor, *El Código Penal español de 1848*, p. 911–914; by the same author, "La proyección hispanoamericana del Código Penal español de 1848", *Actas de Derecho Indiano, XIII Congreso del Instituto Internacional de Historia de Derecho Indiano*, II, *Estudios* (Luis González Vale, ed.) (San Juan de Puerto Rico: Oficina del Historiador de Puerto Rico, 2003), pp. 493–521.

[76]Iñesta-Pastor, *El Código Penal español de 1848*, pp. 105–106; also, about, the politic system used for the presentation to the Parliament, "The Spanish Parliament and legislative delegation (1844–1849)", *Parliaments, Estates and Representation* 30, 1 (2010), pp. 41–56.

especially by Francesco Rossi's criminal eclecticism,[77] favoured by the association of our theological culture with the foundation of criminal law science on moral law, and by the generalisation of the ideas of 'retributive and expiatory punishment' amongst experts in criminal law.[78]

The drafters, commentators of the Code and Spanish experts in criminal law admit that the 1848 Code is based on Rossi's eclecticism, even though it keeps reminiscences of the previous utilitarianism.[79]

4.2 *The Criminal Code of the Two Sicilies as a Model for the 1848 Spanish Criminal Code*

The 1848 Spanish criminal Code arose at a time when other consolidated criminal law texts already existed in Europe, which allowed its drafters to take advantage of previous experiences in order to incorporate the advances made in the area of criminal law and to prepare a more refined Code than the already existing ones; as it was explicitly recognised by one of its drafters, Manuel Seijas Lozano: "we are writing after the other nations and we have the obligation not to move back."[80]

As said above, it is acknowledged that the drafters of the 1848 Spanish text drew their inspiration from the following models: the 1803 Austrian criminal Code, the 1810 French code, that of the Two Sicilies of 1819, the 1822 Spanish criminal code, and the 1830 Brazilian code, the last three of which clearly derived from the French criminal code.[81]

Nevertheless, amongst all of them prevailed the influence exerted by the Brazilian Code, inspired in the 1822 Spanish Code and that of the Two Sicilies. That is the reason why they were particularly studied and followed as models.[82] A preference is declared for the Code of the Two Sicilies over the French one:

[77]Rossi's influence upon Spanish criminal doctrine and criminal law in Iñesta-Pastor, "La interpretación del eclecticismo en la doctrina y en la legislación penal de la España del siglo XIX," pp. 212–219. See Sect. 2 of this paper and the bibliography of footnotes 23 to 28.

[78]Alfonso Cardenal Murillo, *La Responsabilidad por el resultado en el Derecho Penal* (Madrid, Edersa, 1990), p. 47.

[79]Jiménez de Asúa, "Don Joaquín Francisco Pacheco en el Centenario del Código Penal español," pp. 29–30. Ruperto Núñez Barbero, *La Reforma penal de 1870* (Salamanca: Universidad de Salamanca, 1969), p. 13.

[80]This was recognised by one of its authors, Manuel Seijas Lozano. ACGC, ACP, October 2nd 1844, leg. 6, fol. 2 v.; Iñesta-Pastor, *El Código penal español de 1848*, p. 79.

[81]About the foreign code models, see Iñesta-Pastor, *El Código penal español de 1848*, pp. 294–303; Ramón Revuelta Benito "El Código penal de 1848 y su gran comentarista don Joaquín Francisco Pacheco," *REEP* 40 (1948), pp. 8–13, pp. 12–13.

[82]See Sect. 1 and its corresponding footnotes; Iñesta-Pastor, *El Código penal español de 1848*, pp. 79.

"...even though that country was ruled by an absolutist government when it was published, it largely outperformed the French Code in its drawing-up and in its structure."[83]

The direct influence exerted by the code of the Two Sicilies upon the process that led to the drawing-up of the 1848 Spanish Code consequently becomes clear by the fact that its own personality was acknowledged –and with advances compared to the French Code.[84] However, it also had its direct influence through the Brazilian Code, in which doctrine also underlines the influence of the Two Sicilies. That is how Jiménez de Asúa explained it: "... The Brazilian criminal Code..., inspired by the Neapolitan one... served as a paradigm for our 1848 Code".[85]

4.3 The Specific Influences Exerted by the 1819 Criminal Code of the Two Sicilies upon the 1848 Spanish Criminal Code

4.3.1 In the General Part

The Principle of Non-retroactivity of Criminal Law

One of the aspects deriving from the principle of legality is the principle of non-retroactivity of criminal law (Article 19). This is one of the innovations introduced by the Neapolitan Code which influenced the Spanish one.[86]

It was the object of several sessions during the discussion of the Bill because it was considered unnecessary and redundant. Seijas Lozano's proposal, which was supported on humanity criteria, finally succeeded.[87]

It was justified by doctrine as a complement to Article 2: "no punishments will be imposed upon acts or omissions other than those which the law has previously categorised as offences and misdemeanours" for the purpose of restricting the adjudication of judges.[88] It is additionally necessary to bear in mind that it was a constitutional-rank principle in the 1837 and 1845 constitutions which were in force at the time when the

---

[83]DSC. Congreso, 1847–48, March 10th 1848. pp. 1715–1716; *ibid.*, pp. 80.

[84]ACGC, ACP, April 24th 1845, leg. 6, fol. 84rv. Antón Oneca, *Derecho Penal. Parte General*, p. 76.

[85]Luis Jiménez de Asúa, *Un viaje al Brasil* (Madrid, Ed. Reus, 1929), p. 99; also, *Tratado de Derecho Penal*, I, p. 1330.

[86]CPE 1848, Articles 1, 2 and 19. It already appears in the 1822 Spanish Criminal Code, as well as in the drafts of 1830, 1831 and 1834. CPDS 1819, Article 60; Rodríguez Devesa, *Derecho Penal Español. Parte General*, pp. 138–139; Iñesta-Pastor, *El Código penal español de 1848*, pp. 322–328.

[87]ACGC, ACP, October 29th 1844, leg. 6, fol. 66rv.

[88]José de Castro y Orozco & M. Ortiz de Zúñiga, *Código penal explicado para la común inteligencia y fácil explicación*, I (Granada: Librería de Manuel Sanz, 1848), p. 129; Pacheco, *El Código penal concordado y comentado*, I, pp. 310–331.

Code was drawn up.[89] Contemporarily, Antón Oneca highlights the singularity of the 1848 Code when it comes to the restriction of judges' adjudication expressed in the rules for penalty application as a consequence of this principle.[90]

The Concept of Offence

The Spanish text defines an offence as "any voluntary action or omission punished by the law" (Article 1.1st).[91] It was widely debated upon by the General Codification Commission, where Rossi's influence has been attested.[92] The influence exerted by the 1830 Brazilian code is generally accepted when, in fact, it already appeared in the 1822 Spanish criminal Code. Nevertheless, Álvarez and Vizmanos stress the influence of the Code of the Two Sicilies at this point.[93]

It can be easily inferred from the different speeches or expositions carried out during the discussion about the concept of offence that an essential element thereof is intent, wilful misconduct,[94] with allusions being made to the Neapolitan code with the aim of defending the identification of voluntary action as equivalent to mischievous in the interpretation about the definition of offence contained in Article 1, during Vila's speech to reject Luzuriaga's proposal to put voluntary action on a level with any free action.[95]

Failed Attempt and Attempted Offence

The 1848 criminal Code declares the imperfect forms of offence execution in Article 3 as punishable: "not only a committed offence but also attempted offences and failed attempts are punishable"—with a distinction being drawn between: Attempted offence and failed attempt.[96]

This is yet another influence of Italian criminal law doctrine on Spanish criminal law codification, since the 1848 legislator echoed Romagnosi's doctrinal contribution,[97] maintained by Rossi too.[98]

The complexity involved in the treatment of failed attempt and attempted offence led the Commission to dedicate a total of 9 sessions between October 1944 and April 1945 to its drawing-up.[99] The discussions clearly reveal the influence exerted

[89]Iñesta-Pastor, *El Código penal español de 1848*, pp. 327–328.

[90]Antón Oneca, *Derecho Penal. Parte General*, p. 110.

[91]It is one of the contributions of the 1848 Spanish Criminal Code preserved in the subsequent codes; José Cerezo Mir, (6ª ed), II, *Teoría Jurídica del delito* (Madrid: Tecnos, 1998), p. 18; Iñesta-Pastor, *El Código penal español de 1848*, pp. 328–355.

[92]ACGC, ACP, October 5th 1844, leg. 6, fol. 19r.

[93]Vizmanos & Álvarez Martínez, *Comentarios al Nuevo Código* Penal, I, p. 7.

[94]ACGC. ACP, October 8th 1844, leg. 6, fol. 22v. Iñesta-Pastor, *El Código penal español de 1848*, pp. 334–341.

[95]ACGC, ACP, October 11th 1844, leg. 6, fol. 32rv; *ibid.*, pp. 341–342.

[96]CPE 1848, Article 3. CPDS 1819, Articles 69–73.

[97]Rodríguez Devesa, *Derecho Penal. Parte General*, p. 662.

[98]Rossi, *Tratado de Derecho penal*, I, p. 409.

[99]Evolution of the drafting of the failed attempt and attempted offence, Iñesta-Pastor, *El Código penal español de 1848*, pp. 369–383.

by the Code of the Two Sicilies upon the distinction between attempted offence and failed attempt –unlike what happens in the French and Brazilian codes.[100] The proposal defended by Domingo María Vila to follow the Two Sicilies system and to include failed attempt in a specific title was not successful.[101]

Attempted offence arose when dealing with the penalty imposed upon authors, accomplices and accessories. It reappeared during the treatment of attempted homicide and its distinction with injuries and wounds, when it became obvious that it had been covered neither by the French code nor by the Brazilian one.[102]

Once again drawn up by Manuel Seijas Lozano, attempted offence was going to form part of Article 3, distinguishing between committed offence, attempted offence and failed attempt with a penalty reduction following the Code of the Two Sicilies.[103]

Minority

The model set by the 1819 Code of the Two Sicilies was followed in this case, fixing some general guidelines on which discussion was not allowed and leaving others to the sensible judgment of courts.[104] This was explicitly stated by Cirilo Álvarez Martínez: "The Code… of the Two Sicilies… is entirely the same as what has been decided in the Spanish Code."[105]

Pursuant to the above, the 1848 legislator considers that a child below 9 years of age and one older than 9 and younger than 15 are not responsible unless it is attested that they acted with discernment—which must be declared by the Court (Article 8, 1st, 2nd and 3rd).[106] Finally, in the event that the Court should appreciate discernment, it was also necessary to take into account the provisions contained in

[100]Vizmanos & Álvarez Martínez, *Comentarios al Nuevo Código Penal*, I, pp. 279–284. Failed attempt already appeared in arts. 5 and 7 of the 1822 Spanish Criminal Code, but Manuel Seijas Lozano preferred to mention the Brazilian text in the minutes; the 1830 Brazilian punished failed attempt and complicity with the same penalties, and attempted complicity with one third, Articles 34–35; *Código Criminal del Imperio del Brasil*, 1830. *Colección de Códigos penales modernos*, Madrid, 1848; Alvarado Planas, *La Codificación penal en la España Isabelina*, p. 47; Iñesta-Pastor, *El Código penal español de 1848*, pp. 376.

[101]ACGC, ACP, leg. October 5th 1844, leg. 6, fol. 19rv.; *ibid.*, p. 377.

[102]ACGC, ACP, October 24th 1844, leg. 6, fol. 59rv. April 11th 1845, leg. 6, fol. 35r.; *ibid.*, pp. 380.

[103]ACGC, ACP, April 14th and 16th 1845, leg. 6, fols. 49–50 and 57–58. Pacheco, *El Código penal concordado y comentado*, I, pp. 102–108; Vizmanos & Álvarez Martínez. *Comentarios al Nuevo Código Penal*, I, pp. 279–284; Iñesta-Pastor, *El Código penal español de 1848*, pp. 369–376, 381–383.

[104]CDS 1819, Article 64. CPE 1848, Articles 8, 2nd, 3rh and 72. Evolution of the drafting of the minority, Iñesta-Pastor, *El Código penal español de 1848*, pp. 405–413.

[105]Vizmanos & Álvarez Martínez. *Comentarios al Nuevo Código Penal*, I, p. 71.

[106]In this case the Spanish Criminal Code departed from the French Criminal Code, the call to discernment could already be found in the 1822 Spanish criminal Code, Article 23; Iñesta-Pastor, *El Código penal español de 1848*, pp. 405–408.

Article 72, 1st, which imposed "a discretional penalty, but always inferior in two degrees."[107]

A third age-period was additionally distinguished between the ages of fifteen and eighteen, during which a moderation of the general penalty foreseen in the law was established (Article 72)—which entailed the prohibition of imposing death penalty.[108]

The discussion took place in the course of the session held on October 11th 1844; no other proposals inspired in the French Code were admitted, and neither was that of Peña Aguayo, who suggested the age of seven years because betrothals were permitted and sacraments were received at that age. All commissioners agreed with the drawing-up except for a proposal made by Seijas to exempt under-25 s from death penalty. In Zúñiga's opinion, such a system would encourage the use of youngsters to commit offences. Luzuriaga found that it was contradictory with emancipation at eighteen years of age and marriage at fourteen. Strong repression was supported by Peña Aguayo as well, whereas others preferred to replace it by imprisonment.[109]

Preterintentionality

The extenuating circumstances envisaged in the 1848 Code include the case of someone who intended to cause harm, though not the harm really caused by that person but another less serious one (Article 9, 3rd). The code consequently contemplates those events in which offenders did not have the intention of causing all the harm which they eventually produced.[110]

This is one of the most significant contributions made by the 1848 Criminal Code because few codes include it except for Latin American ones due to the influence of the Spanish text.[111] Nevertheless, criminal lawyers highlight that a specific mitigation in homicide appears both in the 1822 Spanish criminal Code and in the 1819 Code of the Two Sicilies.[112]

The Code refers to the case known in modern criminal law theory as *preterintentionality* or *preterintentional offence*. It is Joaquín Francisco Pacheco who best defines this case: "Here we deal exclusively with facts that exceed the purpose but which derive from a criminal purpose."[113]

---

[107] *Ibid.*, p. 409.

[108] *Ibid.*, pp. 409, 462–463.

[109] ACGC, ACP, October 11th 1844, leg. 6, fols. 34–6r.; *ibid.*, pp. 410–413.

[110] Castro y Orozco & Ortíz de Zúñiga, *Código penal explicado*, I, pp. 65–66.

[111] José Antonio Martos Nuñez, "La preterintencionalidad," *RDPCrim.* 3 (1993), pp. 553–575, pp. 556–557; Iñesta-Pastor, *El Código penal español de 1848*, pp. 463–465.

[112] CPE 1822, Article 626. CPDS 1819, Article 355. CPE 1848, Article 9, 3rd; Jiménez de Asúa, *Tratado de Derecho Penal*, IV, pp. 35–49; Iñesta Pastor, *El Código penal español*, pp. 463–465.

[113] Pacheco, *El Código penal concordado y comentado*, I, p. 209.

Recidivism

Article 10 considers it an aggravating factor "when the culprit has been previously punished for an offence to which the law assigns an equal or higher penalty"[114] in its 17th item; and "being a reoffender in an offence of the same kind" in its 18th item. Persistence in the offence is punished in such cases because it is seen as a threat to society, hence why it receives a harsher punishment.[115]

Cirilo Álvarez considered the regulation of the 1819 Neapolitan Code more suitable.[116] He objects to introducing recidivism as an aggravating circumstance as is done in the Code. In his opinion, it would have been more appropriate to place recidivism and repetition in a chapter specifically dedicated to them.[117]

Complicity and Cover-up

Article 11 in the 1849 Spanish text draws a distinction between authors, accomplices and accessories, describing them, as "criminally responsible for the offences and misdemeanours."[118]

It reflects a new system which derives from the progress made in criminal law science,[119] moving away both from previous Spanish models[120] and from contemporary codes too.[121] Amongst them all, the one which comes closer is the criminal Code of the Two Sicilies when distinguishing between author and accomplice, reducing the penalty for the latter in specific cases.[122]

Manuel Seijas Lozano pointed out during the discussion about criminal involvement inside the Codes Commission that he had tried to achieve a middle ground between the systems followed by European Codes. The discussion about involuntary homicide along with the concealment and illegal burial of corpses

---

[114]The evolution of the configuration of aggravating circumstances, Iñesta-Pastor, *El Código penal español de 1848*, pp. 480–536.

[115]Francisco de Cárdenas, "Observaciones y Comentarios sobre los artículos del Código Penal que tratan de las agravantes," *El Derecho Moderno* VI, (Madrid: 1848), pp. 234–135.

[116]CPDS 1819, Articles 78 and 79. CPE 1848, Article 10, 17th, 18th.

[117]Vizmanos & Álvarez Martínez, *Comentarios al Nuevo Código Penal*, I, pp. 146–147; *ibid.*, p. 524–527.

[118]Detailed study of complicity and cover-up, Iñesta-Pastor, *El Código penal español de 1848*, pp. 544–552.

[119]Francisco Tomás y Valiente, *El Derecho Penal de la Monarquía Absoluta (siglos XVI, XVII y XVIII)* (Madrid: Tecnos, 1969), p. 291; Juan Sainz Guerra, *La evolución del Derecho Penal en España* (Jaén: Universidad de Jaén, 2004), pp. 183–208.

[120]The 1822 Spanish Criminal Code characterises authorship, complicity and assistance as three involvement modes which entail an activity occurring prior or simultaneously to the offence, Articles 12–20. The same happens in the Draft Criminal Codes before 1848; Iñesta-Pastor, *El Código penal español de 1848*, pp. 538–539.

[121]The 1810 French Criminal Code, Article 59–63, punishes the accomplice and the author with the same penalty. The 1830 Brazilian Code drew a distinction between author and accomplice, including the accessory in the latter, Articles 4–6.

[122]CPDS 1819, Article 74. CPE 1848, Article 13, 64; María de Vizmanos & Álvarez Martínez, *Comentarios al Nuevo Código Penal*, I, p. 160; Iñesta-Pastor, *El Código penal español de 1848*, pp. 544–545.

makes the cover-up issue reappear.[123] It was going to be in the following session, on April 25th 1845, that the debate focused once again on cover-up. Luzuriaga's argument is interesting insofar as he clarifies that the term 'cover-up' refers to an event subsequent to the offence without knowledge thereof and which, no matter how serious it is, it has no relationship with the event that happens afterwards; hence his suggestion of making an exception to the general rule so as not to punish the father, mother, etc. as accessories. The wording prepared by Seijas Lozano was ultimately approved.[124]

Determination and Enforcement of Penalties

The 1848 legislator adopted a complicated system of rules for the determination of penalties adapted, on the one hand, to the configuration of a penalty with a retributive or intimidating character following Rossi's eclecticism; and on the other hand, to the need to put an end to the Ancien Regime's judicial arbitrariness and, finally, closely linked to the principles of legality and proportionality between the penalty and the offence.[125]

Therefore, one of the most complex systems in its geographical environment was elaborated following the model of the 1819 Code of the Two Sicilies.[126] The system resulted in complex mathematical operations meant to determine scales and degrees applicable according to the nature and number of concurrent circumstances. It is the so-called "criminal metrics or arithmetic" which has led to the categorisation of this system as a "doctrine which mechanises the judicial function."[127] This led to strong criticism of criminal metrics.[128]

Penalty Catalogue

It is an outstanding feature of the 1848 Code that it contains an extensive catalogue of penalties stipulated in Article 24, which lists up to twenty-nine main penalties and eight accessory ones, thus illustrating the obsession with finding an analogy between offence and penalty.[129] The projection of the criminal Code of the Two Sicilies can be observed in the distinction between afflictive, correctional and mild penalties, common to the three previous types, and accessory penalties. This

---

[123]ACGC, ACP, October 22nd 1844, leg. 6, fols. 54r–56r and April 24th 1845, leg. 6, fols. 91v–92v.; *ibid.*, pp. 552–555.

[124]ACGC. leg. 3 of Criminal Code, fold. 3, doc. 1, Manuscript A, fol. 17.

[125]Vizmanos & Álvarez Martínez, *Comentarios al Nuevo Código Penal*, I, pp. 279–280.

[126]Mercedes García Arán, *Los criterios de determinación de la pena en el Derecho español* (Barcelona: Edicions de la Universitat de Barcelona, 1982), p. 32; Iñesta-Pastor, *El Código penal español de 1848*, pp. 593–632. Emilia Iñesta-Pastor, "Influencias extranjeras en la configuración de la pena en los códigos penales españoles decimonónicos", *La codificación penal española tradición e influencias extranjeras: su contribución al proceso codificador (Parte General)* (Aniceto Masferrer, ed.) (Madrid: Aranzadi, 2017), pp. 401-599, pp. 454-469.

[127]CPE 1848, Articles 60–85; Manuel Gallego Díaz, *El sistema español de determinación legal de la pena*, p. 236; *ibid.*, pp. 599–600.

[128]DSC. Congreso, 1847–48, March 15th 1848, pp. 1789–1791.

[129]Iñesta-Pastor, *El Código penal español de 1848*, p. 558–559.

classification corresponded to serious offences, less serious ones and misdemeanours. The distinction between them is based on their duration, as well as on the conditions and the place where they are enforced.[130]

The influence of the Code of the Two Sicilies becomes evident in the diversity of penalties involving deprivation of liberty. However, the Spanish legislator went much further because the distinction of three degrees in each penalty multiplied their number. They likewise coincide in the absence of the idea of correction and amendment since, although they mentioned correctional penalties, their content did not fit in with that heading. Both fail to comply with the declaration of not to recognise infamous penalties, by collecting the ring penalty, degradation or penalties involving deprivation of rights such as disqualification, suspension and civil interdiction.[131] Despite the debates that these penalties raised during the drawing-up of the Bill, especially the ring penalty for regicide and parricide, they were kept in the final wording.[132]

It was Seijas who wrote the general penalty scale in Article 24 justifying it for reasons of legal security, because thanks to it, death penalty application was reduced and the criminal's correction was encouraged because:

> ...you can never move cruelty further away than increasing the penalty catalogue because injustice is condemned in that way.[133]

Gradual Scales in a Penalty and Its Division in Degrees

One of the consequences of the system adopted by the 1848 legislator was the need to bear in mind the connection between different penalties and to establish a scale between them according to their respective superiority or inferiority.[134]

As can be checked in the minutes of the Codes Commission[135], the model adopted was the Code of the Two Sicilies, which established three scales to mark the passage from a serious penalty to another less serious one, and another five scales in the opposite direction.[136] The Spanish Code introduces gradual scales according to the nature and analogy of penalties, from the most serious to the least serious one (Article 79). To this was added a subdivision of each penalty into three degrees: maximum; medium; and minimum, which triple the content of scales, insofar as each degree is regarded as a different penalty (Article 83). It is possible to

---

[130]CPDS 1819, criminal penalties, Article 3; correctional penalties, Article 21 and ff.; common penalties, Articles 29–35; police penalties, Articles 36–39; and common provisions, Articles 40–51.

[131]CPE 1848, ring penalty (Articles 52 and 113); disqualification (Articles 29 and 51); degradation (Article 114). CPDS 1819, Article 8, chain penalty; disqualification, Articles 14–18, 27–28, and 41.

[132]ACGC. ACP, October 29th 1844, leg. 6, fol. 73r.; *ibid.*, pp., 562–563.

[133]ACGC. ACP, October 2nd 1844, leg. 6, fol. 4rv.; *ibid*, 561–562.

[134]José Antonio Elías, *Aplicación práctica del Código penal de España, acompañada de tablas sinópticas* (Barcelona: Imprenta de Ramón Martínez Indar, 1848), p. 44.

[135]ACGC. ACP, December 10th 1845, leg. 6, fol. 170v.

[136]CPDS 1819, Articles 55–58; Iñesta-Pastor, *El Código penal español de 1848*, pp. 601–604.

go up to a more serious penalty or to go down to a less serious one within each scale; moving from one scale to another is not possible, though.[137]

Determination of the Penalty According to the Degrees of Execution and Involvement in the Offence

It reflects the conviction about the existence of lesser guilt in cases of *failed attempt, attempted offence, complicity* and *cover-up* compared to authorship. This system was adopted following above all the model of the Code of the Two Sicilies,[138] though structuring it in a more accurate and rigid way in accordance with the criminal law metrics system.[139]

Therefore, the 1848 Spanish text reduces the penalty in one degree for attempted offence, failed attempt and complicity (Article 61, 62 and 63) and in two degrees for accessories (Article 64). However, exceptions were foreseen in cases "especially punished by the law" (Article 65). This referred to offences such as treason, theft, falsehood or arson, which showed the special protection granted to attacks against political authority and property, the special harshness in their treatment matching the Sicilian text as well.[140] These rules have remained largely unchanged in the subsequent criminal Codes up to the present day.[141]

The Enforcement of Death Penalty

A feature shared by the 1848 Spanish criminal Code and that of the Two Sicilies is the detailed regulation of death penalty, accompanied by a whole series of actions that had a clearly intimidating nature.[142] Amongst them stands out the change of colours in convicts' clothes depending on the offence committed.[143] The projection of the Sicilian text is clearly visible in cases of regicide and parricide where it was foreseen that the convict had to wear "yellow clothes and a cap in the same colour, with red spots."[144]

Both exemplarity and the intimidating purpose in death penalty enforcement become obvious in the discussion about the Draft Code. Proposals of great severity such as cutting off the offender's right arm after having died and the public exhibition of the corpse were actually made for regicide and parricide

[137]Pacheco, *El Código penal concordado y comentado*, I, p. 442.; *ibid.*, pp. 605–609.

[138]CPDS 1819, failed attempt and attempted offence in Articles 69 and 70, complicity in Article 75.

[139]Vizmanos & Álvarez Martínez, *Comentarios al Nuevo Código Penal*, I, p. 248.

[140]Castro y Orozco & Ortiz de Zúñiga, *Código penal explicado*, p. 173; Iñesta-Pastor, *El Código penal español de 1848*, pp. 610–612.

[141]Manuel Gallego Díaz, *El sistema español de determinación legal de la pena*, pp. 358–360.

[142]The influence exerted by Bentham and Filangieri was proved.

[143]CPE 1848, Articles 89–92. A widespread issue in every Code; it already appeared in the 1822 Spanish Code (Articles 40 and 42).

[144]CPDS 1819, Article 6. CPE 1848, Article 91; José Arias Brime, "Asesinato y parricidio: la pena de muerte antes estos delitos," *Revista General de Legislación y Jurisprudencia* 39 (1871), pp. 338–334; for the configuration of the death penalty, see Iñesta-Pastor, *El Código penal español de 1848*, pp. 564–579.

cases.[145] Especially strong criticism was addressed to the sentence by which a convict's accomplice had to witness the execution tied to a piece of wood with a ring around his neck (Article 52).[146]

4.3.2 Innovations in the Special Part

Untruths

The 1848 Code introduces a new scheme in these issues,[147] following the Neapolitan text in a case-based regulation, in 38 articles and six chapters, dedicated to the forgery of stamps and marks, coins, banknotes, State credit documents, sealed paper and documents[148] Also false testimony as well as slanderous accusation and reports,[149] and the usurpation of functions, false names and positions, and common provisions.[150] Its content was going to be maintained with only very slight variations in the subsequent 1870, 1932 and 1944 codes.[151]

Offences Committed by Civil Servants

The model of the criminal Code of the Two Sicilies was followed using the term "civil servant" instead of "official,"[152] presenting the definition of what has to be regarded as such for criminal law purposes as a novelty.[153] The extension and meticulousness in the regulation are outstanding in both cases.[154]

---

[145]ACGC. ACP, October 29th 1844, leg. 6, fols. 68v–69r.

[146]ACGC. ACP, October 29th 1844, leg. 6, fols. 68v–69r.

[147]José González Serrano, *Apéndice a los comentarios al Código penal de Don Francisco Pacheco* (Madrid: Imprenta de Manuel Tello, 1889), p. 270. An study of the Untruths, Iñesta-Pastor, *El Código penal español de 1848*, pp. 564–579.

[148]CPDS 1819 Articles 186–195. CPE 1848, Articles 234–242.

[149]CPDS 1819, Libro II, título V, *De los crímenes contra la fe pública* with a structure and section which closely resembled the Spanish text, Articles 263–286, imposing life imprisonment penalties, CPE 1848, Articles 207–233.

[150]CPDS 1819, Articles 263–286, CPE 1848, Articles 243–245.

[151]Juan Antonio Alejandre, "Estudio histórico del delito de falsedad documental," *AHDE* 42 (1972), pp. 117–187, p. 185.

[152]This terminology was going to be kept until the 1928 code; instead, the Sicilian text refers to "official" and "civil servant." ACGC. ACP, December 15th 1845, leg. 8, fols. 185r–193v. About these crimes, Iñesta-Pastor, *El Código penal español de 1848*, pp. 670–682.

[153]CPE 1848, Article 322: "*Se reputa empleado todo el que desempeña un cargo público aunque no sea de real nombramiento, ni reciba sueldo del Estado*". Se incluyen los eclesiásticos "[The consideration of employee is given to every person who has a public position even if they have not been appointed by the king or receive a salary from the State]," Ecclesiastics are included.

[154]Chapter VIII with 11 Titles, 17 chapters and 60 articles (Articles 262–322). The Neapolitan Code dedicates 50 articles to it, Chapter IV, *De los abusos de la autoridad*, seven sections (Articles 196–246).

It is recorded in the minutes of the Codes Commission how José María Claròs drew up these offence categories, with plenty of details and examples, which was in keeping with the other European Codes and showed the concern about such issues.[155] June 19th 1845 was devoted to lawyers' malfeasance following the Neapolitan Code, the text of which does not appear in the minutes.[156]

Special attention deserves to be paid to the case of an official who sexually abused an imprisoned woman under his custody and the declaration in this respect by García Goyena, who considers it a double offence which had to be punished with utmost severity.[157]

Offences Against Property

They are regulated very accurately as a reflection of clear individualism and also of the defence of rural bourgeoisie as the socially and politically dominant population segment. It is worth highlighting the harshness in their punishment adopting as a criterion the economic value of the physical object or the damage suffered.[158] The model followed was basically the French code, but references are also made to the Neapolitan one in the penalisation of theft according to the amount corresponding to what had been stolen. Jose Maria Claròs had prepared a case-based regulation in this respect with the aim of preventing judges' adjudication. Tomás María de Vizmanos objected to this recalling Bentham's theories, according to which the seriousness of offences did not depend on the amount but on the person to whom the damage was caused.[159]

4.4 Injuries and Supposition of Births

The 1848 legislator establishes the offence of injuries independently from offences against individuals. He configures it pursuant to the result produced, laying the foundation of a criminal law regulation which has remained up to the 1995 criminal Code currently in force. Doctrine highlights at this point the precedents set by the

[155]ACGC. leg. 4 Criminal Code, 7th fold: Ponencia de Claròs: Proyecto de Título 7°, De los delitos de los funcionarios públicos [Presentation: Draft Title 7th, Of the offenses of public officials].

[156]ACGC. ACP, June 19th 1845, leg. 6, fols. 83r–84r. CPDS 1819, Article 206 and ff.

[157]ACGC. ACP, June 22nd 1845, leg. 6, fols. 98v–99r.

[158]José María Rodríguez Devesa, "Consideraciones generales sobre los delitos contra la propiedad," *AHDE* 13 (1960), pp. 37–65, pp. 38–41; Iñesta-Pastor, *El Código penal español de 1848*, pp. 730–758. About the projection of these offences in Latin America, see Emilia Iñesta-Pastor, "Los delitos contra la propiedad en la codificación penal hispanoamericana: la pervivencia jurídica indiana", *Actas del XVIII Congreso del Instituto internacional de Historia del Derecho Indiano*, Córdoba, Argentina, 2012 (Alejandro Agüero & Pedro Yanzi Ferrerira, eds.), (Córdoba, Argentina: 2016), pp. 1287–1327.

[159]ACGC, ACP, May 28th 1845, leg. 6, fols. 185–186; Iñesta-Pastor, *El Código penal español de 1848*, pp. 755–756.

Code of the Two Sicilies in the consideration of the injury caused in addition to healing time according to José María Clarós's wording.[160]

The Spanish code punished the supposition of birth and the substitution of one child for another, as well as the concealment or exhibition of a legitimate son for the purpose of making him lose his civil status.[161]

It was punished with a prison penalty justifying this not only by the individual harm but also by the social alarm generated. In the case of concealment, the punishment has to do with the usurpation of the rights that correspond to someone by birth or of the benefits that might eventually correspond to them through the inheritance of their parents or relatives.[162]

5 The Journey to Latin America

Codification was utilised by most European countries in the 19th century while the Liberal State simultaneously became consolidated; this will give rise to a network of codes stemming from a model Code.

In addition to its projection in the 1848 Spanish Criminal Code and in the subsequent Italian criminal codes, the Code of the Two Sicilies also exerted a direct influence upon Latin America, on the 1830 Brazilian Code. According to doctrine, the latter —"inspired by the Neapolitan Code"—served as the model for the 1848 Code.[163]

The Brazilian Criminal Code additionally reveals the influence both of the 1822 Spanish Criminal Code[164] and of the 1803 Austrian Code[165]—influences which would be incorporated into the 1848 Spanish Criminal Code via the 1830 Brazilian Code. Hence why the influence exerted by the Brazilian Criminal Code has come to be regarded as the paradigm of mutual influence between Spanish and Latin American criminal codification.[166]

---

[160]CPDS 1819, Articles 377–392. CPE 1848: Articles 332–338 and 470–471; Miguel Ángel Morales Payan, *La configuración legislativa del delito de lesiones en el Derecho histórico español* (Madrid: Comunidad de Madrid, 1997), p. 53; Iñesta-Pastor, *El Código penal español de 1848*, pp. 693–697.

[161]CPE 1848, Article 382. CDS 1819, Article 346.

[162]Pacheco, *El Código penal concordado y comentado*, I, pp. 214–216.

[163]Jiménez de Asúa, *Un viaje al Brasil*, p. 99.

[164]See Sect. 1 and footnotes.

[165]Bernardino Bravo Lira, "Bicentenario del Código penal de Austria. Su proyección desde el Danubio a Filipinas," *Revista de Estudios Histórico-Jurídicos*, 26 (2004), pp. 115–155, p. 119.

[166]Luis Jiménez de Asúa y Francisco Carsi Zacarés, *Códigos penales iberoamericanos. Estudio de legislación comparada* (Caracas: Editorial Andrés Bello, 1946). Antonio Quintano Ripollés, *La influencia del Derecho español en las legislaciones hispanoamericanas*, Madrid, Ediciones de Cultura Hispánica, 1953. Manuel de Rivacoba y Rivacoba & Eugenio Raúl Zaffaroni, *Siglo y medio de Codificación Penal en Iberoamérica*, (Valparaíso, 1980). See bibliography and scope of the influence on the different Latin America countries in Emilia Iñesta-Pastor, "La proyección hispanoamericana del Código Penal español de 1848," pp. 493–521 pp. 502–505.

The projection of the 1848 Spanish Criminal Code cannot be denied either; it not only influenced the Spanish codes but also reached Latin America, either directly or through the subsequent drawing-ups of 1850, 1870, 1932 and 1944. The 1848 Spanish model will survive in the criminal Codes of Peru (1863), Venezuela (1863 and 1873), El Salvador (1859 and 1881), Chile (1874), Honduras (1880 and 1889), Costa Rica (1880), Guatemala (1889), Nicaragua (1891) Mexico [Criminal Code of State Veracruz Llave (1868) and Criminal Code of District and federal territories ('Distrito y territorios federales') (1871)], Colombia (1906), despite moving away from it to some extent, reminiscences of the aforementioned 1848 model also exist in the Criminal Code of Guatemala (1936) and in a number of articles of other Codes, as exemplified by the regulation of legitimate defence in Argentina and Cuba.[167]

We thus find ourselves before a system of codes where, starting from the widespread adoption of the 1810 French Criminal Code, the successive contributions made by the different codes—the 1819 Two Sicilies Code, the 1822 Spanish Code, the 1830 Brazilian Code and the 1848 Criminal Code—eventually gave rise to a chain of codes as an expression of what could be referred to as "travelling codes."

6 Conclusion

The comparative analysis about the Criminal Code of the Two Sicilies exemplifies the influence capacity of a code drawn up in an absolute monarchy within the context of a Liberal State.

The Code of the Two Sicilies results not only from the adoption of the 1810 French criminal code as a model, but also from the complex political and legal evolution operated during Napoleonic rule and Murat's Government in the Italian territories of Naples and Sicily. It is the influence exerted by the Italian criminal law doctrine of the Enlightenment, by authors such as Beccaria, Filangieri, Pagano, Briganti and Romagnosi that will most significantly contribute to the unique nature of this 1819 code, which in turn explains its projection amongst Italian pre-unitary

[167]Iñesta-Pastor, "La proyección hispanoamericana del Código Penal español de 1848". *Actas de Derecho Indiano, XIII Congreso del Instituto Internacional de Historia de Derecho Indiano, II, Estudios* (Luis González Vale, ed.) (San Juan de Puerto Rico: Oficina del Historiador de Puerto Rico, 2003), pp. 493–521. By the same author, "El Código Penal chileno de 1874," *Revista Chilena de Historia del Derecho*, 19 (Santiago de Chile, 2006), pp. 293–328. Also, "La reforma penal del Perú independiente: El Código Penal de 1863," *Actas XV Congreso del Instituto Internacional de Historia del Derecho Indiano*, II, *Córdoba, España, 2005*, (Manuel Torres Aguilar, coord.) (Córdoba: Universidad-Diputación, 2008), pp. 1071–1098. Equally, "Antecedentes histórico-jurídicos del Código penal chileno de 1874", *Derecho, Instituciones y Procesos históricos, XIV Congreso del Instituto Internacional de Historia del Derecho Indiano*, III (José De La Puente Brunke y Armando Guevara Gil, eds.) (Lima: Instituto Riva Agüero, Universidad Pontificia de Lima, 2008), pp. 203–242; see also "Los delitos contra la propiedad en la codificación penal hispanoamericana: la pervivencia jurídica indiana," already cited.

codes. However, its influence even also reached the codes elaborated in the other European countries as well as in Latin American ones, either directly, as it happened in the case of the 1830 Brazilian Code, or in an indirect way, through the 1848 Spanish Code. The latter undoubtedly served as a model, with contributions that were incorporated into the subsequent Spanish criminal codes of 1850, 1870, 1928, 1932 and 1944, the reforms of 1863 and 1983, and up to the 1995 Code, currently in force.

Issues such as the distinction between accomplices, authors and accessories; the distinction between failed attempt and attempted offence, and recidivism. The catalogue of circumstances modifying responsibility, such as minority, dementia or insurmountable fear; preterintentionality, and legitimate defence are precepts the regulation of which was improved by the 1848 Criminal Code on the basis of the Two Sicilies text, thus achieving greater consistency and coherence.

The Code of the Two Sicilies largely influenced the penalty determination system too, the distinction of scales and degrees in penalties according to the principle of legality and proportionality between the offence and the penalty. The Code of the Two Sicilies will thus favour the construction of the so-called Spanish "arithmetic or metrics" system. This is one of the characteristic features of the 1848 Criminal Code that will adopt one of the most legalist systems for the determination of penalties within the European context.

It likewise deserves to be highlighted that the influence exerted by the Neapolitan legislation is inseparable from the arrival of Italian criminal law doctrine in Spain. One cannot deny in this respect the relevance of the doctrine developed by Beccaria, and that of Filangieri, which inspired the first Spanish criminal code in 1822, along with those of Romagnosi and Pellegrino Rossi—the latter determining the doctrinal orientation in the codes of 1848 and 1870.

Finally, on the basis of the 1810 French Code and the contributions of Italian criminal doctrine, the 1819 Criminal Code of the Two Sicilies made significant innovations in criminal Law. These innovations were going to be received in the 1848 Spanish criminal Code and, through it, projected to Latin America, giving rise to an important succession of Codes as the expression of a set of "travelling codes."

References

Actas de las sesiones de la Comisión General de Codificación, 1828–1994 (Madrid: Ministerio de Justicia, 2007).

Agüero, Alejandro, and Lorente, Marta, "Penal enlightenment in Spain: from Beccaria's reception to the first criminal code," *Forum Historiae Iuris*, (15 November 2012), http://www.forhistiur.de/2012-11-aguero-lorente/.

Alejandre, Juan Antonio, "Estudio histórico del delito de falsedad documental," *Anuario de Historia del Derecho Español*, 42 (1972), pp. 117–187.

Alimena, Bernardino, "Derecho penal de Italia", Franz Von Liszt, *La legislación penal comparada*, I. *El Derecho criminal de los Estados europeos* (translation Alberto Posada) (Madrid-Berlín, 1896), pp. 500–531.

Alvarado Planas, Javier, "La Codificación penal en la España Isabelina: la influencia del Código penal del Brasil en el Código penal español de 1848", *España en la época de la Fundación de la Guardia Civil. V. Seminario Duque de Ahumada*, Madrid, UNED, (1994), pp. 43–82.
Andrea Romano, *Difesa dei diritti e diritto alla difesa nell'esperienza del "Codice per lo Regno delle Due Sicilie," De la Ilustración al liberalismo. Symposium en honor al profesor Paolo Grossi* (Madrid: Centro de Estudios Constitucionales, 1995), pp. 317–359.
Antón Oneca, José, "El Código penal de 1848 y D. Joaquín Francisco Pacheco," *Anuario de Derecho Penal y Ciencias Penales*, 18 (1965), pp. 473–495.
Antón Oneca, José, "Historia del Código penal de 1822," *Anuario de Derecho Penal y Ciencias Penales*, 17 (1965), pp. 262–278.
Antón Oneca, José, *Derecho penal. Parte General* (2ª ed.), (Madrid: Akal, 1986).
Antón Oneca, José, Estudio Preliminar al *Discurso sobre las penas* de Manuel de Lardizábal, *Revista de Estudios Penitenciarios*, 174 (1966), pp. 597–626.
Arias Brime, José, "Asesinato y parricidio: la pena de muerte antes estos delitos," *Revista General de Legislación y Jurisprudencia*, 39 (1871), pp. 338–334.
Astigarraga, Jesús, "La ilustración napolitana imputada. Críticas y censuras a la Scienza della legislazione de G. Filangieri en la España de finales del siglo XVIII," *Nuevo Mundo Mundos Nuevos* (online), Colloques, 18 juin 2007, http://nuevomundo.revues.org/6911.
Asúa Batarrita, Adela, "Reivindicación o superación del programa de Beccaria," *El Pensamiento penal de Beccaria: su actualidad* (Adela Asúa Batarrita coord.) (Bilbao: Universidad de Deusto, 1990).
Barbero Santos, Marino, *Política y Derecho penal en España* (Madrid: Tucar, 1977).
Baró Pazos, Juan, "Historiografía sobre la Codificación del Derecho Penal en el siglo XIX," (Germán Rueda (ed.), *Doce Estudios de Historiografía contemporánea*, (Santander: Universidad de Santander, 1991), pp. 1–40.
Beccaria, Cesare, *De los delitos y las penas*, translation of Juan Antonio de las Casas, introduction, appendix and notes by Juan Antonio del Val, (Madrid: Alianza ed., 1968).
Bravo Lira, Bernardino, "Bicentenario del Código penal de Austria. Su proyección desde el Danubio a Filipinas," *Revista de Estudios Histórico-Jurídicos*, 26 (2004), pp. 115–155.
Bravo Lira, Bernardino, "Bicentenario del Código penal de Austria. Su proyección desde el Danubio a Filipinas," *Revista de Estudios Histórico-Jurídicos*, 26 (2004), pp. 115–155, p. 119.
Calabro, G., "Beccaria e la Spagna," *Atti del Convegno Internazionale sul Cesare Beccaria, Torino 2–6 ottobre 1964 (Torino: Accademia delle Scienze,* serie 4, No. 9, 1966) pp. 101–120.
Cañizares-Navarro, Juan Benito, "El Código penal de 1822: sus fuentes inspiradoras. Balance historiográfico (desde el s. XX)," *Glossae, European Journal of Legal History*, 10 (2013), pp. 109–136 (http://www.glossae.eu).
Carbasse, Jean Marie, "État autoritaire et justice répressive. L'évolution de la législation penale de 1789 au Code Pénal de 1810," *All'ombra dell'Aquila Imperiale. Transformazioni e continuità instituzionali nei territorio sabaudi in età napoleónica (1802–1814).* Atti del Convegno, Torino 15–18 ottobre 1990, (Roma: Ministero per i beni culturali e ambientali, Ufficio centrale per i beni archivistici, 1994), I, pp. 313–333.
Carbasse, Jean Marie, *Introduction historique au droit pènal* (Paris: PUF, 1990).
Cardenal Murillo, Alfonso, *La Responsabilidad por el resultado en el Derecho Penal* (Madrid, Edersa, 1990).
Cárdenas, Francisco de, "Observaciones y Comentarios sobre los artículos del Código Penal que tratan de las agravantes," *El Derecho Moderno*, VI, (Madrid: 1848), pp. 234–135.
Casabó Ruiz, José Ramón, "Los orígenes de la Codificación penal en España: el plan de Código Criminal de 1787," *Anuario de Derecho Penal y Ciencias Penales*, 22 (1969), pp. 313–342.
Casabó Ruiz, José Ramón, *El Código penal de 1822*, Unpublished Doctoral Thesis (Valencia, 1968).
Castejón, Federico, "Las ideas penales en la época del Código penal de 1870," *Conmemoración del centenario de la Ley provisional sobre organización del Poder Judicial y del Código penal de 1870* (Madrid: Real Academia de Legislación y jurisprudencia, 1970).
Castro y Orozco José de & Ortiz de Zúñiga, Manuel, *Código penal explicado para la común inteligencia y fácil explicación*, I (Granada: Librería de Manuel Sanz, 1848).

Cavanna, Adriano, *Le leggi penali di Giuseppe Bonaparte per il Regno di Napoli (1808)*, facsimile edition with comments by S. Vinciguerra, (Padova: Cedam, 1988), pp. CCCXC–CCCXCIII.

Cerezo Mir, José, *Derecho Penal*, II, *Teoría Jurídica del delito* (Madrid: Tecnos, 6ª ed., 1998).

Chieregati Costa, V., *Codificaçao e formaçao do Estado-nacional brasileiro: o Código Criminal de 1830 e a positiaçao das leis na pós-Independência*. (Dissertaçao de mestrado. Universidade de Sao Paulo, Istituto de Estudos Brasileiros, Sao Paulo, 2013).

Clavero, Bartolomé, *Manual de Historia Constitucional de España* (Madrid: Alianza ed. 1989).

Códice per lo Regno delle Due Sicilie. Parte Seconda, Leggi Penali, Prima edizione originale e uffiziale (Napoli: Dalla Real Tipografia del Ministero di Reato della Cancelleria Generale, 1819).

Codice per lo Regno delle Due Sicilie (1819), Parte seconda, Leggi Penali (Presentazione di Mario da Passano, Aldo Mazzacane, Vicenzo Patalano & Sergio Vinciguerra) (Padova: Cedam, 1996).

Código Penal de España, Madrid, Imprenta Nacional, 1848.

Código Penal de las Dos Sicilias (1819). Colección de Códigos penales de los Estados Modernos, Madrid, 1848.

Código Penal del Imperio Francés. (Traslation Don Benito Redondo de Toledo) (Paris: Imprenta de P.N. Rougeron, 1810).

Código Criminal del Imperio del Brasil, 1830. *Colección de Códigos penales modernos*, Madrid, 1830.

Comellas, José Luis, *Los Moderados en el poder (1844–1854)* (Madrid: Consejo Superior de Investigaciones Científicas, 1979).

Cuello Calón, Eugenio, "Centenario del Código penal de 1848. Pacheco penalista y Legislador. Su influjo en este cuerpo legal," *Información Jurídica*, (1948), pp. 5–15.

Da Passano, Mario, "La codification du droit pénal dans l'Italie jacobine et napoleonienne," *Revolutions et justice en Europe. Modeles français et traditions nationales (1780–1830)* (X. Rousseaux, M.-S. Dupont-Bouchat, C. Vael, dirs.) (Paris: L'Harmattan, 1999), pp. 85–100.

Da Passano, Mario, *Emendare o intimidare. La codificazione del Diritto penale in Francia e in Italia durante la Rivoluzione e l'Impero* (Torino: Giappichelli ed. 2000), pp. 176–182.

De Martino, Armando, *Illuminismo e codificazione, La codificazione del diritto dall'atlantico al moderno* (Napoli: Scientifica ed., 1998).

Delmas Saint-Hilaire, Jean Pierre, "1789: un nouveau droit pénal est né...," *Liber Amicorum. Etudes offertes à Pierre Jaubert* (Gérard Aubin, ed.) (Bourdeaux: Presses Universitaires de Bordeaux, 1992), pp. 161–177.

Diario de Sesiones de las Cortes, Congreso de los Diputados, legislatura 1847–48.

Elías, José Antonio, *Aplicación práctica del Código penal de España, acompañada de tablas sinópticas* (Barcelona: Imprenta de Ramón Martínez Indar, 1848).

Feola, Raffaele, *Dall'Illuminismo alla Restaurazione, Donnato Tommasi e la legislazione delle Sicilie* (Napoli: Jovwne editore, 1977).

Filangieri, Gaetano, *Scienzia della legislazione*, Nápoles, 1780–1785, translation of J. Rubio, Madrid, 1822.

Galindo Ayuda, Fernando, "La Scienza della legislazione en España," *Gaetano Filangieri e l'Illuminismo Europeo, Atti del Convengo «Gaetano Filangieri e l'Illuminismo Europeo,»* (Nápoles: Guida ed. 1991), pp. 375–401.

Gallego Díaz, Manuel, *El sistema español de determinación legal de la pena, Estudio de las reglas de aplicación de penas del Código penal* (Madrid: ICAI, 1985).

García Arán, Mercedes, *Los criterios de determinación de la pena en el Derecho español* (Barcelona: Universitat de Barcelona, 1982).

González Serrano, José, *Apéndice a los comentarios al Código penal de Don Francisco Pacheco* (Madrid: Imprenta de Manuel Tello, 1889.

Groizard, Alejandro, *El Código penal de 1870, concordado y comentado*, II (Burgos: Esteban hermanos impresores, 1870).

Gutiérrez Fernández, Benito, *Examen histórico del Derecho Penal* (Madrid: Imprenta de Antonio Peñuelas, 1866).

Guzmán Dálbora, José Luis, "«Código Penal francés de 1791», Traducción y nota introductoria," *Revista de Derecho Penal y Criminologia*, 3ª época, nº 1, 2009, pp. 481–517.
Hélie, Faustin, *Traité de Droit Pénal* of Pellegrino Rossi, *Introduction* (Paris: Librairie de Guillaumin et Cie, 1863).
Iñesta-Pastor, Emilia, "La proyección hispanoamericana del Código Penal español de 1848," *Actas del XIII Congreso del Instituto Internacional de Historia de Derecho Indiano*, II, Estudios, (González Vale, ed.) (San Juan de Puerto Rico, 2003), pp. 493–521.
Iñesta-Pastor, Emilia, "El Código Penal chileno de 1874," *Revista Chilena de Historia del Derecho*, 19 (Santiago de Chile, 2006), pp. 293–328.
Iñesta-Pastor, Emilia, "Antecedentes histórico-jurídicos del Código penal chileno de 1874", *Derecho, Instituciones y Procesos históricos, XIV Congreso del Instituto Internacional de Historia del Derecho Indiano*, III (José De La Puente Brunke y Armando Guevara Gil, eds.) (Lima: Instituto Riva Agüero, Universidad Pontificia de Lima, 2008), pp. 203–242.
Iñesta-Pastor, Emilia, "La Comisión General de codificación (1843–1976). De la codificación moderna a la descodificación contemporánea," *Anuario de Historia del Derecho Español* 83 (Madrid, 2013), pp. 65–103.
Iñesta-Pastor, Emilia, "La reforma penal del Perú independiente: El Código Penal de 1863," *Actas XV Congreso del Instituto Internacional de Historia del Derecho Indiano*, II, *Córdoba, España, 2005*, (Manuel Torres Aguilar, coord.) (Córdoba: Universidad-Diputación, 2008), pp. 1071–1098.
"The Spanish Parliament and legislative delegation (1844–1849)", *Parliaments, Estates and Representation*, 30, 1 (2010), pp. 41–56.
Iñesta-Pastor, Emilia, *El Código Penal español de 1848* (Valencia: Tirant lo Blanch, 2011).
Iñesta-Pastor, Emilia, "La interpretación del eclecticismo en la doctrina y en la legislación penal de la España del siglo XIX," *Ius Fugit*, 19 (2016), pp. 209–230.
Iñesta-Pastor, Emilia, "Los delitos contra la propiedad en la codificación penal hispanoamericana: la pervivencia jurídica indiana," *Actas XVIII Congreso del Instituto Internacional de Historia del Derecho Indiano, Córdoba, Argentina, 2012* (Alejando Agüero & Pedro Yanzi Ferreira eds.) (Córdoba, Argentina, 2016), pp. 1287–1327.
Jiménez de Asúa, Luis, *Un viaje al Brasil* (Madrid, Ed. Reus, 1929)
Jiménez de Asúa, Luís, "Don Joaquín Francisco Pacheco en el Centenario del Código Penal español", *El Criminalista*, (Buenos Aires), 9 (1951), pp. 13–33.
Jiménez de Asúa, Luis, *Tratado de Derecho Penal*, I (Buenos Aires: Losada, 1964).
Jiménez de Asúa, Luis, *Tratado de Derecho Penal*. VI, (Buenos Aires, Losada, 1964).
Jiménez de Asúa, Luis, y Carsi Zacarés, Francisco, *Códigos penales iberoamericanos. Estudio de legislación comparada* (Caracas: Editorial Andrés Bello, 1946).
Lalinde Abadía, Jesús, "El eco de Gaetano Filangieri en España," *Gaetano Filangieri e l'Illuminismo Europeo, Atti del Convengo «Gaetano Filangieri e l'Illuminismo Europeo,»* (Nápoles: Guida ed. 1991), pp. 453–506.
Landi, Guido, *Istituzioni di diritto pubblico del Regno delle Due Sicilie (1815–1861)*, (Milano: A. Giuffrè, 1977).
Lasso Gaite, Juan Francisco, *Codificación Penal. Crónica de la Codificación Española*, V, I, (Madrid: Ministerio de Justicia, 1970).
López Barja de Quiroga, Jacobo, Rodríguez Ramos, Luis y Ruiz de Gordezuela López, Lourdes, *Códigos penales españoles, 1822, 1848, 1850, 1928, 1932, 1944. Recopilación y concordancias* (Madrid: Akal, 1988).
Lorente Sariñena, Marta, "De la suerte normativa de la ciencia de la legislación: Filangieri y la codificación moderna en la España decimonónica," *Nuevo Mundo Mundos Nuevos* (online), Colloques, 28 janvier, 2007, http://nuevomundo.revues.org/3510
Martos Nuñez, José Antonio, "La preterintencionalidad," *Revista de Derecho Penal y Criminología*, 3 (1993), pp. 553–575.
Masferrer, Aniceto & Sánchez González, María del Mar, "Tradición e influencias extranjeras en el Código penal de 1848," *La codificación española. Una aproximación doctrinal e historiográfica a sus influencias extranjeras y a la francesa en particular* (Aniceto Masferrer, ed.) (Pamplona: Thomson-Aranzadi, 2014).

Masferrer, Aniceto, "La codificación española y sus influencias extranjeras. Una revisión en torno al alcance del influjo francés," *La codificación española. Una aproximación doctrinal e historiográfica a sus influencias extranjeras, y a la francesa en particular* (Aniceto Masferrer, ed.), (Pamplona: Thomson-Aranzadi, 2014), pp. 21–52.

Masferrer, Aniceto, "The Napoleonic *Code Pénal* and the Codification of Criminal Law in Spain," *Le Code Pénal. Les Métamorphoses d'un Modèle 1810–2010. Actes du colloque international Lille/Ghent, 16–18 décembre 2010* (Chantal Aboucaya & Renée Martinage, coords.) (Lille: Centre d'Histoire Judiciare, 2012), pp. 65–98

Mastroberti, Francesco, *Codificazione e Giusticia Penale nelle Sicilie dal 1808 al 1820*, (Napoli: Jovene editore, 2001).

Mazzacane, Aldo, "Una Sciencia per due Regni", *Codice per lo Regno delle Due Sicilie (1819),* Parte Seconda, *Leggi penali* (Presentazione di Mario da Passano, Aldo Mazzacane, Vicenzo Patalano & Sergio Vinciguerra) (Padova, Cedam, 1996), pp. XXVII–XLIV.

Meissel, Franz-Stefan, "Le code de 1810 et le droit pénal en Europe Centrale," *Bicentenaire du Code Pénal. 1810–2010, Bicentenaire du Code Pénal. 1810–2010, Les colloques du Sénat, 25–26 novembre 2010* (Paris, Sénat, 2010), pp. 113–124 (*available at* https://www.senat.fr/colloques/actes_bicentenaire_code_penal/actes_bicentenaire_code_penal.pdf), pp. 125–138.

Monti, Annamaría, "L'influence du Code Pénal français de 1810 sur les conceptions de la peine en Italie", *La dimensión historique de la peine* (1810–2010), *Bicentenaire du Code Pénal de 1810, Colloque International de Strasbourg, 27–28 mai 2010* (Ives Jeanclos, dir.) (Paris: editeur Economica), 2011, pp. 277–292.

Morales Payan, Miguel Ángel, *La configuración legislativa del delito de lesiones en el Derecho histórico español* (Madrid: Comunidad de Madrid, 1997.

Novarese, Daniela, *Costituzione e codificazione nella Sicilia dell'Ottocento. Il progetto di códice penale del 1813* (Milano: A. Giuffrè 2000).

Novarese, Daniela, *Istituzioni e proceso di codificazione nel Regno delle Due Sicilie* (Milano: Giuffré, 2000.

Núñez Barbero, Ruperto, *La Reforma penal de 1870* (Salamanca: Universidad de Salamanca, 1969), p. 13.

Pacheco, Joaquín Francisco, *El Código penal concordado y comentado*, I (Madrid: Imprenta de Santiago Saunaque, 1848).

Pacheco, Joaquín Francisco, *Estudios de Derecho Penal* (3ª ed.), 2 vols. (Madrid, Viuda de Jordán e Hijos, 1868).

Patalano, Vicenzo, "Sulle leggi penali contenute nella parte seconda del Códice pero lo Regno delle Due Sicilie", *Codice per lo Regno delle Due Sicilie (1819),* Parte Seconda, *Leggi penali*, Presentazione di Mario Da Passano, Aldo Mazzacane, Vicenzo Patalano & Sergio Vinciguerra) (Padova: Cedam, 1996), pp. XLV–LXVIII.

Pelleriti, Enza, 1812–1848. *La Sicilia fra due costituzioni* (Milano: A. Giuffrè 2000).

Pene Vidari, Gian Savino, *Constitutzioni e Codici* (Torino: Giappichelli, ed. 1996), p. 90.

Pene Vidari, Gian Savino, *La Codificazione e i codici: Genni*, *Storia del Diritto contemporáneo* (Enrico Genta and G. S. Pene Vidari), (Torino: Giappichelli ed. 2005).

Pessina, Enrico, "Il diritto penale in Italia da Cesare Beccaria sino alla promulgazione del códice penale vigente (164–1890)," *Enciclopedia del Diritto penale italiano* (Enrico Pessina, dir.), (Milano, 1906).

Pessina, Enrico, *Elementos de Derecho Penal*, (translation of Hilarión González), (Barcelona, ed. Reus, 1919), pp. 283–4.

Prieto Sanchís, Luis, "*La filosofía penal de la Ilustración española,*" *Homenaje a Dr. Barbero Santos, in memoriam* (L., Fuente Arroyo Zapatero e I. Berdugo de la Torre, drs.) (Cuenca: Universidad de Castilla la Mancha, Universidad de Salamanca, 2001), pp. 489–510.

Quintano Ripollés, Antonio, *La influencia del Derecho español en las legislaciones hispanoamericanas* (Madrid, Ediciones de Cultura Hispánica, 1953).

Ramos Vázquez, Isabel & Cañizares-Navarro, Juan Benito, "La influencia francesa en la primera codificación penal española: el Código penal francés de 1810 y el Código penal español de 1822," *La codificación española. Una aproximación doctrinal e historiográfica a sus influencias extranjeras y a la francesa en particular* (Aniceto Masferrer, ed.) (Pamplona: Thomson-Aranzadi, 2014), pp. 193–270, pp. 224–225.

Revuelta Benito, Ramón, "El Código penal de 1848 y su gran comentarista don Joaquín Francisco Pacheco," *Revista de la Escuela de Estudios Penitenciarios*, 40 (1948), pp. 8–13, pp. 12–13.

Risco, Antonio, "Présence de Beccaria dans l'Espagne des Lumières," *Becccaria et la culture juridique des Lumières. Actes du colloque européen de Genève, 25–26 novembre 1995* (Michel Porret, ed.) (Genève: Droz, 1997), pp. 149–167.

Rivacoba y Rivacoba, Manuel de, "Lardizábal, un penalista ilustrado," *Anuario del Instituto de Investigaciones Históricas de la Universidad Nacional del Litoral*, 7 (1964), pp. 210–248.

Rivacoba y Rivacoba, Manuel de & Zaffaroni, Eugenio Raúl, *Siglo y medio de Codificación Penal en Iberoamérica* (Valparaíso, 1980).

Rodríguez Devesa, José María, "Consideraciones generales sobre los delitos contra la propiedad," *Anuario de Historia del Derecho Español*, 13 (1960), pp. 37–65, pp. 38–41.

Rodríguez Devesa, José María, *Derecho Penal Parte General* (Madrid: 1976).

Rossi, Pellegrino, *Tratado de Derecho penal*, (traducción de Cayetano Cortés), (Madrid: Imprenta de José María Repullés, 1839).

Sainz Cantero, José Antonio, "El informe de la Universidad de Granada sobre el Proyecto que dio lugar al Código penal de 1822," *Anuario de Derecho Penal y Ciencias Penales*, 20 (1967), pp. 509–538, pp. 512–513.

Sainz Guerra, Juan, "José María Calatrava o la Codificación penal a comienzos del siglo XIX," *Estudios de Historia de las Ciencias Criminales en España* (J. Alvarado y A. Serrano Maíllo, eds.) (Madrid: Dykinson 2007), pp. 351–384.

Sainz Guerra, Juan, *La evolución del Derecho Penal en España* (Jaén: Universidad de Jaén, 2004).

Saldaña, Quintiliano, *Historia del Derecho Penal en España*, Adiciones al *Tratado de Derecho Penal* de Von Listz (Madrid: Instituto editorial Reus, 3ª ed., s.f.).

Sanchez Blanco, Francisco, *Europa y el pensamiento español del siglo XVIII* (Madrid: Alianza ed. 1991).

Sánchez González, María del Mar, *Historiografía penal española (1808–1870): La Escuela Clásica*, (J. Alvarado y A. Serrano Maíllo, (eds.), *Estudios de Historia de las Ciencias criminales* (Madrid: Boletin Ofical del Estado), 2007, pp. 69–129.

Sánchez González, María del Mar, *La Codificación penal española: los Códigos de 1848 y 1850* (Madrid: Centro de Estudios Políticos y Constitucionales, 2004).

Sánchez Osés, José, "Gaetano Filangieri," *Anuario de Derecho Penal y Ciencias Penales*, 19, (1966), pp. 413–438.

Sbriccoli, Mario, "*Pellegrino Rossi et la Science Juridique*," *Des libertés et des peines. Actes du Colloque Pellegrino Rossi organisé à Gen*ève, 23–24 novembre de 1979 (Genève, Librairie de l' Université, 1980), pp. 179–184.

Silvela, Luis, *El Derecho español estudiado en principios y en la legislación vigente en España*, (2nd ed.), II (Madrid: Establecimiento Tipográfico de Ricardo Fe, 1903).

Spiritto, Ugo, *Storia del Diritto penale italiano* (Firenze: Sansoni, 1974), p. 65.

Stevens, Fred, "La codification pénale en Belgique. Heritage français et debats neerlandais (1781–1867)", *Le pénal dans tous ses Etats. Justice, Etats et Sociétés en Europe (XIIe XXe siècles)* (Rousseaux, X. Levy, R., dirs.) (Bruxelles: Facultés Universitaires Saint-Louis, 1997), pp. 287–302.

Stile, Alfonso M., *Il codice penale del 1819 per lo Regno delle due Sicilie*, en *Diritto penale del Ottocento. Il codici preunitari e il códice Zanardelli* (S. Vinciguerra coord.) (Milano: Cedam, 1993), pp. 183–195.

Teruel Carralero, Domingo, "El Código del 48 en su Centenario," *Revista de la Escuela de Estudios Penitenciarios*, 40 (1948), pp. 8–13.

Tomás y Valiente, Francisco, *El Derecho Penal de la Monarquía Absoluta (siglos XVI, XVII y XVIII)* (Madrid: Tecnos, 1969).

Torres Aguilar, Manuel, *Génesis parlamentaria del Código penal de 1822*, (Messina, Sicania-University Press, 2008).

Vinciguerra, Sergio, "L' influence du code de 1810 en Italie," *Bicentenaire du Code Pénal. 1810–2010, Les colloques du Sénat, 25–26 novembre 2010* (Paris, Sénat, 2010), pp. 113–124 (*available at* https://www.senat.fr/colloques/actes_bicentenaire_code_penal/actes_bicentenaire_code_penal.pdf).

Vinciguerra, Sergio, "Una técnica giuridica raffinata al servizio dell'assolutismo regio: «le leggi penale» delle Due Sicilie," *Codice per lo Regno delle Due Sicilie (1819)*, Parte Seconda, *Leggi penali*, Presentazione di Mario da Passano, Aldo Mazzacane, Vicenzo Patalano & Sergio Vinciguerra) (Padova: Cedam, 1996), pp. VII–XXVI.

Vinciguerra, Sergio, *Diritto penale italiano*, I (Milano: Padova, 1999).

Vizmanos, Tomás María de & Álvarez Martínez, Cirilo, *Comentarios al Nuevo Código Penal* (Madrid: Establecimiento tipográfico de J. González y A. Vicente, 1848), 3 t.

VV. AA. *Des libertés et des peines. Actes du Colloque Pellegrino Rossi organisé à Genève, 23–24 novembre de 1979* (Genève: Université de Genève, 1980).

VV. AA. *Un Liberale europeo: Pellegrino Rossi (1787–1848)* (a cura de Luigi Lachè) (Milano: 2001).

Zaffaroni, Eugenio Raúl, "La influencia del pensamiento de Cesare Beccaria sobre la política criminal en el mundo," *Anuario de Derecho Penal y Ciencias Penales*, 42 (1989), pp. 135–149.

Emilia Iñesta-Pastor graduated and Ph.D. in Law with an Extraordinary Doctorate Award by the University of Alicante and Graduated in History by the University of Valencia. She is currently Associate professor in History of Law at the Law Faculty of the University of Alicante. Her main line of research is the study of Spanish criminal law codification in the nineteenth century: *El Código penal español de 1848* (Valencia, Tirant lo Blanch, 2011), 951 pp.; "La Comisión General de Codificación (1843–1976). De la codificación moderna a la descodificación contemporánea," *Anuario Historia del Derecho Español*, 83 (2013), pp. 65–103; "La interpretación del eclecticismo en la doctrina y en la legislación penal de la España del siglo XIX," *Ius Fugit*, 19 (2016), pp. 209–230. Among the works dealing with the influence of Spanish codification in Latin America stand out: "La proyección Hispanoamericana del Código penal español de 1848, Actas y Estudios," *XIII Congreso del Instituto Internacional de Historia del Derecho Indiano, II Estudios* (E. González Vales, coord.) (San Juan, Puerto Rico: 2003), pp. 493–521; "El Código penal chileno de 1874," *Revista Chilena de Historia del Derecho*. 19 (2006), pp. 293–328; "El Derecho penal del Perú independiente: El Código penal de 1863," *XV Congreso del Instituto Internacional de Historia del Derecho Indiano, II*, (Manuel Torres Aguilar, coord.). (Córdoba: 2008), pp. 1071–1098; "Antecedentes histórico-jurídicos del Código penal chileno de 1874", *Derecho, Instituciones y procesos históricos, III* (José de la Puente Brunke & Jorge Armando Guevara Gil, eds.) (Lima, 2008), Vol. III, pp. 203–242; "Los delitos contra la propiedad en la codificación penal hispanoamericana: la pervivencia jurídica indiana," *XVIII Congreso del Instituto Internacional de Historia del Derecho Indiano*, (Pedro Yanzi Ferreira & Alejandro Agüero, coords.), (Córdoba, Argentina: 2016), pp. 1287–1327. A third field of study refers to the History of the nineteenth-century Spanish Parliament: "The Spanish Parliament and the legislative delegation (1844–1849)," *Parliaments, Estates and Representation*, vol. 30 No. 1, April 2010, pp. 41–56, ISSN 0260–6755. Legal powers of the Spanish Senate during the Moderate Decade (1844–1854) in *Separation of powers and Parliamentarism. The Past and the Present, Law, Doctrine, Practice* (Warsaw: 2007), pp. 534–553; "The Spanish parliament and woman's penal condition during the legislative period of 1847–1849," *Parliaments: The Law, the practice and the presentations. From the Middle Age to the present day* (Da Cruz Coelho, M.H; Tavares Ribeiro, M.M, coords.) (Lisbon: 2010), pp. 151–160. Professor Iñesta has also explored the criminal law tradition in the Crown of Aragón. She is a member of international committees such as: Sociètè Internationale d'Histoire du Droit; International Commission for the History of Representative & Parliamentary Institutions and Instituto Internacional de Historia del Derecho Indiano.

Part III
Latin America

The 'Code Pénal' in the Itinerary of the Criminal Codification in America and Europe: 'Influence' and Circularity of Models

Diego Nunes

Abstract The work aims to analyse the circulation of ideas contained in the French Code Pénal (1810) in some Latin American contexts, especially the Brazilian one but also another experiences in the 19th Century. The analysis method was the historical, and the main sources gathered to explain this were the texts of some criminal codes in Europe and America, the Brazilian lawyers who studied the Brazilian Criminal Code (1830) and other lawyers who studied those foreign criminal codes. The result obtained was the French Criminal Code is a model really utilized, but so many others too: most important to verify an influence it was understand the ways to circulation of French and other codes, as the Brazilian one.

1 Introduction

This work aims to analyse the legacy of the French model in Latin America from the Brazilian perspective. The original idea it was to verify how present are some elements (general rules as well as crime species) of the Napoleon's "Code Pénal de l'Empire Français" (French Empire's Criminal Code) of 1810[1] in the Latin American Criminal Codes of the nineteenth century is due to the dissemination of the "Codigo Criminal do Imperio do Brazil" (Brazilian Empire's Criminal Code) of 1830.[2]

In your "historical introductions" to the handbooks of Criminal Law, until nowadays the Brazilian jurists (for example, Siqueira[3]) frequently tried to find in

[1]France, *Code Pénal de l'Empire Français* (available at http://gallica.bnf.fr/ark:/12148/bpt6k57837660?rk=21459;2).
[2]Brasil, *Lei de 16 de dezembro de* 1830*: Manda executar o Codigo Criminal* (available at http://www.planalto.gov.br/ccivil_03/leis/lim/LIM-16-12-1830.htm).
[3]Galdino Siqueira, *Direito penal brazileiro* I, (Rio de Janeiro: Jachinto, 1921).

D. Nunes (✉)
Universidade Federal de Santa Catarina, Florianópolis, Brazil
e-mail: nunes.diego@ufsc.br

A. Masferrer (ed.), *The Western Codification of Criminal Law*, Studies in the History of Law and Justice 11, https://doi.org/10.1007/978-3-319-71912-2_10

certain rules performed in other countries an "origin" of some rules contained in the national criminal codes. However, some rules as the duty of indemnity *ex delicto* in a criminal code gave status of Brazilian legacy (for example, Costa e Silva[4]).

The few historiographical works done, so far report that Latin American criminal codes from the Spanish speaking area, looked closely at the codification process in Spain. And this same historiography (prof. Masferrer,[5] himself, in Spain, but also prof. Bravo Lira[6] in Chile) informs me that the Spanish penal codification of 1848 was based on the Brazilian Imperial Criminal Code of 1830.

To exemplify that, this study will start from here, trying to understand if the Brazilian Criminal Code of 1830 it was an autonomous model or a version of the French Penal Code. After, I will discuss on the other possible models of the Brazilian Criminal Code and its relationship with the construction of the Spanish Criminal Code of 1848 who supposedly spread the "French model" to the Latin American countries.

This research approaches the sources by the "history of legal dimensions of justice".[7] The goal is understand how the legal instruments, as codes and specially your relations as models or copies, could to grow an ideal of Criminal Law. It could be give an interesting interface between the Legal and Political History, and understand if criminal codes contributed to build national identity or to collaborate for hybridization of legal culture in an original perspective,[8] recognizing the autonomy of each legal space.[9]

---

[4]Antonio José da Costa e Silva, *Código penal dos Estados Unidos do Brasil* (Brasília: Senado Federal, [1930] 2004; available at http://www2.senado.leg.br/bdsf/item/id/496204).

[5]Aniceto Masferrer, "The Liberal State and Criminal Reform in Spain in Sellers", *The Rule of Law in comparative perspective* (edited by Mortimer Sellers and Tadeusz Tomaszwski) (London; New York: Springer, 2010).

[6]Bernardino Bravo Lira, "Bicentenario del Código Penal de Austria: Su proyección desde el Danubio a Filipinas", *Revista de estudios histórico-jurídicos* 26 (2004) (available at http://www.scielo.cl/scielo.php?script=sci_arttext&pid=S0716-54552004002600005); Bernardino Bravo Lira, "La fortuna del Código Penal español de 1848. Historia en cuatro actos y tres continentes: de Mello Freire y Zeiller a Vasconcelos y Seijas Lozano", *Anuario de Historia del Derecho Español* 74 2004 (available at https://dialnet.unirioja.es/descarga/articulo/2056658.pdf).

[7]Massimo Meccarelli, "La protección jurídica como tutela delos derechos: reducciones modernas del problema de la dimensión jurídica de la justicia", *Forum Historiae Iuris* (Retrieved 05 August 2014; available at http://www.forhistiur.de/fr/2014-08-meccarelli/); Massimo Meccarelli, "La storia del diritto in America Latina e il punto di vista europeo. Prospettive metodologiche di un dialogo storiografico", *Forum Historiae Iuris* (Retrieved 24 August 2009; available at http://www.forhistiur.de/es/2009-08-meccarelli/?l=it and http://www.seer.ufu.br/index.php/revistafadir/article/viewFile/34420/18268 [Portuguese translation]).

[8]Thomas Duve, "Entanglements in Legal History: Introductory Remarks", *Entanglements in Legal History: Conceptual Approaches* (edited by Thomas Duve) (Frankfurt am Main: Max Planck Institute for European Legal History, 2014; available at http://dx.doi.org/10.12946/gplh1).

[9]Massimo Meccarelli and Paolo Palchetti, "Derecho en movimiento: una cuestión teórica nada convencional", *Derecho en movimiento: personas, derechos y derecho en la dinámica global* (edited by Massimo Meccarelli and Paolo Palchetti) (Madrid: Dykinson, 2015).

2 The Brazilian Imperial Criminal Code of 1830: Autonomous Model or Version of 'Code Pénal'?

Luis Jiménez Asúa, important criminal jurist and Spanish republican, on a trip made to Brazil in 1928 (a few years later was exiled to Latin America, settling definitively in Argentina), wrote:

> For a Spanish, Brazilian criminal laws have the prestige of the old model. The Brazilian Penal Code, December 16th 1830, inspired by the Neapolitan style and composed by the General Assembly on the basis of the projects did by Bernardo Pereira de Vasconcellos and Clemente Pereira, served as a paradigm for our code of 1848 which through reforms lasted for 80 years.[10]

It was certain that the "Criminal Code of the Brazilian Empire" enacted in 1830 enjoyed great prestige among Brazilian and foreign jurists.

But now let us direct attention to the comments of national jurists during the Brazilian Empire (1822-1889). Pimenta Bueno said that "*our criminal code honors the intelligence which organized it.*"[11] It was a clear and direct reference to Vasconcellos. The latter made the project (unlike what it was said by Asúa) prevalently based on parliamentary proceedings that resulted in the imperial code "*based on the criteria of justice and equity*", as stated in the 1824 Constitution (Art. 179, XVIII).[12]

However, the success of the Brazilian code does not necessarily mean that it is due to its similarities to the French codification. Every now and then, it showed exactly the opposite. Braz Florentino[13] pointed out, in his "*Lessons of criminal law*", the fact that the Brazilian codification did not follow the tripartite classification of criminal offenses (crimes, delicts and contraventions). Interestingly, this

[10]"*Para un español tienen las leyes penales brasileñas el prestigio de viejo modelo. El Código penal del Brasil, de 16 de Diciembre de 1830, inspirado en el napolitano y compuesto por la Asamblea general a base de los Proyectos elaborados por Bernardo Pereira de Vasconcellos y Clemente Pereira, sirvió de paradigma para nuestro Código de 1848, que a través de dos reformas ha vivido en España ochenta años.*" (Luis Jiménez De Asúa, *Un viaje al Brasil*, (Madrid: Reus, 1929) p. 99).

[11]"O nosso codigo criminal honra a intelligencia que o organizou [...]" (José Antonio Pimenta Bueno alias Marquês de São Vicente, *Direito publico brasileiro* (Rio de Janeiro: J. Villeneuve, 1857), p. 417).

[12]"Art. 179. A inviolabilidade dos Direitos Civis, e Politicos dos Cidadãos Brazileiros, que tem por base a liberdade, a segurança individual, e a propriedade, é garantida pela Constituição do Imperio, pela maneira seguinte [...] XVIII. Organizar–se-ha quanto antes um Codigo Civil, e Criminal, fundado nas solidas bases da Justiça, e Equidade." (Brasil, *Constituição Politica do Imperio do Brazil (De 25 de Março de* 1824*)* (available at https://www.planalto.gov.br/ccivil_03/constituicao/constituicao24.htm)).

[13]Braz Florentino Henrique de Souza, *Lições de direito criminal* (Brasília: Senado Federal, [1872] 2003), p. 10–11.

fact was criticized by French Victor Foucher[14] when he translated the Brazilian code, part of a collection that includes the Austrian penal code of 1803 and Neapolitan of 1810, regarded as important pillars of the criminal code of the nineteenth century.

By the end of the 1800s, A. Paula Ramos Jr. welcomed the code "*that honors our country and its authors.*" But despite this, he wondered if "*the time had come to examine the work of the wise men of the 1830s?*" The answer: "*We do not hesitate in face of affirmative statement,*"[15] because the nineteenth century was the age of penal reforms, and made reference to all changes occurred in several European countries.

Heredity but also autonomy; local resourcefulness, in all. Other commentators sought to do a similar exercise, as Antonio Tinoco[16] and Vicente de Paula,[17] who brought the differences of some particular rules into focus. But there were those who were silent about the argument, but perhaps only because of the scope of their works, such as notes made to the code by Antonio Carlos Cordeiro[18] and José Marcelino Pereira de Vasconcelos.[19]

The pragmatic nature of Brazilian criminal scholarship of the nineteenth century is a factor to be taken into account. The most common style of the comments to the code did not allow room for a self-analysis of the origins and the influences of the Criminal Code of 1830. The truth was that a lot had been discussed about the French Penal Code of 1810, since works of foreign criminalists which were read in Brazil at that time circulated almost all in French language (including, for example, translations of Bentham or Pellegrino Rossi's[20] work).

---

[14]Victor Foucher, *Code criminel de l'empire du Brésil* (Paris: Imprimierie Royale, 1834; available at http://gallica.bnf.fr/ark:/12148/bpt6k4262610?rk=64378;0); Victor Foucher, *Code pénal général de l'empire d'Autriche* (Paris: Imprimierie Royale, 1833; available at http://catalogue.bnf.fr/ark:/12148/cb33965081m); Victor Foucher, *Lois de la procédure criminelle et lois pénales du royaume des Deux-Siciles* (Paris: Imprimierie Royale, 1836; available at http://catalogue.bnf.fr/ark:/12148/cb31138208j).

[15]"Ha mais de quarenta e quatro annos vivemos sob o regimen d'esse monumento legislativo de penalidade que honra nossa pátria e seus autores. Será porem chegado o tempo de rever a obra dos sábios de 1830? Estaremos preparados para tão importante trabalho pelas licções da experiência, e reclamos instantes dos costumes e da civilisação que, segundo Bonneville, são as melhores e mais sabias conselheiras de quaesquer modificações e reformas penaes? Não hesitamos diante da affirmativa." (Antonio de Paula Ramos Jr., *Comentários ao código criminal brazileiro* (Rio de Janeiro: Tip. e Lit. Carioca, 1875), p. VIII).

[16]Antônio Luiz Tinôco, *Código criminal do Império do Brazil annotado* (Brasília: Senado Federal, [1886] 2003; available at http://www2.senado.leg.br/bdsf/item/id/496203).

[17]Vicente Alves de Paula Pessoa, *Código criminal do Império do Brazil annotado* (Rio de Janeiro: Livraria Popular, 1877; available at http://www2.senado.leg.br/bdsf/item/id/227311).

[18]Carlos Antonio Cordeiro, *Código criminal do Império do Brazil* (Rio de Janeiro, Typ. de Quirino, 1861).

[19]José Marcelino Pereira de Vasconcelos, *Código criminal do Império do Brazil* (Rio de Janeiro: Em Casa de Antonio Gonçalves Guimarães & C, 1860).

[20]Pellegrino Rossi, *Traité de droit pénal* (Bruxelles: L. Hauman et compagnie, 1835; available at http://cujas-num.univ-paris1.fr/ark:/45829/pdf0600027793).

Because of that it is possible to ask in a deeply way why the reforms in Criminal Law between the eighteenth (*Ancién Regime* and Enlightment) and the nineteenth (Liberalism) century. According to Tarello, we had the dawn of "the penal problem".[21] Basically, the heritage of Enlightment had spread during the nineteenth century in Brazil as a way to scape of "terrible" Book V of *Ordenações Filipinas* on crimes, punishments and procedure by *Ancién Regime* style. But, as explained Masferrer,[22] the penal forms had no changed so much; the difference is the philosophical regard pointed out by Tarello, resumed in five questions: there is a right to punish? Who have it? How apply it? What actions are punished? What the relation between action and punishment?[23] In fact, the history of penal practice is different of the history of penal thought.

Analysing the characters of the penal reforms (systematization, secularization and humanization) it is clear a new regarding respect to *Ancién regime*, even we can see some of these aspects before. Criminal codes in the nineteenth century are a reform, not a revolution, because this is occurred a century before.[24] The characters of these reforms it was rationalism, in a modern view. The "Enlighted codes" played with (a) the nationalism in the liberal regimes, the tensions between (b) the principle of legality and the natural law, and (c) the sovereignty (and participation) of parliament and the (legal) role of constitutions.

Moreover, we cannot refute the mythical power of the Napoleonic codification model in the Brazilian context. France it was the first one to finish this project, with a complete codification of law in modern sense.

This situation in Brazil, although it was seen as original, it was perceived as periphery in relation to Europe and North America. Despite the Spanish and Portuguese cultural (and legal) background in Latin America, the revolutions in France and United States did the American countries look out in these realities basis to your legal codification process.[25]

Let us conclude this itinerary with the germanophile's analyse (at that time in Brazil, an exception) Tobias Barreto:

> That the code falls short of what it should be, at the present time, the criminal law of any country that takes part in the feast of modern culture, even though, as we are, those who

[21]Giovanni Tarello, "O problema penal no século XVIII" [1975], *História do direito penal entre medievo e modernidade* (edited by Arno Dal Ri Jr. and Ricardo Sontag) (Belo Horizonte: Del Rey, 2011).

[22]Aniceto Masferrer, "La ciencia del derecho penal en la codificación decimonónica: una aproximación panorámica a su contenido y rasgos fundamentales", *Estudios de Historia de las ciencias criminales en España* (edited by J. Alvrado Planas and A. Serrano Maíllo) (Madrid; Dykinson, 2017).

[23]Giovanni Tarello, "O problema penal no século XVIII" [1975], *História do direito penal entre medievo e modernidade* (edited by Arno Dal Ri Jr. and Ricardo Sontag) (Belo Horizonte: Del Rey, 2011), p. 219.

[24]Aniceto Masferrer, *Spanish Legal Traditions* (Madrid: Dykinson, 2012).

[25]Juan Carlos González Hernández, *Influencia del derecho español en América* (Madrid: Mapfre, 1992).

> stayed for the second table; that the Code, in a word, is incomplete and flawed, why should it be repeated or highlighted? What matters, especially, if it is not sure to stay in the puerile belief that the Brazilian Criminal Code was received directly from the hands of Egeria nympha, it is also no longer to stress the numerous defects, which are beginning to be visible to the eyes of those who see little.[26]

"Peripheral" self-conscience, raging look to the "center", models myth surrounding the 1830 code: if at the end of Empire age we began to see some critics as Barreto, in the new Republican era a novel criminal code we can verify a reborn of the traditional ideas.

3 The Models of the Model: About the Construction of the Brazilian 'Codigo Criminal' of 1830

This debate gained strength in the Republic, especially on the criminal code. The bad reputation of the Brazilian Penal Code of the new regime, of 1890, it was said "*the worst code of the world*",[27] led to many reform projects on this from one party, but controversially it was observed a rise in prestige of the replaced Code of 1830.

The Republican scholarship began to worry about rebuilding a history of coding, narrative based on the release of the "terrible" Book V of Philippine Ordinances,[28] the originality of Vasconcellos' project (and even Pereira's), and finally the use of comparative models to demonstrate the awareness of Brazilian academics about what was the most modern penal legislation at the time. Arguments were already found in writings of the imperial jurists, but here they take a sharper tone.

In this sense, it can be observed as stated the by the republican criminal jurist Galdino Siqueira:

> Brazil anticipated, with the codification of criminal law, Portugal, Spain and several American republics, and even prominently as conforming to that period and its state of science, the code stood out as a legislative monument [...] the merits of the code, with its flaws, were evidenced by several foreign writers [...] adopting as the main source the

[26]Que o Código está muito aquém do que deve ser, na época actual, a legislação penal de qualquer paiz, que toma parte no banquete da cultura moderna, ainda mesmo sendo, como somos, dos que ficaram para a segunda mesa; que o Código, em uma palavra, é lacunoso e incompleto, para que mais repetil-o e accenlual-o? O que importa, sobretudo, se não é de certo permanecer na crença pueril de que o Código Criminal brazileiro foi recebido diretamente das mãos da nympha Egeria, já não é também tratar somente de sublinhar-lhe os inúmeros defeitos, que começam a ser visiveis até aos olhos dos que pouco vêem. (Tobias Barreto, *Menores e loucos em direito criminal* (Brasília: Senado Federal, [1886] 2003; available at http://www2.senado.leg.br/bdsf/item/id/496216), p. 1).

[27]"[...] *peior de todos os códigos conhecidos* [...]" (João Monteiro et al., "Parecer da congregação da faculdade de Direito de São Paulo (projecto João Vieira de Araújo n. 250/1893)", *Revista da faculdade de Direito de São Paulo* 2 (1894), p. 10).

[28]Candido Mendes de Almeida, *Codigo Philippino, ou, Ordenações e leis do Reino de Portugal: recopiladas por mandado d'El-Rey D. Philippe I* (Rio de Janeiro: Typ. do Instituto Philomathico, [1603] 1870) (available at http://www1.ci.uc.pt/ihti/proj/filipinas/ordenacoes.htm).

French Penal Code, from which deviates in important points […] More than the French legislator, Brazilian was influenced by Bentham's philosophical principles.[29]

Siqueira also admits that the importance of the 1830 code led to a wide range of criticism about the 1890 code.[30] Nevertheless, by observing the "*historical foundations of the Brazilian criminal law*", there was a law of "*coordination*" and "*rigorous technique*" being therefore "*incomplete*" and "*worsened*" in what it was changed from the imperial legislation.[31] Great compliment were seen in prominent Republican jurists, as Vicente Piragibe[32] and Costa e Silva,[33] but at least they were more lenient to the Republican encoding.

Nor should we forget that in 1913 Siqueira gave to the government a new penal code draft to replace the 1890.[34] In 1932, Piragibe, in turn, consolidated the republican criminal laws which was recognized as official by the Vargas regime.[35] Different destinations of their work that—perhaps—appointed to various tones of criticism.

From these criminalists (in the Republic, in full, as stated by Sontag in the book "*Criminological Code?*"[36]), unlike the multifaceted "bachelors" of the empire, who one could not say "professionals" criminalists, civilists or publicists one started the search for the source and the destiny of the 1830 Code. And here we return to the argument about the circularity of models.

In this, each author will try to make his list of scientific and regulatory models to approach the code of 1830. It is not said here that they were arbitrary choices; on

[29]"*O Brazil antecipava-se, com a codificação das leis penaes, a Portugal, a Hespanha e a diversas republicas americanas, e ainda salientemente, porque, attendendo á época e ao estado da sciencia, o código se destacava como um monumento legislativo* […] *Os méritos do código, como suas falhas, foram, evidenciados por vários escriptores extrangeiros* […] *Adoptando como fonte principal o código penal francez, dele se desvia em pontos importantes* […] *Mais que o legislador francez, o brazileiro se deixou influenciar pela orientação philosophica de BENTHAM.*" (Galdino Siqueira, *Direito penal brazileiro* I (Rio de Janeiro: Jachinto, 1921), p. 10).

[30]Ricardo Sontag, *"Código Criminológico"? Ciência jurídica e codificação penal no Brasil* (Rio de Janeiro: Revan, 2015).

[31]"*Se manteve em geral os fundamentos históricos do direito penal brazileiro, como estavam corporificados no anterior codigo e em leis posteriores, muito embora em forma nem sempre perfeita, nessa preoccupação de emendar, trouxe innovações, colhidas em leis extrangeiras, ms, em regra, com desvos para peior das fontes procuradas*" (Galdino Siqueira, *Direito penal brazileiro* I (Rio de Janeiro: Jachinto, 1921), p. 14).

[32]Vicente Piragibe, *Legislação penal do Brasil e do estrangeiro: 1º Volume: Codigo penal brasileiro (completado com as leis modificadoras em vigor)* (São Paulo: Saraiva, 1932).

[33]Antonio José da Costa e Silva, *Código penal dos Estados Unidos do Brasil* (Brasília: Senado Federal, [1930] 2004).

[34]Galdino Siqueira, *Projeto de Código Penal brasileiro* (Rio de Janeiro: Jornal do Brasil, Revista da Semana, 1913).

[35]Brasil, *Decreto n. 22.213, de 14 de dezembro de 1932. Aprova a Consolidação das Leis Penais, de autoria do Sr. Desembargador Vicente Piragibe* (available at http://www2.camara.leg.br/legin/fed/decret/1930-1939/decreto-22213-14-dezembro-1932-516919-publicacaooriginal-1-pe.html).

[36]Ricardo Sontag, *"Código Criminológico"? Ciência jurídica e codificação penal no Brasil* (Rio de Janeiro: Revan, 2015).

the contrary, the effort seems exactly to understand and express attributes such as clarity, strength and durability of the imperial text. The English Bentham,[37] the American Livingston,[38] the Portuguese Mello Freire[39] and also the German Feuerbach[40] are often quoted; likewise, the French Code was accompanied by the Austrian, Bavarian[41] and Neapolitan. All of these references, however, were not quoted properly—unfortunately—it was a characteristic of the literary style of that period not to mention sources accurately. Thus, depending on the author's background, we can realise more or less the "influence" of certain authors, models and/or doctrines. Also, these comments made by the republican jurists are always descriptive, without a background analysis, as could be expected of the monarchy lawyers.

By analysing, however, the Brazilian parliamentary acts, we can observe references to the French code from the start and the Livingston project in the last year. In the same way, by watching the Spanish parliamentary acts,[42] the reference to the Brazilian code occurs all the time, either by Seijas[43] (the true intellectual "father" of the 1848 code, if we do not recognize this—likewise in the Brazilian case—as

[37]In French translation: Jeremy Bentham, *Théorie des peines et des recompenses par M. Jérémie Bentham, rédigée en françois, d'après les manuscrits, par M. Ét. Dumont* (Londres: B. Dulau, 1811; available at http://catalogue.bnf.fr/ark:/12148/cb30375787c).

[38]Edward Livingston, *Rapport sur le projet d'un code pénal, fait à l'assemblée générale de l'État de la Louisiane, par M. Édouard Livingston, suivi des Observations sur les conditions nécessaires à la perfection d'un code pénal, par M. Mill, avec une introduction et des notes, par M. A.-H. Taillandier* (Paris: A.-A. Renouard, 1825 available at http://catalogue.bnf.fr/ark:/12148/cb308250471).

[39]Paschoal José de Mello Freire, *Codigo criminal intentado pela Rainha D. Maria I: Segunda edição, castigada dos erros* (Lisboa: Typographo Simão Thaddeo Ferreira, 1823; available at http://bibdigital.fd.uc.pt/C-16-8/C-16-8_item2/C-16-8_PDF/C-16-8_PDF_01-C-R0120/C-16-8.pdf).

[40]Paul Johann Anselm von Feuerbach, *Lehrbuch des gemeinen, in Deutschland geltenden peinlichen Rechts* (Gießen: 1801).

[41]Gottes Gnaden König von Baiern, *Strafgesetzbuch fuer das Koenig reich von Baiern* (available at (http://www.koeblergerhard.de/Fontes/StrafgesetzbuchfuerdasKoenigreichBaiern1813.pdf).

[42]According to Javier Alvarado Plamas (*Manual de Historia del Derecho y de las Instituciones* (Madrid, Sanz y Torres, 2006), p. 819): "Se percibe la influencia del Código Penal francès de 1810, el Código Penal de Nápoles de 1819 y el Código Penal de Brasil de 1830. Para Seijas 'en el de Brasil me entusiasmó su estructura y en el de Napoleón su precisión'. Luzuriaga era más devote del Código Penal del Brasil por su claridad, sencillez y método; 'el más perfecto de cuantos se conocen'. Sobre la influencia de este Código brasileño, Pacheco afirmará que 'en esta ley es en la que encontró nuestra Comisión el modelo artístico… Y nadie la culpara de ser imitadora, si lo que limitava era digno de ser seguido'."

[43]Alejandro Martínez Dhier, "Un tránsito del Antiguo Régimen al estado liberal de derecho en España" *Revista de estudios histórico-jurídicos* 30 (2008), p. 425–464. (available at https://dx.doi.org/10.4067/S0716-54552008000100015); Francisco Candil Jimenez, Manuel Seijas Lozano, "miembro de la Comision General de Codigos", *Anuario de Derecho Penal y Ciencias Penales* 34 (1981) (available at https://www.boe.es/publicaciones/anuarios_derecho/abrir_pdf.php?id=ANU-P-1981-20041300432_ANUARIO_DE_DERECHO_PENAL_Y_CIENCIAS_PENALES_Manuel_Seijas_Lozano,_miembro_de_la_Comisi%F3n_General_de_C%F3digos).

teamwork, full of various contributions in the parliament) as by Pacheco (already acclaimed father of this code, but now recognized as who popularized it by spreading its writings[44]).[45] If our working hypothesis was only the circularity of the code, as it is done, for example, by the Brazilian criminal jurist Heleno Fragoso in a conference at the Max-Planck-Institut in Freiburg,[46] we would not have problems: in fact, models circulate, a lot.

The problem concerns the idea of "influence". How could it be possible to measure to what extent would a code be a "copy" of another, or rather, "from where does it come?" In this regard, it is worth noting the results of historiography, so as to ask if "how much?" (in other words, influence) would matter more than "how?" (that means, the use of these models in each historical reality).

If you read carefully the historian of the Chilean legal system Bernardino Bravo Lira, he insists more than once in the Austrian inheritance of the Brazilian model. Therefore, he presents a series of elements to convince us of this conclusion. Of which: (I) the approach between the Central European and Iberian models, less radical with respect to the French one; (II) the similarity in comparing some articles listed by him; and (III) even the Habsburg origin of Brazilian empress.[47]

However it seemed to us difficult to confirm such hypotheses because we have not found so far references or by Vasconcellos, not even by the parliament on the use of the Austrian Code of 1803, either in its original version or by its Italian translation (1815).[48] These documents were available before 1830, as the French translation of Foucher (in the same collection in which was included the Brazilian code of 1830 in the 1836) was only published in 1833. At the end, the similarity does not occur apart from intuition as we shall see next.

There are two other works that seem more reliable, because they face sources more closely. We refer to the Brazilian translation of the Treaty on Penal Law by the Argentinian Eugenio Zaffaroni (in practice, a different book, because of the important contribution of the Brazilian criminal jurist Nilo Batista[49]), and the recent

---

[44]Joaquin Francisco Pacheco, *El código penal concordado y comentado* (Madrid, Imp. Manuel Tello, [1849] 1881) (available at http://fama2.us.es/fde/ocr/2007/codigoPenalConcordadoT1.pdf).

[45]José Antón Oneca, "El Código penal de 1848 y D. Joaquin Francisco Pacheco", *Anuario de derecho penal y ciencias penales* 18, 3 (1965), p. 473–496 (available at https://dialnet.unirioja.es/servlet/articulo?codigo=2783080).

[46]Heleno Fragoso, "O direito penal comparado na América Latina", *Revista de Direito Penal* 24 (1977), p. 17–25 (available at http://www.fragoso.com.br/eng/arq_pdf/heleno_artigos/arquivo30.pdf).

[47]Bernardino Bravo Lira, "Bicentenario del Código Penal de Austria: Su proyección desde el Danubio a Filipinas", *Revista de estudios histórico-jurídicos* 26 (2004) (available at http://www.scielo.cl/scielo.php?script=sci_arttext&pid=S0716-54552004002600005).

[48]Austria, *Codice penale universale austriaco: coll'appendice delle più recenti norme generali* (Milano: Regia Stamperia, 1815) (available at https://babel.hathitrust.org/cgi/pt?id=hvd.hnky6w;view=1up;seq=2).

[49]Eugenio Raúl Zaffaroni, Nilo Batista, Alejandro Alajia, Alejandro Slokar, *Direito Penal Brasileiro* (Rio de Janeiro: Revan, 2003).

dissertation of Vivian Costa (supervised by political historian Monica Dantas, who worked on the relation between the Criminal Code and slavery[50]).[51]

Zaffaroni and Batista say they have had control over the main models that were mentioned above. In their view, the French Penal Code presented itself as dominant. In addition, they observed some elements of the theories of Bentham and the Livingston project; and at the end, they refuted the presence of Mello Freire project and the Bavarian and Neapolitan codes.

According to them, when they wrote this section of the treaty, a decade ago, the question of the origins and heredity of the 1830 code was still open. And not by chance, the recent work of the Brazilian historian Costa refuted one of the conclusions of South American criminalists: "*the parliamentary discussion based on Clemente Pereira and Vasconcelos project was theoretical and politically very poor*".[52] In fact, Costa's goal was precisely to demonstrate the importance of the efforts made in codification to the formation of the Brazilian Nation-State in the early nineteenth century.

In order to prove this speech, Costa made comparative tables between: (I) Vasconcellos project; and (II) the Brazilian code in confront with ten other codes or contemporary projects. The results are very interesting: from the 334 articles comprising Vasconcellos project, 32 were based "*unquestionably*"—according to Costa —in the Spanish penal code of 1822, 24 about the French Penal Code and 10 in Melo Freire project.[53] In the final version of the code were added another 88 articles with respect to Vasconcellos project. On these 20 resulted from "*effective*" grafts—also here Costa points out—of rules set out in the comparative table: 17 of the Louisiana project, two still of the French Penal Code, and finally one of Melo Freire project.[54]

And guess what: (I) the Spanish Code of 1822,[55] as always regarded as peripheral, whether in parliamentary debate, or in historiography contradicts also

[50]Monica Dantas, "Dos statutes no código brasileiro de 1830: o levante de escravos como crime de insurreição", *R.IHGB* 452 (2011).

[51]Vivian Costa, *Codificação e formação do estado-nacional brasileiro: o código criminal de 1830 e a positivação das leis no pós-independência* (São Paulo: USP, 2013).

[52]"[...] a discussão parlamentar sobre as bases do projeto de Clemente Pereira e Vasconcelos foi teoricamente e politicamente muito pobre", (Eugenio Raúl Zaffaroni, Nilo Batista, Alejandro Alajia, Alejandro Slokar, *Direito Penal Brasileiro* (Rio de Janeiro: Revan, 2003), p. 429).

[53]Vivian Costa, *Codificação e formação do estado-nacional brasileiro: o código criminal de 1830 e a positivação das leis no pós-independência* (São Paulo: USP, 2013), p. 241.

[54]Vivian Costa, *Codificação e formação do estado-nacional brasileiro: o código criminal de 1830 e a positivação das leis no pós-independência* (São Paulo: USP, 2013), p. 244.

[55]According to Javier Alvarado Plamas (*Manual de Historia del Derecho y de las Instituciones* (Madrid, Sanz y Torres, 2006), p. 819), the Spanish Criminal Code of 1822 it was discussed by jurists (in academic and praxis worlds) and parliament, mixing old traditions and the French code. Juan Antonio Alejandre (*Temas de historia del derecho: el derecho del constitucionalismo y de la codificación* (Sevilla, Universidad de Sevilla, 1978) pointed out the fact who the penal code, the first one, it was an exception in Spain: constitutions had orders to make codes, but it was hard to did it. It was occurred because your relationship with the possibilities of solution in social organization referring to the powers of state and your titularity (Antonio Merchán Álvarez, *Las épocas del derecho español*, (Valencia, Tirant lo Blanch, 1998)).

the myth that the Brazilian legal culture does not communicate with the "Hispanic"; (II) a confirmation: the "*Code of Offences and Punishments*" by Livingston (already studied by political historian Dantas), widely used in the final period of the preparatory work. Finally, an observation: the French Penal Code, which really was one of the protagonists (but not alone) in all stages of the discussion.

But attention: If we look at the Costa's calculations in reverse, in Vasconcellos project, over two hundred articles are not "unquestionably" based on some specific model of comparative law, and in the final version, more than sixty rules remain still deprived of models reference. It would confirm the compliments paid for the originality and resourcefulness of the Brazilian legislator of the nineteenth century, as the criminalists referred to in the early twentieth century?

To some extent, yes; however, we follow the warning of Cavanna: "*We can thus enunciate a physiology of codification of law which is not trivial and even less approximative to how much one might think: codes rise from codes*."[56] Contradiction?

4 Conclusion

Let us give a further explanation. In a debate in Brazilian parliament (recovered by the magistrate Vicente Azevedo, in a commemorative writing to the 1830 Code's centennial[57]), held in 1839, when it was discussed in Senate a code reform bill due to several revolts during the Regency period (between the abdication of Pedro I and the enthronement of Pedro II).

The Minister of Justice Lopes Gama went to Senate in order to defend this code reform bill. As an argument, he maintained that "*our Criminal Code is a patchwork quilt* […] *therefore; I do not say that the Code is useless; there are many defects that have been noted in these codes from which it originate.*" Senator Nicolau Vergueiro's answer, who attended the 1830 text discussion, refutes this assertion. Allow me to quote: "*The code is a patchwork?! A code* [the Brazilian code of 1830] *which since its creation is subject to a system, it must be treated so, because it contains rules that are in other codes? Where is it possible to make new laws? The excellence of our code is in the system, because, in relation to rules, necessarily, one will find them employed in other legislation.*"[58] That means, similar rules, however, in original system.

[56]"*Possiamo così enunciare uma legge di fisiologia della condificazione per nulla banale e assai meno approssimativa di quanto si possa pensare: i codici nascono dai codici.*" Adriano Cavanna, *Storia del diritto moderno in Europa* II (Milano: Giuffrè, 2005), p. 321.

[57]Vicente Azevedo, "O centenário do código criminal", *Justitia* 109 ([1930] 1980; available at http://www.revistajustitia.com.br/revistas/b2bxb6.pdf).

[58]"*o nosso Código Criminal é uma manta de retalhos* […] *portanto, não digo que o Código não preste para nada; tem muitos defeitos que têm sido notados nesses códigos de onde tira a sua origem*"; "*Pois o código é uma manta de retalhos?! Um código* [o de 1830] *que desde o seu princípio é subordinado a um sistema, deve ser assim tratado, porque contém disposições que se*

The Senator concludes his reasoning in another session: "*But will our code be a patchwork quilt because it has ideas of Bentham, the French Code and others* [as Livingston project for Louisiana]*? I think that's not enough to draw here the conclusion that it is patchwork; because, gentlemen, how can we do a systematic code, without this code between the thinking of jurists and the experience of other codes?*"[59]

From the French Penal Code to the Brazilian Criminal Code, passing through the Spanish penal code of 1822; getting to the Spanish Code of 1848, and from there onwards to the Latin American criminal codes—and perhaps rediscover the French Penal Code? We could intuit heredity, as did Bernardino Bravo Lira; or even measure it, as Vivian Costa.

The codes implied a brake in the legal thought? In Brazil the answer is affirmative. The myth of Imperial Criminal Code it was fundamental to the State building and to create a legal tradition. It was possible to see the "nationalization" of legal thought. Of course the foreign models played a special role. It was hard to understand from where the ideas are come from. Some "travel (criminal) codes", as the French one of 1810, the Spanish one of 1822 and the Brazilian one of 1830, found a good way and moment to circulation of ideas.

But find out from where does a code come—its origin—and then understand where it goes—its influence—it does not seem so important to verify the way it has been living in every historical reality. The experience or rather, the use of these models seems the aspect of originality required to make grow the recent and lively historiography of the Brazilian Criminal Law.

References

Adriano Cavanna, *Storia del diritto moderno in Europa* II (Milano: Giuffrè, 2005).

Alejandro Martínez Dhier, "Un tránsito del Antiguo Régimen al estado liberal de derecho en España" *Revista de estudios histórico-jurídicos* 30 (2008), p. 425–464. (available at https://dx.doi.org/10.4067/S0716-54552008000100015).

Aniceto Masferrer, "La ciencia del derecho penal en la codificación decimonónica: una aproximación panorámica a su contenido y rasgos fundamentales", *Estudios de Historia de*

encontram em outros códigos? Onde é possível fazer legislação nova? Onde esta a excelência do nosso código é no sistema, porque quanto às disposições, necessariamente se hão de encontrar muitas empregadas em outras legislações." (Vicente Azevedo, "O centenário do código criminal", *Justitia* 109 ([1930] 1980; available at http://www.revistajustitia.com.br/revistas/b2bxb6.pdf), p. 34).

[59]"*Mas será o nosso código uma manta de retalhos porque tem ideias de Bentham, do Código Francês e de outros* [como o projeto de Livingston para a Louisiania]*? Creio que isso não é bastante para se tirar aqui a conclusão de que é manta de retalhos; pois, Senhores, como se há de fazer um código sistemático, sem que entre nesse código o pensamento dos jurisconsultos e a experiência dos outros códigos?*" (Vicente Azevedo, "O centenário do código criminal", *Justitia* 109 ([1930] 1980; available at http://www.revistajustitia.com.br/revistas/b2bxb6.pdf), p. 36).

las ciencias criminales en España (edited by J. Alvrado Planas and A. Serrano Maíllo) (Madrid: Dykinson, 2017).

Aniceto Masferrer, "The Liberal State and Criminal Reform in Spain in Sellers", *The Rule of Law in comparative perspective* (edited by Mortimer Sellers and Tadeusz Tomaszwski) (London; New York: Springer, 2010).

Aniceto Masferrer, *Spanish Legal Traditions* (Madrid: Dykinson, 2012).

Antonio de Paula Ramos Jr., *Comentários ao código criminal brazileiro* (Rio de Janeiro: Tip. e Lit. Carioca, 1875).

Antonio José da Costa e Silva, *Código penal dos Estados Unidos do Brasil* (Brasília: Senado Federal, [1930] 2004; available at http://www2.senado.leg.br/bdsf/item/id/496204).

Antônio Luiz Tinôco, *Código criminal do Império do Brazil annotado* (Brasília: Senado Federal, [1886] 2003; available at http://www2.senado.leg.br/bdsf/item/id/496203).

Antonio Merchán Álvarez, *Las épocas del derecho español*, (Valencia, Tirant lo Blanch, 1998).

Austria, *Codice penale universale austriaco: coll'appendice delle più recenti norme generali* (Milano: Regia Stamperia, 1815) (available at https://babel.hathitrust.org/cgi/pt?id=hvd.hnky6w;view=1up;seq=2).

Bernardino Bravo Lira, "Bicentenario del Código Penal de Austria: Su proyección desde el Danubio a Filipinas", *Revista de estudios histórico-jurídicos* 26 (2004; available at http://www.scielo.cl/scielo.php?script=sci_arttext&pid=S0716-54552004002600005).

Bernardino Bravo Lira, "La fortuna del Código Penal español de 1848. Historia en cuatro actos y tres continentes: de Mello Freire y Zeiller a Vasconcelos y Seijas Lozano", *Anuario de Historia del Derecho Español* 74 (2004; available at https://dialnet.unirioja.es/descarga/articulo/2056658.pdf).

Brasil, *Constituição Politica do Imperio do Brazil (De 25 de Março de 1824)* (available at https://www.planalto.gov.br/ccivil_03/constituicao/constituicao24.htm).

Brasil, *Decreto nº 847, de 11 de outubro de1890. Promulga o Codigo Penal* (available at http://www.planalto.gov.br/ccivil_03/decreto/1851-1899/d847.htm)

Brasil, *Decreto n. 22.213, de 14 de dezembro de 1932. Aprova a Consolidação das Leis Penais, de autoria do Sr. Desembargador Vicente Piragibe* (available at http://www2.camara.leg.br/legin/fed/decret/1930-1939/decreto-22213-14-dezembro-1932-516919-publicacaooriginal-1-pe.html).

Brasil, *Lei de 16 de dezembro de 1830: Manda executar o Codigo Criminal* (available at http://www.planalto.gov.br/ccivil_03/leis/lim/LIM-16-12-1830.htm).

Braz Florentino Henrique de Souza, *Lições de direito criminal* (Brasília: Senado Federal, [1872] 2003).

Candido Mendes de Almeida, *Codigo Philippino, ou, Ordenações e leis do Reino de Portugal: recopiladas por mandado d'El-Rey D. Philippe I* (Rio de Janeiro: Typ. do Instituto Philomathico, [1603] 1870) (available at http://www1.ci.uc.pt/ihti/proj/filipinas/ordenacoes.htm).

Carlos Antonio Cordeiro, *Código criminal do Império do Brazil* (Rio de Janeiro, Typ. de Quirino, 1861).

Edward Livingston, *Rapport sur le projet d'un code pénal, fait à l'assemblée générale de l'État de la Louisiane, par M. Édouard Livingston, suivi des Observations sur les conditions nécessaires à la perfection d'un code pénal, par M. Mill, avec une introduction et des notes, par M. A.-H. Taillandier* (Paris: A.-A. Renouard, 1825; available at http://catalogue.bnf.fr/ark:/12148/cb308250471).

Eugenio Raúl Zaffaroni, Nilo Batista, Alejandro Alajia, Alejandro Slokar, *Direito Penal Brasileiro* (Rio de Janeiro: Revan, 2003).

France, *Code Pénal de l'Empire Français* (available at http://gallica.bnf.fr/ark:/12148/bpt6k57837660?rk=21459;2).

Francisco Candil Jimenez, Manuel Seijas Lozano, "miembro de la Comision General de Codigos", *Anuario de Derecho Penal y Ciencias Penales* 34 (1981) (available at https://www.boe.es/publicaciones/anuarios_derecho/abrir_pdf.php?id=ANU-P-1981-20041300432_ANUARIO_

DE_DERECHO_PENAL_Y_CIENCIAS_PENALES_Manuel_Seijas_Lozano,_miembro_de_la_Comisi%F3n_General_de_C%F3digos).

Galdino Siqueira, *Direito penal brazileiro* I, (Rio de Janeiro: Jachinto, 1921).

Galdino Siqueira, *Projeto de Codigo Penal brasileiro* (Rio de Janeiro: Jornal do Brasil, Revista da Semana, 1913).

Giovanni Tarello, "O problema penal no século XVIII" [1975], *História do direito penal entre medievo e modernidade* (edited by Arno Dal Ri Jr. and Ricardo Sontag) (Belo Horizonte: Del Rey, 2011).

Gottes Gnaden König von Baiern, *Strafgesetzbuch fuer das Koenig reich von Baiern* (available at http://www.koeblergerhard.de/Fontes/StrafgesetzbuchfuerdasKoenigreichBaiern1813.pdf).

Heleno Fragoso, "O direito penal comparado na América Latina", *Revista de Direito Penal* 24 (1977), p. 17–25 (available at http://www.fragoso.com.br/eng/arq_pdf/heleno_artigos/arquivo30.pdf).

Javier Alvarado Plamas, *Manual de Historia del Derecho y de las Instituciones* (Madrid, Sanz y Torres, 2006).

Jeremy Bentham, *Théorie des peines et des recompenses par M. Jérémie Bentham, rédigée en françois, d'après les manuscrits, par M. Ét. Dumont* (Londres: B. Dulau, 1811; available at http://catalogue.bnf.fr/ark:/12148/cb30375787c).

João Monteiro et al., "Parecer da congregação da faculdade de Direito de São Paulo (projecto João Vieira de Araújo n. 250/1893)", *Revista da faculdade de Direito de São Paulo* 2 (1894).

Joaquin Francisco Pacheco, *El código penal concordado y comentado* (Madrid, Imp. Manuel Tello, [1849] 1881) (available at http://fama2.us.es/fde/ocr/2007/codigoPenalConcordadoT1.pdf).

José Antón Oneca, "El Código penal de 1848 y D. Joaquin Francisco Pacheco", *Anuario de derecho penal y ciencias penales* 18, 3 (1965), p. 473–496 (available at https://dialnet.unirioja.es/servlet/articulo?codigo=2783080).

José Antonio Pimenta Bueno alias Marquês de São Vicente, *Direito publico brasileiro* (Rio de Janeiro: J. Villeneuve, 1857).

José Marcelino Pereira de Vasconcelos, *Codigo criminal do Império do Brazil* (Rio de Janeiro: Em Casa de Antonio Gonçalves Guimarães & C, 1860).

Juan Antonio Alejandre, *Temas de historia del derecho: el derecho del constitucionalismo y de la codificación* (Sevilla, Universidad de Sevilla, 1978).

Juan Carlos González Hernández, *Influencia del derecho español en América* (Madrid: Mapfre, 1992).

Luis Jiménez De Asúa, *Un viaje al Brasil*, (Madrid: Reus, 1929).

Massimo Meccarelli and Paolo Palchetti, "Derecho en movimiento: una cuestión teórica nada convencional", *Derecho en movimiento: personas, derechos y derecho en la dinámica global* (edited by Massimo Meccarelli and Paolo Palchetti) (Madrid: Dykinson, 2015; available at http://e-archivo.uc3m.es/bitstream/id/92449/derecho_HD33_2015.pdf).

Massimo Meccarelli, "La storia del diritto in America Latina e il punto di vista europeo. Prospettive metodologiche di un dialogo storiografico", *Forum Historiae Iuris* (Retrieved 24 August 2009; available at http://www.forhistiur.de/es/2009-08-meccarelli/?l=it and http://www.seer.ufu.br/index.php/revistafadir/article/viewFile/34420/18268 [Portuguese translation]).

Massimo Meccarelli, "La protección jurídica como tutela delos derechos: reducciones modernas del problema de la dimensión jurídica de la justicia", *Forum Historiae Iuris* (Retrieved 05 August 2014; available at http://www.forhistiur.de/fr/2014-08-meccarelli/).

Monica Dantas, "Dos statutes no código brasileiro de 1830: o levante de escravos como crime de insurreição", *R.IHGB* 452 (2011; available at https://drive.google.com/file/d/0B_G9pg7CxKSsbGd3aXNjU2kxb2s/view).

Paschoal José de Mello Freire, *Codigo criminal intentado pela Rainha D. Maria I: Segunda edição, castigada dos erros* (Lisboa: Typographo Simão Thaddeo Ferreira, 1823; available at http://bibdigital.fd.uc.pt/C-16-8/C-16-8_item2/C-16-8_PDF/C-16-8_PDF_01-C-R0120/C-16-8.pdf).

Paul Johann Anselm von Feuerbach, *Lehrbuch des gemeinen, in Deutschland geltenden peinlichen Rechts* (Gießen: 1801).
Pellegrino Rossi, *Traité de droit pénal* (Bruxelles: L. Hauman et compagnie, 1835; available at http://cujas-num.univ-paris1.fr/ark:/45829/pdf0600027793).
Ricardo Sontag, *"Código Criminológico"? Ciência jurídica e codificação penal no Brasil* (Rio de Janeiro: Revan, 2015).
Thomas Duve, "Entanglements in Legal History: Introductory Remarks", *Entanglements in Legal History: Conceptual Approaches* (edited by Thomas Duve) (Frankfurt am Main: Max Planck Institute for European Legal History, 2014; available at http://dx.doi.org/10.12946/gplh1).
Tobias Barreto, *Menores e loucos em direito criminal* (Brasília: Senado Federal, [1886] 2003; available at http://www2.senado.leg.br/bdsf/item/id/496216).
Vicente Alves de Paula Pessoa, *Codigo criminal do Império do Brazil annotado* (Rio de Janeiro: Livraria Popular, 1877; available at http://www2.senado.leg.br/bdsf/item/id/227311).
Vicente Azevedo, "O centenário do código criminal", *Justitia* 109 ([1930] 1980; available at http://www.revistajustitia.com.br/revistas/b2bxb6.pdf).
Vicente Piragibe, *Legislação penal do Brasil e do estrangeiro: 1° Volume: Codigo penal brasileiro (completado com as leis modificadoras em vigor)* (São Paulo: Saraiva, 1932).
Victor Foucher, *Code criminel de l'empire du Brésil* (Paris: Imprimierie Royale, 1834; available at http://gallica.bnf.fr/ark:/12148/bpt6k4262610?rk=64378;0).
Victor Foucher, *Code pénal général de l'empire d'Autriche* (Paris: Imprimierie Royale, 1833; available at http://catalogue.bnf.fr/ark:/12148/cb33965081m).
Victor Foucher, *Lois de la procédure criminelle et lois pénales du royaume des Deux-Siciles* (Paris: Imprimierie Royale, 1836; available at http://catalogue.bnf.fr/ark:/12148/cb31138208j)
Vivian Costa, *Codificação e formação do estado-nacional brasileiro: o código criminal de 1830 e a positivação das leis no pós-independência* (São Paulo: USP, 2013; available at http://www.teses.usp.br/teses/disponiveis/31/31131/tde-04112013-164930/pt-br.php).

Diego Nunes is Associate Professor at Universidade Federal de Santa Catarina (Brazil), and teaches Legal History. He earned his Ph.D. in Legal History (2011–2014) at the Università degli Studi di Macerata (Italy). He was Visiting Professor at the Università degli studi di Milano (2015) and Stipendiat at Max-Planck-Institut für europäische Rechtsgeschicht (2012 and 2014), and a leader of the Ius Commune Research Group on Legal Culture History. His major research interests concern legal history, especially history of criminal law, constitutional history, history of international law and the history of criminal justice. Current projects are dealing with the comparative legal history, history of political crimes and terrorism, history of justice and the history of human rights. In the last years he has recently published articles in journals and collected volumes on: Legislative Proceedings outside Parliament in Authoritarian States (Sequência 37, 2016; and Beiträge zur Rechtsgeschichte Österreichs 2, 2013), Inter American Convention on Human Rights in the Brazilian Constitucionalism (Direito Internacional em expansão, Belo Horizonte 2016), The expulsion of Olga Benario Prestes before the Brazilian Supreme Court ((Wo)Men in Legal History, Lille 2016; Questões de Direito Internacional, Curitiba, 2017 and Quaderni del Dipartimento Jonico 1, 2015), National Security laws in Brazil and terrorism (Revista Brasileira de Ciências Criminais 22, 2014) and the role of European Legal experience in the Brazilian Estado Novo regime (European traditions, Nijmegen 2012).

Codifying the Criminal Law in Argentina: Provincial and National Codification in the Genesis of the First Penal Code

Alejandro Agüero and Matías Rosso

Abstract This essay analyzes the gradual process of criminal reform in the territories that would form Argentina throughout the 19th century. After the independence and in spite of different attempts for establishing a new republican system, the reform of the criminal laws did not have the revolutionary pace that one could expect. The Spanish colonial law persisted during the first half of the 19th century. The first national penal code was enacted in 1886, two decades after the constitutional organization of the country (1853–1860). We will describe the process of coding the criminal law, paying attention to the inherent complexity derived from the hybridism of the Argentinean constitutional model (half Federal, half Unitarian). In order to get a better comprehension of the way in which actors of the time understood the codification process, we will look at the archives, focusing our view in the experience of the Province of Cordoba, the second district in population and territory of the country. These primary sources help us to understand the way in which the daily justice administration gradually encompassed the codification process. Finally, we cast some doubts about the efficacy of the first national penal code for achieving the sought after legal uniformity.

1 Introduction: The Criminal Reform in the Hispanic Tradition

By the last quarter of the eighteenth century, the reform of the criminal justice system was one of the recurring themes among enlightened thinkers, lawyers and councilors who gathered around the Spanish King's Court. However, unlike the more radical writings of foreign figures like Beccaria or Voltaire, who claimed for a

A. Agüero
Universidad Nacional de Córdoba, Córdoba, Argentina
e-mail: aaguero@derecho.unc.edu.ar

M. Rosso (✉)
Universidad Empresarial Siglo XXI, Córdoba, Argentina
e-mail: mjrosso@hotmail.com

A. Masferrer (ed.), *The Western Codification of Criminal Law*, Studies in the History of Law and Justice 11, https://doi.org/10.1007/978-3-319-71912-2_11

completely new system of law that should set a *tabula rasa* with the past, Spanish reformers found it more reasonable to undertake a gradual adjustment of traditional laws. This is evident in the pages of the most significant book of the time concerned with the criminal laws reform in Spain: the *Discourse on Punishments* by Manuel de Lardizábal y Uribe (1782).[1]

The *Discourse on Punishments* shows, like other writings of the era, that a radical reform was irreconcilable with the Catholic and historicist foundations of the Spanish Monarchy; foundations that no one reformer was willing to criticize. For this reason, they looked at the past as the standpoint for reform, recognizing the high value of historical laws like the medieval *Siete Partidas* –renamed by this time as "the Spanish Code of Partidas".[2] In his prologue, Lardizábal made it clear that he had tried to apply the "new maxims and principles to the current criminal laws", pointing out those that deserved to be reformed and supporting, at the same time, the new maxims and principles "on the authority of the said laws". Furthermore, he asserted that some maxims adopted as useful and new, "have been approved and enshrined from immemorial times in our homeland laws".[3]

There was no opportunity during the Spanish *Ancient Régime* for adopting the gradual reforms suggested by authors like Lardizábal. The experience of the French revolution was a deterrent for Spanish reformers; years later, the imperial and constitutional crisis of 1808 opened a new era, setting a watershed in the history of both, Spain and her former colonies.

In this study, we will focus on the criminal reform in some of the territories of the former Viceroyalty of Río de la Plata that would form Argentina throughout the 19th century. We will show how, in spite of proclaiming independence and attempts for establishing a new republican system, the reform of the criminal law and justice did not have the revolutionary pace that one could expect. In other words, concerning the criminal law reform, the leaders of the new country seemed to share the same moderate gradualism expressed by reformers of the enlightened despotism.

Firstly, we will summarize the cultural patterns and the persistence of the colonial laws after the independence during the first half of the 19th century; in the second place, we will describe the process of coding the criminal law with the inherent complexity of a hybrid constitutional model (half Federal, half Unitarian). In order to get a better comprehension of the way in which actors of the time understood the codification process, we will look at the archives, focusing our view in the experience of the Province of Cordoba, the second district in population and territory in the newborn Argentine Confederation, then the Argentine Nation (from 1860 onwards).

---

[1]Agüero, Alejandro and Marta Lorente, "Penal enlightenment in Spain: from Beccaria's reception to the first criminal code", in Jesús Astigarraga (ed.), *The Spanish Enlightenment Revisited*, (Oxford, The Voltaire Foundation of Oxford University, 2015.), pp. 235–264.

[2]Clavero, Bartolomé, 'La idea de código en la Ilustración jurídica', in *Historia, instituciones, documentos*, (nº 6, 1979), pp. 72–73.

[3]Lardizábal y Uribe, Manuel, *Discurso sobre las penas contraído a las leyes criminales de España para facilitar su reforma*, (Madrid, Imp. Joaquín Ibarra. 1782). 'Prologue', pp. xii–xiii.

2 The Persistence of Spanish Legal Traditions After the Independence in Rio de la Plata

After the revolution of May 1810, some of the provinces of the former Viceroyalty of Rio de la Plata (1776–1810) fought for their independence from Spain, while they looked for a new political organization. In 1816, they declared the independence of the "United Provinces of South America". However, different attempts of establishing a general government upon the base of a common written constitution (1813, 1819, and 1826) failed. In this context, each province declared her own independence and from 1820 onwards, most of them adopted local Constitutions. Each province claimed to be a sovereign state and, by means of pacts, they gave birth to the "Argentine Confederation". The provinces kept their sovereignty and domestic government as independent republics, while the Governor of Buenos Aires, Juan Manuel de Rosas, acted as common delegate for foreign affairs. Rosas was, in fact, more than a mere common delegate of the provinces. Particularly after 1835, he exerted his political and military influence over the whole territory. This confederative regimen lasted until the constituent moment of 1853/1860.[4]

During the confederative system, there were few changes to the criminal justice inherited from colonial times.[5] At the beginning of the revolutionary period, some symbolic reforms were passed, like abolishing judicial torture and Inquisition courts (1813). However, the lack of a common authority after 1820 conditioned the effectiveness of these general reforms adopted in the first decade after the revolution. Deeper reforms were undertaken within each provincial territory after 1820. However, they were rather aimed at setting basic constitutional aspects and territorial organization, than at reforming the criminal substantive or procedural law.

The first glimpse of codification appeared in Buenos Aires, among a set of reforms projected by Minister Rivadavia. He announced the intention of the Government to enact a Criminal Code for the province. There was even a draft code presented in 1822 by the French lawyer Guret Bellemare. The text is lost, though considering the nationality of the author, scholars suggest that the French Code of 1810 inspired the draft.[6] In 1824, during the preludes of the general constituent convention, the Governor of Buenos Aires appointed a commission of three jurists to produce a Penal Code, but the task was never fulfilled. These are the few references concerning the criminal law codification in this period.

[4]For an overview, Goldman, Noemí (dir.), *Revolución, República, Confederación. Nueva Historia Argentina*, (vol. III, 2 ed. Buenos Aires. 2005).

[5]Levaggi, Abelardo, *Historia del Derecho Penal Argentino*, (Buenos Aires, Perrot, 1978); Agüero, Alejandro, "Formas de continuidad del orden jurídico. Algunas reflexiones a partir de la justicia criminal de Córdoba (Argentina), primera mitad del siglo XIX", in *Nuevo Mundo Mundos Nuevos*, (Published online March 23, 2010. Available at: http://nuevomundo.revues.org/59352.).

[6]Levaggi, Abelardo, *El derecho Penal Argentino en la Historia*, (Buenos Aires. Eudeba, 2012), p. 39.

From a general point of view, we can say that during the first half of the 19th century, besides the aforementioned reforms and the persistence of the Spanish law, the courts and judges, slowly and casuistically adjusted the criminal justice administration to the new republican context. New regulations affected mostly the structure of courts and the institutions for the control of rural population.[7] However, neither the substantive nor the procedural laws were thoroughly reformed. Some studies have shown the persistent use of the Spanish colonial laws and doctrines, moderated by the so-called "prudent discretion of judges".[8] Certainly, the old legal tradition had to work in a self-recognized republican system. For this reason, some scholars have stressed that, during the confederative system, the reinforcement of the justice administration would have had a key role in spreading republican values.[9] However, in these provinces-republics during the confederative system, there was no room for political dissension and governors usually got "extraordinary powers" that authorized them to pursue political adversaries and to act, in most cases, as court of justice- in the same way that it had been the practice for centuries during the colonial era.[10]

3 Federal Constitution and National Codification

The confederative system collapsed in 1852. A new constituent convention passed the first Federal Constitution in 1853. While the federal structure was assumed as part of the historical legacy (supported with the exemplary model of the United

[7]Barreneche, Osvaldo. *Dentro de la Ley TODO. La justicia criminal de Buenos Aires en la etapa formativa del sistema penal moderno de la Argentina.* (La Plata, Al Margen. 2001), For this point see especially Chapter IV, pp. 75–101. Also, Romano, Silvia, "Instituciones coloniales en contextos republicanos: los jueces de la campaña cordobesa en las primeras décadas del siglo XIX y la construcción del estado provincial autónomo", en *Revolución. Política e ideas en el Río de la Plata durante la década de 1810*, (Fabián Herrero comp) (Buenos Aires, Ediciones Cooperativas, Colección: Politeia de Ciencias Sociales, 2004). By the same author, "Las nuevas fuentes de legitimación del poder y sus protagonistas en la configuración del sistema republicano y representativo en la provincia de Córdoba (1821–1855)", en *Córdoba Bicentenaria. Claves de su historia contemporánea.* (César Tcach coord) (Córdoba, Editorial de la UNC—CEA, 2010), pp. 15–35. See too, Sedeillan, Gisela, *La justicia penal en la provincia de Buenos Aires*, (Buenos Aires,1ª ed., Biblos, 2012).

[8]Agüero, Alejandro, "Formas de continuidad del orden jurídico…" Cit.

[9]Salvatore, Ricardo, Wandering Paysanos. State order and subaltern experience in Buenos Aires during the Rosas era, (Durham—London, Duke University Press, 2003).

[10]Upon the problem of the republicanism in this context, Myers, Jorge, *Orden y Virtud. El discurso republicano en el régimen rosista,* (Buenos Aires, 1995). See also, Chiaramonte, José C., *Raíces históricas del federalismo latinoamericano*, Buenos Aires. A critical review, in Agüero, Alejandro (2016), Ancient Constitution or Paternal Government? Extraordinary Powers as Legal Response to Political Violence (Río De La Plata, 1810–1860) (April 1, 2016, *Max Planck Institute for European Legal History Research Paper Series*, No. 2016-10. Available at SSRN: https://ssrn.com/abstract=2841769).

States of North America), the goal of setting a uniform legal system among very unequal provinces encouraged the convention to adopt the system of national codification of substantive law (inspired by the continental European experience). The Constitution granted the National Congress the power for enacting the Civil, Commercial, Criminal and Mining Law Codes (art. 64, inc. 11). Thus, while the provinces retained their political identities, with their local governments, courts systems (including their own procedural law), they were supposed to share the same national substantive codified law.

J. B. Alberdi, one of the fathers of the Argentinean Constitution of 1853, said that the Argentina constitutional model was an original solution that he called "the mixed system".[11] It was a hybrid model meant to overcome the old tensions between the Federal and the Unitarian factions. The need of imposing a common law over the whole country was as compelling for the elite as the historical legacy was in order to adopt the federal structure and preserve the provincial identities. The deep cultural and economic differences amongst the provinces and the lack of lawyers in many of them were strong reasons for setting the national codification of substantive law. Even before the Constitution was passed, General Urquiza exerting as Interim Director of the country, issued a decree in 1852 designating the commissions for drafting codes. Regarding the still current Spanish criminal laws, General Urquiza considered them as:

> … Absolutely irrelevant [… because they were …] cruel and extravagant, so the judges, not to incur in the infamy or the ridiculousness of executing them, legislate each case for themselves; and their discretion, […] becomes a positive, compared with the abuse of imposing such penalties. [12]

With these words, Urquiza gave voice to the thoughts of several contemporaries who claimed for enacting a Penal Code to end with the judicial discretion that had become unavoidable for moderating the cruelty of the old laws.[13] Nonetheless, this early attempt of codification was unsuccessful. Buenos Aires, the strongest province, had broken relationship with the rest of the provinces in 1852 and did not recognize the Constitution of 1853. Instead, it passed its own Constitution as independent state in 1854. The secession of Buenos Aires lasted until 1860. After two historical battles, Buenos Aires accepted joining the Argentine Federation upon the condition of reforming the National Constitution of 1853.

Inspired by Buenos Aires's interests, the amendment of 1860 reinforced the federal patterns of the 1853 text, although maintained the established system of

[11]Alberdi, Juan B., *Bases y puntos de partida para la organización política de la República Argentina.* (Buenos Aires. "La Nueva Cultura Argentina". 1915), p. 118.

[12]Tau Anzoátegui, Víctor, *La codificación en la Argentina (1810–1870). Mentalidad social e ideas jurídicas*, (Buenos Aires: Perrot. 1977), p. 315.

[13]Yangilevich, Melina, "Leyes antiguas para un estado moderno. Prácticas jurídicas en la provincia de Bueno Aires durante el período de la codificación". *Justicia y Fronteras. Estudios sobre historia de la justicia en el Rio de la Plata. Siglo XVI–XIX.* (Darío Barriera compilador), (Murcia, ediciones de la universidad de Murcia), pp. 205–223.

national codified substantive law. However, a subtle modification was introduced to ensure that the new national codes could not "alter local jurisdictions".[14] Thus, it was assured the intangibility of the jurisdictional powers of the provinces to apply the substantive codes, including—as it was interpreted—the powers to legislate on procedural matters too. Besides this, the text of 1860 kept in force the norm that forbade the provinces to "enact civil, commercial, criminal, or mining codes after Congress had enacted them".[15] The norm was interpreted as a temporary authorization to the provinces to enact their own substantive law codes while the National Congress had not done it.[16]

As the National Congress was not able to enact a common penal code until 1886 (despite having the first draft by 1867 and other one by 1881), most of the provinces kept in force their traditional laws and after 1877, many of them passed their own local codes. These provincial codes—actually adaptations of the drafts for the national code—were current law until the enforcement of the first national penal code in 1887. Before analyzing the way in which the provinces dealt with this transitional moment, let us briefly describe the different drafts prepared for the national penal code, their sources and the problems to get their enactment.

4 First Attempts of Passing a National Penal Code: The Two Draft

The constitutional amendment of 1860- with the incorporation of Buenos Aires- finally set the conditions to carry out the national coding of substantive laws among other actions addressed to begin the modern state building. In 1863, the President named the committees responsible for preparing the different draft codes. Dr. Carlos Tejedor, professor at Buenos Aires University, was commissioned with drafting the Penal Code. Tejedor introduced the General Section of his draft in 1865 and the Special Section in 1867.[17] However, it took almost twenty years for the National Congress to enact the National Penal Code.[18]

---

[14]"Article 67- Congress is empowered… Inc. 11.- To enact the Civil, Commercial, Criminal, and Mining Codes… provided that such codes do not alter local jurisdictions, and their enforcement shall correspond to the federal or provincial courts depending on the respective jurisdictions for persons or things… ". The constitutional texts, with their respective amendments, are available in http://bib.cervantesvirtual.com/portal/constituciones/constituciones.shtml.

[15]"Article 108. The provinces do not exercise the power delegated to the Nation. Provinces shall in no case enter into any partial treaty of political nature; enact laws dealing with commerce… enact civil, commercial, criminal, or mining codes after Congress had enacted them…".

[16]Tau Anzoátegui, Víctor, *La codificación en la Argentina (1810–1870)*... Cit. P. 333.

[17]Levaggi, Abelardo. *Historia del Derecho Penal Argentino.* (Buenos Aires. Perrot. 1978), p. 184.

[18]By Law No. 1920 of December 7, 1886, enacting the Criminal Code of the Nation, issued by the Honorable National Congress of Argentina.

During that time, the commission that should revise the Tejedor's draft proposed a completely new draft in 1881. Besides technical considerations, and bureaucratic delays, political circumstances interfered in this process too. Dr. Tejedor came to be governor of Buenos Aires in 1878. Later, while competing for president, he leaded a revolt against the national authorities that has declared the city of Buenos Aires as federal district and capital of the country. Tejedor was defeated in the battle camp. The next year, the parliamentary Commission presented the new Draft, shelving the Tejedor's draft.[19] The two drafts had significant role in the history of the transition to a criminal law codification system in Argentina.

4.1 *Tejedor's Draft (1867)*

It is a common place to say that Tejedor took the base for his draft from the Bavarian Code of 1813—written by von Feuerbach—as he himself declared. It is also known that Tejedor acceded to that Code not through the original German version, but via the French translation released by Charles Vattel in 1852.[20] The imprints of the Bavarian Code may seem evident in the systematic structure of the General Section, though there are also traces of the French law as the triple classification of the offenses into contraventions, delicts, and crimes. However, analyzing the Special Section, Thomas Duve concluded that contrary to what Tejedor declared, the draft was not primarily based on the Bavarian Code, but on the contemporary North and South American Codes of the era, particularly on the Peruvian Code of 1863. Duve has also pointed out the problems of understanding derived of the French translation of the Bavarian Code.[21]

According to Levaggi, other sources for the Tejedor's draft were the Spanish Codes of 1848 and 1850, the French Code of 1810 and those of the Two Sicilies, Austria and Prussia. He also finds traces of the Penal Codes of Bolivia, Brazil, New York, and Louisiana.[22] It is worth noting here that Tejedor did not set aside the traditional Spanish laws, including references to the medieval *Siete Partidas* and

[19]Zaffaroni, Eugneio and Corxatto, Guido, "El pensamiento penal en el derecho penal argentino", in *Rechtsgeschichte Legal History*, (nº 22, 2014), pp. 192–212.

[20]Zaffaroni, Eugenio, Alagia, Alejandro and Slokar, Alejnadro [2000,], *Derecho Penal – Parte General*, 2da ed., (Buenos Aires, Ediar, 2002), p. 249. Levaggi, Abelardo, *El derecho Penal Argentino...*, cit. P. 276.

[21]Duve, Thomas, "¿Del absolutismo ilustrado al liberalismo reformista? La recepción del Código penal Bávaro de 1813 de Paul J. A. von Feuerbach en Argentina y el debate sobre la reforma del derecho penal hasta 1921", En *Revista de historia del Derecho, Nº 27,* (Buenos Aires, Tau Anzoátegui, Víctor, 1999), pp. 125–152.

[22]Levaggi, Abelardo, *El derecho Penal Argentino en la Historia...* cit. pp. 276–277.

Leyes de Estilo, to the early modern Castilian *Nueva Recopilación* (1567) and to the Spanish *Novisima Recopilación* (1805).[23]

Let us add, that the author pointed out in footnotes the possible concordances between the articles of his draft and the Roman law, the Castilian law, the new Argentinean laws and the doctrines of the time. At this point, it is interesting to remark on some traditional imprints that may show how far Tejedor was from the utilitarian individualist values that guided the radical codification thinking.[24] Consider, in example, the sixth article of the second book, which prohibits the capital execution of more than one convicted for the same offense. Who should be executed in that case? It was a matter of fortune. A raffle among the convicted should decide who would suffer the death penalty, while the rest had to undergo a life sentence in "presidio", after witnessing the execution of their accomplice. In the footnote, Tejedor related this article to the Peruvian Code (V. art. 70), the Bolivian Code (arts. 56 and 58) and to the medieval *Siete Partidas*, according to which, he recalled, when there are many convicted for the same crime, "justice must be softened, punishing only the leaders."[25]

Regarding the death penalty, Tejedor supported a process of gradual abolitionism. In the line of the moderate Spanish reformers,[26] he claimed for reducing the application of the death penalty, reserving it for the most "horrible crimes". He was against torture and any other kind of torments, limiting the capital execution to the "simple death".[27] However, he trusted in a progressive substitution of the death penalty by the use of "presidios" and penitentiaries according to the improvements in the customs and conditions of the country.[28] Some years before, by the time when he wrote his Course of Criminal Law (1860), he said that it would have been

[23]Laplaza, Francisco, "El proceso histórico de la codificación penal argentina", en *Revista de Historia del Derecho "Ricardo Levene"*, Nº 21, (Buenos Aires, Imprenta de la universidad, 1978), pp. 59–92.

[24]On the "ideology of codification", Tarello, Giovanni, *Cultura jurídica y política del derecho*, (México, Fondo de Cultura Económica, 1995), pp. 39–56; see also, Inge Kroppenberg and Nikolaus Linder, Coding the Nation. Codification History from a (Post-) Global Perspective, in *Entanglements in Legal History: Conceptual Approaches*, (Tomas Duve ed.), (Frankfurt, Max Planck Institute for European Legal History, 2014), pp. 67–99.

[25]Tejedor, Carlos, *Proyecto de Código Penal para la República Argentina,* (Buenos Aires, Imprenta del Comercio del Plata, 1866), p. 97.

[26]Scandellari, Simonetta (2007) "La difusión del pensamiento criminal de Gaetano Filangieri en España", in *Nuevo Mundo Mundos Nuevos*, (Coloquios, 2007), (Puesto en línea el 28 janvier 2007. Available at http://nuevomundo.revues.org/index3484.html).

[27]"En el fondo, he conservado la pena de muerte, pero limitada a los crímenes más espantosos, respecto de los cuales la conciencia de todo hombre razonable reclama el último suplicio, y eso mismo rodea a tales condiciones, que su aplicación será rarísima. Nada tampoco de tormentos o refinamientos, ni aun aparentes. Este Código no reconoce más que la muerte simple". Letter sent by Tejedor to the Minister of Justice, December of 1865. In Tejedor, Carlos, *Proyecto de Código Penal*... cit, p. II.

[28]Tejedor, Carlos, *Proyecto de Código Pena*... cit, pp. II y III.

crazy to abolish the death penalty considering the lack of penitentiaries and the current conditions of the local jails.[29]

The Tejedor draft has had a huge impact on the history of the Argentinean criminal law. The extensive footnotes that describe the normative concordance and doctrinal precedents, offered a set of doctrinal sources for interpretation very useful for lawyers and magistrates, accomplishing this way a pedagogic task also in this field of knowledge. On the other hand, it was the model of the first criminal code of the Nation, after a turbulent course at the National Congress.

4.2 The Commission's Draft (1881)

In 1868, the President appointed a commission of three jurists to examine the draft Criminal Code submitted by Tejedor. The Commission had to present a report detailing every point of the project, so that the Congress could take the corresponding resolution. After twelve years of work and countless jurists having taken part in it, the Commission raised its conclusions to the Minister of Justice in 1881.[30]

The Commission's report was critical of the Tejedor's draft. If, on the one hand, it recognized the expertise of the author, on the other, it remarked on the fact that the models considered by Tejedor were mostly codes enacted during the first half of the century. Thus, the Commission observed that Tejedor could not have had in mind the new "general movement of coding throughout the world, which—the report said—still continues existing, particularly in relation to penal matters". The report referred to Denmark, Switzerland, Belgium, Germany, Portugal, Spain, the United States, Louisiana, Chile, Italy, Austria, the Netherlands, Mexico and Venezuela, as cases of new codes or projects that had to be considered in order to improve the draft. According to the report, "…the Commission had to take into account these codes or draft Codes and comments, because they contain the science of each country".[31]

The Commission virtually reformed the whole of the Tejedor Project, creating, in fact, a new draft.[32] According to Zaffaroni, the new draft was mostly inspired

[29]Tejedor, Carlos, *Curso de Derecho Criminal,* Parte Primera, (Buenos Aires, Imprenta Argentina, 1860), p. 83.

[30]Moreno, Rodolfo, *El Código Penal y sus antecedentes.* (Buenos Aires. T. I. Editor H. A. Tommasi. 1822–1923).

[31]*Proyecto de Código Penal presentado al Poder Ejecutivo Nacional por la Comisión nombrada para examinar el proyecto redactado por el Dr. D. Carlos Tejedor compuesta por los Dres. Sisto Villegas, Andrés Ugarriza y Juan Agustín Garcia.* (Buenos Aires, Imprenta de El Nacional. 1819), pp. VII–VIII.

[32]Ruiz Moreno, Isidoro. *El derecho penal en la República Argentina.* (Paraná, Ed. Gutemberg. 1898).

by the Spanish code of 1870.[33] The Commission Draft suppressed the division of the offenses in contraventions, delicts and crimes, explaining that it was no longer in use in the world and that those terms were synonymous in many laws, being the said classification a source of confusion and uncertainty.[34] The draft maintained the death penalty, considered by the Commission as a necessary and unavoidable punishment "given the current state of the civilization".[35] Thus, the Commission supported the exceptional use of the death penalty asserting that it was admitted in the laws of almost all civilized nations of the world, referring, as exemplary cases, to Spain, Mexico, Brazil, Bolivia, Peru, France, Denmark, Austria, Naples, Parma, Sardinia and even the Pontifical States. They also mentioned the case of Switzerland that had abolished the death penalty and notwithstanding that, two million people had voted for its restoration in a plebiscite.[36]

As we said, the Commission presented the new draft by 1881. The President sent it to the National Congress but it would take still five year more for the enactment of the first Penal Code. According to the project, the Supreme and the federal courts should report to the Minister of Justice all doubts and problems that may follow due to the application of the Code and the possible gaps in its content.[37] This clause may suggest that the notion of codification was open to the feedback provided by the courts. On the other hand, admitting possible gaps, would mean that this codification was far from the formal definition of crime and, therefore, that there was still active an ontological notion of offence that could be discovered in the daily praxis. However, what do we know about the praxis in that time?

In accordance with the National Constitution of 1853 and the amendment of 1860, justice administration in ordinary cases competed to the provincial courts; therefore, we must look at the provincial archives to have an idea about the way in which they dealt with the problem of carrying out criminal justice in this transitional moment. Moreover, because of the delay of the National Congress, the majority of the provinces adopted their local penal codes. We think this is a worthy transitional experience scarcely studied due to the national dimension of the Penal Code in Argentina.

[33] Zaffaroni, Eugenio, Alagia, Alejandro and Slokar, Alejnadro [2000,] 2002, *Derecho Penal...* cit., p. 249.

[34] *Proyecto de Código Penal presentado al Poder Ejecutivo Nacional por la Comisión...* cit, p. X.

[35] *Proyecto de Código Penal presentado al Poder Ejecutivo Nacional por la Comisión...* cit, p. XX.

[36] *Proyecto de Código Penal presentado al Poder Ejecutivo Nacional por la Comisión...* cit, p. XXV.

[37] *Proyecto de Código Penal presentado al Poder Ejecutivo Nacional por la Comisión...* cit, p. XL.

5 The Provincial Codes: Justice Administration During the Coding Process

In order to grasp the provincial dimension of the history of codification, we have focused on the experience of the Province of Cordoba, the second territory in population of the country, with a lasting cultural traditions rooted in the Spanish values. In order to see the law in action, we have taken a random sample of criminal cases pursued at the provincial courts during few years before the enactment of the first National Penal Code. We have considered the period that runs from 1883 to 1886 with a sample of the 30% over a universe of 403 cases preserved for those years in the Archive.[38] We have chosen that period because we wanted to test the impact of the enactment, in 1882, of the first provincial penal code that was based on the national Commission's Draft of 1881.

5.1 *Codification Without "Code Culture"*

Before the codification of criminal law, judges continued in Córdoba performing justice according to the Castilian-colonial tradition, using as referential texts the *Siete Partidas* of Alfonso X (13th century). This was a common praxis in the whole region. However, the new political discourse had enshrined the legality principle and it was not easy to observe literally the wording of a five centuries old law. In many cases, the clauses of the *Siete Partidas* had become disproportionate regarding the new sensibilities and the new standards of relationship between crime and punishment. Being legalist with an old-fashioned law could lead to all sort of cruelties. For this reason, it became a common practice among judges to impose a "reasonable punishment", adjusting casuistically their sentences, in accordance with diverse criterions, lessening this way the severity of such old laws.

Therefore, against the legality principle proclaimed at the rhetorical level, that praxis implied a clear revalidation of judicial discretion, maintaining the traits of a system that still relied on the wisdom of the judges rather than on the laws; a justice of judges rather than laws, as the Hispanic tradition has been defined.[39] Aggravating or mitigating circumstances were usually invoked for adjusting the law to the new context. At the same time, the normative field was still construed in a

[38]The records belong to the Crime Series of the Historical Archive of the Province of Córdoba, hereafter quoted as AHPC for its acronym in Spanish.

[39]Lorente, Marta (coord.), *De justicia de Jueces a Justicia de leyes: hacia la España de 1870*, (Madrid, Consejo General del Poder Judicial, 2007).

pluralist sense, allowing the magistrates and parties to invoke diverse kinds of norms and precepts, taken from very different sources (from the Bible to police regulations).[40]

By the decade of 1880, lawyers and judges in Córdoba began studying the drafts discussed at the National Congress. The two texts were soon integrated into that open universe of normativity, providing arguments for the daily task of carrying out justice, regardless the fact that they were still mere drafts. In a case for abduction, pursued in 1882, the defense of one accused requested a reduction of the punishment, invoking the Article 1, title 3, paragraph 4, of the Tejedor's draft.[41] In the plea of another accused, the defender criticized the *Siete Partidas* because of mingling the responsibility of the authors and accomplices; at the same time, he referred to the Tejedor's draft and to the Commission's one. He requested the judge to apply "either of the two drafts", excluding the law of *Partidas*. His argument regarding the sentence was as follows:

> (…)[The punishment] to be applied to my client is discretionary; the Code of Dr. Tejedor and the 1881 Draft which have been presented should be taken into account, as even if their contents are not law, it is at least a doctrine of legal advisers, whose authoritative words enjoy the confidence of the government…[42]

The case offers a strong testimony concerning the way in which the law was still conceived. Its binding force relied in its value as doctrine rather than in the formal proceedings of enactment. The draft codes could run like current law in order to carry out justice, no matter they were still only drafts. Moreover, this traditional way of comprehending the authority of the law seems to have been a lasting cultural pattern, even after the enactment of the Codes. Some scholars called this "codification without code culture".[43] The brief transitional period in which the provinces enacted their own local codes provides us with a fruitful observatory to analyze this feature.

5.2 *The Experience of the Provincial Penal Code of Córdoba (1882–1887)*

Faced with the delay of the National Congress to enact the Criminal Code, the provinces assumed their remaining powers to do it in accordance with the

[40]On that kind of pluralism, from a comparative perspective, see (Seán Patrick Donlan and Dirk Heirbaut eds.), *The Law's Many Bodies. Studies in Legal Hybridity and Jurisdictional Complexity, c. 1600–1900*, (Berlin, Duncker & Humblot, 2015).

[41]AHPC, Criminal 1882, Leg. 438, Exp. 2 fs. 58.

[42]AHPC, Criminal 1882, Leg. 438, Exp. 2 fs. 67.

[43]For the Latin American context, on this topic see Garriga, Carlos and Andréa Slemian, "Em trajes brasileiros": justiça e constituição na América ibérica (c. 1750–1850), *Revista de história são paulo*, N° 169, p. 181–221, (JULHO/DEZEMBRO 2013), pp. 207.

interpretation given to the Federal Constitution. Between 1877 and 1882, the provinces adopted either the Tejedor draft or the Commission's one, as provincial codes. Among the 14 existing provinces, 11 chose the Tejedor draft as provincial code, while Córdoba enacted the Commission's draft in 1882. The provinces of Jujuy and Santiago maintained the traditional Castilian law until the enactment of the National Penal Code in December 1886.[44]

In his dispatch submitted to the local legislature, the Governor of Cordoba expressed that "while the National Congress takes its time to enact the Penal Code, the draft submitted to the National Government by the Commission integrated by Dr. Sixto Villegas, Dr. Andrés Ugarriza and Dr. Juan A. García, is declared as provincial law". At the same time, the local Executive assumed the commitment of preparing an "official edition" for the province.[45] Thus, the Commission's draft of 1881—with light modifications—became the penal code of Córdoba in 1882. It was in full force until the First Penal Code of the Nation came into force on 1 March 1887.

The records of the daily justice administration show that the enforcement of the provincial penal code did not mean the end of the traditional normative pluralism. Moreover, the new code did not repeal precedent local regulations that overlapped one another in several aspects, such as the "Rural justice and police regulation" of 1856 and the Cattle Rustling Act issued the same year. After the enactment of provincial penal code, in 1885, the Legislature of Cordoba passed a "Rural Code", which included a set of typified offences as "rural delicts", adding one more element of complexity. In addition, records show that lawyers and judges kept using the *Siete Partidas* among other historical laws. The normative complexity was, in turn, in the hands of a set of overlapping jurisdiction managed by different authorities, such as justices of the peace, criminal court judges, correctional judges, etc. The new code was but one more piece in that complex puzzle. Some examples taken from the archive should help us to describe this context.

In 1886, Eusebia Guevara was accused of killing her newborn son in a small village of the rural area of Cordoba; her sister, Mauricia Guevara, was accused of burying the corpse. Eusebia said that the baby was stillborn and that she had called her sister to bury him. The prosecutor argued that there was no evidence that the child had been born alive, so the mother could not be punished for murder. He held that the case should be dismissed. The judge stated that even when there were some suspicions that the accused had killed the baby, they were not enough "*to form the necessary legal awareness of guilt*" attributed to the accused. The judge quoted the Law 12 title 14, *Partida* 3, according to which suspicions or indirect evidence were not enough to condemn, and the Law 26 title 1 Partida 7, that is to say, the classical formulation of the *in dubio pro reo* principle.[46] For the judge, there was no reason

[44]Levaggi, Abelardo, *El derecho Penal Argentino*... cit, p. 279.

[45]AHPC, Gobierno, t. 259 "A", 1882, fs. 467.

[46]See Law 12 title 14, *Partida* 3 and Law 26 title 1 *Partida* 7.

not to believe the mother. Therefore, he dismissed the case "... *according to what is taught by the practices and the rulings of the courts*."[47]

There was no need to refer to the new constitutional texts nor to the new codes to sustain those axiomatic principles of the procedural law. They were still interpreted in the same way they had been enshrined in the practice and in the traditional Spanish law- as Lardizábal had claimed a century before. Combined with the ancient laws, some traditional manners persisted as well. In 1883, a man was accused of stealing three steers. The justice of the peace (appointed for rural districts) imposed a punishment of three years of public service (one year per animal, according to the Cattle Rustling Act of 1856). The sentence was submitted to the city judges, where the prosecutor invoked two articles of the Penal Code to ask a penalty of eighteen months' imprisonment or military service. Meanwhile, the defendant was released by grace of the Governor due to the celebration of the "Mercedes" feast. The judge decreed to shelve the case.[48] Alongside with the overlapping normativity, the case also shows the persistence of the praxis of pardoning crimes during religious holidays.

The actors of this transition moment were well aware of the provisional nature of the provincial criminal code, and this character provided an argument to reinforce the ongoing judicial discretion. In a case for cattle rustling of 1883, the defender argued that the local code was defective as it was "nothing but a light and ill-considered draft". The lawyer criticized the provincial penal code because it lacked of a scale to adjust the punishments according to the seriousness of the crime. He pointed out the article 317 that set a punishment of 2–4 years to whom steal "a movable thing". However, he wondered, "how to equate he who steals 500 pesos with he who steals a pen or an ordinary thimble". Certainly, he added, "the legislator could not have such an absurd intention" and in case of doubt, he concluded, "it must be conceded to the magistrate the discretionary faculties that the new provisory law had not deprived him".[49]

Besides the ongoing confidence in the judicial discretion, the allegation also shows the perplexities triggered by the inherent process of abstraction that made it possible to simplify the codified law, in the mind of those who were used to deal with a more casuistic judicial tradition.[50] On the other hand, the aforementioned case shows us another persistence. The accused was sentenced to eight months in prison by the justice of the peace. When the sentence was submitted for its

---

[47]AHC, Criminal 1886, Leg. 480, Exp. 9.

[48]AHC, Criminal 1883, Leg. 453, Exp. 5.

[49]AHC, Criminal 1883, Leg. 458, Exp. 9.

[50]On the abstraction as an inherent feature of the process of coding the law, Caroni, Pio, *Escritos sobre la Codificación*, (Madrid, Universidad Carlos III, 2012). Also Tarello, Giovanni, *Storia della cultura giuridica moderna. Assolutismo e codificazione del diritto.* (Bologna, Il Mulino. 1976). By the same author, *Le ideologie della codificazione nel secolo XVIII*, (Génova, ECIG, 1976). On the traditional casuistic praxis, Tau Anzoategui, Víctor. *Casuismo y sistema. Indagación histórica sobre el espíritu del Derecho Indiano. Instituto de Investigaciones de Historia del Derecho*, (Buenos Aires, 1992).

confirmation at the city courts, the criminal judge released the defendant considering the imprisonment he had suffered during the judicial proceedings.[51] The judge did not provide any legal ground for his decision. He did not need to do it as he was following a long lasting praxis.

Commuting the sentence and releasing the accused for the prison suffered during the judicial proceedings had been a usual way of closing a criminal case since the colonial times and, as we can see, it was still in use after the penal code enforcement.[52] For what we have seen in the records, this praxis is observable in the overwhelming majority of cases. Sometimes it served to release the accused, sometimes to dim the resultant punishment; moreover, judges proceeded this way without expressing any positive legal ground to justify the decision.

Another colonial persistence that is easy to observe after the provincial code enactment is the "visit" to the local jail by judges and other authorities. Taken from the medieval law, *la visita de cárcel* (the visit to the jail) was a well-defined praxis in the colonial law. Levaggi has characterized the jail visit as a "clemency institution", alongside with the royal pardons, pardons of the offended and the asylum in the Church.[53] The visit was meant to check out the conditions of imprisonment and the state of the jails. At the same time, it also served to decide in situ some cases, reducing the sentences, releasing temporary or definitively the inmate, according to the time suffered in prison, the type of crime, the quality or quantity of evidences, etc.[54]

In 1883, Juan Mañanan was acquitted after a jail visit. The criminal judge considered that the death of a boy caused by Mañanan's carriage on the street had been an accident, giving his judgment in accordance with the paragraph 6, article 93 of the Penal Code. The provincial Supreme Court confirmed the sentence.[55] The same year, Isabel Carranza, accused of killing her newborn son, was released after a jail visit. In this case, the provincial Supreme Court adopted the decision in a session held the day after the visit, considering she had purged the crime.[56]

Some cultural elements with deep traditional roots, like the belief in a natural social hierarchy, were also resilient to the abstraction encouraged by the coding ideology. This may help to explain the observable fact that, in spite of the formal tenor in which the new law referred to the subjects—as the Tarellian unique subject of the law -, subjective conditions had still high incidence in the sense of judicial decisions. Thus, it is not rare to find arguments based on such hierarchies, like stating that the testimony of a laborer is irrelevant to condemn.

[51]AHC, Criminal 1883, Leg. 458, Exp. 9.

[52]About the described praxis in colonial times, Alejandro Agüero, *Castigar y perdonar cuando conviene a la República. La justicia penal de Córdoba del Tucumán, siglos XVII y XVIII*, (Madrid, Centro de Estudios Políticos y Constitucionales, 2008), p. 256 ss.

[53]Levaggi, Abelardo, (2012), *El derecho Penal Argentino…*, cit.

[54]Levaggi, Abelardo, (2012), *El derecho Penal Argentino…*, cit, p. 164.

[55]AHC, Criminal 1883, Leg. 454, Exp. 10.

[56]AHC, Criminal 1883, Leg. 457, Exp. 3.

That is what a justice of the peace did in a case for cattle rustling, in 1886. He also invoked the law of cattle rustling of 1856 and the *Siete Partidas* to add that two witnesses were necessary to condemn when the defendant had not confessed the crime. At the city court, where the sentence of the justice of the peace had to be confirmed, a new discussion had place. The prosecutor argued that there was enough evidence to condemn, pleading for the application of the article 31 of the Penal Code. In turn, the defender asked the confirmation of sentence of the justice of the peace invoking, nonetheless, the article 17 of the Constitution of the Province. Finally, the criminal judge of the city confirmed the justice of the peace decision.[57] The case may also suggest that while in the hinterland the lay justices of the peace kept using traditional laws, the learned lawyers and judges at the city courts looked more familiarized with the new language of the penal code and the constitution. This is just a research hypothesis that needs further evidence.

However, regarding the incidence of social hierarchies in the judicial decisions, we have some more evidences, particularly related to another colonial persistence: the praxis of sentencing the convicted to undergo to work for a particular master that would watch over his behavior. The master had also to instruct the convicted for a job and report to the judge about his conduct. In 1883, a man was accused of counterfeiting currency by given silver aspect to bronze coins. The prosecutor pleaded for the application of the article 185 of the Penal Code, which punished the crime of fraud. Nonetheless, considering the insignificant amount of the fraud and the young age of the accused, he argued that the crime was purged and that the defendant should be released on the condition of undergoing work for his former master who would watch out for his conduct. This is what the judge sentenced.[58] In another case, a 15 year-old minor was accused of stealing money. The stolen money was recovered and given back to the victim. A man submitted a pleading to the judge offering himself as "master" of the accused. He assumed the compromise of preparing the boy for a job and of reporting on his conduct. The judge conceded.[59]

As we can see, the judicial praxis exceeded the limits of the provincial penal code and different customs persisted beyond the boundaries of the codification. Judicial discretion was part of such customs. Sometimes it is hard to found legal grounds for judicial decisions. For example, in a case of a death boy who suffer a carriage accident, both the prosecutor and the judge considered that the accused were not guilty. The judge said that they were innocent and that there had not been negligence on their part. Still, he decided to give them the "city as jail" (la ciudad por cárcel). This was a traditional formula used to restrict the freedom of the accused when, for his privileges, was exempt of going to the common jail. This institution, inherited from the colonial times, was not in the penal code. We will

[57]AHC, Criminal 1885, Leg. 476, Exp. 11.
[58]AHC, Criminal 1883, Leg. 456, Exp. 1.
[59]AHC, Criminal 1883, Leg. 456, Exp. 5.

never know why the judge decided to impose this measure when both accused had been regarded innocent.[60]

Finally, we have to mention that alongside with traditional customs, the lasting normative pluralism also contributed to uphold the judicial discretion. As we said, the provincial penal code was one among many different competing laws that, in several aspect, overlapped one each other. The laws enacted for "rural police" offer the most evident case of such complexity. In some cases, it is not easy to discern between crimes of the penal code and contraventions of the "rural code". Legislating on "contraventions" was regarded an expression of the police power of the province; therefore, they were conceptually excluded of the "penal code" and of the faculty given to the National Congress to legislate in criminal matters.[61] Actually, in order to avoid competence conflicts after the National Penal Code entered in force in 1887, the Rural Code was modified in Córdoba, replacing the terms "rural delicts" by the expression "rural infringement".[62]

Even when there is a lack of archive studies referred to most of the provinces, we could say that the experience of the provincial penal codification in Córdoba does not differ too much from the other cases. We suppose that provincial codifications were assumed as a transitional experience that did not end the traditional pluralism of legal sources and the judicial discretion inherently linked to this latter feature. Actually, we could say that the only difference that characterized the case of Córdoba is just a minor detail. The legislature of Córdoba adopted as provincial penal code the national draft of 1881, while other 11 provinces enacted as provincial code the Tejedor's Draft of 1867. In a context of normative pluralism, this would have been a minor detail, as it was in many relevant aspects. However, the fact that the majority of provinces had adopted the Tejedor's Draft was determinant for the history of the first penal codification in Argentina.

6 Enactment of the First National Penal Code: A Code Enshrined from the Base

Four years after the Commission had presented its draft, the Congress finally decided to discuss the enactment of the national penal code. This issue was the first item in the agenda for the sessions of 23 of October 1885.[63] In the dispatch of that day, the committee of the House of Deputies declared to have studied the two draft

[60]AHC, Criminal 1886, Leg. 479, Exp. 6.

[61]The interpretation on the power of issuing contravention is still a matter of discussion. See Zaffaroni, Alagia, Slokar, *Derecho Penal...* cit., p. 177.

[62]Provincial Law 3586 modifying the Law 1005 passing the Rural Code of the Province of Córdoba.

[63]*Diario de sesiones de la Cámara de Diputados. Año 1885. Sesión de 23 de Octubre.* En Moreno, Rodolfo. *El Código Penal y sus antecedentes.* Tomo I. (Buenos Aires, Ed. H.A. Tommasi. 1922), p. 70.

(Tejedor 1867 and Commission's 1881) remarking on the fact that the Tejedor Draft was already "*in force in the whole country because of its enactment by the provincial legislatures*".[64] Upon this argument, the new committee would propose to enact the Tejedor Draft with some minor modifications.

In the discussion about which of the two draft should be considered as base for the national penal code, the members of the committee unanimously vote for the Tejedor Draft. They criticized the Commission Draft of 1881 pointing out its lack of coherence and confusions. On the other hand, they pondered the fact that the Tejedor Draft had been enacted in most of the provinces and that with some modifications it could offer a solid base for the national criminal code. As first measure, the committee proposed to eliminate the triple classification of offenses into contraventions, delicts and crimes that Tejedor had taken from the French Law. About this point, the committee considered that this classification was confused for the Argentinean Law because, among other reasons, the Federal Constitution referred to treason "as delict and not as crime" and there is—they argued—no more serious and horrible offense than treason.[65]

The Minister of Justice expressed his opinion before the Congress. He said that the Tejedor Draft was defective, though he recognized it was current law in most of the provinces and that the modifications introduced had improved it.[66] In order to urge the Congress to pass the penal code, the Minister mentioned a report he had received from the Courts exposing the "clamorous differences" and disproportionate relations between crimes and punishments among the provinces. He claimed for the Congress to stop such "legal monstrosities" in which the judges frequently incurred so in "this enlightened capital" (that is to say, Buenos Aires) as in the provinces.[67]

The Minister of Justice had to insist before the Senate, where an attempt of postposing the issue had been submitted. Thanks to the insistence of the Minister of Justice, the Senate finally accepted to approve the draft. Senator Pizzaro, supporting the insistence of the Minister, argued that existed a fundamental reason to proceed immediately to enact the modified Tejedor Draft as national penal code expressing that, along the country there were two different criminal law systems: the traditional Spanish one and the Tejedor Draft. As we have seen, this was not exactly like that; however, the assertion was convincing. Senator Pizarro added that the modified

[64]Moreno, Rodolfo *Diario de sesiones de la Cámara de Diputados. Año 1885...* Cit, p. 70.

[65]*Fragmento de la 19° sesión de prórroga del 23 de Octubre de 1885. Comisión de códigos.* En Aguirre, J "*Código Penal de la República...*", cit., prologo, p. XXV. The article 103 of the National Constitution read, "Treason against the Nation shall only consist in rising in arms against it, or in joining its enemies, supplying them with aid and assistance…".

[66]Diario de sesión de la Cámara de Diputados. Año 1886. Tomo II, p. 686. En Moreno, Rodolfo. *El Código Penal y sus...*, cit., p. 73.

[67]*Fragmento de sesión de prórroga del 15 de Noviembre de 1886. Comisión de códigos.* En Aguirre, J, *Código Penal de la República...*, cit., prologo, p. XXXVI.

draft would allow achieving the legislative unity, avoiding that the same fact could be qualified as "crime" in a district and not in other.[68]

For a government and political elite that held a more Unitarian vision of the progress and of the state building, the enactment of the Penal Code meant a significant achievement of national policy. It was a way of enforcing the constitutional "mixed system", conceived more than thirty year before and recently consolidated by the enactment of the Civil Code (1869). On the other hand, in a federal-structured country with such unequal provinces -most of them poor and almost dessert territories- that Unitarian perspective of the progress was the only way out for local elites to share the welfare of the most powerful member of the federation, namely Buenos Aires.[69]

This was how the first Penal Code, based on the modified Tejedor Draft, was finally enacted in December 1886 and came into effect in 1887. However, the clamorous differences, the so-called "legal monstrosities" persisted for a long time after that. When the Minister of Justice had claimed against that problem, he did not take into account the ostensible fact that by the time, before 1886, most of the provinces had already adopted the same text as provincial penal code. This may indicate two important notes to underline:

(A) The first Argentinean Penal Codification did not proceed like a top-down imposition of common standards as usually happened in other coding experiences. On the contrary, it only became possible once the provinces had adopted as local law the draft that would be later enacted by the National Congress. For this reason we may suggest that it was a codification enshrined from the bottom.

(B) The fact that the differences had persisted after the enforcement of the national penal code, confirms that the national penal codification was a necessary condition, but not a sufficient one, in order to achieve the sought-after legal unity.

The second point compels us to look at under the surface of the formal substantive law. It is a common place to say that the substantive penal law does not "touch the accused" as yes it does it the procedural law.[70] We also know that the normative senses are not set in the textual formulations of the principles and rules but in their interpretation.[71] Therefore, the way in which criminal justice is/was carried out does not depend as much as on the penal code but on the interpretative

---

[68]*Fragmento de la 20° sesión de prórroga del 25 de Noviembre de 1886.* En Aguirre, J, *Código Penal de la República…*, prologo, p. XLII.

[69]On the convergence of provincial elite's interests in the nation state building in this context, see Botana, Natalio, *El orden conservador. La política argentina entre 1880 y 1916*, 2da ed., (Buenos Aires, 1985), pp. 85 ss.

[70]The German jurist Ernst von Beling said that the penal law "does not touch even a hair of the defendant, as yes it does it the procedural law". Nuñez, Ricardo. *Manual de Derecho Penal.* Pate General, (Córdoba, Lerner 1999), p. 18.

[71]Garriga, Carlos, "Continuidad y Cambio del Orden Jurídico", en, *Historia y Constitución. Trayectos del constitucionalismo hispano*, (Garriga, Carlos coord.) (México, Instituto Mora-CIDE, 2010), p. 60.

praxis determined by the procedural law and the courts systems. These latter elements, according to the Argentinean "mixed system", remained within the scope of the provincial powers, alongside with other powerful device for the social control of subaltern population: the contraventions issued by the police regulations of the provinces.[72]

Moreover, according to the Constitution and to the Federal Justice Act of 1863, the application of the national codes by the provincial courts was explicitly out of the list of "federal issues" in which the National Supreme Court could act as court of last resort.[73] Consequently, the observance of the national substantive codes in Argentina depended on the willingness of the provincial governments to establish adequate courts systems and good procedural laws. In some way, one could think that the old tradition according to which the general standards had to pass by the interpretative filter of the local jurisdictions was still in mind.[74] Let us add that in 1865 the provinces had rejected the proposal from the National Government to enact a common procedural code for criminal justice, arguing that it was against their local customs, that affected their autonomy, and that it was even contrary to the "nature of things".[75] This argument shows the naturalized tenor of the localization of jurisdictional powers.[76]

By the last decades of the nineteenth century, there was in Argentina a national codification without any centralized instance to watch out for the respect and right understanding of the national codes. It would still take a long time to create a mechanism for harmonizing the way of carrying out criminal justice in the

---

[72]Zaffaroni has recently called attention upon the importance of contraventions for social control, remarking on the lack of studies on this repressive device and the lack of interest from the penal sciences on this issue. Zaffaroni, R. Eugenio (2015), "La importancia de la mirada histórica para la investigación y la enseñanza del derecho penal en la Argentina". *Working paper delivered at the Seminario Historia del Ordenamiento Jurídico-Penal en América Latina. Aproximaciones históricas y conceptuales*, (Frankfurt am Main, Max Planck Institute For European Legal History, July 2015).

[73]Carrió, Genaro and Carrió, Alejandro, *El Recurso Extraordinario por Sentencia Arbitraria*, (Buenos Aires: Abeledo-Perrot, 1995), p. 23.

[74]For this argument, Agüero, Alejandro. Law and criminal justice in the Spanish colonial order: the problematic enforcement of the legality principle in the early criminal law in Argentina. In *From the Judge's Arbitrium to the Legality Principle. Legislation as a Source of Law in Criminal Trials*. (Berlin, Ed. Duncker & Humblot GmbH. 2013), pp. 229–252.

[75]Levaggi, Abelardo, La codificación del procedimiento criminal en la Argentina en la segunda mitad del siglo XIX. In *Revista de Historia del Derecho N° 11*. (Buenos Aires, INHIDE. 1983), p. 131.

[76]Agüero, Alejandro, "Local Law and Localization of Law. Hispanic legal tradition and colonial culture (16th–18th centuries)", in, *Spatial and Temporal Dimensions for Legal History: Research experiences and Itineraries*, (Massimo Meccarelli – Julia Solla Sastre eds.), (Frankfurt am Main, Max Planck Institute for European Legal History, 2016), pp. 101–129.

provinces. The National Supreme Court assumed this function casuistically. Broadening its competence, the Court began to admit an extraordinary action against "arbitrary sentences", as a last resort for cases involving, among other reasons, manifest violations to the substantive codes by the provincial courts.[77]

For all this reasons, we can suggest that the enforcement of the first national penal code (1887) and its subsequent reforms and replacement (1906, 1916, and 1921) are not the end but the beginning of a truly history of the criminal codification in Argentina. We need to know what happened in the daily work of provincial courts. Otherwise, we shall keep moving in the field of the formal history of law. We know that, even today, there are crass divergences in the interpretation of the current penal code in the different provinces. The "legal monstrosities" are still alive.

The province of Córdoba enacted its first procedural penal code in November 1887, based on the national one passed the same year. The authors of the draft, Dr. Ibañez and Dr. Bialet Massé, expressed that the still current Spanish procedural laws were contradictory in many aspects with the Constitution, compelling the judges to use their prudential discretion. The same argument that had been in the air for years with relationship to the penal code itself. The provincial procedural code was modified two year later, in 1889, because of the "shortcomings observed in the judicial praxis", as the Governor expressed it in his message to the legislature.[78]

At this moment, we do not have enough archive evidence to measure the incidence of both the national penal code and the provincial procedural code in the judicial praxis of Córdoba during the last decade of the 19th century. For what we have been able to see until now, it seems that ostensible changes in the daily praxis responded much more to the last reform of the procedural law than to the previous enforcing of the national penal code. However, we are still working in order to confirm this hypothesis.

7 Conclusions

If we were allowed to utter a counterfactual assertion, we could suggest that if the Spanish Empire had not fallen in 1808, the reform of the criminal laws in its former dominions would have followed the gradual process proposed by the 18th century's moderate reformers like Lardizabal. Al least, this could have been the case of the provinces of Rio de la Plata.

The experience of the criminal codification in Argentina tells us about the syncretic, gradual and progressive character with which the ideology of codification

[77]Carrió, Genaro and Carrió, Alejandro, *El Recurso Extraordinario…* Cit. Also, Zavalía, Clodomiro, *Historia de la Corte Suprema de Justicia de la República Argentina en relación con su modelo Americano.* (Buenos Aires, Talleres "Casa Jacobo Peuser, 1920).

[78]Mensaje del gobernador de la Provincia al abrirse las sesiones legislativas de 1890. *Compilación de leyes, decretos y demás disposiciones de carácter público.* Tomo 15. 1890, pp. 55–56.

was assimilated into the legal culture of a country emerged from the colonial collapse. That ideology was neither a priority nor even a goal of the revolutionary elite at the beginning of the emancipation process. Even when it was mentioned by the decade of 1820 in Buenos Aires, it was not until the second half of the 19th century -once the old provinces concurred into a nation making process- when the ideal of coding the law became a real goal of national policy.

Once assumed the need of codification, the coding process had to face the persistence of traditional elements such as the normative pluralism and the judicial discretion that were not easy to deal with, as they reinforced each other. On the other hand, the peculiar hybridism of the constitutional "mixed system" added a note of complexity. For political circumstances, Argentina was one of the latest countries of the region in passing a penal code. Zaffaroni has noted that the delay also shows that the national penal code was not necessary for the social control exerted by local elites.[79] Things seem to have changed twenty years later, when a national elite conformed by provincial elements too, undertook the task of the state building adopting a Unitarian perspective of progress and development. In this context, homogenizing the law became an urgent goal for the national policy.

The first national penal code was passed in December of 1886 -twenty year later than the first Draft had been submitted to the Congress. Besides the delay and the two competing drafts, one striking feature of the Argentinean criminal law codification is the criterion that determined which draft should be the base for the national code. It was not a matter of technical regards. It was the consummate fact that the overwhelming majority of the provinces had adopted one of the two draft as local penal code. In this sense, it was not a top-down imposition of a common law but a codification enshrined from the base. For this reason, it is important to remark on the provincial dimension of this history.

The study of the case of Córdoba has helped us to understand the way in which the daily justice administration gradually encompassed the codification process. At first, they used the drafts as if they were current law. Then, the adoption of the provincial penal code did not involve making a clean sweep of the past; rather it coexisted with other standards such as the Rural Code, the Law of cattle rustling and the old Spanish legislation. The code was never assumed as repealing the preexisting laws. On the other hand, the national codification did not achieve the sought after legal uniformity. Our provisional observations at the archive indicate that it was necessary the procedural law reform to change the judicial praxis. We need further investigations focused on the provincial courts activity to figure out the pace in which the national penal codification took real effect in the whole country.

From the point of view of the substantive law, as the first penal code was an old draft by the time of its enactment, new reforms became necessary in the short term. It was not until 1921 that Argentina had a national penal code at the level of the criminal law developments of the time. It has been in force until the present, despite

[79]Zaffaroni, Eugenio, *"La importancia de la mirada histórica para la investigación y la enseñanza del derecho penal*...cit., p. 2.

a huge amount of reforms and spare criminal laws. Since the decade of the 1940',[80] a "dogmatic penal science" fueled by university scholars- much of them also magistrates and lawyers- works for the right interpretation of the penal code and the respect of the constitutional guarantees. Putting aside the periods of de facto governments, that task is becoming everyday harder due to the increasing trend to enact spare penal laws for whatever social problem that politicians have to deal with, distorting the systematic of the penal code.

References

Agüero, Alejandro, *Castigar y perdonar cuando conviene a la República. La justicia penal de Córdoba del Tucumán, siglos XVII y XVIII,* (Madrid. Centro de Estudios Políticos y Constitucionales. 2008).

Agüero, Alejandro, "Formas de continuidad del orden jurídico. Algunas reflexiones a partir de la justicia criminal de Córdoba (Argentina), primera mitad del siglo XIX", in *Nuevo Mundo Mundos Nuevos.* (2010), (Available at http://nuevomundo.revues.org/59352).

Agüero, Alejandro, (2011) Tradición jurídica y derecho local en época constitucional: El "Reglamento para la Administración de justicia y policía en la campaña" de Córdoba, 1856". *Rev. hist. derecho* [online]. Nº.41, (Buenos Aires, 2011), pp. 1–43. Available at: http://www.scielo.org.ar/scielo.php?script=sci_arttext&pid=S1853-17842011000100001.

Agüero, Alejandro. "Law and criminal justice in the Spanish colonial order: the problematic enforcement of the legality principle in the early criminal law in Argentina". In *From the Judge's Arbitrium to the Legality Principle. Legislation as a Source of Law in Criminal Trials.* (Berlin, Ed. Duncker & Humblot GmbH. 2013), pp. 229–252.

Agüero, Alejandro and Lorente, Marta, "Penal enlightenment in Spain: from Beccaria's reception to the first criminal code", in *The Spanish Enlightenment Revisited,* (Jesús Astigarraga ed.), (Oxford, The Voltaire Foundation of Oxford University. 2015), pp. 235–264.

Agüero, Alejandro, "Local Law and Localization of Law. Hispanic legal tradition and colonial culture (16th–18th centuries)", in, *Spatial and Temporal Dimensions for Legal History: Research experiences and Itineraries,* (Massimo Meccarelli – Julia Solla Sastre eds.), (Frankfurt am Main, Max Planck Institute for European Legal History, 2016), pp. 101–129.

Agüero, Alejandro, Ancient Constitution or Paternal Government? Extraordinary Powers as Legal Response to Political Violence (Río De La Plata, 1810–1860). (Agüero, Alejandro) (Max Planck Institute for European Legal History Research Paper Series, No. 2016-10. 2016.) (Available at SSRN: https://ssrn.com/abstract=2841769).

Aguirre, Julián, *Código Penal de la República Argentina,* (Buenos Aires: Ed. Félix Lajouane. 1887).

Alberdi, Juan B., *Bases y puntos de partida para la organización política de la República Argentina.* (Buenos Aires. "La Nueva Cultura Argentina". 1915).

Barreneche, Osvaldo, *Dentro de la ley, todo. La justicia criminal en buenos aires en la etapa formativa del sistema penal moderno de la Argentina,* (Buenos Aires, Ediciones al margen. 2001).

[80]We can consider the issuing of the Treaty of Criminal Law by Sebastian Soler as the first step in order to create a dogmatic science in Argentina. See Soler, Sebastián, [1940,] *Derecho Penal Argentino,* 5ta ed. 10ª reimpresión, (actualizado por Guillermo Fierro), (Buenos Aires, Tipográfica Editora Argentina, 1992), pp. V–X.

Botana, Natalio, *El orden conservador. La política argentina entre 1880 y 1916, 2da ed.*, (Buenos Aires, 1985).

Caroni, Pio, *Lecciones catalanas sobre la historia de la codificación*. (Trad. Aquilino Iglesias Ferreirós.) (Madrid: Ed. Marcial Pons. 1996).

Caroni, Pio, *Escritos sobre la Codificación*, (Madrid: Universidad Carlos III. 2012).

Carrió, Genaro, and Carrió, Alejandro, *El recurso extraordinario por sentencia arbitraria: en la jurisprudencia de la Corte Suprema*, (Buenos Aires. Abeledo-Perrot, 1995).

Chiaramonte, José C., *Raíces históricas del federalismo latinoamericano* (Buenos Aires: Sudamericana, 2016).

Clavero, Bartolomé "La idea de código en la Ilustración jurídica", in *Historia, instituciones*, (documentos, nº 6. 1979).

Garriga, Carlos, "Continuidad y Cambio del Orden Jurídico", en *Historia y Constitución. Trayectos del constitucionalismo hispano,* (Garriga, Carlos coord.), (México, Instituto Mora-CIDE, 2010) pp. 59–106.

Garriga, Carlos, Slemian, Andréa, "Em trajes brasileiros": justiça e constituição na América ibérica (c. 1750–1850), *Revista de história são paulo*, Nº 169, (JULHO / DEZEMBRO 2013), pp. 181–221.

Donlan, Patrick and Heirbaut, Dirk (eds.), *The Law's Many Bodies. Studies in Legal Hybridity and Jurisdictional Complexity, c. 1600–1900,* (Berlin, Duncker & Humblot, 2015).

Duve, Thomas, "¿Del absolutismo ilustrado al liberalismo reformista? La recepción del Código penal Bávaro de 1813 de Paul J. A. von Feuerbach en Argentina y el debate sobre la reforma del derecho penal hasta 1921", En *Revista de historia del Derecho*, Nº 27, (Buenos Aires, Tau Anzoátegui, Víctor. 1999) , pp. 125–152.

Goldman, Noemí (dir.), *Revolución, República, Confederación. Nueva Historia Argentina,* vol. III, 2 ed., (Buenos Aires. Ed. Sudamericana. 2005).

Kroppenberg, Inge and Linder, Nikolaus, Coding the Nation. Codification History from a (Post-) Global Perspective, in *Entanglements in Legal History: Conceptual Approaches*, (Tomas Duve ed.), (Frankfurt, Max Planck Institute for European Legal History, 2014), pp. 67–99.

Laplaza, Francisco, "El proceso histórico de la codificación penal argentina", en *Revista de Historia del Derecho "Ricardo Levene",* Nº 21, (Buenos Aires, Imprenta de la universidad, 1978), pp. 59–92.

Lardizábal y Uribe, Manuel. *Discurso sobre las penas contraído a las leyes criminales de España para facilitar su reforma,* (Madrid, Imp. Joaquín Ibarra. 1782).

Levaggi, Abelardo, (1978), *Historia del Derecho Penal Argentino*, (Buenos Aires Perrot, 1978).

Levaggi, Abelardo, "La codificación del procedimiento criminal en la Argentina en la segunda mitad del siglo XIX." In *Revista de Historia del Derecho Nº 11*. (Buenos Aires. INHIDE. 1983).

Levaggi, Abelardo, *El derecho Penal Argentino en la Historia*, (Buenos Aires: Eudeba. 2012).

Lorente, Marta (coord.), *De justicia de Jueces a Justicia de leyes: hacia la España de 1870*, (Madrid, Consejo General del Poder Judicial. 2007).

Melo, Carlos R., *Constituciones de la Provincia de Córdoba*, (Córdoba: Imprenta de la Universidad Nacional de Córdoba. 1950).

Moreno, Rodolfo, *El Código Penal y sus antecedentes*. (Buenos Aires: T. I. Editor H. A. Tommasi. 1922).

Myers, Jorge, *Orden y Virtud. El discurso republicano en el régimen rosista*, (Buenos Aires. 1995).

Nuñez, Ricardo. *Manual de Derecho Penal. Pate General*, (Córdoba, Lerner. 1999).

Romano, Silvia, "Instituciones coloniales en contextos republicanos: los jueces de la campaña cordobesa en las primeras décadas del siglo XIX y la construcción del estado provincial autónomo", en *Revolución. Política e ideas en el Río de la Plata durante la década de 1810*, (Fabián Herrero comp.) (Buenos Aires Ediciones Cooperativas, Colección: Politeia de Ciencias Sociales. 2004).

Romano, Silvia, "Las nuevas fuentes de legitimación del poder y sus protagonistas en la configuración del sistema republicano y representativo en la provincia de Córdoba (1821–1855)", en *Córdoba Bicentenaria. Claves de su historia contemporánea.* (César Tcach coord) (Córdoba. Editorial de la UNC - CEA, 2010). pp. 15–35.

Ruiz Moreno, Isidoro, *El derecho penal en la República Argentina,* (Paraná: Ed. Gutemberg. 1898).

Salvatore, Ricardo, *Wandering Paysanos. State order and subaltern experience in Buenos Aires during the Rosas era,* (Durham y London. Duke University Press, 2003).

Scandellari, Simonetta, "La difusión del pensamiento criminal de Gaetano Filangieri en España", in *Nuevo Mundo Mundos Nuevos*, (Puesto en línea el 28 janvier 2007).(Available at: http:// nuevomundo.revues.org/index3484.html).

Sedeillan, Gisela, *La justicia penal en la provincia de Buenos Aires*, (Buenos Aires, 1ª ed., Biblos, 2012).

Sodero, Bladimiro, *Código Rural de la Provincia de Córdoba*, (Córdoba: Marcos Lerner. 1983).

Soler, Sebastián, [1940] *Derecho Penal Argentino, 5ta ed. 10ª reimpresión*, (actualizado por Guillermo Fierro), (Buenos Aires, Tipográfica Editora Argentina, 1992).

Tarello, Giovanni, *Storia della cultura giuridica moderna. Assolutismo e codificazione del diritto.* (Bologna. Il Mulino. 1976).

Tarello, Giovanni, *Le ideologie della codificazione nel secolo XVIII*, (Génova: ECIG. 1976).

Tarello, Giovanni, *Cultura jurídica y política del derecho*, (México: Fondo de Cultura Económica, 1995).

Tau Anzoátegui, Víctor, *La codificación en la Argentina (1810–1870). Mentalidad social e ideas jurídicas*, (Buenos Aires: Perrot. 1977).

Tau Anzoategui, Víctor. *Casuismo y sistema. Indagación histórica sobre el espíritu del Derecho Indiano.* (Bueno Aires. Instituto de Investigaciones de Historia del Derecho, 1992).

Tejedor, Carlos, *Curso de Derecho Criminal, Parte Primera*, (Buenos Aires. Imprenta Argentina. 1860).

Vivas, Mario Carlos, "El proyecto nacional de 1881 como Código Penal de la Provincia de Córdoba", en *Revista de Historia del Derecho*, Núm. 4, (Buenos Aires: Instituto de Investigaciones de Historia del Derecho. 1976). pp. 305–323.

Yangilevich, Melina, "Leyes antiguas para un estado moderno. Prácticas jurídicas en la provincia de Bueno Aires durante el período de la codificación", En *Justicia y Fronteras. Estudios sobre historia de la justicia en el Rio de la Plata. Siglo XVI-XIX.* (Darío Barriera compilador) (Murcia, ediciones de la universidad de Murcia. 2009). pp. 205–223.

Zaffaroni, Eugenio, Alagia, Alejandro and Slokar, Alejnadro, *Derecho Penal – Parte General,* 2da ed., (Buenos Aires, Ediar. 2002).

Zaffaroni, Eugneio and Corxatto, Guido, "El pensamiento penal en el derecho penal argentino", *in Rechtsgeschichte Legal History, nº 22.* (2014).

Zaffaroni, R. Eugenio, "La importancia de la mirada histórica para la investigación y la enseñanza del derecho penal en la Argentina". Working paper delivered at the Seminario *Historia del Ordenamiento Jurídico-Penal en América Latina. Aproximaciones históricas y conceptuales,* (Frankfurt am Main. Max Planck Institute For European Legal History. 2015).

Zavalía, Clodomiro, *Historia de la Corte Suprema de Justicia de la República Argentina en relación con su modelo Americano.* (Buenos Aires. Talleres "Casa Jacobo Peuser. 1920).

Alejandro Agüero teaches legal history at the National University of Córdoba (Argentina). From 2007, he is scientific researcher of the National Council for Scientific and Technical Research (CONICET) of Argentina. He has been professor of legal history and history of constitutionalism at the Universidad Autónoma de Madrid (2001–2006). His major research interests concern history of criminal justice administration, constitutional history, and the history of the state building process in Argentina. Currently he leads a research project on this issue, titled "Legal tradition and political discursivity in the 19th century. The emergence of a "state culture". Río de la Plata—Argentina, 1808–1910", supported by the National Agency for Scientific Promotion (Argentina), PICT 2014/3408 (2015–2018). He was awarded with the international prize to the best work on colonial law for his book on colonial criminal justice (Castigar y perdonar cuando conviene a la República. La justicia penal de Córdoba de Tucumán, siglos XVII y XVIII, Madrid, 2008). His recent relevant articles include "On Justice and "Home Rule" Tradition in the Spanish Colonial Order", in Quaderni Fiorentini, n. XLI, 2012; "Law and criminal justice in the Spanish colonial order: the problematic enforcement of the legality principle in the early criminal law in Argentina", in Georges Martyn, Anthony Musson, Heikki Pihlajamäki (eds.) From the Judge's Arbitrium to the Legality Principle. Legislation as a Source of Law in Criminal Trials, Berlin, 2013; (with Marta Lorente) "Penal enlightenment in Spain: from Beccaria's reception to the first criminal code", in Jesús Astigarraga (ed.), The Spanish Enlightenment Revisited, The Voltaire Foundation of Oxford University, Oxford, 2015; "Local Law and Localization of Law. Hispanic legal tradition and colonial culture (16th–18th centuries)", in Massimo Meccarelli—Julia Solla Sastre (eds.), Spatial and Temporal Dimensions for Legal History: Research experiences and Itineraries, Max Planck Institute for European Legal History, Frankfurt am Main, 2016.

Matías Jorge is assistant Professor of Argentinian legal history at the Facultad de Derecho de la Universidad Nacional de Córdoba (Argentina), Virtual Professor of Argentinian History of Law in Universidad Empresarial Siglo XXI, Córdoba (Argentina) and Professor of Argentinian legal history at the Universidad Empresarial Siglo XXI, Córdoba (Argentina). He studied Law at the Universidad Nacional de Córdoba (Argentina), a European Master in "Storia e comparazione delle istituzioni politiche e giuridiche dei paesi dell'Europa mediterranea", Universidad de Messina (Italy). He is currently a Ph.D. Candidate at the Universidad Nacional de Córdoba. He is scientific researcher of the Secretaría de Ciencia y Técnica (SeCyT). His major research interests concern history of criminal justice administration and history of Criminal law codification. He has published some boos reviews—e.g. Abelardo Levaggi's book, "El derecho penal argentino en la historia", published by Eudeba, Buenos Aires, 2012, in Revista de Historia del Derecho, 44, 2012—and an article entitled "Codificación Penal Provincial. Aplicación del Código Penal de la Provincia de Córdoba (1883–1886)", Prologos, Revista de historia, política y sociedad, Universidad Nacional de Lujan (forthcoming). He participates in a research project on the "Ideas jurídicas y religión en la Universidad de Córdoba (1808–1853): clérigos y juristas para justificar el orden nuevo", led by Marcela Aspell and coordinated by Esteban Llamosas.

From Free Will to Social Defense (or from Cesare Beccaria to Cesare Lombroso): Julio Herrera and the Criminal Law Codification in Argentina (1903–1922)

Jorge A. Núñez

I believe that [...] our Criminal Code is one of the worst codes in the world and is in desperate need of reform, not a partial but a full, fundamental, all-encompassing reform, from the definition of offense to that of punishment, consistent with the significant advancements in the field of criminal science, the science which has undergone the most transformations in the last third of the previous century.[i]

...it is a great honor for us, the Argentine people, to have approved a code that compares or even surpasses the most remarkable proposals drafted as of late, suiting the most demanding requirements of modern criminal science, and that [...] will be a true homage to our nation's juristic culture. Such honor falls mainly upon the noted criminal law jurist who drafted the proposal, Rodolfo Moreno, upon the patriotic, erudite members of the legislative committees for devoting all their knowledge and efforts to studying it and, last but not least, upon our Honorable Congress for approving it.[ii]

Abstract This paper aims to scrutinize the views of Julio Herrera—one of the most prominent Argentine criminal law jurists of the first half of the 20th century, oddly overlooked by legal historiography—on two criminal codes. First, in 1903, before his fellow senators, Herrera harshly questioned the code in force at the time (styled

[i]*Discurso pronunciado por el Senador Don Julio Herrera en la discusión del proyecto sobre reforma al Código Penal*, (Buenos Aires, El Comercio, 1903), pp. 3–4.

[ii]*Conferencias pronunciadas los días 28 de Junio y 4 de Julio por el Dr. Julio Herrera. Facultad de Derecho y Ciencias Sociales*, (Buenos Aires, s/e, 1922), p. 48.

J. A. Núñez (✉)
CONICET (Consejo Nacional de Investigaciones Científicas y Tecnológicas),
Buenos Aires, Argentine Republic
e-mail: jorgealber75@gmail.com

J. A. Núñez
INHIDE (Instituto de Investigaciones de Historia del Derecho),
Buenos Aires, Argentine Republic

A. Masferrer (ed.), *The Western Codification of Criminal Law*, Studies in the History of Law and Justice 11, https://doi.org/10.1007/978-3-319-71912-2_12

"Tejedor Code" after its author) for being based on the ideas of the Classical School of Criminology and suggested a complete overhaul. Some years later, in 1922, in a series of lectures delivered in Buenos Aires and Córdoba, he praised the criminal code then in force—approved a year earlier—in which he noticed the influence of the new ideas of the Italian Positivist School and the German Criminal Policy doctrine. Despite giving a favorable opinion on the code's general part, he strongly criticized many of its specific sections. We believe that an analysis of Herrera's remarks before the Senate, in his lectures at the two most prominent law schools in the country, as well as those views contained in his written work, especially La reforma penal, published in 1911, will provide us with some insight on the prevailing ideology at the time, the foreign influences, discussions and transformations Criminal Law in Argentina was subject to during the first decades of the 20th century.

1 Introduction

This paper follows a line of research centered upon the analysis of a set of ideas and practices promoted by a group of Argentine jurists and penitentiarists from 1890 to 1955.[1]

Such ideas and practices can be found in the management of correctional facilities (the Penitenciaría Nacional and the Presidio de Ushuaia, symbols of the Argentine prison reform); in Criminal Law academic courses; in the holding of conferences (such as the First National Prison Congress, held in Buenos Aires in 1914); in doctoral theses on prison matters; in the publication of specialized journals (*Revista Penitenciaria* and *Revista Penal y Penitenciaria* among others) and in the work carried out in Congress.

In this paper, we will analyze the involvement of Julio Herrera, one of Argentina's most distinguished criminal law jurists of the first half of the 20th century, who has oddly not been paid much attention by legal historiography.

In 1903, before his fellow senators, Herrera questioned a proposal that introduced a series of amendments to the existing criminal code, underscoring the need to reform it completely to make it more consistent with popular new ideas on criminal law. Even though his proposal failed to gain support and such questioned amendments were introduced a year later through Law number 4189, the Executive formed a committee to draft a new criminal code reform proposal, finally submitted in 1906.

[1]A line of investigation I am pursuing within CONICET and in two collective projects: the *Revista de Historia de las Prisiones*-http://www.revistadeprisiones.com and the *Criminología Argentina* collection, which reissues rare classic writings of local criminology with accompanying preliminary research to provide context on the author and the work, with six volumes published to date.

This new proposal was also harshly criticized by Herrera in a book called *La reforma penal*, published in 1911. Herrera's objections, raised both in the Senate and in his book, had a considerable influence on Rodolfo Moreno, the "father" of the criminal code approved in 1921. A year after that new code entered into force, Herrera gave a series of lectures at the Buenos Aires and Córdoba law schools in which he dissected the new legislation, praising its general part while harshly criticizing dozens of provisions (which had been taken from the 1906 proposal).

Thus, we believe that an analysis of such contributions by Julio Herrera will allow us to gain some insight into the prevailing ideology of the first decades of the 20th century in Argentina in connection with Criminal Law.

This paper is structured as follows: first, we will briefly introduce Julio Herrera, focusing on his administration as governor of Catamarca (a northwestern Argentine province). Then, we will examine the main aspects of the 1887 criminal code then under discussion and the most relevant points of Herrera's remarks before Congress in 1903. Finally, we will look at Herrera's objections to the 1906 proposal and his observations on the criminal code of 1921, which, albeit a few amendments, is the legislation currently in force in Argentina.

2 Biographical Facts About Julio Herrera

The son of Próspero Andrés Herrera and Azucena González, Julio Herrera was born in Catamarca on June 28, 1856, within a traditional *criollo* family.[2] He received his secondary education diploma at the age of fifteen from the Colegio Nacional de Catamarca.[3] Unexpected family circumstances—losing his father at a very young age—prevented him from pursuing higher education. This situation led Herrera, isolated from the main cultural hubs yet equipped with a high degree of self-discipline, to become a self-taught young man.

In 1874, at the age of 18, he was appointed clerk of the Federal Court presided over by Joaquín Quiroga, a notable jurist from the Argentine northwest with whom he developed a lasting friendship. According to the literature on the subject, this task aroused in Herrera an early fondness for the study of legal science.[4]

A few years later, he became involved in local politics when Governor José Dulce appointed him Minister of Treasury. In 1890, at the age of 34, he was elected to represent the province of Catamarca at the Argentine Chamber of Deputies,

[2]Marcelo Gershani Oviedo, "Notas sobre la ascendencia del Gobernador Julio Herrera" (unpublished conference).

[3]Armando Raúl Bazán, "Gobernador Julio Herrera: el hombre y su tiempo", in *Revista de la Junta de Estudios Históricos de Catamarca,* (Año XV, 2005–2006), p. 44.

[4]Bazán, "Gobernador Julio Herrera: el hombre y su tiempo", cit.

remaining in office for four years. Once his congressional term came to an end, he was appointed governor of his province for three years.[5]

The few pieces of research dealing with the life of Julio Herrera highlight his administration as governor of Catamarca. Here we will touch upon three aspects: (1) his progressive administration; (2) the emphasis laid on education; and (3) transformations brought about in the province's codification and constitution.

As for his administration, Herrera worked to bring electricity, street lighting and tap water to a large sector of the population, putting the needs of the underprivileged first, and enacted a law concerning land expropriation for public use. He also created the Office of Vital Records, established free access to public office, with good behavior and ability as the only requirements.[6] He also addressed the needs of the prison population, improving existing correctional facilities and building new ones, and put a religious congregation in charge of the women's prison.

Herrera's work in education was truly remarkable as well. Despite the province's continuous lack of resources, he created the City of Catamarca Public Library, known for its rich inventory.[7] He also founded the General Education Board, in charge of managing all schools, as "...free, public, basic education is a fundamental duty of governments and of the Argentine people as a whole, who are compelled to contribute to that effort," he stated.[8]

Concerned over a materialistic attitude spreading across Argentine society, Herrera fought the closing of educational facilities in his province and lack of concern over education. As part of his efforts, he doubled the number of students enrolled in schools compared to the previous administration. He thought that

[5]Some biographical facts on Julio Herrera can be found in: Cornelio Sánchez Oviedo, "Apuntes biográficos del Dr. Julio Herrera", en *Boletín de la Junta de Estudios Históricos de Catamarca*, (Catamarca, 1944), pp. 20–55, Soria, Manuel: *Fechas catamarqueñas*, (Catamarca, Propaganda, 1920); Ricardo Piccirilli & Francisco L. Romay, *Diccionario Histórico Argentino*, (Buenos Aires, Ediciones Históricas Argentinas, 1953); Vicente Cutolo, *Nuevo Diccionario biográfico argentino (1750–1930)*, (Buenos Aires, Ediciones Elche, 1978), and Diego Monllau, "La ley es el resorte del progreso de los pueblos": Julio Herrera: un hombre de convicción y principios", *La generación del Centenario y su proyección en el Noroeste argentino (1900–1950)*, (Tucumán, Fundación Miguel Lillo, 2000), pp. 240–252.

[6]Sánchez Oviedo, "Apuntes biográficos del Dr. Julio Herrera", cit.

[7]*Discurso pronunciado en la inauguración de la Biblioteca Provincial por el Gobernador Julio Herrera y el Presidente de la comisión de la misma Doctor Joaquín Quiroga* (*25 de mayo de 1895*), Catamarca, Publicación oficial, 1895, p. 2. Nowadays, the library bears his name: http://www.cultura.catamarca.gov.ar/index.php?option=com_content&view=article&id=95&Itemid=337

[8]*Discurso pronunciado en la inauguración de la Biblioteca Provincial por el Gobernador Julio Herrera y el Presidente de la comisión de la misma Doctor Joaquín Quiroga (25 de mayo de 1895*), (Catamarca, Publicación oficial, 1895), p. 2.

"Without civilization and freedom, all there is left are the brutal, servile, corrupted dregs of society, burdened by social squalor."[9]

During his term in office, Julio Herrera introduced long-lasting constitutional and legal reforms for his province. First of all, he advanced a constitutional reform which remained in force until 1965, being the longest standing constitution in the history of Catamarca. He extended the governor's term in office to four years, created the office of vice-governor and promoted administrative centralization and the submission of the municipal administration to the Executive, which was now charged with appointing municipal mayors, justices of the peace and district judges. In connection with legal reforms, he founded the Provincial Law School and drafted the Civil Code of Procedure, the Rural Code and the Police Code.

In 1897, upon the end of his term in office, he was appointed Supreme Court Justice for the province of Catamarca. Then, from 1898 to 1907, he served as senator for that province. In 1907, President José Figueroa Alcorta proposed him as candidate for president of the Court of Appeals for Criminal and Correctional matters of the Federal Capital, but Herrera turned it down, not wanting to access that privilege without a college degree.

Throughout the 1910s, he wrote a series of works of immense significance on the subject of criminal law. Prominent among them is *La reforma penal*, published in 1911, in which he scrutinizes the criminal code proposal submitted in 1906. In 1917, he also published *Anarquismo y Defensa Social*, which included a comprehensive outline of the evolution of the anarchist doctrine as well as the legal devices employed to fight it (Residency Act and Social Defense Act). During those years, he participated actively in several scholarly conferences, such as the National Prison Congress (1914) and the Congress of Social Sciences of the Americas (1916).

In 1922, following the approval of the new criminal code, Herrera gave a series of lectures at the University of Buenos Aires and the National University of Córdoba law schools. There, he offered a thorough analysis of the new criminal legislation.

On February 9, 1927, while traveling from Córdoba to Buenos Aires, Julio Herrera encountered death. In a series of heartfelt obituaries, the press commented on the late jurist's praiseworthy intellectual, moral and public qualities. The newspaper *La Nación* wrote that he was "both a prominent scholar of Criminal Law and a staunch soldier of the Republic".

Although Herrera is practically unknown to today's law historians (and positive law scholars), back in his time, however, he was praised by renowned jurists both local (Sebastián Soler, Eusebio Gómez, Osvaldo Magnasco, etc.) and foreign (Jiménez de Asúa and Enrico Ferri). His knowledge of legal matters was also appreciated by the political elite, including President Julio Argentino Roca and President Roque Sáenz Peña.

---

[9]*Discurso pronunciado en la inauguración de la Biblioteca Provincial por el Gobernador Julio Herrera y el Presidente de la comisión de la misma Doctor Joaquín Quiroga (25 de mayo de 1895)*, cit. On the increase in school enrollment rates, Bazán, Armando Raul: "Gobernador Julio Herrera: el hombre y su tiempo", cit.

In 1939, over ten years after Herrera's passing, a bill was brought before the Argentine Chamber of Deputies to increase his widow's pension. Alfredo Palacios, a distinguished leader of the Argentine Socialist Party and one of the promoters of the proposal, stated, "Herrera has been one of the most eminent men in the country due to his talent and virtues. He broke ground in this Senate by promoting new trends in criminal law that took hold in our country."[10] In the statement of motives, it was pointed out that "Herrera belonged [...] to a generation of productive men who had no other interest but the wellbeing of our nation, disdaining the allure of authority and the fascination of fortune [...] [Herrera] devoted his life to his nation and the science of law, and it is now our duty to pay tribute to him, affirming that, after Carlos Tejedor, he is the Argentine jurist who has gone the farthest into the depths of criminal law, quoting in his honor the following very appropriate statement by Von Ihering: a governor, a representative, a senator, a judge, a professor, a publicist, he died surrounded by the dignity of his poverty and the respect of his fellow citizens."[11]

3 The 1903 Criminal Code Reform. Previous Codes and Reform Proposals

The first criminal code proposal in Argentina was drafted in the early 1860s by *classical* jurist Carlos Tejedor. However, it was not until twenty years later that Congress finally approved it, not without some severe criticisms directed at it shortly after.[12]

By 1890, on the initiative of President Miguel Juárez Celman, a committee was established that proposed amendments to the code. The committee, composed of three distinguished jurists—Norberto Piñero, Rodolfo Rivarola and José Nicolás Matienzo-submitted the bill, which, after slowly progressing through different legislative bodies, was finally treated and approved by the Argentine Chamber of Deputies in September 1900. Once brought before the Senate, the Legislation Committee, made up of Carlos Pellegrini (senator for Buenos Aires), Dámaso Palacio (senator for Santiago del Estero), and Manuel Mantilla (senator for Corrientes), argued that its approval was a matter of urgency.

Among the arguments deployed by the Legislation Committee were the country's rapid growth (in terms of population and wealth), the existing legal voids, and

[10]Vicente Cutolo, *Nuevo Diccionario biográfico argentino (1750–1930)*, cit.

[11]Diego Monllau, "La ley es el resorte del progreso de los pueblos": Julio Herrera: un hombre de convicción y principios", cit.

[12]Zaffaroni and Arnedo argue that it is incorrect to speak of the "Tejedor bill" while the "Tejedor code" is an accurate statement, as the code was gradually and successively approved by most provinces—except for Córdoba-before being passed by the Argentine Congress. See Eugenio Zaffaroni & Miguel A. Arnedo, *Digesto de codificación penal argentina*, (Buenos Aires, AZ Editora, 1996), p. 123.

the rate at which crimes that the law had failed to contain or limit were being committed, all of which stressed the pressing need for the bill's approval.

The Committee further argued that it was imperative to: (a) tighten repression of punishable acts, considering the rate at which such actions were being perpetrated, enforcement actions under the existing code were inadequate when it came to preventing or lessening them, which made it necessary to leave judges ample room to adjust punishments or sentence times for each offense. Therefore, sentence times had to be conducive to preserving the order, restoring the rights violated by the offense in question, and maintaining the rule of justice over the social collective; (b) eliminating the concept of degrees of complicity and sentencing ranges, as it became necessary to increase punishment for accomplices, though not putting them on a par with principal perpetrators; (c) punishing *association*, the most effective and dangerous form of offense back then; (d) introducing the punishment of deportation for repeat offenders, i.e. segregating people with a marked tendency towards crime from populated areas; (e) removing the provisions from the Tejedor Code which established that recidivists were so deemed only if their repeat crimes were of the same kind; and, finally, (f) tightening punishment for excesses committed by striking workers-agitators who assaulted other workers who chose not to become involved in their struggle and protesters who disturbed public gatherings, religious or related ceremonies.

Once the main arguments were offered, an immediate approval was requested.

Then, Senator Julio Herrera asked for the floor to voice his opinion on the proposal, and, during sessions held on July 2nd, 4th and 11th of 1903, he cited an endless list of authors and foreign statutes in order to make it very clear that the proposal ought to be dismissed and that the criminal code had to be fully reformed, from the definition of offense to the concept of punishment. He also argued that, given its many amendments, the Tejedor Code had lost its essential core, becoming a collection of articles following seriously inconsistent criteria.

4 Julio Herrera's Criminal Code Reform Proposal

Herrera stated that the criminal code had to be completely overhauled in order to contribute to solving the criminal justice issue and become an effective tool in containing the increasing crime wave sweeping the country.

The first criticism was directed at the ideas behind the Tejedor Code, which reflected the state of the science before 1850, a period dominated exclusively and indisputably by the tenets of the *Classical School*. However, in 1876, following the publication of Cesare Lombroso's *Criminal Man*, "…the second great revolution in criminal law began, one of great significance, marking the beginning of a highly productive period in the legislative and scientific fields."[13]

---

[13]*Discurso pronunciado por el Senador Don Julio Herrera en la discusión del proyecto sobre reforma al Código Penal*, cit, p. 5.

For Herrera, even though the classical notion of offense—based on the principle of free will and its objective and factual qualities, ignoring the agent responsible for such offense—had been proven false, this idea was still present in the Tejedor Code, which stated that "…the factuality of the action is everything; the offender is disregarded as an unrelated factor, to the point in which his punishment has been established beforehand without even knowing him. The judge opens the code and determines the punishment. He has all the necessary elements: he does not need to know the criminal, his background or what has led him to such actions. It is true that a punishment so dictated will turn a first-time offender into a recidivist, corrupt the occasional offender, and put a defenseless society at the mercy of the incorrigible. But the punishment is fair and sufficient! The law, which aims at being equal for all, behind this purported equality, a merely formal equality, allows for the most brutal injustice!"[14]

For Herrera, social defense—i.e. society's right and responsibility to defend itself from any attackers to ensure its normal functioning—had to be the aim of the punishment, which also had to take the perpetrator into account (personal background, moral character, more or less dangerous nature, reasons for committing the crime, etc.). This new approach, which originated in Germany, was termed *Criminal Policy* and had achieved its ultimate recognition by being enshrined in the most advanced legislations around the world. Thus, "…the offender is no longer an abstraction, an algebraic quantity, but an actual being, with vices, passions, atavistic or morbid germs—with a soul, ultimately—who could, perhaps, be regenerated and whom the judge must get to know in order to apply the punishment he deserves as an individual."[15]

After expressing his overall objections to the Tejedor Code, Herrera moved on to give a thorough analysis of the proposal submitted by the Legislation Committee, stating that it ought to be completely dismissed as "…it does not tend towards individualizing the punishment, [which would foster] a more reasonable, humane, effective, moralizing justice system. […] Therefore, the Argentine criminal justice problem persists, and punishment will continue to be the same instrument of injustice, corruption and recidivism it has always been."[16]

4.1 Tightening of Punishment

With regard to imposing more severe punishments, Herrera argued that crime would not be reduced by adding a few years to prison sentences but by taking the

[14] *Discurso pronunciado por el Senador Don Julio Herrera en la discusión del proyecto sobre reforma al Código Penal*, cit, p. 14.

[15] *Discurso pronunciado por el Senador Don Julio Herrera en la discusión del proyecto sobre reforma al Código Penal*, cit, p. 9.

[16] *Discurso pronunciado por el Senador Don Julio Herrera en la discusión del proyecto sobre reforma al Código Penal*, cit, p. 45.

repressive legislation in a different direction to be more consistent with advancements made by developed countries in the field of criminal science. Herrera thought it necessary to introduce three principles into the new criminal code: (a) the individualization of punishment, (b) conditional release, and (c) conditional sentencing.

4.2 Individualization of Punishment, Conditional Release and Sentencing

Herrera claimed that, during the time in which the tenets of the *Classical School* were the dominant doctrine, punishments were abstractly and unfairly imposed, with all offenders being judged by the same standards without considering the nature and character of that person who had been driven to crime. Instead, Herrera thought that the aim of punishment could not be to counter the harm caused by the offense with another harm; it should serve a noble, deeper purpose, being an instrument for good, aiming at the offender's rehabilitation—whenever possible—and the protection of society at all times. Therefore, he advocated for the individualization of punishment, as an abstractly applied sentence could only lead to negative results, not only allowing for abusive actions by those who imposed that punishment for no other reason than to cause the offender suffering but also not bringing any benefits whatsoever to society.[17]

Conditional sentencing meant imposing punishment on law breakers without actually enforcing it during a so-called testing period. If, during such period, offenders maintained good behavior, that time was to be subtracted from their sentence. If they relapsed into crime, however, they were forced to serve both sentences combined. For Herrera, conditional sentencing represented the highest degree of individualization of the punishment and had already proven successful in more advanced countries.

As for conditional release, which had also proven successful in more developed countries, Herrera argued that it had to be implemented immediately, as the possibility of early release for convicts serving time in prison would act as an incentive for the rehabilitation of offenders. Unlike the irrevocable nature of the pardon contained in the Tejedor Code, conditional release would be granted provided that, in case of recidivism, second-offenders would have to serve a full sentence without subtracting the time served on conditional release. On the contrary, if they maintained good behavior, offenders could acquire the right to a definite release. In this scenario, no one but the offender would have an interest in maintaining good behavior, contributing to reduce levels of criminal recidivism, which used to occur during the first months following the release, prompted by difficulties in finding a job or occupation. Along the same lines, he drew attention to the role to be played

[17] *Discurso pronunciado por el Senador Don Julio Herrera en la discusión del proyecto sobre reforma al Código Penal*, cit, p. 47.

by associations for ex-offenders (*patronatos de liberados*) in providing those ex-offenders and their families with necessary resources.

4.3 Similar Punishment for Perpetrators and Accomplices

In connection with this point, Herrera began by arguing that "...the one principle in criminal law that has triumphantly prevailed over the centuries, outliving the most diverse civilizations, surviving through the deep revolution started by the great Beccaria and carried on today by the Positivist School, is that of imposing different punishments on perpetrators and accomplices. One fact that is strongly rooted in human consciousness—and we know that nothing takes root in the hearts of the people unless it is based on truth and justice—is the imposition of different punishments on participants in a crime."[18]

Herrera believed that this provision not only was in conflict with the criminal legislation but was also unpolitical, which is why he claimed that it sounded as if it had been suggested by the offenders themselves, offering an incentive to crime by making every gang member's wish come true: making the danger equal for everyone. The law needed to set the perpetrators apart from the accomplices, as their physical and moral nature, their character and passions, as well as the unequal, uneven danger their impunity would imply, drew a clear line between them. In response to the proposal made by the Legislation Committee—punishing attempted complicity even if not conducive to the commission of the crime—Herrera argued that complicity needed to be punished when it actually contributed to the success of the crime, claiming that punishing attempted complicity constituted a legal aberration.

4.4 Deportation of Repeat Offenders

Herrera criticized the use of deportation as a weapon to fight recidivism. He claimed that deportation was a "new, exotic form of punishment with no history in our legal system and a high cost," which had failed in every system where it was introduced and had even been suppressed by the despotic Russian regime. The 1890 proposal had adopted it when its effectiveness had yet to be assessed; however, fifteen years later, its usefulness could no longer be justified.

Deportees, he added, were lazy libertines, incompetent workers who would rather be subject to any punishment than having to humble themselves to a job. Besides, this punishment implied providing food, clothing, housing and watching

---

[18]*Discurso pronunciado por el Senador Don Julio Herrera en la discusión del proyecto sobre reforma al Código Penal*, cit, p. 54.

over deportees on land and water. Moreover, he questioned the geographical efficiency of Tierra del Fuego, where a correctional facility to house the most dangerous offenders was being built, as it was right next to the most populated area in Argentina and to the neighboring country of Chile.

In Herrera's opinion, the evil had to be nipped in the bud, in its causes and not in its effects. Thus, the main cause of recidivism was brought about by the inadequate prison system, in addition to the multiplicity of sentences (arrest, jail, prison, correctional facility), which, given the provinces' lack of funds, ended up being served all in the same facilities, housing "…thieves, murderers, political prisoners, petty offenders, detainees and even children."[19] Prisons, he claimed, were schools of crime, corruption and vice, where you came in an honest man, perhaps, but inevitably came out a recidivist doomed to a life of crime.

4.5 The Arbitrariness of the Judge

The last point in the proposal addressed by Herrera was the role the judge was expected to play in issuing a sentence. The proposal gave judges ample room to adjust punishment or sentence times for each offense by claiming mitigating and aggravating factors. Herrera thought this posed two problems: on the one hand, the category of mitigating and aggravating factors had to be removed, as it was impossible to outline them all. Besides, these factors were applied on a purely objective basis to all defendants, and were ultimately determined by the judge only, which is, supposedly, what was trying to be avoided. Finally, he pointed out that Argentine courts often took an arbitrary individualization approach, issuing completely unjustified acquittals or leaving crimes deserving a conviction unpunished.

Herrera concluded his long statement by saying that the proposal at hand had to be completely dismissed, deeming it unacceptable both in its overall concept and in its details. "Should that happen—and I do not hold my hopes high," he claimed, "I would propose submitting a request to the Executive to have a committee of notable criminal justice specialists appointed to draft a new criminal code proposal, based on the one drafted by Rivalora, Piñero and Matienzo, which has many useful provisions, […] on the one drafted by Mr. Segovia, which I assume to be quite good judging by its author's background, even though I am not acquainted with it, as well as on the latest European codes of law and […] on the many proposals drafted in almost every European country, all of which should make it quite easy to produce a solid criminal code."[20]

---

[19]*Discurso pronunciado por el Senador Don Julio Herrera en la discusión del proyecto sobre reforma al Código Penal*, cit, p. 85.

[20]*Discurso pronunciado por el Senador Don Julio Herrera en la discusión del proyecto sobre reforma al Código Penal*, cit, pp. 103–4.

As we know, Herrera's arguments failed to persuade legislators, who, influenced by the socio-political climate in Argentina (rise of anarchism within the labor movement, attacks and general strikes, etc.) and the high crime rates, voted with a sweeping majority in favor of the highly repressive proposal submitted by the Legislation Committee and passed through Law Number 4189.[21]

5 Julio Herrera and His Criticism of the 1906 Committee Proposal

Apparently, Herrera's strong objections to the 1903 proposal did not fall on deaf ears. Soon after, on December 19, 1904, President Manuel Quintana appointed a committee to draft a new criminal code proposal. Such committee was made up of jurists Rodolfo Rivarola, Norberto Piñero, Cornelio Moyano Gacitúa and Diego Saavedra, Federal Capital Chief of Police Francisco Beazley, Doctor José María Ramos Mejía, with José Luis Duffy (head of the Prison for the Prosecuted, a provisional correctional facility) as secretary. The bill was submitted on March 10, 1906. The Executive forwarded it to Congress for it to be properly treated, but it never was.

In 1911, Herrera released a book called *La reforma penal* in which he harshly questioned the 1906 proposal.[22] He claimed that it took a conservative approach, presenting a classical view of offense and punishment, based on retributive principles. Such a code, he thought, which ignores new trends in criminal science—although it adopted new principles such as conditional release and sentencing, it did not alter the core ideas—would not counter the threat of crime or properly contribute to fulfilling the country's aims.

The proposal considered crime only in its factual aspect, ignoring the character of its perpetrator. Under this conception, the punishment served purely expiatory purposes without aiming at moral rehabilitation or contributing to social and individual wellbeing.[23]

---

[21]Miguel Ángel Lancelotti, *La criminalidad en Buenos Aires, al margen de la estadística (1887 a 1912)*. (Buena Vista Editores, Córdoba, 2012) and Cornelio Moyano Gacitúa, *La delincuencia argentina ante algunas cifras y teorías* (Buena Vista Editores, Córdoba, 2012).

[22]Regarding this work, renowned criminal law specialist Juan P. Ramos claimed that "[…] it was the best, most comprehensive systematization of the most essential problems in criminal science published in Argentina," while Carlos Octavio Bunge pointed out that "…the most eminent and authoritative representative of criminal law in Argentina is Julio Herrera, the author of the very thorough and elaborate book *The Criminal Reform*." Cfr. Diego Monllau, "La ley es el resorte del progreso de los pueblos": Julio Herrera: un hombre de convicción y principios", cit, p. 248.

[23]*La reforma penal. Estudio de la parte general del proyecto de código penal redactado por los Dres. Saavedra, Beazley, Rivarola, Moyano Gacitúa, Piñero y Ramos Mejía. Principios fundamentales en que debe inspirarse. Por Julio Herrera. Ex Senador Nacional. Miembro de la Corte Suprema de Justicia de Catamarca. Con un prólogo del Dr. Osvaldo Magnasco* (Buenos Aires. Librería e Imprenta de Mayo. 1911).

While acknowledging the intellectual qualities of the members of the committee, Herrera believed that their juristic background prevented them from dismissing certain ideas they viewed as undisputed truths—the fact that offenders must be punished because they deserve to be, because they are morally guilty, because the absolute principle of duty is imposed on man and he is free to fulfill it, etc. Those were ideas they had been taught at university, which had been uttered by eminent scholars, which inspired many codes in the civilized world, which they had absorbed throughout the years. Thus, he pointed out that "...they forgot that such law had to apply to men who were radically different from each other, that criminal justice is relative and essentially practical and only pertains to actual facts and living realities."[24]

6 Remarks by Julio Herrera on the New Criminal Code Approved in 1921

In 1916, Representative Rodolfo Moreno found the proposal submitted by the Committee in 1906 and brought it before the Chamber of Deputies, which led to the establishment of a special committee that included the Radical Civic Union, the Socialist Party and the Conservative Party (the three parties represented in Congress).[25] He had previously conducted a survey among criminal law judges, professors and specialists to get their opinions on the proposed reform.

The final draft of the proposal by the Special Committee on Criminal and Correctional Legislation was written by Rodolfo Moreno, Antonio de Tomaso, Carlos M. Pradere, Gerónimo del Barco and Delfor del Valle. After being submitted to the Chamber of Deputies by Moreno, it was approved without discussion. It was delayed in the Senate, as the Codes Committee did not communicate its decision until 1920. After sending the bill back to the Chamber of Deputies, it was passed through Law Number 11179 on September 30, 1921.[26]

Scholars highlight the work of Moreno, who acted as compiler, systematizer and updater, pointing out that the new code did not fully adopt the dominant Italian

[24]Herrera supported his own arguments by explaining that great reformers had not been jurists- or at least not only jurists-and cited Beccaria, Bentham, Kant, Voltaire, Lombroso and Ferri as examples. Cfr. *La reforma penal. Estudio de la parte general del proyecto de código penal redactado por los Dres. Saavedra, Beazley, Rivarola, Moyano Gacitúa, Piñero y Ramos Mejía. Principios fundamentales en que debe inspirarse. Por Julio Herrera. Ex Senador Nacional. Miembro de la Corte Suprema de Justicia de Catamarca. Con un prólogo del Dr. Osvaldo Magnasco,* cit, p. 15.

[25]Eugenio R. Zaffaroni & Guido L. Croxatto, "El pensamiento alemán en el derecho penal argentino", in *Rechtsgeschichte Legal History,* (n° 22, 2014) pp. 192–212.

[26]Thomas Duve, "¿Del absolutismo ilustrado al liberalismo reformista? La recepción del Código Penal Bávaro de 1813 de Paul J. A. von Feuerbach en la Argentina y el debate sobre la reforma del Derecho penal hasta 1921", in *Revista de Historia del Derecho*, (Buenos Aires, 1999, n° 27), pp. 125–152.

Positivist School ideas, as it included three points more in line with the liberal ideology: (a) rejecting the death penalty; (b) establishing conditional sentencing; (c) avoiding a dangerousness-based approach.[27]

The criminal code entered into force on April 30, 1922. Shortly after, Julio Herrera was invited by the University of Buenos Aires School of Law to give two lectures on the newly-approved legislation.

There, he stated that the new code was one of the most advanced criminal codes in the world, marking the transition from the principle of free will to that of social defense. Punishment was no longer of an expiatory nature and now tended towards individualization—taking into account the agent who perpetrated the offense. In his exposition, Herrera detached himself from the determinism of the Italian Positivist School, considering his ideas to be closer to Von Liszt's Criminal Policy doctrine. So he outlined an action plan in order for the new code to solve the pressing problem of criminality. The plan consisted in (a) eliminating short prison sentences, which did not rehabilitate the offender but "contaminated" him, and proposed to replace sentences shorter than three months with a conditional release, a pardon, an admonition, a monetary fine or court-ordered job; (b) creating special facilities for young offenders, separate from adults; (c) focusing on the nature of the offender: occasional offender or permanent deviant; (d) establishing security measures for alcoholic, demented and degenerate convicts.[28]

Herrera classified offenders into four categories: young offenders, who had to be sent to juvenile detention centers; occasional offenders, who had to receive intimidation punishment without incarceration; offenders who showed an underlying immorality and could be rehabilitated through treatment based on a three-prong approach: employment, education, religion[29]; and incorrigible offenders, career criminals who had to be sent away for good (life imprisonment) for society's sake.[30]

Even though, as was previously stated, Herrera praised the general part of the new code, he also criticized some specific provisions quite sharply. He believed the fact that the general part had been drafted by Rodolfo Moreno while the specific sections had been hastily based on the 1906 proposal, which he had deeply

---

[27]Raúl Guillermo López Camelo & Gabriel Darío Jarque, *Curso de Derecho Penal. Parte General* (Bahía Blanca. Universidad Nacional del Sur, 2004).

[28]*Conferencias pronunciadas los días 28 de Junio y 4 de Julio por el Dr. Julio Herrera.* Facultad de Derecho y Ciencias Sociales, cit, p. 5.

[29]Herrera thought religion was, "…one of the most powerful factors in the reformation of criminals or, that is, the only one that prompts a full reformation. […] Only religion, going as deep as the consciousness, enlightening it, offering a glimpse into a new reality that ends the misery of earthly life to open the soul to endless horizons, can work the miracle of making vice loathly and virtue lovable. If this is is so, the teaching of religion must have a substantial place in any correctional facility, where all worship ceremonies must be conducted," cfr. *Conferencias pronunciadas los días 28 de Junio y 4 de Julio por el Dr. Julio Herrera.* Facultad de Derecho y Ciencias Sociales, cit. p. 5.

[30]*Conferencias pronunciadas los días 28 de Junio y 4 de Julio por el Dr. Julio Herrera.* Facultad de Derecho y Ciencias Sociales, cit. p. 5.

criticized, could account for this inconsistency. Moreover, he questioned the state of the prison system, which he called "an insult to civilization and good sense," suggesting the use of penal labor to build new correctional facilities, as was done in more developed countries.

A month later, at the University of Córdoba, he gave three lectures on the new code, thoroughly analyzing it section by section, highlighting mistakes and flaws that impaired its quality. Again, he praised the code, which was written in a clear language for everyone to understand, claiming it was "…excellent, even better than the 1921 Italian proposal", and drew attention to the new justification for punishment-social defense—as it contributed to a single objective: protecting society from the dangers of crime.[31]

7 Conclusions

This paper has been an attempt to shed light on the transformations criminal law codification in Argentina underwent during the first decades of the 20th century through the contributions made by Julio Herrera, a distinguished—yet overlooked by legal historiography-criminal law jurist, as a senator and an author.

Through Julio Herrera's perspective—a partial one, of course—we have gained insight into the transition from the supremacy of the Classical School ideas—retributive nature of punishment, free will, crime as a legal abstraction, etc.—to the partial dominance of principles formulated by the Italian Positivist School and the German Criminal Policy doctrine—social defense, individualization of punishment, reform and reeducation of offenders, incorrigibility, etc.

References

Baigún, David, "Ideas político-criminales del Código de 1921", in *Nueva Doctrina Penal* (Buenos Aires, 1997), pp. 3–32.

Bazán, Armando Raúl, "Gobernador Julio Herrera: el hombre y su tiempo", in *Revista de la Junta de Estudios Históricos de Catamarca* (Año XV, 2005–2006), pp. 43–49.

Bazán, Armando Raúl, *Historia de Catamarca* (Buenos Aires, Plus Ultra, 1996).

Caimari, Lila, "Ciencia y sistema penitenciario", in *Nueva Historia de la Nación Argentina.* (Buenos Aires, Planeta, 2001), pp. 471–496.

Caimari, Lila, "Entre el panóptico y el pantano: avatares de una historia de la prisión argentina", in *Política y Sociedad*, (volumen 46, n° 3, 2009), pp. 135–147.

[31]Julio Herrera, *El nuevo código penal. Conferencias pronunciadas en la Facultad de Derecho y Ciencias Sociales de la Universidad de Córdoba durante el mes de Octubre de* 1922, *a solicitud de sus autoridades* (Serie III, Volumen II, s/f/), p. 25.

Cesano, José Daniel, "Aproximación al encuadramiento ideológico de la legislación penitenciaria nacional: una perspectiva histórica", in *Horizontes y Convergencias. Lecturas Históricas y Antropológicas sobre el Derecho* (available in http://horizontesyc.com.ar/).

Cesano, José Daniel, "Notas para la comprensión de una hipótesis interpretativa sobre la libertad condicional (cuando desde la Historia de las Ideas se analiza el discurso jurídico), in *Horizontes y Convergencias. Lecturas Históricas y Antropológicas sobre el Derecho* (available in http:// horizontesyc.com.ar/).

Cesano, José Daniel, *En el nombre del orden. Ensayos para la reconstrucción histórica del control social formal en la Argentina* (Córdoba, Alveroni, 2005).

Conferencias pronunciadas los días 28 de Junio y 4 de Julio por el Dr. Julio Herrera (Facultad de Derecho y Ciencias Sociales. Universidad de Buenos Aires. Septiembre 1922).

Cutolo, Vicente, *Nuevo Diccionario biográfico argentino (1750–1930)* (Buenos Aires, Elche, 1978).

Discurso pronunciado en la inauguración de la Biblioteca Provincial por el Gobernador Julio Herrera y el Presidente de la comisión de la misma Doctor Joaquín Quiroga (25 de mayo de 1895), (Catamarca, Publicación oficial, 1895).

Discurso pronunciado por el Senador Don Julio Herrera en la discusión del proyecto sobre reforma al Código Penal, (Buenos Aires, El Comercio, 1903).

Duve, Thomas, "¿Del absolutismo ilustrado al liberalismo reformista? La recepción del Código Penal Bávaro de 1813 de Paul J. A. von Feuerbach en la Argentina y el debate sobre la reforma del Derecho penal hasta 1921", in *Revista de Historia del Derecho*, (Buenos Aires, 1999, n° 27), pp. 125–152.

Gershani Oviedo, Marcelo, "Notas sobre la ascendencia del Gobernador Julio Herrera" (unpublished conference).

Herrera, Julio, *El nuevo código penal. Conferencias pronunciadas en la Facultad de Derecho y Ciencias Sociales de la Universidad de Córdoba durante el mes de Octubre de 1922, a solicitud de sus autoridades* (Serie III, Volumen II, s/f/).

Levaggi, Abelardo, "Esbozo de las ideas penales argentinas en la década de 1890", in *Revista de Historia del Derecho "Ricardo Levene"*, (n° 30, Buenos Aires, 1995), pp. 233–241.

Levaggi, Abelardo, *Historia del Derecho Penal Argentino*, (Buenos Aires, Editorial Perrot. 1977).

Levaggi, Abelardo, *Las cárceles argentinas de antaño (Siglos XVIII y XIX). Teoría y realidad*, (Buenos Aires, Ad-Hoc, 2002).

Monllau, Diego, "La ley es el resorte del progreso de los pueblos": Julio Herrera: un hombre de convicción y principios", in AA.VV, *La generación del Centenario y su proyección en el Noroeste argentino (1900–1950)*, (Tucumán, Fundación Miguel Lillo, 2000).

Moreno, Rodolfo, *El código penal y sus antecedentes*, (Buenos Aires, H.A. Tomassi, 1922).

Piccirilli, Ricardo y Francisco L. Romay, *Diccionario Histórico Argentino* (Buenos Aires, Ediciones Históricas Argentinas, 1953).

Ramos, Juan P., *Concordancias del proyecto de código penal de 1917. Trabajos del curso de seminario de derecho penal de los años 1919 y 1920* (Buenos Aires, Ediciones de la Facultad de Derecho y Ciencias Sociales, 1921).

Sánchez Oviedo, Cornelio, "Apuntes biográficos del Dr. Julio Herrera", in *Boletín de la Junta de Estudios Históricos de Catamarca* (Catamarca, 1944), pp. 20–55.

Soria, Manuel, *Fechas catamarqueñas* (Catamarca, Propaganda, 1920).

Zaffaroni, Eugenio y Miguel A. Arnedo, *Digesto de codificación penal argentina*, (Buenos Aires, AZ, 1996).

Zimmermann, Eduardo, *Los liberales reformistas. La cuestión social en la Argentina 1890–1916* (Buenos Aires, Sudamericana, 1995).

Jorge A. Núñez has a doctoral degree in Law from the University of Valladolid (Spain), a Master's degree in Political Science from the Autonomous University of Madrid (Spain), and a degree in Secondary and Higher Education History Teaching from the University of Buenos Aires (Argentina). He is an assistant researcher at CONICET (National Scientific and Technical Research Council of Argentina), he was an associate researcher at the Max-Planck Institute for European Legal History (Frankfurt am Main, Germany) where he has done six research stays. He has been granted scholarships by the National Agency for Scientific and Technological Promotion-Argentina and the Ministry of Education of Argentina, as well as Fundación Carolina (Spain). His research focuses mainly on penitentiary reform in Argentina and Spain during the 1890–1955 period. He is co-director of the Revista de Historia de las Prisiones (Journal on the History of Prisons, www.revistadeprisiones.com) and of the Colección Criminología Argentina (Argentine Criminology collection), which has eight volumes so far. He has released over twenty five papers on penitentiary matters in both local and foreign publications. In 2014, he published his first book, Fernando Cadalso y la reforma penitenciaria en España (1883–1939) through Editorial Dykinson (Madrid). Together with co-author José Daniel Cesano, he published Visiones de la criminología argentina. Una aproximación historiográfica (1903–1924). He created the Jornadas de Jóvenes Investigadores en Historia del Derecho (Conferences for Young Researchers of Legal History), which has met uninterruptedly every year since 2009. He is secretary of the Instituto de Investigaciones de Historia del Derecho (Buenos Aires). He teaches Social History of Argentina at the University of Buenos Aires, School of Social Sciences.

The 1830 Criminal Code of the Brazilian Empire and Its Originality

Ignacio Maria Poveda Velasco and Eduardo Tomasevicius Filho

Abstract After the Independence in 1822, the newly created Brazilian Empire launched into building its legal framework. The 1824 Constitution, granted by Emperor D. Pedro I, established, as soon as possible, the enactment of a Civil and a Criminal code. The first one took nearly a century to come up, in 1916. The second one, the Criminal Code of the Empire, came into force in 1830, and was considered by scholars as the model of the Criminal Code in Latin America in the nineteenth century. Among the possible reasons for the speed of its draft and enactment, historians and jurists mention the rise of Beccaria's and Bentham's ideas that forced to replace the anachronistic homeland Criminal Law embodied in the Book V of the Philippines Ordinances. This quickly put the question to what extent the new law is an original creation or was mere use of ideas stemmed overseas. The studies for the preparation of a draft to be discussed by the National Assembly began in the first days of the legislative session of 1826. That year, José Clemente Pereira offered to the House of Representatives a kind of 'basis' for the Code draft, whose full text would be presented by him in 1827, some days after the proposal sent by Bernardo Pereira de Vasconcellos. The mentioned drafts were submitted for analysis of a Committee constituted by the House of Representatives, which left the text that came to be finally enacted in 1830. The scope of this paper is to investigate to what extent the Criminal Code of the Empire incorporated Bernardo Pereira de Vasconcellos' draft, as is often alleged, or to what extent it is the result of an innovative work of the House of Representatives' Committee. In addition to this goal, the other most important is presented: whether the 1830 Criminal Code was, as repeatedly stated, truly innovative or consisted only in the application of the ideas of the 1803 Austrian Code or the 1810 French Code. And yet, to what extent it would have been model for the 1848 Spanish Code, which is considered, in turn, the pattern of Latin American criminal law in the nineteenth Century.

I. M. Poveda Velasco · E. Tomasevicius Filho (✉)
University of São Paulo Law School, São Paulo, Brazil
e-mail: tomasevicius@usp.br

A. Masferrer (ed.), *The Western Codification of Criminal Law*, Studies in the History of Law and Justice 11, https://doi.org/10.1007/978-3-319-71912-2_13

1 Statements About the Brazilian Criminal Code of 1830

The rivalry between Brazil and Argentina is a long history and quite intense about a wide range of subjects. In 2013, the 'dispute' between Argentinians and Brazilians was about the election of the new Pope of the Catholic Church. When it comes to soccer, the rivalry, rather fierce, is about which of the two countries had the greatest player of all times, which team plays the most beautiful soccer, who has won more times the Libertadores Cup, or even who won the most World Cups titles. Tempers were even more tense in 2014, the year the World Cup was held in Brazil and 'los hermanos', a term used by Brazilians to refer to Argentines, tried to achieve three-time champions in Maracanã Stadium.

However, not all has been dispute between the two countries, and sometimes there has been some recognition of merit. Thus, in 1930, year of the first World Cup in Uruguay, the argentine Ladislau Thót, a professor at the National University of La Plata, Argentina, wrote a paper entitled 'The Brazilian Criminal Code of 1830', in which he stated that the Brazilian Criminal Code '*was one of the happiest legislative creations*', whose importance can be seen '*from several points of view, as the national, the American, the comparative law and the criminal policy*', reason why he proposed to build '*a perfect historical compilation, worthy flagged the importance of 1830 Code in the progress of the criminal codification*'.[1]

Throughout his paper, dedicated to the celebration of the centenary of this legal text, promulgated by the Law of 16 December 1830, Ladislau Thót pointed out that this code was a result of the representative José Clemente Pereira's draft and '*regarding the other Latin American Republics, we must say that the 1830 Code was the first independent and autonomous Criminal Code of Latin America, because the three that preceded it, the codes of Bolivia (1831), San Salvador and Haiti (1826), were the adoption of the 1822 Spanish Criminal Code and the 1810 French Code, respectively. Herein lies the significance and importance of the Brazilian Code to the Latin American Codification*'.[2]

Another important statement made by Thót was about the influence of the Brazilian Code in other countries: '*Regarding the new legislation, it was thought about the 1830 Brazilian Code, in a way that most of the sanest political-criminal ideas from the new 1848 Spanish Criminal Code, which was the successor of the 1822 Criminal Code, are due to the 1830 Brazilian Criminal Code*' and '*As to Argentina, the famous draft by the jurist Carlos Tejedor, presented to the Republic*

[1]Ladislau Thót, 'O Código Criminal Brasileiro de 1830' (*Archivo Judiciário - Publicação quinzenal do Jornal do Commercio*, Rio de Janeiro. volume XV). 1930, p. 39.

[2]*Ladislau Thót. Idem.* p. 40. The first Bolivian Code, approved by the Congress of that country in 1830 to become effective in 1831, as mentioned by Thót, was based on a draft which was a copy of the Spanish Criminal Code of 1822, presented by the jurist Facundo Infante, in 1826. See: Jorge Machado. 'Historia del Derecho Penal Boliviano y sus Reformas'. Available at: http://jorgemachicado.blogspot.com.br/2009/03/historia-del-derecho-penal-bolivianoy.html#_Toc224636917. Access on: 09 July 2015. Despite the anachronism, maybe that's the reason why the Argentinian professor placed him among those who 'preceded' the 1830 Brazilian Code.

government in 1866 was also based, in many points of view, in both the 1830 Brazilian Criminal Code and the 1850 Spanish Code'.[3] According to Thót, the importance of the Brazilian Code was, in fact, in being '*one of the few nineteenth century codes with an accentuated political-criminal orientation*', reason why '*from the historical-dogmatic point of view, the Code of the Empire was, in Latin America, the first Criminal Code actually proper and national.*[4]

Besides Ladislau Thót, Professor Luis Jiménez Asúa, criminal law professor at the University of Buenos Aires and the University of Madrid, asserted in a few lines that '*The Brazilian Criminal Code, from December 16, 1830, had many aspects from the 1819 Neapolitan Code and also the 1810 French Code. Its basis was composed, by the General Assembly, by the drafts prepared by Bernardo Pereira de Vasconcellos and Clemente Pereira. This Brazilian Code has, in its turn, inspired the 1848 Spanish Penal Code*'.[5]

On the opposite way, the Brazilian jurist Nelson Hungria, in his extensive doctrinal work, makes only one reference, in a footnote, about the 1830 Brazilian Code, as follows: '*The 1830 Code was the initial stage of the Brazilian criminal law (because before it, even after the independence in 1822, it ruled in Brazil the 'liber terribilis' from Philippines Ordinations, borrowed from Portugal). It was indeed the first autonomous Code in Latin America. Although lacking originality (aside from, inspired by Bentham's doctrines, considering the 'pactum sceleris' as a generic aggravating circumstance), it was no copy or pure imitation of European Codes. It followed the ideas of the Enlightenment. It is undeniable that, in its time, was a remarkable piece of legislation and, as pointed out by the illustrious Ladislau Thót, exerted an influence on almost all Latin American criminal law, throughout the 1848, 1850 and 1870 Spanish Codes, which, in many aspects, were inspired by the Brazilian standard and, in its turn, served as a model to the Codes of spanish-speaking countries of America. One should not, however, by mere spirit of patriotism, seeing the merit of our first Code. The news assigned to it were only authentic antiques ....*'.[6]

This curious difference of opinions, with great Argentine professors valuing the Brazilian Criminal Code while one of the greatest Brazilian criminalists considers this same Code a work without originality, indicates one more case of tension between memory and history about the past.[7]

---

[3]Ladislau Thót. *Idem*, p. 41 e 42. The Spanish Criminal Code of 1850 was nothing else than a reformed edition of the code of 1848. See: Ladislau Thót. *Idem*, p. 42.

[4]Ladislau Thót. *Idem*. p. 51.

[5]Luis Jiménez de Asúa. *Tratado de Derecho Penal. Tomo I. Concepto de derecho penal y de la criminología, historia y legislación penal comparada*, 5ª ed. actualizada. (Buenos Aires, Editorial Losada, S.A, 1992), p. 1330.

[6]Nelson Hungria. *Comentários ao Código Penal*, v. 1, tomo 1. 3ª ed. revista e atualizada (Rio de Janeiro, Forense, 1955), p. 38.

[7]About the tension between memory and history, cf. Eduardo Tomasevicius Filho. *Entre a memória coletiva e a história de cola-e-tesoura: as intrigas e os malogros nos relatos sobre a Fábrica de Ferro de São João de Ipanema*. (Dissertation, Master in Social History, University of São Paulo, Philosophy, Litteracy and Human Sciences Faculty, São Paulo. 2012).

This controversy was rekindled with the important work of Bernardino Bravo Lira, on the 1803 Austrian Code. This author agrees with the general opinion that the 1830 Brazilian Criminal Code was the matrix of the Spanish Penal Code of 1848, which, in turn, served as a model for Latin American criminal codifications. On the other hand, Bravo Lira states a lack of originality of the 1830 Brazilian Criminal Code, because this code was supposedly drafted from the 1803 Austrian Criminal Code,[8] due to the proximity between the Brazilian and Austrian courts, because Leopoldina, the first Brazilian empress, was Francis I of Austria's daughter.[9]

Therefore, this imposes reflections on the development of the 1830 Brazilian Criminal Code and its influences in other countries.[10]

2 The Development of the Brazilian Criminal Code of 1830

With the independence of Brazil in 1822 from Portugal, proclaimed by D. Pedro I, son of King John VI, the creation of new laws for the country was required, since the Ordinations by King Philip I from Spain were still effective in Brazil, complemented by other Portuguese legislation enacted at that time. In fact, it was not easy developing a new legal order in such a short time. The only possibility was keeping effective the Portuguese law, which occurred by the Law of 20 October 1823. In the following year, Pedro I granted the first Brazilian political constitution, which, in its Article 179, XVIII, ordered the following: 'As soon as possible, a Civil

[8]Bernardino Bravo Lira, 'La fortuna del Código Penal español de 1848: historia en cuatro actos y tres continentes: de Mello Freire y Zeiller a Vasconcellos y Seijas Lozano', *Anuario de Historia del Derecho Español*, Madrid, 2004, p. 27: 'There are at least three things that should be clarified. Firstly, how the Austrian code was known in Brazil (…). Then, the reasons why it was adopted as a model with preference to others: the French, the Bavarian, the Spanish of 1822, and the Louisiana project. Last but not least, a question to explain: why this imperial code of Brazil, (..), whose origin is Vasconcelos' project, was imposed so generally in the rest of the world Hispanic, through the Spanish code of 1848(..)'. Furthermore (p. 45): 'This history culminates with the 1848 Spanish Criminal Code, and the other its derivatives. It is simpler than the previous one. After examining the European and American codes, drafters agreed to take the Brazilian Code as a model. They made a thorough review of their text. As the Brazilian Imperial code was only a corrected and augmented reworking of the Austrian Code, Spanish Code was only a revised version of the Brazilian Code'.

[9]Bravo Lira, 'La fortuna del Código Penal español de 1848', p. 39: 'We do not know accurately why the [1803 Austrian Criminal Code] became known in Brazil. But it is not difficult to suppose it, if you take into account the ties that joined Rio de Janeiro and Vienna's Courts'.

[10]This matter was recently studied by Vivian Chieregati Costa, *Codificação e formação do Estado-nacional brasileiro: o Código Criminal de 1830 e a positivação das leis no pós-Independência*. (Dissertation, Master in Brazilian Studies, University of São Paulo, Brazilian Studies Institute, São Paulo, 2013).

and Criminal Codes, based on the strong foundations of justice and equity, shall be drafted and enacted'.

The fulfillment of this constitutional command in Brazil resulted in a peculiar codification process that is relatively distinct of those occurred both in Europe and in America. Concerning the private law codification, it is a story of almost sixty years, which only ended with the enactment of the 1916 Civil Code, which repealed by antinomy the Book IV of Philippines Ordinations. In this story, the pioneer was the jurist Augusto Teixeira de Freitas, who developed, in 1857, the 'Consolidação das Leis Civis', a work destined to organize the private law in force at that time in Brazil, and his draft of the Civil Code, known as the 'Esboço de Código Civil', unfinished because of its attempt to achieve by itself the unification of the entire Brazilian private law, yet in the nineteenth century.[11]

Regarding Criminal Law, the events that culminated in the enactment of a Criminal Code were held over a shorter period, due to relevant reasons that required the fast enactment of new legislation.

The first point to be considered is that, unlike private law, that was enough to rule the population' needs and had been applied in Brazil until the twentieth century, the criminal law needed urgently to be replaced. The Book V of Philippines Ordinations, which legislated about crimes, punished the conducts with severity, it means, with the death penalty or banishment overseas, including to Brazil...

The second point is that the Enlightenment ideas in criminal matters, defended mostly by Beccaria and Bentham, made criminal laws anachronistic even at that time. Therefore, the criminal law came to have an underlying philosophy. As examples, it can be mentioned the ideas of proportionality between the conduct practiced and the corresponding sanctions, as well as the ineffectiveness of torture as evidence and the death penalty as a mean to dissuade criminals.

The third point is that, in the decades of 1810 and 1820, there were insurrections and civil wars claiming for the independence of the Brazilian crown, which were strongly suppressed, and their leaders sentenced to death penalty. Among them was Frei Caneca, who participated at the Confederation of Ecuador, a separatist movement which claimed to establish a republic in northeastern Brazil. Some Brazilian representatives were directly or indirectly involved in these separatist movements and, thus, they were interested in the elimination of the death penalty for political reasons.[12]

---

[11]Several studies on the Brazilian Civil Code, focusing on Teixeira de Freitas were conducted in Brazil and in Italy. The most relevant works on this subject are: Silvio Meira. *Teixeira de Freitas: o jurisconsulto do Império. Vida e obra.* (Brasília, Cegraf, 1983); Sandro Schipani (org). *Augusto Teixeira de Freitas e il diritto latioamericano.* (Padova, Cedam, 1988); Ignacio Maria Poveda Velasco. 'Augusto Teixeira de Freitas' (verbete). In: R Domingo (org). *Juristas Universales.* V. 3. (Madrid, Marcial Pons, 2004); Estevan Lo Re Pousada. *Preservação da tradição jurídica luso-brasileira: Teixeira de Freitas e a introdução à Consolidação das Leis Civis.* (Dissertation, Master in History of Law, University of São Paulo, Law School, São Paulo, 2006).

[12]Gislene Neder. 'Degredo e pena de morte no Brasil Império'. In: *ANAIS DO XXV SIMPÓSIO NACIONAL DE HISTÓRIA – ANPUH.* Fortaleza, 2009. Available at: http://anpuh.org/anais/?p=18520. Access on: 15.dez.2013.

It is still possible to highlight other two points: the Brazilian population at the time was also composed by slaves, therefore, subject to corporal punishment established by their masters, and another considerable portion of the population lived in economic misery and cultural ignorance.

The history of the Criminal Code's development, which came to replace the Philippines Ordinations, is still surrounded by doubts about the work and leadership of two representatives involved in the preparation of this new text: José Clemente Pereira and Bernardo Pereira de Vasconcellos. Before analyzing the preparatory process of this important code, it must be presented a short biography of them.

José Clemente Pereira was born in 1787 at the village of Castelo-Mendo, Portugal. He joined the University of Coimbra, where he obtained the bachelor degree in law and in canons. As a military, he participated of the Anglo-Portuguese resistance army against France during the Napoleonic invasion in 1808. In 1815, with twenty-eight years old, he moved to Brazil. He practiced law until he was nominated to the position of judge at the Praia Grande Village (current city of Niterói), in 1819. He was known for his works at building and developing streets and water supply for the city. In 1821, he became a judge outside the Court and, shortly after, was elected president of the City Council. At the practice of this function he became in charge of presenting, on 9 January 1822, the request for D. Pedro I not return to Portugal, episode known as the 'Dia do Fico'.[13] He was also responsible for the order dated 17 September 1822, which demanded the young prince to promise to maintain and defend the future Constitution of Brazil. He was elected as representative, and participated of the development of the Criminal Code draft. As a public administrator, he was provider of the Santa Casa of Rio de Janeiro (The 'Holy House' Hospital of Rio de Janeiro) and made great effort in fundraising for the foundation of the Pedro II Asylum in 1852, seeking to build it as one of the most modern in the world at the time. With that in mind, he sought assistance from great experts in the field, also following the teachings of the French doctor Philippe Pinel, as well as the named 'great French alienists'. He also participated in the development of the Commercial Code draft. Elected representative and senator for various provinces, he was the first president of the Commercial Court, created by the Commercial Code, in 1850. He died in 1854, at sixty-seven years old.[14]

Bernardo Pereira de Vasconcellos was born in Vila Rica, Brazil, known today as Ouro Preto, on 27 August 1795. His father had a law degree from Coimbra and practiced law in Ouro Preto, holding first the position of prosecutor and later the role of criminal judge in Rio de Janeiro. One of his maternal uncles was a minister in Portugal and the other maternal uncle, dean of the University of Coimbra. With twelve years old, he was sent to Portugal, but never got to land in the metropolis, as tensions between England and France were at their peak: the ship he was in was seized and the route diverted to England, what forced him to return to Brazil. Just in

---

[13]In a literal translation: the day when Peter said officially: 'I will remain in Brazil!'.

[14]Sébastien Auguste SISSON. 'José Clemente Pereira'. In: SA SISSON. *Grandes Brasileiros Ilustres*. Volume I. (Brasília, Senado Federal, 1999), pp. 41–46.

1813, with eighteen years old, he was able to go to Portugal to study law at Coimbra. He returned to Brazil in 1820, with twenty-five years old. He began his career as an attorney, but ended up being nominated to the position of outside judge of Guaratingueta village and, later, Chief Justice of the Court of Maranhão. As the elections to the National Assembly began, he was elected representative by the Province of Minas Gerais. During this period, he worked at the development of the Criminal Code. Due to his liberal opinion, he became Minister of Finance in 1831. He was assigned to elaborate the Additional Act to the Constitution of the Empire. From 1834 and on, he changed his political leanings, becoming a conservative and thus, offering great opposition to the Standing Regency of Priest Diogo Feijó, his former colleague in political matters. In 1838 he was elected senator. In 1840, Pereira de Vasconcellos founded the School Pedro II and, in 1842, became State Councilor. He participated in the reform of the Criminal Procedure Code of the Empire and also the creation of the Law on Lands. He died in 1850 at 55 years old, due to the yellow fever epidemic that affected Rio de Janeiro.[15]

3 Clemente Pereira's 'Basis' Proposed in 1826

The first step on the Brazilian process of criminal codification was taken at the session on 3 June 1826, when Clemente Pereira presented a draft called by him as 'basis' for a future Criminal Code.[16] In fact, this draft corresponds to the 'First Book' on crimes and penalties, consisted of forty-five sections, which should come into force when the entire Criminal Code was enacted and also be composed by those elements. There are no historical references about the reasons that led him to file this draft, neither on the methodology used on it. The only references about this subject are two Clement Pereira's speeches on 17 August 1826 and 16 May 1827,[17] in which he claimed to have presented these 'basis' to obtain the opinion of the House of Representatives about what he had already done and avoiding unnecessary work, in the event of not getting it approved.[18] However, one possible hypothesis is that Clement Pereira wanted to control the development of the Criminal Code, because the other books, prepared by him or a by a third part,

[15]José Murilo de Carvalho (in cooperation with Patrícia Souza Lima). 'Introdução'. In: JM Carvalho (Org.). *Bernardo Pereira de Vasconcellos.* (São Paulo, Ed. 34, 1999). pp. 9–34.

[16]Brazil. House of Representatives. *Sessão em 3 de junho de 1826.* In: Brazil (Empire). *Annaes da Câmara dos Deputados.* pp. 16–18. Available at: http://imagem.camara.gov.br/pesquisa_diario_basica.asp Access on: 13.dez.2013.

[17]Brazil. House of Representatives. *Sessão em 16 de maio de 1827.* In: Brazil (Empire). *Annaes da Câmara dos Deputados.* p. 97. Available at: http://imagem.camara.gov.br/pesquisa_diario_basica.asp Access on: 13.dez.2013.

[18]Brazil. House of Representatives. *Sessão de 17 de agosto de 1826.* In: Brazil (Empire). *Annaes da Câmara dos Deputados.* p. 173. Available at: http://imagem.camara.gov.br/pesquisa_diario_basica.asp Access on: 13.dez.2013.

could not fail to take into consideration his work eventually approved by the House of Representatives.

As for the content of these 'basis', it consisted in the proposition to adopt a new model at the time of structuring a criminal code. Several articles of these 'basis' were very similar to the provisions of the 1810 French Criminal Code, as for example, definitions of crime, attempt, misdemeanor, authorship, as well as the principle of anteriority in criminal law and the classification of punishments in cruel and infamous or only cruel punishments, the first being the death, denaturalization, perpetual work and life imprisonment, while the latter were the perpetual or temporary banishment, temporary jobs, temporary imprisonment, suspension of political rights and fine.[19] On the other hand, in the same direction of the 1813 Bavarian Criminal Code, it recognized that crimes should be charged in three degrees: minimum, medium and maximum. According to section 18 of the 'basis', the minimum degree would be the simple crime 'as, for example, the industrious theft of an ounce of gold'; the average degree 'qualifies the offense accompanied by aggravating circumstances, as, for example, the theft made breaking in'; the maximum degree 'qualifies the crime accompanied by even worse aggravating circumstances, such as theft done with armed force'.

The House of Representatives, before receiving this draft, sent it to the Legislation, Civil and Criminal Justice Committee, which produced two reviews about the issue. The first review, transcribed on the records of the session made in 1 August 1826, recognized that the draft was 'constitutional', meaning that it was in accordance with the provisions of section 179, XVIII, but did not recommend that this draft was attached to subsequent code, as the one by Clemente Pereira or others by third parties, who could wish to develop a full draft of Criminal Code, because it could 'hobble the geniality and preclude the nation of achieving the best code'.[20] The second review suggested granting a prize for who, within two years, presented the best draft, which would be examined by a committee of jurists. The winning work would be printed and submitted for public consultation of the courts, lawyers and sages of the nation.[21] These reviews were discussed at the session of 17 August 1826. On that day, the representative Bernardo Pereira de Vasconcellos pointed out the inconclusiveness of the review, because on one hand it praised the draft, but on the other, it did not recommend to bind the draft to the subsequent work. In his opinion, the draft should return to the Committee, which would continue the work to produce a final draft of Criminal Code. During this debate, it was mentioned that

---

[19]Brazil. House of Representatives. *Sessão de 3 de junho de 1826*. In: Brazil (Empire). *Annaes da Câmara dos Deputados*. pp. 16–18. Available at: http://imagem.camara.gov.br/pesquisa_diario_basica.asp Access on: 13.dez.2013.

[20]Brazil. House of Representatives. *Sessão de 1º e agosto de 1826*. In: Brazil (Empire). *Annaes da Câmara dos Deputados*. p. 17. Available at: http://imagem.camara.gov.br/pesquisa_diario_basica.asp Access on: 13.dez.2013.

[21]Brazil. House of Representatives. *Sessão de 1º e agosto de 1826*. In: Brazil (Empire). *Annaes da Câmara dos Deputados*. p. 16. Available at: http://imagem.camara.gov.br/pesquisa_diario_basica.asp Access on: 13.dez.2013.

the entire draft was ready, but the intention was to approve the 'basis' firstly. The discussion diverged to scathingly criticize the commission that reviewed the draft and the time to be spent in the same discussion. Finally, it was decided to return the matter to the Committee, which should present a full draft of the Criminal Code.[22]

4 The Two Criminal Code Drafts of 1827

Due to the end of the previous legislature, the second step in the preparation of a Criminal Code occurred at the session on 4 May 1827, when Bernardo Pereira de Vasconcellos presented a draft that contained not only the criminal part, but also the procedural part.[23] This draft, according to its author, contained three parts: '*The first part deals with crimes that can be committed in society, and the application of the corresponding penalties; the second deals with legal matters, and the third with the order of the process.*' Clemente Pereira, in his turn, presented his draft at the session on 16 May 1827, and it corresponded only to the criminal part, excluding the procedural rules.[24] At this same session, it was decided to remit both drafts to a special committee for analysis.[25]

Clemente Pereira's draft was divided into four books. From the first book, similar to the 'basis' presented in 1826 in terms of structure, it was suppressed the chapters of denaturalization penalty, exile and the suspension of political rights. The first crime specified was the one committed against the religion of the Empire. Were also specified crimes such as lampoons, challenges, sodomy, bestiality, as well as crimes against public trade, which included the falsification of goods to sell, and the use of false or falsified weights, measures weighting or scales, which was also classified in the Philippines Ordinations. Moreover, it regulated police and good public order misdemeanors.[26]

On the other way, Bernardo Pereira de Vasconcellos' draft was composed by 334 sections and divided into four parts. The first part (Title I) was about the crimes

[22]Brazil. House of Representatives. *Sessão de 17 de agosto de 1826*. In: Brazil (Empire). *Annaes da Câmara dos Deputados*. p. 174. Available at: http://imagem.camara.gov.br/pesquisa_diario_basica.asp Access on: 13.dez.2013.

[23]Brazil. House of Representatives. *Sessão de 17 de agosto de 1826*. In: Brazil (Empire). *Annaes da Câmara dos Deputados*. p. 174. Available at: http://imagem.camara.gov.br/pesquisa_diario_basica.asp Access on: 13.dez.2013.

[24]Brazil. House of Representatives. *Sessão de 5 de maio de 1827*. In: Brazil (Empire). *Annaes da Câmara dos Deputados*. p. 97. Available at: http://imagem.camara.gov.br/pesquisa_diario_basica.asp Access on: 13.dez.2013.

[25]Brazil. House of Representatives. *Sessão de 16 de maio de 1827*. In: Brazil (Empire). *Annaes da Câmara dos Deputados*. p. 97. Available at: http://imagem.camara.gov.br/pesquisa_diario_basica.asp Access on: 13.dez.2013.

[26]The access to this draft was not possible, since it was microfilmed at the National Library in Rio de Janeiro, where access is restricted to the consultant. The summary of this draft is attached to the work of Vivian Chieregati Costa. *Idem*. pp. 328–329.

and penalties; the second part (Title II) referred to the police crimes; the third part (Title III) was about private crimes and the fourth part (Title IV) regulated public offences.

Regarding the content, the first section of Bernardo Pereira de Vasconcellos' draft presented some innovation: the figure of crime was equated with felony in section 1: '*It is a crime or offence (synonyms in this code)*: …'. It was established that crime would also be the disobedience to the determinations of the competent authorities, the abuse of power, the threat and the refusal to aid who was in great danger notwithstanding who could get saved. The principle of legality was set in section 2 as follows: '*There is no crime without a previous law to qualify it and without bad faith, that is, without knowledge of evil and intent of to practice it*'.

Mentally disabled people were considered unable to be punished, except in periods of lucidity, and criminal liability was set in this draft to fourteen years old. Still on this subject, another innovation: in case of criminal conduct practiced by madmen or children under fourteen years old, they would be withdrawn to houses built to people on these conditions or left to their families, at the discretion of the judge.

Following philosophical tendencies on punishment individualization, the draft established the criminal liability in case of multiple criminals regarding their guilt (section 5): '*When two or more people together commit the crime, or to it they compete, they are named partners in crime and perpetrators or accomplices, according to the greater or lesser part they had on committing it. It will never be imposed to accomplices the same penalties as to the perpetrators*'. It is worth noticing that the draft considered partners in crime the civil servants, bailiffs, those who executed orders opposed to the letter of the Constitution, those who hid and protected criminals without bail and those who hid stolen things. Another interesting provision was about crimes committed by many people: '*Section 9. When there are many offenders, only those who committed the crime will be punished*'.

The causes of withdrawn the wrongfulness of conducts were subject to regulation. It would not be considered crime the conduct against oneself or with the victim's consent, as well as the state of necessity and self-defense or defense of third parties. It was also not considered crime the moderate punishment of fathers on sons, masters on slaves and husbands on their wives, if they were not against any existing laws.

Pereira de Vasconcellos' draft ruled the definition of aggravating and mitigating circumstances of the offenses, as already set out in the Bavarian and Spanish codes. However, the hypotheses were not the same of the European codes, meaning that the draft only used the idea of quantifying the penalty for each specific case. It was settled that crimes would be punished with sentences in maximum, medium or minimum degrees, according to the aggravating or mitigating circumstances. Then, the draft brought twenty-three aggravating circumstances and eight mitigating circumstances, number significantly higher to those found in other codes. The draft also provided that, in the application of penalty, it should be considered the sensitivity of the offender, variable according to age, gender, social representation, education, usual occupation and religious profession. This would allow the judge to switch the type of penalty. Furthermore, it established that the penalty basis should be set in medium degree.

Various rules on repairing damages were established on the draft, including dispositions on parents' obligation to repair the damage caused by their children, also the husband liability for damages caused by his wife and the masters' liability for the damage caused by their slaves, when they are negligent in their education and management. Another interesting disposition on this matter is that the satisfaction of the damage should be done by the government when the offender had no resources to do so, notwithstanding, he could be asked to perform different types of work in jails for the reimbursement of the public treasure.

In the same direction as the French Code, the penalties were settled in the following manner: '*1st. Death penalty; 2nd. Galley labor; 3rd. Imprisonment with labor; 4th. Imprisonment; 5th. Penalty of banishment; 6th. Banishment; 7th. Penalty of infamy; 8th. Fine; 9th. Loss of objects of the crime; 10th. Deposit; 11th. Surveillance of justice*'.

The death penalty would be executed by hanging, twenty four hours after the final judgment of the sentence. The draft also ruled about the possibility of cutting off the head and the hands of the convicted to be affixed where the offense took place, such as was also occurring in Brazil. The convicted should walk through the most public streets and squares until the place of execution, wearing a white liturgical robe with a label on the back, indicating his crime, with his hands tied and a noose around his neck. The body of the hanged should be handed over to the family, that could not bury him with pomp, under the penalty of imprisonment from one month to one year, as ruled in the French Code. Moreover, it would only be allowed the hanging of a recent mother after fifteen days of delivery.

The penalty of galley labor consisted of submitting the convicted to forced labor, with iron rings tied at their feet, also bound with chains. They should be dressed with a label on their back to indicate their crimes, facilitating identification. Women could not be sentenced with such penalty. Also, people under seventeen years old or over seventy years old could not be convicted to this sentence. According to the Bavarian Code, this penalty could not last less than two years. However, the draft prevised the construction of proper buildings fort those sentenced with imprisonment with forced labor. Nonetheless, until they were built, these sentences should be commuted to galley labor, simple imprisonment or banishment.

The nineteenth-century Brazilian society was still marked by slavery. The treatment assigned to slaves was different from the one established to free people. The draft ruled that, if a slave practiced committed a capital crime, he would suffer the death penalty; otherwise he would be scourged and hand into his master.

Pereira de Vasconcellos' draft settled limitation and forgiveness of penalties. It established the prompt of ten years for attempted crimes and crimes with no aggravating circumstances. The Emperor could forgive or reduce the penalties. However, reparation of the damage would not be affected by limitation or by forgiveness.

The following books, tough, were *sui generis*. They were different from the first part both in terms of editorial technique but also in content. At times, it mingled specified conducts with corresponding penalties, and on other moments, they used the quirk 'it's a crime…'. For example, Section 241: '*The one who, to collect taxes or legitimate rights, voluntarily employ against the taxpayer more onerous means than those prescript in laws or regulations and higher orders, or make him suffer unfare vexations, shall be suspended from his job for 6 to 18 months and shall compensate the losses and damages caused, notwithstanding any other penalty that may be incurred by vexation*' and also section 185: '*It's a crime against property to destroy or damage something of any value or immediately, or by persons or things. Penalty – Fine of one third of the value of the thing destroyed or damaged. And in case of aggravating circumstances, the penalty will be the one predicted to theft*'.

Another Bernardo Pereira de Vasconcellos' *sui generis* proposition was the establishment of the law of talion (penalty of retaliation), although there were no specific details about how exactly this would be applied. For example, the last figure of the section 231 on official misconduct: '*If the official misconduct consist of criminal procedure against those who knew did not deserve, shall also incur the penalty of retaliation*'; also, section 234 on bribery: '*The same penalty shall incur the justice of law or fact, or arbitrator to give fair sentence because of bribery; if unfair, the imprisonment shall be from six month to two years, and if criminal conviction, the subordinated will suffer the penalty of talion*' and section 238: 'The calumniator incurs in the penalty of retaliation'.

As to the crime of slander, the penalty consisted of the defendant's reading of his own sentence: 'Section 162: There is calumny or slander when in a public place, in some authentic act, engraving, printed writing, lithographed or not printed, in any manner that is distributed by more than ten persons: (…) Penalty – Reading or repeating the sentence in audience, done by the defendant aloud. Imprisonment from one month to one year and the corresponding fine.'

Interesting aspect is that the copyright protection was predicted in section 194: 'Section 194. It is theft to print, record or lithograph, any patterns or writings, which have been composed or translated by Brazilians, while they live and ten years after their death, if they leave heirs. Penalties - loss of all copies to the author, translator or his heirs. Fine of six times the value of the copies'.

The special committee organized to analyze the presented drafts elaborated a report, which was read at the session of 14 August 1827. After praising both drafts presented by Clemente Pereira and Bernardo Pereira de Vasconcellos, highlighting their patriotism and their lights, the committee opined that both drafts needed changes because 'not always the beauty of the theory corresponds to the usefulness in practice (…)' and, therefore, one alternative could be to merge both drafts in a single text, since the design of Clement Pereira's draft had better structure and could supply the lack of clarity, order and innovation of Pereira de Vasconcellos' draft. However, the commission recommended the receipt of both drafts and their printing for consideration of representatives, though, '*to enter the regular discussion as determined by our work schedule, we prefer the Mr. Vasconcellos' draft, due to its wideness in the development of reasonable equitable legal maximums, and on the other hand, to its straightness in the division of the penalties, which wise variety contributes to their well-regulated distribution, it could easily lead to perfection with fewer touches, considering the ones already done by the commission in accordance with the illustrious author'.*[27] It was decided then to only print the drafts, without giving preference to Bernardo Pereira de Vasconcellos' draft.

5 The Rewriting of Criminal Code's Draft and the Parliamentary Debates

The discussion about the Criminal Code was held truly only from 1829, with the reading of the joint committee's report, which reviewed the amendments to Clemente Pereira and Bernardo Pereira de Vasconcellos' drafts. On 31 August 1829, the committee declared that they had remodeled the draft, which was divided into four parts, according to the disposition of the French Criminal Code, therefore moving away from the division proposed by Bernardo Pereira de Vasconcellos:

> The 1st part is about crimes and penalties in general; it brings the qualification of criminal actions, and set the rules to (…) the imputation; regulates the reparation of the damage; defines the penalties adopted and determine the general rules for their establishment and execution. It can be said that this 1st part contains the system theory that is developed through the other parts into a classification box of all crimes. The 2nd part sets the crimes against the general interests of the nation. The 3rd is about crimes against the individuals' interests. And the 4th comprehends the crimes committed by police, which the public authority must carefully conceal to prevent greater evils.[28]

Moreover, the suggestion of the committee was to abolish the death penalty:

> The committee wanted to suppress the death penalty, which usefulness rarely compensates the horror caused in its use, especially between people of tender costumes, such as Brazilians, but the current status of our population, which does not has primary education as a general reality, can lead to hypothesis in which the death penalty would be necessary; reason why we must console of this sad necessity and defend the maintenance of this rule, though it is forbidden the execution of such penalty without the consent of the moderating power, which surely will refuse it when a replacement is founded and suits well.[29]

It was also emphasized that the then current set of disjointed laws in Brazil, established in ancient times, were influenced by superstition and equaled to the Dracon in barbarity, including by extending the penalty to innocents. Therefore, it was used in the sentencing guidelines the 'cardinal principle of utility', aiming the

---

[27]Brazil. House of Representatives. *Sessão de 14 de agosto de 1827*. In: Brazil (Empire). *Annaes da Câmara dos Deputados*. pp. 130–131. Available at: http://imagem.camara.gov.br/pesquisa_diario_basica.asp Access on: 13.dez.2013.

[28]Brazil. House of Representatives. *Sessão de 31 de agosto de 1829*. In: Brazil (Empire). *Annaes da Câmara dos Deputados*. p. 84. Available at: http://imagem.camara.gov.br/pesquisa_diario_basica.asp Access on: 13.dez.2013.

[29]Brazil. House of Representatives. *Sessão de 31 de agosto de 1829*. In: Brazil (Empire). *Annaes da Câmara dos Deputados*. p. 85. Available at: http://imagem.camara.gov.br/pesquisa_diario_basica.asp Access on: 13.dez.2013.

fairness of goods and evils result of criminal actions. Finally, the committee suggested the printing of this reviewed Criminal Code draft, so that it could be presented the necessary amendments.

Another year passed and, on the end of 1830, the legislature was up to finish. The representatives found themselves pressed by time and decided to vote the text urgently. The atmosphere was that it would be better to enact an imperfect code, than to seek perfection of a code that would take many years to be enacted.

The discussion on the Criminal Code was resumed in September 1830. Because of the shortness of time, discussions were synthesized by initiative of the representatives, as they predicted the delay the review of all proposed amendments would cause, and it was feared that they could disfigure the original text, breaking the inherent system of the code, by the internal contradictions that would be created in the final text.[30] The representatives agreed to discuss only the desirability or not of maintaining the death penalty and the penalty of galley labor, which allowed the recognition of great familiarity between the writers and philosophers of the time with parliamentary speeches.

Therefore, it's illustrative the speech by the representative Rebouças:

> I heard from another honorable representative that those who advocated the abolition of the death penalty seemed only to have read Beccaria, leaving aside the notes of Diderot. We really would be late if we limited ourselves to the work on crimes and punishments; however, I observe that the honorable representative may not want to take into account what other students of Beccaria said, such as Morelet and Bielfeld; and yet about Diderot that he saw only the side that looked flattering to him.[31]

Most speeches defended the abolition of these severe punishments. The most incisive representative was the previously mentioned Rebouças, who argued, based on the idea of social contract, that people transfer their personal freedoms, but not their being, to social coexistence.[32] The death penalty was not supported by natural law, besides being unconstitutional, because Brazil had adopted Catholicism as the official religion. He remembered that Cain was not killed when he murdered Abel, but he was banished, and that Jesus Christ had forgiven all men. He pointed out that the Constitution abolished beatings, torture, hot iron brands and all the severe and cruel punishments, and that it would be unfair to eliminate a young person; moreover, rather than imposing work to the offender on the benefit of his family,

---

[30]Brazil. House of Representatives. *Sessão de 11 de setembro de 1830*. In: Brazil (Empire). *Annaes da Câmara dos Deputados*. p. 490. Available at: http://imagem.camara.gov.br/pesquisa_diario_basica.asp. Access on: 13.dez.2013.

[31]Brazil. House of Representatives. *Sessão de 15 de setembro de 1830*. In: Brazil (Empire). *Annaes da Câmara dos Deputados*. p. 516. Available at: http://imagem.camara.gov.br/pesquisa_diario_basica.asp Access on: 13.dez.2013.

[32]Brazil. House of Representatives. *Sessão de 11 de setembro de 1830*. In: Brazil (Empire). *Annaes da Câmara dos Deputados*. p. 493. Available at: http://imagem.camara.gov.br/pesquisa_diario_basica.asp Access on: 13.dez.2013.

the children would be threw to orphan houses.[33] He indicated that the law of war imposed the least harm possible and it would be a profound shame to society to enforce security through annihilation of its people, since if it was possible to tame a tiger or a lion, it would also be possible to tame a man. Finally, he argued that the death penalty was not able to dissuade those who really wanted to commit any crime, because it did not allow the cooling of hate.[34] Reinforcing this position, he noticed that the abolition of the death penalty in Tuscany had reduced homicides, unlike in Naples and Rome.

Another argumentative line against the death penalty argued about the responsibility of the State for bad examples in face of population, as well as neglecting on attending human needs. Also advocate of this point of view, the representative Carneiro da Cunha made opposition to the death penalty because, throughout history, only the innocent victims and the underprivileged were punished, while the idle rich, the nobles, the courtiers, the parasites and perfidious ministers lived in peace enjoying the fruits of their iniquities.[35] He held that the killers lurking on the roads would become even crueler if they were sure that their end would be death. In his view,

> The lack of repression of small offences leads the offenders to higher crimes; how many have initiated with small thefts and gradually become the greatest thief. Shall the government protect public moral by choosing well the employees and the fair magistrates; by distributing with impartiality and fairness prizes and punishments; by saving the nation incomes to not burden the poor with heavy tributes and increase the primary instruction, spreading the lights through the empire, and, in result, soon these awful crimes among us will disappear: soon the Brazilians, better instructed in their duties, will not only respect the laws, but their superiors, and then grateful will bless the humans legislators and philanthropists who predict this wicked and atrocious penalty (…).[36]

Elsewhere, the same representative argued that:

> Mr. President, the Brazilians are guilty of allowing the old Portuguese government to introduce the corruption in public administration, selling jobs, not punishing magistrates, protecting and supporting violence and oppression, closing ears to the complaints of the persecuted, not distributing justice and authorizing the powerful people to practice their wickedness, greed and revenge, succeeded by our misfortune that prevails, since the Brazilian government, even after independence, remains in the same traitor system,

[33]Brazil. House of Representatives. *Sessão de 11 de setembro de 1830*. In: Brazil (Empire). *Annaes da Câmara dos Deputados*. p. 494. Available at: http://imagem.camara.gov.br/pesquisa_diario_basica.asp Access on: 13.dez.2013.

[34]Brazil. House of Representatives. *Sessão de 11 de setembro de 1830*. In: Brazil (Empire). *Annaes da Câmara dos Deputados*. p. 495. Available at: http://imagem.camara.gov.br/pesquisa_diario_basica.asp Access on: 13.dez.2013.

[35]Brazil. House of Representatives. *Sessão de 11 de setembro de 1830*. In: Brazil (Empire). *Annaes da Câmara dos Deputados*. p. 497. Available at: http://imagem.camara.gov.br/pesquisa_diario_basica.asp Access on: 13.dez.2013.

[36]Brazil. House of Representatives. *Sessão de 11 de setembro de 1830*. In: Brazil (Empire). *Annaes da Câmara dos Deputados*. p. 497. Available at: http://imagem.camara.gov.br/pesquisa_diario_basica.asp Access on: 13.dez.2013.

stalking, murdering and deporting free writers, while their oppressors were protected and rewarded? If there were no such penalty, we would not remember with pain these mourning and bitter days, when exhale the last breath suffering from the political inquisition one Antonio Henrique, the Satyros, the Canecas and other martyrs of the homeland who courageously will sacrifice themselves defending our rights, our independence and freedom.[37]

Another argument against death penalty was raised by the representative Ernesto, for whom besides being usurpation of divine power to decide on the life or death of a person, the death penalty carried out impunity, since no person wants to compete for the death of the criminal and, thus, the witnesses do not want to testify and the judge is afraid to give this kind of sentence.[38]

On the other hand, the representative Rego Barros argued that the death penalty could be abolished in political cases, but not in cases of homicide and of contention of slaves' rebellions.[39] The representative Paula Cavalcanti emphasized that, when entering into society, the person does not grant the right to imprison her, but the imprisonment is possible; the same consideration could be extended to the death penalty. '*I do not doubt the mankind feeling demands the abolishment of this penalty; but what can we do in Brazil, with such barbarous customs? In the Brazilian country side, there are professional murderers, and in some provinces we have crimes, and not as few as is wanted to believe*'.[40]

Bernardo Pereira de Vasconcellos declared his discordance with the death penalty, but it should be kept in the draft he presented as an answer to few cases. He pointed out that section 27 of the Constitution of the Empire recognized the death penalty.[41] He proposed the following strategy: the House of Representatives should suggest the cases in which the death punishment was allowed, under the penalty of the Senate multiply it to several hypothesis, making shorter the distance between the Code and the Philippines Ordinations.[42]

---

[37]BRAZIL. House of Representatives. *Sessão de 15 de setembro de 1830*. In: Brazil (Empire). *Annaes da Câmara dos Deputados*. p. 517. Available at: http://imagem.camara.gov.br/pesquisa_diario_basica.asp Access on: 13.dez.2013.

[38]Brazil. House of Representatives. *Sessão de 13 de setembro de 1830*. In: Brazil (Empire). *Annaes da Câmara dos Deputados*. p. 506. Available at: http://imagem.camara.gov.br/pesquisa_diario_basica.asp Access on: 13.dez.2013.

[39]Brazil. House of Representatives. *Sessão de 15 de setembro de 1830*. In: Brazil (Empire). *Annaes da Câmara dos Deputados*. p. 512. Available at: http://imagem.camara.gov.br/pesquisa_diario_basica.asp Access on: 13.dez.2013.

[40]Brazil. House of Representatives. *Sessão de 15 de setembro de 1830*. In: Brazil (Empire). *Annaes da Câmara dos Deputados*. p. 512. Available at: http://imagem.camara.gov.br/pesquisa_diario_basica.asp Access on: 13.dez.2013.

[41]'Article 27. No Senator, or Representative, during the mandate, shall be imprisoned by any authority, except by order of the respective Chamber, unless in case of flagrant crime punished by death penalty'.

[42]Brazil. House of Representatives. *Sessão de 15 de setembro de 1830*. In: Brazil (Empire). *Annaes da Câmara dos Deputados*. p. 512. Available at: http://imagem.camara.gov.br/pesquisa_diario_basica.asp Access on: 13.dez.2013.

The representative Paula e Sousa defended the death penalty in a few cases, because its abolishment only made sense in an entirely new population, but not to an existing one with its own customs, since no punishment, ultimately, is effective and also, only the death penalty would stop a two million slaves rebellion.[43] He argued that, abolished the penalties of death and galley labor, slaves would prefer the idle of prisons, as they are a prize to people.[44] He gave the example of Pennsylvania, where people committed crimes just to be imprisoned during winter, which led the government to intentionally worsen the treatment inside that prison.

As for the galley labor, in the opinion of representative Rebouças, it would not improve the criminal. Instead, it depraved him, because in prison he would found his first school of depravity and in the galley labor he would find his academy. '*As a result, not only they will demoralize themselves, but by depravation they will learn how to commit all crimes without horror and successfully, given the knowledge acquired of prevent and frustrate all precautions and efforts that are opposed and employed to them*'.[45] Bernardo Pereira de Vasconcellos, as he had already done in his draft, suggested the survival of the penalty of galley labor while were not built the proper establishments for convicts to work.[46]

On 16 September 1830, the draft was voted at the joint commission, so they could get orientation about the matter when adopting or not the amendments to the Criminal Code draft. As a result, it was approved the proposal of Rego Barros for maintaining the penalties of death and galley labor.[47]

Although discussions were most about these severe penalties, there were some—but a few—comments on other aspects of the draft. The representative Ferreira França, for example, advocated the rejection of the draft and all amendments, because he saw on it '*a set of crimes and guilty individuals, many accomplices, many adherents. (…) The penalties should be reduced to the least possible number. All legislative that imposes a penalty to each mistake, who wants only to find criminals, certainly is not worthy of the name 'man'; is a tiger worthy only to*

[43]Brazil. House of Representatives. *Sessão de 15 de setembro de 1830*. In: Brazil (Empire). *Annaes da Câmara dos Deputados*. p. 514. Available at: http://imagem.camara.gov.br/pesquisa_diario_basica.asp Access on: 13.dez.2013.

[44]Brazil. House of Representatives. *Sessão de 14 de setembro de 1830*. In: Brazil (Empire). *Annaes da Câmara dos Deputados*. p. 507. Available at: http://imagem.camara.gov.br/pesquisa_diario_basica.asp Access on: 13.dez.2013

[45]Brazil. House of Representatives. *Sessão de 14 de setembro de 1830*. In: Brazil (Empire). *Annaes da Câmara dos Deputados*. p. 507. Available at: http://imagem.camara.gov.br/pesquisa_diario_basica.asp Access on: 13.dez.2013.

[46]Brazil. House of Representatives. *Sessão de 16 de setembro de 1830*. In: Brazil (Empire). *Annaes da Câmara dos Deputados*. p. 518. Available at: http://imagem.camara.gov.br/pesquisa_diario_basica.asp Access on: 13.dez.2013.

[47]Brazil. House of Representatives. *Sessão de 16 de setembro de 1830*. In: Brazil (Empire). *Annaes da Câmara dos Deputados*. p. 518. Available at: http://imagem.camara.gov.br/pesquisa_diario_basica.asp Access on: 13.dez.2013.

legislate for ferocious beasts (...)'.[48] The representative Maia, on the other hand, condemned the rule of conspiracy, because it treated all persons indistinctly, without regard to the culpability of each.[49]

On 19 October 1830, the opinion of the responsible committee for summarizing the proposed amendments to the Criminal Code draft was read. The impossibility to analyze all the amendments led to the option of reviewing only a few. The main changes proposed by the commission were: '*for all crimes there is a classification based on degrees, and only to the crime of homicide, with certain aggravating circumstances, and also to the crimes of theft and slaves insurrection (when there is always atrocious homicides), there is the possibility of death penalty, but even in these hypothesis the death penalty would be possible only when in the maximum degree. The committee highlighted all the dispositions in the code related to the expression of thought, leaving them in a special law (...). The committee finally adopted the suppression of some crimes and changed the classification of others, always keeping in mind what seemed the best*'.[50]

On 23 October 1830, the draft with all its amendments was voted, approved and sent to the Senate,[51] that did not make any changes and sent it to sanction, being enacted on 16 December 1830.[52]

6 The Structure of the Criminal Code

The 1830 Criminal Code, although based on Bernardo Pereira de Vasconcellos' draft, underwent major changes in the House of Representatives, towards its structure and its content, as indicated on the opinions of the special committees that reviewed it. It is impossible to ascertain who was the author of each accepted amendment. It is only possible to know the reasons that led to the maintenance of the death penalty and galley labor.

On its final version, the enacted Criminal Code was divided into four parts. The first one corresponds to general rules on crimes and penalties, comprehending

---

[48]Brazil. House of Representatives. *Sessão em 11 de setembro de 1830*. In: Brazil (Empire). *Annaes da Câmara dos Deputados*. p. 489. Available at: http://imagem.camara.gov.br/pesquisa_diario_basica.asp Access on: 13.dez.2013.

[49]Brazil. House of Representatives. *Sessão em 11 de setembro de 1830*. In: Brazil (Empire). *Annaes da Câmara dos Deputados*. p. 489. Available at: http://imagem.camara.gov.br/pesquisa_diario_basica.asp Access on: 13.dez.2013.

[50]Brazil. House of Representatives. *Sessão em 19 de outubro de 1830*. In: Brazil (Empire). *Annaes da Câmara dos Deputados*. p. 612. Available at: http://imagem.camara.gov.br/pesquisa_diario_basica.asp Access on: 13.dez.2013.

[51]Brazil. House of Representatives. *Sessão de 23 de outubro de 1830*. In: Brazil (Empire). *Annaes da House of Representatives*. p. 617. Available at: http://imagem.camara.gov.br/pesquisa_diario_basica.asp Access on: 13.dez.2013.

[52]Brazil (Empire). *Lei de 16 de dezembro de 1830. Manda executar o Código Criminal*. Available at: http://www.planalto.gov.br/ccivil_03/leis/lim/lim-16-12-1830.htm. Access on: 15.dez.1830.

'crimes and criminals', the 'justifiable crimes', the 'aggravating and mitigating circumstances of the crime', the reparation of the damage, the quality of the penalties and the way they should be enforced and carried out.

Quite interesting was the consecration of the principle of legality in section 1: 'There is no crime or offense (synonyms in this Code) without a previous law that qualifies it'. On the other hand, the code, in its section 5, did not distinguish the culpability on conspiracy, equating the conduct of agents and accomplices when setting the penalty. Differently from Bernardo Pereira de Vasconcellos' draft, it was decided who would be considered an accomplice, for example, those who received, concealed or bought things obtained by criminal means or those who had given asylum to criminals or lend their own house to the offenders' meeting.

Press crimes, not predicted in Bernardo Pereira de Vasconcellos' draft, were specified as an offense in the Criminal Code. Already on its first part, it brought some general provisions on the subject, such as to establish, in section 7, the criminal liability of the printer, engraver or lithographer, if there were no identified editor; who would be criminally punished, unless it could be proved that the author was responsible for the writings. It was also considered a criminal the seller or distributor of the prints or patterns, when there was no mention of the printer or, if identified, the work had been printed abroad and, finally, the one who communicated for more than fifteen people the writings not printed and with no identification of the author. On section 8 it was established that in these crimes, the analysis should be made according to the hermeneutical rules, not taking into consideration isolated or highlighted phrases. It was not considered crime the printing or circulating parliamentary speeches, reasonable analysis of principles, religious uses, as well as the use of the Constitution and existing laws, since it was done in vigorous, decent and restrained terms, not inciting disobedience and censorship to government acts and public administration.

The legal age was fixed at fourteen years old. However, unlike Bernardo Pereira de Vasconcellos' draft, in case of offence committed by minors, they should be collected to houses of correction and not to their family home, as determined in section 14:

> '*If it is proved that the under fourteen years old, who have committed crimes, behave with discernment, they shall be collected to houses of correction, by the time the court defines, as long as the carrying out of the penalty does not exceed the age of seventeen years old*'. The draft was maintained regarding the insane people who committed crimes, establishing that they would be collected to houses designed to them or handed into their families, at the discretion of the judge.

On the matter of legal excuse, the text approved did not follow the proposed by Bernardo Pereira de Vasconcellos. It was excluded the hypothesis of misconduct against the person herself or with the victim's consent, but were added the resistance situations when facing the execution of illegal orders, the regular exercise of law, and the moderate punishment of the disciple by the master.

The Criminal Code maintained the idea of aggravating and mitigating circumstances. However, it did not establish the criteria of minimum, medium and maximum degrees, but rather, the imposition of the penalty between the limits predicted in the text. Twenty-two aggravating circumstances and ten mitigating circumstances were established. Nonetheless, differently from Bernardo Pereira de Vasconcellos' draft, it did not remain the subjective criteria for application of the penalty, defined as 'sensitivity of the offended'.

Regarding the reparation of the damage, there were changes when compared to the draft by Bernardo Pereira de Vasconcellos. The liability of parents and husbands did not remain. The liability of the master for the damage caused by his slaves was limited to its value. The possibility of public treasure supplies the satisfaction of the damage was withdrawn, being this responsibility solely and exclusively attributed to the offender.

As to the penalties, the Criminal Code maintained most of it: (a) death penalty; (b) galley labor; (c) imprisonment with labor; (d) simple imprisonment; (e) banishment; (f) fine. The penalty of infamy became a penalty of suspension from employment and slave whipping, followed by branding with hot iron.

The rules on the death penalty did not change, except for the new prohibition of hanging a mother before the period of forty days since the delivery. The galley labor penalty was also maintained, although it was prohibited to label the prisoners and everyone under twenty-one years old could not be sentenced to this type of penalty. The convicted who completed sixty years old would have his sentence commuted to imprisonment with work. Thus, as for the penalty of imprisonment with work, it should be carried out in public prisons that provided greater convenience, security and proximity to the place of the offense. However, when the prison did not have these characteristics, the penalties should be commuted to simple imprisonment, added the sixth time, differently from what Pereira de Vasconcellos provided in his draft.

The penalty for slaves was specified as an offense as follows: '*If the defendant is a slave, and incurs on punishment, other than the capital or the galley labor, he shall be convicted on whipping, being delivered to his master in sequence, which will be required to bring the slave with an iron, by the time and manner the judge designates*'. This was extinct by Law 3, 310 of 1886. However, it remained that the number of whips would be fixed in the sentence, and also that the slave could not suffer more than fifty strokes per day.

Likewise, also differently from Bernardo Pereira de Vasconcellos' draft, the Criminal Code established that all penalties were unlimited, following the orientation of the positive school, that no crime should go unpunished.[53]

The second part of the Code specified public offenses, encompasses the crimes against the State, such as the offense opposed to the independence or integrity of the empire, the restraint of the free exercise of political powers or political rights of citizens, the conspiracy, the rebellion, riot, the insurrection, the resistance, besides the crimes against public administration, such as official misconduct, bribery,

[53]Ladislau Thót. *Idem.* p. 50.

authority abuse, undue influence peddling, falsehood and perjury, and finally offenses against the treasury, such as peculation, counterfeit money and contraband.

The third part specified private crimes, which corresponded to crimes against individual freedom, crimes against individual security (homicide, infanticide, slander, threat, break into someone else's house, opening of letters), crimes against the security of honor (rape, kidnapping, calumny and slander), crimes against the security of civil and domestic state (polygamy, adultery, alleged birth) and crimes against property (theft, bankruptcy, embezzlement, theft and damage).

The last part was about police crimes, which refers to the practice of unofficial religions, secret societies, unlawful gatherings, vagrancy and panhandling, use of weapons of defense, fabrication of tools for the commitment of crimes, improper use of name or title and misuse of company.

Concerning the content of these last three books, there was improvement on the writing quality, as stated by the committee in charge of systematization of the final text. Penalties were softened when compared to the draft, maintaining the death penalty and the penalty of galley labor only in case of insurrection, homicide, theft and robbery, according to the circumstances of the offense. In contrast, it was increased the number of hypothesis of imprisonment, including the possibility of converting the galley labor into confinement.

It is also worth noticing the mildness of the penalties for crimes committed by employees of the public administration, when facing the parliamentary debates, that pointed out the corruption as one of the causes of criminality in Brazil. For example, the crime of official misconduct, on section 129, was punished with the dismissal of the position for the period of one year and a fine equivalent to six months, when in the maximum degree. The medium degree resulted in the loss of the job and the same fine; and in the minimum degree, the suspension for three years and a fine of three months. The crime of bribery was punished as the disposed on sections 130 and 133, with the loss of the job or a fine equal to six times the bribery or even the imprisonment from three to nine months. The crime of concussion was punished with suspension from the job for six months to two years. The penalties for the crime of embezzlement, provided by section 170, were the loss of employment or imprisonment with work for two months to four years or a fine of five to twenty percent of the amount of the value taken, spent or lost.

7 The Originality of 1830 Criminal Code

As already seen, Bernardo Pereira de Vasconcellos' draft, as well as the final draft that resulted in the 1830 Criminal Code, although have been influenced by criminal codes enacted at that time, are not literal reproductions of them. There was no explicit mention in the debates in the House of Representatives to the greater or lesser influence of these codes in Brazil, in contrast to what was observed in terms of criminal law philosophy, especially the work of Cesare Beccaria.

Both Bernardo Pereira de Vasconcellos and the committee in charge of remodeling his draft, as well as other Brazilians members of Congress, most of them graduated in law, had access to such legislation. This influence was due to the fact that the nineteenth century was a period of consolidation of a new model of criminal code, reason why the Brazilian code adopted this new paradigm. Thus, the greater or lesser approximation of the Brazilian code to its European counterparts is the result of the contemporary interpretation arising from the comparison between these texts.

Traces of three codes can be noticed in the final version of the Brazilian Criminal Code. These are: the 1810 French Criminal Code,[54] the 1813 Bavarian Criminal Code[55] and the 1822 Spanish Criminal Code.[56] Although Luiz Jiménez Asúa has pointed out that the 1830 Criminal Code is a reproduction of the Neapolitan code, whose original title is Code of the Kingdom of the Two Sicilies, enacted in 1819,[57] its reading leads us to the conclusion that no provision of this code has been used in Brazil.

Similarly, it is hard to recognize the influence of the 1803 Austrian Criminal Code in the elaboration of the 1830 Brazilian Criminal Code.[58] In spite of the importance of the 1803 Austrian Code for the history of criminal law, it seems that this code is not the main dividing line between criminal law prior to the Enlightenment and the Criminal Codes enacted under the influence of ideas of such great thinkers as Bentham and Beccaria. The rupture of an ancient criminal law into a modern criminal law certainly occurred with the 1810 French and the 1813 Bavarian Criminal Codes. This statement is based on the analysis of the text of the 1803 Austrian Criminal Code,[59] whose widely descriptive, doctrinal and detailed writing is closer to the Portuguese Philippine Ordinations or to many other similar texts than to a modern Criminal Code. The types of penalties provided for in the 1803 Austrian Criminal Code do not resemble those provided for in the 1830 Brazilian Criminal Code. Also in the 1803 Austrian Code, the prediction of crimes is mixed with what is meant by the "General Part" of a Criminal Code, in addition to the fact that, except for the most common crimes, such as homicide, robbery, etc., are not original contributions of the 1803 Austrian Criminal Code, as well as the

---

[54]France. *Code Penal de 1810*. Available at: http://ledroitcriminel.free.fr/la_legislation_criminelle/anciens_textes/code_penal_de_1810.htm. Access on: 15.dez.2013.

[55]Bavaria (Kingdom). *Code Penal du Royaume de Bavière*; traduit du allemand avec des explications tirées du commentaire officiel (exposé des motifs) et appendice par Ch. Vatel. (Paris, Auguste Durand, Libraire-Editeur, 1852).

[56]Spain (Kingdom). *Código Penal Español decretado por las Cortes en 8 de junio, sancionado por el Rey, y mandado promulgar en 9 de julio de 1822*. (Madrid, Imprenta Nacional, 1822).

[57]Sicily (Kingdom). *Códice pel il Regno delle Due Sicilie*. Parte seconda. (Napoli, Tipografia del Ministro dello Stato della Cancillleria Generale, 1819).

[58]Bravo Lira, 'La fortuna del Código Penal español de 1848', cited in fn n. 9.

[59]Austrian Empire. *Codice dei Delitti e delle gravi trasgressioni politiche*. (Vienna, Appresso Gio. Tomasso Nob de Trattern. Stampatore e Librajo di S. M. Imp. e Reale, 1803).

purpose of insurrection crimes in the 1803 Austrian Criminal Code was distinct of the Brazilian Code, as there was also no provision for the crime of mourning in the 1830 Austrian Criminal Code. Likewise, the existence of aggravating and mitigating circumstances in the 1803 Austrian Criminal Code does not mean that this was the origin of similar prediction in the 1830 Brazilian Criminal Code. Therefore, the eventual influence of the 1803 Austrian Criminal Code was indirect, by means of the other codes promulgated between the decades of 1810 and 1820.

Regarding the 1810 French Penal Code, the influence can be recognized on the disposition of the subjects. The draft proposed by Bernardo Pereira de Vasconcellos followed with imperfections the order of the Bavarian Code, reason why representatives considered necessary to correct the draft, aiming to obtain better clarity. The used the order established by the French Code, which consisted in dividing the code into four parts: crimes and penalties, public offenses, private offenses and police crimes. Another influence of the French Code—although is not exclusivity of this code—is the existence of the first book, about crimes and penalties. Moreover, the order of disposition of the types of penalties was similar both in the draft and in the final text that was converted into the code. Certain public offences were similar. On the same way, the understanding of Pereira de Vasconcellos on the individualization of punishment in case of conspiracy was not followed, being ruled the same liability for all agents, as predicted in the French Code.

On the other hand, the aspects of the Brazilian Criminal Code that does not resemble to the dispositions of the French Code are those arising from the approximation to the codes of Bavaria and Spain. The main issue was the definition of aggravating and mitigating circumstances, brought by these two European codes. This point is very important because the French Criminal Code was widely criticized at the time for being too severe and not give leeway to the judge on the sentencing guideline.[60]

The similarities with the Code of Bavaria result from the content preserved from Bernardo Pereira de Vasconcellos' draft. This approximation was noticed on the length of the penalty of galley labor, which could not be applied to people over sixty years old, but also on the penalty of whipping, which could not exceed fifty strokes. The ideas of legal excuse also came from this source, as well as the definition of certain public offenses.

However, the 1830 Brazilian Code distances itself from the Bavarian Code because it does not adopt the idea of degrees of complicity, neither the clear distinction between crimes and felonies, nor the difference between intentional and culpable crimes as well as it adopts the distinction between criminal penalties and civil penalties. It did not follow the rules of criminal limitation or limitation for crimes itself, also did not follow the same order of exposition of specification of offenses,

[60]"Article 65. No crime or offense may be justified, nor the penalty shall it be mitigated, except in those cases and circumstances in which the law declares that the fact is defensible or that it allows the application of a less severe penalty."

since the Bavarian Code detailed the conduct of agents for each criminal offense. Finally, the 1830 Brazilian Code did not brought the idea of civil death, nor the various hypothesis of death penalty held in that text, and refused the idea of indeterminate penalties.

Yet, the 1822 Spanish Criminal Code,[61] which is similar in some aspects to the Bavarian Code, especially on the long essay of articles, was an influence to the Brazilian code on the existing rules of aggravating and mitigating circumstances, as well as the rules on reparation of damages caused by a criminal act. Some types of crimes are also similar, such as the ones practiced by employees of public administration and the offensives against prisons. On the other hand, the Brazilian code did not follow the rules on granting pardon—unlike the contemporary Brazilian criminal law—and prescription, both established in the Spanish code.

Despite the influences, it is possible to assert some degree of originality both in the Bernardo Pereira de Vasconcellos' draft and in the final draft that resulted in the Criminal Code. Thus, the first aspect lies in the equalization between crimes and felonies, treated as synonyms. Also, the Brazilian Code innovates when does not follow the distinction between cruel and infamous punishments from merely cruel punishment. It is also novelty in the Criminal Code of the Empire the inclusion of the principle of legality as one of the foundations of criminal law, brought by section 1.

Although death penalty was allowed, its discipline was different from the one established in other codes of that time. As already seen, the death penalty was considered cruel by the representatives, but it was admitted for practical reasons, restricted to a few hypotheses. Still, there was an effort to correct the severity of the penalties brought by Bernardo Pereira de Vasconcellos—also existent in European codes, which ruled the death penalty for more than thirty circumstances—by setting up milder penalties, granting the proportionality between the legal interests protected and the corresponding penalties. This certainly was a differential for the time.

Other important aspects in terms of originality of the 1830 Brazilian Criminal Code lies on the discipline of 'justifiable crimes', on the reparation of the damage, including a detailed discipline of mitigating and aggravating circumstances, besides the criminal impunity of minors and insane people, who should be referred to houses intended for them or, also be sent to the family (only insane people had this option). It is precisely these points that were incorporated into the 1848 Spanish Penal Code,[62] which represented a break of style and arrangement of subjects when compared to its antecessor of 1822.

---

[61]In the opinion of Vivian Chieregati Costa. (*Idem.* p. 249), the Brazilian Code is deeply influenced by the 1822 Spanish Criminal Code and has received some influence from the Louisiana Criminal Code, developed by Edward Livingston.

[62]Spain (Kingdom). *Código Penal de España.* Ediciòn oficial reformada. (Madrid, Imprenta Nacional, 1850).

8 Conclusion

In the first years of the Brazilian Empire, the change of criminal legislation determined in Article 179, XVIII, of the 1824 Constitution, was also necessary, since authors like Beccaria and Bentham clarified the criminal law, making the Book V of the Philippines Ordinations become anachronistic, known for its cruelty in the application of punishments. Also in the nineteenth century, permeated with romanticism and insurgent and nationalist movements, punishments for political crimes were no longer accepted.

In Brazil, this change was a result of the work of two important jurists graduated at the University of Coimbra: José Clemente Pereira and Bernardo Pereira de Vasconcellos. The first had an outstanding political role in Brazil between the decades of 1820 and 1850 and, Bernardo Pereira de Vasconcellos, born in Minas Gerais, also had a relevant political activity. In 1826, they both became representatives and worked to develop a Criminal Code.

José Clemente Pereira took the first step by presenting, in 1826, his 'basis for a future criminal code, followed by the submission of a complete draft in the following year. In that same month of May, in 1827, Bernardo Pereira de Vasconcellos presented another criminal code draft.

The House of Representatives, through a special committee, worked on developing a third draft from what had already been presented. This third draft became the Criminal Code, enacted in 1830. Thus, it is clear that the Criminal Code is not a result of exclusive work by Bernardo Pereira de Vasconcellos. Although his work has been the basis to the final Code, the committee was not bounded to it. Still, it is important to emphasize the parliamentary discussions about this relevant Code, because they reveal the deep knowledge of the representatives about the philosophy of criminal law at the time, brought by Beccaria and Bentham, highlighting the arguments about the inconvenience of the death penalty, also in a country like Brazil.

Although one can identify the influence of the 1810 French Penal Code, the 1813 Bavarian Criminal Code and the 1822 Spanish Criminal Code, fact that forbids to qualify the 1830 Brazilian Criminal Code as a totally original text, it can be said that it was, indeed, an advanced and unique text for the time. It has not received any influence of the Criminal Code of the Kingdom of the Two Sicilies, though the opposite of this truth is sometimes heard. The most relevant Brazilian contributions were the treatment of crimes and felonies as synonyms; the inclusion of the principle of legality; the reduction on the number of hypothesis of application of death penalty, when compared to European codes; and the detailed discipline of aggravating and mitigating circumstances.

Thus, Ladislau Thót had certain reason when he defended that the 1830 Criminal Code was effectively a national and proper code, meaning that it was not a faithful reproduction of European codes, since it was a result of the work of two brilliant jurists and representatives, prepared for heading discussions on the subject, at a high level of knowledge and depth about it.

Nelson Hungria was not able to recognize all the advances brought by the Criminal Code, which were not restricted to the *pactum sceleris* as generic aggravating circumstance, even though he gave some importance to the Code. With all due respect, one understands that he was mistaken in defending that the novelties presented were 'authentic antique', because these changes did not exist in the most famous European criminal codes, promulgated after the works of those two philosophers who most influenced the criminal law in the world. Thus, the drafters of the 1830 Criminal Code of the Empire had some merit in becoming the first people in the world to incorporate these allegedly 'old' ideas.

References

Bravo Lira, B. 'La fortuna del Código Penal español de 1848: historia en cuatro actos y trés continents: de Mello Freire y Zeiller a Vasconcellos y Seijas Lozano'. (Anuario de Historia del Derecho Español, Madrid, 2004), pp. 23–57.

Carvalho, JM (in cooperation with LIMA, PS). 'Introdução'. In: CARVALHO, JM (Org.). *Bernardo Pereira de Vasconcellos*. (São Paulo, Ed. 34, 1999). pp. 9–34.

Costa, VC. *Codificação e formação do Estado-nacional brasileiro: o Código Criminal de 1830 e a positivação das leis no pós-Independência*. (Dissertation, Master in Brazilian Studies, University of São Paulo, Brazilian Studies Institute, São Paulo, 2013).

Hungria, N. *Comentários ao Código Penal*. v. 1. tomo 1. 3ª ed. revista e atualizada. (Rio de Janeiro, Forense, 1955).

Jiménez de Asúa, L. *Tratado de Derecho Penal. Tomo I. Concepto de derecho penal y de la criminologia, história y legislación penal comparada*. 5ª ed. actualizada. (Buenos Aires, Editorial Losada, S.A, 1992).

Machado, J. 'Historia del Derecho Penal Boliviano y sus Reformas'. Available at: http://jorgemachicado.blogspot.com.br/2009/03/historia-del-derecho-penal-boliviano-y.html#_Toc224636917. Access on: 09 July 2015.

Meira, S. *Teixeira de Freitas: o jurisconsulto do Império. Vida e obra*. (Brasília, Cegraf, 1983).

Neder, G. 'Degredo e pena de morte no Brasil Império'. In: Anais do XXV Simpósio Nacional de História - Anpuh. Fortaleza, 2009. Available at: http://anpuh.org/anais/?p=18520. Access on: 15.dez.2013.

Pousada, ELR. *Preservação da tradição jurídica luso-brasileira: Teixeira de Freitas e a introdução à Consolidação das Leis Civis*. (Dissertation, Master in History of Law, University of São Paulo, Law School, São Paulo, 2006).

Poveda Velasco, IM. 'Augusto Teixeira de Freitas' (verbete). In: R Domingo (org). *Juristas Universales*. V. 3. (Madrid, Marcial Pons, 2004).

Schipani, S (org). *Augusto Teixeira de Freitas e il diritto latioamericano*. (Padova, Cedam, 1988).

Sisson, SA. 'José Clemente Pereira'. In: SISSON, SA. *Grandes Brasileiros Ilustres*. Volume I. (Brasília, Senado Federal, 1999), pp. 41–46.

Thót, L. 'O Código Criminal Brasileiro de 1830'. (*Archivo Judiciário*. Rio de Janeiro. volume XV). 1930. pp. 39–51.

Tomasevicius Filho, E. *Entre a memória coletiva e a história de cola-e-tesoura: as intrigas e os malogros nos relatos sobre a Fábrica de Ferro de São João de Ipanema*. (Dissertation, Master in Social History, University of São Paulo, Philosophy, Litteracy and Human Sciences Faculty, São Paulo. 2012).

Sources

Austrian Empire. *Codice dei Delitti e delle gravi trasgressioni politiche.* (Vienna, Appresso Gio. Tomasso Nob de Trattern. Stampatore e Librajo di S. M. Imp. e Reale, 1803).

Bavaria (Kingdom). *Code Penal du Royaume de Bavière; traduit du allemand avec des explications tirées du commentaire officiel (exposé des motifs) et appendice par Ch. Vatel.* (Paris, Auguste Durand, Libraire-Editeur, 1852).

Brazil (Empire). '*Sessão em 3 de junho de 1826'. Annaes da Câmara dos Deputados.* pp. 16–18. Available at: http://imagem.camara.gov.br/pesquisa_diario_basica.asp Access on: 13.dez.2013.

Brazil. House of Representatives. 'Sessão em 1° e agosto de 1826'. *Annaes da Câmara dos Deputados.* p. 17. Available at: http://imagem.camara.gov.br/pesquisa_diario_basica.asp Access on: 13.dez.2013.

Brazil. House of Representatives. 'Sessão em 17 de agosto de 1826'. *Annaes da Câmara dos Deputados.* p. 173. Available at: http://imagem.camara.gov.br/pesquisa_diario_basica.asp Access on: 13.dez.2013.

Brazil. House of Representatives. 'Sessão em 4 de maio de 1827'. *Annaes da Câmara dos Deputados.* p. 16. Available at: http://imagem.camara.gov.br/pesquisa_diario_basica.asp Access on: 13.dez.2013.

Brazil. House of Representatives. 'Sessão em 5 de maio de 1827'. *Annaes da Câmara dos Deputados.* p. 23. Available at: http://imagem.camara.gov.br/pesquisa_diario_basica.asp Access on: 13.dez.2013.

Brazil. House of Representatives. 'Sessão em 16 de maio de 1827'. *Annaes da Câmara dos Deputados.* p. 97. Available at: http://imagem.camara.gov.br/pesquisa_diario_basica.asp Access on: 13.dez.2013.

Brazil. House of Representatives. 'Sessão em 14 de agosto de 1827. *Annaes da Câmara dos Deputados.* pp. 130–131. Available at: http://imagem.camara.gov.br/pesquisa_diario_basica.asp Access on: 13.dez.2013.

Brazil. House of Representatives. 'Sessão em 31 de agosto de 1829'. *Annaes da Câmara dos Deputados.* p. 84. Available at: http://imagem.camara.gov.br/pesquisa_diario_basica.asp Access on: 13.dez.2013.

Brazil. House of Representatives. 'Sessão em 11 de setembro de 1830'. *Annaes da Câmara dos Deputados.* p. 490. Available at: http://imagem.camara.gov.br/pesquisa_diario_basica.asp Access on: 13.dez.2013.

Brazil. House of Representatives. 'Sessão em 13 de setembro de 1830'. *Annaes da Câmara dos Deputados.* p. 506. Available at: http://imagem.camara.gov.br/pesquisa_diario_basica.asp Access on: 13.dez.2013.

Brazil. House of Representatives. 'Sessão de 14 de setembro de 1830'. *Annaes da Câmara dos Deputados.* p. 507. Available at: http://imagem.camara.gov.br/pesquisa_diario_basica.asp Access on: 13.dez.2013.

Brazil. House of Representatives. 'Sessão em 15 de setembro de 1830'. *Annaes da Câmara dos Deputados.* p. 516. Available at: http://imagem.camara.gov.br/pesquisa_diario_basica.asp Access on: 13.dez.2013.

Brazil. House of Representatives. 'Sessão em 16 de setembro de 1830'. *Annaes da Câmara dos Deputados.* p. 518. Available at: http://imagem.camara.gov.br/pesquisa_diario_basica.asp Access on: 13.dez.2013.

Brazil. House of Representatives. Sessão em 19 de outubro de 1830. In: BRASIL (Empire). *Annaes da Câmara dos Deputados.* p. 612. Available at: http://imagem.camara.gov.br/pesquisa_diario_basica.asp Access on: 13.dez.2013.

Brazil. House of Representatives. 'Sessão de 23 de outubro de 1830'. *Annaes da Câmara dos Deputados.* p. 617. Available at: http://imagem.camara.gov.br/pesquisa_diario_basica.asp Access on: 13.dez.2013.

Brazil. House of Representatives. Lei de 16 de dezembro de 1830. Manda executar o Código Criminal. Available at: http://www.planalto.gov.br/ccivil_03/leis/lim/lim-16-12-1830.htm. Access on: 15.dez.2013.

Spain (Kingdom). *Código Penal Español decretado por las Cortes en 8 de junio, sancionado por el Rey, y mandado promulgar en 9 de julio de 1822*. (Madrid, Impreta Nacional, 1822).

Spain (Kingdom). *Código Penal de España*. Edición oficial reformada. (Madrid, Imprenta Nacional, 1850).

France. *Code Penal de 1810*. Available at: http://ledroitcriminel.free.fr/la_legislation_criminelle/anciens_textes/code_penal_de_1810.htm. Access on: 15.dez.2013.

Sicily (Kingdom). *Códice pel il Regno delle Due Sicilie*. Parte seconda. (Napoli, Tipografia del Ministro dello Stato della Cancillleria Generale, 1819).

Ignacio María Poveda Velasco LL.B Degree in Law at the University of São Paulo Law School. LL.M and S.J.D. in Civil Law (emphasis in Roman Law) at the University of São Paulo Law School. Full Professor of History of Law at the University of São Paulo Law School. Former Dean of the Ribeirao Preto University of Sao Paulo Law Scchool. General-Secretary of the University of Sao Paulo. Professor Poveda Velasco is also a researcher about Latin American Codification for the "Direto das Fontes" Research Group, linked to the Civil Law Department of the University of São Paulo Law School.

Eduardo Tomasevicius Filho LL.B Degree in Law at the University of São Paulo Law School. M.Sc. in Social History at the University of São Paulo Philosophy, Literacy and Human Sciences Faculty and S.J.D. in Civil Law at the University of São Paulo Law School. Associate Professor of History of Law and Civil Law at the Civil Law Department of the University of Sao Paulo Law School. Professor Tomasevicius Filho is also a researcher about Latin American Codification for the "Direto das Fontes" Research Group, linked to the Civil Law Department of the University of São Paulo Law School.

The Mexican Codification of Criminal Law: Its Foreign Influences

Oscar Cruz Barney

Abstract This chapter analyzes the influence of the French Penal Code among others on the Mexican codification efforts in this area. Also the presence of other influences and the Mexican legal tradition itself reflected on the criminal legislation of the nineteen century. The authors of the Mexican codification did not intend to do an original work or copy a foreign model, but to collect and reformulate Castilian law, as a part of Mexican legal tradition. The Mexican codification started early in the nineteen century (1827) and has its best results in 1871 with the Penal Code of 1871 for Mexico City.

1 Introduction

In 1789 and thanks to the *Declaration of the Rights of Man and the Citizen*,[1] instead of the legal concept of the old regime, there were two political-constitutional values: the individual and the law as an expression of the sovereignty of the nation. Maurizio Fioravanti argues that the term 'law' in the Declaration contains along with the meaning of 'limit' to the exercise of liberties, the one of submission, ensuring that individuals can no longer be bound by any authority other than that of the legislator, "Legitimate interpreter of the general will".[2]

In this sense, the law is conceived by the French revolutionaries as a value, rather than a mere instrument, thanks to which the rights and freedoms of all are made possible.[3] The validity of legal norms will depend on their forms of

[1]On the background of the *Declaración* see Jean Louis Gazzaniga, "La dimension historique des libertés et droits foundamentaux", Cabrillac, Remy, Marie-Anne Frison-Roche & Thierry Revet (Coords.), *Libertés et droits fondamentaux* (Paris: Dalloz, 2002, 8th ed.), pp. 16–23.
[2]Maurizio Fioravanti, *Los derechos fundamentales. Apuntes de Historia de las Constituciones* (trans. by Manuel Martínez Neira) (Madrid: Ed. Trotta, 2000, 3rd ed.), p. 58.
[3]*Ibid.*, p. 62.

O. Cruz Barney (✉)
Instituto de Investigaciones Jurídicas, UNAM, México City, Mexico
e-mail: ocbarney@unam.mx

A. Masferrer (ed.), *The Western Codification of Criminal Law*, Studies in the History of Law and Justice 11, https://doi.org/10.1007/978-3-319-71912-2_14

production; its legality will no longer depend on its intrinsic justice or rationality, but on its positivity, that is, on the fact that it is issued by a competent authority in the manner provided for it.[4] The subjection of the powers of the State to the law will consist in the regulation by the law of the relations between the State and the society, by supposing that the State acts according to laws and through them.[5]

From the eighteenth century, it will be increasingly considered that the legislative produced norms are the only legitimate source of law, the only one capable of expressing the general will and therefore imposing itself above any other form of legal production, weakening the others, "the old legal pluralism, which had behind it, although with several vicissitudes, more than two thousand years of life, is suffocated in a rigid monism."[6] In this sense, the division of powers will be the foundation to assign legal production to the Legislative Branch, which is identified as the holder of popular sovereignty. Thus, the general will (or *voluntas*) will be expressed through the Representation and this is expressed through the Law, "material basis of its place in the normative hierarchy."[7] The codification supports the idea of overcoming legal particularism and affirms the authority of the State.[8]

It is a "comprehensive law, systematically constructed, expressed in clear principles, which orders at least a whole sphere of life, if not the whole life of a given society."[9] The Code must order and guide the freedom and equality of individuals required by Natural Law. From a formal point of view, the code must be systematic and clear in its expression, departing from casuistic particularisms and subtleties; it must contain principles. Codification became a symbol of modernity in the Western world, a source of personal prestige for the sovereign and in this sense can be seen as an expression of the power of the governor,[10] and as the expression of a 'national right' to which it affirms, and which tries to be more vigorous and efficient than the old *Ius Commune*.[11]

The codification of law is a process initiated in the eighteenth century and developed fully in the nineteenth, which leads to the removal of legal structures of the old regime based on the *Ius Commune*, replacing it with a new legal regime.

---

[4]Luigi Ferrajoli, *Derechos y garantías. La ley del más débil* (trand. by Perfecto Andrés Ibáñez y Andrea Greppi) (Madrid: Ed. Trotta, 1999), p. 66.

[5]Carlos de Cabo Martín, *Sobre el concepto de ley* (Madrid: Ed. Trotta, 2000), p. 19.

[6]Paolo Grossi, *Mitología jurídica de la modernidad* (trad. by Manuel Martínez Neira) (Madrid: Ed. Trotta, 2003), p. 75.

[7]Carlos de Cabo Martín, *Sobre el concepto…*, p. 20.

[8]Renzo Dickmann, "Codificazione e processo legislativo", Costanzo, Pasquale (Coord.), *Codificazione del diritto e ordinamento costituzionale,* (Napoli: Facoltá di Giurisprudenza della Universitá di Camerino, 1999), p. 61.

[9]Helmut Coing, *Derecho privado europeo. I: Derecho común más antiguo (1500–1800)* (translation and notes by de Antonio Pérez Martín) (Madrid: Fundación Cultural del Notariado, 1996), vol. I, p. 113.

[10]See Bruno Oppetit, *Essai sur la codification* (Paris: Presses Universitaires de France, 1998), p. 8.

[11]Carlos Ramos Núñez, *El Código Napoleónico y su recepción en América Latina* (Lima: Pontificia Universidad Católica del Perú – Fondo Editorial, 1997), p. 51.

It begins with humanism and continues with rationalistic naturalism,[12] "Codification is the logical consequence of the ideology of the Enlightenment; Through the Codes, iusnaturalism finds the most graphic form of expression of the ideas coined by Domat, Tomasio, Pothier, Loysel, Püfendorf".[13] The rise of rationalism and the development of Nation-States led to the decay of the old legal structures.[14]

Grossi maintains that iusnaturalism thus leads to a very heavy legal positivism and the Code, although bearer of universal values, is reduced to being the voice of the national sovereign: the positive law of the State.[15]

However, it must be clear that the codification did not mean innovation of the contents of the law, but instead of its modes of creation, conservation, manifestation and fixation. As has been stated,

> [t]he codification is not limited to gathering preexisting legislative materials as formulated in their time and to systematize them, which was the method of the previous collections. The codes, from the end of the eighteenth century and to the present day, imply a new formulation of the legal norm.[16]

The Codes reflect traditional law and accommodate new institutions, reforming and adapting to each other. As Abelardo Levaggi points out, "although modern codification was presented as a break with the romanic tradition, it was only partial: much more formal than material".[17] Guzmán Brito sees the codification from two points of view: as an evolutionary stage of the *Ius Commune*, so that the codification of the law actually means codification of the *Ius Commune*; and as an operation intended to replace the *Ius Commune* in terms of its form and to express it taking advantage of its contents in the new codes.[18] The Spanish historiography has developed this line of thought, applying it to the codification of law in general,[19] and in the criminal law province in particular.[20]

---

[12]Abelardo Levaggi, *Manual de Historia del Derecho Argentino* (Buenos Aires: Depalma, 1998), vol. I, General Part, p. 185, n. 61.

[13]Juan Baró Pazos, *La codificación del Derecho Civil en España (1808–1889)* (Santander: Universidad de Cantabria, 1992), pp. 11–12.

[14]Reinhard Zimmermann, *Estudios de derecho privado europeo* (trans. by Antoni Vaquer Aloy) (Madrid: Civitas, 2000), p. 20.

[15]Grossi, *Mitología jurídica…*, p. 74.

[16]Agustín Motilla, "La codificación como técnica de producción legislativa", *Revista de Derecho Privado* 71 (1987), p. 546.

[17]Levaggi, *Manual de historia del derecho…*, p. 187, n. 61.

[18]Alejandro Guzmán Brito, *La codificación civil en Iberoamérica. Siglos XIX y XX* (Santiago de Chile: Editorial Jurídica del Chile, 2000), p. 23.

[19]See, for example, Aniceto Masferrer (ed.), *La Codificación española. Una aproximación doctrinal e historiográfica a sus influencias extranjeras, y a la francesa en particular* (Aniceto Masferrer, ed.) (Pamplona: Aranzadi–Thomson Reuters, 2014).

[20]On this matter, see several works by Aniceto Masferrer, *Tradición y reformismo en la Codificación penal española. Hacia el ocaso de un mito. Materiales, apuntes y reflexiones para un nuevo enfoque metodológico e historiográfico del movimiento codificador penal europeo*,

With codification, Latin ceased to be the universal language of the European and Ibero-American jurists, with the national languages becaming the way to express the legislation and the doctrine.[21]

What was truly new in the codification was "the political ideology of the code, individualistic liberal and egalitarian, expressed with a full legal sense."[22] The enlightened legislators presented to their subjects a codification, "while at the same time exhaustive and grounded in natural reason, which should allow them to know more intelligibly their rights and obligations within the State".[23] In this sense, codification can be seen as an attempt to rationalize and technify legislative activity.[24]

2 México and the Idea of Codification

In Mexico the codification[25] task was seen as the organization of "a simple and philosophical legislation at the same time, where without losing sight of the luminous principles of Roman law, those of the natural law are developed."[26] The codification was considered necessary for the purpose of making "quicker, stronger and more effective the action of justice," hence its fault was considered to be one of the great evils that Mexican society suffered in 1862.[27] There was, yes, an

Universidad de Jaén, 2003; "Codification of Spanish Criminal Law in the Nineteenth Century. A Comparative Legal History Approach", *Journal of Comparative Law* Vol. 4, no. 1 (2009), pp. 96–139; "The Napoleonic *Code pénal* and the Codification of Criminal Law in Spain", *Le Code pénal. Les metamorphoses d'un modèle 1810-1820. Actes du colloque international Lille/ Gand 16-18 décembre 2012*. Textes réunis et présentés par Chantal Aboucaya et Renée Martinage (Lille: Centre d'Histoire Judiciaire, 2012), pp. 65–98.

[21]Ramos Núñez, *El Código Napoleónico...*, p. 52.

[22]*Ibid.*, p. 192.

[23]Zimmermann, *Estudios de derecho...*, p. 20.

[24]Motilla, "La codificación como técnica de producción legislativa", p. 546.

[25]For a general view of the codifiaction process in Mexico see Oscar Cruz Barney, *La codificación en México* (México: Ed. Porrúa – Instituto de Investigaciones Jurídicas, UNAM, 2010); see also Oscar Cruz Barney (Coord.), *La Codificación* (México: Ed. Porrúa, Universidad Iberoamericana, 2006).

[26]"Códigos", *El Observador Judicial y de Legislación. Periódico que contiene todas las leyes y decretos dados por el Exmo. Señor Presidente Provisional D. Antonio López de Santa-Anna, desde la época de nuestra regeneración política. Establecido á impulso del Exmo. Señor Ministro de Justicia é Instrucción Pública, Don Crispiniano del Castillo* (México: Imprenta de Vicente García Torres, 1842), vol. II, p. 98.

[27]José María Pérez Hernández, *Estadística de la República Mejicana* (Guadalajara: Tip. del Gobierno, a cargo de Antonio de P. González, 1862), p. 259.

awareness that the codification could not be the work of a year or two, as indeed it happened, "no matter how efficient may be the hands to which they have been entrusted."[28]

In the early nineteenth century Mexico, the law was considered the 'symbol of order', 'the bond that identifies the universe.' In 1878 it was stated: "Who said man, said society; who said society, said law."[29]

It should be noted, however, that the authors of the codification did not intend to do an original work or copy a foreign model.[30] "His work consists primarily in collecting and reformulating Castilian law".[31]

In January of 1874 Luis Méndez maintained, with respect to the civil code, the code of civil procedures and the penal code recently approved that they were[32]:

> Bodies of dispositions in which, retaining much of the good that contained the old codes, has adopted everything that has seemed good of the modern laws of several countries of Europe and even of America, the Mexican codes demand to be well understood, a deep knowledge, as well as vast, of all those elements.

The codification meant the creation of a formal equality of society, without being able to erase an existing material inequality.[33]

---

[28]"Leyes Bárbaras", *El Observador Judicial y de Legislación. Periódico que contiene todas las leyes y decretos dados por el Exmo. Señor Presidente Provisional D. Antonio López de Santa-Anna, desde la época de nuestra regeneración política. Establecido á impulso del Exmo. Señor Ministro de Justicia é Instrucción Pública, Don Crispiniano del Castillo* (México: Imprenta de Vicente García Torres, 1843), vol. III, p. 97.

[29]Eduardo Esponda, "La Ley", *El Foro, Periódico de Jurisprudencia y de Legislación* (México) vol. IV, 2nd Epoch, Num. 79, (Saturday, 19 October 1878), p. 310.

[30]On this matter, see, for example, Aniceto Masferrer, "La Codificación española y sus influencias extranjeras. Una revisión en torno al alcance del influjo francés", *La Codificación española. Una aproximación doctrinal e historiográfica a sus influencias extranjeras, y a la francesa en particular* (Aniceto Masferrer, ed.) (Pamplona: Aranzadi–Thomson Reuters, 2014), pp. 19–43; more recently, Aniceto Masferrer, "Codification as Nationalization or Denationalization of Law: The Spanish Case in Comparative Perspective", *Comparative Legal History* 4.2 (2016), pp. 100–130; see also the bibliography cited in the fn. n. 21.

[31]Bernardino Bravo Lira, "Codificación y derecho común en Europa e Hispanoamérica. Disociación de los derechos nacionales del derecho común", Bernardino Bravo Lira & Sergio Concha Márquez de la Plata (Eds.), *Codificación y descodificación en Hispanoamérica* (Santiago de Chile: Escuela de Derecho – Universidad Santo Tomás, 1998), p. 17.

[32]Luis Méndez, "Introducción", *El Foro, Periódico de Jurisprudencia y de Legislación* (México), vol. II, Num. 1, (Thursday, 1 January 1874), pp. 1–2.

[33]In this sense Víctor Tau Anzoategui, *La codificación en la Argentina, 1810–1870. Mentalidad social e ideas jurídicas* (Buenos Aires: Librería-Editorial Emilio J. Perrot, 2008, 2nd ed.), p. 18.

3 The Mexican Codification of Criminal Law in the Western Context

3.1 Liberal Criminal Law Reforms and Codification in Europe: Spain and France

A series of reforms in criminal matter were carried out around the *Constitution of Cadiz,* as they are the one of 22 April 1811[34] with the abolition of the torment in the prisons; on 17 August 1813[35] and 8 September 1813,[36] the abolition of the punishment of whipping in schools and to the Indians, and the replacement, on 24 January 1812,[37] of the hanging by the *garrote* (death by strangulation) in the execution of the death penalty.[38]

Almost all of the special jurisdictions were abolished by the *Constitution of Cadiz,* with the exception of the ecclesiastical and the military, circumstance that subsisted in the independent Mexico until 23 November 1855 by the named *Juárez Law*[39] (*Law of administration of justice and organic of the Courts of the Federation*). The privileges for the civil matters were suppressed and the

[34]*Decreto de 22 de Abril de 1811, Abolición de la tortura, y de los apremios, y prohibición de otras prácticas aflictivas,* en *Colección de los decretos y ordenes de las Cortes de España, que se reputan vigentes en la República de los Estados-Unidos Mexicanos,* (México: Imprenta de Galván, á cargo de Mariano Arévalo, 1829), Edición facsimilar y estudio introductorio por Oscar Cruz Barney, (México: Suprema Corte de Justicia de la Nación, 2005), pp. 8–9.

[35]*Decreto de 17 de Agosto de 1813, Prohibición de la corrección de azotes en escuelas y colegios,* en *Colección de los decretos y ordenes de las Cortes de España, que se reputan vigentes en la República de los Estados-Unidos Mexicanos,* (México: Imprenta de Galván, á cargo de Mariano Arévalo, 1829), Edición facsimilar y estudio introductorio por Oscar Cruz Barney (México: Suprema Corte de Justicia de la Nación, 2005), p. 104.

[36]*Decreto del 8 de Septiembre de 1813, Abolición de la pena de azotes: se prohibe usar de este y otros castigos con los indios,* en *Colección de los decretos y ordenes de las Cortes de España, que se reputan vigentes en la República de los Estados-Unidos Mexicanos,* (México: Imprenta de Galván, á cargo de Mariano Arévalo, 1829), Edición facsimilar y estudio introductorio por Oscar Cruz Barney, (México: Suprema Corte de Justicia de la Nación, 2005), p. 105.

[37]*Decreto del 24 de enero de 1812, Abolición de la pena de horca,* en *Colección de los decretos y ordenes de las Cortes de España, que se reputan vigentes en la República de los Estados-Unidos Mexicanos,* (México: Imprenta de Galván, á cargo de Mariano Arévalo, 1829), Edición facsimilar y estudio introductorio por Oscar Cruz Barney (México: Suprema Corte de Justicia de la Nación, 2005), p. 25.

[38]Miguel S. Macedo, *Apuntes para la historia del derecho penal mexicano* (México: Editorial Cultura, 1931), pp. 131–132.

[39]*Ley de administración de justicia y orgánica de los tribunales de la Federación, 23 de noviembre de 1855,* in Manuel Dublán and José María Lozano, *Legislación Mexicana, Colección Completa de las Disposiciones Legislativas expedidas desde la independencia de la República* (México: Imprenta del Comercio, á Cargo de Dublán y Lozano, Hijos, 1877), Tomo VII, pp. 593–606.

ecclesiastical one for the criminal matter was made resignable; this one finally was suppressed on 12 July 1859, with the total separation of Church and State.[40]

The military jurisdiction survived for military crimes. Special courts were banned.

The *Constitution of Cadiz* enshrined a series of guarantees in matters of administration of justice in the criminal, establishing in favor of the subject to process the obligation to form the trials with brevity and without vices, as well as for the prison, the precedence of the summary information prior to any corporal punishment and written order of the judge, except in the crimes *in fraganti*, among others. Torment, coercion, confiscation of property, transcendental punishments and underground dungeons were prohibited.[41]

It should be noted that on 12 February 1810, the *French Penal Code* was decreed, which was promulgated the following 22.[42] Divided into 484 articles and four books that are:

- Book One: Of the penalties in criminal and correctional matter and its effects.
- Second Book: Of the punishable, excusable or responsible people, for crime or for crimes.
- Book Three: Of the crimes, of the crimes and of its punishment.
- Book Four: Police contraventions and their sentences.

The first *Spanish Penal Code*, dated 9 July 1822,[43] first published in 1821 as a Draft,[44] was the basis for later Mexican codes in this area, although in Mexico it was not possible to consolidate the criminal codification until the *Criminal Code of the Federal District* of 1871.

---

[40]See Article 3 of the *Ley de nacionalización de los bienes eclesiásticos*, in Manuel Dublán and José María Lozano, *Legislación Mexicana, Colección Completa de las Disposiciones Legislativas expedidas desde la independencia de la República*, (México: Imprenta del Comercio, á Cargo de Dublán y Lozano, Hijos, 1877), Tomo VIII, pp. 680–683.

[41]*Ibid.*, pp. 193–194.

[42]We use the edition contained in *Les Cinq Codes de L'Empire Français* (Paris: Chez Amable Costes, Libraire, 1812).

[43]*Código Penal Español, decretado por las Córtes en 8 de junio, sancionado por el Rey, y mandado promulgar en 9 de julio de 1822* (Madrid: En la Imprenta Nacional, 1822).

[44]*Proyecto de Código Penal, presentado a las Córtes por la Comisión Especial nombrada al efecto*. Impreso de órden de las mismas, (Madrid: Imprenta de Don Mateo Repullés, 1821).

3.2 Criminal Law Reforms and Codification in México

The *Decree of the General and Extraordinary Courts of the Kingdom on the Arrangement of Courts and their Powers* of 9 October 1812[45] contains, in Roa Bárcena's opinion, the general bases on which the later laws have rested.[46]

In the independent Mexico and during the government of the Emperor Don Agustín de Iturbide, the penal legislation tended to repress the remarkable increase in the criminality levels.

On 22 January 1822,[47] the Sovereign Provisional Governmental Council of the Mexican Empire, with the intention of preparing some papers to aid the work of Congress, appointed the commissions responsible for the formation of civil, criminal, trade, mining, agricultural and arts codes, the military (including the navy), the national treasury system and a study education plan. The commission appointed to undertake the work of criminal codification was made up of Messrs. Don Juan Jose Espinosa de los Monteros and Don Antonio de Gama and Córdoba, members of the Sovereign Junta; Don Nicolás Oláez, rapporteur of the Audiencia; Don Juan Arce, Don Jose Ignacio Alva, regidores. As in the case of the commission responsible for civil codification, the effort in criminal matters did not produce any results.[48]

On 13 May 1822,[49] the crime of conspiracy against independence was equated with that of lese human majesty; the proceedings against conspirators were

[45]*Decreto de las Cortes Generales y Extraordinarias del Reyno sobre arreglo de Tribunales y sus Atribuciones* del 9 de octubre de 1812, Reimpreso en México en virtud de órden del Excmo. Sr. Virey de 19 de Marzo de 1813 á consequencia de la de la Regencia de la Monarquía de 4 de Noviembre del año próximo anterior, en que S.A.S. se sirvió autorizar a S.E. para que dispusiese su reimpresion en este Reyno, (México: Por. D. Manuel Antonio Valdes, Impresor de Cámara de S.M., 1813).

[46]Rafael Roa Bárcena, *Manual Razonado de Práctica Criminal y Médico-Legal Forense Mexicana* (México: Imprenta de Andrade y Escalante, 1860), p. 11.

[47]*Decreto XXXI de 22 de Enero de 1822, Nombramiento de Comisiones que preparen algunos trabajos para auxiliar al próximo Congreso*, en *Colección de órdenes y decretos de la soberana junta provisional gubernativa, y soberanos congresos generales de la nación mexicana.* (1821–37), (México: Imprenta de Galván, a cargo de Manuel Arévalo, 1829), 4 vols. Estudio Introductorio de Oscar Cruz Barney, (México: Tribunal Superior de Justicia, 2010), Tomo 1, pp. 95–96.

[48]"Reseña histórica de la codificación en México.- Discusión de los códigos", en *El Derecho, Periódico de Jurisprudencia y Legislación* (México) (Sábado 23 de abril de 1870), Tomo IV, Núm 17, p. 336.

[49]*Decreto de 13 de mayo de 1822, Pena impuesta por delito de conspiración contra la Independencia*, en *Colección de órdenes y decretos de la soberana junta provisional gubernativa, y soberanos congresos generales de la nación mexicana.* (1821–37) (México: Imprenta de Galván, a cargo de Manuel Arévalo, 1829), 4 vols. Estudio Introductorio de Oscar Cruz Barney, (México: Tribunal Superior de Justicia, 2010), Tomo 1, pp. 45–46.

regulated by provisions of 28 August 1823[50]; and in 2 October 1823[51] the Executive was authorized by the Congress to dispose of persons suspected of disturbing the public tranquility, confining them to places deemed convenient, without prejudice to the respective judicial processes. On 27 September 1823,[52] for a period of four months, a summary procedure was instituted to try road robbers, thieves in depopulation, and criminals who made resistance, submitting them to military jurisdiction. This decree was extended by others from 6 April 1824[53] and 3 October 1825,[54] until its repeal, 18 December 1832.[55]

It should be noted that at the session of 9 October 1824, introduced by Mr. Barbabosa, a draft of the Military Penal Code was read for the first time, without any subsequent news being found about it.[56]

During the first federal period, it was constitutionally guaranteed, in arts. 146 to 153 of the *Federal Constitution of 1824*, the prohibition of imposing retroactive laws, as well as the freedom to write, print and publish political ideas without the

---

[50]*Decreto de 28 de Agosto de 1823, Medidas para el breve despacho de las causas de conspiración*, en *Colección de órdenes y decretos de la soberana junta provisional gubernativa, y soberanos congresos generales de la nación mexicana* (1821–37) (México: Imprenta de Galván, a cargo de Manuel Arévalo, 1829), 4 vols. Estudio Introductorio de Oscar Cruz Barney, (México: Tribunal Superior de Justicia, 2010), Tomo 2, pp. 164–166.

[51]*Decreto del 2 de Octubre de 1823, Sobre providencias del alta policía*, en *Colección de órdenes y decretos de la soberana junta provisional gubernativa, y soberanos congresos generales de la nación mexicana.* (1821–37), (México: Imprenta de Galván, a cargo de Manuel Arévalo, 1829), 4 vols. Estudio Introductorio de Oscar Cruz Barney, (México: Tribunal Superior de Justicia, 2010), Tomo 2, p. 185.

[52]*Decreto del 27 de Septiembre de 1823, Que los reos de algunos delitos sean juzgados militarmente. Reglas para observar el despacho de las causas de los mismos reos, cuando sean juzgados por la jurisdicción ordinaria*, en *Colección de órdenes y decretos de la soberana junta provisional gubernativa, y soberanos congresos generales de la nación mexicana.* (1821–37), (México: Imprenta de Galván, a cargo de Manuel Arévalo, 1829), 4 vols. Estudio Introductorio de Oscar Cruz Barney (México: Tribunal Superior de Justicia, 2010), Tomo 2, pp. 182–183.

[53]*Decreto del 6 de Abril de 1824, Prorogacion de la ley de 27 de Septiembre de 1823*, en *Colección de órdenes y decretos de la soberana junta provisional gubernativa, y soberanos congresos generales de la nación mexicana.* (1821–37) (México: Imprenta de Galván, a cargo de Manuel Arévalo, 1829), 4 vols. Estudio Introductorio de Oscar Cruz Barney, (México: Tribunal Superior de Justicia, 2010), Tomo 3, p. 40.

[54]*Decreto del 3 de Octubre de 1825, Estension de la ley de 27 de Septiembre de 823 sobre ladrones juzgados militarmente*, en *Colección de órdenes y decretos de la soberana junta provisional gubernativa, y soberanos congresos generales de la nación mexicana.* (1821–37), (México: Imprenta de Galván, a cargo de Manuel Arévalo, 1829), 4 vols. Estudio Introductorio de Oscar Cruz Barney, (México: Tribunal Superior de Justicia, 2010), Tomo 4, pp. 5–6.

[55]*Decreto de 18 de Diciembre de 1832, Ley. Cesan las leyes que expresa relativas á ladrones y otros reos que deben ser juzgados militarmente*, in Manuel Dublán and José María Lozano, *Legislación Mexicana, Colección Completa de las Disposiciones Legislativas expedidas desde la independencia de la República*, (México: Imprenta del Comercio, á Cargo de Dublán y Lozano, Hijos, 1876), Tomo II, pp. 470–473.

[56]See Juan A. Mateos, *Reinstalación del Primer Congreso Mexicano Nombrado en 1822 y disuelto por el Golpe de Estado del Emperador Iturbide, Historia de sus sesiones,* (México: Imprenta de J.F. Jens, 1878), p. 968.

need for any license, revision or approval,[57] although the freedom of the press was restricted by provisions of 14 May 1831[58] and 23 May 1835,[59] with which it was decreed that the aggrieved by printed defamatory libels could choose the action for insults or for abuse of freedom of Printing, preventing printers who do not admit responsive letters of vagrants, prisoners, indigents or persons of unknown domicile and way of life, under penalty of pecuniary fines and imprisonment of up to a year and a half.

Early on, even before the State of Veracruz, whose *Criminal Code* of 28 April 1835 was considered the first Code of the matter in our country, the State of Chihuahua adopted, promulgated and published as its own on 11 August 1827 the *Spanish Penal Code* of 9 July 1822.[60] It is the *Código penal presentado por las Cortes de España en 8 de junio de 1822, y mandado observar provisionalmente por el Congreso Constitucional del Estado de Chihuahua en 11 de agosto de 1827*, in 132 pages.[61]

The *Spanish Penal Code* of 1822, which—as said—was called to be the basis for later Mexican codes, contained elements from both the Spanish criminal law tradition and foreign influences (particularly from lawyers like Bentham, Beccaria, Filangieri and Bexon).[62]

---

[57]Macedo, *Apuntes…*, p. 223.

[58]*Ley sobre libelos infamatorios impresos, Mayo 14 de 1831*, in Manuel Dublán and José María Lozano, *Legislación Mexicana, Colección Completa de las Disposiciones Legislativas expedidas desde la independencia de la República*, (México: Imprenta del Comercio, á Cargo de Dublán y Lozano, Hijos, 1876), Tomo II, pp. 326–327.

[59]*Ley de 23 de Mayo de 1835, Prevenciones relativas á responsabilidad de imprenta,* in Manuel Dublán and José María Lozano, *Legislación Mexicana, Colección Completa de las Disposiciones Legislativas expedidas desde la independencia de la República*, (México: Imprenta del Comercio, á Cargo de Dublán y Lozano, Hijos, 1876), Tomo III, p. 51.

[60]Oscar Cruz Barney, "La codificación del derecho en el Estado de Chihuahua", en Becerra Ramírez, Manuel et al., *Obra en Homenaje a Rodolfo Cruz Miramontes,* (México: Instituto de Investigaciones Jurídicas, UNAM, 2008), tomo II, p. 201; a reference to it in Rafael Lozoya Varela, "La prescripción en nuestro Código de Defensa Social", in *Lecturas Jurídicas*, (Chihuahua: Universidad Autónoma de Chihuahua, Escuela de Derecho, Enero- Marzo, 1965), Núm. 22, pp. 10–11.

[61]*Código penal presentado por las Cortes de España en 8 de junio de 1822, y mandado observar provisionalmente por el Congreso Constitucional del Estado de Chihuahua en 11 de agosto de 1827,* (México: Imprenta á cargo de Mariano Arévalo, 1827). The bibliographic description of it is the following: CODIGO PENAL/PRESENTADO POR LAS CORTES DE ESPAÑA/EN 8 DE JUNIO DE 1822;/Y MANDADO OBSERVAR PROVISIONALMENTE/POR EL CONGRESO CONSTITUCIONAL/DEL ESTADO/DE CHIHUAHUA/EN 11 DE AGOSTO DE 1827/VIÑETA HORIZONTAL/MEXICO: 1827./LINEA/Imprenta de Galvan á cargo de Mariano Arevalo/Calle de/Cadena núm 2. (En cuarto, 132 páginas).

[62]On this matter, see Isabel Ramos Vázquez & Juan B. Cañizares-Navarro, "La influencia francesa en la primera Codificación española: el Código penal francés de 1810 y el Código penal español de 1822", *La Codificación española. Una aproximación doctrinal e historiográfica a sus influencias extranjeras, y a la francesa en particular* (Aniceto Masferrer, ed.) (Pamplona: Aranzadi–Thomson Reuters, 2014), pp. 153–212.

It is clarified by the government of the state that the adoption was made, in everything that did not oppose to the system of government, *Act of the Federation, General Constitution of 1824*, the particular of the State of Chihuahua, and the laws and decrees given after of the publication of the *Penal Code*.

On 22 February 1832,[63] the prisoners for rebellion were held jointly and *in solidum* responsible with their own property in respect of the sums that they themselves or their chiefs violently took. It was also guaranteed that the penalty of infamy would not exceed the offender, the prohibition of confiscation of property as well as retroactive laws, among others.[64]

On 29 October 1835,[65] it was established that those responsible for robbery or homicide were to be tried throughout the Republic by an ordinary court-martial. It also regulated the carrying of arms and the use of alcoholic beverages, suppressed vagrancy and begging and attempted to organize the police.[66]

Prohibition of personal torment was issued in 1814,[67] and new regulations were issued in 1820[68] and 1826.[69] Provisions on the subject were issued on 9 March

[63] *Ley del 22 de Febrero de 1832, Responsabilidad de los que, en caso de pronunciamiento, tomen propiedad ajena*, in Manuel Dublán and José María Lozano, *Legislación Mexicana, Colección Completa de las Disposiciones Legislativas expedidas desde la independencia de la República*, (México: Imprenta del Comercio, á Cargo de Dublán y Lozano, Hijos, 1876), Tomo II, p. 411.

[64] See also José Ángel Ceniceros, "Historia del derecho penal mexicano", en *La Justicia*, (México: 1977), junio, t. XXXIV, núm. 566, p. 28.

[65] *Ley de 29 de Octubre de 1835 sobre el modo de juzgar á los ladrones homicidas y sus cómplices*, in Manuel Dublán and José María Lozano, *Legislación Mexicana, Colección Completa de las Disposiciones Legislativas expedidas desde la independencia de la República* (México: Imprenta del Comercio, á Cargo de Dublán y Lozano, Hijos, 1876), Tomo III, pp. 92–93.

[66] Macedo, *Apuntes...*, pp. 251 and 258.

[67] *Real Cédula de S.M. y Señores del Consejo de 25 de julio de 1814, por la qual se manda que en adelante no puedan los jueces usar de apremios ni de género alguno de tormento personal para las declaraciones y confesiones de los reos ni de los testigos, quedando abolida la práctica que había en ello con los demás que se expresa* (Madrid: En la Imprenta Real, 1814).

[68] *Decreto del 11 de septiembre de 1820, Haciendo varias aclaraciones para poder procederá la prisión ó detención de cualquier español*, in *Colección de los decretos y órdenes de las Cortes de España, que se reputan vigentes en la República de los Estados-Unidos Mexicanos* (México: Imprenta de Galván, á cargo de Mariano Arévalo, 1829), Edición facsimilar y estudio introductorio por Oscar Cruz Barney, (México: Suprema Corte de Justicia de la Nación, 2005), p. 129.

[69] *Decreto del 20 de Mayo de 1826, Ningún condenado por ladrón será aplicado al servicio de las armas*, in Manuel Dublán and José María Lozano, *Legislación Mexicana, Colección Completa de las Disposiciones Legislativas expedidas desde la independencia de la República* (México: Imprenta del Comercio, á Cargo de Dublán y Lozano, Hijos, 1876), Tomo I, pp. 794–795.

1824,[70] regarding establishment of arts and crafts workshops in prisons on 11 April[71] and on Mexico City security on 6 May 1833.[72]

On 6 July, a *Law on the way to judge thieves, murdererers and slayers* was issued under the presidency of Don José Joaquín Herrera.[73]

In the State of Veracruz, on 15 September 1832, the First Part of a Draft Criminal Code was sent to the Fourth Constitutional Congress of the State,[74] signed on 1 September of that year. On 15 November of the same year, the Second Part was delivered. The project was prepared and signed by a Committee of Deputies: Bernardo Couto,[75] Manuel Fernández Leal, José Julián Tornel and Antonio María Salonio.[76]

On 28 April 1835, the *Draft Criminal Code* of 1832 entered into force, constituting the second Mexican Penal Code (the first was that of Chihuahua in 1827, adopting the Spanish of July 9, 1822); in 1849 was modified.

The *Criminal Code* of 1835 was composed of three parts, with the same distribution of the *Spanish Penal Code* of 1822:

- Part One, 'Punishment and Crimes in General';
- Second Part, 'Offenses Against Society,' and
- Third Part, referred to 'Crimes against individuals.'

[70]*Decreto de 9 de Marzo de 1824, Amnistía por opiniones políticas*, in Manuel Dublán and José María Lozano, *Legislación Mexicana, Colección Completa de las Disposiciones Legislativas expedidas desde la independencia de la República* (México: Imprenta del Comercio, á Cargo de Dublán y Lozano, Hijos, 1876), Tomo I, pp. 703–704.

[71]*Circular de la Secretaría de Justicia del 11 de Abril de 1833, Reglamento aprobado por el supremo gobierno, para el establecimiento de talleres de artes y oficios en la cárcel nacional*, in Manuel Dublán and José María Lozano, *Legislación Mexicana, Colección Completa de las Disposiciones Legislativas expedidas desde la independencia de la República* (México: Imprenta del Comercio, á Cargo de Dublán y Lozano, Hijos, 1876), Tomo II, pp. 504–506.

[72]*Bando del 14 de Mayo de 1833, Prevenciones de policía, de aseo, limpieza y seguridad*, in Manuel Dublán and José María Lozano, *Legislación Mexicana, Colección Completa de las Disposiciones Legislativas expedidas desde la independencia de la República* (México: Imprenta del Comercio, á Cargo de Dublán y Lozano, Hijos, 1876), Tomo II, pp. 517–518.

[73]*Ley del 6 de julio de 1848 sobre el modo de juzgar a los ladrones, homicidas y heridores*, in Manuel Dublán and José María Lozano, *Legislación Mexicana, Colección Completa de las Disposiciones Legislativas expedidas desde la independencia de la República* (México: Imprenta del Comercio, á Cargo de Dublán y Lozano, Hijos, 1876), Tomo II, pp. 401–406.

[74]*Proyecto de Código Penal, presentado al Cuarto Congreso Constitucional del Estado de Veracruz. Primera Parte* (Jalapa: Impreso en la Oficina del Gobierno por Aburto y Blanco, 1832).

[75]About this jurist see Oscar Cruz Barney, "Don José Bernardo Couto y Pérez y la formación del Estado Mexicano", in Oscar Cruz Barney, Héctor Fix Fierro and Elisa Speckman Guerra (Coordinadores), *Los abogados y la formación del Estado mexicano* (México: Instituto de Investigaciones Jurídicas, Instituto de Investigaciones Históricas, Ilustre y Nacional Colegio de Abogados de México, 2013).

[76]Celestino Porte Petit Candaudap, *Evolución legislativa penal en México* (México: Editorial Jurídica Mexicana, 1965), p. 12.

On behalf of the Veracruz State Legislature of 1848, José Julián Tornel, Minister of the Supreme Court of Justice of the Nation, formulated a *Draft Criminal and Penal Code*, composed of 689 articles, of which 189 corresponded to the General Part and the remainder, from 190 to 689, to the Special Part. He delivered it to the aforementioned Legislature in November 1851 and January 1852, but was not received by the legislators, who returned it to its author on 14 July 1853.[77]

By means of article 9 of the *Provisional Organic Law of the Administration of Justice* of 26 September 1855[78] it was established that to sentence in criminal trials the judges should be subject to the provisions of the abovementioned *Penal Code* of 1835, which was declared effective in the State.

Provisions that completed the Penal Code of 1835 were published on 1 November 1855.[79]

Medina and Ormaechea maintains that unity in legislation in Mexico was terminated on 5 May 1869 for the observance in the State of Veracruz of the codification formed by Don Fernando de Jesus Corona.[80]

As can be seen, during the period from 1823 to 1857 the most important problem in criminal matters is that of procedural law, since most of the provisions referred to jurisdiction and to make more effective the repression of crimes,[81] although the need for an "illustrated criminal code" was made clear by D. Juan José Espinoza de los Monteros, Secretary of State and the Universal Office of Justice and Ecclesiastical Affairs in the Chamber of Deputies on January 19, 1829[82] stating that it would have to ensure that such criminal code:

> To pacify the peoples of the District and Territories, to remove them from those species of crimes to which they are most frequently and repetitively delivered, to redeem them from

[77]About this draft Code see Oscar Cruz Barney, "El Proyecto de Código Criminal y Penal de 1851-1852 de José Julián Tornel", in Martín Gabriel Barrón Cruz (Coord.), *Cinco ordenamientos penales del siglo XIX* (México: Instituto Nacional de Ciencias Penales, Ilustre y Nacional Colegio de Abogados de México, 2010).

[78]*Ley Orgánica Provisional de la Administración de Justicia* de 26 de septiembre de 1855, en *Leyes, Decretos y Circulares del Estado de Veracruz Llave, Año de 1855* (Jalapa: Imprenta del Gobierno del Estado, 1889).

[79]See the *Decreto de 1 de Noviembre, restableciendo el juzgado de 1ª instancia de los Tuxtlas, y declarando vigentes varios decretos para aclarar y completar la ley número 54 del año de 1848 y el Código Penal del Estado,* en *Leyes, Decretos y Circulares del Estado de Veracruz Llave, Año de 1855* (Jalapa: Imprenta del Gobierno del Estado, 1889).

[80]Antonio A. Medina y Ormaechea, *Código Penal Mexicano. Sus motivos, concordancias y leyes complementarias* (México: Imprenta del Gobierno, 1880), tomo I, p. IV.

[81]Ceniceros, "Historia…", pp. 28–29. An overview of the legislation applicable in criminal matters prior to codification in Roa Bárcena, *op. cit.*, pp. 1–11.

[82]*Memoria que en cumplimiento del Artículo 120 de la Constitución Federal de los Estados Unidos Mexicanos leyó el Secretario de Estado y del Despacho Universal de Justicia y Negocios Eclesiásticos en la Cámara de Diputados el día 19, y en la de Senadores el día 20 de enero de 1829, sobre los ramos del Ministerio de su cargo*, en José Luis Soberanes Fernández (Comp.), *Memorias de la Secretaría de Justicia* (México: Universidad Nacional Autónoma de México, Instituto de Investigaciones Jurídicas, 1997), pp. 54–55.

the prolonged delays of incommensurate unequal processes and penalties, and unadaptable to the principles of our system, on wich the old indigestible legislation abounds, which passes as it is still valid… It would be a superior expediency for a commission of three or four persons to be prepared, for now and as more urgent, of the criminal code.[83]

3.3 The Mexican Criminal Code of 1871: Promulgation and Foreign Influences

Under the presidency of Benito Juárez, the State of Veracruz was ordered to appoint a commission to draft a Criminal Code. The elaboration of it and one of procedures was ordered in the beginning to D. Juan Antonio de la Fuente, without success.[84] Later on, the Minister of Justice, Jesus Terán, formed, on 6 October 1862,[85] a commission made up of the jurists Urbano Fonseca, José María Herrera y Zavala, Ezequiel Montes, Manuel Zamacona and Antonio Martínez de Castro. Time later Carlos Ma. Saavedra replaced Ezequiel Montes. The commission worked until 1863, and had to interrupt its work by the French invasion that leads to the instauration of the Second Mexican Empire under Maximilian of Habsburg.

During the Second Mexican Empire, Emperor Maximilian of Habsburg appointed a commission formed by Teodosio Lares, Jose Urbano Fonseca and Juan B. Herrera, to draft a *Penal and Penal Procedures Code*.[86] The work carried out did not come to light due to the fall of the Empire and reestablishment of the Republic. Provisions were also issued in criminal and penitentiary matters such as the *Bases for the Organization and Arrangement of the Prisons* of 24 December

---

[83]*Idem.* As read in the *Memoria que en cumplimiento del Artículo 120 de la Constitución Federal de los Estados Unidos Mexicanos leyó el Secretario de Estado y del Despacho Universal de Justicia y Negocios Eclesiásticos en la Cámara de Diputados el día 18, y en la de Senadores el día 22 de marzo de 1830, sobre los ramos del Ministerio de su cargo*, in José Luis Soberanes Fernández (Comp.), *Memorias de la Secretaría de Justicia* (México: Universidad Nacional Autónoma de México, Instituto de Investigaciones Jurídicas, 1997), p. 74, there was established "a group of enlightened and practical subjects to whom this precious, useful, delicate and laborious task of the codification was entrusted."

[84]*Memoria que el Secretario de Estado y del Despacho de Justicia e Instrucción Pública presenta al Congreso de la Unión, en marzo de 1868*, in José Luis Soberanes Fernández (Comp.), *Memorias de la Secretaría de Justicia* (México: Universidad Nacional Autónoma de México, Instituto de Investigaciones Jurídicas, 1997), pp. 262–263.

[85]See *Proyecto de Código Penal para el Distrito y Territorio de la Baja-California sobre Delitos del Fuero Común; y para toda la República sobre Delitos contra la Federación* (México: Imprenta del Gobierno, En Palacio, 1871), p. I.

[86]On this topic See Fernando Arilla Baz, "Proyecto de Codificación Penal de Maximiliano de Habsburgo. Apuntes para la historia del Derecho Penal Mexicano", *Criminalia* (México: Mayo, 1957), Año XXII, pp. 358–359.

1865,[87] la *Ley para la Organización del Ministerio Público* de 19 de diciembre de 1865,[88] y la *Ley para la concesión de indultos y amnistías* de 25 de diciembre de 1865.[89]

Meanwhile, the French *Codes of Criminal Instruction* and *Penal Codes* of 1808 and 1810 respectively (whose translation into Spanish, ordered by Maximilian, was carried out by General Manuel Zaval, Colonel Jose Ignacio Serrano and Lieutenant Colonel Prudencio Mesquia) were applied in Mexico.[90]

Once the Republic was reestablished, President Juarez, through the Minister of Justice, Ignacio Mariscal, ordered on 28 September 1868 to integrate and reorganize the drafting commission of the future *Penal Code*, in order to continue the work that had been interrupted. The appointments fell on the people of Antonio Martínez de Castro as president, and Manuel Zamacona, Jose Maria Lafragua, Eulalio María Ortega as members of the same and Indalecio Sánchez Gavito, as secretary.[91]

It should be noted that in the *Political Constitution of the United Mexican States* of 1857, articles 13–24 established a series of guarantees concerning criminal matters, referring to the fact that nobody could be tried by private laws or special courts; suppression of privileges, with the exception of military jurisdiction; prohibition of retroactive laws; prohibition of being tried by laws subsequent to the criminal act; accurate application of the law; prohibition of being apprehended by authorities that were not competent; imprisonment only for crimes that deserve corporal punishment; the obligation of leting the accused know the reason for the procedure; etc.

By November 1869 the first book of the Penal Code had already been completed and had been sent to the Chamber of Deputies for its examination, since "of the reforms or modifications that may be made to this book, are depending the rest of the works to be done on the rest of the project".[92]

---

[87] *Bases para la Organización y arreglo de las Cárceles* de 24 de diciembre de 1865, in *Boletín de las Leyes*, (México: Diciembre de 1865), Núm. 10.

[88] See the *Ley para la Organización del Ministerio Público* de 19 de diciembre de 1865, in *Boletín de las Leyes* (México: Diciembre de 1865), Núm. 10.

[89] *Ley para la concesión de indultos y amnistías* de 25 de diciembre de 1865, in *Boletín de las Leyes* (México: Diciembre de 1865), Núm. 10.

[90] José de Jesús Ledesma Uribe, "Panorama del derecho mexicano en el siglo XIX", in *Jurídica, Anuario del Departamento de Derecho de la Universidad Iberoamericana* (México: Universidad Iberoamericana, Departamento de Derecho, 1981), núm. 13, t. II, p. 644. See *Código Penal Francés, Traducido al castellano de Orden de S.M. el Emperador Maximiliano I, por el General graduado, coronel D. Manuel Zavala; coronel retirado, D. José Ignacio Serrano y el coronel graduado, teniente coronel D. Prudencio Mesquia, que compusieron la comisión nombrada al efecto* (México: Imprenta de A. Boix, a cargo de M. Zornoza, 1866).

[91] Celestino Porte Petit Candaudap, *Apuntamientos de la parte general de derecho penal I* (México: Ed. Porrúa, 1989, 2nd ed.), pp. 43–46.

[92] *Memoria que el Secretario de Estado y del Despacho de Justicia e Instrucción Pública presenta al Congreso de la Unión, en marzo de 1868*, in José Luis Soberanes Fernández (Comp.),

The second book was concluded in December. According to Medina and Ormaechea, two years and five months used the Commission to form the draft code.[93]

The sources of the *Penal Code* of 1871 were, according to Martinez de Castro and in the Commision minutes, the *Belgian penal code* of 1867, the *Draft Penal Code of Portugal* of 1864, the *Portuguese Penal Code* of 1852, the *Luissiana Code*, the *Code of Baviera* of 1813, the *Code of Prussia* of 1851, the *Spanish Penal Code* of 1848,[94] the *Novísima Recopilación* of 1805, the *Civil Code of Veracruz*, the *Spanish Civil Code*, the ideas of Mittermaïer[95] (in his article on Duel, inserted under number XVIII of the *Revue des revues de droit* of 1838, Renazzi (*Elementa iuris criminalis*),[96] Julio Claro (*Praxis*),[97] Joseph Louis E. Ortolan,[98] Rossi (*Droit Penal*),[99] Chauveau and Hélie (*Théorie du code penal*),[100] Bentham, Edouard

Memorias de la Secretaría de Justicia (México: Universidad Nacional Autónoma de México, Instituto de Investigaciones Jurídicas, 1997), p. 280.

93Medina y Ormaechea, *Código Penal Mexicano...*, tomo I, p. V.

94See *Actas de la comisión del Código Penal de 1871. Reproducción del ejemplar de la biblioteca privada del Lic. Indalecio Sánchez Gavito* (México: s/f.), pp. 12 ff.

95In Mexico, two books of Carl Joseph Anton Mittermaier were printed: *La pena de muerte considerada según las investigaciones de la ciencia, los progresos de la legislación y los resultados de la experiencia*, (Trad. por Manuel Rivera y Río), (México: J. Rivero, hijo, 1873) y Carl Joseph Anton Mittermaier, *Tratado de la prueba en materia criminal, ó exposición comparada de los principios en materia criminal, y de sus diversas aplicaciones en Alemania, Francia, Inglaterra, &c.* (Trad. por un abogado del Ilustre Colegio de Madrid), con un apéndice sobre la legislación criminal de España, relativa á la prueba, (México: R. Rafael, 1853).

96This is the well-known work: Philippi Mariae Renazzi J.C., *Elementa iuris criminalis* (Venetiis: sumptibus Heredis Nicolai Pezzana, 1776).

97It is: Giulio Claro, *Opera omnia, sive, Practica civilis atque criminalis/Ivlii Clari Alexandrini ; cum doctissimis addtionibus perillustrium Ioan Baptistae Baiarde parmensis, Bernardini Rosignoli Mediol. Hier. Giacharii Lugiensis, Ioan. Gviotii Niuernensis, Anton. Drochii è Castro Lauro, hisque nouissimè accesserunt natae, [et] animaduersiones doctorum inter germanos sublimium DD. Ioan. Harprecti, et Manfredi Goveani* (Genevae: Sumptibus Samuelis Chovet, 1666).

98Joseph Louis Elzéar Ortolan, *Éléments de Droit Pénal* (Paris: Plon, 1855).

99Pelegrino Rossi, *Traité de Droit Pénal* (H. Fournier, 1829), 3 vols.

100Adolphe Chauveau, et Faustin Hélie, *Théorie du code pénal*, 3 éd., rev. et mise en rapport avec la législation et la jurisprudence (Paris: Cosse, Succ. de Cosse et No., Delamotte, 1852).

Laboulaye,[101] A. de Tocqueville and Gustave de Beaumont,[102] Leon Vidal, Boneville, Philippe Antoine Merlin,[103] and Sourdat.[104]

Also, the *Italian Civil Code* of 1865,[105] the *Penal Code of Austria* of 1803, Nicola Nicolini[106] (Derecho Penal), Ferraroti (Comentario al Código Italiano), Gregori (Proyecto de Código Universal), the *Siete Partidas*, Fournell, Plaza, Prospero Farinacio,[107] *Civil Code of Portugal*, Diego de Covarrubias y Leyva,[108] Antonio Gomez,[109] Luis de Molina,[110] Joannes Voet,[111] Pedro Gómez de la Serna

[101]Edouard Laboulaye *Essai sur les lois criminelles des Romains concernant la responsabilité des magistrats* (Paris: A. Durand, Libraire, 1845).

[102]Gustave de Beaumont, *On the penitentiary system in the United States, and its application in France; winth an appendix on penal colonies, and also statistical notes / By G. de Beaumont and A. de Tocqueville ... Tr. from the French, with an introduction, notes and additions. By Francis Lieber* (Philadelphia: Carey, Lea & Blanchard, 1833).

[103]Philippe Antoine Merlin, *Recueil alphabétique des questions de droit qui se présentent le plus fréquemment dans les tribunaux* (Paris: Garnery, Lib., 1827–1930), 8 vols.

[104]See Antonio Martínez de Castro, *Exposición de motivos del Código Penal vigente en el Distrito Federal y Territorio de la Baja California dirigida al Supremo Gobierno por el Ciudadano Antonio Martínez de Castro, Presidente de la Comisión encarada de formar el Código expresado* (México: Imprenta de Francisco Díaz de León, 1876), pp. 3–66.

[105]See *Actas de la comisión del Código Penal de 1871. Reproducción del ejemplar de la biblioteca privada del Lic. Indalecio Sánchez Gavito* (México: s/f.), p. 17.

[106]Nicola Nicolini, *Principes philosophiques et pratiques de Droit pénal,* (Schneider: 1851). They use the mexican edition: Nicola Nicolini, *Principios filosóficos y prácticos de derecho penal/ estractados y traducidos al francés de las obras de Niccola Nicolini; y precedidos de una introducción sobre las opiniones filosóficas del autor; por Eugenio Flotard* (Trad. al español por Ignacio Otero) (México: J. Abadiano, 1864).

[107]Prospero Farinacci, *Decisiones rotae CXL: criminvm materiam in praecedentibvs praesertim consilius pertractatam respicientes* (Ed. postrema), (Lvgdvni: Sumptibus Horatij Cardon, 1610).

[108]Diego de Covarrubias y Leyva, *Opera omnia : jam post varias editiones correctiora, & cum veteribus ac melioris notae exemplaribus* de novo *collata & ab innumeris mendis seriò repurgata / Didaci Covarruvias de Leyva Toletani; accesserunt* de novo *Joannis Uffelii, in variarum resolutionum libros* (Genevae: Sumptibus Fratrum de Tournes, 1734), 2 vols.

[109]Antonio Gómez, *Compendio de las varias resoluciones de Antonio Gomez : en que se contiene todo lo substancial de estas, y se ponen muchas notas de las más útiles é importantes del Atillon y Suarez con otras diversas no ménos necesarias que comprueban, ilustran, corrigen ó explican la doctrina epitomada: habiéndose tenido presentes para unas y otras las novedades introducidas en nuestro derecho hispánico, ya por la práctica contraria, y ya por las órdenes, cédulas, pragmáticas y decretos que hasta el dia se han promulgado / compuesto en obsequio de los jóvenes facultativos por el licenciado Don Joseph Márcos Gutierrez* (Madrid: En la Imprenta de Don Benito Cano, 1789).

[110]Luis de Molina, *De justitia et jure: opera omnia, tractatibus quinque, tomisque totidem comprehensa,* Ed. novissima (Coloniae Allobrogum: Sumptibus Fratrum de Tournes, 1759).

[111]Joannes Voet, *Commentarius ad pandectas: in quo praeter romani juris principia ac controversias illustriores, ejus etiam hodiernum, & praecipuae fori quaestiones excutiuntur / Johannis Voet JCti & antecessoris in Academiâ Lugduno-Batavâ* (Ed. sexta), (Hagae-Comitum: Apud Petrum de Hondt, 1731–1734), 2 vols.

y Juan Manuel Montalbán,[112] Robert Joseph Pothier,[113] Jean Jacques Gaspard Foelix,[114] Henry Wheaton,[115] Boneville, Florencio García Goyena[116] and the *French Civil Code*.

The sources used that are mentioned or quoted (the number indicates the number of mentions) in the minutes of the commission are the following:

- *Penal Code of Austria* of 1803: 4
- *Draft Penal Code of Portugal* of 1864: 10
- *Civil Code of Portugal:* 2
- *Italian Civil Code* of 1865: 4
- *Luissiana Code:* 1
- *Code of Baviera* of 1813: 4
- *Code of Prussia* of 1851: 1
- *French Penal Code*: 4
- *French Civil Code*: 1
- *Spanish Penal Code* of 1848: 7
- *Spanish Civil Code:*
- *Novísima Recopilación* of 1805: 2
- *Civil Code of Veracruz:* 2
- Adolphe Chauveau and Faustin Hélie: 18
- Antonio Gomez: 1
- Boneville: 3
- Carl Joseph Anton Mittermaïer: 1
- Diego de Covarrubias y Leyva: 1
- Jean Jacques Gaspard Foelix: 1
- Ferraroti: 2
- Florencio García Goyena: 1
- Gregori: 1
- Henry Wheaton: 2
- Joseph Louis Elzéar Ortolan: 16
- Luis de Molina: 1
- Philippe Antoine Merlín:1

---

[112]Pedro Gómez de la Serna y Juan Manuel Montalbán, *Elementos del derecho civil y penal de España: precedidos de una reseña histórica / por los doctores Pedro Gómez de la Serna y Juan Manuel Montalbán,* Edición: 6ª ed. nuevamente corregida y aumentada por los autores (Madrid: D. F. Sánchez, 1861), 3 vols.

[113]Robert Joseph Pothier, *Oeuvres de Pothier / annotées et mises en corrélation avee le Code civil et la législation actuelle, par M. Bugnet* (Paris: Cosse et N. Delamontte, 1846).

[114]Jean Jacques Gaspard Foelix, *Tratado de Derecho internacional privado, ó del conflicto de las leyes de diferentes naciones en materia de derecho privado* (Imp. de la Revista de Legislación: 1860–1861), 2 vols.

[115]Henry Wheaton, *Elements du droit international*, (3e. ed.), (Leipzig: F. A. Brockhaus, 1858), 2 vols.

[116]Florencio García Goyena, *Código criminal español, comparado con el penal de 1822, el francés y el inglés* (R. Callejas: 1843), 2 vols.

- Nicola Nicolini: 2
- Pelegrino Rossi: 1
- Plaza: 1
- Robert Joseph Pothier: 1
- Prospero Farinacio: 1
- Pedro Gómez de la Serna y Juan Manuel Montalbán: 1
- Joannes Voet: 1

It is interesting to note that the most cited authors were Adolphe Chauveau and Faustin Hélie (18 times) and Joseph Louis Elzéar Ortolan (16 times), followed by the *Draft Portuguese Penal Code* of 1864 (10 times), the *Spanish Penal Code* of 1848 (7 times) and the *Criminal Codes* of Austria, Italy, Bavaria and France (4 times).

As of in March 1871, the press was given the *Proyecto de Código Penal para el Distrito y Territorio de la Baja-California sobre Delitos del Fuero Común; y para toda la República sobre Delitos contra la Federación* (México, Imprenta del Gobierno, En Palacio, 1871)[117] and on 7 December 1871 the *Código Penal para el Distrito Federal y territorio de la Baja California sobre delitos del fuero común, y para toda la República sobre delitos contra la Federación* was promulgated,[118] and began its publication in the Official Gazette the following 14 December, and was sent to the governors of the States of the Republic for its possible adoption.[119]

The *Criminal Code* of 1871 was divided into four Books and 1152 articles plus a Transitory Law of 28 articles. The structure of the Code in four books is closer to the *French Criminal Code*, although in the internal distribution of the first three books it resembles the first two of the *Spanish Penal Code* of 1848,[120] which was

[117]The minutes of the commission were published facsimilarly. See *Actas de la comisión del Código Penal de 1871. Reproducción del ejemplar de la biblioteca privada del Lic. Indalecio Sánchez Gavito* (México: s/f.).

[118]*Código Penal para el Distrito Federal y territorio de la Baja California sobre delitos del fuero común, y para toda la República sobre delitos contra la Federación* (México: Imprenta del Gobierno, en Palacio, 1871).

[119]"Hechos Diversos", *El Foro, Periódico de Jurisprudencia y de Legislación* (México), Tomo III, Núm. 125, (Viernes 27 de noviembre de 1874), p. 499.

[120]We used the *Código Penal de España*, (Madrid: en la Imprenta Nacional, 1848), also the *Código Penal Reformado, Mandado publicar provisionalmente, en virtud de autorización concedida al Gobierno por Ley de 17 de junio de 1870* (Edición Oficial), (Madrid: Imprenta del Ministerio de Gracia y Justicia, 1870); on the Spanish criminal code of 1848, see Mª Dolores del Mar Sánchez González, *Los Códigos Penales de 1848 y 1850* (Madrid, 2003); Emilia Iñesta-Pastor, *El Código penal de 1848* (Valencia: tirant lo blanc, 2010); on the contribution of both the tradition and the foreign influences of this code, see Aniceto Masferrer & Mª Dolores del Mar Sánchez González, "Tradición e influencias extranjeras en el Código penal de 1848. Aproximación a un mito historiográfico" (con Aniceto Masferrer), *La Codificación española. Una aproximación doctrinal e historiográfica a sus influencias extranjeras, y a la francesa en particular* (Aniceto Masferrer, ed.), Pamplona: Aranzadi–Thomson Reuters, 2014, pp. 213–274; for the impact of the Spanish Penal Code of 1848 in Latin America see Emilia Iñesta-Pastor, "La proyección hispanoamericana del Código Penal Español de 1848", *XIII Congreso del Instituto Internacional de Historia del Derecho Indiano: San Juan, 21 al 25 de mayo de 2000* (Luis E.

used by the commission and mentioned by the same (and thus the reformed version of 1870).[121] The Fourth Book seems to have a greater influence of the *French Penal Code*, at least in the structure.[122] It is important to bear in mind the influence of Francisco Pacheco's thinking on the authors of the Penal Code of 1871.[123]

The Code, by virtue of its transitory article, began to apply on 1 April 1872. It is known as the *Martinez de Castro Code*, for having been one of the most outstanding members of the commission drafting it. At the time, there were discussions about the appropriateness of having a unified Penal Code for the Republic.[124]

According to José Diego Fernández, the work of Martínez de Castro "considered in his capital ideas, encloses the progress of science, the constant idea of regenerating society and the delinquent; this one with the punishment, the society with the example".[125]

This Code underwent modifications in 1884 in the area of theft, injury, homicide, adultery, and others.[126]

In matters of criminal procedure under the presidency of Ignacio Commonfort, D. Mariano Contreras was charged with determining whether or not to establish a jury in criminal matters, and then proceed with the elaboration of a *Code of Criminal Procedure*, without success.[127]

On 4 February 1871, the Executive appointed a commission composed of Manuel Dublán, Manuel Ortiz de Montellano and Luis Méndez to form a *Draft Code of Criminal Procedure*, based on the *Penal Code*. José Linares, Manuel

González Vale, coord.) (San Juan, Puerto Rico: Instituto Internacional de Historia del Derecho Indiano; Oficina del Historiador Nacional de Puerto Rico, 2003), vol. II, Estudios, pp. 493–520.

[121]See *Actas de la comisión del Código Penal de 1871. Reproducción del ejemplar de la biblioteca privada del Lic. Indalecio Sánchez Gavito* (México: s/f.), pp. 12, 39.

[122]See in the Appendix the structure of the Mexican Criminal Code of 1871.

[123]See Iñesta-Pastor, p. 495.

[124]See "Hechos Diversos", *El Foro, Periódico de Jurisprudencia y de Legislación*, (México), Tomo III, Núm. 126, (Sábado 28 de noviembre de 1874), pp. 503–504.

[125]José Diego Fernández, "Estudio sobre el Código Penal", *El Foro, Periódico de Jurisprudencia y de Legislación* (México), Tomo VI, Núm. 50 (Jueves 16 de marzo de 1876), p. 197.

[126]*Decreto que reforma los arts. 46, 199, 376, 380, 407, 527, 528, 552, 553, 816, 819 y 912 del Código Penal para el Distrito Federal y territorio de la Baja California* (México: Imprenta de Francisco Díaz de León, 1884).

[127]*Memoria que el Secretario de Estado y del Despacho de Justicia e Instrucción Pública presenta al Congreso de la Unión, en marzo de 1868*, en José Luis Soberanes Fernández (Comp.), *Memorias de la Secretaría de Justicia*, (México), (Universidad Nacional Autónoma de México, Instituto de Investigaciones Jurídicas, 1997), p. 267.

Siliceo and, as secretary, Pablo Macedo became part of the commission also.[128] The commission began its work and on 18 December 1872 presented to the Ministry of Justice a project for review.[129] This was carried out in the house of José Díaz Covarrubias from the Ministry of Justice. The project was then reviewed by the Attorney General, Protasio Tagle, and modified according to his observations by Manuel Dublán and Pablo Macedo. The project thus modified was printed for his knowledge and opinion in 1873.[130]

The project generated several discussions and proposals, so, on 12 May 1874, a proposal was presented to the Executive, elaborated by the Supreme Court of Justice on modifications to the *Draft Code of Criminal Procedure*. The proposal included amendments to articles 7, 9, 10, 11, 12, 13, 15, 44, 45, 47, 48, 49, 52, 53, 56, 57, 58, 59, 61, 64, 66-68, 70, 73, 79, 86-89, 91, 92, 102, 118 and 125. It was also suggested to delete Articles 96 to 101 and 104 to 116.[131] The commission in charge of forming the Code initiated the revision of the project in May of 1875 based on the commentaries made to it. In September 1878, the Ministry of Justice continued to work on the project.[132]

Later, in 1879, the *Draft Code of Criminal Procedure* was published,[133] and being Secretary of Justice in 1880 D. Ignacio Mariscal the work was resumed on the same, again with the intervention of Dublán and Macedo, as well as D. Emilio Monroy, then Fiscal Prosecutor and the third Chamber of the Superior Court of

[128]*Memoria que el encargado de la Secretaría de Justicia e Instrucción Pública presenta al Congreso de la Unión en 15 de septiembre de 1873,* in José Luis Soberanes Fernández (Comp.), *Memorias de la Secretaría de Justicia,* (México: Universidad Nacional Autónoma de México, Instituto de Investigaciones Jurídicas, 1997), p. 307. Also *Memoria que el Secretario de Justicia e Instrucción Pública presenta al Congreso de la Unión y Comprende del 1 de enero de 1878 al 15 de septiembre de 1881,* in José Luis Soberanes Fernández (Comp.), *Memorias de la Secretaría de Justicia* (México: Universidad Nacional Autónoma de México, Instituto de Investigaciones Jurídicas, 1997), p. 347. Also Ignacio Mariscal, *Ministerio de Justicia e Instrucción Pública (Exposición de Motivos al Código de Procedimientos Penales de 1880)* (México: septiembre, s/e, 1880), p. 2.

[129]On criticisms to the Project see Pablo Macedo, "Apuntes sobre el Código de Procedimientos Criminales", *El Foro, Periódico de Jurisprudencia y de Legislación,* (México), Tomo II, Núm. 97, (Domingo 3 de mayo de 1874).

[130]See *Proyecto de Código de Procedimientos Criminales para el Distrito Federal y el Territorio de la Baja California, formado por encargo del Supremo Gobierno, por los licenciados Manuel Dublán, José Linares, Luis Méndez y M. Siliceo* (México: Imprenta del Gobierno, en Palacio, 1873).

[131]See Suprema Corte de Justicia, "El Código de Procedimientos Criminales", *El Foro, Periódico de Jurisprudencia y de Legislación* (México), Tomo III, Núm. 78, (Viernes 2 de octubre de 1874), pp. 310–311; "El Código de Procedimientos Criminales", *El Foro, Periódico de Jurisprudencia y de Legislación,* (México), Tomo III, Núm. 80, (Domingo 4 de octubre de 1874), p. 319, y "El Código de Procedimientos Criminales", *El Foro, Periódico de Jurisprudencia y de Legislación,* (México), Tomo III, Núm. 81, (Martes 6 de octubre de 1874), p. 322.

[132]*Código de Procedimientos Criminales, El Foro, Periódico de Jurisprudencia y de Legislación* (México), Tomo IV, 2ª Epoca, Núm. 62, (Jueves 26 de septiembre de 1878), p. 243.

[133]*Proyecto de Código de Procedimientos Penales* (México: Imprenta del Gobierno, en Palacio, 1879).

Justice of the Federal District.[134] The authorization from 7 December 1871 for Executive Power for the promulgation of the Code of Procedure was renewed, through a new one as of 1 June 1880. Finally, the *Code of Criminal Procedures of the Federal District and Territory of the Baja California* was promulgated on 15 September 1880, and entered into force on 1 November of that year. Described as "a monument of national pride for the advancement of its principles, the goodness of its method and its clear and correct diction",[135] which established in the examination of the evidence and in terms of the trial three important conditions: "contradiction, orality and publicity [...] harmonizing the legal protection of the State with individual freedom, it guarantees at the same time, as a logical and inevitable consequence, the social interest and the rights of the accused".[136] The Code was divided into four books, these in titles and 687 articles, eight of which were transitory. Among the reforms introduced by this Code are the precise establishment of rules for the substantiation of criminal proceedings; the indication of which authorities and under what circumstances restrictions on freedom can be imposed: the regulation of home visits; interim release; improvement of the institution of the jury, the resources, etc.[137] On the jury, it is important the *Law of Jurors* of 24 June 1891.

The *Code of Criminal Procedure* of 1880 was repealed by the *Code of Criminal Procedure of the District and Federal Territories* of 6 July 1894.[138] Rafael Rebollar, F. G. Puente, Pedro Miranda and J. Agustín Borges participated as drafters. The Secretary of Justice, Joaquín Baranda created the commission. Its sources were the procedural laws and codes of France, Spain, Italy, Belgium, Portugal, Germany and Japan, as well as the works of Pacheco, Robles Pozo, H. Marcy, Faustin Helié, J. Bollié, G. Timmermans, E. Roguin and others.[139]

On 2 October 1929, the *Code of Organization, Jurisdiction and Procedures in Criminal Matters for the Federal District and Territories* was issued. It was published in the *Official Gazette of the Federation* on 7 October, and entered into force on 15 October. It replaced the previous one, of 6 July 1894. It is composed of 726

---

[134]Ignacio Mariscal, *Ministerio de Justicia e Instrucción Pública (Exposición de Motivos al Código de Procedimientos Penales de 1880)* (México: septiembre, s/e, 1880), p. 2.

[135]*Memoria que en cumplimiento del precepto constitucional presenta al Congreso de la Unión en C. Lic Joaquin Baranda Secretario de Estado y del despacho de Justicia e Instrucción Pública, 31 de marzo de 1887,* in José Luis Soberanes Fernández (Comp.), *Memorias de la Secretaría de Justicia* (México: Universidad Nacional Autónoma de México, Instituto de Investigaciones Jurídicas, 1997), p. 379.

[136]See Ricardo Rodríguez, *El procedimiento penal en México, Primera Parte Legislación Comparada* (México: Oficina Tip. de la Secretaría de Fomento, 1898), p. 13.

[137]See the Explanatory Memorandum made by Ignacio Mariscal al *Código de Procedimientos Penales,* (México: Imprenta del Comercio, de Dublán y Compañía, 1880), pp. 1–13.

[138]*Código de Procedimientos Penales del Distrito y Territorios Federales* (México: Edición del Boletín Judicial, Imprenta y Litografia, 1894).

[139]*Exposición de Motivos con que fue presentado a la Secretaría de Justicia el proyecto de reformas al Código de Procedimientos Penales del Distrito y Territorios Federales* (México: Edición del Boletín Judicial, Imprenta y Litografia, 1894), pp. V y XLVII.

articles distributed in eight titles and these in turn, in chapters, plus 13 transitory articles.[140]

The *Federal Code of Penal Procedures* was published[141] on 16 December 1908, which came into force on 5 February 1909; it was divided into seven titles, these in chapters and 489 articles, four transients.

4 The Criminal Codification in the States of the Republic and the Adoption of the Criminal Code of 1871 of the Federal District

The criminal codification in the States of the Mexican Republic followed parallel roads in occasions and in others divergent to the codification of the Federal District. The States that adopted with or without modifications the *Criminal Code of the Federal District* of 1871 were, in alphabetical order[142]:

- Aguascalientes, by law of 14 June 1879.
- Campeche, by decree of 21 October 21 1872.
- Chiapas, by decree of 13 December 1872.
- Chihuahua, by decree of 28 April 1883.
- Coahuila, by decree of 20 August 1874.
- Colima, by decree of 22 June 1878.
- Durango, by decree of 17 December 1880.
- Guerrero, by decree of 26 June 1872.
- Hidalgo, by decree of 5 February 1875.
- Jalisco, by decree of 23 August 1885.
- Mexico, by decree of 12 January 1875.
- Morelos, by decree of 30 May 1879.
- Nuevo León
- Oaxaca, by decree of 15 December 1878.
- Puebla, by decree of 30 November 1875.
- Querétaro, by decree of 4 June 1877.
- San Luis Potosí, by decree of 7 December 1872.
- Sinaloa, by decree of 11 November 1874.
- Sonora, by decree of 5 March 1885.

[140] *Código de organización, de competencia y de procedimientos en materia penal, para el Distrito Federal y Territorios* del 2 de octubre de 1929, in *Diario Oficial de la Federación* (lunes 7 de octubre de 1929).

[141] *Código Federal de Procedimientos Penales* (Edición Oficial), (México: Imprenta de Antonio Enríquez, 1908).

[142] See Oscar Cruz Barney, "La recepción del Código Penal de Martínez de Castro en los estados de la República", in *Iter Criminis, Revista de Ciencias Penales* (México: Instituto Nacional de Ciencias Penales, Enero-Febrero, 2010), Número 13, Cuarta Época.

- Tabasco, by decree of 22 June 1883.
- Tamaulipas, by decree of 12 June 1873.
- Tlaxcala, by decree of 18 February 1879.
- Yucatan, by decree of 2 October 1871.
- Zacatecas, by decree of 2 December 1872.

The States that did not adopt the Code of the Federal District were Veracruz, Guanajuato and Michoacán.

The *Code of Veracruz* of 1868 or *Code Corona* is divided not in four but in three Books, whereas the *Code of Guanajuato* of 1870 or *Code Tovar* and the one of Michoacan of 1880 or Code Martínez-Flores are divided in only two Books.

We have then three structures or models with a variant of Penal Code in Mexico from the triumph of the Republic that are:

(1) The Criminal Code of Distrito Federal of 1871 in Four Books and 1152 articles.
(2) The Criminal Code of Veracruz of 1868 or *Código Corona* in Three Books ans 761 articles.
(3) The Guanajuato Penal Code or *Código Tovar* of 1871 in Two Books and 361 articles.
(4) In the case of the Michoacán Criminal Code or the Martínez-Flores Code in two books and 687 articles, it is a Code that follows in its structure, but not necessarily in its content, the model of the Tovar Code of Guanajuato of 1871 with elements from the Code od Distrito Federal of 1871. The influence of the Guanajuato criminal codification in the Michoacan one is announced by Alejandro González Gómez who states that "Although there is no express reference to these works (the Leon Tovar Project and the Montesdeoca Project), the reduced Extension of the alternative project (451 arts.), could well be taken into account by the Commission drafter of the *Penal Code of Michoacan* of 1880".[143]

5 A New Criminal Codification for Mexico City: 1929, 1931 and 2002

The revision of the *Penal Code* of 1871 began in 1903, and lasted until 1912. It was done by Miguel S. Macedo, Pimentel and Olivera Toro who sought to incorporate new doctrines that could benefit and adjust to the social situation, such as

[143]Alejandro González Gómez, *Consideraciones básicas en torno al origen y evolución de la legislación penal michoacana* (Morelia, Michoacán: Universidad Michoacana de San Nicolás de Hidalgo, Facultad de Derecho y Ciencias Sociales, División de Estudios de Posgrado, Supremo Tribunal de Justicia, Instituto de Especialización Judicial, 2003), p. 31, fn n. 6. González Gómez is not mistaken in the indicated influence, although it will be necessary to make the respective comparative exercise between the codes in order to identify the origins of each article.

conditional sentence, protection of the property of electrical energy, preventive seclusion of alcoholics, as well as eliminate the obscurities, imperfections and inconsistencies of the text. The results of this reviewing task could not be immediately reflected in the Code, due to the outbreak of the Mexican Revolution in 1910. The *Draft Penal Code Reform* was published in 1914 in four volumes, whith the proposed changes indicated.[144]

On 15 December 1929, a new *Penal Code* came into force,[145] work of José Almaráz Harris, which replaced the previous one of 1871. The new Penal Code was divided into three books, titles and articles (a total of 1228 plus five transients). It was a widely criticized text because of its complexity and extension, described as very crazy and voluminous, "that gives the sensation, [...] of being written for another planet"[146] which motivated the revision of the same and finally the elaboration of a new one.[147]

The works to prepare the new code that replaced the one of 1929 were carried out by a commission integrated by Alfonso Teja Zabre, Luis Garrido, Ernesto G. Garza, Jose Angel Ceniceros, Jose López Lira and Carlos Ángeles. It was published in the *Official Gazette of the Federation* on 14 August 1931 and entered into force on 17 September of that same year.[148] To this was added a *Code of Criminal Procedures*, of the same year.

The Code of 1931 underwent various modifications, among others, in the following matters: Conditional sentence; Juvenile delinquency; vague and evil; prohibited games; sexual harassment, sexual abuse, rape and rape; rapture; blows and other simple physical violence; injury and defamation; crimes committed by merchants subject to banckrupcy, electoral crimes and in matters of National Registry of Citizens.

The *Penal Code* of 1931 was abrogated in 2002 by a new *Penal Code* consisting of two Books, 32 Titles, 147 Chapters and 365 Articles. The new Code, adopted in

---

[144]See Secretaría de Justicia, Comisión Revisora del Código Penal, *Trabajos de Revisión del Código Penal, Proyecto de Reformas y Exposición de Motivos* (México: Tip. de la Oficina Impresora de Estampillas, Palacio nacional, 1914), Tomo IV.

[145]*Código Penal para el Distrito y Territorios Federales* (Edición Oficial), (México: Secretaría de Gobernación, Talleres Gráficos de la Nación, 1929).

[146]See Jiménez de Asúa, according to Porte Petit Candaudap, *Evolución legislativa*..., p. 35.

[147]One of the main critics was precisely José Ángel Ceniceros, whose journalistic articles were published in his work: *El nuevo Código Penal de 13 de agosto de 1931 en relación con los de 7 de diciembre de 1871 y 15 de diciembre de 1929* (México: Talleres Gráficos de la Nación, 1931). See the introductory note thereto by Octavio Mendoza González.

[148]*Ibid.*, pp. 36–37. See *Código Penal para el Distrito y Territorios Federales en materia de Fuero Común, y para toda la República en materia de Fuero Federal*, 13 de agosto de 1931, in *La Legislación Mexicana* (México: La Legislación Mexicana, Sociedad Editora, Agosto de 1931), Publicación mensual autorizada por la Secretaría de Gobernación.

June and promulgated on 11 July 2002, entered into force in October of that year.[149] It was published in the *Official Gazette of the Federal District* on 16 July 2002.

6 Concluding Remarks

We cannot say that there was a clear use of the French Criminal Code as a model of Mexican criminal codification. In fact, the drafters of the Code of 1871 did not include it in the list of sources of the same in the explanatory statement, although—as we said—the drafters of the Mexican Criminal Code used the French Code in just 4 occasions, in comparison with the 16 occasions in which the Portuguese codification was used.

Although an influence of French criminal law existed in Mexican law, many other sources were used, both legislative and doctrinal in the drafting of the Criminal Code of 1871.

In fact, French influence can be clearly seen in the constant use of doctrine, rather than in the invocation or reception of the French Penal Code, particularly in the Criminal Code of the Federal District of 1871. It is remarkable the use of the works by authors like Adolphe Chauveau, Faustin Hélie, Boneville, Jean Jacques Gaspard Foelix, Joseph Louis Elzéar Ortolan, Philippe Antoine Merlin and Robert Joseph Pothier, whose works were used for the teaching of law in Mexico well into the twentieth century.

The authors of the Mexican codification did not intend to do an original work or copy a foreign model, but to collect and reformulate Castilian law, as a part of Mexican legal tradition.

The influence of the Spanish penal codes of 1822, 1848/50 and its version of 1870 is much more clear and evident. Even the State of Chihuahua adopted, promulgated and published as its own on 11 August 1827, the *Spanish Penal Code* of 1822.

Appendix: The Structure of the Mexican Criminal Code of 1871

- **Preliminary Title**
- **First Book**
- **Of the Crimes, Faults, Delinquers and Penalties in General**

[149]See *Nuevo Código Penal* (México: Tribunal Superior de Justicia del Distrito Federal, Instituto de Investigaciones Jurídicas de la UNAM, 2003). The background to the formulation of the new Penal Code is included in pages XXVIII and XXIX of the cited edition.

- **Title One**. Crimes and faults in general

  Chapter I. General rules on crimes and misdemeanors
  Chapter II. Degrees of intentional crime
  Chapter III. Accumulation of crimes and faults—Recidivism
  Chapter XII. Subjection to the surveillance of political authority—Prohibition to go to a certain place, District or State, or to reside in them
  Chapter XII. Subjection to the surveillance of political authority—Prohibition to go to a certain place, District or State, or to reside in them

- **Second Title**. Of the criminal responsibility—Circumstances that exclude it, attenuate or aggravate it.—Responsible persons

  Chapter I. Criminal responsibility
  Chapter II. Circumstances that exclude criminal responsibility
  Chapter III. Preventions common to attenuating and aggravating circumstances
  Chapter IV. Mitigating Circumstances
  Chapter V. Aggravating circumstances
  Chapter VI. Of the people responsible for the crimes

- **Third Title**. General rules on penalties—Enumeration of them—Aggravations and attenuators Preparatory freedom

  Chapter I. General rules on penalties
  Chapter II. Enumeration of penalties and some preventive measures
  Chapter III. Mitigating and aggravating penalties
  Chapter IV. Preparatory freedom

- **Title Four**. Exposure of penalties and preventive measures

  Chapter I. Loss, in favor of the Treasury of instruments, effects or objects of a crime
  Chapter II. Missing—Warning
  Chapter III. Penalty fee
  Chapter IV. Minor and major arrest
  Chapter V. Imprisonment in a correctional institution
  CHAPTER VI. Ordinary prison
  Chapter VII. Confinement—Simple detention—Banishment of the place of residence—Banishment of the Republic—Death—Extraordinary imprisonment
  Chapter VIII. Suspension of any civil, family or political right. Disqualification to exercise some civil family, or political right
  Chapter IX. Suspension of position, employment or honor—Removal of them—Disqualification to obtain them—Disqualification for all kinds of jobs, honors or positions

Chapter X. Preventive Detention in Correctional Education Establishment—Preventive Detention in a School of Deaf-Mutes—Preventive Detention in a Hospital
Chapter XI. Caution not to offend—Protest of good conduct—Warning
Chapter XII. Subjection to the surveillance of political authority—Prohibition to go to a certain place, District or State, or to reside in them

- **Title Fifth**. Application of penalties—Substitution, reduction and commutation of them—Execution of sentences

Chapter I. General rules on the enforcement of sentences
Chapter II. Application of penalties to crimes of guilt
Chapter III. Application of penalties for conviction, attempted crime, felony and consummate offense
Chapter IV. Application of penalties in case of accumulation and in case of recidivism
Chapter V. Application of penalties to accomplices and concealers
CHAPTER VI. Application of penalties to those over nine years of age who do not reach eighteen and to the deaf-mute, when they commit an offence with discernment
Chapter VII. Application of penalties when there are extenuating or aggravating circumstances
Chapter VIII. Replacement, reduction commutation of feathers
Chapter IX. Execution of the sentences

- **Title Six**. Extinction of criminal action

Chapter I. Preliminary Rules
Chapter II. Death of the accused—Amnesty
Chapter III. Forgiveness and consent of the offended
Chapter IV. Prescription of criminal actions
Chapter V. Irrevocable Judgment

- **Title Seven**. Extinction of sentence

Chapter I. Causes that extinguish the sentence
Chapter II. Death of the accused—Amnesty—Rehabilitation
Chapter III. Pardon
Chapter IV. Prescription of sentence

- **Book Two**
- **Civil Liability in Criminal Matters**

Chapter I. Extension and requirements of civil liability
Chapter II. Computation of civil liability
Chapter III. Civilly responsible persons
Chapter IV. Division of civil liability among those responsible
Chapter V. How to make civil liability effective
CHAPTER VI. Extinction of civil liability and actions to sue

- **Third Book**
- **Of the Crimes in Particular**

  - **Title One**. Crimes against property

    Chapter I. Theft—General rules
    Chapter II. Robbery without violence
    Chapter III. Robb people with violence
    Chapter IV. Trust abuse
    Chapter V. Fraud against property
    CHAPTER VI. Fraudulent bankruptcy
    Chapter VII. Disposal of immovable property or waters
    Chapter VIII. Threats—Feints—Physical violence
    Chapter IX. Destruction or deterioration caused by property or fire
    Chapter X. Destruction or deterioration caused by flood
    Chapter XI. Destruction, deterioration or damage caused in property of others by other means

  - **Second Title**. Crimes against persons, committed by individuals

    Chapter I. Hits and other simple physical violence
    Chapter II. Injuries—General rules
    Chapter III. Simple injuries
    Chapter IV. Qualified injuries
    Chapter V. Homicide. General rules
    CHAPTER VI. Simple homicide
    Chapter VII. Qualified homicide
    Chapter VIII. Parricide
    Chapter IX. Abortion
    Chapter X. Infanticide
    Chapter XI. Duel
    Chapter XII. Exposure and abandonment of children and the sick
    Chapter XIII. Plagiarism
    Chapter XIV. Attacks committed by individuals against individual freedom —burglary

  - **Third Part**. Offenses against reputation

    Chapter I. Injury—Defamation—Extrajudicial calumny
    Chapter II. Judicial calumny

  - **Title Four**. Falsehood

    Chapter I. Forgery of currency and alteration of it
    Chapter II. Falsification of shares, bonds or other documents of public credit, interest vouchers or dividends, and blank bills
    Chapter III. Falsification of stamps, punches or dies, punches, marks, weights and measures
    Chapter IV. Forgery of authentic public documents and private documents

Chapter V. Falsification of certifications
CHAPTER VI. Falsification of keys
Chapter VII. False judicial statements and in reports given to an authority
Chapter VIII. Concealment or variation of name
Chapter IX. Falsehood in telegraphic dispatches
Chapter X. Usurpation of public or profession. Misuse of decoration or uniform

- **Title Fifth**. Disclosure of secrets

  Single chapter

- **Title Six**. Offense against the order of families, public morals or good customs

  Chapter I. Offenses against the civil status of persons
  Chapter II. Outrage against public morality, or morality
  Chapter III. Attacks against the modesty—Rape—Violence
  Chapter IV. Corruption of minors
  Chapter V. Abduction
  CHAPTER VI. Adultery
  Chapter VII. Bigamy or double marriage and other illegal marriages
  Chapter VIII. Provocation to a crime—Apology of this or some vice

- **Title Seven**. Crimes against public health

  Single chapter

- **Title Eight**. Crimes against public order

  Chapter I. Vagance—Begging
  Chapter II. Lotteries—Raffles
  Chapter III. Prohibited games
  Chapter IV. Infringement of laws and regulations on burials
  Chapter V. Violence of graves. Profanation of a human corpse
  CHAPTER VI. Breach of stamps
  Chapter VII. Opposition to the execution of any public work or work
  Chapter VIII. Crimes of *asentistas* and suppliers
  Chapter IX. Disobedience and resistance of individuals
  Chapter X. Offense and attacks against public officials
  Chapter XI. Riot
  Chapter XII. Habitual drunkenness
  Chapter XIII. Crimes against industry or commerce, or against freedom in public auction

- **Title Nine**. Crimes against public safety

  Chapter I. Evasion of prisoners
  Chapter II. Breach of conviction
  Chapter III. Prohibited weapon

Chapter IV. Associations formed to deal with people or property

- **Title Tenth**. Attacks against constitutional guarantees

Chapter I. Crimes committed in popular elections
Chapter II. Crimes against freedom of the press
Chapter III. Crimes against freedom of worship
Chapter IV. Crimes against freedom of conscience
Chapter V. Violation of correspondence of the post office and telegraphic offices—Suppression of these
CHAPTER VI. Attack to the individual freedom—Burglary of dwelling—Registration or seizure of papers
Chapter VII. Violation of certain other guarantees and rights granted by the Constitution

- **Eleventh Title**. Offenses of public officials in the exercise of their functions

Chapter I. Anticipation or extension of public functions. Exercise of those that do not compete an official—Abandonment of commission, position or employment
Chapter II. Authority abuse
Chapter III. Coalition of civil servants
Chapter IV. Bribery
Chapter V. Peculum and concussion
CHAPTER VI. Crimes committed in civil criminal matters
Chapter VII. On some crimes of the high officials of the Federation

- **Title Twelfth**. Offenses of attorneys, assignees and trustees

Single chapter

- **Title Thirteenth**. Crimes against the external security of the Nation. Single chapter.

Betrayal and other offenses against foreign security

- **Title Fourteenth**. Crimes against internal security

Chapter I. Rebellion
Chapter II. Sedition

- **Title Fifteenth**. Crimes against the law of nations

Chapter I. Piracy
Chapter II. Violation of immunity
Chapter III. It deals with the slave trade
Chapter IV. Violation of the duties of humanity in prisoners, hostages, wounded or hospitals

- **Book Four**
- **Of the Faults**

  Chapter I. General rules
  Chapter II. First class faults
  Chapter III. Second class faults
  Chapter IV. Third class faults
  Chapter V. Fourth class faults

- **Transitory Law**

Bibliography

"Códigos", *El Observador Judicial y de Legislación. Periódico que contiene todas las leyes y decretos dados por el Exmo. Señor Presidente Provisional D. Antonio López de Santa-Anna, desde la época de nuestra regeneración política. Establecido á impulso del Exmo. Señor Ministro de Justicia é Instrucción Pública, Don Crispiniano del Castillo* (México: Imprenta de Vicente García Torres, 1842), vol. II.

"El Código de Procedimientos Criminales", *El Foro, Periódico de Jurisprudencia y de Legislación* (México), Tomo III, Núm. 80, (Domingo 4 de octubre de 1874).

"El Código de Procedimientos Criminales", *El Foro, Periódico de Jurisprudencia y de Legislación* (México), Tomo III, Núm. 81, (Martes 6 de octubre de 1874).

"Hechos Diversos", *El Foro, Periódico de Jurisprudencia y de Legislación* (México), Tomo III, Núm. 125, (Viernes 27 de noviembre de 1874).

"Hechos Diversos", *El Foro, Periódico de Jurisprudencia y de Legislación* (México), Tomo III, Núm. 126, (Sábado 28 de noviembre de 1874).

"Leyes Bárbaras", *El Observador Judicial y de Legislación. Periódico que contiene todas las leyes y decretos dados por el Exmo. Señor Presidente Provisional D. Antonio López de Santa-Anna, desde la época de nuestra regeneración política. Establecido á impulso del Exmo. Señor Ministro de Justicia é Instrucción Pública, Don Crispiniano del Castillo* (México: Imprenta de Vicente García Torres, 1843), vol. III.

"Reseña histórica de la codificación en México.- Discusión de los códigos", en *El Derecho, Periódico de Jurisprudencia y Legislación* (México), (Sábado 23 de abril de 1870), Tomo IV, Núm 17.

Arilla Baz, Fernando, "Proyecto de Codificación Penal de Maximiliano de Habsburgo. Apuntes para la historia del Derecho Penal Mexicano", *Criminalia*, (México: Mayo, 1957), Año XXII.

Baró Pazos, Juan, *La codificación del Derecho Civil en España (1808-1889)* (Santander: Universidad de Cantabria, 1992).

Beaumont, Gustave de, *On the penitentiary system in the United States, and its application in France; winth an appendix on penal colonies, and also statistical notes / By G. de Beaumont and A. de Tocqueville ... Tr. from the French, with an introduction, notes and additions. By Francis Lieber*, (Philadelphia: Carey, Lea & Blanchard, 1833).

Bravo Lira, Bernardino, "Codificación y derecho común en Europa e Hispanoamérica. Disociación de los derechos nacionales del derecho común", Bernardino Bravo Lira & Sergio Concha Márquez de la Plata (Eds.), *Codificación y descodificación en Hispanoamérica* (Santiago de Chile: Escuela de Derecho – Universidad Santo Tomás, 1998).

Cabo Martín, Carlos de, *Sobre el concepto de ley* (Madrid: Ed. Trotta, 2000), p. 19.

Ceniceros, José Ángel, "Historia del derecho penal mexicano", *La Justicia* (México: 1977), junio, t. XXXIV, núm. 566.

Ceniceros, José Ángel, *El nuevo Código Penal de 13 de agosto de 1931 en relación con los de 7 de diciembre de 1871 y 15 de diciembre de 1929* (México: Talleres Gráficos de la Nación, 1931).
Chauveau, Adolphe et Faustin Hélie, *Théorie du code pénal*, 3 éd., rev. et mise en rapport avec la législation et la jurisprudence (Paris: Cosse, Succ. de Cosse et No., Delamotte, 1852).
Claro, Giulio, *Opera omnia, sive, Practica civilis atque criminalis / Ivlii Clari Alexandrini; cum doctissimis addtionibus perillustrium Ioan Baptistae Baiarde parmensis, Bernardini Rosignoli Mediol. Hier. Giacharii Lugiensis, Ioan. Gviotii Niuernensis, Anton. Drochii è Castro Lauro, hisque nouissimè accesserunt natae, [et] animaduersiones doctorum inter germanos sublimium DD. Ioan. Harprecti, et Manfredi Goveani* (Genevae: Sumptibus Samuelis Chovet, 1666).
Coing, Helmut, *Derecho privado europeo. I: Derecho común más antiguo (1500-1800)* (translation and notes by Antonio Pérez Martín) (Madrid: Fundación Cultural del Notariado, 1996), vol. I.
Covarrubias y Leyva, Diego de, *Opera omnia : jam post varias editiones correctiora, & cum veteribus ac melioris notae exemplaribus de novo collata & ab innumeris mendis seriò repurgata / Didaci Covarruvias de Leyva Toletani; accesserunt de novo Joannis Uffelii, in variarum resolutionum libros* (Genevae: Sumptibus Fratrum de Tournes, 1734), 2 vols.
Cruz Barney, Oscar (Coord.), *La Codificación* (México: Ed. Porrúa, Universidad Iberoamericana, 2006).
Cruz Barney, Oscar, "Don José Bernardo Couto y Pérez y la formación del Estado Mexicano", in Oscar Cruz Barney, Héctor Fix Fierro and Elisa Speckman Guerra (Coordinadores), *Los abogados y la formación del Estado mexicano* (México: Instituto de Investigaciones Jurídicas, Instituto de Investigaciones Históricas, Ilustre y Nacional Colegio de Abogados de México, 2013).
Cruz Barney, Oscar, "El Proyecto de Código Criminal y Penal de 1851-1852 de José Julián Tornel", in Martín Gabriel Barrón Cruz, (Coordinador), *Cinco ordenamientos penales del siglo XIX* (México: Instituto Nacional de Ciencias Penales, Ilustre y Nacional Colegio de Abogados de México, 2010).
Cruz Barney, Oscar, "La codificación del derecho en el Estado de Chihuahua", in Becerra Ramírez, Manuel *et. al*, *Obra en Homenaje a Rodolfo Cruz Miramontes* (México: Instituto de Investigaciones Jurídicas, UNAM, 2008), tomo II.
Cruz Barney, Oscar, "La recepción del Código Penal de Martínez de Castro en los estados de la República", *Iter Criminis, Revista de Ciencias Penales* (México: Instituto Nacional de Ciencias Penales, Enero-Febrero, 2010), Número 13, Cuarta Época.
Cruz Barney, Oscar, *La codificación en México* (México: Ed. Porrúa – Instituto de Investigaciones Jurídicas, UNAM, 2010).
Dickmann, Renzo, "Codificazione e processo legislativo", Costanzo, Pasquale (Coord.), *Codificazione del diritto e ordinamento costituzionale* (Napoli: Facoltá di Giurisprudenza della Universitá di Camerino, 1999).
Esponda, Eduardo, "La Ley", *El Foro, Periódico de Jurisprudencia y de Legislación* (México) vol. IV, 2nd Epoch, Num. 79, (Saturday, 19 October 1878).
Farinacci, Prospero, *Decisiones rotae CXL : criminvm materiam in praecedentibvs praesertim consilius pertractatam respicientes* (Ed. postrema), (Lvgdvni: Sumptibus Horatij Cardon, 1610).
Fernández, José Diego, "Estudio sobre el Código Penal", *El Foro, Periódico de Jurisprudencia y de Legislación* (México), Tomo VI, Núm. 50, (Jueves 16 de marzo de 1876).
Ferrajoli, Luigi, *Derechos y garantías. La ley del más débil* (trand. by Perfecto Andrés Ibáñez y Andrea Greppi) (Madrid: Ed. Trotta, 1999).
Fioravanti, Maurizio, *Los derechos fundamentales. Apuntes de Historia de las Constituciones* (trans. by Manuel Martínez Neira) (Madrid: Ed. Trotta, 2000, 3rd ed.).
García Goyena, Florencio, *Código criminal español, comparado con el penal de 1822, el francés y el inglés* (R. Callejas: 1843), 2 vols.

Gaspard Foelix, Jean Jacques, *Tratado de Derecho internacional privado, ó del conflicto de las leyes de diferentes naciones en materia de derecho privado,* (Imp. de la Revista de Legislación: 1860-1861), 2 vols.
Gazzaniga, Jean Louis, "La dimension historique des libertés et droits foundamentaux", Cabrillac, Remy, Marie-Anne Frison-Roche & Thierry Revet (Coords.), *Libertés et droits fondamentaux* (Paris: Dalloz, 2002, 8th ed.).
Gómez de la Serna, Pedro y Juan Manuel Montalbán, *Elementos del derecho civil y penal de España: precedidos de una reseña histórica / por los doctores Pedro Gómez de la Serna y Juan Manuel Montalbán,* Edición: 6ª ed. nuevamente corregida y aumentada por los autores, (Madrid: D.F. Sánchez, 1861), 3 vols.
Gómez, Antonio, *Compendio de las varias resoluciones de Antonio Gomez : en que se contiene todo lo substancial de estas, y se ponen muchas notas de las más útiles é importantes del Atillon y Suarez con otras diversas no ménos necesarias que comprueban, ilustran, corrigen ó explican la doctrina epitomada: habiéndose tenido presentes para unas y otras las novedades introducidas en nuestro derecho hispánico, ya por la práctica contraria, y ya por las órdenes, cédulas, pragmáticas y decretos que hasta el dia se han promulgado / compuesto en obsequio de los jóvenes facultativos por el licenciado Don Joseph Márcos Gutierrez* (Madrid: En la Imprenta de Don Benito Cano, 1789).
González Gómez, Alejandro, *Consideraciones básicas en torno al origen y evolución de la legislación penal michoacana* (Morelia, Michoacán: Universidad Michoacana de San Nicolás de Hidalgo, Facultad de Derecho y Ciencias Sociales, División de Estudios de Posgrado, Supremo Tribunal de Justicia, Instituto de Especialización Judicial, 2003).
Grossi, Paolo, *Mitología jurídica de la modernidad* (trad. by Manuel Martínez Neira) (Madrid: Ed. Trotta, 2003).
Guzmán Brito, Alejandro, *La codificación civil en Iberoamérica. Siglos XIX y XX* (Santiago de Chile: Editorial Jurídica del Chile, 2000).
Iñesta-Pastor, Emilia, "La proyección hispanoamericana del Código Penal Español de 1848", *XIII Congreso del Instituto Internacional de Historia del Derecho Indiano: San Juan, 21 al 25 de mayo de 2000* (Luis E. González Vale, coord.) (San Juan, Puerto Rico: Instituto Internacional de Historia del Derecho Indiano; Oficina del Historiador Nacional de Puerto Rico, 2003), vol. II, Estudios.
Iñesta-Pastor, Emilia, *El Código penal de 1848* (Valencia: tirant lo blanc, 2010).
Laboulaye, Edouard, *Essai sur les lois criminelles des Romains concernant la responsabilité des magistrats,* (Paris: A. Durand, Libraire, 1845).
Ledesma Uribe, José de Jesús, "Panorama del derecho mexicano en el siglo XIX", in *Jurídica, Anuario del Departamento de Derecho de la Universidad Iberoamericana,* (México: Universidad Iberoamericana, Departamento de Derecho, 1981), núm. 13, t. II.
Levaggi, Abelardo, *Manual de Historia del Derecho Argentino* (Buenos Aires: Depalma, 1998), vol. I, General Part.
Lozoya Varela, Rafael, "La prescripción en nuestro Código de Defensa Social", en *Lecturas Jurídicas,* (Chihuahua: Universidad Autónoma de Chihuahua, Escuela de Derecho, Enero-Marzo, 1965), Núm. 22.
Macedo, Miguel S., *Apuntes para la historia del derecho penal mexicano* (México: Editorial Cultura, 1931).
Macedo, Pablo, "Apuntes sobre el Código de Procedimientos Criminales", *El Foro, Periódico de Jurisprudencia y de Legislación* (México), Tomo II, Núm. 97, (Domingo 3 de mayo de 1874).
Mariscal, Ignacio, *Ministerio de Justicia e Instrucción Pública (Exposición de Motivos al Código de Procedimientos Penales de 1880)* (México: septiembre, s/e, 1880).
Martínez de Castro, Antonio, *Exposición de motivos del Código Penal vigente en el Distrito Federal y Territorio de la Baja California dirigida al Supremo Gobierno por el Ciudadano Antonio Martínez de Castro, Presidente de la Comisión encarada de formar el Código expresado* (México: Imprenta de Francisco Díaz de León, 1876).
Masferrer, Aniceto & Mª Dolores del Mar Sánchez González, "Tradición e influencias extranjeras en el Código penal de 1848. Aproximación a un mito historiográfico" (con Aniceto Masferrer),

La Codificación española. Una aproximación doctrinal e historiográfica a sus influencias extranjeras, y a la francesa en particular (Aniceto Masferrer, ed.), Pamplona: Aranzadi–Thomson Reuters, 2014.
Masferrer, Aniceto, "Codification as Nationalization or Denationalization of Law: The Spanish Case in Comparative Perspective", *Comparative Legal History* 4.2 (2016).
Masferrer, Aniceto, "Codification of Spanish Criminal Law in the Nineteenth Century. A Comparative Legal History Approach", *Journal of Comparative Law* Vol. 4, no. 1 (2009).
Masferrer, Aniceto, "La Codificación española y sus influencias extranjeras. Una revisión en torno al alcance del influjo francés", *La Codificación española. Una aproximación doctrinal e historiográfica a sus influencias extranjeras, y a la francesa en particular* (Aniceto Masferrer, ed.) (Pamplona: Aranzadi–Thomson Reuters, 2014).
Masferrer, Aniceto, "The Napoleonic *Code pénal* and the Codification of Criminal Law in Spain", *Le Code pénal. Les metamorphoses d'un modèle 1810-1820. Actes du colloque international Lille/Gand 16-18 décembre 2012*. Textes réunis et présentés par Chantal Aboucaya et Renée Martinage (Lille: Centre d'Histoire Judiciaire, 2012).
Masferrer, Aniceto (ed.), *La Codificación española. Una aproximación doctrinal e historiográfica a sus influencias extranjeras, y a la francesa en particular* (Aniceto Masferrer, ed.) (Pamplona: Aranzadi–Thomson Reuters, 2014).
Masferrer, Aniceto, *Tradición y reformismo en la Codificación penal española. Hacia el ocaso de un mito. Materiales, apuntes y reflexiones para un nuevo enfoque metodológico e historiográfico del movimiento codificador penal europeo*, Universidad de Jaén, 2003.
Mateos, Juan A., *Reinstalación del Primer Congreso Mexicano Nombrado en 1822 y disuelto por el Golpe de Estado del Emperador Iturbide, Historia de sus sesiones* (México: Imprenta de J.F. Jens, 1878).
Medina y Ormaechea, Antonio A., *Código Penal Mexicano. Sus motivos, concordancias y leyes complementarias* (México: Imprenta del Gobierno, 1880), tomo I.
Méndez, Luis, "Introducción", *El Foro, Periódico de Jurisprudencia y de Legislación* (México), vol. II, Num. 1, (Thursday, 1 January 1874).
Merlin, Philippe Antoine, *Recueil alphabétique des questions de droit qui se présentent le plus fréquemment dans les tribunaux* (Paris: Garnery, Lib., 1827-1930), 8 vols.
Mittermaier, Carl Joseph Anton, *La pena de muerte considerada según las investigaciones de la ciencia, los progresos de la legislación y los resultados de la experiencia*, (Trad. por Manuel Rivera y Río), (México: J. Rivero, hijo, 1873).
Mittermaier, Carl Joseph Anton, *Tratado de la prueba en materia criminal, ó exposición comparada de los principios en materia criminal, y de sus diversas aplicaciones en Alemania, Francia, Inglaterra, &c.* (Trad. por un abogado del Ilustre Colegio de Madrid), con un apéndice sobre la legislación criminal de España, relativa á la prueba (México: R. Rafael, 1853).
Molina, Luis de, *De justitia et jure : opera omnia, tractatibus quinque, tomisque totidem comprehensa,* Ed. novissima, (Coloniae Allobrogum: Sumptibus Fratrum de Tournes, 1759).
Motilla, Agustín, "La codificación como técnica de producción legislativa", *Revista de Derecho Privado* 71 (1987).
Nicolini, Nicola, *Principes philosophiques et pratiques de Droit pénal* (Schneider: 1851).
Nicolini, Nicola, *Principios filosóficos y prácticos de derecho penal / estractados y traducidos al francés de las obras de Niccola Nicolini; y precedidos de una introducción sobre las opiniones filosóficas del autor; por Eugenio Flotard* (Trad. al español por Ignacio Otero) (México: J. Abadiano, 1864).
Oppetit, Bruno, *Essai sur la codification* (Paris: Presses Universitaires de France, 1998).
Ortolan, Joseph Louis Elzéar, *Éléments de Droit Pénal* (Paris: Plon, 1855).
Pérez Hernández, José María, *Estadística de la República Mejicana* (Guadalajara: Tip. del Gobierno, a cargo de Antonio de P. González, 1862).
Porte Petit Candaudap, Celestino, *Apuntamientos de la parte general de derecho penal I* (México: Ed. Porrúa, 1989, 2nd ed.).

Porte Petit Candaudap, Celestino, *Evolución legislativa penal en México* (México: Editorial Jurídica Mexicana, 1965).
Pothier, Robert Joseph, *Oeuvres de Pothier / annotées et mises en corrélation avee le Code civil et la législation actuelle, par M. Bugnet* (Paris: Cosse et N. Delamontte, 1846).
Ramos Núñez, Carlos, *El Código Napoleónico y su recepción en América Latina* (Lima: Pontificia Universidad Católica del Perú – Fondo Editorial, 1997).
Ramos Vázquez, Isabel and Juan B. Cañizares-Navarro, "La influencia francesa en la primera Codificación española: el Código penal francés de 1810 y el Código penal español de 1822", *La Codificación española. Una aproximación doctrinal e historiográfica a sus influencias extranjeras, y a la francesa en particular* (Aniceto Masferrer, ed.) (Pamplona: Aranzadi–Thomson Reuters, 2014).
Renazzi J.C., Philippi Mariae, *Elementa iuris criminalis* (Venetiis: sumptibus Heredis Nicolai Pezzana, 1776).
Roa Bárcena, Rafael, *Manual Razonado de Práctica Criminal y Médico-Legal Forense Mexicana* (México: Imprenta de Andrade y Escalante, 1860).
Rodríguez, Ricardo, *El procedimiento penal en México, Primera Parte Legislación Comparada* (México: Oficina Tip. de la Secretaría de Fomento, 1898).
Rossi, Pelegrino, *Traité de Droit Pénal*, (H. Fournier, 1829), 3 vols.
Sánchez González, Mª Dolores del Mar, *Los Códigos Penales de 1848 y 1850* (Madrid, 2003).
Secretaría de Justicia, Comisión Revisora del Código Penal, *Trabajos de Revisión del Código Penal, Proyecto de Reformas y Exposición de Motivos* (México: Tip. de la Oficina Impresora de Estampillas, Palacio nacional, 1914), Tomo IV.
Suprema Corte de Justicia, "El Código de Procedimientos Criminales", *El Foro, Periódico de Jurisprudencia y de Legislación*, (México), Tomo III, Núm. 78, (Viernes 2 de octubre de 1874).
Tau Anzoategui, Víctor, *La codificación en la Argentina, 1810-1870. Mentalidad social e ideas jurídicas* (Buenos Aires: Librería-Editorial Emilio J. Perrot, 2008, 2nd ed.).
Voet, Joannes, *Commentarius ad pandectas: in quo praeter romani juris principia ac controversias illustriores, ejus etiam hodiernum, & praecipuae fori quaestiones excutiuntur / Johannis Voet JCti & antecessoris in Academiâ Lugduno-Batavâ*, (Ed. sexta), (Hagae-Comitum: Apud Petrum de Hondt, 1731-1734), 2 vols.
Wheaton, Henry, *Elements du droit international* (Leipzig: F. A. Brockhaus, 1858, 3rd ed.), 2 vols.
Zimmermann, Reinhard, *Estudios de derecho privado europeo* (trans. by Antoni Vaquer Aloy) (Madrid: Civitas, 2000).

Sources

Actas de la comisión del Código Penal de 1871. Reproducción del ejemplar de la biblioteca privada del Lic. Indalecio Sánchez Gavito (México: s/f.).
Bando del 14 de Mayo de 1833, Prevenciones de policía, de aseo, limpieza y seguridad, in Manuel Dublán and José María Lozano, *Legislación Mexicana, Colección Completa de las Disposiciones Legislativas expedidas desde la independencia de la República* (México: Imprenta del Comercio, á Cargo de Dublán y Lozano, Hijos, 1876), Tomo II.
Bases para la Organización y arreglo de las Cárceles de 24 de diciembre de 1865, in *Boletín de las Leyes*, (México: Diciembre de 1865), Núm. 10.
Circular de la Secretaría de Justicia del 11 de Abril de 1833, Reglamento aprobado por el supremo gobierno, para el establecimiento de talleres de artes y oficios en la cárcel nacional, in Manuel Dublán and José María Lozano, *Legislación Mexicana, Colección Completa de las Disposiciones Legislativas expedidas desde la independencia de la República* (México: Imprenta del Comercio, á Cargo de Dublán y Lozano, Hijos, 1876), Tomo II.

Código de organización, de competencia y de procedimientos en materia penal, para el Distrito Federal y Territorios del 2 de octubre de 1929, in *Diario Oficial de la Federación* (lunes 7 de octubre de 1929).

Código de Procedimientos Criminales, El Foro, Periódico de Jurisprudencia y de Legislación, (México), Tomo IV, 2ª Epoca, Núm. 62, (Jueves 26 de septiembre de 1878).

Código de Procedimientos Penales del Distrito y Territorios Federales (México: Edición del Boletín Judicial, Imprenta y Litografia, 1894).

Código Federal de Procedimientos Penales (Edición Oficial) (México: Imprenta de Antonio Enríquez, 1908).

Código Penal de España (Madrid: en la Imprenta Nacional, 1848).

Código Penal Español, decretado por las Córtes en 8 de junio, sancionado por el Rey, y mandado promulgar en 9 de julio de 1822, (Madrid: En la Imprenta Nacional, 1822).

Código Penal Francés, Traducido al castellano de Orden de S.M. el Emperador Maximiliano I, por el General graduado, coronel D. Manuel Zavala; coronel retirado, D. José Ignacio Serrano y el coronel graduado, teniente coronel D. Prudencio Mesquia, que compusieron la comisión nombrada al efecto (México: Imprenta de A. Boix, a cargo de M. Zornoza, 1866).

Código Penal para el Distrito Federal y territorio de la Baja California sobre delitos del fuero común, y para toda la República sobre delitos contra la Federación, (México: Imprenta del Gobierno, en Palacio, 1871).

Código Penal para el Distrito y Territorios Federales en materia de Fuero Común, y para toda la República en materia de Fuero Federal, 13 de agosto de 1931, in *La Legislación Mexicana*, (México: La Legislación Mexicana, Sociedad Editora, Agosto de 1931), Publicación mensual autorizada por la Secretaría de Gobernación.

Código Penal para el Distrito y Territorios Federales (Edición Oficial), (México: Secretaría de Gobernación, Talleres Gráficos de la Nación, 1929).

Código penal presentado por las Cortes de España en 8 de junio de 1822, y mandado observar provisionalmente por el Congreso Constitucional del Estado de Chihuahua en 11 de agosto de 1827 (México: Imprenta á cargo de Mariano Arévalo, 1827).

Código Penal Reformado, Mandado publicar provisionalmente, en virtud de autorización concedida al Gobierno por Ley de 17 de junio de 1870, (Edición Oficial), (Madrid: Imprenta del Ministerio de Gracia y Justicia, 1870).

Decreto de 1 de Noviembre, restableciendo el juzgado de 1ª instancia de los Tuxtlas, y declarando vigentes varios decretos para aclarar y completar la ley número 54 del año de 1848 y el Código Penal del Estado, en *Leyes, Decretos y Circulares del Estado de Veracruz Llave, Año de 1855* (Jalapa: Imprenta del Gobierno del Estado, 1889).

Decreto de 13 de mayo de 1822, Pena impuesta por delito de conspiración contra la Independencia, en *Colección de órdenes y decretos de la soberana junta provisional gubernativa, y soberanos congresos generales de la nación mexicana.* (1821-37) (México: Imprenta de Galván, a cargo de Manuel Arévalo, 1829), 4 vols. Estudio Introductorio de Oscar Cruz Barney, (México: Tribunal Superior de Justicia, 2010), Tomo 1.

Decreto de 17 de Agosto de 1813, Prohibición de la corrección de azotes en escuelas y colegios, en *Colección de los decretos y ordenes de las Cortes de España, que se reputan vigentes en la República de los Estados-Unidos Mexicanos*, (México: Imprenta de Galván, á cargo de Mariano Arévalo, 1829), Edición facsimilar y estudio introductorio por Oscar Cruz Barney (México: Suprema Corte de Justicia de la Nación, 2005).

Decreto de 18 de Diciembre de 1832, Ley. Cesan las leyes que expresa relativas á ladrones y otros reos que deben ser juzgados militarmente, in Manuel Dublán and José María Lozano, *Legislación Mexicana, Colección Completa de las Disposiciones Legislativas expedidas desde la independencia de la República*, (México: Imprenta del Comercio, á Cargo de Dublán y Lozano, Hijos, 1876), Tomo II.

Decreto de 22 de Abril de 1811, Abolición de la tortura, y de los apremios, y prohibición de otras prácticas aflictivas, in *Colección de los decretos y ordenes de las Cortes de España, que se reputan vigentes en la República de los Estados-Unidos Mexicanos* (México: Imprenta de Galván, á cargo de Mariano Arévalo, 1829), Edición facsimilar y estudio introductorio por Oscar Cruz Barney (México: Suprema Corte de Justicia de la Nación, 2005).

Decreto de 28 de Agosto de 1823, Medidas para el breve despacho de las causas de conspiración, en *Colección de órdenes y decretos de la soberana junta provisional gubernativa, y soberanos congresos generales de la nación mexicana.* (1821-37), (México: Imprenta de Galván, a cargo de Manuel Arévalo, 1829), 4 vols. Estudio Introductorio de Oscar Cruz Barney, (México: Tribunal Superior de Justicia, 2010), Tomo 2.

Decreto de 9 de Marzo de 1824, Amnistía por opiniones políticas, in Manuel Dublán and José María Lozano, *Legislación Mexicana, Colección Completa de las Disposiciones Legislativas expedidas desde la independencia de la República* (México: Imprenta del Comercio, á Cargo de Dublán y Lozano, Hijos, 1876), Tomo I.

Decreto de las Cortes Generales y Extraordinarias del Reyno sobre arreglo de Tribunales y sus Atribuciones del 9 de octubre de 1812, Reimpreso en México en virtud de órden del Excmo. Sr. Virey de 19 de Marzo de 1813 á consequencia de la de la Regencia de la Monarquía de 4 de Noviembre del año próximo anterior, en que S.A.S. se sirvió autorizar a S.E. para que dispusiese su reimpresion en este Reyno (México: Por. D. Manuel Antonio Valdes, Impresor de Cámara de S.M., 1813).

Decreto del 11 de septiembre de 1820, Haciendo varias aclaraciones para poder procederá la prisión ó detención de cualquier español, in *Colección de los decretos y órdenes de las Cortes de España, que se reputan vigentes en la República de los Estados-Unidos Mexicanos* (México: Imprenta de Galván, á cargo de Mariano Arévalo, 1829), Edición facsimilar y estudio introductorio por Oscar Cruz Barney, (México: Suprema Corte de Justicia de la Nación, 2005).

Decreto del 2 de Octubre de 1823, Sobre providencias del alta policía, en *Colección de órdenes y decretos de la soberana junta provisional gubernativa, y soberanos congresos generales de la nación mexicana* (1821-37) (México: Imprenta de Galván, a cargo de Manuel Arévalo, 1829), 4 vols. Estudio Introductorio de Oscar Cruz Barney, (México: Tribunal Superior de Justicia, 2010), Tomo 2.

Decreto del 20 de Mayo de 1826, Ningún condenado por ladrón será aplicado al servicio de las armas, in Manuel Dublán and José María Lozano, *Legislación Mexicana, Colección Completa de las Disposiciones Legislativas expedidas desde la independencia de la República* (México: Imprenta del Comercio, á Cargo de Dublán y Lozano, Hijos, 1876), Tomo I.

Decreto del 24 de enero de 1812, Abolición de la pena de horca, en *Colección de los decretos y ordenes de las Cortes de España, que se reputan vigentes en la República de los Estados-Unidos Mexicanos* (México: Imprenta de Galván, á cargo de Mariano Arévalo, 1829), Edición facsimilar y estudio introductorio por Oscar Cruz Barney, (México: Suprema Corte de Justicia de la Nación, 2005).

Decreto del 27 de Septiembre de 1823, Que los reos de algunos delitos sean juzgados militarmente. Reglas para observar el despacho de las causas de los mismos reos, cuando sean juzgados por la jurisdicción ordinaria, en *Colección de órdenes y decretos de la soberana junta provisional gubernativa, y soberanos congresos generales de la nación mexicana* (1821-37), (México: Imprenta de Galván, a cargo de Manuel Arévalo, 1829), 4 vols. Estudio Introductorio de Oscar Cruz Barney (México: Tribunal Superior de Justicia, 2010), Tomo 2.

Decreto del 3 de Octubre de 1825, Estension de la ley de 27 de Septiembre de 823 sobre ladrones juzgados militarmente, en *Colección de órdenes y decretos de la soberana junta provisional gubernativa, y soberanos congresos generales de la nación mexicana.* (1821-37), (México: Imprenta de Galván, a cargo de Manuel Arévalo, 1829), 4 vols. Estudio Introductorio de Oscar Cruz Barney, (México: Tribunal Superior de Justicia, 2010), Tomo 4.

Decreto del 6 de Abril de 1824, Prorogacion de la ley de 27 de Septiembre de 1823, en *Colección de órdenes y decretos de la soberana junta provisional gubernativa, y soberanos congresos generales de la nación mexicana* (1821-37), (México: Imprenta de Galván, a cargo de Manuel Arévalo, 1829), 4 vols. Estudio Introductorio de Oscar Cruz Barney (México: Tribunal Superior de Justicia, 2010), Tomo 3.

Decreto del 8 de Septiembre de 1813, Abolición de la pena de azotes: se prohibe usar de este y otros castigos con los indios, en *Colección de los decretos y ordenes de las Cortes de España, que se reputan vigentes en la República de los Estados-Unidos Mexicanos* (México: Imprenta de Galván, á cargo de Mariano Arévalo, 1829), Edición facsimilar y estudio introductorio por Oscar Cruz Barney (México: Suprema Corte de Justicia de la Nación, 2005).

Decreto que reforma los arts. 46, 199, 376, 380, 407, 527, 528, 552, 553, 816, 819 y 912 del Código Penal para el Distrito Federal y territorio de la Baja California (México: Imprenta de Francisco Díaz de León, 1884).

Decreto XXXI de 22 de Enero de 1822, Nombramiento de Comisiones que preparen algunos trabajos para auxiliar al próximo Congreso, en *Colección de órdenes y decretos de la soberana junta provisional gubernativa, y soberanos congresos generales de la nación mexicana* (1821-37), (México: Imprenta de Galván, a cargo de Manuel Arévalo, 1829), 4 vols. Estudio Introductorio de Oscar Cruz Barney (México: Tribunal Superior de Justicia, 2010), Tomo 1.

Exposición de Motivos con que fue presentado a la Secretaría de Justicia el proyecto de reformas al Código de Procedimientos Penales del Distrito y Territorios Federales (México: Edición del Boletín Judicial, Imprenta y Litografia, 1894).

Les Cinq Codes de L'Empire Français (Paris: Chez Amable Costes, Libraire, 1812).

Ley de 23 de Mayo de 1835, Prevenciones relativas á responsabilidad de imprenta, in Manuel Dublán and José María Lozano, *Legislación Mexicana, Colección Completa de las Disposiciones Legislativas expedidas desde la independencia de la República* (México: Imprenta del Comercio, á Cargo de Dublán y Lozano, Hijos, 1876), Tomo III.

Ley de 29 de Octubre de 1835 sobre el modo de juzgar á los ladrones homicidas y sus cómplices, in Manuel Dublán and José María Lozano, *Legislación Mexicana, Colección Completa de las Disposiciones Legislativas expedidas desde la independencia de la República*, (México: Imprenta del Comercio, á Cargo de Dublán y Lozano, Hijos, 1876), Tomo III.

Ley de administración de justicia y orgánica de los tribunales de la Federación, 23 de noviembre de 1855, in Manuel Dublán and José María Lozano, *Legislación Mexicana, Colección Completa de las Disposiciones Legislativas expedidas desde la independencia de la República*, (México: Imprenta del Comercio, á Cargo de Dublán y Lozano, Hijos, 1877), Tomo VII.

Ley de nacionalización de los bienes eclesiásticos, in Manuel Dublán and José María Lozano, *Legislación Mexicana, Colección Completa de las Disposiciones Legislativas expedidas desde la independencia de la República* (México: Imprenta del Comercio, á Cargo de Dublán y Lozano, Hijos, 1877), Tomo VIII.

Ley del 22 de Febrero de 1832, Responsabilidad de los que, en caso de pronunciamiento, tomen propiedad ajena, in Manuel Dublán and José María Lozano, *Legislación Mexicana, Colección Completa de las Disposiciones Legislativas expedidas desde la independencia de la República* (México: Imprenta del Comercio, á Cargo de Dublán y Lozano, Hijos, 1876), Tomo II.

Ley del 6 de julio de 1848 sobre el modo de juzgar a los ladrones, homicidas y heridores, in Manuel Dublán and José María Lozano, *Legislación Mexicana, Colección Completa de las Disposiciones Legislativas expedidas desde la independencia de la República* (México: Imprenta del Comercio, á Cargo de Dublán y Lozano, Hijos, 1876), Tomo II.

Ley Orgánica Provisional de la Administración de Justicia de 26 de septiembre de 1855, en *Leyes, Decretos y Circulares del Estado de Veracruz Llave, Año de 1855* (Jalapa: Imprenta del Gobierno del Estado, 1889).

Ley para la concesión de indultos y amnistías de 25 de diciembre de 1865, in *Boletín de las Leyes* (México: Diciembre de 1865), Núm. 10.
Ley para la Organización del Ministerio Público de 19 de diciembre de 1865, in *Boletín de las Leyes* (México: Diciembre de 1865), Núm. 10.
Ley sobre libelos infamatorios impresos, Mayo 14 de 1831, in Manuel Dublán and José María Lozano, *Legislación Mexicana, Colección Completa de las Disposiciones Legislativas expedidas desde la independencia de la República* (México: Imprenta del Comercio, á Cargo de Dublán y Lozano, Hijos, 1876), Tomo II.
Memoria que el encargado de la Secretaría de Justicia e Instrucción Pública presenta al Congreso de la Unión en 15 de septiembre de 1873, in José Luis Soberanes Fernández (Comp.), *Memorias de la Secretaría de Justicia* (México: Universidad Nacional Autónoma de México, Instituto de Investigaciones Jurídicas, 1997).
Memoria que el Secretario de Estado y del Despacho de Justicia e Instrucción Pública presenta al Congreso de la Unión, en marzo de 1868, in José Luis Soberanes Fernández (Comp.), *Memorias de la Secretaría de Justicia* (México: Universidad Nacional Autónoma de México, Instituto de Investigaciones Jurídicas, 1997).
Memoria que el Secretario de Justicia e Instrucción Pública presenta al Congreso de la Unión y Comprende del 1 de enero de 1878 al 15 de septiembre de 1881, in José Luis Soberanes Fernández (Comp.), *Memorias de la Secretaría de Justicia* (México: Universidad Nacional Autónoma de México, Instituto de Investigaciones Jurídicas, 1997).
Memoria que en cumplimiento del Artículo 120 de la Constitución Federal de los Estados Unidos Mexicanos leyó el Secretario de Estado y del Despacho Universal de Justicia y Negocios Eclesiásticos en la Cámara de Diputados el día 19, y en la de Senadores el día 20 de enero de 1829, sobre los ramos del Ministerio de su cargo, en José Luis Soberanes Fernández (Comp.), *Memorias de la Secretaría de Justicia* (México: Universidad Nacional Autónoma de México, Instituto de Investigaciones Jurídicas, 1997).
Memoria que en cumplimiento del Artículo 120 de la Constitución Federal de los Estados Unidos Mexicanos leyó el Secretario de Estado y del Despacho Universal de Justicia y Negocios Eclesiásticos en la Cámara de Diputados el día 18, y en la de Senadores el día 22 de marzo de 1830, sobre los ramos del Ministerio de su cargo, in José Luis Soberanes Fernández (Comp.), *Memorias de la Secretaría de Justicia* (México: Universidad Nacional Autónoma de México, Instituto de Investigaciones Jurídicas, 1997.
Memoria que en cumplimiento del precepto constitucional presenta al Congreso de la Unión en C. Lic Joaquin Baranda Secretario de Estado y del despacho de Justicia e Instrucción Pública, 31 de marzo de 1887, in José Luis Soberanes Fernández (Comp.), *Memorias de la Secretaría de Justicia* (México: Universidad Nacional Autónoma de México, Instituto de Investigaciones Jurídicas, 1997).
Nuevo Código Penal, (México: Tribunal Superior de Justicia del Distrito Federal, Instituto de Investigaciones Jurídicas de la UNAM, 2003).
Proyecto de Código de Procedimientos Criminales para el Distrito Federal y el Territorio de la Baja California, formado por encargo del Supremo Gobierno, por los licenciados Manuel Dublán, José Linares, Luis Méndez y M. Siliceo (México: Imprenta del Gobierno, en Palacio, 1873).
Proyecto de Código de Procedimientos Penales (México: Imprenta del Gobierno, en Palacio, 1879).
Proyecto de Código Penal para el Distrito y Territorio de la Baja-California sobre Delitos del Fuero Común; y para toda la República sobre Delitos contra la Federación (México: Imprenta del Gobierno, En Palacio, 1871).

Proyecto de Código Penal, presentado a las Córtes por la Comisión Especial nombrada al efecto. Impreso de órden de las mismas, (Madrid: Imprenta de Don Mateo Repullés, 1821).
Proyecto de Código Penal, presentado al Cuarto Congreso Constitucional del Estado de Veracruz. Primera Parte (Jalapa: Impreso en la Oficina del Gobierno por Aburto y Blanco, 1832).
Real Cédula de S.M. y Señores del Consejo de 25 de julio de 1814, por la qual se manda que en adelante no puedan los jueces usar de apremios ni de género alguno de tormento personal para las declaraciones y confesiones de los reos ni de los testigos, quedando abolida la práctica que había en ello con los demás que se expresa (Madrid: En la Imprenta Real, 1814).

Oscar Cruz Barney Doctor in Law with honors from the Universidad Panamericana and law degree with honors from the Universidad Iberoamericana. Law degree from the Ministry of Education, Culture and Sport of Spain. Diploma on Orientation in American Law by the University of California, campi Davis and Berkeley. Former President of the Illustrious and National Collegium of Lawyers of Mexico, founded in 1760 for the periods 2008–2010 and 2010–2012. Admitted to the Bar Association of Madrid in 2012. Former Senator of the Unión Iberoamericana de Colegios y Agrupaciones de Abogados UIBA. Former Counselor of the Presidency of the Union internationale des Avocats, Paris, France. International Arbitrator. Panelist of the Chapter XIX Dispute Settlement Mechanism of the North American Free Trade Agreement (NAFTA) on antidumping. Arbitrator of the International Chamber of Commerce in Paris. He was Vice President of the Commission of Foreign Trade of the Confederation of Industrial Chambers of Mexico (CONCAMIN). Honorary Academician of the Royal Academy of Jurisprudence and Legislation of Madrid. Foreign Corresponding Academician of the Colombian Academy of Jurisprudence. Researcher at the Institute of Legal Research of the National Autonomous University of Mexico where he is Director of the Mexican History of Law Review and Coordinator of the Legal History Section. National Researcher Level III in the National System of Researchers of CONACYT (National Council of Science and Technology). Among its international decorations he is Knight of Merit of the Sacred Military Constantinian Order of St. George; Distinguished Cross First Class of the Order of St. Raymond of Peñafort by the Ministry of Justice in Spain; he is Great Cross of Merit in the Service to the Spanish Advocacy awarded by the General Council of Spanish Lawyers; he is San Ivo Cross by the Royal and Illustrious Bar of Zaragoza; he received the Medal of Honor of the Bar Association of Madrid; he received the Honorable Mention of the Bar Association of Seville; Collegiate of Honor at the Bar Association of Valencia and received the Medal of Merit of the Bar Association of Oviedo. Academic seat number 36 of the Mexican Academy of Jurisprudence and Legislation; Academic seat 39 of the International Academy of Customs Law; Member of the International Institute of History of Derecho Indiano. He has been invited as international lecturer to the United States (by the USDA and the Vance Center and by the USDA), Peru, Chile, Colombia, France, Spain, Germany, Italy and Finland.

Part IV
Prison Law Reform

European and US Influences on the 19th Century Prison Reform

Isabel Ramos Vázquez

Abstract On 19th century, imprisonment became the principal penalty of western societies due to the triumph of Enlightenment movement for humanization of punishments and Rationalist philosophy. Prison reform became an international issue, and liberal states had to build from nothing a new penalty system, transforming the ancient and obsolete Old Regime's punishments. Social reality and new legal principles promoted this important legislative reform in the United States of America and many European countries, which reciprocally analysed and studied their different penitentiary laws and models in order to transplant or adapt their major achievements. This paper aims to draw the main European an US influences at this early stage of prison reform.

1 The Origins of Prison Reform in Europe

The origins of prison reform in most European countries concurred with the criminal codification process, and it was inspired gradually by Howard's humanism, Beccaria's individualism, and Bentham's utilitarianism.[1] However, the first European criminal Codes did not clearly bet on this new type of punishment against the archaic Old Regime's penology (the triumph of imprisonment in contemporary

[1]Michel Foucault, *Vigilar y castigar: nacimiento de la prisión* (Madrid, 1992), Luis Jiménez de Asúa, *Tratado de derecho penal I* (Buenos Aires, 1964), Marcelo Tomás Maestro, *Voltaire and Beccaria as reformers of Criminal Law* (Nueva York, 1942), Norval Morris y Rothman, *The Oxford history of the prison* (Oxford, 1995), Peter O'Brien, "Prison reform in France and other European countries in the nineteenth century", *Institutions of confinement: hospitals, asylums, and prisons in Western Europe and North America. 1500-1950* (Cambridge, 1996), pp. 297–298, Pedro Frailes, *Un espacio para castigar. La cárcel y la ciencia penitenciaria en España (siglos XVIII-XIX)* (Madrid, 1999), o Clive Emsley, "Law reform and penal reform in England in the age of the French revolution", *Révolutions et justice pénale in Europe* (London, 1999).

I. R. Vázquez (✉)
University of Jaén, Jaén, Spain
e-mail: iramos@ujaen.es

A. Masferrer (ed.), *The Western Codification of Criminal Law*, Studies in the History of Law and Justice 11, https://doi.org/10.1007/978-3-319-71912-2_15

criminal codes was not immediate). Neither the first Criminal Code contemporary, the French Code of 1791, nor the *Code des délits et des peines* of 1795, raised imprisonment to a prominent place.[2] It is true that they contained some secondary penalties of this type, inherited from the Old Regime, as forced labour or deportation to colonies, and that they anticipated other new imprisonment penalties, like the so-called *"peine de la gene"*, reclusion or arrest. But these penalties were only the natural evolution of eighteenth century secondary and utilitarian punishments, and they were still far from being placed as the main or structural penalties of the penal system.

We should note also that there still were not enough facilities or institutions for prisoner's reclusion (although they started to be built, reusing as well old jails or deposits), and any prison system had not even been developed, so the most sentences in France at this time were to death, deportation to the colonies or forced labour, like in the old times.[3]

Consequently, the actual origin of imprisonment in French criminal codification would not occur until the promulgation of the Napoleonic Penal Code of 1810, in which Bentham's influence is remarkable.[4] Imprisonment gained prominence in it by the penalties of forced labour, deportation to the colonies, banishment, reclusion in *"maison de force"* for more than five years, imprisonment from six days to five years, and arrest from one to five days, which became the main penalties in the code. They were the general framework from which prison reform actually began in France through legislative development and an important comparative work.

Municipal or departmental prisons (*"maisons d'arrêt"*), and central prisons (*"maisons centrales"*), began to be built in the Napoleonic era. A significant Ordinance of 1816 divided them into *"maisons du force"* for those sentenced to reclusion, and *"maisons de correction"* for those sentenced to corrective penalties.[5] All of this prisons practiced obligatory labor, tried to separate men, women and children, and some of them attempted to apply as well the Philadelphia's cellular

---

[2]Jean-Marie Carbasse, "État autoritaire et justice répressive. L'évolution de la législation pénale de 1789 au Code pénal de 1810", *All'ombra dell'aquila imperiale. Trasformazioni e continuità istituzionali nei territori sabaudi in età napoleónica* (Rome, 1994), pp. 313–333, André Laingui, *Histoire du droit pénal* (París, 1993), vol. 1, pp. 121–123, Renée Martinage, *Histoire du droit pénal en Europe* (Paris, 1998), pp. 75–76, Jean-Marie Carbasse, *Histoire du droit pénal et de la justice criminelle* (París, 2000), pp. 243–247, José Luis Guzmán Dalbora, "Código penal francés de 1791", *Revista de Derecho Penal y Criminología*, 3° ep., n°1 (2009), pp. 481–517.

[3]Robert Allen, *Les tribunaux criminels sous la Révolution et l'Empire. 1792-1811* (Rennes, 2005).

[4]Renée Martinage, *Histoire du droit pénal en Europe* (Paris, 1998), p.76, Jean-Marie Carbasse, "État autoritaire et justice répressive. L'évolution de la législation pénale de 1789 au Code pénal de 1810", *All'ombra dell'aquila imperiale. Trasformazioni e continuità istituzionali nei territori sabaudi in età napoleónica* (Rome, 1994), pp. 313–333, and Jean-Marie Carbasse, "Code pénal", *Dictionnaire de culture juridique* (París, 2003), pp. 210–216.

[5]Marcel le Clère, "Prisons et bagnes en France du Directoire aux Cent-Jours", *Revue de l'Institut Napoléon*, 1974, n° 130, pp. 33–43, and Jacques-Guy Petit, Claude Faugeron, Michel Pierre, *Histoire des prisons en France. 1789-2000* (Rennes, 2002).

system imported from the United States of America.[6] The Parisian prisons of Roquette or Mazás could be some early examples.

The same way, England tried to do at that time its own prison reform apart of any codification, and based on the American experience. After the first failed project represented by the *Penitentiary Act* of 1779, that was approved by Parliament following the ideas of Howard, in 1816 was founded the *Society for the Improvement of Prison Discipline and for the Reformation of Juvenile Offenders*, supporting both the ideas of Howard and Bentham's, and trying to promote knowledge of others prisons realities in Europe and the United States.

The American separate or cellular system attracted the attention of reformers in United Kingdom and led to the creation of Millbank Prison in 1816, followed by other attends of separate prisons in Belfast, Glasgow, Paisley, Liverpool, Wakefield, Parkhurst or Pentonville. Furthermore, Robert Peel's *Gaols Act* of 1823 tried to impose uniformity in the country prisons, convicts began to be classified according to types, and they were kept separate and treated differently. *Gaols Act* of 1823 and *Prison Act* of 1835, introducing among other things inspection in prisons, were the final green light for the English prison reform.

Meanwhile, the failure of the first Spanish Criminal Code of 1822 neither prevented the starting of prison reform in this country. Humanization and rationalization of penalties had become an international target, and, before the enactment of the next Penal Code of 1848 (in which a large number of imprisonment penalties was finally consolidated), the most important nineteenth-century prison law in Spain was enacted: the *Ordenanza General de Presidios* of 1834.

The *Ordenanza General de Presidios* of 1834, and subsequent penitentiary laws as the *Ley de prisiones* of 1849, promoted the penitentiary reform in Spain based mainly on the analysis of foreign policies and experiences. Others European countries, like Switzerland, Belgium, Italy and Prussia, also participated in this international movement, using law as instrument for social development, and following different penitentiary influences known through comparative prison law studies.

2 Foreign Experiences and Influences Promoting Prison Reform on 19th Century

Probably the first study of comparative prison law in Europe was the well-known work of John Howard, *The State of the Prisons in England and Wales*, first published in London in 1777. John Howard, who was a philanthropist and the first

[6]François Alexandre Frédéric de La Rochefaucault-Liancourt, *Des Prisons de Philadelphie par un Européen*, Filadelfia, 1796 (2° ed., París, 1799).

English prison reformer,[7] not only described prisons in England and Wales, but also many other prisons, hospitals and correction houses existing in Europe in the late eighteenth century, known in successive trips to Scotland, Ireland, Netherlands, Germany, Denmark, Sweden, Russia, Poland, Silesia, Italy, Switzerland, Austria, Portugal, Spain, and France.

Howard's work widely circulated by many other European countries, and it started an important discussion on the state of prisons and the need for its reform at the end of the eighteenth century.[8] This move towards the humanization of punishment already had important antecedents in England, like Geffrey Mynshull,[9] or the philanthropists Sollom Elym, George Ollyffe, Thomas Robe, William Blackstone or William Eden.[10] In fact, along with John Howard, Willian Eden has been considered one of the intellectual leaders of the English prison reform,[11] which was finally promoted in the Parliament with the approval of the *Penitentiary Act* in 1779. The *Penitentiary Act* provided the classification of prisoners, women's prisons, religious instruction and daily work, but unfortunately it did not get to fulfil expectations.[12]

The comparative labour continued in England with *A Visit to the Philadelphia Prison* (Philadelphia, 1796), by Robert J. Turnbull. This work described the solitary confinement of prisoners in individual cells applied in the Pennsylvania's prison (*separate system*), and inspired the creation of the prisons of Belfast in Ireland, Glasgow and Paisley in Scotland, and Liverpool, Wakefield, Pentonville, Parkhurst and Millbank in England, in the early nineteenth century.[13]

---

[7]Arthur Gordon Rose, *The Struggle for Penal Reform: the Howard League and its Predecessors*, (London, 1961), Tessa West, *The curious Mr. Howard: legendary prison reformer* (Hampshire, 2011), and Sergio García Ramírez, "John Howard: la obra y la enseñanza", *El estado de las prisiones en Inglaterra y Gales* (México, 2003), pp. 49–50.

[8]Hepworth Dixon, *John Howard and the Prison-World of Europe. From Original and Authentic Documents* (Massachusset, 1852).

[9]Geoffrey Mynshull, *Essays and Character of a Prison and Prisoners* (London, 1618).

[10]Sollom Elym, *State Trials* (London, 1730), Thomas Ollyfe, *An essay humbly offer'd, for an Act of Parliament to prevent capital crimes, and the loss of many lives; and to promote a desirable improvement and blessing in the nation* (London, 1731), Thomas Robert, *Some Considerations for rendering the Punishment of Criminals more effectual* (London, 1733), William Blackstone, *Commentaries on the laws of England* (Oxford, 1766–1769), and William Eden, *Principles of Penal Law* (London, 1711).

[11]Jonas Hanway, *Solitude in Imprisonment* (London, 1779), John Leroux, *Thoughts on the Present State of the Prisons of this Country* (London, 1780), Paul George Onesiphorus, *A State of the proceedings on the subjecto of a Reform of prisons* (London, 1783), John Jebb, *Thoughts on the Polity and Construction of Prisons with Hints for Their Improvement* (London, 1785), or Thomas MacDonald, *A treatise on civil imprisonment in England* (London, 1791).

[12]Randall McGowen, "The Well-Ordered Prison: England, 1780-1865", *The Oxford History of the prison. The practice of punishment in Western Society*, (Oxford-New York, 1998), p.80.

[13]Michael Ignatieff, *A just measure of pain: the penitentiary in the Industrial revolution (1750-1850)* (New York, 1978), and Adam J., Hirsch, *The Rise of the penitentiary. Prisons and punishment in Early America*, (New Haven/Londres, 1992).

Pennsylvania's system was created in the seventeenth century in the Quaker community led by William Penn in the English colonies of America. This community was the first, in 1682, abolishing the corporal punishment characteristic of that time (death, mutilation and flogging), and setting in place a new prison or confinement penalty, that aimed correction of the individual through isolation and reflection.[14] The system tried to improve in 1790 with the creation of Walnut Street Prison, and soon the states of New York, Maryland, Massachusetts, Maine, New Jersey and Virginia joined it.

Nevertheless, the lack of satisfactory results, and growing criticism for the damages that isolation produced on the health of inmates, promoted a series of discussions and prisons reforms in the United States of America, where a second prison system appeared: the mixed system of Auburn (*silent system*).[15] The Auburn system was based on isolation at night, and daily common work and religious instruction under the rule of silence. A year after its establishment, in 1824, an inspection commission did a very favourable report about Auburn prison, and its director Elam Lynds (whom historiography wanted to point out as the main ideologue of the system), directed the construction of Sing Sing prison, inspired in the same principles.[16]

From that moment, other American projects followed the silent system, and a great controversy arose in the United States of America, which was mainly aided by the confrontation between the *Bostonian Society*, supporting Auburn's system, and the *Society of Philadelphia*, supporting the benefits of isolation or cellular system.

When the controversy came to Europe, cellular system was beginning to be used in some prisons in the United Kingdom, and also in other continental prisons as La Roquette in Paris. It was known mostly thanks to a new comparative work, *Des Prisons de Philadelphie par un Européen*,[17] written in France by La Rochefaucault-Liancourt, who travelled to the United States between 1795 and 1797 to study this system, and whose ideas spread rapidly throughout Europe by different translations. In Spain, for example, the work was acknowledged by the early translation of Ventura de Arquellada *Noticia del estado de la cárcel de Filadelfia* (1801),[18] which together with Bentham's works helped to promote a very first and unsuccessful prison reform during the Liberal Triennium (1820–1823).

---

[14]Abel Téllez Aguilera, *Los sistemas penitenciarios y sus prisiones. Derecho y realidad* (Madrid, 1998), pp. 89–97, or Fernando Tercero Arribas, "Sistemas penitenciarios norteamericanos", *Historia de las prisiones. Teorías economicistas* (Madrid, 1997), pp. 149–157.

[15]David J. Rothman, "Perfecting the prison. United States 1789-1865", *The Oxford history of the prison: the practice of punishment in western society*, (New York, 1995), pp. 111–129; y Mark Kann, *Punishment, prisons, and patriarchy liberty and power in the early American republic* (New York, 2005).

[16]Enoch C. Wines, *The State of Prisons and of Child-Saving* (Cambridge, 1880), p.119.

[17]François Alexandre Frédéric de La Rochefaucault-Liancourt, *Des Prisons de Philadelphie par un Européen*, Filadelfia, 1796 (2° ed., París, 1799).

[18]Ventura de Arquellada, *Noticia del estado de la cárcel de Filadelfia* (Madrid, 1801), Madrid, 1916.

Philadelphia's regime was also known in Spain by the works by Marcial Antonio López *Descripción de los más célebres establecimientos penales de Europa y Estados Unidos* (1832),[19] and Ramón de la Sagra, *Cinco meses en los Estados Unidos de América del Norte (desde el 20 de abril al 23 de septiembre de 1835*) (1836),[20] which, although won the public opinion approval, also failed to implement the system for lack of financial means.

The support for the new Auburn's model in Europe, also comes first in France with the work of the renowned criminal lawyer Charles Lucas,[21] *Du système pénitentiaire en Europe at aux Etats-Unis* written between 1828 and 1830.[22] Charles Lucas based his work on statistical data provided by the *Boston Prison Discipline Society*, headed by Louis Dwight in favour of silent system, and that did not coincide at all with the data offered by the *Philadelphia Society for Alleviating the Miseries of Public Prisons*, supporting cellular system.

Confusion of statistical data roused controversy both in the United States and Europe. In Europe, the work by the Prussian Nikolaus Heinrich Julius, *Du système pénitentiarie américaine en 1836*,[23] was widely recognized, and Alexis de Tocqueville and Gustave de Beaumont confronted Charles Lucas with a new work, *On the Penitentiary System in the United States and Its Application in France*, (Philadelphia, 1833),[24] in favor of the cellular system. Their followers were more than those of Charles Lucas, and they got the publication of several new prisons laws in France, approved between 1841 and 1848, and based on the isolation model.

Charles Lucas' project was rejected in the House of Representatives. But it did not stop some very interesting initiatives influenced by his ideas, pointing out the foundation of Mettray Penal Colony, just north of the city of Tours. Mettray Penal

---

[19]Marcial Antonio López, *Descripción de los más célebres establecimientos penales de Europa y Estados Unidos, seguida de la aplicación práctica de sus principios y régimen interior a las Casas de Corrección, Fuerza y Reconciliación que pudieran plantearse en España*, (Valencia, 1832), 2 tomos.

[20]Ramón de la Sagra, *Cinco meses en los Estados Unidos de América del Norte (desde el 20 de abril al 23 de septiembre de 1835)* (París, 1836).

[21]Andre Normandeu, "Pioneers in criminology: Charles Lucas, opponent of capital punishment", *Journal of Criminal Law and Criminology*, vol. 61, issue 2 (1970), pp. 218–228.

[22]Charles Lucas, *Du système pénitentiaire en Europe at aux Etats-Unis*, (Paris, 1828–1828) 3 vols. See also Charles Lucas, *Exposé d'un Système de Legislation criminelle pour l'État de la Lousiane et pour les États-Unis d'Amerique por Edward Livingston*, (París, 1872) 2 vols., and *Des moyens et des conditions de la réforme pénitentiaire en France* (París, 1848).

[23]Nicolaus Heinrich Julius, *Du système pénitentiarie américain en* 1836 (Rennes-París-Geneve-Bruxelles, 1837), and Nicolaus Heinrich Julius, *Leçons sur les prisons présentées en forme de Cours au Public de Berlin, en l'Année 1827, I et II*, (París- Bruxelles, 1831).

[24]Wilson Pierson, G., *Tocqueville in America*, (New York, 1938), Juan Manuel Ros, y Julián Sauquillo, "Un sistema penitenciario traído del viaje," *Del sistema penitenciario en Estados Unidos y su aplicación en Francia* (Madrid, 2005); and Julián Sauquillo, "Un descubrimiento judicial de la democracia: el viaje de Tocqueville y Beaumont a América (1831-1832)", *Jueces para la democracia*, 2008, nº 62, pp. 92–103.

Colony, supported as well by Frédéric-Auguste Demetz and Guillaume-Abel Blouet,[25] was a private reformatory in the countryside, opened in 1840 for the rehabilitation of young male delinquents aged between 6 and 21.

The progressive way in which the Colony was organized anticipated the later reformatory system in United States, United Kingdom or Spain.[26] But at the time of its foundation it was a uniqueness in France, where still predominated the congregation system characteristic of Old Regime, regardless of any cellular experience such as prisons of La Roquette, and Mazas in Paris, or some departmental prisons that were built with a new plant according to the cell model between 1841 and 1851.[27]

At this time, under the *Gaols Act* of 1823 and the *Prision Act* de 1835, and with the support of reformers like Samuel Romilly, Thomas Buxton, Samuel Gurney, Whitworth Russell, Robert Peel or William Crawford, Secretary of the *London Prison Discipline Society* who wrote *Report of William Crawford on the Penitentiaries of the United States* (London, 1834), England lived a second stage in its prison reform movement.[28]

Pentoville prison, inspired by the cellular system, remained a reference in the country[29]; but the hard results of the absolute isolation models (suicides, serious psychological and physical damages etc.), urged the search for other models abroad. Thus, the mixed or silent system of Auburn was anew analyzed in works as the one of Tellkampf, *Reform of punishment and prisons* en *Essays on law reform, commercial policy, Banks, penitentiaries,* etc. *in Great Britain and the United*

[25]Frédéric-Auguste Demetz, and Guillaume-**Abel** Blouet, M., *Rapports a M. le Comte de Montalivet sur les pénitenciers des États-Unis* (París, 1837).

[26]Luc Forlivesi, Georges-François Pottier, and Sophie Chassat, *Éduquer et punir. La colonie agricole pénitentiaire de Mettray (1839-1937)* (Rennes, 2005).

[27]Jean-Marie Carbasse, *Histoire du droit pénal et de la justice criminelle* (París, 2000), pp. 266–267, or André Zysberg, *Politiques du bagne.* 1820-*1850. L'impossible prison: recherches sur le système pénitentiaire au XIXe siécle* (París, 1980), pp. 175–188.

[28]Francis C. Gray, *Prison Discipline in America* (London, 1847), Joseph Adshead, *Prisons and Prisoners* (London, 1845), Dorothea Lynde Dix, *Remarks on Prisons and Prison Discipline in the United States*, (London, 1845), John Field, *Prison discipline: and the advantages of the separate system of imprisonment, with a detailed account of the discipline now pursued in the new County Gaol, at Reading*, 2 vols. (London, 1848), y Joshua Jebb, *Observations on the Separate System of Discipline submitted to the Congress assembled at Brussels, on the subjects of Prison Reform, on the 20 September 1847* (London, 1847).

[29]Beatrice and Shaw Webb, *English prisons under local government* (London, 1922), Ursula R. Q Henriques, "The rise and decline of the separate system of prison discipline", *Past & Present*, vol. 54, (1972), pp. 61–93, William James Forsythe, "The beginnings of the separate system of imprisonment 1835-1840", *Social Policy & Administration*, vol. 13.2 (1979), pp. 105–110, Heather Tomlinson, "Design and reform: the 'separate system' in the nineteenth century English prison", *Buildings and Society: Essays on the Social Development of the Built Environment*, (London, 1984), pp. 94–119, Christopher Hadign, *Imprisonment in England and Wales: A concise History* (London, 1985), o Peter Spierenburg, *The prison experience* (London, 1991).

States of America (1859)[30]; and others European experiences were studied by authors like Patrick Joseph Murray, *Reformatory Schools In France And England* (1854).[31]

Mettray Penal Colony and other Reformatory institutions, as Ruysselède's School in Belgium (created by Inspector General Ducpétieux in 1849 and known as the "Belgian Mettray"), or some others Dutch, Swiss, or Polish Farm institutions, became then the main focus of attention,[32] which moved from the United States to Europe. In England, they became an ideal for philanthropists and reformers like the aforementioned Joseph Patrick Murray, Wheatley-Balme, Lord Leigh or Davenport Hill, who influenced the publication of the *Youthful Offenders Act* in 1854, promoting the creation of this type of Penal Colonies or Reformatories. Few years earlier, in 1850, the *English Philanthropic Society* had already founded an Farm Reformatory for young people in Red Hill (Surrey) directed by Sidney Turner, and Thomas Barwick Lloyd-Baker also founded and direct his own Farm Reformatory shortly after.[33]

This shift towards the most innovative European models can also be noted in Spain in the second half of the nineteenth century, both in the Parliament's discussions and in the comparative prisons law studies sponsored by the government, as the one by Francisco Murube y Galán in 1860,[34] or the one of Andrés Borrego Moreno in 1873.[35] Borrego especially liked the new so-called *progressive system* implemented by Walter Crofton in Ireland that became another leading model at the time.

In addition to the penal colonies or reformatories inspired in some kind of progressive system to gradually reintegrate young offenders in society, other progressive experiences starred in the international discussion. The main criminal schools of the time urged solutions for amendment of the offenders, not only their punishment or separation from society, and for this purpose the progressive experiences carried out by Captain Maconochie in Australia, Sir Walter Crofton in

---

[30]Johann Louis Tellkampf, *Reform of punishment and prisons* en *Essays on law reform, comercial policy, Banks, penitenciaries, etc in Great Britain and the United States of America* (London-Edimburgh, 1859).

[31]Patrick Joseph Murray, *Reformatory Schools In France And England* (London, 1854).

[32]Frédéric-Auguste Demetz, *Report on Reformatory Farm institutions*, traduc. E.B Wheathley (London, 1856).

[33]Ben Elliot, "The Provision of Reformatory Schools, the Landed Class, and the Myth of the Superiority of Rural Life in Mid-Victorian England: a Footnote", *History of Education*, 1980, vol. 9, nº1, pp. 63–74, and Johan A. Stack, "Reformatory and industrial schools and the decline of chils imprisonment in mid-Victorian England and Wales", *History of Education*, 1994, vol. 23, nº1, pp. 59–73.

[34]Francisco Murube y Galán, *Tratado de las prisiones y sistemas penales de Inglaterra y Francia, con observaciones generales sobre lo que conviene saber para la reforma de las de España* (Santiago de Compostela, 1860).

[35]Andrés Borrego, *Estudios penitenciarios. Visita de los principales establecimientos penales de Europa, ejecutada de orden del Gobierno, seguida de la exposición de un sistema aplicable a la reforma de las cárceles y presidios de España* (Madrid, 1873).

Ireland, Counselor Von Obermaier in Munich, or Colonel Montesinos in Valencia, became the leading models. All these *progressive* experiences consisted of dividing the duration of the sentence in several periods of absolute isolation, common work and conditional freedom, with the aim of gradually integrating the inmate in society.

European models, Mettray Penal Colony and Irish progressive prisons basically, reached the United States when the old discussion between cellular system or mixed system was already overcome. They were thoroughly analyzed in the Cincinnati Prison Congress of 1870, organized by the Secretary of the *Prison Association of New York*, Enoch Cobb Wines and Zebulon Reed Brockway.[36] There, from the conjunction between the two referred models resulted precisely a new kind of prison system: the *"reformatory system"*.[37]

Reformatory system was described by Zebulon Reed Brockway[38] in his report to Cincinnati Congress *The ideal of a true prison reform system*[39]:

> The penitentiary exists for the infliction of punishment; the reformatory exists for the reformation of the offender. The reformatory system assumes that men can be reformed, and that it is the duty of society to invoke those influences which shall lead to reformation. Its not concerned with the simple question of a punitive theory. [...] In a system purely retributive, obligation to the criminal is either disparaged or ignored. In a system purely sentimental, the protection of the society may be sacrificed to a misplaced pity. The reformatory system is neither retributive nor sentimental. It assumes that society must be protected; it is organized and administered with this end in view.[40]

Briefly, this new system consisted in a progressive programme with rewards and punishments for the amelioration of offenders, the indeterminate sentence instead of the fixed one, and the purpose of rehabilitating the offender by work and learning. The idea was enthusiastically welcomed in Cincinnati Congress, and six years after

---

[36]Francesco Federico Falcó, *La obra de los congresos penitenciarios internacionales* (La Habana, 1906), pp. 5–6, or Leon Radzinowicz, "International collaboration in criminal science", *The modern approach to criminal law. Collected essays*, London, 1945, pp. 467–497.

[37]Abel Téllez Aguilera, *Los sistemas penitenciarios y sus prisiones. Derecho y realidad*, Madrid, 1998; Fernando Tercero Arribas, "Sistemas penitenciarios norteamericanos", *Historia de las prisiones* (Madrid, 1997), pp. 149–157.

[38]See Zebulon R. Brockway, *Fifty years of prison service: an autobiography* (New York, 1912), or "The American Reformatory Prison System", *American Journal of Sociology*, vol. 15, nº 4 (Jan., Jan 1910), pp. 454–477. Also Harry Allen and Clifford E. Simonsen, *Corrections in America: An Introduction* (New Jersey, 2001), pp. 76–84, James J. Beha, "Redemption to Reform: The Intellectual Origins of the Prison Reform Movement", *New York University Annual Survey of American Law*, vol. 3 (2007–2008), pp. 773 y ss, or Todd R. Clear, George F. Cole, and Michael D. Reisig, *American Corrections* (Nueva York, 2009), pp. 50–53.

[39]Zebulon R. Brockway, *The Ideal of a True Prison System for a State. a Paper Read Before the National Congress on Penitentiary and Reformatory Discipline at Cincinnati*, on October 12, 1870.

[40]Samuel J. Barrows, *The reformatory system in the United States. Reports prepared for The International Prison Commission*, S.J. Barrows, commissioner for the United States, Washington, 1900 (House of representatives, 56th Congress, 1st Session, document n.459), p.8.

it was put into effect with the foundation of Elmira Reformatory, under the direction of Zebulon Reed Brockway since its opening in 1876 till 1900.[41]

The *reformatory* model in the United States represented a significant evolution versus the *penitentiary model*,[42] and, though the first of them were founded for young people, similar establishments for women and men appeared soon (for example, the *Massachusetts Reformatory Prison for Women* in 1877), in the belief that the progressive system was convenient for all of them. Differences between the ones for young offenders and the other mainly were the kind of work required of convicts and the greater attention paid to the education of young people. But they all applied the progressive system in three periods (isolation period to observe and classify inmates, common life for their education and training, and pre-release period to put them in contact with society by short exit licenses), the third of which could be divided in a fourth period of probation or conditional release out of prison. The list of reformatories operating in 1899 in United States amounted to 65, with a total of 19,410 inmates.[43]

The "American-type" reformatory system began to be introduced in the late nineteenth century in some of the European central prisons or agricultural colonies.[44] Not too many, since in most European prisons (especially municipal, provincial or departmental) remained the congregation system, and only a few have developed the new prison principles. However, in addition to the reformatories for juvenile offenders who were established following the example of Mettray (especially the Ruysselade and Beernem reformatories in Belgium, and the more than forty juvenile reformatories founded in England and Ireland[45]), they can be mentioned as pioneering examples of this influence the Reform School of St. Hilaire,

---

[41]Samuel J. Barrows, *The reformatory system in the United States. Reports prepared for The International Prison Commission* (Washington, 1900), *Reformatory. Hand Book of the New York State Reformatory at Elmira* (New York, 1906), Zebulon R. Brockway, *Fifty years of prison service: an autobiography*, New York, 1912, or Pisciotta, A.W., *Benevolent Repression: Social Control and the American Reformatory-Prison Movement* (New York, 1994).

[42]Samuel J. Barrows, *The reformatory system in the United States…*, p.7: *"The reformatory system in the United States is an illustration of evolution in penology (…). The names of Machonochie and Crofton, in England and Ireland; and of Brockway, Tufts, Scott, McClaughry, and Ellen C. Johson, in our own country, will always be remembered and associated with the practical development of the reformatory system in the United States(…). The germ of the American system may be found in the ideas and experiments tried in Ireland and England by Machonochie and Crofton, but it was in the United States that these ideas were destined to find more thorough application and a more complete development".*

[43]Samuel J. Barrows, *The reformatory system in the United States…*, p.225.

[44]Norman Morris, and David J. Rothman, (eds.), *The Oxford History of the Prison: The Practise of Imprisonment in Western Society* (Oxford and New York, 1995), Peter O'Brien, "Prison reform in France and other European countries in the nineteenth century", *Institutions of confinement: hospitals, asylums, and prisons in Western Europe and North America. 1500-1950*, German Historical Institute/Cambridge University Press, 1996, pp. 297–298; and Emsley Clive, *Crime, police, and penal policy. European experiences 1750-1940* (Oxford, 2007).

[45]Eugenio Cuello Calón, "El tratamiento actual de la criminalidad de los menores", *La Lectura. Revista de Ciencias y Artes*, mayo 1912, nº137, pp. 1–16.

the Penal Colony of Belle-Ille-Mer, the Penal Colony of Aniane, the Correctional Colony of Eysses and the prison for women of Saint-Lazare in France; or the central prisons of Louvain and Ghent in Belgium, which carried out an interesting moral accounting system, and an advanced system of work and moral education for the inmates.

Countries such as Switzerland or Germany preferred another system for young offenders: the family houses, emerged from the *Rahue Haus* experience in Hamburg. But England, France, Holland, Italy or Spain, even also put up interesting initiatives of family or correctional houses, accused a greater influence of the American reformatory system, and tried to push it not only for young offenders, but also for adults and women. Their major problems were economic, technical (it was difficult to undertake a good inmates classification system), and social, due to the absence of an adequate network of industrial or manufacturing work.[46]

Otherwise, *Progressive system* managed to achieve great success both in United States and in Europe, and reformation the offenders by the institution prevailed throughout the twentieth century, developed by laws as the English Prison Act of 1877, the French law of 14 August 1885, or the Spanish *Real Decreto de 3 de junio de* 1901. Probation or conditional sentence, that was another feature of the Reformatory system, also succeed over time, promoted by laws as the English Act of 1907, the French law of 26 March 1991 or the Spanish *Ley de Libertad Condicional* of 23 July 1914.

3 Conclusions

Philosophy and legal science led a new international culture towards the humanization and rationalization of penalties on nineteenth century. Imprisonment was considered the most humane, equal and proportional punishment, able to be individualized for each offender, and it prevailed above the ancient corporal, economic or infamous punishment characteristics of the Ancient Regime.

Changes in the penalty system were used as an engine of social and legal modernization by liberal states, but they had to decide how to do them without any background, and for this purpose they began an important comparative labour. This way, penitentiary laws were commonly inspired by foreign policies and experiences, following common lines of influence in Europe and United States.

So far, we have especially talked of American influence in Europe. There were the Pennsylvania's prison model (*separate system*) and the mixed system of Auburn (*silent system*) that inspired the creation of a significant number of prisons in US and Europe, it is been said. But as we have seen, European Penal Colonies and progressive system also had a direct influence on the emergence of American

[46]Álvaro Navarro de Palencia, *Las prisiones extranjeras (Francia, Bélgica e Italia)* (Madrid, 1918), p.145.

reformatory system and the development of the conditional sentence. Influences were reciprocal and global, although each country developed their own models.

References

ADSHEAD, J., Prisons and Prisoners, London, 1845.

ALLEN, R., *Les tribunaux criminels sous la Révolution et l'Empire. 1792–1811*, Rennes, 2005.

ALLEN, H.E. and SIMONSEN, C., Corrections in America: An Introduction, New Jersey, 2001.

Álvaro Navarro de Palencia, *Las prisiones extranjeras (Francia, Bélgica e Italia)* (Madrid, 1918), p. 145.

ARQUELLADA, V. de, Noticia del estado de la cárcel de Filadelfia (Madrid, 1801), Madrid, 1916.

BARROWS, S.J., The reformatory system in the United States. Reports prepared for The International Prison Commission, S.J. Barrows, commissioner for the United States, Washington, 1900 (House of representatives, 56th Congress, 1st Session, document n.459).

BEHA, J. J., "Redemption to Reform: The Intellectual Origins of the Prison Reform Movement", New York University Annual Survey of American Law, vol. 3 (2007–2008), pp. 773–792.

BLACKSTONE, W., Commentaries on the laws of England, Claredon Press, Oxford, 1766–1769.

BORREGO, A., Estudios penitenciarios. Visita de los principales establecimientos penales de Europa, ejecutada de orden del Gobierno, seguida de la exposición de un sistema aplicable a la reforma de las cárceles y presidios de España, Madrid, 1873.

BROCKWAY, Z.R., The Ideal of a True Prison System for a State. a Paper Read Before the National Congress on Penitentiary and Reformatory Discipline at Cincinnati, on October 12, 1870.

BROCKWAY, Z.R., "The American Reformatory Prison System", *American Journal of Sociology*, vol. 15, nº 4 (Jan., 1910), pp. 454–477.

BROCKWAY, Z.R., Fifty years of prison service: an autobiography, New York, 1912.

CARBASSE, J.M., "État autoritaire et justice répressive. L'évolution de la législation pénale de 1789 au Code pénal de 1810", *All'ombra dell'aquila imperiale. Trasformazioni e continuità istituzionali nei territori sabaudi in età napoleonica*, Rome, 1994.

CARBASSE, J.M., Histoire du droit pénal et de la justice criminelle, París, 2000.

CARBASSE, J.M., "Code pénal", *Dictionnaire de culture juridique*, París, 2003.

CHARLES LUCAS, Du système pénitentiaire en Europe at aux Etats-Unis, 3 vols., París, 1828–1830.

CHARLES LUCAS, De la réforme des prisons ou de la théorie de l'emprisonnement, 3 vols., 1836–1838.

CHARLES LUCAS, Des moyens et des conditions de la réforme pénitentiaire en France, París, 1848.

CHARLES LUCAS, Exposé d'un Système de Legislation criminelle pour l'État de la Lousiane et pour les États-Unis d'Amerique por Edward Livingston, 2 vols., Guillaumin et Cie., París, 1872

CLEAR, T.R., COLE, G.F., and REISIG, M.D., American Corrections, Nueva York, 2009.

CLIVE, E., Crime, police, and penal policy. European experiences 1750–1940, Oxford Univ. Press, Oxford, 2007.

DEMETZ, F.A., Report on Reformatory Farm institutions, traduc. Wheathley, E.B., London, 1856.

DEMETZ, M. and ABEL BLOUET, M., Rapports a M. le Comte de Montalivet sur les pénitenciers des États-Unis, París, 1837.

DIXON, H., John Howard and the Prison-World of Europe. From Original and Authentic Documents, Massachusset, 1852.

EDEN, W., Principles of Penal Law, London, 1771.
EMSLEY, C., "Law reform and penal reform in England in the age of the French revolution", en Révolutions et justice pénale in Europe, London, 1999.
ELLIOT, B., "The Provision of Reformatory Schools, the Landed Class, and the Myth of the Superiority of Rural Life in Mid-Victorian England: a Footnote", History of Education, 1980, vol.9, nº1, pp.63–74.
ELYM, S., State Trials, London, 1730.
Eugenio Cuello Calón, "El tratamiento actual de la criminalidad de los menores", *La Lectura. Revista de Ciencias y Artes*, mayo 1912, nº137, pp. 1–16
FALCO, F.F., La obra de los congresos penitenciarios internacionales, La Habana, 1906.
FIELD, J., Prison discipline: and the advantages of the separate system of imprisonment, with a detailed account of the discipline now pursued in the new County Gaol, at Reading, 2 vols., London, 1848.
FORSYTHE, W.J., "The beginnings of the separate system of imprisonment 1835–1840", Social Policy & Administration, vol. 13.2 (1979), pp. 105–110.
FORLIVIESI, L., POTTIER, G.F., and CHASSAT, S, *Éduquer et punir. La colonie agricole pénitentiaire de Mettray (1839–1937)*, Rennes, 2005.
FOUCAULT, M., Vigilar y castigar: nacimiento de la prisión, ed. Madrid, 1992.
FRAILES, P., Un espacio para castigar. La cárcel y la ciencia penitenciaria en España (siglos XVIII–XIX), Madrid, 1999.
GARCÍA RAMÍREZ, S., "John Howard: la obra y la enseñanza", El estado de las prisiones en Inglaterra y Gales, México, 2003.
GRAY, F.C., Prison Discipline in America, London, 1847.
GUZMAN DALBORA, J.L., "Código penal francés de 1791", Revista de Derecho Penal y Criminología, 3º ep., nº1 (2009).
HADING, C., Imprisonment in England and Wales: A concise History, London, 1985, o SPIERENBURG, P., The prison experience, London, 1991.
HANWAY, J., Solitude in Imprisonment, London, 1779.
HENRIQUES, U. R. Q., "The rise and decline of the separate system of prison discipline", Past & Present, vol. 54, (1972), pp. 61–93.
HIRSCH, A.J., The Rise of the penitentiary. Prisons and punishment in Early America, Yale University Press, New Haven/Londres, 1992.
IGNATIEFF, M., A just measure of pain: the penitentiary in the Industrial revolution (1750–1850), New York, 1978.
JEBB, J., Thoughts on the Polity and Construction of Prisons with Hints for Their Improvement, Bury St Edmund's, 1785.
JEBB, J., Observations on the Separate System of Discipline submitted to the Congress assembled at Brussels, on the subjects of Prison Reform, on the 20 September 1847, London, 1847.
JIMÉNEZ de ASÚA, L., Tratado de derecho penal I, Buenos Aires, 1964.
JULIUS, N.H., Leçons sur les prisons présentées en forme de Cours au Public de Berlin, en l'Année 1827, I et II, F.G. Levrault, París-Bruselas, 1831.
JULIUS, N.H., Du système pénitentiarie américain en 1836, Rennes-París-Geneve-Bruxelles, 1837.
KANN, M.E., Punishment, prisons, and patriarchy liberty and power in the early American republic, New York, 2005.
LA ROCHEFAUCAULT-LIANCOURT, Des Prisons de Philadelphie par un Européen, Filadelfia, 1796 (2º ed., París, 1799).
LAINGUI, A., Histoire du droit pénal, 2ª ed. París, 1993.
LEROUX, J., Thoughts on the Present State of the Prisons of this Country, London, 1780.
LÓPEZ, M.A., Descripción de los más célebres establecimientos penales de Europa y Estados Unidos, seguida de la aplicación práctica de sus principios y régimen interior a las Casas de Corrección, Fuerza y Reconciliación que pudieran plantearse en España, 2 tomos, Valencia, 1832.

MARCEL LE CLÈRE, "Prisons et bagnes en France du Directoire aux Cent-Jours", *Revue de l'Institut Napoléon,* 1974, n° 130, pp. 33–43.
MAcDONALD, A treatise on civil imprisonment in England, London, 1791.
MAESTRO, M.T., Voltaire and Beccaria as reformers of Criminal Law, Nueva York, 1942.
MARTINAGE, R., Histoire du droit pénal en Europe, Paris, 1998.
MORRIS, N, and ROTHMAN, D. J. (eds.), The Oxford History of the Prison: The Practise of Imprisonment in Western Society, Oxford and New York, Oxford University Press, 1995.
MURRAY, P.J., Reformatory Schools In France And England, London, 1854.
MURUBE y GALÁN, F., Tratado de las prisiones y sistemas penales de Inglaterra y Francia, con observaciones generales sobre lo que conviene saber para la reforma de las de España, Santiago de Compostela, 1860.
MYNSHULL, G., Essays and Character of a Prison and Prisoners, London, 1618.
NORMANDEAU, A., "Pioneers in criminology: Charles Lucas, opponent of capital punishment", Journal of Criminal Law and Criminology, vol. 61, issue 2 (1970).
O'BRIEN, P., "Prison reform in France and other European countries in the nineteenth century", Institutions of confinement: hospitals, asylums, and prisons in Western Europe and North America. 1500-1950, German Historical Institute/Cambridge University Press, 1996, pp. 297–298.
OLLYFE, G., An essay humbly offer'd, for an Act of Parliament to prevent capital crimes, and the loss of many lives; and to promote a desirable improvement and blessing in the nation, London, 1731.
PAUL, G.O., A State of the proceedings on the subjecto of a Reform of prisons, London, 1783.
PETIT, J.G., FAUGERON, C., PIERRE, M., Histoire des prisons en France. 1789–2000, Rennes, 2002.
RADZINOWICZ, L., "International collaboration in criminal science", The modern approach to criminal law. Collected essays, London, 1945, pp. 467–497.
Randall McGowen, "The Well-Ordered Prison: England, 1780-1865", *The Oxford History of the prison. The practice of punishment in Western Society*, (Oxford-New York, 1998), p. 80.
ROBERT, T., Some Considerations for rendering the Punishment of Criminals more effectual, London, 1733.
ROS, J.M., y SAUQUILLO, J., "Un sistema penitenciario traído del viaje," *Del sistema penitenciario en Estados Unidos y su aplicación en Francia*, Madrid, 2005.
ROSE, G., The Struggle for Penal Reform: the Howard League and its Predecessors, Stevens, 1961.
ROTHMAN, D. J., "Perfecting the prison. United States 1789-1865", The Oxford history of the prison: the practice of punishment in western society, New York Press, 1995.
ROUSSEAUX, X., DUPONT-BOUCHAT, M.S., CARBASSE, J.M., *Histoire du droit pénal et de la justice criminelle*, 1ª ed. París, 2000.
SAGRA, R. de la, Cinco meses en los Estados Unidos de América del Norte (desde el 20 de abril al 23 de septiembre de 1835), París, 1836.
SAUQUILLO, J., "Un descubrimiento judicial de la democracia: el viaje de Tocqueville y Beaumont a América (1831-1832)", *Jueces para la democracia*, 2008, nº 62, pp. 92–103.
STACK, J., "Reformatory and industrial schools and the decline of chils imprisonment in mid-Victorian England and Wales", History of Education, 1994, vol. 23, nº1, pp. 59–73.
STAFFORD-SMITH, T.W., The curious Mr. Howard : legendary prison reformer, Hook, Hampshire, 2011.
TÉLLEZ AGUILERA, A., Los sistemas penitenciarios y sus prisiones. Derecho y realidad, Madrid, 1998.
TELLKAMPF, J.L., Reform of punishment and prisons en Essays on law reform, comercial policy, Banks, penitenciaries, etc in Great Britain and the United States of America, London-Edimburgh, 1859.
TERCERO ARRIBAS, F., "Sistemas penitenciarios norteamericanos", Historia de las prisiones. Teorías economicistas, Madrid, 1997. pp. 149–157.

TOMLINSON, H., "Design and reform: the 'separate system' in the nineteenth century English prison", Buildings and Society: Essays on the Social Development of the Built Environment, (Routledge), 1984, pp. 94–119.

WEBB, S. and B., English prisons under local government, London, 1922.

WILSON PIERSON, G., Tocqueville in America, Oxford University Press, New York, 1938.

WINES, E.C., The State of Prisons and of Child-Saving, Cambridge University Press, Cambridge, 1880.

ZYSBERG, A., Politiques du bagne. 1820-1850. L'impossible prison: recherches sur le système pénitentiaire au XIXe siécle, Paris.

Isabel Ramos Vázquez is Professor of Legal History in the Faculty of Social and Legal Sciences, University of Jaén. Doctor of Laws (Universidad de Jaén, 2001), and Doctor of History (Universidad Nacional de Educación a Distancia, Madrid, 2013), her research main outlines are about the history of criminal and penitentiary law, the institutional history of public administration, and the history of social or labour law. She has worked as visiting researcher in the University of Granada, the University of Catania, and the Max-Planck Institut für europäische Rechtsgeschichte in Frankfurt/M. She has also participated in national research projects about institutional history and criminal law history, with seven books and more than thirty articles or other publications on these subjects. Finally, she has carried out institutional labor as Vice Dean of Law (2008–2015), Academic Secretary (2015–2016), and Dean in the Faculty of Social and Legal Sciences, University of Jaén, since April 2016.

Kolibri 360 GmbH
Ferdinand-Jühlke-Straße 7
99095 Erfurt, Deutschland
produktsicherheit@kolibri360.de